EDITED BY WILLIAM E. KASDORF

The Columbia Guide to Digital Publishing

Columbia University Press • New York

Columbia University Press
Publishers Since 1893
New York Chichester, West Sussex

Library of Congress Cataloging-in-Publication Data
The Columbia guide to digital publishing / edited by William E. Kasdorf.
p. cm.
Includes bibliographical references and index.
ISBN 0–231–12498–8 (alk. paper) — ISBN 0–231–12499–6 (pbk. : alk. paper)
1. Electronic publishing I. Kasdorf, William E.
Z286 .E43C65 2003
070.5'797—dc21 2002041462

Columbia University Press books are printed on
permanent and durable acid-free paper.
Printed in the United States of America
c 10 9 8 7 6 5 4 3 2 1
p 10 9 8 7 6 5 4 3 2

Contents

Credits *xliii*
Contributors *xlv*
Preface *liii*

Chapter 1. Introduction: Publishing in Today's Digital Era *1*
William E. Kasdorf, President, Impressions Book and Journal Services, Inc.

Today, virtually all publishing is digital to some extent, whether content is delivered electronically or in print. But every publishing family is digital in its own way. Some, like journals and reference publishers, have moved so far toward electronic publishing that they are beginning to abandon print. Others, like magazines and catalogs, have focused more on digital production technology and, with newspapers, on integrating workflow for print and online publication. E-books still seem tentative, although they present big advantages, especially to publishers of textbooks and scholarly books. This introduction examines these different sides of publishing today to provide some perspectives on the many aspects of publishing in the digital era that this Guide discusses in depth in subsequent chapters. This overview ends with some suggestions of important technologies that deserve special attention from publishers today.

1.01 Digital publishing is both a given and a goal *1*
(i) The real revolutions have already happened *2*
1.02 Various publishers, various solutions *3*
(i) Journals: the proving ground for electronic publishing *3*
– The problem with print *4*
– Awkward economics *4*
– Moving from print to electronic publication *5*
– Pioneering SGML *5*
– Pricing and delivery models *6*
– Making access ubiquitous *6*

Chapter 2. The Technical Infrastructure *32*
Chris Biemesderfer, Seagoat Consulting

This chapter discusses the basic hardware and software that provide the infrastructure for digital publishing. Becoming familiar with these components will help those involved in digital publishing to better understand technical issues and use tools and techniques more effectively.

William E. Kasdorf, President, Impressions Book and Journal Services, Inc.

Markup enables the various parts and features of a given set of content to be distinguished and named. It provides a way to label, describe, and delimit these in a publication so that processing systems can tell them apart and know how they relate to each other. Markup languages are used to define specific markup schemes. In the past, markup languages were typically proprietary and used only by specialists. The Web gave rise to one of the simplest and most widely used markup languages ever devised, HTML, and also to one of the most flexible and powerful: XML, the Extensible Markup

Language. After a brief overview of earlier markup languages, this chapter focuses on the technologies in the XML family— XML itself, and related standards for defining, styling, linking, transforming, and annotating—that provide the foundation for digital publishing today.

The production and distribution of content are two of the most important functions carried out by publishers. Historically, these publishing functions had only to concern themselves with how to produce and distribute physical items: books, magazines, and journals printed on paper. However, since the mid-1990s publishers have recognized that in order to meet the demands of digital publishing, their publishing processes require radical rethinking. The traditional print requirements must continue to be fulfilled, but the additional demands of digital publishing must also be met. The content must be available electronically—usually on-line. It must be consistently produced to a high standard, available at the same time or ahead of print, and it must provide maximum functionality—which often means linking both internally and externally, and sometimes means including nonprint content. Of course, all of this must be achieved at minimum added cost to the publisher.

Chapter 5. Data Capture & Conversion *179*

Mark Gross, President, Data Conversion Laboratory

This chapter discusses the ins and outs of converting and upgrading textual data and related information from all kinds of formats into markup languages for publishing purposes. While the issues and approaches apply to all markup languages, particular emphasis is given to the issues of converting documents into XML, SGML, and HTML. The chapter looks at the issues surrounding the capture of data from sources such as paper and microfilm, word processors, publishing systems, PDF, and ASCII—the main issue being the need to untangle content from structure.

Publishing in the digital era, to an overwhelming degree, still means publishing in print. More often than not what is published electronically today first started as print. While much of the energy in digital publishing has shifted to the electronic conveyance and display of information, the bulk of the economic activity still centers on print-based publishing. Electronic publishing is the future of the industry, but print publishing pays today's bills. Today's digital tools, technologies, and techniques are as often used in print as in electronic publishing. Mastering print publishing demands knowledge of a broad range of processes and technologies surrounding composition, design, and graphics. Print publishing has reached the intersection of 500 years of analog craft and a new era in digital computer graphics. Publishing practitioners require an appreciation of both. This chapter is a broad overview of the processes and technologies that comprise the practice of print publishing in the era of digital publishing. We focus on the digital technologies that are moving the process forward into the future, and the traditional craft-based skills still important in the digital era that optimize quality in everyday work.

Frederick Bowes, III, Electronic Publishing Associates

Digital publishing technologies offer publishers and other content providers a new dimension in shaping their publications. Well-constructed digital content can be configured to be used with a wide range of accessibility tools, including specialized software such as text-to-speech programs, designed to help people with disabilities gain access to published materials that would otherwise be unavailable to them. This has not been lost on disability advocates, who have driven recent federal and state legislation that puts increasing pressure on publishers to provide their products in formats accessible to people with a variety of disabilities. This chapter will inform the reader of key issues, problems, and opportunities in content accessibility and what publishers must do, operationally, to meet accessibility needs. It also contains strategic suggestions about factoring accessibility requirements into product and business plans.

Chapter 8. Digital Printing *369*

George Alexander, Executive Editor, the Seybold Report

The technology that is used to print books digitally has been evolving rapidly. Initially, sheetfed monochrome laser printers were the only technology available. But today, high-speed roll-fed devices are often used, full color is becoming more economical, and other printing technologies (such as inkjet) are coming into use. This chapter describes the available printing and binding options and some of the new publishing options they create.

Florian Brody, President and CEO, Brody Inc.

Since the format of the book evolved from the continuous scroll to the page-oriented folio, no change in the practice of publishing texts has had such an impact on the way we perceive and use a book as electronic publishing. This paradigm shift changes the way text is perceived in time and space and the integration of text, video, and audio into a multimedia product is a logical step in an electronic medium. Yet it is not the technology that undergoes the biggest change, but the role of the publisher, who has to re-emerge as the agent of a new medium, still in statu nascendi. In the first phase of multimedia, everybody seemed to be empowered by the new tools and technologies to become a multimedia producer. Most multimedia publications do not live up to the promise of an interactive and integrated experience, but remain an exploration into technologies without a clear goal. It is the publisher who needs to act as the integrator of multiple media types, multiple experts, and multiple industries in order to do his job—to turn an idea into a product and make it public. This chapter gives an overview of the different technologies, standards, and business issues to be considered when extending electronic publishing into multimedia.

This chapter tackles two subjects—the process of publishing on the Web, and the technology called content management that has emerged to address Web publishing. Publishers who have moved to the Web have found it brings all the challenges of print publishing—and some new challenges that are unique to the Web. Content management technology has grown to meet these challenges, but has also brought with it technical complexity that is new for some publishers. This chapter outlines the technical issues regarding content management, and gives the readers a framework for understanding how content management technology can help their publishing processes.

(ii) Proprietary CMS development issues *447*
- Application service providers (ASP) *448*
(iii) "Your mileage may vary"—opting for open source *449*
- Advantages of an open source CMS *450*
- Disadvantages of an open source CMS *450*
- Cost *451*
- Control *451*
- Support *451*
(iv) Commercial content management systems: additional factors for consideration *452*
- Price, Size, Scale *452*
  - Upper-tier content management systems *453*
  - Mid-market content management systems *453*
  - Low-priced content mangement systems *453*
- Technology *453*
- Industry specialization *453*
10.06 Post-implementation issues *454*

Chapter 11. Electronic Books & the Open eBook Publication Structure *455*

Allen Renear, University of Illinois, Urbana-Champaign
Dorothea Salo, University of Wisconsin, Madison

Electronic books, or e-books, will soon be a major part of electronic publishing. This chapter introduces the notion of electronic books, reviewing their history, the advantages they promise, and the difficulties in predicting the pace and nature of e-book development and adoption. It then analyzes some of the critical problems facing both individual publishers and the industry as a whole, drawing on our current understanding of fundamental principles and best practice in information processing and publishing. In the context of this analysis the Open eBook Forum Publication Structure, a widely used XML-based content format, is presented as a foundation for high-performance electronic publishing.

11.01 Introduction *455*
11.02 OEBPS in a nutshell *457*
(i) Basic description of OEBPS *457*
- What it is *457*
- What it does *458*
- Who developed it *458*
- What it is for *458*

Maintaining ownership of commercially viable digital assets is increasingly important. As digital files have become the de facto standard for use and reuse of products published both in print and electronic formats, libraries and publishers are working to create a viable way to store and preserve digital assets. Publishers have additional reasons for creating the process and infrastructure for storing their digital materials: the potential for reduced operating costs and increased profit margins associated with reusable content and the increased revenue derived from licensing, selling, or otherwise making available content that is centrally available. This chapter will focus on the issues facing publishers, but will also provide an overview of the wider issues involving archiving.

The purpose of this chapter is to give a succinct overview of the various legal doctrines that apply to digital publishing and to make the concepts and basic rules as accessible as possible. This chapter does not substitute for legal advice on any specific matter that the reader may encounter; rather, it is intended to help the reader be more alert to legal issues that may arise, and be a more informed consumer of legal services. It does not, of course, purport to address all the legal issues that a publisher will encounter. Publishers are businesses, and must deal with all the laws that affect businesses of every kind. Nor does this chapter address some issues that are common to everyone who does business on the Internet, such as the laws of consumer privacy, e-commerce, and the like. The main focus is on copyright, as that creates the property that is the currency of publishing. This chapter will also deal with other intellectual property principles and with some other concerns, such as libel, that are uniquely central to publishing.

Chapter 14. International Issues *587*

Robert E. Baensch, Director, Center for Publishing, New York University

This chapter highlights the twelve key elements that are most important for international communications, online publishing, and e-commerce on the Internet. The size of organization or location of country is irrelevant, because the World Wide Web is a stateless network and framework that goes beyond the physical location of electronic resources and information by connecting millions of computers into a seamless global network. Statistics on Internet users worldwide, with a focus on Europe, Asia, and South America, establish a meaningful framework for what it really means to publish globally. A review of the international publishing activities of professional, legal, scientific, technical, and medical journal publishers offers realistic working examples for publishers who are considering the development of their international on-line business. A concise analysis of geographic, cultural, language, economic, technological, and legal factors provides perspective on the global environment for digital publishing.

One of the promises of the digital revolution in publishing is that it has the potential to give owners of content—authors, publishers, aggregators—new, robust tools for more intelligent, efficient, and effective management of their content. Nowhere have the benefits of new technology been more eagerly awaited than in the area of rights management. However, content owners have been groping not only for the right technology but for the right applications of competing technologies—as well as dealing with changing business models, customer resistance, legal challenges, and implementation questions. This chapter explores the fundamentals of Digital Rights Management and the different DRM technologies available in order to help publishers and their partners implement the right technology in the right manner.

Credits

Columbia University Press
William B. Strachan *Publisher*
Linda Secondari *Creative Director, Manufacturing and Technology*
Stephen H. Sterns *Editor, Electronic Reference*
Richard Hendel *Designer*
Paul Berk *Copyeditor*

Impressions Book and Journal Services
William E. Kasdorf *President*
David Nelson *Electronic Publishing Manager*
Christie Pinter *Project Coordinator*
Chris Cott *Systems Specialist/Senior Pagination Specialist*
Sharon Hughes *Indexer*

Open Book Systems
Laura Fillmore *President*
Dee Landergren *Vice President of Systems*
Sunny Gleason *Manager of Programming*
David G. Cassidy *Project Lead*
Mircea Baciu *Programmer*
Danielle Hull *Information Designer*
Kendall Dawson *HTML programmer*

Contributors

George Alexander

Alexander is executive editor of *The Seybold Report* and has been involved with publishing technology since 1977. He began his career in publishing as systems manager for a daily newspaper and later served as director of publishing systems for Harper & Row. During his twenty years with the Seybold organization, he has written articles and done consulting projects on many areas of publishing technology. His particular areas of interest include digital printing, computer-to-plate systems, color management, cross-media publishing, and systems to support large-scale publishing. His consulting clients have included many well-known publishing organizations, including the *New England Journal of Medicine,* World Book, Scholastic, and HarperCollins.

Robert Baensch

Baensch is Associate Professor of Publishing and the Director of the Center for Publishing, New York University. Before joining NYU, he was a publishing consultant and president of Baensch International Group Ltd. New York. He was senior vice president for marketing for Rizzoli International Publications, Inc. Prior to that as director for publishing at the American Institute of Physics from 1988 to 1991, he was responsible for over 60 journals, a book program and database information services. From 1983 to 1988, Baensch was vice president-marketing of Macmillan Publishing Company where, in addition to a full range of marketing and sales responsibilities, he directed the Macmillan Software Company and English as a Second Language Multimedia Program. Before 1983, he was president of Springer Verlag New York, and from 1968 to 1980 vice president and director of the International Division of Harper & Row Publishers, Inc. Baensch started his publishing career with the McGraw-Hill Book Company, where he was manager of the Translation Rights Department and editorial director of the International Division. He has served on the Board of Directors of the Association of American Publishers and the Society of Scholarly Publishers. He is currently on the Board of the Book Industry Study Group and serves as the Editor for the *Publishing Research Quarterly* journal. Baensch received his B.A. from Johns Hopkins University, and a degree of SEP from Stanford University Graduate School of Business.

Chris Biemesderfer

Biemesderfer, principal of Seagoat Consulting, consults for numerous professional societies and academic publishers in the area of information dissemination via computer networks. He is a member of the team that developed several electronic journals for the American Astronomical Society. He has offices in Washington, DC and Tucson.

Frederick Bowes, III

Bowes is president of Electronic Publishing Associates, a consultancy for publishers addressing the many strategic and operational challenges related to implementing electronic publishing technologies. A major area of current focus for EPA is on solving problems relating to curriculum accessibility for students with learning, physical and other disabilities. Rick has been publisher of the *New England Journal of Medicine* and president of both Macmillan New Media and Cadmus Digital Solutions. He founded PubList.com (now part of Infotrieve, Inc.) and served as co-director of CAST's Universal Learning Center (ULC), a non-profit Web-based service being developed to provide digital content and software to meet the curriculum needs of individual learners, especially those with disabilities. Rick is a past president of the Society for Scholarly Publishing and is an active member of the Electronic Information Committee of the Association of American Publishers' Professional and Scholarly Publishing Division.

Florian Brody

Brody has more than fifteen years experience in electronic publishing and digital media technology, working both in Europe and the United States. He has provided his expertise to many Fortune 500 companies, including Kodak, Apple Computer, and Andersen Consulting. He has worked as a strategic consultant in new media for the Austrian Federal Ministry of Science, was an advisor for the Multimedia Task Force of the European Commission DG III, launched Philips CDi in Austria, and developed the Web presence for *Der Standard,* Vienna, the first German-language newspaper on the Internet in 1995. The co-inventor in 1991 of Voyager's Expanded Books, the first electronic books to be read on a laptop, Brody has also provided strategic electronic publishing consulting to Zinio Inc., a developer of digital magazines; InterTrust Technologies; and Themestream, an e-mail newsletter service, where he served as executive director for product management. In 1999 he co-founded AlcheMe Inc., a personalized, user-side "infomediary" on the Internet, and served as its CEO. Brody studied at the University of Vienna, and he frequently teaches at Art Center College of Design in Pasadena, Ca., and the Vienna University. He held the chair for multimedia at the MultiMediaArt College in Salzburg, Austria, and was visiting professor at the Universidad de las Palmas de Gran Canaria. He frequently keynotes at events and is published in the field of digital media and electronic publishing.

Mark Gross

Gross, founder of Data Conversion Laboratory, Inc. (http://www.dclab.com), is a recognized authority on automated data conversion. Prior to founding DCL in 1981, Mark was with the consulting practice of Arthur Young & Co. He has also taught at the New York University Graduate School of Business, the New School, and Pace University. Mark has a BS in Engineering from Columbia University and an MBA from New York University. He is a frequent speaker on the topic of automated conversions to XML and SGML. He has authored numerous articles on the topic which may be found on the DCL Web site, as well as the chapter on "Planning for Document Conversion" in *The XML Handbook,* second and third editions.

Michael Gross

Gross is Chief Technology Officer, Data Conversion Laboratory, Inc. Michael Gross (not related to Mark Gross) is responsible for solution engineering at Data Conversion Laboratory, Inc. (http://www.dclab.com). Mike has been solving digital publishing conversion problems at DCL for almost twenty years, where he has overseen thousands of legacy conversion projects, and is the chief architect of DCL's document conversion tool set, including its proprietary hub and spoke technology. Prior to joining DCL in 1986, Mike managed the development of a U.S. Air Force Software Development Tool Set for Advanced Computer Techniques Corporation. He holds a B.S. in Computer Engineering from the Case Institute of Technology at Case Western Reserve University, and is a frequent contributor to DCLnews, DCL's monthly e-journal newsletter, where he writes about the technical issues that arise in the world of digital publishing conversion and structured markup.

Paul Hilts

Hilts is a publishing and media analyst who has been involved with technical publishing for nontechnical people since 1970, beginning with Popular Mechanics Books. He was with *OMNI* Magazine for ten years, five as managing editor, and was technology editor for *Publishers Weekly* for more than ten years, writing about printing, binding, electronic books and computer books. He is also adjunct faculty at the University of Virginia's Publishing Institute, and has been an advisor and track chairman for Seybold Seminars for five years.

Bill Kasdorf

Bill Kasdorf is president of Impressions Book and Journal Services (http://www.impressions.com)—a composition and publishing services firm that designs, edits, and produces books and journals in print and electronic forms, with special expertise in XML workflows—and vice president of IoFlex, Inc., a software development firm that specializes in image processing and workflow tools. He is Past President of the Society for Scholarly Publishing, and lives in Ann Arbor, MI.

Heather Malloy

Malloy is the Digital Archive Manager at John Wiley & Sons, Inc., and has also held various print and electronic publishing positions at *Scientific American,* Greenwood Publishing Group, and Southern Connecticut Newspapers.

Thad McIlroy

McIlroy is an electronic publishing analyst and author, and president of Arcadia House (http://www.arcadiahouse.com), founded in 1988 and based in San Francisco and Toronto. In 1990 he co-founded (with Miles Southworth) The Color Resource, a publishing and distribution company devoted to books and training materials on color design, imaging and prepress. A well-established expert in the technology and marketing issues surrounding electronic publishing, color imaging, and the Internet, he has written a dozen books—including *Using Color Management Systems for Push-Button Color* (co-author; 1993: Smart Color and The Color Resource), *Inside Photo CD: Market Opportunities in a Leading Edge Technology* (1993: The Color Resource), *The Color Resource Color Desktop Publishing Product Annual* (1992–93: The Color Resource), *The Complete Color Glossary* (1992: The Color Resource)—and over 160 articles. McIlroy is a contributing editor to *Printing Impressions* magazine and *The Future Image Report* and a member of the Technical Association of the Graphic Arts, and until recently, served as Program Director for Seybold Seminars, the publishing industry's premier technology conference. He is also a frequent speaker at national and international conferences.

Allen Renear

Allen Renear is an Associate Professor in the Graduate School of Library and Information Science at the University of Illinois, Urbana-Champaign, where he is head of the Electronic Publishing Research Group and teaches courses in knowledge representation and electronic publishing. Prior to joining GSLIS he was Director of the Brown University Scholarly Technology Group. Renear has been involved in electronic publishing projects and electronic publishing research for over twenty years and has published widely on topics in document engineering, text ontology, and markup semantics. He has served as President of the Association for Humanities Computing and on the Advisory Board of the Text Encoding Initiative, and was a Distinguished Visiting Fellow at the Oxford University Humanities Computing Unit. Renear was involved in the original development of the Open eBook Publication Structure (OEBPS) and has been Chair of the OeBF Publication Structure Working Group since its formation. Currently the research team he leads at the University of Illinois is applying techniques from logic and artificial intelligence to improve the functionality and efficiency of publishing systems.

Frank Romano

Romano's career has spanned over forty years in the printing and publishing industries. He is the author of thirty-nine books, co-author of the Pocket Pal, contributor to major encyclopedias and dictionaries, and the author of numerous articles. He has founded eight publications, serving as publisher or editor or both for *TypeWorld*, now *Electronic Publishing,* founded in 1977. He lectures extensively throughout the United States and Canada and has consulted for major corporations, publishers, government, and other users of digital publishing technology. He has been quoted in the *New York Times, Wall Street Journal, USA Today, Business Week, Forbes,* and many other newspapers and publications, as well as on TV and radio. Professor Romano now teaches digital publishing and digital printing at the Rochester Institute of Technology, College of Imaging Arts and Sciences.

Bill Rosenblatt

Rosenblatt is president of GiantSteps Media Technology Strategies, a management consultancy that helps its clients, media companies and digital media technology vendors, achieve growth through business strategy and technology architecture expertise. Bill is a recognized authority on digital media technologies, including content management, digital rights management, cross-media publishing, and content production systems. He has written several articles and contributed to technology standards initiatives in these areas, and he is the author of *Digital Rights Management: Business and Technology* (John Wiley & Sons). He was one of the architects of the Digital Object Identifier, an emerging standard for on-line content identification and digital rights management. Bill has twenty years of experience in technology business development, architecture, and marketing; publishing; new media; and online education. He has been a business development executive at a leading technology vendor, an IT executive at major publishing companies, and chief technology officer of an e-learning startup.

Dorothea Salo

Salo served two years as scribe to the Open eBook Forum's Publication Structure Working Group, and edited the 1.0.1 release of the Open eBook

Publication Structure. She is currently working with the Puerto Rican Census Project at the University of Wisconsin Survey Center.

John Shreeve

Shreeve is a U.K.-based writer and journalist, and is also editor of DCLnews, newsletter of Data Conversion Laboratory, Inc. (http://www.dclab.com/dclnews.asp). John writes for a diverse range of publications, including the *Financial Times, Guardian,* and *Aviation Maintenance* magazine (U.S.). He also writes a popular Internet marketing column for *EDP Business* magazine, published in eastern England. Under a pseudonym, he wrote an acclaimed novel set around blues music and hoodoo for St. Martins Press. John also writes and sells e-books over the Web. http://www.johnshreeve.com

John Strange

Strange is a Member of the Institute of Printing, and has been in the printing and publishing industry for over thirty years. Having spent fifteen years in Educational Publishing (at Pearson Education) responsible for global production, prepress and administrative systems etc; for the last ten years he has been responsible for the global production strategy and implementation in academic publishing (at Blackwell Publishing). For many years John has lectured on scheduling and professional production control, etc. at the Publishing Training Centre together with presentations at various industry seminars.

William S. Strong

Strong has practiced in the fields of copyright, publishing, and trademark law for over twenty-five years. (He describes his practice as "cradle to grave: registration, licensing, and litigation.") He is the author of *The Copyright Book: A Practical Guide* (Cambridge, The MIT Press), now in its fifth edition, the leading guide to copyright law for non-specialists, and of the "Copyright" chapter of the *Chicago Manual of Style.* His articles include "Database Protection After Feist v. Rural Telephone Co." [*Journal of the Copyright Society of the U.S.A.,* 42, no. 1 (Fall 1994)], and "Copyright in a Time of Change" [*Journal of Electronic Publishing,* 5 (March, 1999)]. Mr. Strong was Adjunct Professor of Copyright Law at Franklin Pierce Law Center, 1987–1996; he is also active in the Intellectual Property Law Section of the American Bar Association, where he served on the governing Council, 1997–2001, and in the Copyright Society of the U.S.A., most recently serving as Chair of the New England Chapter.

William Trippe

Trippe is president of New Millennium Publishing, a Boston-based consulting practice formed in 1997. Bill has more than twenty years of technical and management experience in electronic publishing, content management, XML, and related technologies. He brings a unique blend of strategic and hands-on knowledge of the products and trends that are shaping the publishing and content technology marketplace. In addition to his role at New Millennium, Bill is associate editor of *The Gilbane Report,* the XML columnist for *Transform,* a Consulting Associate with the consulting and market research firm CAP Ventures, and a regular contributor to the magazine, *EContent.* He recently co-authored *Digital Rights Management: Business and Technology* (John Wiley & Sons) and is the co-author of the new book, *SVG for Designers* (Osborne/McGraw-Hill). Samples of Bill's writing and presentations can be found at http://www.nmpub.com.

Mark Walter

Walter is a consultant for the Seybold Consulting Group and a senior editor at Seybold Publications (http://www.SeyboldReports.com), since 1970 a leading provider of media technology guidance to publishers and their suppliers. A twenty-year publishing industry veteran, Walter's consulting work has focused on helping both commercial and corporate publishers implement technologies that improve their business processes. Since 1987 he has spearheaded Seybold's coverage of SGML and XML, and in 1998 he directed the editorial team that launched XML.com, the leading Web resource for XML professionals. In his role as a senior editor for The Seybold Report, he has written extensively on publishing standards and reviewed scores of products, ranging from XML-based authoring tools and e-books to digital rights management and large-scale content-management systems. Prior to joining Seybold, Walter worked at McGraw-Hill, where he was part of the development team that introduced Datapro's information service on electronic publishing. He began his career at Temple University Press and later served as a production editor at Editing, Design & Production, shepherding college and medical textbooks through the publishing process.

Preface

Today's digital landscape feels perilous to most people in the publishing industry. Technology is evolving at a breathtaking pace; new developments continually emerge that force us to reexamine where we're going, while well-publicized setbacks stop us in our tracks. The blizzard of information (for which, ironically, we have digital publishing to thank) sometimes seems only to blur the view. And the paths seem to shift before the maps can be drawn.

We need a guide. That's the role *The Columbia Guide to Digital Publishing* is designed to fill. It's intended to be helpful, authoritative, and comprehensive. It's written by people who are both expert and experienced, with thorough knowledge of the topics they cover and with direct personal and professional involvement in the realities of making it all work.

A good guide takes you where *you* want to go. This is not a handbook or a manual; the information it provides is not of the "how-to-do-it" sort. It was created with the understanding that different publishers have very different needs, as do all the various participants in the publishing process. It is designed to help you explore, to find the path that's best for you. It offers a broad array of subjects and perspectives, and it is structured so that it not only provides quick answers to concrete questions, but puts those answers into meaningful contexts that help lead you to things you might not have thought to ask about.

One of the most profound effects of the digital revolution is the broadening of the concept of what it means to be a publisher. In the analog era, it was relatively clear who a "publisher" was—although the average person still often confuses "publisher" with "printer." Even then, there were a host of contributors to the publishing process—authors, freelance editors and designers, production services, printers, distributors, booksellers—but these parties were all quite separate, not particularly involved in or knowledgeable about each other's work. The same is true of the consumers: we picture a reader sitting in a chair by the fire with a novel and tend to forget about the even larger numbers of students and teachers, business people and their employees (training or being trained, documenting or using documentation), and public and private institutions (especially libraries) who buy and use what is published. In the digital era, all of these people—from the authors and editors and designers who create the publications, through the typesetters and printers and Web developers who produce them, to the booksellers and corporations and libraries and others who provide access to them—are linked: what each of them does can affect and be affected by what the others do. The Guide is designed to be helpful to all these people.

Although its authors were encouraged to be open-minded and comprehensive, acknowledging various approaches and points of view, they were not discouraged from taking stands as appropriate. A good guide doesn't just say "well, there are two paths up the mountain, Path A and Path B, which one do you want to take?" It's the guide's responsibility to point out that Path A may take twice as long, but has a beautiful waterfall and stunning views, or that far more people have died attempting Path B. People don't die from taking the wrong path in publishing, but companies do.

Where the Guide authors agree, that agreement is totally unsolicited. There are a number of common themes, often from authors writing on quite different topics; this unanimity warrants more than passing attention. Most acknowledge that the future will be characterized by multiple modes of publication, print and electronic; it is not a matter of one mode "winning," but of many coexisting. Most acknowledge that publishing is becoming more democratic and more international. Most emphasize the importance of workflow, advocating a much more integrated process from writing and editing to production and distribution than what is common today. Most see XML, the Extensible Markup Language, as fundamental to accomplishing this. Most see the evolution of digital technology as improving both the process and the products, making them more efficient and more effective over time. Although there are many paths, we all seem to be climbing the same mountain.

A good guide also speaks your language. Despite the technical nature of many of their topics, the authors have been encouraged to write in a way accessible to a broad range of people in publishing and related fields. Although the chapters are intended to be authoritative, they are not intended to be the ultimate reference on their subjects. They are designed to provide clear explanations of a broad range of topics related to publishing in the digital era. A typical reader might well be expert in one aspect of digital publishing but need this Guide for insight into other aspects. An experienced graphic designer will already know what this book has to say about graphic file formats, but may need to know more about XML and metadata. An editor may already have a good grasp of those subjects, but need to know the difference between TIFF, JPEG, and SVG (three graphic file formats). Both of them may need to know more about making their publications more accessible, or how a content management system could help them. If the Guide has done its job well, it will not only give those people the information they need, but point them to other resources, in print or online, where they can find more information.

The Guide is designed to be consulted when people in publishing have questions and need quick answers, but it is also designed to be *read*—when what is needed is not just information but insight. It is not an A-Z encyclopedia of topics (although the Glossary does provide that sort of help); rather, it is written in cohesive, contiguous chapters that not only cover a broad array of topics but put those topics in context, to show how they relate to each other. The section below on "How to use this book" discusses a variety of ways in which this Guide can be approached. It's no accident that it is published both in print and online: these formats should reinforce each other, providing both a dynamic, richly linked electronic resource and the convenience of a physical book that can be kept within easy reach for a quick look-up or an extended reading.

Finally, a guide goes along with you. A conscientious effort was made to produce this book in ways that demonstrate, and take advantage of, the technologies and techniques of digital publishing. From writing and editing through the production of both the print and online versions of the Guide, the process was (and is) digital. Rather than attempting to be "cutting edge," the emphasis was on the practical application of technologies available today. The section below on "How this book was done" tells this story in some detail.

It's a story that is not finished: an essential aspect of the Guide is that it will be continually augmented and updated. Although it is not intended to be a source of news or product information, it will be kept current as new technologies evolve, as new developments in the industry or the marketplace affect publishing in the digital era. Users of the online version will always see the most recent version; new print editions will be issued periodically as demand warrants. Does this mean the print editions are "dated"? No more than any other such printed reference book, and less than most. The digital process used to edit and produce the Guide is extremely efficient, which means that once the decision is made to issue a new print edition, that edition will be available very quickly as a "snapshot" of the content of the Guide upon publication. Because the emphasis is on discussion and explanation of fundamental issues and core topics in digital publishing, rather than being a news service, it should be an enduring resource.

HOW TO USE THIS BOOK

There are many ways to approach the content of this Guide, whether in print or online. While it was written in contiguous chapters designed to be able to be read from start to finish—and that's the best way to really understand the issues that each of the chapters covers—these chapters are highly "granular," carefully structured and liberally marked with four levels of subheads that are intended to be helpful both for browsing and for locating specific topics. These subheads are all spelled out in a lengthy, detailed Table of Contents that provides a topical, structured method of entry to the Guide.

Another good point of entry is the Glossary. As each of the chapters was written and edited, key terms were highlighted for inclusion in the Glossary, which provides a quick, one- or two-sentence definition of each. It is expected that this Glossary will be one of the most-used features of the Guide; not only for print readers or online subscribers, the Glossary is being made freely available on the Web. This is intended not only to provide a handy resource in itself, but also to point people to relevant sections of the Guide. Each Glossary entry concludes with a reference (or a link, for online subscribers) to the section of the Guide where that topic is discussed.

In the text of the Guide, a number of things are highlighted. The editors have selected instances of ***glossary terms*** where consulting the glossary—and, through it, the relevant section of the Guide—might be most helpful; these are linked online and typeset in bold italic in print, as are the words "glossary terms" above. In addition, **cross references**, typeset in bold roman, direct the reader to sections of the Guide where those topics are discussed in more depth. The referenced section is linked online and cited by number in print. These numbers begin with the chapter number and progressively cite sections and subsections; so, for example, [1.2] simply refers to the second main section of Chapter One, while [1.2.iii.4] refers to the fourth sub-subsection of the third subsection of the second section of the first chapter. The running foot at the bottom of each right-hand page keeps track of the current subhead level on that page.

The third major avenue into the Guide is the Index. This is a particularly notable feature of the Guide. Indexes are taken for granted in print and, unfortunately, rarely provided online. Whereas the Glossary provides a shallow, topical view of the content, and the Table of Contents provides a logical, structured view, a good index provides an intellectual view of the content unavailable by any other means. It is the result of an intelligent reading by an indexer trained in recognizing and documenting the interrelationships of the intellectual content; the indexer not only notes topics and subtopics, but also makes judgments about them, selecting the most important and relevant sections to direct readers to. Simple searching for terms does not substitute for this; it provides too many inappropriate or unhelpful hits, and can miss the most relevant section if the term does not occur in it. Much effort continues to be made to compensate for this in search engines, but these only approximate the function of a well-made index like the one print or online users of this Guide have available.

In addition to the Table of Contents, the Glossary, the Index, and cross references—which are available in print and online—subscribers to the online version of this Guide have additional features at their disposal. One, of course, is the ability to search electronically; although this is not a substitute for an index, it is a very useful function, and one that the Guide provides at all times. Another online-only feature is a large collection of examples that augment or demonstrate topics discussed in the text. These range from simple images, to extensive text-based examples that would be impractical to include in print, to multimedia examples not possible at all in print. When these are referred to in the text, they are linked; and at the end of each chapter online, a list of all available examples is provided, not only identifying them but documenting, for downloadable files, the nature and size of the files and the software required to view or otherwise access them. The online version of the Guide will be continually enriched over time as new examples are added. Online users of the Guide also have access to an index of companies, products, and organizations named in the text; each indexed name is highlighted and linked to contact information, usually a URL which is then linked from the Name Index to the referenced Web page. Best of all, online users can customize their interface to the Guide (called "My Guide") to make it easy to find and refer to sections of special interest and to be alerted to updates to those sections.

Finally, both print and online users of the Guide are directed to other resources for further information. Many URLs are provided in the text, to allow for convenient access to the cited Web sites; these, of course, are linked in the online version. In addition, extensive bibliographic information is provided to print and online resources. These are provided at the end of each chapter; in addition, they are collected into a consolidated Bibliography at the back of the book. This, too, will be an increasingly valuable resource as it is expanded in the online version over time.

HOW THIS BOOK WAS DONE

If there is anything that characterizes publishing in the digital era, it's collaboration. The writing, editing, production, and publication of this Guide was an example of a dynamic collaboration between three primary organizations—the publisher, Columbia University Press; the compositor, Impressions Book and Journal Services; and the developer of the content management system, Open Book Systems (OBS)—designed to demonstrate the practical application of today's digital technologies. It was by no means an attempt to experiment or to use a technology for its own sake; instead, the intention was to use methods and tools generally available to most publishers today, to produce the Guide in both print and online forms as efficiently, as economically, and as effectively as possible, using today's technology in ways that will adapt well as technology evolves in the future.

There are two key aspects to the technology behind this project: a content management system (CMS) developed by Open Book Systems and an XML infrastructure (with associated editing and composition tools) developed by Impressions. The architecture and functionality of both of these aspects are a result of ongoing collaboration between OBS, Impressions, and the Press, from the development of the initial concepts to the ultimate implementation. In a traditional workflow, each of these parties might have worked quite independently of each other, with little knowledge of or concern for the other parties' methods or processes. In this case, these parties had not just knowledge of but involvement in each other's work; and that collaboration is ongoing.

The original content was written in Microsoft Word using a custom Authoring Template that provides a set of styles corresponding to the elements needed in the Guide and custom toolbars designed to make it easy to apply those styles. A second, Editing Template—designed to be used in conjunction with the electronic editing system Impressions had created for Columbia University Press—was used to clean up irregularities in the authors' files, provide more functions to the editors, and to generate XML as an output. (Consistent with the general observation that such templates are better used by editors than authors, the editors made extensive and exclusive use of the Editing Template, whereas only about half of the authors used the features of the Authoring Template to any great extent.)

Four XML DTDs were used for the Guide. (DTDs are Document Type Definitions—the chapter on Markup explains all these XML-related terms and concepts.) The differences between them are instructive. First of all, what is output from the Word templates is what is known as Well-Formed XML. A Base DTD serves as an initial assessment tool; it is very flat and permissive, enabling a sort of inventory of the chapter while tolerating some structural irregularities. Prior to importing the text into the CMS, an Import DTD that imposes more structure on the text is used to parse the file, allowing the editor to correct any irregularities before the content enters the system. When the content is being managed by the CMS, instead of having XML tags, it is organized in a database. This provides powerful functionality for the system. The CMS keeps track of every chunk of content at the paragraph level, provides a mechanism for editing and adding content, and manages a host of metadata and structural relationships essential to the Guide, such as the numbering for each level of subhead, cross-reference and glossary links, and online examples. It also manages access to the content: a chapter author can change only his or her chapter (accessing it in a browser over the Web); the general editor has access to all of them; and the editor at Columbia not only has access but has final approval of all content before it is published. All of this intricate structure is described by the third DTD: the Archival DTD. If the Guide were ever to be transferred out of this CMS to some other system, the Archival DTD would help define what all the components are and how they relate. It is also the basis for generating other forms of publication, such as future possible e-book versions.

When it is time to produce a print edition, the CMS generates XML in a form defined by the fourth XML DTD: the Composition DTD. This form of XML is designed to exploit the capabilities of the high-end XML-based composition system used for the Guide. This system is capable of using richly tagged, deeply structured XML as input coding, and the Comp DTD calls for the intricate relationships within the Guide to be expressed as attributes that handle the section numbering, cross-referencing, etc. The XML handles the structure; the composition system make use of the XML to present the content and structure as specified by the designer. The actual composition of a chapter from the Comp XML generated by the CMS is lightning fast, because it is 100 percent coded, and the DTD makes sure it is coded correctly.

The proofing process used for the Guide was entirely digital as well. The composition process produced PDF files which were FTP'd to Columbia and e-mailed to the general editor and authors, who reviewed them and returned them with any corrections to Columbia. The editor at Columbia made all the changes in the CMS and exported corrected Comp XML, which was again FTP'd to Impressions. When the pages were finalized, final PDF files were FTP'd to the book manufacturer, Edwards Brothers.

Another interesting aspect of this project is the indexing. It was done with a special process developed by Impressions which enables a professional indexer to create the index with her preferred high-end indexing software (in this case, CINDEX™), and to do so at any stage. (In this case, it was done with first-pass composition proofs.) The index is maintained independently of the XML or the text in the CMS; rather than having index terms embedded in the XML, the content maintained in the CMS contains markers delineating the places the index entries refer to—not to a page number, but to the actual pertinent section of text, whether one paragraph or several pages worth. This Integrated Indexing™ process then generates an index from the XML used to compose each edition of the book, after the composition system has determined the page breaks. This not only allows the Guide's index to adapt to changes over time, it also enables it to adapt to different formats and pagination. Plus it provides a very useful map to the content online.

Digital technology was used not just in the writing, editing, production, and online publication of the Guide, but in the printing as well. The digital era offers publishers a range of options; it is important to realize that no one option is always the best solution. In this case, the initial print edition of the Guide was needed in a quantity of several thousand books, so it made sense to use offset printing (though making full use of modern digital prepress technology). Because Edwards Brothers offers a combination of offset and digital printing, it is possible to optimize the printing technology to suit the circumstances. Subsequent editions of the Guide will be printed in smaller quantities as needed—also from PDF files—at Edwards Brothers' Digital Book Center.

ACKNOWLEDGMENTS

In keeping with the collaborative nature of this project, I would like to thank a number of people instrumental to the process. At Columbia University Press, Stephen Sterns was (and is) the perfect editor for this project: technically knowledgeable (he can read a DTD better than I can), extremely hard working (largely writing the Glossary himself, and working many late nights as the deadline loomed), unfailingly cheerful and supportive, and most important, charged up about the vision of this Guide. Also at Columbia, Linda Secondari championed this project and the very special process needed to produce it from beginning to end, putting together the collaborative team and keeping things moving forward; she was the steady hub around which all the activity revolved. And finally, thanks to James Raimes, who conceived of this book and got the project underway just before his retirement. At Open Book Systems, Laura Fillmore contributed far more than her firm's work on the CMS; her insight and experience played a major role in shaping all aspects of the Guide, and much of its success is due to her creativity and flexibility. Her staff has been wonderful to work with; three deserving special mention are David Cassidy, who managed the project with incredible professionalism and good cheer, and Dee Landergren and Sunny Gleason, who were instrumental in the system design and programming. At Impressions, David Nelson worked tirelessly on the infrastructure, writing and rewriting DTD after DTD as the project took shape and evolved, always striving to make it better. Much of what I know about publishing in the digital era, and especially about XML, I learned from David and his staff; four of them who were particularly helpful on this project were David Niergarth (whose expert review and thoughtful insights were invaluable), Daniel Grossberg (who along with the two Davids contributed significantly to the Bibliography), and Christina Sulkowski and Jason Kivela (who did much of the work on the online examples). The XML composition wizardry was performed by the incomparable Chris Cott. I would also like to thank Christie Pinter and Jennifer Gibeaut, who so ably coordinated the project. And of course most of all, I want to thank the authors who created the content that the Guide was built to convey: they are a stellar group of very knowledgeable, very busy people, and I am extremely grateful for the time they took out of their demanding lives to share their knowledge and their insights with us.

—Bill Kasdorf
November 10, 2002

Introduction: Publishing in Today's Digital Era

WILLIAM E. KASDORF
President, Impressions Book and Journal Services, Inc.

Today, virtually all publishing is digital to some extent, whether content is delivered electronically or in print. But every publishing family is digital in its own way. Some, like journals and reference publishers, have moved so far toward electronic publishing that they are beginning to abandon print. Others, like magazines and catalogs, have focused more on digital production technology and, with newspapers, on integrating workflow for print and online publication. E-books still seem tentative, although they present big advantages, especially to publishers of textbooks and scholarly books. This introduction examines these different sides of publishing today to provide some perspectives on the many aspects of publishing in the digital era that this Guide discusses in depth in subsequent chapters. This overview ends with some suggestions of important technologies that deserve special attention from publishers today.

1.1 DIGITAL PUBLISHING IS BOTH A GIVEN AND A GOAL

The digital revolution in publishing is both overestimated and underappreciated.

When it's compared to the revolution of Gutenberg's time—and that's an apt comparison—expectations are high. Reality can't help but fall short. People scoff at today's e-books and claim they don't want to read on a screen, even though many of us spend a significant portion of our time doing just that. Most of us prefer to read newspapers and magazines on paper, and we can't imagine ever wanting to do otherwise (although our children can, and do), yet we've come to take for granted that the readiest source of information—whether we're looking for a stock price or a statistic, a new shirt or breaking news—is the Web. When we've bought some published content in digital form—a story, a song, a movie, maybe even a book—we expect to be able to enjoy it effortlessly and at no additional cost on any appropriate digital device, existing or yet to be invented, despite the fact that we thought nothing of buying CDs of the very same music that we previously bought on cassette tapes and, before that, on vinyl. To most people today, "digital" implies "free and easy," and whenever we encounter obstacles, whether technological, legal, or commercial, we take it as proof that the digital revolution isn't all it's cracked up to be.

We also fail to appreciate how deeply and broadly the digital revolution has affected the way printed publications are produced. That comforting paper book we love to take to bed or the beach—which we may have found and bought over the Web—was created, most likely, as a word processing file on its author's computer. The book's pages were almost surely typeset digitally, too; but ironically, because all-digital editorial workflows have not yet become universal, there's a good chance that the author's manuscript was edited on paper and scanned or retyped in India or the Philippines—digitally transmitted halfway around the world and back again. Although some books are even printed digitally, most likely the one we take to bed or the beach was printed on an offset press; but all the prepress processes leading up to the ink transferring from plate to paper were digital. The same is true of the newspapers and magazines we read every day; the *New York Times* we read this morning in Ann Arbor or Omaha was a digital file bouncing off a satellite last night, images and all—unless we're in a generation that has come of age with the Web, in which case we more likely read it online.

(i) THE REAL REVOLUTIONS HAVE ALREADY HAPPENED

Although it may feel as if we're witnessing the birth of a new era, the real revolutions have already happened. The most fundamental is the realization that the published content is independent of the physical products that convey it to us. This was always the case, of course; but it was not until the digital era that we fully appreciated that a book or article is not inextricably bound up in the stacks of paper on which we read it. This is profoundly liberating.

There are two essential consequences of this, both involving an explosion of options, a wealth of opportunities: there are many new things to publish, and there are many new ways to publish them.

Even when we just want to publish print pages, the digital revolution offers many ways to do that, and makes those options not as mutually exclusive as they seemed to be in the past. Sometimes, we want to publish the identical pages, with all their typography and images and layout and other graphical features preserved, in a variety of modes—printed by offset, printed digitally, even delivered over the Web to be viewed or printed locally by the recipient. (***PDF***, Adobe's Portable Document Format, is the core technology for that.) Other times, we want to reformat the pages—to publish them in different shapes and sizes, to reflow them in a Web browser or a Palm ***PDA***, perhaps some day to publish them as an e-book, and even to license the content to some other publisher. (***XML***, the Extensible Markup Language, is the core technology for that.) The digital era gives us a never ending set of new modes for publishing our pages—and gives us a new appreciation of the digital files used to create them.

But the digital era also liberates us from the page altogether. We're no longer limited to what can be printed in ink on paper; we're no longer constrained by what can be manufactured, inventoried, sold, and distributed efficiently or economically in physical form. We can include color images when we could only afford to print black and white ones. We can publish works too big or too small to be accommodated by traditional print media. We can include multimedia content where it enhances our publications—an audio clip of Dr. Martin Luther King's "I Have a Dream" speech, a video of a complicated procedure for a surgeon or a chef or an auto repair technician. We can provide supporting data or executable software that not only supports our content but stimulates the creation of more. And perhaps most taken for granted in the electronic environment, we can link our publications to others—continuing to enrich that web of knowledge that is so rapidly enriching us.

1.2 VARIOUS PUBLISHERS, VARIOUS SOLUTIONS

The digital revolution takes various forms—and is proceeding at various paces—for various kinds of publishers. The concerns of trade book publishers are very different from those of textbook publishers; the revolution is very different in the context of magazines as compared to scholarly journals. We read for many reasons: entertainment, instruction, reference, revelation. Doesn't it make sense that there would be many modes in which to publish as well? What the digital revolution gives us, most of all, is an ever-expanding wealth of alternatives. It has opened up a virtually unlimited future. Today's familiar print media—books, magazines, newspapers—are not obsolete; they are being supplemented, not replaced, by new media, and those new media will enable us to publish in new ways. We have entered the most exciting era to work in publishing that the world has ever known.

(i) JOURNALS: THE PROVING GROUND FOR ELECTRONIC PUBLISHING

Many aspects of the digital publishing revolution either originated or were first widely implemented in the field of scholarly—and especially scientific—journal publishing. While legal and reference information-retrieval resources date back to the 1960s and 1970s (today's LexisNexis originated as the Data Corporation in 1966, and Medline, an important medical reference service, started in 1971), the first major print journals were published in full text online in the early 1980s (*Annals of Internal Medicine* and the *New England Journal of Medicine* almost simultaneously in the summer of 1984). That was well before the Web—which, not incidentally, was originally created for the exchange of scientific papers: Tim Berners-Lee began working on creating HTML at CERN, the European particle physics laboratory, in 1989; ***HTTP*** (the transfer protocol the Web is based on) was published in 1990; and ***HTML*** 1.0 was published in 1992.

The chapter **Organizing, Editing, and Linking Content** [4] provides an in-depth discussion of journals in this context; but an overview of the journal experience provides a useful orientation to the subject of publishing in the digital era in general.

1. The problem with print

There are many reasons why journals took the lead in digital publishing and electronic delivery, but there is one fundamental reason: scientists are impatient with print. They want (most would say *need*) to exchange their research rapidly and fluidly. Although many scientists appreciate and respect the well-established processes of print publishing—responsible peer review; thorough editing; professional composition; and printing and publishing in a recognized, reliable, and archival form—that doesn't mean they like them. When these processes are done on paper with analog technologies, they are often frustratingly slow; papers commonly take many months to be published. Physicists were the first to subvert this in a big way: arXiv.org—the Los Alamos E-Print Archive started in 1991 by Paul Ginsparg at Los Alamos and moved to Cornell in 2001 (http://arXiv.org/)—put papers online as soon as they were written. The community of particle physicists came to depend on the speed and ready access to current papers, and the eventual publication of those papers (or some of them), after peer review and editing and professional publishing, became almost an archival function. Most disciplines did not follow the physicists' model; but in almost every discipline journals felt pressure to publish electronically.

2. Awkward economics

A peculiarity of scientific journal publishing (and most scholarly publishing in general) is that the originators and the consumers do not perceive a direct personal compensation or cost. Authors may get prestige or promotions from being published, but they don't get paid; sometimes authors even have to pay "page charges" when their articles are accepted. (The research leading to the article was likely to have been funded by a grant.) Most readers of these papers don't pay for them personally, because they have access through their libraries, their universities, or their labs. These journals are primarily published by two kinds of publishers—big commercial publishers and scholarly societies—and they are primarily paid for by library subscriptions or society memberships.

The skewed economics of this situation breeds resentment on all sides: the commercial publishers are burdened by having to make a profit while publishing both print and electronic versions of their journals; they raise prices, which stresses library budgets, leading to dropped subscriptions (not to mention decimating the budgets for acquiring scholarly monographs); authors and readers—and in a given discipline, the authors *are* the readers—resent having to pay for the results of their own research and think electronic publication should cost little or nothing (despite the fact that printing is a small fraction of the cost of publishing a journal); and the societies, who exist to serve their members, are squeezed in the middle, often without the financial resources and technical expertise—or the clout—of the commercial publishers.

3. Moving from print to electronic publication

Nothing stimulates innovation like stress. Throughout the 1990s journal publishers struggled to find solutions. (Two of the pioneering projects were ***TULIP***, Elsevier's experiment in collaboration with several major universities, and ***Red Sage***, a project led by Springer Verlag in partnership with Bell Labs and the University of San Francisco.) The solutions—the underlying technologies—already existed, for the most part; it was a matter of figuring out how to implement them, how to make them commercially viable, and how to manage the transition from print-only publishing to print-plus-electronic to electronic-only. Whereas in the mid-1990s journal publishers saw electronic publishing as an expensive but necessary burden, by 2002 many of them have come to see *print* as the expensive burden—and sometimes no longer a necessary one.

4. Pioneering SGML

Many of the technologies we use today were first successfully implemented (if not originated) by these publishers. Scientific journal publishers were some of the first major users of ***SGML***, the Standard Generalized Markup Language, which liberated their content from proprietary markup and file formats and enabled it to be exchanged between unrelated systems. The consistency of format and clarity of structure that these journals enjoy helped make this possible—unlike books or magazines, every article in a given journal looks like almost every other, and most such journals from most publishers resemble each other in fundamental ways. On the other hand, some of these journals, full of complex mathematics and tabular material and heavily illustrated layouts, are some of the most difficult publications to produce, whether in print or electronic form; they continue pushing these technologies to evolve. (The

Astrophysical Journal, produced by the University of Chicago Press in an SGML-based workflow since 1994, is a cardinal example: when it came time to publish this journal online in 1995, the Press was able to convert its SGML files programmatically to HTML, publishing this huge and complex journal on the Web in three weeks at little additional cost.) Today, more than any other area of publishing, journals have widely implemented SGML or its successor technology, XML.

5. Pricing and delivery models

Journals pioneered some of the commercial aspects of the digital revolution as well. They experimented with a variety of pricing and delivery models. While they were developing and implementing SGML- and XML-based infrastructures, they made PDFs of their print pages available electronically; even as full text became available as HTML (ideally, generated from an SGML or XML source), PDFs continue to be a popular option because the user can print out the paper in exactly the form in which it appears in the print journal. Some journals make it possible to buy individual articles; some provide electronic access along with a print subscription; some charge extra for electronic access, some don't; many offer electronic-only subscriptions; and some big publishers have experimented with "big deals" to libraries where for a fixed price (often tied to the library's existing print subscriptions) they get access to many or all of a publisher's journals in electronic form (but not print).

Because journals are historically subscription-based, that model has succeeded. During the dot-com mania of the late 1990s, when many ambitious but now vanished ventures were giving away content for free to attract "eyeballs" and hoped-for advertising revenue, scholarly journals were quietly making a go of it. Today, most journals are available electronically by subscription; many users, especially scientific ones, no longer even want the printed copies; and some of these publishers are making plans to phase out print altogether. Most are also aggressively digitizing their back issues—sometimes only as scanned images, others as full text SGML or XML—with the goal of making not only recent literature but the historical record of each discipline electronically available. The result is that in the field of scholarly journals an astonishing amount of content has been made accessible online in an amazingly short time.

6. Making access ubiquitous

As more journals have become available electronically, users expect not only to access them but to *find* them electronically as well. Commercial publishers have created services for aggregating not only their own electronic content, but that of other publishers; third party aggregators offer a range of electronic services to publishers (one of the most prominent, HighWire, originated at the Stanford University Library—an early example of libraries becoming more actively involved in the publishing process, a trend that will accelerate in the coming years); and abstracting and indexing services provide bibliographic information to huge numbers of scholarly publications. As these venues and services proliferate, users expect not only to be able to link to other resources within a publication or a collection, but between publications: they want to click on a reference at the end of one journal article and link immediately to the cited paper, no matter when or where it was published.

1. DOI AND CROSSREF

Two other important innovations grew out of this: the Digital Object Identifier (***DOI***) and ***CrossRef***. The DOI is a way to permanently and unambiguously identify any kind of digital content (unlike a URL, which can be unstable and ambiguous) and to provide a "discovery mechanism" for locating the owner of the rights to that content (even if ownership changes over time). Scholarly journal publishers were the main driving force behind the development of the DOI and the first major users of it. The use of the DOI in journals really exploded with the creation of CrossRef, an innovative collaboration between a number of leading publishers to create a cross-publisher linking mechanism. Publishers participating in CrossRef use the DOI to identify their own published articles and provide metadata "headers" which enable these articles to be searched for systematically; and they retrieve from CrossRef the DOIs of other publishers' papers that are *cited* in their publications and embed them in the reference sections at the ends of the articles. CrossRef provides the mechanism for linking up the reference and the cited article. First implemented for scholarly journals—and including nearly five million articles in its first two years—CrossRef has been expanded to accommodate reference, book, and other content as well.

7. It's real

Anyone doubting whether electronic publishing is viable need only look at scholarly journals to realize that it is very emphatically here to stay.

(ii) MAGAZINES AND CATALOGS: WHERE GRAPHICS BECAME DIGITAL

Just as many aspects of electronic *publishing* technology first succeeded in the context of scientific journals, catalogs and magazines (and the advertisements appearing in them) drove the development of digital *production* technology. Although the benefits of the progress made by electronic journals are yet to be widely felt outside that world, the changes in production technology first widely used for magazines and catalogs (and commercial printing in general) have had an enormous impact on almost every kind of publishing. Tools now taken for granted by writers of term papers and holiday letters were beyond the reach of all but the most professional publishers and their suppliers before the mid-1980s. The result is a dramatic decrease in the costs needed to achieve dramatically increased quality and sophistication.

1. PostScript + PC = DTP

The technology at the heart of this production revolution (though not the only one) is ***PostScript***; and what made that technology able to proliferate so widely was the development of the personal computer. PostScript and the personal computer were the foundation of the desktop publishing revolution of the late 1980s. (The chapter on **composition and graphics** [6] discusses this subject in detail.)

Before desktop publishing, creating a page of a magazine or a catalog was a complex process requiring a labor-intensive workflow involving highly trained specialists working on expensive equipment performing very discrete tasks. Now, although the best pages are still produced by professionals, those artists use tools costing a tenth or even a hundredth as much—and able to do much more, much faster. And amateurs can use the same tools.

2. A whole new way to work

This has obviously simplified and democratized the process of producing pages; but, most important from the professional point of view, it has *lubricated* the process. Artists no longer have to sketch type and layouts, then spec type and photos and wait for proofs to be delivered, and then cut and paste these into pages—and wish there were time to change the style of a headline or the size of an image, but having to make do with what's in hand. Now, pages are designed with real type, over which the artist has complete control, and real images, which the artist can resize to her heart's content. She can perform almost any conceivable graphic manipulation of the elements on her page, creating effects beyond the budgets and even the capabilities of the pre-PostScript world. A case in point: a good quality scanner can be purchased today for less than half what it cost to buy just one film color separation of a photograph twenty years ago—and the software to manipulate the images acquired from that scanner is on every artist's desktop, able to achieve results that would have required a $250,000 system in 1985.

3. It's all about print

More than most other areas of publishing, magazines and catalogs are especially print-centric. They exist not just to *say* but to *show:* the visual aspects of their pages are essential to what they are all about. Their publishers constantly strive for new eye-catching effects; they struggle for just the right shade of red in a pair of lips or a plate of cherry pie, the right font to express a feeling or a point of view; they plan the flow from page to page to page, from image to text, from article to ad. They need to be able to change their minds about any of these things at the last minute. And they need to trust that once they have everything just right, nothing can go wrong with those lovely pages.

This is a tall order. It used to be simply impossible. But there's one other thing magazines and catalogs have that most other kinds of publishing lack: money. That comes from the huge audiences some of them enjoy. Major magazines are printed in the millions, and companies spend many thousands of dollars to place ads in them; they want those ads to look perfect. Those lips can't look too pink or too purple; they can't look even a little bit pink or purple. Big catalogs are printed in the millions, too; when the plate is on the press but the supplier of the sweater on the cover calls to say that they can't deliver, the presses stop and the cover gets re-designed. Fast. And the color of the new sweater that gets featured instead had better be exactly right, or returns will be devastating. Digital technology made this possible—and practical.

Not every magazine or catalog publisher has a huge budget, of course. But this is a case where everybody wins: the needs and resources of the big players have benefited the little ones. The technologies to create those beautiful pages and punch up the color in those dazzling images and stabilize the proofing and printing processes required huge investments at first, but once the fundamental technological problems had been solved the solutions proliferated rapidly to shrink-wrapped software accessible to almost anybody.

What are some of these technological improvements?

- *Fonts and font technology*—now thousands of fonts are widely available, and new fonts can easily be created or customized.
- *Scanning technology*—capturing ever better image data at ever lower costs.
- *Page layout software*—desktop publishing puts professional tools on almost any Mac or PC.
- *Illustration and image manipulation*—led by Adobe's Illustrator and Photoshop.
- *PostScript and PDF*—sophisticated page description languages that enable pages to be viewed on monitors, printed out on laser printers, and put through professional prepress workflows without the application programs that created them.
- *Color management systems and standards*—resulting in more reliable rendering of colors on monitors, on proofing systems, and in the pressroom.

- *Proofers and printers*—producing photographic quality images on ink-jets, enabling proofing of color without traditional film proofs.

These technologies and many others—discussed in depth in the chapter on **composition and graphics** [6]—are widely available and unbelievably accessible, both in terms of cost and in terms of usability. They can't make an amateur automatically produce professional results, of course; but they make it so much easier for both the amateur and the professional to produce the best results they're capable of. The tools virtually never hold us back, if we know what they are and how to use them.

4. What about electronic publishing?

Magazines have been slow to develop on the Web—partly for technical reasons (it's hard to reproduce the magazine-reading experience online, especially for a graphically sophisticated magazine dependent on page-flipping, although the new Zinio system does just that) and partly for commercial ones (the combination of the early expectation that content on the Web should be free coupled with the failure of Web advertising to meet admittedly overblown expectations). Plus, Web users expect interactivity and rich linking; the systematic approach that worked for scientific journals doesn't work in the fast-paced deal-dominated environment of magazine publishing.

Catalogs, on the other hand, are ideal for the Web. Whereas print pages have physical limitations—for example, the bigger the pictures or the longer the descriptions, the fewer items can fit on a page—the Web enables an almost endlessly layered structure that lets users "drill down" from initial browsing to more and more in-depth information to an actual ordering and payment mechanism. Once past people's initial wariness of making payments over the Web—and we have the pioneering merchants like Amazon.com (who started with books) to thank for that—the Web captures an impulse and an order much more effectively than a print catalog can. Not only that, it has the ability to link to related items—other books by the same author, a shirt that goes with the chosen sweater—and to get to "know" an individual customer's preferences. Most importantly, it offers the ability to customize and update: that sweater on the cover suddenly unavailable from the factory is gone with a few keystrokes; the overstock of purple parkas can get marked down in March, further still in April, and on and on until they're sold. Many of the advances in e-commerce have come out of contexts like these.

1. PRINT PRODUCTION TOOLS FOR ONLINE USES

Some of the digital technologies developed to improve the production of print pages have turned out to be extremely useful in electronic publishing as well. The tools used to manipulate images for print can also be used to manipulate them for the screen; although the designer of the print page may produce a high-resolution image optimized for offset printing and the designer of the Web page may tweak the image for the screen, they probably both use Photoshop. Common desktop programs like Photoshop and Illustrator enable images to be created in saved in a variety of formats for either print or online use. Although Adobe's Acrobat software started out as a program for exchanging office documents, its first great success was producing a print page format, PDF, that is now a common method of displaying pages online as well. It would be incorrect to attribute all of this to magazine and catalog publishing, of course; but the demands of those markets were the major force behind many of these technologies in the first place.

5. Content management and digital asset management

Magazines and catalogs were also the two areas of publishing most responsible for the advances in technologies for managing digital assets. Even when limited to the print world, they need to keep track of an enormous number of images, for example; when these images came to exist only in digital form, systems were necessary to organize, store, browse, search, and access them—along with key information about them. The catalog publisher needs to quickly locate the right picture of that purple parka by product number; the magazine publisher may need to find a picture of mountains in Peru, choose among several available, and make sure the proper rights to that image are secured. These needs led to the development of **digital asset management** [6.12.12] systems (DAM). As the workflow for producing catalogs and magazines became more digital, it became necessary to keep track not just of images but Word files or Quark files or XML files—perhaps even managing the flow of articles throughout the editorial and production process. And as these publications needed to be produced not just for print but online as well, systems for automating the generation of HTML and for keeping a Web site up to date needed to be developed. (The corporate market was also instrumental in this latter development, streamlining the production and maintenance of corporate Web sites.) We now enjoy a wide range of content management technologies—as discussed in detail in the chapter **Content Management and Web Publishing** [10].

(iii) TEXTBOOKS: A TOUGH TRANSITION TO ELECTRONIC PUBLISHING

Textbooks seem to be obvious candidates as e-books. They are extremely expensive to produce: especially as a result of the intense competition between publishers of major school and college textbooks through the 1980s and 1990s, such textbooks require lavish use of color, elaborate layouts, and a wealth of ancillary materials for students and teachers. Plus, they are big, typically many hundreds of pages long, and are printed in very large quantities—making the manufacturing, warehousing, and distribution of them a challenge. Not only is this a huge investment for a textbook publisher, it is a risky one. A paragraph offending an interest group in a key state can kill the adoption of a major school textbook, resulting in the loss of millions of dollars in sales. A competing textbook even a year or two more up-to-date can be a big threat. Finally, there is the timing issue: despite the fact that it is a long-term team effort to get most textbooks to market, that market is very seasonal and driven by critical dates; being available at the right time in the right quantities can make or break a textbook's success.

Electronic publishing addresses a lot of these issues. Color doesn't cost extra in the electronic world. Size doesn't matter as much: the "manufacturing" cost of an electronic book doesn't increase as the length of the book does (although of course editorial and production costs do), and even very large electronic books don't add any weight to students' already-overburdened backpacks. They can be searched electronically, for more effective study. They can be linked to outside resources, dynamically broadening their scope. They can even be supplemented by multimedia content—that audio clip of King's "I Have a Dream" speech, the demonstration of a lab procedure, a molecule rendered in 3-D. They require no physical inventory, carry no risk of making more copies than will be sold, have minimal storage and distribution costs, and they can be delivered instantly to the end user. They can be issued in versions for people with various forms of disabilities—as the chapter **Accessibility** [7] points out, state and federal accessibility requirements will have their first major effects on textbook publishers. Most important, they can be updated and customized relatively easily. This raises obvious ethical issues—is it okay to edit one paragraph for Texas, a different one for California?—but obvious opportunities as well, foremost the ability to tailor a textbook to a school's or an individual professor's specific needs.

1. The obstacles to electronic publishing

Why, then, haven't textbooks taken off yet electronically? The fundamental issue is the turning-the-battleship problem. Producing a major textbook is a major undertaking. It involves a large number of people working over a long span of time and requires major investment. This is true not only for the publisher itself but also for a host of suppliers and partners involved in developing, editing, producing, manufacturing, marketing, and distributing textbooks. In this environment, electronic publishing is a disruptive technology. The participants in the process have well-established infrastructures, staffs, and workflows; there are well-established expectations of what each will be provided to work with and what each is required to provide; and there are well-established cost and price structures. Turning this battleship in the direction of electronic publishing is not easily done.

There are other reasons as well. The nature of the textbooks themselves is an obstacle. Many of these books are extremely complex in structure, full of sidebars and exercises and tips and questions for study; this is much harder to express in an XML DTD than it is to do so for a journal article or an encyclopedia entry or a chapter of a scholarly monograph. Moreover, major textbooks tend to be highly designed, with a premium on originality—they are not cookie-cutter production tasks, so they are much harder to automate and to translate into various presentation media. PDF might seem to be the obvious solution (and for many textbooks it is); but even when a publisher can simply make PDFs of the pages created for print, the issues of rights and security flare up. With the huge investments involved in textbooks, their publishers are rightfully cautious about releasing them in a form that might easily be copied and pirated or given away.

None of these problems is insurmountable; in fact, the solutions to many of them already exist. It will take some time to turn this battleship, but it will eventually happen, and it will be worth the trouble. The problems associated with large print textbooks and the appeal of the solutions offered by electronic publishing are too compelling. And although the market may fluctuate as baby booms and boomlets move through the schools and colleges, the market for these books will always be a large and important one, even expanding as it encompasses other aspects of continuing education and training. At this writing no major textbook publisher would say they've accomplished the transition, but it is also safe to say that every one of them is convinced that it is essential to do so and is in the process of figuring out how.

2. Custom publishing and coursepacks

One area where textbook publishers have pioneered is in the creation of custom versions. Until recently, these have usually been in print form, and the technology used to produce them has largely not been digital in any meaningful way. This is primarily a college phenomenon, originating with the practice of professors providing photocopies of book chapters, journal articles, notes, and other resources for their courses. A small industry grew up on college campuses to provide these "***coursepacks***," which are usually produced by local copy shops. Some have done so responsibly, requesting and paying for permission from the original publishers to reproduce the various components. Others have not, and this has led to some of the key rights battles in the industry—battles that continue to the present day. A famous case in the late 1990s drove the leading copy shop chain, Kinko's, out of the coursepack business; it was too much trouble to track down and pay for the rights, and the legal liability for not doing so was too great. But the need is still there: professors want to shape their courses to their own visions, and thus don't always want to use a textbook in its entirety or in exactly the sequence the publisher intended. And they need to supplement the textbook with other relevant readings.

The major textbook publishers saw a big opportunity in this. Most of them have a wealth of material from which to draw: textbooks in related fields or at different levels, other books or publications offering relevant material. The pioneering venture of this sort was one begun in 1990 and still maintained by McGraw-Hill called Primis (http://www.mhhe.com/primis/)—an ambitious enterprise for producing custom textbooks tailored to individual college courses, based on a large repository of digital content from which professors can pick and choose. Other publishers followed this lead, and the technology gradually evolved to help it along—especially the development of PDF, which allowed stable digital page images to be stored and recombined easily.

The first custom textbooks were really glorified coursepacks; the pages were unaltered from their original form—with the exception, perhaps, of new page numbers. A better solution would be a true custom textbook, where the fifth chapter would be numbered "Chapter 5" even if it had been Chapter 8 in the original publication, and all references to chapter numbers would be updated (e.g., "see Figure 8.3" would become "see Figure 5.3," and the number on the figure itself would be changed, too). This is far from trivial; and the more you delve into the implications of real customization the more complicated it becomes.

The ultimate solution to this, of course, is to have richly tagged ***XML*** files with stylesheets to enable the automatic revision and reformatting of the pages as desired. That way, when the professor wants to eliminate only Section 2 of Chapter 6, not the whole chapter, or wants to add two more learning objectives to the list at the head of the chapter, she can. And of course, the resulting custom books can be published electronically even more easily than in printed form: the ability to customize is one of the most compelling factors pushing textbook publishing in an electronic direction. This is another case where many of the solutions to the problems are already available, but it will take quite some time to make them a practical reality. Once editorial and production workflows make the transition to XML, these advances will be much easier to accomplish; but in the current environment, where much editing is still done on paper and most pages are composed in QuarkXPress, they seem like a pipedream.

(iv) SCHOLARLY MONOGRAPHS: SAVED BY PRINT-ON-DEMAND AND E-BOOKS

The scholarly monograph is widely considered to be the most endangered species in publishing. Although it is the primary mode by which scholarship is communicated outside the sciences (where journal articles rule)—offering a scholar the space for an extended consideration of a subject, thoroughly researched, meticulously documented, thoughtfully examined, and compellingly argued—the monograph has become almost impossible to sustain economically in its traditional form. These books are caught in a vise, pressed on one side by increasing editorial, production, and manufacturing costs and on the other by diminishing demand. Libraries, already squeezed by declining budgets and rising journal prices, find it hard to justify acquiring monographs of interest primarily to a handful of specialists. Many of these titles are published in quantities of less than a thousand—and sold in quantities of a few hundred, leaving hundreds of copies to take up inventory space and tie up capital for years.

Most monographs are published by university presses (augmented by a few brave commercial scholarly houses). In the past, these presses were seen as essential parts of their universities' missions, advancing scholarship by publishing books that might not be commercially viable but which were intellectually vital. Far from being vanity presses for the local faculty, most of these presses had—and have—an idealism, a seriousness of purpose, that sets them apart from their more commercial colleagues. They publish important books, and they often publish them elegantly (these are some of the typographically finest books published). But through the 1970s and 1980s these presses endured not only the shrinking of library budgets but the shrinking of subsidies from their parent institutions as well. They were like the well-bred sons and daughters of the gentry forced to open the manor house to the public: they suddenly had to pay their way. They rolled up their sleeves and rose to the occasion, developing excellent lines of regional titles, trade books, midlist books given short shrift by the big bestseller-obsessed trade houses—and still struggled to bring out those important monographs when they knew full well they'd be lucky to sell 300 copies of some of them.

Digital technology came along in the nick of time. Although at present we are in the early stages of the transition, the solutions are clear: print-on-demand and e-books.

1. Print-on-demand

The demand for scholarly monographs may be small, but it can be intense. Maybe only 300–500 people will ever read a given title; but of those, there might be 100–200 who absolutely *must* read it. In fact, they may not just need to read it (which they could do in a library) but need to own it—so they can scribble disagreements in the margins, and fold down corners, and pull it from their bookshelves to refer to or lend to a colleague or a student.

This is a perfect situation for print-on-demand (***POD***, discussed in detail in the chapter **Digital Printing** [8]). POD is based on digital printing, which evolved out of copier technology. Unlike offset printing (which is how most monographs are printed), digital presses do not use a plate with a fixed image on it which is then duplicated on paper; instead, each page is, in a sense, an original, imaged from a digital file. (They can be thought of as large, high-speed, high-volume laser printers.) Although their cost to print each page is higher than that of offset printing when the latter produces sufficient quantities, their cost to print the first copy—because they have virtually no setup costs—is very close to their cost to print the fiftieth or the five-hundredth. Offset, on the other hand, requires at least a few hundred copies to cover its setup costs, and most publishers find that they need to order one or two thousand copies to achieve viable unit costs for a monograph. What this means is that scholarly publishers typically print that many, sell the first few hundred, and keep the rest in inventory in the hope that they will eventually sell out. But many such books don't come close.

Print-on-demand enables these publishers to print either in very low quantities (just as many as they realistically can sell at a given time) or literally one-by-one as the orders come in. True, the unit costs of these books are typically higher than those of the offset printed books in inventory. But they have not tied up capital, space, or other resources; the publisher has not risked costs beyond the editorial and production costs. And because the monograph's small market may be so committed, the publisher may be able to charge a premium. (This is most common for scientific and medical monographs, which can sometimes sell for very high prices.) Certainly this doesn't mean that these monographs are cheap to produce; their editorial and production costs are as high as ever, which means a certain income still needs to be achieved. What print-on-demand accomplishes most in this context is that it allocates the manufacturing costs appropriately, minimizing waste and not requiring the publisher to risk money second guessing a very unpredictable market. It also allows the publisher to keep the books "in print" forever; there is no point in calling a book out of print when there's no cost to keeping it alive and when there's a profit, if a small one, every time a copy is bought.

2. E-books

Although print-on-demand may offer an immediate way for publishers to cut their risk on monographs while continuing to offer them in their traditional form, the ultimate solution to the monograph dilemma is likely to be ***e-books***.

Unlike textbooks, monographs are generally simple in format and structure, making it easy to adapt them to various devices or technologies. They're relatively small, so the cost to create an "electronic master" is low. (Ideally, this would be XML from which various outputs, especially ***OEBPS***, the Open e-Book Publication Structure, can be generated. See the chapter **Electronic Books and the Open eBook Publication Structure** [11] for an in-depth discussion of this.) They cost little to store and distribute. They can easily be adapted to new technologies that become available. Libraries are becoming increasingly adept with electronic resources. And because their market is so small, monographs are less threatened by piracy than most other kinds of books are. If the publisher can make a profit selling a few hundred at an accessible price to libraries and the scholars in the field, there is little expectation of additional sales to be undermined. That is not to say these publishers won't be concerned about rights, but they will be more willing to take the plunge because the benefits outweigh the risks.

The resistance to reading monographs on screen is likely to decline as display technologies improve and as more and more scholarship is available electronically. Scholars increasingly do research online; in fact, the time is not far off when those who read monographs will *expect* them to be available in electronic form and accessible online, just as scholarly journal readers do now. Not only will this make them more "discoverable," it will make them more useful as well. Scholars don't just read, they study; they take notes, they document and annotate, they perceive links to related works and need to cite them; and they quote from the works they study. All of these things are easier to do when the book is in electronic form than when it is only in print.

A few far-sighted scholarly publishers have begun testing the waters with e-books. Some university presses have made a good number of their books available through netLibrary, one of the near casualties of the dot-com debacle, which was rescued by OCLC, a library consortium. Baker and Taylor, a leading distributor of scholarly books, is also beginning to distribute e-books. Ebrary and Questia offer services and systems that are well suited to scholarly monographs. Some university presses are teaming up with their university library systems to make monographs accessible electronically to their university communities. The National Academy of Sciences has long made the full text of all its titles available electronically, and has found that this has actually stimulated the sales of print books. Because many scholarly monographs are relatively obscure and don't warrant much marketing, making them available online can be a huge boost: rather than languishing in the stacks and the catalogs of a couple hundred libraries, they are suddenly visible to anybody searching for their subject matter online. More than anything else, this is likely to save the day for the scholarly monograph.

(v) TRADE BOOKS: THE RIGHTS BATTLEGROUND

If scholarly monographs are relatively easy to turn into e-books, most trade books are easier still. Certainly fiction is as easy as it gets: sometimes, the only tags needed are for chapter numbers and paragraphs and an italic word here and there. Many non-fiction titles are almost that easy; not only do they have simple structures, their users have simple expectations. Whereas the scholar wants to annotate and search and link, most readers of trade books simply want to read. These books have relatively large markets, too, making it worth the risk to invest in a new way to publish them—especially when that new way virtually eliminates manufacturing, inventory, and distribution costs.

1. E-book trials, failures, and partial successes

Certainly the present inability to widely publish trade books electronically is not due to lack of trying. Since well before the Web, the dream of a device the size of a paperback that could hold a number of interchangeable titles and display them conveniently has been a compelling one. Progress has proceeded in fits and starts, often stirred by the introduction of a specific device or technology—the Sony Bookman in 1991, the Softbook and the Rocket eBook in 1998, Glassbook in 1999 (now part of the Adobe eBook Reader), Franklin's eBookman and Microsoft's big splash with its Reader in 2000, Adobe's PDF-based eBook Reader in 2001—only to wane as the public seemed not to be very interested.

Actually, as the chapter on **e-books** [11] discusses, many of the common objections to e-books are not the obstacles they seem to be. As more of us begin to take reading on a screen for granted, and as those screens improve (especially as e-paper displays roll out), the likelihood of our wanting to read on a laptop or a PDA or some other device will grow. And of course the perception that e-books have not succeeded ignores the many areas where they have: in reference books, guidebooks, computer books, and certain trade areas like science fiction, e-books, especially on Palm devices, have developed a significant audience that appears to have growth potential. A huge number of public-domain books, from classic literature to obscure popular literature of the past, has been published in e-book form, led by Project Gutenberg and the University of Virginia's Electronic Text Center. The Open eBook Forum continues to advance standards, reducing the risk of producing e-books in a format that might fail in the marketplace. Most publishers, especially the largest, expect it to be only a matter of time before they are able to sell many titles as e-books.

2. Wrangling over rights

Nevertheless, it's undeniable that e-books have not caught on in the mainstream. Certainly, a key factor is that the broad public does not yet have a device and a display technology that it finds sufficiently compelling or convenient to use for pleasure reading. Another important factor, however, is the rights issue. Trade book authors actually make a living—or at least some meaningful income—from what they write, and what they earn is based on their books' success in the marketplace, whereas royalty income for authors of most non-trade works is secondary income, if it exists at all. And publishing trade books is a bigger gamble than most other publishing: many books struggle to make a profit; even big bestsellers sometimes fail to produce much return after costs for advances, marketing, manufacturing, and distribution are covered. Trade publishers make a disproportionately large part of their profit from a disproportionately small number of their titles. The authors and publishers of these books have a lot to gain and a lot to lose. Protecting copyright is critical to them.

1. AUTHORS VS. PUBLISHERS

The battle first starts between the authors and the publishers themselves. Despite the fact that they are so dependent on each other, they often act more like adversaries than allies. The chapter **The Legal Framework** [13] discusses two important recent cases: the *Tasini* case (in which periodical publishers were prevented from licensing content to new collective works published as electronic databases when they had not explicitly obtained that right from the writers) and the *Rosetta Books* case (in which book publishers who had obtained the rights to publish works "in book form" were judged not to have the right to publish them in e-book form unless the contracts specifically said so). Now that the publishing landscape has become so complex, contracts have, too; authors and publishers now rarely neglect to spell out electronic rights.

This is not as simple as it might seem. When most of the income from a book comes from the sales of the print edition, and when most publishers do not yet have an internal mechanism to market and sell electronic versions, electronic sales are often treated as ancillary income like subsidiary rights, foreign sales, etc., which are usually split fifty-fifty between author and publisher. This won't work if most of the income comes from electronic sales. Although this is not an immediate prospect for most trade books today, authors and publishers are distinctly aware of the potential. It will take a while for the economics of this to get sorted out; in the meantime, coming up with contracts that satisfy both parties is a struggle.

2. PUBLISHERS VS. READERS

From there, the battle moves to a new front: between the publisher and its customers. In the past, before the distinction between content and its physical manifestation was so clear, publishers seemed to be selling products—books.

They manufactured them, marketed them, shipped them to retailers, and sold them. The purchasers "owned" them—at least the copy they had bought—and could lend it, give it away, or sell it to somebody. (They couldn't copy the whole book and sell it or give it away, though.) If the purchaser happened to be a library, the whole point was lending the book; but it could only lend that single copy, and was trusted not to let people photocopy more than a few pages at a time.

3. THE PERFECT COPY PROBLEM

Electronic publishing undermines all this because it makes it so easy to create and distribute a perfect copy of the whole book. Photocopying a print book has been possible for decades, but it's not worth the trouble: it results in an inferior copy that can cost more than simply buying the "real" book. Libraries exist to lend books, but they buy multiple copies of those they lend frequently. And although the resale of used books has always undermined the publisher (and the author, who gets no royalty), it wasn't much of an issue except to textbook publishers until the Web made it so easy to connect buyers and sellers. Now, what publishers fear most is "Bookster," a book-industry repeat of the music industry's Napster debacle: the widespread exchange of digital copies of books between individuals, and an ensuing battle that makes the publisher's customer its enemy. In this climate, it is somewhat of a relief that there is not yet an e-book format as convenient and universal as MP3 is for music.

Of course that's exactly what readers want—the book equivalent of MP3. Not that most trade books won't continue to be sold in print; it's hard to beat the pleasure of reading a well-designed printed book, and they look so nice on bookshelves and coffee tables. But there is no doubt that there would be a demand for them electronically as well, especially with a convenient medium that readers could use at their discretion. The physicality of a nice thick book that is such a pleasure in a chair by the fire is a problem to lug on a plane; and a backlit e-book with an adjustable font size is actually easier to read in bed. Wouldn't it be nice to leave that lovely print copy on the coffee table and take a digital copy on a trip?

4. LEARNING HOW TO *MANAGE* DIGITAL RIGHTS

This is what digital rights management is all about. Physical copies can be owned, but digital copies must be licensed. Rather than buying a copy of a book, the reader of the future will likely buy certain rights, ideally similar to the rights commonly associated with the physical book: the right to lend the book (but not duplicate it), the right to sell it (at which point rights pass from seller to buyer), and so forth. As the chapter **Digital Rights Management** [15]-

(***DRM***) discusses, many of the mechanisms to do this have already been created.

In fact, the digital world offers appealing options not possible in print. Wouldn't it be good for a publisher if a reader were able to lend a friend a *copy* of a book, as long as that copy carried with it a purchase mechanism, perhaps with the ability to be viewed for free for a short time? That sort of viral marketing could be a bonanza for some books—and with some DRM technologies, it's possible today. Wouldn't it be good for a reader if the copy bought for one device (perhaps a laptop) could be transferred to another device (like a PDA), and if the book would be able to adapt to the capabilities of each of those devices? (That's what the Open eBook Publication Structure is working to make possible.) Wouldn't it be nice if the publisher could sell and the reader could buy whatever rights were appropriate for a given situation—to read for a short time, to read perpetually but not copy and print, to make encrypted copies, to make pass-along copies, etc.?

It is not inconceivable that at some point in the not too distant future every print book will be available in digital form as well. As publishers move to all-digital workflows, especially those based on XML and OeB, the obstacles will not be as much technical as commercial and legal. The next few years will see if publishers succeed in implementing good pricing models and DRM solutions (with a fair price and a convenient mechanism, most readers won't steal); if they do, the result could be a book trade that is both more dynamic and more profitable than the one we have today.

(vi) REFERENCE: WHERE METADATA MATTERS MOST

The most obvious segment of publishing to benefit from electronic access is reference publishing—and indeed, reference publishers were the pioneers, some of them selling electronic access long before the Web was born. More than any other kind of publisher, they sell pure information; liberating that information from physical constraints, though certainly disruptive, has enormous benefits. Even in the days when that information could only be displayed as plain text on a monochrome screen, the ability to zero in on just the right chunk of information was a compelling case for the computer. Of course many reference books—especially encyclopedias designed for school and public libraries—are still published in print; but their publishers either already offer electronic versions or plan to. And many reference works, from encyclopedias and dictionaries to legal, medical, and scientific references, are now available only electronically.

1. Isn't it all free on the Web?

In fact, many people assume it is reference publishers who are the endangered species. Isn't everything available on the Web these days? Now that "google" has become a verb, can't you find pretty much anything you want in a flash, and for free? The answers, of course, are "no" and "no." One problem is that there is *too much* information on the Web; despite the sophistication of the best portals, and despite users' increasing ability to refine their search criteria, unmediated searching on the Web—while a wonderful way to find a lot of information—is not the best way to find everything you need to know. Another problem is that what you find on the Web is not always reliable—or understandable. Sometimes it is worth paying for information that is especially trusted, or especially current, or presented in an especially useful way.

2. Metadata makes it really work

The task for reference publishers is to make the information they sell ever more useful to their customers. Note that this implies a process: static information withers and dies. To thrive, it must be continually updated and enriched. That means updating the content itself over time; but it also means updating information *about* that content, including its internal and external relationships (cross-references, links). The key to this is metadata—information about the published content. (Metadata is discussed in the chapters on **markup** [3] and on **organizing, editing, and linking** [4].)

Metadata is increasingly important to all kinds of publishing, of course; but it is critical to reference publishing. Reference works are typically highly granular: they are composed of a large number of small chunks of information, sometimes tied together in a narrative flow (as this Guide is), sometimes not (like a dictionary or a gazetteer). To access these chunks efficiently, it is necessary first to uniquely identify them; metadata (often in the form of "dumb number" IDs—which can easily become DOIs) is used for this. It is also useful to describe them: to classify them according to a fixed set of categories (historical periods, geographical areas, fields of study) or a controlled vocabulary (facilitating systematic search and analysis), or by using a more free-form description like keywords. Relationships between the chunks are important to delineate: sequential relationships, cause-and-effect relationships, parent/child relationships, and so forth. How does the given body of information being published relate to external resources—are there sources to be cited, or resources for further study? Metadata is used for all of these purposes. It's also used for activities "under the hood," not directly accessed by a user: recording the origin of the information and documenting when it was edited, and by whom; perhaps grouping it into various saleable categories or "virtual products"; keeping track of rights and permissions; and managing the myriad details having to do with the access and sale of the information.

3. Adding intelligence adds value

Reference publishers are realizing that their metadata can be as valuable as the published content it describes. When done well (which usually involves people knowledgeable about the subject matter), it can provide a significant competitive advantage, making that content much more accessible and useful. But the job is never finished: unlike more ephemeral publications (which don't last long enough to warrant updating or augmenting) or more archival ones (once a journal article or a book chapter is published, it's not likely to change), reference publications must change or die—and that means their metadata must be continually updated and enriched. Plus, it is impossible, except for very simple sorts of publications, to scope out everything up front: new categories and classifications and keywords will emerge, the need for new links will become apparent.

Fortunately, ***XML***, the Extensible Markup Language, and its related technologies (especially ***XLink***, ***XPointer***, and ***XPath***—all of which are described in the chapter on **markup** [3.3]) are designed to accommodate this. Not only do they make it easier for the published content to change over time (compared to when it was locked up in proprietary databases or markup schemes), they are designed to adapt to future changes in technology and information science tools and techniques. Far from being a perilous time to be a reference publisher, this turns out to be a particularly good time to be one.

(vii) NEWSPAPERS: PUTTING IT ALL TOGETHER

Newspapers are so complex and are produced with such speed that it's a miracle they can be done at all. They deliver an amazing assortment of information: international, national, and local news; advertisements ranging from a cashmere sweater at a classy boutique to the price of peaches in the local supermarket; feature articles and entertainment, from science to sports, from fashion to the Sunday comics; an amalgam of "who, what, and where" information of interest to their communities, from school board and city council meetings to movie listings to the holiday schedule for trash pickup; classified ads for people looking for jobs, cars, or companionship; and much more. Imagine the varied sources of all that information, the varied ways it's structured and presented, and the varied audiences it's aimed at. Plus, it's very time sensitive: not only can't a paper get by with publishing yesterday's news, the ads are timely too—the price of those peaches was picked more recently than the peaches themselves were.

Just keeping track of all that is a daunting task; actually writing, editing, illustrating, typesetting, and assembling it so all the pieces fit together to make the paper day after day is amazing. And the result is very much "a paper"—

the printed format is by no means accidental or incidental. Readers want to flip to the sports or the TV listings without having to wonder where they'll be that day; advertisers depend on the news and information being mixed with their ads to pull readers through, page by page. Although much of the information in the paper (especially "look up" features like movie listings or classified ads) translates well to the electronic medium, the display ads don't—they're too easy to skip. Yet the pressure for newspapers to publish online is great: not only does it offer the ability to stay virtually up-to-the-minute, it also helps them fulfill their missions as the central source of information for their local communities.

1. Digital technology makes it easier, not more complicated

The good news is that some of the leading advances in digital publishing and production have come in the newspaper industry. After a rocky transition from the days of hot-metal composition on Linotypes to photocomposition and offset printing, newspapers have capitalized more effectively on the advances offered by digital technology. Digital photography was a natural, for example. Once that technology reached an adequate level of quality and cost, film-based photography seemed to disappear almost overnight. Today, virtually all pictures in the newspaper are shot on digital cameras, transmitted from almost anywhere in the world. Text is acquired digitally too, of course; ***NewsML*** was one of the first concrete applications of XML to be widely used, and standards like ***ICE*** help smooth the handling of syndicated stories. The ads are digital as well; standards like ***TIFF/IT*** and ***PDF/X*** make it easier to trust that they'll come out right when there's no time to see a proof.

2. Beyond managing content to managing workflow

The most significant advance, however, has been in the development of true digital workflows. Although magazines and catalogs pioneered ***DAM*** (keeping track of all those pictures and pieces of text), and corporate publishing pushed the envelope for content management of large Web sites, newspapers needed to do both and then some. The first large-scale systems for integrating the whole workflow—from creation and acquisition of content to publishing in print and online—were developed to address this need. On such systems, writers don't just write and editors don't just edit; they write and edit *to fit*. They must do more than create content and tag it properly; they need a system that tells them how that content will look when it is typeset for the page (if not actually yet laid out on the page). Then that content must be assembled into pages—very large and very complex pages, mixed with all those digital photos and digital ads. The systems have to make it possible to revise those pages up until the last minute, to accommodate breaking news and shifting priorities. Then they must deliver that content not only to a manufacturing plant that images the pages and prints the paper, but increasingly to a Web site as well. All of this must be tightly integrated and happen lightning fast.

These systems are perhaps the best real-world examples of the way virtually all the digital technologies in use today—XML and HTML, TIFF and PDF, systems for authoring and editing and composition and layout and imaging and Web publishing—can come together in an integrated workflow. Not all newspapers have such systems, of course, but some do and many are getting close. Some day, perhaps most kinds of publishing will be produced in managed workflows like this. It should encourage publishers of simpler content that some newspapers—complex and demanding as they are—can do this today.

1.3 WHAT NEXT?

Although it should be clear by now that the digital revolution in publishing is not just a fond dream, we are still in the early stages of making it a practical reality. Certain technologies are well established enough, and based on such firm foundations, that they can be considered givens. Others are works in progress. Still others *are* fond dreams, or a twinkle in a programmer's eye. There will be failures and frustrations; these are part of the process by which technologies evolve from being "what ifs" to being taken for granted. As a summary, here are some suggestions about a few at each such stage.

(i) SOME GIVENS

1. The Internet

The ***Internet*** is so taken for granted that we forget that it is not just the Web. It is central to much of what we do today, from the e-mails we use in our daily business to the ***FTP*** (File Transfer Protocol) by which digital files for our printed publications are transmitted around the world while in production. Its effect is essentially democratic, removing the physical barriers that kept many of the world's people out of the game. It radically alters the time and space in which we work. Almost no publishing happens today without involving the Internet to some extent.

2. The Web

The ***Web*** is a given for most professionals in the developed world, and it's rapidly reaching many others. It's the visible face of the Internet, where we increasingly look for information and entertainment. It is taken for granted, most of all, by the young; and the young don't stay young for long.

3. XML

XML, the Extensible Markup Language is designed to accommodate variation and change. It's not a static solution to a problem, it's a way to create solutions. In its short lifetime so far it has become the fundamental way to tag everything from news feeds and syndicated stories to scientific journals and encyclopedias; it is also fundamental to much of today's software development and e-commerce. It has spawned a host of related technologies by which we structure, format, transform, and link what we publish. Like the palm trees that survive the hurricane, it's built to bend. XML is here to stay.

4. PDF

Although not the universal, nonproprietary standard XML is, Adobe's Portable Document Format (***PDF***) has become the standard way to describe the visual aspects of a page, and increasingly accommodates other information about that page as well (including tags, metadata, and workflow information). XML purists might argue that evolving standards like ***XSL-FO*** could eventually replace it, but PDF has become so essential to composition and layout, to prepress and printing, and to Web delivery and display, that although work will still be done to evolve and improve it, PDF can be considered a given in the digital production and publishing world for the foreseeable future.

5. DOI

Less obvious and less well established than the technologies listed above, the Digital Object Identifier (***DOI***) nevertheless has the reach and the real-world implementations to qualify it as a given. Like XML, it's designed to be adaptable; it's the only numbering scheme that can adapt to all other numbering schemes, and it adapts to any system of metadata as well. It provides a permanent, reliable way to find the current owner of a digital asset, and allows that owner to control any resulting transaction. Mostly a future given, but a given.

6. Unicode

A near-universal system of character encoding, ***Unicode*** is fundamental to XML. It provides a stable, unique identifier for the huge number of characters in many of the world's languages. As the chapter **International Issues** [14] discusses, the Internet makes all publishing international in potential, if not yet in fact. Unicode is at the heart of that.

(ii) SOME WORKS IN PROGRESS

1. The personal computer

It may be surprising not to see the PC listed as a given, but so much has changed about computer architecture in so short a time that what we now think of as the personal computer is not as likely to persist in its current form as long as the technologies listed above are. What makes a PC a PC is a combination of hardware and software and their architecture; currently, Windows rules this domain—but the rules of the game could change. Not long ago computing was dominated by "dumb" terminals linked to minicomputers and mainframes in which the software resided. Some may remember "timesharing." The new push toward Web services, where applications are hosted on servers and accessed via the Web rather than being resident in the user's computer as they are in the PC model, might have a "back to the future" aspect to it. In the most grand vision, the Internet becomes the computer.

2. E-books

Much of what we read today, we read on computer screens, but much progress still needs to be made before ***e-books*** can be considered a given. Unlike DOI, which is likely to remain stable and just needs time to be widely implemented, the current instability in the e-book world will go on for a while. It's safe to say e-books will become mainstream if you can avoid predicting when.

3. DRM

Progress in Digital Rights Management (***DRM***) is necessary before e-books can really succeed. A lot of the fundamental problems, however, have been identified, and many have been addressed. In a sense, DRM and e-books are joined at the hip: each needs progress from the other to make progress itself. As today's high school and college students come of age, the demand for a practical solution to DRM issues will become compelling.

4. Linking

Although we take linking for granted (as it has been implemented in HTML) and although the linking technologies in the XML family are well defined and mostly published, there will be a significant change in how linking is actually done in the next few years. As more content is available in XML, the XML linking technologies will make it possible to link to points in documents without requiring embedded link anchors, and will enable "linkbases" to be maintained outside the documents they link.

5. Metadata

There will be an explosion in the use of metadata in the next few years. Publishers will find that it is both essential (they'll be forced to use certain metadata if they want to stay in the game) and useful (metadata will shift from being a necessary evil to being a significant source of value). It will become somewhat demystified as well, more easily able to be captured and used at various points in the authoring, editing, production, and distribution process.

6. JDF

The Job Definition Format (***JDF***) is an XML-based standard for specifications and statistical data relevant to the printing process—job ticket information, process instructions and controls, in-process measurements, and so forth. When more widely and thoroughly implemented, it promises to dramatically improve automation of the printing process, producing more predictable results with less human intervention and error.

7. Digital printing

Significant strides have been made since the introduction of the Xerox DocuTech in 1990, and significant research and development continues. The effect of digital printing on publishing will be to enable shorter and shorter runs to be economical, to enable distributed printing (printing closer to or at the point of use), and to enable content customization and personalization.

8. Broadband

Broadband connections to the Web exist today, of course; the work in progress is to make it more universally available. Despite the recent traumas in the telecommunications industry (caused in part by massive investments in fiber that haven't had a chance to pay off yet), broadband connections will become increasingly common. College students already take them for granted. The World Wide Wait will get shorter.

9. Accessibility

Currently, printed publications are made available to the visually impaired and people with other disabilities only rarely, and often laboriously and crudely. As publishers implement more systematic workflows that produce more consistently structured and well-tagged publications, they will be able to generate accessible versions more easily. They will find that much of what is desirable for accessibility—clearly linked text flows, consistently tagged elements, images with verbal descriptions, and so forth—will enhance their publications in general.

(iii) SOME FUTURE PROSPECTS

1. The Semantic Web

Currently, search engines find content on the Web by looking for words and patterns in ***terabytes*** of mostly unstructured, unlabeled content. As XML is used more widely to structure documents meaningfully and as metadata is used more effectively to annotate those documents or portions of them, a much more dynamic and powerful discovery process will be possible—a Semantic Web.

2. Web services

As mentioned above, Web services involve "renting" access to applications over the Web. By maintaining the software on a central server and enabling users to access it with their familiar browsers, problems of user interface design, supporting multiple versions, and even barriers to usage such as initial investment and training can be reduced. This is not just for the Microsofts of the world; in fact, it could turn out to be most useful to the small developer with specialized software who can offer it as a Web service both as a source of ongoing income and to provide a "try before you buy" option to its customers.

3. XSL-FO

Extensible Stylesheet Language—Formatting Objects (***XSL-FO***) provides a universal and nonproprietary way to specify how content should be presented, just as XML does for how content should be structured. As formatting and rendering engines are developed which can interpret XSL-FO specifications, it will be possible to create pages without having to use coding proprietary to a particular composition or presentation technology. This will enable a new level of flexibility in composition and Web or e-book display.

4. E-paper

Electronic paper, a display technology that provides a number of advantages over today's ***CRT***s and ***LCD***s—high contrast, high resolution, low power usage (none, when the image is static), and able to be implemented on lightweight, flexible materials—will eventually eliminate many of today's obstacles to e-books. Imagine unrolling a 6-inch x 9-inch screen (the size of a typical book page) like a window shade from a device the size of a fountain pen, and seeing type and images almost as clear and sharp as those printed on paper. This technology exists today; although its first implementations will be for signage and cell phones, books won't be far behind.

5. XMP

The Extensible Metadata Platform (***XMP***) was created by Adobe but immediately made available as a nonproprietary standard. It provides a way to embed metadata right in the binary files associated with specific applications—a Photoshop image, a diagram created in Illustrator, a page laid out with InDesign. As more vendors incorporate XMP capabilities in their products and as applications develop to make use of the embedded metadata, XMP could become a very valuable technology to publishers.

6. SVG

Scalable Vector Graphics (***SVG***) is a way to describe image information in XML. Unlike common bitmap formats like TIFF and JPEG, it provides the ability for images to adapt to the resolution of any output or display device and to be enlarged and reduced without loss of quality. The fact that it uses a nonproprietary standard like XML to do this opens it up for creative uses by developers of all sorts.

7. Taxonomies

Once publishers accomplish the task of describing the structure of their publications, they will need to think about structuring information *about* those publications. The next few years will see a lot of work on the development of *information taxonomies,* ways to systematically describe the published information that will make them more accessible and more useful.

8. Mapping information

As our understanding of our information assets becomes more comprehensive and complicated, describing them with text-based methods will become more cumbersome. The map metaphor will become increasingly useful to describe these information assets. A graphical representation can communicate much more at a glance—relative proportions, relationships, affinities and distinctions, and so forth—than a text description can. It can also communicate taxonomy, ways to structure or look at that information. Expect to see more such graphical interfaces replacing conventional directory or folder structures in the future.

1.4 DIVE IN!

Digital technology in publishing is here to stay—but it won't stand still. Although it may seem daunting at first, it's both exhilarating and empowering. We can accomplish so much more in the digital world: digital technology enables us to publish much richer content, in so many more ways, and to do so more effectively and efficiently than ever before. Certainly, it's possible to stumble and go astray; not every experiment works, not every venture pays off. But when digital technologies are implemented well, they make life easier, and when they are exploited to their full potential, they pay off handsomely in the long run. This Guide is here to help you along the way.

2 The Technical Infrastructure

CHRIS BIEMESDERFER
Seagoat Consulting

This chapter discusses the basic hardware and software that provide the infrastructure for digital publishing. Becoming familiar with these components will help those involved in digital publishing to better understand technical issues and use tools and techniques more effectively.

2.1 OVERVIEW

Digital publishing presupposes computers: it is the use of the modern digital computer that makes our publishing operations today "digital." This chapter will improve familiarity with the fundamental notions and components behind the digital computing and networking environment.

Today's computing and networking environment is technologically complex and rapidly changing. Rather than attempt to be either a product survey or a how-to manual, this chapter categorizes a large cross-section of that technology, organizing the discussion around the components' overall functions.

Throughout, definitions of important terminology are provided. Basic definitions appear at the beginnings of the sections in which they are most relevant, although a number of fundamental terms will be defined in the first section.

2.2 THE BASICS OF COMPUTER ARCHITECTURE

(i) THE ANTHROPOMORPHIZED COMPUTER

Almost since the advent of computers, we have both longed for and dreaded the day when computers might be as capable as human beings. In real life, we are thrilled to have an "intelligent" microwave oven that produces perfectly browned and crispy roast chicken without requiring our constant attention. In the movies, HAL 9000 and its ilk make terrific villains.

For better or worse, we have come to regard computers as surrogates for ourselves. This chapter will do the same by categorizing the computer's components in terms of their anthropomorphic traits and using these traits, or functions, as the framework to organize the material.

1. Thinking: processors, memory, and the processing environment

Computers transform the representation of information, and sometimes convey new information in the process. These operations are carried out in aggregations of ***transistors*** (tiny semiconductor switches) mounted in ***chips***; the aggregated transistors are sometimes called ***integrated circuits.***

Integrated circuits can be designed for many purposes, but the two main types relevant to digital publishing are *processors,* which actively transform **bytes** [2.2.2.1], and *memory,* which passively holds bytes.

Computers often contain chips that perform various specialized kinds of processing. The master processor, the most complex collection of integrated circuits, is called the ***central processing unit*** (CPU).

The kind of memory used in computers today is called ***random access memory*** (RAM) because each of its storage locations can be addressed (i.e., selected) directly, as opposed to having to be accessed in order (which would be called *sequential access*). The direct approach—that is, being able to select memory locations at random—is far more efficient for the retrieval of the stored entity. (This is also true of physical storage facilities, such as your attic.)

The collections of bytes that processors operate on (and memory stores) can be grouped into two main types that correspond to the chips' primary function. Some bytes constitute *instructions* for the processor, directing the operation or transformation being performed, while others, by far the majority, are *data,* the information being operated upon. The distinction between instructions and data is akin to the arithmetic concepts of operator and operand.

Instructions are typically gathered together in sets so that when they are executed as a group, an always interesting, sometimes useful, result is produced. Such a collection is singly referred to as a ***program***; the array of programs collaborating to make a computer function is referred to as the ***processing environment***.

2. Showing: display technology

Computers present information to us in two principal ways: on paper and on the screen. Both of these technologies are important to publishers; the display devices used for presentation are discussed **below** [2.4], and printing technology is covered in the chapter on **digital printing** [8] as well as the chapter on **composition and design** [6].

The most important difference between print and on-screen presentation, from a reader's perspective, is the ability to interact with the content in some way that changes the presentation. One can't fundamentally change a print presentation—one can hide it or destroy it, but once the information is rendered on paper, it is fixed.

This crucial difference is a consequence of the fact that computer displays are controlled electronically, hence they are changeable quickly and precisely.

3. Saving: storage technology

Information is stored (more or less permanently) by computers using technologies that are magnetic or optical in nature. These sorts of devices are crucial because they retain data almost indefinitely when computer power is turned off, as opposed to memory or displays, which require a current flow. Details on data storage are found **below** [2.5].

The modern computer's ability to store and retrieve data is at least as important as its ability to perform calculations quickly and accurately. When information is recorded digitally, it can be reproduced with full fidelity; digital data do not degrade over time. The consequences of being able to perfectly recreate works time and again affects our culture profoundly. Other chapters in this Guide discuss the **legal** [13] and **international** [14] issues.

4. Talking: communication and data transfer

A computer system consists of numerous devices; networks consist of many computers. All the components are linked together by communications circuits, which are either electromagnetic or optical in nature.

Many of these circuits have to carry communications between multiple devices, that is, numerous different "conversations" between devices have to be multiplexed onto the same channel. Order is maintained (most of the time) on these channels by requiring the communications to proceed according to ***protocols***, which are simply rules that must be followed when exchanging data. More about **data communications below** [2.6].

(ii) A FEW BASIC TERMS AND DEFINITIONS

1. Bits and bytes

According to legendary technology humor, computers wreak havoc extremely effectively because they are at once immensely stupid and incomprehensibly fast. The reference to their stupidity arises from the fact that they only understand two things: one and zero.

A system that has only two states is called a binary system. Those states can be represented in many ways: electrically (voltage on or voltage off), magnetically (N polarization or S polarization), or logically (true or false). They can also be represented numerically with digits such as one and zero, and this is how computers represent state—with a *binary digit,* a term whose contraction is ***bit***. When we gather bits together in groups, we can convey more information than simply "on" or "off."

Modern computers group bits eight at a time; a sequence of eight bits is called a ***byte***. A byte can represent a numeric value (from zero to 255), and these values can be interpreted in many ways: for example, as a letter in an alphabet or as a level of gray in an image.

The size of the byte is not arbitrary. To expedite processing and communication within computers (on chips and printed circuit boards) the various devices operate on several signals at once. To facilitate addressing, processors are designed to work with powers of two (the number of states in a binary system). The first microprocessor operated on four bits at a time; the first widely used microprocessor, Intel's 8080, operated on eight. As a consequence of the 8080's popularity, early computing devices used ***communications buses*** that could transmit eight digital (on/off) signals concurrently (in parallel). We say that such a bus is eight bits "wide." A grouping of eight parallel bits constitutes a byte.

Other groupings of bits have been employed as well. Univac produced computers that used 9-bit bytes in the 1970s, for instance. The 8-bit architecture of Intel was by far the most successful, however, and virtually all devices today operate on some multiple of eight bits at a time.

2. Input and output

Computers receive input many ways in many forms, and they dispense output in diverse forms through varied channels. This chapter focuses on the kinds of input and output that are associated with the exchange of information between or among computing resources, rather than physical devices such as keyboards and mice, printers, and audio devices. The kinds of input that humans give to express our instructions, or to originate information ourselves, are surely crucial, but not necessarily relevant for our purpose. When we need to refer to them, we will call them ***I/O devices***.

3. Digital vs. analog

Digital computer technology takes advantage of a binary state machine that expresses state as a one or a zero. It is important to recognize that there is no in-between: to paraphrase the popular punch line, "it's *only* ones and zeroes." We add resolution by stringing bits together and interpreting all the possible combinations of ones and zeroes as a spectrum of states, but in the end there is still a finite number of states with steps between them.

Our experience in the real world differs. We are used to things that vary smoothly: the amount of flame under a kettle on our gas range, or the speed of our car as we accelerate onto the freeway. These changes occur continuously through an infinite number of states. Systems that behave this way are called ***analog***.

In mathematics, these notions are represented by number sets or functions that are *discrete,* in contrast to those that are *continuous.*

2.3 THE PROCESSING ENVIRONMENT

The processing environment that is presented to the user depends on the type of computer system and the blend of ***operating system*** (OS) and application software that is installed. The distinction between operating system and application is blurring, even though in what follows the two will be treated separately, as if they were independent of each other. We can still distinguish between application software and operating system, by considering applications as software optimized for the purposes of some "high-level" task, while operating system software is concerned with the operation of the computer itself.

(i) OPERATING SYSTEMS

At its deepest, most arcane level, the ***operating system*** is how a computer moves bits and bytes among its components: processors, memory, and I/O devices. These functions are still at the core of any OS, and the core piece of an OS with such responsibilities is often called the ***kernel*** of the OS. It is the part of the OS that is most tightly bound to the details of the component mix and architecture of the computing machine.

The complete modern OS is vastly more complex than its kernel: it consists of a staggering number of layers that combine to offer ever more complicated functions. The connection points between these layers are called ***interfaces***; the computing and networking environment in which we work is a panoply of interfaces.

Applications are software programs that perform tasks at a higher level of abstraction: they do things that are typically useful for the computer user, and produce concrete results for us in the real world. These things include preparing a memo, determining a budget, balancing a checkbook, or retouching a digital photograph.

1. Unix

Unix is an operating system that has been in existence for over 30 years. The system as we know it today was devised by Ken Thompson and Dennis Ritchie at Bell Telephone Laboratories in the early 1970s. The ***Linux*** system is a Unix derivative created by Linus Torvalds in the early 1990s. Released into the wider development community, Linux has evolved at the hands of many programmers and has been adopted by such leading companies as Sun and IBM.

Work on this type of multitasking OS had been going on in industry and academia since the 1960s. One of the prominent implementations was carried out at MIT by Fernando Corbató and his collaborators. It was known as Multics, which stood for Multiplexed Information and Computing Service. Bell Labs was an early participant in the Multics project, but began to withdraw in the late 1960s, for a variety of reasons. When Thompson and Ritchie's group developed their kernel on a DEC PDP-7 computer, they called it Unix, a play on the word Multics.

Unix became popular in the 1980s as the OS of choice for "scientific and engineering workstations," personal desktop-sized systems that were more potent than PCs for solving complex technical problems. Two main "flavors" of Unix flowered at that time, the version that evolved at AT&T Bell Labs, which was known as ***System V*** (the roman numeral "five"), and a version that was developed at the University of California at Berkeley, which was known as ***BSD***. The NIST/IEEE standard known now as ***POSIX*** appeared in the late 1980s as an attempt to reconcile these two different versions through a common programming interface.

Linux, as popular as it is today, is not really a new variety of Unix. Like most Unixes on the market today, it is a hybrid of BSD and System V interfaces (Linuxes tend to be more like System V), with a healthy dose of POSIX interfaces. Linux's technological achievement is that it is an efficient kernel for the Intel 32-bit chip architecture. Combined with a vast array of software tools from the Free Software Foundations' GNU project and other like-minded sources, Linux is extremely popular in small and large enterprises alike, especially for Web-based services.

2. Apple Macintosh

Steve Jobs and Steve Wozniak started Apple to build personal computers, and they were very successful with their second offering, the Apple II, in the late 1970s. They moved into grander, more sophisticated machines around 1980, after seeing a pair of new workstations at Xerox's Palo Alto Research Center (PARC).

The scientists at PARC had developed systems (called the Star and the Alto) that had user interfaces that were *graphical,* rather than being based on commands typed at a console prompt. The computer displays were bit-mapped, which means that each pixel on screen was individually addressed, and in addition to a keyboard for input, there was a pointing device called a ***mouse***.

All of today's graphical user interfaces (the acronym ***GUI*** is pronounced "gooey") employ design abstractions conceptualized in the 1950s and which Xerox researchers brought to fruition in the 1970s at PARC. While the Star and Alto workstations were not great commercial successes, the GUI proved to be revolutionary.

Apple's graphical workstation was called the ***Lisa***, and was arguably the first commercially successful workstation to employ a GUI. Lisa was *tres* cool and *tres* expensive.

Apple raised the bar for personal computers' capabilities when the ***Macintosh*** debuted in 1984—ushered into the commercial sensibility by the critically acclaimed Superbowl XVIII advertisement, directed by Ridley Scott (see the bibliography at the end of the chapter). Like the Lisa, the user interface for the Macintosh was graphical, but the Mac was a much more affordable implementation ($2,500 as opposed to $10,000, in 1984 dollars).

The ***operating system*** for the Macintosh has been referred to as simply ***Mac OS*** almost since its inception, even though the official name of the system was System *N*, where *N* was a number. System 7 was officially christened Mac OS in the mid-1990s.

Mac OS's abiding strength has always been its capacity for handling graphics at the core, an efficiency requirement for a system that presents a graphical user interface. Mac OS was designed and built to take advantage of the 32-bit architecture of Motorola's 68000 line of processors. It supported Small Computer System Interface (**SCSI** [2.6.1.2.5]) peripherals at an early stage, because the Mac's compact design meant that there were frequently outboard devices to be managed.

For most of its life, Mac OS evolved fairly smoothly and incrementally, to take advantage of improvements in Motorola's processor line, or to add enhancements to support more sophisticated devices. In 1999, after years of gradual change through version 9, Mac ***OS X*** was released (and Apple switched from Arabic to Roman numbering systems).

Mac OS X is based on Unix (a POSIX-compliant, Berkeley flavor), and retains its graphics savvy, while adding many sophisticated kernel features. The kernel of OS X is based on a Unix implementation called Darwin.

3. Microsoft Windows

Microsoft has been in the ***operating system*** business for a long time. Bill Gates and Paul Allen started the company writing game software for the Altair, a machine based on Intel's 8080 processor, and usually regarded as the first personal computer. In the early 1980s, Microsoft licensed a disk-based OS (or DOS) to IBM for that company's evolving personal computer line. Microsoft's DOS was a third-party clone of another OS called ***CP/M*** (which IBM was unable to license); Microsoft bought the (cloned) system in one of the innumerable masterful acquisitions that have characterized the company's growth.

Gates and Co.'s capacity to capitalize on good ideas (their own as well as those of others) is legendary. Mr. Gates had also been inside Xerox PARC in the late 1970s, so Microsoft was also aware of the revolutionary workstations that had been built there. The success of the Mac OS made it evident that a graphical face for DOS was needed.

When ***Windows*** debuted in 1985, it was almost literally a graphical interface layered on top of DOS. The core functions stabilized with the release of Windows 3.1, and native networking capability was added in the subsequent Windows for Workgroups product.

In the early 1990s, as Windows' evolution drove it toward what would become Windows 95, a new operating-system effort at Microsoft produced a native 32-bit kernel to take advantage of the 32-bit architecture of Intel's 80x86 microprocessor line. This strain of Windows became known as Windows ***NT*** (New Technology), and has been the heart of Microsoft's "enterprise" OS line since NT version 3.5 (1994).

The two Windows lines continued to evolve along nominally convergent paths, Windows 95 becoming Windows 98 and then Windows ME (for Millennium Edition, evidently signaling the abandonment of numeral systems altogether), while NT 4.0 followed 3.5 and eventually became Windows 2000.

Windows ***XP*** is Microsoft's converged form of Windows, and has versions for home consumers as well as enterprise users. The home editions blend ease-of-use features from the original Windows line with the newer, more robust NT line. The enterprise editions extend the NT line with new Microsoft initiatives for advanced network services.

4. Other operating systems

1. LARGE: MAINFRAMES AND SUPERCOMPUTERS

Mainframe computers, and to a considerable extent supercomputers, are large and imposing machines. Consequently, they are sometimes referred to as "big iron."

They are large because, historically, one had to confront large computing problems with sheer size: more memory and more processors. By having large amounts of the thinking components, these large computers could solve large (difficult) problems fairly fast.

The operating systems tailored for mainframe computers are optimized for ***batch processing***, as opposed to the interactive computing environments we typically work in today. This optimization was an expedient: these large problems still take a long time to compute. Consequently, an operator typically wants to specify the input and output parameters and all the other constraints when the process, or *job,* is initialized. Then the operator goes away and does something else while the computer works on the problem.

This notion of *batch,* or unattended, processing persists today in many circumstances, some well known to publishers. We still use batch pagination and hyphenation/justification (H&J) systems.

Another approach to making computers faster is to use highly efficient materials and specialized designs that capitalize on semiconductor properties or even fundamental physics. Seymour Cray's supercomputers were cylindrical so the components could be arranged radially around the central processing core and communications bus, thus minimizing the distances that signals had to travel within the machine. Other supercomputers use liquid nitrogen or other elements to keep components as cold as possible, since electrical resistance is a function of temperature and diminishes in direct proportion to the temperature of the conductor.

At extremely low temperatures, many materials become ***superconductors*** in which electric currents flow virtually unimpeded, that is, with practically no resistance. Handling very cold liquids is difficult, which makes computers constructed this way cumbersome to install and maintain, so the prospect of finding materials with superconductive properties at higher temperatures is appealing. This is one of the reasons why research in "room-temperature superconductors" continues to be an important area of applied physics research.

Supercomputing resources can also take the form of an amalgam of computing resources (individual computers or processors) that are combined to address a problem. One way to do this is to wire together many individual processors (chips) in a single computer. This kind of computer is called a ***multiprocessor***, or sometimes, a ***parallel processing*** computer.

Another approach is to utilize processors in different computers that are connected via network communications. Nowadays these kinds of efforts are referred to as ***grid computing***, or distributed computation, and they are being used to determine very large prime numbers, to scan radio signals from outer space for signs of intelligent life, and to find effective new pharmaceuticals to fight disease.

2. TINY: HANDHELD AND EMBEDDED

While there is still a need for massive, big-iron computers, a more prevalent trend today is for computing devices to be made smaller, and in many cases, more specialized in function. Certain of these devices are more "programmable" than others, although the programming interface may not always be as straightforward as the typical desktop computer. Familiar examples would include ***PDA***s (such as Palm Pilot, Handspring Visor, and Pocket PC) and cellular phones.

Other types of devices perform specific tasks; the computing hardware and software that is built into such devices is sometimes called an ***embedded system***. Examples of this sort of system might be a GPS navigation device in your car or your boat, or an environmental monitoring and control module for your refrigerator, or that clever microwave oven that roasts chicken perfectly.

It may seem irrelevant to mention this latter sort of embedded system in a guide for publishing, but as wireless communications technology becomes more robust, some of those systems in certain environments will surely come to have generalized interfaces, akin to a browser, for accessing resources on the Internet.

(ii) APPLICATION SOFTWARE

We distinguish application software as those programs that perform high-level tasks, operations that produce useful outcomes in our real world. There are innumerable ways to classify applications, and we will consider them in terms of canonical office automation tools.

1. Concurrent calculation: spreadsheets

Spreadsheets are fancy adding machines, *very* fancy adding machines. Spreadsheets are designed to automate the function of a bookkeeper or an accountant performing tabulations on a columnar pad. Indeed, it is like having an adding machine in each one of those little boxes on a sheet of columnar paper.

The spreadsheet is laid out as a grid of boxes, called *cells*. Each cell contains either a value (text or a number) or a formula that generates a value. The cells are referred to by their positions in the grid, according to what row and column they are in. Rows are typically referred to by number, while columns are usually labeled with letters of the alphabet. One therefore addresses cells in the spreadsheet the way one locates towns on a map: with a letter-number combination that identifies a grid-square location, "B5," for example.

When you specify formulas in a cell that contains a calculation, you can have the formula operate either on numbers that you type into the formula directly, or on the contents of other cells that you refer to by grid-square address. Since you may refer to a cell whose contents are themselves the result of another calculation, you can chain operations together in order to build a complex array of interrelated values.

Spreadsheets' other potent capability is that all the linked formula cells are automatically recalculated any time one of the preceding cells in the chain is altered. Consequently, entire pages of figures can be adjusted as parameters are varied. This makes spreadsheets valuable tools for all kinds of scenario evaluation, forecasting, and modeling.

Spreadsheet programs typically accommodate collections of worksheets, and permit the user to address cells on different sheets, rather like referring to boxes on other pages in a columnar pad. Many also provide graphic capabilities that make it possible also to portray the data visually in various types of graphs.

2. Storage, search, and retrieval: databases

When we want to store a collection of related facts so that we can compare them at a later time, we often record them in a table. Each column of the table contains a certain kind of information, such as color, size, material, or price. There is then a row of these related facts for each item we are concerned with, articles of clothing or pieces of furniture, for instance. These facts tend all to be fairly independent of one another, which means that changes to one fact in a table generally do not change any other fact.

This sort of tabular approach to data organization and storage is the essence of the modern ***database***. Database tables have ***fields*** for each kind of information (analogous to our columns above); the field data for each item is stored in a ***record*** of the table, which is analogous to our rows.

A ***relational database*** is one in which groupings of data stored in different tables are related to each other by some crucial element, which is called the *key*. Data are segregated into several tables when they have to do with different contexts, such as business processes, or when there are many instances of certain sets of properties for a single item.

For instance, a bookstore might keep the bibliographic information (e.g., title and ISBN) about a book separate from the inventory information (e.g., number of copies and unit price). Each book would have a key value that identifies it uniquely, and the same key value would be used to identify records in both the bibliography table and the inventory table. This key is the link between the two tables that allows the bookstore owner to know how many copies of a certain title are in stock.

A database can store immense quantities of information, so ***database management systems*** (***DBMS***s) are the programs that we typically use to manipulate databases. In order to expedite the search and retrieval of relevant records, these systems *index* the data in its tables. Like the index for a book, the purpose of these indexes is to order the information so it is easy to find; however, a database table index is a set of numeric values that are the result of a sophisticated calculation.

Information is retrieved from a database by making a ***query*** to the DBMS. A query identifies the source of the data, which particular fields are desired, and may also set limits or constraints for the values. These specifications can get rather complex, and so we interact with database systems via a ***query language*** that allows us to refine the queries precisely.

Databases provide the core functionality for **content management systems** [10] that track digital assets (e.g., text documents and graphic files) in many digital publishing environments.

3. Manipulation of text: word processing and formatting

As intelligent beings, we humans express ourselves in spoken and written language. We also have an appreciation of art and beauty, and consequently we exert our creativity in the written word. We do that through the words we choose and the turns of phrase we employ, and by changing the appearance of the texts we write. That is, we alter the *content* of what we write and we adjust the *form* of the letters, words, and paragraphs.

The manipulation of the words (content) in a text is an editing function, and the most basic kinds of programs for doing this are called simply ***text editors***. The modification of the appearance (form) of the text is a formatting or layout function; software that specializes in these sorts of functions is called a typesetting, composition, or page layout program, subjects that are discussed in the **composition, design, and graphics chapter** [6.10]. When these functions are combined in a single piece of software, it is typically called a ***word processor***.

A substantial portion of this guide is devoted to the merits of keeping these two functions reasonably well separated. The most common technique for doing so is to identify the component parts that may need to be formatted, or the formatting instructions themselves, in an encoded way, called *markup*. There are many different kinds or dialects of markup, and these are called *markup languages,* because they resemble (in some cases, they actually are) programming languages. Markup languages—especially **XML** [3.3]—are discussed in detail the chapter on markup.

4. Manipulation of nontext: graphics, design, and image/audio processing

Information appears in many forms. In addition to manipulating words and numbers, we use computers to operate on pictures and sounds.

Pictorial forms include photographic images that contain great detail, drawings or cartoons that help illustrate important points, and geometric or abstract shapes that lend emphasis to a publication. Image data, whether photographic or simulated, is manipulated with programs generically called *image processing software,* which often combines a digital photo lab or darkroom and a special effects department. Line drawings and cartoons are typically rendered in *drawing* or *illustration* programs; these kinds of programs can also be used to create abstract shapes or logos. Programs that are used to manipulate many of these elements at one time are typically called *design* or *layout* software. Layout programs frequently also handle text in sophisticated ways. The subject of graphics is treated in detail in on **composition and graphics** [6.8].

Audio processing software ranges from straightforward recording and playback programs to elaborate digital studio editing systems. *Synthesizer* software is used to create digital waveforms; *sequencer* programs play digital sounds in particular order or according to prescribed algorithms. Digital abstractions of visual and aural information are not limited to one or two dimensions—indeed, sound is inherently three-dimensional (with pitch, amplitude, and time)—and we can add dimensions to image data. Three-dimensional spatial data can be rendered through stereographic techniques or by permitting someone to manipulate the data cube with *visualization* software. When a time dimension is added to image data, *movies* or *animations* result; when sound is added to this, it is called *entertainment.* (See chapters on **digital rights management** [15] and **multimedia** [9] topics.)

5. Combinations: accounting packages, content/asset management, and more

Sophisticated software programs and systems have evolved to automate complex business and engineering functions. If we take a reductionist perspective, we can see these systems as elaborate combinations of numerical calculation, database management, and text and image processing.

1. ACCOUNTING

The typical accounting package, for example, is essentially a collection of specific-purpose spreadsheets combined with database functions. The spreadsheets compute profit and loss, calculate taxes and withholdings, display account balances, total up assets and liabilities, and so forth. To these are added database tables of vendors, employees, and income and expense categories. The software package melds these functions in a system that enables a financially untrained person or a professional accountant to manage fiscal affairs.

2. CAD: COMPUTER AIDED DESIGN

Computer aided design (***CAD***) systems combine drawing programs with database and spreadsheet capabilities. Engineers and draftsmen are able to create and organize all the design schematics for an automobile or aircraft.

The schematic diagrams and engineering details from a CAD system can be combined with explanatory text so that an interactive, on-line airplane maintenance manual is produced. Such a system integrates image processing, text processing, and database functions—for example, by generating diagrams precisely from numerical data instead of requiring them to be "drawn."

3. CONTENT MANAGEMENT

Content-management systems combine database and text processing capabilities; asset-management systems merge image processing and database management. Both systems could employ spreadsheet-like calculations to manage version control and to compute aging.

Not to detract from these systems' complexity, the task of integrating these basic functions into a useful and *usable* whole is difficult and resource-consuming. However, it can be helpful to remember that we tend to use computers for a handful of straightforward operations.

2.4 DISPLAY

Computers display information on relatively flat two-dimensional surfaces or screens. The nature of the technology differs in these devices, but the screens are all controlled electronically, which allows the information presented to the reader to be changed, often interactively.

(i) TERMS AND DEFINITIONS

1. Bitmaps and rasters

Computer displays are sometimes referred to as bitmapped displays. In its simplest incarnation, a ***bitmap*** is a two-dimensional array of ones and zeroes in which the zeroes represent the background and the ones depict an object—a line, the strokes of a letter, or the outline of some shape. It is literally a map of the object in bits.

A more general interpretation of the term bitmap is to think of it as a grid or matrix of points covering an object, where each cell contains a value or values that describe properties of the object at that point. These cells can be thought of as *picture elements.*

The process of sampling an object or a picture into a matrix of cell values is sometimes called *rasterization,* although a better term is *digitization.* The word ***raster*** refers to a scan line on a television screen, not to an individual point. A complete row of cells in a bitmap corresponds to a raster.

2. Pixels and resolution

The word ***pixel*** is a stylized contraction of the term *picture element.* A picture element is a single dot in the matrix of rows and columns that make up a bitmap, be it a display screen or an image file.

The ***resolution*** of a display screen is a measure of the size of each pixel. It indicates how large (or small) each dot really is, and is usually specified in millimeters; sometimes it is called the *dot pitch.* The smaller the pixels are, the more there are per unit length, and thus the higher (sharper) the resolution.

The number of pixels in the display is frequently stated as the *resolution,* although it is really just a count of how many elements are on the screen.

3. Monochrome, grayscale, and color

The capability to display pictures on screens in color or black and white depends on how much information is recorded at each pixel. A pure bitmap, where the cells contain either a one or a zero, is a ***monochrome*** image. Monochrome means "one color," and the term refers to images in which the pixels are either on or off—there are no shades or intermediate brightness. A line drawing or a cartoon is a monochrome image.

When the value of the cell contains a wider range of values than just one and zero, we can interpret the digitized picture with more subtlety. For example, if several bits are recorded at each sample point, the range of values can be interpreted as a brightness scale or shades of gray. We say that such an image is displayed in ***grayscale***.

We display images in color by measuring intensities in several (typically three) channels or bands. Each channel corresponds to a primary color: red, green, or blue. For computer displays, each cell in the matrix contains three values, where each is interpreted as a measure of one of the three intensities of primary color.

4. Antialiasing

The pixels on a screen have finite size, and a display can be regarded as being made up of a grid of tiny blocks. Lines drawn parallel to the edges of the display are created by rows or columns of pixels that are perfectly aligned. Lines in other orientations have to cross between rows and columns, and because of pixels' finite size, each of these crossings produces a step. Consequently, such lines have jagged edges.

Antialiasing is a software technique applied to lines or paths that are not parallel to one of the edges of the display, so as to smooth the jagged edges of such diagonal lines and curves on a bit-mapped screen. This is achieved by changing the values of the pixels at (or near) the edges of the lines to intermediate values (levels of gray in the case of black and white) so that the eye discerns a smoother transition between the line and its background.

(ii) OVERVIEW OF DISPLAY TECHNOLOGY

Display screens, computer monitors, and televisions generally fall into one of two groups depending on the physics of the device. The big heavy monitors on desktops contain an imaging device called a *cathode-ray tube* (***CRT***). So-called flat-screen monitors and the displays of small, handheld devices utilize a *liquid crystal display* (***LCD***). CRTs take advantage of electromagnetism, while LCDs are in the regime of solid-state physics.

1. CRTs: cathode-ray tubes

CRTs are the meeting place of digital and analog technology. The image on a CRT screen is produced using analog electromagnetic techniques, although the computer generating the image manipulates it as a bitmap. Consequently, there is a device inside the monitor that performs what is called a digital-to-analog conversion.

Cathodes are negatively charged electrodes. Electrons are negatively charged particles, and they are therefore repelled by a cathode. A stream of electrons from a cathode is called a *cathode ray.*

Electrons are emitted from a cathode at the back of a CRT, and travel to the front of the CRT (the screen). The front of a CRT has a fluorescent coating that emits photons (light) when it is struck by electrons.

In order to control the beam of electrons (the cathode ray) accurately, the CRT is evacuated; that is, air is removed so that there is a vacuum inside. Further, the electrons are accelerated to high velocity by a large electrical charge, and they are steered when they pass between other electrically charged surfaces that control the horizontal and vertical movement of the electrons. Because CRTs must support a vacuum and fairly high voltages, CRT monitors are relatively large and heavy.

2. LCDs: liquid crystal displays

LCDs are semiconductor devices. Liquid crystals themselves are long molecules that either pass or block light through a property called *polarization.*

The displays most commonly used nowadays for computers (especially laptops) and handheld devices are called ***active-matrix*** LCDs. There are three transistors—one each for red, green, and blue—at each pixel location on the display surface. They are controlled by low-voltage pulses from components called bonding pads at the edges of the matrix or screen.

In addition to the transistor layer, these displays have a backlighting layer behind the transistors and a color filter layer and polarizing layer in front. All these components are manufactured to microscopically thin tolerances. The transistor layer is usually fabricated as a thin film of amorphous silicon, and is referred to as a thin-film transistor (***TFT***).

3. Touch sensitive displays

Touch sensitive screens are actually not a different sort of display technology. Touch screens are used for applications where a keyboard is not desired, and they find use today in handheld devices and tablet PCs. They operate by adding a layer to a CRT or LCD display, typically a glass panel that responds to the resistive or capacitive properties of one's finger or of a stylus.

4. Electronic ink

Electronic ink, or electronic paper, is a logical extension of thin-film transistor displays, but utilizes technology that enables electronically controlled displays on lightweight flexible screens. The display layer in this kind of device is an extremely thin film in which tiny beads or capsules are distributed. The beads contain particles that respond to an electric charge by showing either light or dark (or light and a color).

The particles in the capsules remain in place until a different electrical charge moves them. Thus, images created on these devices persist even when there is no power being applied to the device.

5. Video signals

Computer displays and televisions look alike, and indeed employ the same physical devices to produce images. However, the signals that are sent to control computer monitors are different from those that control televisions, and you cannot use them interchangeably.

Computer displays are bitmapped, that is, each pixel is managed by the computer, and the graphics adapters in computers send signals that address pixels independently. The signaling protocols are named after the type of the graphics adapter: ***CGA***, ***EGA***, and ***VGA***, for *computer, enhanced,* and *video* graphics adapter, respectively. These methods are largely evolutionary, and most computer displays now utilize an upgraded version called ***SVGA***, which stand for *super video graphics adapter,* and permits a large number of pixels to be addressed with a high degree of color definition.

Television signals are not the same as computer monitor signals. Television evolved before there were digital computers, even before the invention of the transistor, so the analog technology of the cathode ray tube dictated how TVs were controlled. They are inherently raster, or scan-line, based. In the United States, the signalling standard was developed by the National Television Standards Committee and is known as ***NTSC***; the corresponding European standard is called ***PAL***, which stands for phase alternating lines.

As we have moved more and more to digital forms of communication, digital television (***DTV***) standards have been developed. A range of DTV standards from the Advanced Television Systems Committee (ATSC) have been approved. The most complex is called high-definition TV, or ***HDTV***.

2.5 DATA STORAGE

(i) STORAGE DEVICES

Digital data are stored on devices that are magnetic or optical in nature. The devices store substantial amounts of data by having a relatively large surface area on which information can be encoded. The individual areas must be read and written accurately by components called *heads,* and in order to read the entire device, recording surfaces and heads must be moved relative to one another. Consequently, these storage devices have transport mechanisms and moving parts, and they are often called *drives.*

1. Magnetic media

Magnetic media, such as tapes and many kinds of disks, encode bits by affecting the magnetic properties of microscopic areas of the medium. These properties (typically *polarity*) are set and detected by heads that carry an electric current that induces the magnetic effect desired. Setting the polarity of an area is a *write* operation; detecting the polarity is a *read* operation. The transitions in polarity can be made over and over in these kinds of media without appreciable loss of fidelity, so magnetic disks and tapes can be rewritten countless times to store different information.

2. Optical media

Optical media encode bits by modulating an optical property, typically the reflectivity of light from a low-power infrared laser. In the early generations of optical devices, reflectivity was affected by mechanical changes in the medium, microscopic indentations called *pits.* Their pattern alters the way the laser light reflects off the surface, and the changes in intensity are interpreted as ones and zeroes. These pits are effectively cast in plastic, so once written, these kinds of devices can only be read.

In newer optical devices that permit reading and writing several times, the laser's reflected intensity is modulated by other properties of a different kind of medium. This material's state is changed between crystalline and amorphous, crystalline being the more reflective, according to the power applied in a laser pulse. The change from a crystalline state to an amorphous state is called a *phase transition* in solid-state physics, and this technology is known as *phase change recording*. The phase change layer in this type of disk can tolerate many phase transitions, so these media are rewritable.

3. Hybrid media

There are also hybrid storage devices that are called *magneto-optical,* or MO devices. These employ both lasers and magnetic fields. The media are more robust than purely optical, meaning that the substrate will hold its state for a long time and can support many more transitions. Since the bits are magnetically encoded these devices can be read more easily, and the platters can be spun at higher speeds, which results in faster data transfer.

4. Media and format

The storage medium is simply the physical device on which data are stored. Storage media have fundamental physical properties that permit information to be stored and retrieved, and in order to do so, computers communicate with the devices via a device *controller*.

Different kinds of processing environments (operating systems) manage information in subtly different ways. This requires that media be laid out in a *format* that is sensible for the given operating system. The same medium can be formatted differently, depending on the processing environment. Note that it is the operating system that dictates the format, not the physical storage device.

The physical size of a storage device is sometimes referred to as its *form factor*. This is snappy engineering language, assuming that engineering language can be snappy. It is important not to confuse form factor and format; form factor just means "dimensions."

(ii) DISK STORAGE

Disks come in a variety of sizes (form factors), but only one shape: circular and flat. Data are accessed by rotating the disks and reading or writing at different radii and position angles. There are many ways to classify disks, and an important distinction is between disks that are *fixed* as opposed to those that are *removable.*

Computers store data in related groups of bytes using the abstraction of the *file.* When media are formatted so that the operating system (OS) makes sense of them, the result is that an infrastructure is created on the medium so that the OS can quickly locate files. That infrastructure is called a *file system.* There are many, many kinds of file systems, and they are often OS-specific. New file systems are created over time to take advantage of advances in media technology and of enhancements in OSs.

As we have become more dependent on digital data, we have come to expect that digital information will always be available. Fortunately, data storage technology has become increasingly reliable; the typical mean time between failures (***MTBF***) for an "everyday" disk drive is in the tens of thousands of hours (several years).

For many applications, however, it is important that there is never any data loss due to a disk failure. In those instances, a high degree of *fault tolerance* is achieved by having extra disk drives available on a standby basis. Devices that support this kind of operation are called ***RAID*** drives, for redundant array of independent disks.

1. Fixed disks

Fixed disks are usually intended to be installed permanently with a computer. They typically store large quantities of data, and can transfer data to and from the computer at high rates. Storage capacity is increased by creating a stack of individual disk surfaces, called *platters,* which rotate together on a central spindle; by making the heads that read and write data very small, so that smaller spots on the disks are magnetized; and by controlling the positions of the heads very precisely. Data transfer rates are increased through a combination of rotating the disks more rapidly and using faster electronics in the device controllers. Fixed disks are high-performance devices, and are manufactured in ultraclean environments and hermetically sealed, meaning they are airtight and moisture-resistant. The rapidly rotating platters are rigid, and so these devices are sometimes called ***hard disks***.

2. Removable disks

Removable disks are devices in which the medium can be removed from the drive. Early forms of these disks were kept lightweight by making the platters out of semirigid material and the housing out of cardboard. As a result, they were flexible, and a medium of this genre is typically referred to as a ***floppy disk.*** Higher capacity removable disks are now made of more rigid materials, and housed in protective plastic casings; they are sometimes called *disk cartridges.* Removable disks have a number of uses, including data backup (especially for off-site archiving), hard-disk space conservation, and transport of information between computers.

3. Optical disks

Optical disks are sometimes called ***laser disks,*** because they use lasers to read (and in some cases, to write) data on the disk. Laser light has several properties that make it useful for digital purposes. The most familiar types of optical disks are 5¼-inch, "coaster"-size, compact discs (CDs).

1. COMPACT DISCS AND CD-ROM

The ***compact disc*** (CD) was introduced in the early 1980s by Sony Corporation; the application was music recordings. Music on CDs was stored digitally, even if the recording itself was made with analog technology. It was quickly recognized that CDs could also be used to store other kinds of digital information.

The first CDs for data were used for the distribution of software and of large data sets, such as telephone directories. These CDs could only be *read* by the consumer, and so they were referred to as ***CD-ROMs***, for *read-only memory.* CD-ROMs are still used, for largely the same purposes. They are frequently created using the mechanical pitting method, and are often produced in mass quantities by machines that physically stamp, or etch, the surface of the disk.

2. RECORDABLE AND REWRITABLE CD: CD-R AND CD-RW

The newer types of CDs and CD drives that can take advantage of phase change recording allow CDs to be written to by the consumer, with the proper drives. Such drives are called CD-R and CD-RW, for *readable* and *writable;* these are becoming commonplace components on today's computers. Optical disks that have the necessary substrates to take full advantage of phase change recording can be written to and rewritten; they are designated CD-RW disks.

Certain kinds of optical media can be written to only once by a CD-RW drive; these disks are designated ***CD-R***, for *read-only* (even though they can be written once). More prosaically, these disks are known as ***WORM*** disks, for *write-once read-many.*

3. DVD

The entertainment industry led the charge to develop optical disks with higher capacity than conventional CDs, motivated by a desire to distribute motion pictures in digital form on optical media. These efforts bore fruit in the form of the ***DVD***, which stands for ***digital video disc***. The original generation of DVDs has roughly four times the data storage capacity of CDs, on a disk that has the same form factor (is the same size). DVDs are not used much at this point for data or software distribution, since CDs are usually adequate. When DVDs are used for this purpose, they are sometimes called *digital versatile discs.*

(iii) TAPE STORAGE

Tapes are removable magnetic media. The tape itself is a ribbon of plastic with a coating of magnetic material; the form factors are numerous. Most tape subsystems today house the tape in a cartridge or a cassette, although in the past, tapes were contained on open reels. Tape cartridges come in a wide variety of shapes and sizes, and there is a corresponding plethora of acronyms: DAT, DLT, Exabyte, QIC, and more.

The information on a tape is laid out in a linear fashion, from the beginning of the tape to the end. Because the tape has to travel in a line, data stored on tape have to be accessed *sequentially*, so reading and writing operations can take a long time.

For this reason, tape storage has historically been used for archival purposes, or more precisely, for purposes of disaster recovery.

2.6 DATA COMMUNICATIONS

For the purposes of this Guide, we are going to segregate communications among devices into two types, local and network. By local communication, we mean to describe signals used to control devices attached "directly" to the computer; that is, peripherals under that computer's control. When we talk about network communications, we will confine ourselves to communications between computers.

It is well to bear in mind that all this communication is fundamentally the same: it all consists of electrical signals transmitted between two devices for the purpose of managing a transaction. The nature of the signaling techniques differs in subtle, often complex and obtuse, ways. We will try to avoid the more devilish aspects in the details that follow.

(i) LOCAL DEVICE COMMUNICATION

1. Communications channels

The principal distinction we will pay attention to in local device communication is the number of bits communicated at one time. When one bit at a time is sent along a communications channel, we say that the channel employs *serial* communication. Channels that transmit several bits at a time are called *parallel*.

1. SERIAL CHANNELS

Serial communications channels require very few individual electrical connections, or wires if you will. As a consequence, they can typically be made to operate over a greater distance than parallel channels using the same amount of power. Their main drawback is communications efficiency, measured in terms of the data transfer rate. They are relatively slow because they transmit only one bit at a time.

2. PARALLEL CHANNELS

On the other hand, ***parallel*** channels move data at a higher rate, at the cost of some electrical and mechanical complexity. There are more conductors to drive the signals along, so more power is required, more wires are needed in the cable, and the end connectors are more complicated.

Several organizations have been active in developing and advocating standards for serial and parallel device communications over many years.

2. Common examples of device communications standards

1. RS-232

One of the earliest widely adopted serial communications standards was recommended by the Electronic Industries Association (EIA; now called Electronic Industries Alliance) in 1969. It is known simply as ***RS-232*** and was widely used to connect time-sharing terminals to central computers. Many printers can be controlled over this type of serial interface, and it is used to connect modems to computers; for that reason, the serial interface ports on many PCs are called COM ports (for communications, in the sense of long-distance, remote communications).

2. FIREWIRE

Apple originated its own, more efficient serial channel for the Macintosh line. Known as ***FireWire***, this popular communications technology was formalized into a standard issued by the Institute of Electrical and Electronics Engineers (IEEE); it is codified as standard IEEE 1394.

3. USB

A consortium of hardware manufacturers and software vendors collaborated on an improved form of serial communications channel, or bus, in the 1990s. The ***Universal Serial Bus*** (***USB***) has a much higher electrical signaling rate than its predecessors, which permits a higher data transfer rate. It also provides for devices to identify themselves, to bargain (negotiate) for a controller's attention, and devices can draw power from the USB line.

4. PARALLEL PRINTERS

Perhaps the most familiar kind of parallel communications occurs between PCs and printers. Originally a one-way channel designed to transmit many bytes to a printer quickly, the IEEE adopted a two-way (bidirectional) form of this communications (IEEE 1284), which is sometimes called ***BiDi***.

5. SCSI

As computers themselves became smaller, it became necessary for more devices to be "outboard" from the main chassis, and attached via communications cable. Hardware manufacturers and software vendors collaborated to develop the ***Small Computer System Interface*** (***SCSI***—usually pronounced "scuzzy") to address this issue. The first, quite successful form of the SCSI standard was adopted by the American National Standards Institute (***ANSI***) in 1986. Several successive generations of SCSI standard followed. SCSI is a parallel communications channel that is used primarily to communicate between computers and storage devices such as disks, CDs, and tape devices.

6. GPIB

Other kinds of electronic devices (in addition to storage devices and printers) can be attached to and controlled by computers. Motors and actuators, medical equipment, and data collecting instruments, among many others, need to establish communications with a host computer. While some devices have to be developed with highly specialized communications, many kinds of controllers have enough similarities that a common interface can be devised. Hewlett-Packard (HP) developed such a communications bus for its instruments in the 1960s. The interface was generalized and standardized under the auspices of the IEEE. IEEE 488 is the formal standard designation of the General Purpose Interface Bus (***GPIB***).

(ii) NETWORK COMMUNICATIONS

Modern network communications are almost all based upon a style of interaction developed in the 1970s at Xerox PARC. This communications protocol architecture is called ***client/server***.

1. The client/server protocol

The traditional ***client/server*** relationship is akin to seeker/teacher: a client program makes requests, and the server answers requests, either by supplying data or by reporting an error condition. The Web browser/server relationship is easily understood as a typical client/server service, but this has been an enormously successful way to make remote resources accessible for many other specific purposes as well.

What we now think of as ***peer-to-peer*** network services (e.g., Napster and Gnutella) are in fact simply evolved client/server implementations. These kinds of services have both client and server components built into a single piece of software. As a consequence, such programs can both initiate and respond to requests.

Information is transmitted on a network in collections of bytes called ***packets.*** Packets are often likened to envelopes with letters inside. There is an enclosing structure that contains control data, including the originating and destination addresses. The "inner" portion of the packet (the *payload*) contains the information that is really meant to be conveyed.

2. Network topology

The ***topology*** of a network is a designation of the orientation of the various computers (called ***hosts***) to each other on the network. For the most part, any differences in topology are functions of the nature of the circuit wiring, and these arise primarily in local area networks (***LAN***s).

The topologies that one is likely to encounter in LAN deployments are ring, chain or bus, star or hub-and-spoke, and mesh. Most wide-area network (***WAN***) connections are what is called ***point-to-point***, which can be regarded as a simple case of chain topology.

(iii) LINKING COMPUTERS: LANS AND WANS

In order for computers to communicate over a network, they must be connected by some sort of circuit that permits signals to be transmitted. Communications signals are propagated either over metallic cable (usually copper wires), optical fiber, or via radio waves; the latter is also called *wireless* networking. Certain kinds of signaling technologies are good over short distances, and are used in LANs, while others are suitable for transmission over greater distances; they are used for wide-area networking.

1. LAN: local area networks

Local area networks (LANs) deliver communication services for computers that are located physically close to one another. LANs can be assembled with cable, fiber, or wireless technologies, in any of several topologies.

Two widely deployed LAN protocols for cabled networks are called ***Ethernet*** and ***Token Ring***. Ethernet is far more prevalent today than Token Ring. Ethernet was developed at Xerox PARC in the 1970s; Token Ring was developed at IBM. Ethernet now refers to a family of protocols that differ principally in their speed.

The most common way to deploy a LAN is a wired Ethernet in a star topology. Each computer in the network is called a ***node***, and nodes are joined by a cable to a central connection point called a ***hub***. Hubs can be coupled together to build networks of considerable size and complexity.

Optical LANs utilize a protocol called Fiber Distributed Data Interface (***FDDI***). When it was originally developed in the 1990s, it was faster than standard Ethernet, so it was used in installations that had high bandwidth requirements. With the availability today of higher-speed versions of Ethernet, FDDI is less compelling than it used to be.

1. WIRELESS LANS

Wireless technology for the LAN has started to mature, but the market is in flux, so we will be representative rather than comprehensive. A family of standards loosely called wireless Ethernet is being developed under the auspices of the IEEE; this group of specifications is designated 802.11, followed by a letter. The "b" standard has been branded ***WiFi*** (for Wireless Fidelity) by an industry organization known as WECA, and currently there are many WiFi-compliant products available. Apple's wireless AirPort system is 802.11b-compliant.

Other short-range wireless technologies are also interesting. Ericsson's Bluetooth is designed for audio and data transmission between mobile and desktop devices; it is not specifically a networking initiative, but it can provide network connectivity for some kinds of mobile devices. HomeRF is similar in function to Bluetooth.

There is crossover in purpose and function between technologies designed for wireless networking per se and those being developed by the cellular telephone industry. Next generation cellular services (called 3G at present) will probably have 802.11 and Bluetooth compatibility. Over time, we should expect convergence at least in the operational capabilities of a wide range of "mobile" devices.

2. WAN: wide area networks

Wide-area networking (***WAN***) involves the commercial telephone and cable television networks (as opposed to LANs, which employ a private cable plant). Most wide-area technologies are *digital* in nature. However, the most familiar of the wide-area technologies, the dial-up modem circuit, is the odd one out—it uses the analog circuitry of the local telephone loop.

We will talk about the dial-up circuit first, and then turn to the remaining digital WAN technologies. The digital WANs are distinguished by the signal processing technology used to transmit data on the circuits. These differences affect the physical nature of the connection (e.g., how many wires are needed) and the equipment needed at the ends of the circuit.

1. DIAL-UP ANALOG CIRCUITS AND MODEMS

A straightforward way to make a network connection for a computer is by using a modem and a "regular" phone line. The "regular" phone line is what makes this type of connection different from the rest, because the signaling technology in ordinary voice-grade telephone service (sometimes called

POTS, for plain old telephone service) is analog rather than digital. By analog, we mean that the signals on such circuits are electrical waves, and information is conveyed (e.g., your voice is transmitted) by varying, or modulating, the amplitudes or frequencies of the waves. Computers, being far too stupid (see **Bits and Bytes above** [2.2.2.1]) to have mastered even the rudiments of electromagnetic theory, do not do waves—they do bits.

Consequently, in order to transmit digital information (a stream of bits) over an analog circuit, digital signals are transformed into waveform modulations that are carried on the analog line; these waveforms are demodulated and turned back into digital signals by the receiver. The *mo*dulation/*dem*odulation function is where the name ***modem*** is derived.

Since a modem is designed to work with an analog phone circuit, attempts to make ***dial-up*** connections are sometimes thwarted by telephone systems that aren't analog. The most notable example of this is the digital private branch exchange (***PBX***), many of which are used for internal corporate telephone systems. They are occasionally encountered in hotels as well.

2. DIGITAL CIRCUITS

When one acquires a digital circuit from a telecommunications provider, in most cases the circuit is always available for (and frequently dedicated to) network communications. Several of these technologies are familiar to the home and small office user, while others are deployed primarily by larger enterprises.

Since the circuits already operate in the digital regime, a modem per se is not required. However, devices that communicate between the WAN circuitry and the local computer or network are still required. These devices have different names, since they perform different transformations depending on the nature of the wide-area circuit.

In home and small office environments, the digital WAN technologies encountered most frequently are ISDN, DSL, and digital cable. Integrated Services Digital Network (***ISDN***) services were developed in the 1980s, although they were rarely seen prior to the mid-1990s. ISDN operates at two speeds, and small office users usually choose the lower bandwidth (because of its lower price), called the basic rate interface, or ***BRI***. The higher speed primary rate interface (***PRI***) is used by enterprises with greater bandwidth needs. One connects a local network to an ISDN circuit with a pair of devices that are called a network terminator and a terminal adapter; these are sometimes combined in a single chassis or on a single circuit board.

Digital subscriber line (***DSL***) technology is more recently developed than ISDN, and has more manifestations, so there are more choices for the customer. DSL circuits can be set up either in asymmetric or symmetric mode.

Symmetric DSL (***SDSL)*** provides the *same* bandwidth both to the customer and from the customer; asymmetric DSL (***ADSL***) circuits have *higher* bandwidth to the customer than from. The asymmetric form of the circuit makes sense for many home Internet users, since the amount of information downloaded is typically far greater than the requests issued (and uploaded) from the home computer.

DSL can be provisioned over a fairly wide range of bandwidths. Lower bandwidth options cost less, which offers customers the opportunity to tailor their costs to their usage. The device used at the customer end of a DSL circuit is often simply called a DSL router; occasionally a more technical person will refer to it as an ***ATU***, which stands for ADSL transceiver unit.

Cable television operators have upgraded their facilities in recent years in preparation for delivering digital television (***DTV***) signals. As a result, it has become possible for cable companies to offer digital data networking services on their lines as well. Digital cable network service is often called "cable Internet." The device customers install is called a ***cable modem***, although modem is something of a misnomer since the cable signals are already digital.

Larger enterprises typically contract with telecommunications providers for dedicated data circuits that have higher bandwidth as well as a higher degree of reliability. These benefits require more engineering attention to the circuit, and more robust equipment, all of which comes with a substantially higher price tag. The two principal circuit types in this regime are ***frame relay***, which provides moderate to high-speed service on copper cable, and synchronous optical networking, or ***SONET***, which is used for very-high-speed digital transmission on optical fiber. At the very high bandwidths of SONET, a highly scalable packet-switching protocol called asynchronous transfer mode, or ***ATM***, is used to route packets on the network. ATM serves the same function in these wide-area circuits as Ethernet does on a local area network.

3. CIRCUIT SPEED DESIGNATIONS

The lowest digital data rate offered by telecommunications companies is on a 64-kbps (kilobits per second) channel. Such channels have been in service for over 40 years, and originally formed the basis for long-distance voice services. A single 64-kbps channel is called a ***DS0*** circuit; DS stands for digital signal, and the zero simply indicates that it is the base service. The equivalent circuit in ISDN is called a B channel. These channels can be bundled to form circuits of higher capacity, and twenty-four 64-kbps channels comprise a DS1 circuit; 672 channels make up a DS3 circuit.

In the original engineering specification, the DS referred to the signaling standard on the line, and the corresponding equipment used to connect to the lines had a "T" designation. Thus, ***T1*** equipment handled data on DS1 circuits.

TABLE 1. TELECOMMUNICATIONS CHANNELS AND THEIR MAXIMUM SPEEDS

Service	Speed
DS0	64 kbps
DS1 (T1)	1.544 Mbps
DS3 (T3)	44.74 Mbps
OC1	51.84 Mbps
OC3	155.5 Mbps
OC12	622.1 Mbps
OC48	2.488 Gbps
OC192	9.953 Gbps
OC768	39.81 Gbps

We use the DS and T interchangeably now, so we often talk about a "T1 circuit." When twenty-four 64-kbps circuits are combined, a bandwidth of about 1.5 Mbps (megabits per second) is achieved.

Optical fiber has a much higher capacity than copper cable, so the speeds on optical circuits are much higher. The designation for transmission speeds over fiber is ***OC***, for optical carrier. A single OC circuit carries almost 52 Mbps, the equivalent of 28 T1 circuits, and a bit more than a ***T3***. The base rate for optical transmission is called OC1, and the OC number is simply a multiplier for the base rate. Many operational backbones now function at OC192, which is nearly 10Gbps (giga, or billion, bits per second). The primary Internet 2 backbones are OC192. The maximum transmission speeds provided by various services are given in Table 1.

(iv) COMMUNICATION RULES: PROTOCOLS

The rules for communication on circuits are specified in ***protocols***. There are protocols that function at various levels, from those that are concerned with the electromagnetic signals on the physical circuits to those that specify languages for fairly high-level applications. Modern networking architectures are all predicated on the notion of layers, and these layers are built upon one another to form a *protocol stack*. The standard model for the networking stack is called Open Systems Interconnection (***OSI***). The OSI model has seven layers, although not all architectures are that granular. The OSI model is not a technical specification so much as an abstraction, but it is still quite useful.

1. Networking protocols

The networking protocols that we are familiar with today have their roots in architectures that were developed in the 1970s at IBM and Xerox. IBM's Systems Network Architecture (SNA) became available for its computer systems in 1974. Xerox's networking architecture was called XNS, for Xerox Network Services. Novell's NetWare and Banyan's Vines are examples of commercially viable networking implementations that were based directly on XNS.

Other protocol families take advantage of the layered nature of networking stacks by utilizing other lower-level protocols for data delivery and circuit management; they are said to "run on" or "run over" lower-level protocols. For instance, ***AppleTalk*** can run on Ethernet or Token Ring networks, as well as using Apple's own data access protocol called ***LocalTalk***. The native Windows network transport called NetBEUI also operates on Ethernet and Token Ring networks.

The protocol family around which most networking today is based is called ***TCP/IP***, which stands for Transmission Control Protocol/Internet Protocol. It was developed under contract for the U.S. Department of Defense as part of R&D efforts to connect different computer systems. Around 1980, TCP/IP was rolled out for operational testing on the ***ARPAnet***, the Defense Department's research network that connected a number of government laboratories and research universities. The TCP layer handles the transport of packets on a local network, and the IP layer permits the routing nodes on local networks to exchange packets, that is, it supports the internetwork exchange of information. The ARPAnet evolved through the 1980s and 1990s into what we now know as the ***Internet***. It is the use of the TCP/IP protocol suite, especially the IP layer, that gives it its name.

In the late 1990s, a consortium of wireless component and cellular telephone manufacturers collaborated to develop a networking architecture for cell phones and other mobile devices. In 1997, they released the first specification of the Wireless Application Protocol, or ***WAP***. WAP provides a network environment for applications on wireless devices that is like TCP/IP. WAP is not TCP/IP, however, so native TCP/IP applications do not run on WAP devices; they must be rewritten for the WAP environment.

Consequently, the consortium, now called the WAP Forum, has developed a new version of WAP that provides support for TCP/IP applications. During this same period, the Japanese telecommunications company NTT DoCoMo has been very successful at delivering TCP/IP-based applications to cellular customers in Japan through a service called i-mode.

2. Application protocols in TCP/IP

Human beings accomplish tasks that are interesting to them when they use applications designed for useful purposes. It is increasingly important that those applications be able to exchange information among computers, and in order to do that, they are typically built upon TCP/IP interfaces. TCP/IP evolved alongside other networking architectures that used the ***client/server*** paradigm, and that model continues to serve extremely well for applications in all categories.

1. TERMINAL AND FILE SHARING SERVICES

For remotely logging onto other computers there are applications called *terminal emulation* programs. The most familiar of these are ***Telnet*** and ***ssh***. The ssh is shorthand for Secure Shell, because the program that accepts typed commands is called a command line shell. Files can be shared between computers individually with remote copy applications; the most elaborate ones use an application protocol called ***FTP***, for file transfer protocol. File systems can be shared with services like the Network File System (NFS), or the System Message Block (SMB) service.

2. INFORMATION EXCHANGE

Often we think about exchanging information more abstractly than "a file at a time." For instance, we trade messages with each other using electronic mail (***e-mail***) applications, or we want to access someone's contact information in the company directory. E-mail is transmitted on the Internet using protocols called Simple Mail Transfer Protocol (***SMTP***, for sending), the Post Office Protocol (***POP***, for retrieving), and Internet Messaging Access Protocol (***IMAP***, also for retrieving). Entries in the company's phone directory can be looked up and retrieved with the Lightweight Directory Access Protocol, or ***LDAP***. Structured catalog data, for instance of the sort that is found in a library card catalog, is retrievable from remote databases using an ANSI standard protocol called ***Z39.50***.

When we say we are going to find some information "on the Net," we are usually talking about looking for it on the ***World Wide Web***. Nowadays, most people's first interactions with the Internet take place through a Web browser, and it is sometimes hard to make the distinction between the Internet and the Web.

The Web is the global realization of a system of linked text called ***hypertext***. The notion of hypertext was devised in the 1960s by Ted Nelson. The means to link texts together on the Internet was invented in 1989 by Tim Berners-Lee, who was working at the Swiss particle physics laboratory CERN. He developed the TCP-based Hypertext Transfer Protocol, HTTP, so that texts could be requested from remote computers. (He also developed **HTML** [3.2], a simple way to tag that text to format it for the screen.) In 1993, when a research associate at the National Center for Supercomputing Applications by the name of Marc Andreessen created a GUI-based program called ***Mosaic*** that made it easy to navigate and view text and graphics over the Internet, the Web (and the Internet) became a phenomenon.

3. APPLICATION SERVICES AND DISCOVERY

The systems we are building today are complex, and the logical systems are often distributed among many computers, even if we don't originally conceive of them that way. These systems evolve now in an environment where computers communicate directly and autonomously with other computers.

We now have interfaces like ***SOAP***, the Simple Object Access Protocol, that allow programs to request services and functions along the lines of "put these numbers in a payroll spreadsheet" or "format these two paragraphs." In order to discover services that remote machines are offering, systems can use ***WSDL***, the Web Services Description Language.

There is practically no end to the complexity to which we can construct systems that exchange information anywhere in the world, or even in the solar system. We can debate how successful we might be at doing so, or whether it is even a good thing to have access to all this information, but even when we construct relatively simple information delivery systems, it is good to have a firm grasp of the underlying principles.

2.7 ADDITIONAL INTERESTING RESOURCES

The Computer History Museum in Mountain View, California, has an interactive timeline that takes you through the history of computers from a variety of viewpoints. Start browsing at http://www.computerhistory.org/timeline/.

When you want to get to know how microprocessors work, you can visit the Intel Museum on-line exhibits at http://www.intel.com/intel/intelis/museum/exhibit/.

A comprehensive history of the development and technology of the Internet has been compiled by Bill Stewart on the Living Internet Web site at http://www.livinginternet.com/.

For thorough definitions of many technical terms and concepts, as well as for the proper expansions of those pesky acronyms, the folks at CMP Media offer the TechEncyclopedia at http://content.techweb.com/encyclopedia/.

BIBLIOGRAPHY

Corbató, F.J., and V. A. Vyssotsky. "Introduction and Overview of the Multics System." 1965. http://www.multicans.org/fjcc1.html

Foster, I. "The Grid: A New Infrastructure for 21st Century Science." Physics Today 55, no. 2: 42. http://www.physicstoday.org/pt/vol-55/iss-2/p42.html

InterPlaNet Project. "Interplanetary Internet Special Interest Group." http://www.ipnsig.org/home.htm

Richie, Dennis M. "The Evolution of the Unix Time-Sharing System." Lucent Technologies. 1996. http://cm.bell-labs.com/cm/cs/who/dmr/hist.html

Scott, Ridley. *1984*. Apple Macintosh advertisement, 1984. http://www.apple-history.com/1984.html

Webopedia. "Network Topologies." Internet.com. 2002. http://www.webopedia.com/quick_ref/topologies.html

3 Markup: XML & Related Technologies

WILLIAM E. KASDORF
President, Impressions Book and Journal Services, Inc.

Markup enables the various parts and features of a given set of content to be distinguished and named. It provides a way to label, describe, and delimit these in a publication so that processing systems can tell them apart and know how they relate to each other. Markup languages are used to define specific markup schemes. In the past, markup languages were typically proprietary and used only by specialists. The Web gave rise to one of the simplest and most widely used markup languages ever devised, HTML, and also to one of the most flexible and powerful: XML, the Extensible Markup Language. After a brief overview of earlier markup languages, this chapter focuses on the technologies in the XML family—XML itself, and related standards for defining, styling, linking, transforming, and annotating—that provide the foundation for digital publishing today.

3.1 OVERVIEW

(i) WHAT IS MARKUP?

At the most basic level, markup can be thought of as the tags and codes embedded in a given set of content that delineate and describe the component parts of that content. An editor marks up a paper manuscript by labeling a chapter number "CN," a chapter title, "CT," a first-level subhead "H1" or "A," an extracted block quote "EX" or "BQ." Traditionally, this markup has provided the instructions for a typesetter, who inserts a different set of markup (often **proprietary markup** [3.1.1.2]) that controls the composition of that content in a particular format using a particular composition system. (In such a system, the code for a chapter title might be "/CT/" or "@CT:" or "[j2].") That same content, when published on the Web, would be marked up with a different set of tags, most likely using HyperText Markup Language (***HTML***); in that case, the chapter title might be marked as "<H2>." In each of these examples, the markup is not the content to be published, but a guide to how some subsequent person or system should process or present it. (The electronic version of the Guide provides examples of various types of markup applied to the portion of text you are reading.)

In a sense, even punctuation can be thought of as a form of markup. Spaces help us tell words apart; periods and capital letters organize those words into sentences; commas, colons, semicolons, dashes, and parentheses help us distinguish the parts of sentences, tell which are subordinate to others, and signal what they mean and how they relate. (We think of those marks as universal, but they're not; they're specific to certain languages or even certain contexts. What looks like a period in the expression "$2.98" is not a period, but a decimal point, actually part of the language of mathematics; in Europe a comma might be used instead, e.g., "2,98." More on **ambiguous markup** [3.1.1.3] below.) In a strict sense, though, punctuation is part of the character set by which a given set of content is expressed; markup typically uses that same character set, or a subset of it, but exists apart from the content itself. In the chapter title "Welcome Home, Our Sophie Mol" the comma is part of the title, whereas a tag like <CT>, which might be attached to it, is markup.

1. Visual cues

Markup is often thought to be "invisible" because the ultimate reader or viewer of the content typically does not see the markup itself, but only the result of the markup. Just as we take punctuation for granted (except when it's incorrect or ambiguous, or when we don't speak the language), we also take for granted the visual cues that guide us to the structure and meaning of what we read. When reading a book, we don't need to see a <CT> tag to know that the words following the chapter number at the beginning of a new page, set in a larger size and perhaps in a special font, are a chapter title. We can usually tell that a second-level subhead is subordinate to a first-level subhead because it is formatted in a less prominent way. We can tell that an extract is a quotation from some other work because it is indented and separated from the text above and below it; and if it is followed by a name set flush right and perhaps preceded by a dash, we recognize that as the attribution of that quotation. When reading a magazine article, we know that the name following the title of the article and set smaller is the author of the article, even if the word "by" does not precede it. On a Web site, we realize that a word or phrase is linked to another location because it is underscored and perhaps blue. In all of these cases, experience has taught us what these typographic conventions mean, so we don't need to actually see the markup to understand the content properly.

2. Proprietary markup

Although human beings may not need markup to interpret those visual cues, some processing system needed explicit instructions to produce them in the first place. A typesetting system needed codes to tell it what font to set that chapter title in, and how big to make it, and where to position it on the page. A Web browser needed codes to tell it to mark a phrase as a link anchor, and to specify what to link to. The authors probably used a word processor to format the content when they wrote it in the first place, and although they might not have realized it, even when they highlighted a phrase and clicked on a bold B button to make it boldface, the word processing system inserted codes to make that happen.

Each of these processing systems typically has its own proprietary set of codes. Generally, except by people in the business of converting them, these codes are not recognized or understood outside the system they were created for. When an author made that chapter title big and bold and centered it on the page in Microsoft Word, the underlying codes in Word would not produce the same result in a typesetting system. Instead, they would need to be converted into the proprietary markup that particular typesetting system uses. Likewise, when those typesetting files are later used to publish that content on the Web, the typesetting codes (unless they are ***XML***) will not tell the Web browser how to format the content; they will need to be converted into HTML or XML.

In a simpler time, when content was typically published in one and only one form, proprietary markup was not much of a problem. Authors used word processors (or even typewriters) in more or less sophisticated ways (generally less), printed out the result, and sent a stack of paper to a publisher. The publisher edited on paper, marking up the manuscript with codes perhaps unique to that publishing house, and then sent the marked-up stack of paper to a typesetter. If the typesetter worked regularly for that publisher, the typesetting and proofreading staff would probably know what the editor's markup meant; if not, they would have to ask or guess. In any case, the typesetter would mark up the manuscript again, this time with the codes needed for the particular composition system to be used. Then the manuscript would be rekeyboarded, with the typesetting markup embedded in the files, in order to produce the typeset pages. The final product would be paper or film, which would be sent to a printer. Except for the typesetter who had to interpret the editor's markup, nobody in that chain needed to know anything about the codes that the other participants used.

That was a simpler time, but it was not a better time. From the point of view of today's technology, the inefficiency of the old process is obvious. Even when the content is published only in print, it makes sense to edit the electronic file the author created, and to use the editor's file for typesetting, and to use the typesetter's file for printing. Beyond that, it makes sense to use the composition file to create an e-book or to publish on the Web. The obstacle to doing so is proprietary markup. Would any sensible typesetter pay to rekey-board and reproofread if they could just as easily use the editor's file? Would any Web developer rekey and recode the content again if they could easily use the typesetter's file? But these things still happen all too often. Either material is rekeyed and recoded at each step, or laborious and sometimes costly conversions are done to translate from one set of proprietary codes to another, and then to another. This is the problem that led to the development of **nonproprietary markup languages** [3.1.2], the history of which is surveyed below.

3. Rigorous vs. ambiguous markup

Another obstacle to the efficient use of files between unrelated systems is ambiguous markup. A proprietary system can use shortcuts and make assumptions because it is designed to be a closed system. As long as it knows what it is doing, it does not care if other systems can interpret it. In the past, Microsoft Word was notorious for this. Whereas WordPerfect files had codes clearly embedded in the text (and viewable through a reveal codes function), early Word versions parked much of the code that controlled the file at the end of the file, making it very hard to convert. Microsoft developed a system called Rich Text Format (RTF) that provides a version of a Word file with embedded markup interpretable by other systems, but the codes in an RTF file are only consistent if the file was created in the first place in a clear and consistent way. (The chapter **Data Capture and Conversion** [5] treats this subject in depth.)

1. FORMATTING AMBIGUITY

Often, the ambiguity is the result of relying on formatting and styling to communicate meaning and structure. For example, it might be assumed that three indented lines, preceded and followed by blank lines, would be an extract. But it could also be a list with three items. The same character is used to type the period at the end of the sentence and the decimal point in the expression "$2.98." An italicized phrase might be emphasis, or it might be a book title, or it might be a glossary term, or it might be a genus and species. People can usually interpret these things correctly, because they understand the content and context, but computers need much more rigorous markup.

2. STRUCTURAL AMBIGUITY

Even computer-driven systems can be ambiguous. QuarkXPress, for example, uses a markup called XPress Tags. A list in QuarkXPress might be coded in XPress Tags like this:

```
@LFI:List first item
@LMI:List middle item
```

@LMI:List middle item
@LLI:List last item

Note that although there is a clear tag marking the beginning of each element, there is no tag marking the end. That's because Quark assumes that when a new element starts, it ends the previous element. In a flat, styles-based system like QuarkXPress, this is sufficient; but it makes it difficult to tag hierarchical structures where some elements are nested inside others. (Styles-based systems like Word and Quark place elements one after another, whereas most structured markup like XML or even HTML needs to be able to place elements one inside another.) Note, too, that the items in the list are not all coded the same: QuarkXPress needs to know to put extra space above the first item, below the last item, and none around the middle items.

Even in a markup language as simple as HTML, nested coding is required for a list, where a "container element" tagged <UL> (unordered list) contains list items tagged <LI>:

<UL>
<LI>List first item</LI>
<LI>List middle item</LI>
<LI>List middle item</LI>
<LI>List last item</LI>
</UL>

Note that in the HTML example (which could also be an XML example, by the way), the first, middle, and last items are not coded differently (as they usually would be in a composition system); instead, they are all coded the same, and the structure of the list is provided by explicit codes saying where the list begins and ends and where each item begins and ends. Rigorous markup like this is much more powerful, enabling content to be more easily converted—and even to be used by some formatting or processing systems without conversion—or to be transformed into other forms or transplanted into other contexts.

3. MISSING CODES

Another common problem with word processing and composition files is that some coding needed for electronic processing is simply not there at all. Take, for example, a book where the text tells the reader to "see Fig. 5.2." A composition system that can make up pages automatically probably uses a code like [ln5.2], embedded immediately after that figure reference, to signal to the software to go get figure 5.2 and put it at the bottom of the page where it sees the [ln5.2] code (or, if there is not enough room, then the top of the next page). It's very useful to have a code like that in the file, because if that content needs to be reformatted into a different page design—or even a computer screen—there is a marker associating a particular figure with a particular point in the file. Most desktop publishing files would lack such a code. Instead, the desktop operator would simply watch for the figure references in the text (perhaps alerted by the editor's markup in the margins of the manuscript), place the figure where it belongs, and flow the text around it.

It is often naively assumed that the text itself provides sufficient markers. This is rarely the case. Phrases like "see the figure below" or "as figures 5.2–5.5 illustrate" make it difficult or impossible to programmatically derive the proper markup. And pity the poor reference publisher who wants to associate a picture of Washington with every mention of George Washington. Searching for "Washington" will bring up the city or the state; searching for "George Washington" will not only miss all the instances where the first U.S. president is referred to as "Washington" (not to mention "the president" or "General Washington"), it will also connect with references to the George Washington Bridge or George Washington Carver. Only explicit, rigorous markup can resolve these ambiguities. And note that the composition file that *does* have an explicit code marking figure 5.2 only associates that code with the *first* reference to that particular figure. When the same content is published electronically, the publisher will likely want to associate that figure with *every* reference to it. All those other codes are likely to be missing.

4. Separating structure and appearance

The root cause of the ambiguities discussed above is usually that markup systems in the past have focused on appearance. Proprietary typesetting systems are concerned with making all the elements on the page look right: the extracts are indented and have spaces above and below them, the level-one subheads are bold whereas the level-two subheads are italic, the chapter number is in a special font and always starts a new page. Even when such systems began to use generic codes (so that they would mark an extract as EX rather than inserting spacing and indenting codes, or mark a chapter number as CN instead of specifying its font and size), there was rarely anything in the system that ensured that these codes were used properly. Operators could "fix" an H2 that had been improperly coded as an H1 by simply changing it from bold to italic. As long as the page looked right, it didn't seem to matter—until somebody wanted to use that electronic file for another purpose, in which case that subhead would look like an italic H1, not an H2.

The problem of markup for appearance is not confined to composition files. In a fundamental way, most markup for the Web (see **HTML** [3.2] below) is appearance based as well. HTML is basically a system of markup to instruct a Web browser how to format the marked-up content. It offers, for example, a fixed set of subhead tags, but since <H1> is inappropriate for use as a subhead (it would display at too large a size), <H3> might be used in HTML for subheads tagged as <H1> in editing and composition, because an <H3> will look better to the user. In fact, these codes are often supplemented by other formatting codes, or not used at all, because the Web designer wants to use specific fonts and specific spacing to display a certain element, rather than leaving it to the user's browser to format. This is one reason why HTML is not very useful as an archive: it is often tagged for one specific presentation mode (Web display with a certain generation of browsers) and not easily adaptable to others.

The fundamental genius of the family of markup languages that originated with Standard Generalized Markup Language (***SGML***)and its predecessors and that has now evolved into ***XML*** (see below for this **history** [3.1.2]) is that they had the wisdom to separate structure and meaning from appearance. They created a markup method that enabled the various elements in a given body of content to be named and identified with no reference to how they should appear in any particular presentation. A level-two subhead is always and only tagged as an <H2> (if that is the tag defined for that purpose for that content); in one print context it may be 12-point Helvetica Medium and in another it may be 14-point Palatino Italic, in one Web display it may default to HTML's <H4> and in another it may be a particular font and size and color, but in the source XML file it only needs the tag <H2>. The formatting instructions for displaying that subhead in the desired way in each of those contexts are not encoded into the XML file itself; instead, they are supplied separately, in processing systems or stylesheets that know how they are supposed to format an <H2> in their specific environment. The beauty of this is that the source file, with its <H2> and hundreds or thousands of other such tags, does not have to be recoded for use in those various contexts. Instead, the presentation system or environment recognizes the <H2> and formats it properly according to the instructions it has been given. Imagine how much laborious conversion, and complexity, and chance for error, this eliminates!

1. MARKUP FOR STRUCTURE

Without the burden of having to describe the appearance of elements, a markup language like XML is able to describe complex structures composed of elements that contain other elements, each of which might have a different appearance. In a Quark file for a printed book, for example, it may be possible to specify the appearance of a chapter number, and a chapter title, and normal text, and extracts, and subheads, and lists, and all the other things a chapter may contain; but it is not possible to describe the appearance of a chapter. With a markup language like XML, it is possible to define and delimit structural units that contain other structural units, whether or not they look alike or contain a variety of formats: there can be an element called a <CHAPTER>, and inside chapters there can be <SECTION>s (which might contain titles and text and lists and other things), and these might contain <SUBSECTION>s. There might be certain kinds of sections, like introductions or exercises or bibliographies, and these might have to be in certain structural locations: introductions might have to follow the chapter title and precede body text, bibliographies might have to be the last section in a chapter. The ability to classify and specify such structural elements and features is one of the strengths of XML and its relatives.

2. MARKUP FOR MEANING

Perhaps the greatest benefit of eliminating appearance from markup is the ability to make meaningful distinctions between elements that may look identical. A phrase in italic might be a foreign expression, or a book title, or an exclamation, or a genus and species, or any of a number of things; but in typical word processing, composition, or desktop publishing files such items would simply be marked up as italic. When the only use of the marked-up file was to produce a print book, this was not much of a problem; the reader can usually figure out which of those things a given italic phrase is because she understands the content and context. But when such a file needs to be used in an electronic environment, it would be very desirable, for example, to link foreign expressions to a glossary, and book titles to a bibliography, or to enable users to search for a particular genus and species. Markup languages like XML provide the ability to make these distinctions.

Such meaning-based markup can have a profound effect on presentation and electronic delivery. For example, if a given sequence of numbers is marked up as <phone_number>, it might be preceded by the word "Tel:" or "Phone:" in one presentation, or set in a column of such numbers with the heading "Telephone" or "No." in another. If a given passage of text is marked as <ABSTRACT>, it can not only be formatted in a special way, it can also be delivered free to nonsubscribers. Imagine how useful it is to know that a certain name refers to the <AUTHOR> or a certain number is the <PRICE>. This kind of markup for meaning is at the heart of not only the electronic publishing environment but electronic commerce and information management in general.

(ii) A BRIEF HISTORY OF STRUCTURED MARKUP STANDARDS

The father of SGML (and thus the godfather of HTML and the grandfather of XML) is widely acknowledged to be Charles F. Goldfarb. Goldfarb spent most of his career at IBM developing and implementing the two key aspects of generic markup: that it should separate the description of a document's elements and other attributes from instructions for formatting or otherwise processing those documents, and that it should be rigorous. A lawyer who came to programming and publishing quite by accident, Goldfarb was motivated initially not by grandiose ambitions to create some master text database scheme, but by the frustrations he encountered in preparing legal documents (in the mid 1960s, this involved typing, and retyping, and more retyping) and, later, in attempting to exchange documents between various early electronic systems for writing, editing, storage, and typesetting (each of which used different coding schemes and different applications on equipment with incompatible operating systems).

1. GenCode and GML

Goldfarb is quick to credit others for sharing in the creation of generic markup. First of these is William Tunnicliffe, chair of the Composition Committee of the GCA (the Graphic Communications Association, now IDEAlliance), whose 1967 presentation on separating the formatting of documents from information about their content led to the formation of the GCA's GenCode Committee. At that same time, Stanley Rice, a prominent book designer, was developing a thoroughgoing standardized markup scheme for publications that led to two innovative early software products, AutoSpec to streamline book design and specification and AutoCast to automate castoffs (estimates of the how long a manuscript will be when typeset to given specs).

Assigned the task at IBM of coming up with a way to integrate the production of legal documents, Goldfarb worked with Edward Mosher and Raymond Lorie to develop, in 1969, the Generic Markup Language (***GML***—which he acknowledges are not coincidentally the initials of its inventors). In GML, Goldfarb did more than simply extend the work of Tunnicliffe and Rice. He realized (as did they) that there are many different types of documents, which call for different coding schemes; rather than attempting a "master generic coding scheme" that could theoretically apply to all documents, in GML he provided a mechanism for formally defining document types. He also tended to see document structures as nested hierarchies, and built the capability of describing these into GML. Although there is no requirement in GML, SGML, or XML that documents be defined in a nested, hierarchical fashion (XML requires proper nesting, but this does not preclude a single level where all elements simply follow one another, as they do in a typical word processing file; there are many situations where such nonhierarchical definitions are more useful), this predisposition to define nested structures is an important design philosophy in many document type definitions.

It is also interesting to note that IBM initially attempted to make GML proprietary, in the context of their Document Composition Facility (***DCF***), the first commercial implementation of GML. When Goldfarb presented a demonstration in 1971 to the GCA, he was not allowed to show technical details. In 1978, almost a decade after the invention of GML, IBM's *DCF GML User's Guide* was the first publication of a formal document type definition. (The example Goldfarb used in that guide was eventually used both in the publication of the SGML standard and as the origin of HTML.) So although GML led to the most idealistic and nonproprietary standards in publishing, it arose both from the practical problems of document creation and from the desire of a commercial enterprise for competitive advantage.

2. SGML: the Standard Generalized Markup Language

The need for a nonproprietary standard, however, was clear. In 1978, the American National Standards Institute (***ANSI***) asked Goldfarb to lead a project—which was also supported by GCA's GenCode committee—to develop a text description language standard based on GML. The first working draft of SGML, the Standard Generalized Markup Language, was published in 1980, and the GCA promoted the sixth draft in 1983 as an industry standard that was used by the U.S. Department of Defense and the Internal Revenue Service. After three more drafts, the project became international in scope with the participation of the International Organization for Standardization (the ***ISO***), overseen by the ISO working group generally known as ***WG8***, and still including the active participation of ANSI and GCA's GenCode committee. When a draft international standard was published in 1985, the SGML Users' Group was founded, and the final text was published as ISO 8879 in 1986.

Note that SGML was being used throughout its development. Although it became a stable, international standard in 1986, its concepts were clear and its technology powerful enough for it to be of value in many contexts throughout the 1980s. One important context in which it was used was the Electronic Manuscript Project of the Association of American Publishers (AAP), an initiative in which SGML was used to develop a system for document interchange between authors and publishers. That work eventually led to the development of one of the most important general-purpose ***Document Type Definitions (DTDs)*** known as ***ISO 12083*** (another international standard), written mainly by Eric van Herwijnen, accommodating books, serials, articles, and math. Seldom used in its pure form in actual publishing environments today, ISO 12083 is nevertheless the basis for many DTDs in common use. Another very important general-purpose DTD is ***TEI*** from the Text Encoding Initiative, actually a modular collection of definitions widely used in scholarship and also the basis for many publisher-specific DTDs. (Both **ISO 12083** [3.3.2.3.1] and **TEI** [3.3.2.3.2] are discussed further below.) Finally, one of the most influential early SGML implementations was done by the U.S. Department of Defense, leading to a standard published in 1988 as MIL-M-28001 and commonly known as CALS (Computer-aided Acquisition and Logistic Support) by which the U.S. military and its thousands of contractors and suppliers can exchange documents. The CALS table model has been particularly influential, and is often incorporated into other DTDs.

3. HTML: HyperText Markup Language

HTML, the HyperText Markup Language, as one of the fundamental technologies of the World Wide Web, is undeniably the most widely used implementation of SGML. At first it was a simple tagging scheme that was based on SGML principles but was not, technically, an SGML application because it lacked a formal DTD. Instead, it was a limited but very useful set of tags for marking up electronic text files in order to enable a browser to render them on a computer screen and to be able to link documents to each other. It was specifically designed for handling by both sophisticated and unsophisticated systems. Its development was begun in 1989 by Tim Berners-Lee and others at CERN, the European Particle Physics Laboratory, where IBM's GML- and then SGML-based Document Composition Facility was in use. HTML 1.0 was published in 1992, and its power and simplicity led to extremely rapid implementation. Browser developers created their own variations of it and implemented some features in different ways (prompting the "browser wars" of the 1990s). The "official" specification for HTML has been periodically revised by the World Wide Web Consortium (W3C). (**HTML** [3.2] is discussed at greater length below.)

4. XML: the Extensible Markup Language

Despite HTML's popularity, and because of its simplicity, it soon became evident that it would not be able to handle all the things people wanted to be able to do over the Web. As a fixed set of tags, it gave publishers and developers no good way to create new tags specifically suited to their needs. At the same time, it seemed that SGML was too complex to be easily implemented in the context of the Web. SGML's very flexibility was part of the problem: since almost anything can be redefined in SGML (even down to the characters that delimit codes: < and > are commonly used, but SGML does not require them), SGML files need sophisticated software to be interpreted properly.

XML was developed as a subset of SGML that would be easy to implement on the Web. By omitting some features of SGML and reducing the flexibility of others—it is more restrictive than SGML—it is much easier to use and to make software tools for. Nevertheless, valid XML documents (those described by a DTD) are also valid SGML documents, or could easily be transformed into SGML. (The reverse is not quite as easy: not all SGML documents are XML documents, although well-constructed SGML documents common to publishers can usually be easily transformed to XML.)

Development of XML began in 1996 under the auspices of a ***W3C*** working group (see below for a description of the **W3C** [3.1.3.2]) chaired by Jon Bosak of Sun Microsystems; its co-editors were Tim Bray and C. M. Sperberg-McQueen, and James Clark was the technical liaison. It was released as an official W3C Recommendation as XML 1.0 in 1998, and it met with both rapid and wide acceptance. XML is now considered a fundamental technology not only for the markup of documents to be published in the conventional sense, but for the exchange of information of all sorts, ranging from data to images to software programs. It is widely used in all types of publishing and e-commerce. It has also led to the development of a host of related technologies, which are discussed below.

(iii) OPEN STANDARDS

The need for standards in publishing is obvious, but it is difficult to develop standards that satisfy a variety of interested parties. Some standards are created by single individuals or organizations, often commercial enterprises, and become standards due to their nearly universal acceptance; these are known as *de facto* standards. ***PostScript*** (and its descendant, ***PDF***) has become the standard page description language, but when it was originally developed it competed in the marketplace with others; even after emerging the obvious victor, it still remains in the control of Adobe Systems, its inventor and owner. Other standards are developed as a result of cooperation between parties who have some common interest, and ideally become freely and publicly available; these are known as *open standards*.

Open standards are generally more difficult to create and to maintain. Cooperation is required between parties who are often in competition with each other; even identifying which parties ought to have a say in the standard is problematic. Satisfying the diverse needs (and opinions) of a big enough set of participants to create a viable standard without resulting in a standard that is either overly complex (trying to be everything to everybody) or overly simplistic (reducing everyone's needs to a basic but barely useful set) is a delicate balancing act. It is interesting to compare SGML, XML, and OeB in this regard.

1. SGML and ISO, the International Organization for Standardization

SGML, while complex, is a very stable, international standard. Its complexity comes from its extreme flexibility: virtually anything can be customized or redefined in SGML. This gives it the power to adapt to the diverse needs of anybody publishing anything; but it also requires customization to a large extent—it is not simply a set of ready-to-use codes. (One publisher might want <FN> to mean "footnote," another might want it to mean "first name," a cloth manufacturer might use it for "fabric number"—and a publisher not publishing in English might not want it to mean any of those.) Its stability comes largely from the elaborate process needed to develop, change, and approve such an international standard. It is governed by the ISO, whose mission is to develop global standards through the consensus of all interested parties within a given industry. ISO, a federation of the national standards bodies of some 140 countries, uses a very thorough process by which standards are proposed, debated internationally, developed by representative committees, subcommittees, and working groups, negotiated between countries of the world, and published only when approved by two-thirds of the ISO members who worked on its development and three-quarters of those who vote. Although SGML, as ISO 8879, has been amended over time (in fact, all ISO standards must be reviewed in no longer than five years), the changes are infrequent and not typically fundamental. The result is a standard that publishers and tool makers can count on not to change much or often.

2. XML and the W3C

The tradeoff for stability is adaptability. The Web operates at "Internet speed": ideas proliferate constantly, develop rapidly, and are implemented while debates are still raging. All of this needs to happen too fast for the thorough but slow ISO process. The ***W3C*** was founded in 1994 by Tim Berners-Lee, the inventor of the Web and now the W3C's director, to provide a governance for the technical evolution of the Web that is responsive enough to keep up with fast-changing technology and representative enough to accommodate a wide range of interest groups. Open to anyone, it is composed of over 500 Member Organizations—product vendors, service providers, publishers, corporations, academic institutions, standards bodies, and governmental organizations—who, through various Working Groups, operate largely by consensus to evaluate and develop proposed technologies for the Web: HTML, XML, and a host of related specifications.

To distinguish their technical specifications from the true international standards issued by ISO, W3C publishes what it calls ***Recommendations***. These are specifications for a given technology that have achieved both consensus within the W3C and the Director's formal approval. Recommendations are considered reliable and stable, so that they can be implemented safely. To get to the recommendation stage, an idea is first published as a "Note" (officially acknowledging the idea); when the W3C commits to work on it, it becomes a "Working Draft." After its specific technical community has come to agreement on it, it is published as a "Candidate Recommendation," inviting wider review and test implementation; when it successfully passes that wider review, it is published as a "Proposed Recommendation," inviting more general comment until it finally achieves Recommendation status. This process is much more thorough and formal than the way de facto standards get thrust into the marketplace, but more flexible and speedy than the full ISO standardization process. It has proved to be an effective way to develop and promote specifications that meet the needs of a wide variety of interest groups; the success of the Web is evidence of its effectiveness.

3. OeB and the Open eBook Forum

The e-book industry has come up with an interesting solution to the dilemma of whether to create a standard that is simple and fixed (but which thus doesn't adapt to variant needs well) or a standard that is totally flexible but which thereby places demands on tools and users to be able to deal with the unknown and unexpected. The Open eBook Publication Structure (***OEBPS***) comes in two versions: ***Basic OEB*** and ***Extended OEB***. Basic OEB is a fixed set of tags that largely conform to XHTML (Extensible HyperText Markup Language), which itself is an XML implementation of HTML 4.01. For software to be considered OeB compliant, it must be able to interpret these tags with no further instructions. This tag set is quite limited; it is a useful output format for presentation, but it does not have the richness needed to make many distinctions (there are no <author> or <chapter> codes, for example). Although it is written in XML, Basic OEB can be thought of as "HTML for e-books." Extended OeB, on the other hand, gives publishers the ability to add XML tags that are not included in the Basic OEB tag set (thus making it, in effect, "XML for e-books"). It stipulates, however, that a CSS stylesheet must be provided to specify the formatting for each such new tag. (The OeB Publication Structure is discussed in detail in the chapter on **e-Books** [11.6].)

The OeB specifications are governed not by ISO or the W3C, but by an industry group called the Open eBook Forum (OeBF) originally convened in 1998 (but not controlled) by the National Institute for Standards and Technology (NIST). Like the W3C, the OeBF is a collaboration of vendors, service providers, publishers, software developers, and others interested in fostering the e-book industry. It is composed of a number of committees that concentrate on specific areas—for example, the Publication Structure Working Group, the Metadata Working Group, the Rights and Rules Working Group, the Accessibility Special Interest Group, and so forth. The main thrust of the OeBF is to publish open, nonproprietary standards for e-books based on open standards like XML and Unicode.

3.2 HTML: HYPERTEXT MARKUP LANGUAGE

If there were a prize for Markup Language of the Millennium, the undisputed winner would be HTML. (That is, for the millennium just ended; for the current millennium, the leading contender would be XML—though if measured by use, HTML is still far in the lead.) In a little over a decade, it has become a fundamental tool for communicating information of all sorts—from scientific research to stock prices, from education to entertainment, from breaking news to the ramblings of anybody with a Web page and some spare time. Virtually everything seen today on the Web uses HTML, even if it started out as XML or some other form of data, because HTML is the markup language used to tell Web browsers how to display HTML-tagged content. That stock price generated dynamically from a database is converted into HTML for viewing; so is the XML for the on-line version of this Guide.

HTML's success is a testament to the value of an effective, simple solution that meets a need—or, arguably, *creates* a need—a solution that gets the job done without attempting to be the *ultimate* solution. HTML never pretended to be more than it is: a simple set of tags that make it easy to mark up content so that it can be displayed as more than plain text. It was not intended to be typographically sophisticated (and it isn't); it was not intended to enable sophisticated labeling and structuring of information (and it doesn't). In fact, it was not even intended to be particularly rigorous: it's notoriously permissive, and the browsers that have been built to render it are notoriously permissive too. XML was created to "correct" these "problems" with HTML; but fundamentally this is a case where the proverbial programmer's excuse is valid: those aren't problems, those are *features*. The fact that HTML makes it so easy to communicate with anybody and everybody is its reason for being.

The term "hypertext" was coined by Ted Nelson in 1965: in an article published by *Literary Machines* (http://www.eastgate.com/catalog/LiteraryMachines.html), he defined it as "nonsequential writing." A research project called *The Electronic Labyrinth* (http://jefferson.village.virginia.edu/elab/contact.html) later defined hypertext as "the presentation of information as a linked network of nodes which readers are free to navigate in a nonlinear fashion." In such an environment, where new connections and links and relationships are continually developing, the creator of information has very little control or even knowledge of the ultimate consumer of the information. A common language that is very clear and simple—and free—has much greater chance of success than something complicated or proprietary.

HTML was first created by Tim Berners-Lee and Robert Caillau, who both worked at CERN, an international center for high-energy physics research in Switzerland. At that time—1989—it was difficult for researchers to exchange documents even within their own organization (not to mention outside organizations) because of the wide variety of hardware and software in use, ranging from simple text-based "dumb terminals" to sophisticated graphical workstations. They understood the principles behind SGML, and recognized that a very simple implementation was needed to work across such a range of systems. Along with the HyperText Transfer Protocol (***HTTP***), they created HTML—and thus laid the foundation for the Web, since HTTP and HTML were useful not just in a local network but over the Internet as well.

By its very simplicity, HTML fueled the initial Web explosion, opening the door to practically all users to become Web publishers. Its interoperability—the capability to be displayed on all browsers, all platforms, all machines—and the fact that it was open source, made it quickly into a standard. Berners-Lee expressed the goal of HTML best: "The Web should be a medium for the communication between people: communication through shared knowledge. For this to work, the computers, networks, operating systems, and commands have to become invisible, and leave us with an intuitive interface as directly as possible to the information" (Realising the Full Potential of the Web: http://www.w3.org/1998/02/Potential.html).

(i) PARTS OF AN HTML DOCUMENT

The formatting of HTML documents depends on markup codes called tags. HTML is a set of 91 tags; these tags define the structure of the document in terms Web browsers can interpret. Each element name is enclosed by angle brackets, such as <H1>, which indicates the start of a level one heading. HTML is not case sensitive: <h1> and <H1> both denote the same thing.

Most tags are used in pairs: a *start tag* tells the browser that a document element is starting; the *end tag* tells the browser an element is ending. The only difference between them is that the end tag contains a forward slash before the element name. For example, the heading start tag <H1> is paired with the heading end tag </H1>. The initial <H1> tag tells the browser a level one heading is starting and the end tag </H1> tells the browser the heading is ending. One of the permissive aspects of HTML is that tag names are not case sensitive; <H1> could be paired with either </h1> or </H1>. In fact, browsers may still display a page (though perhaps incorrectly) even if certain end tags are missing. (XML doesn't let you get away with that.) Again, this is a *feature:* in HTML, it is deemed more important to make a stab at displaying a page even if the coding isn't perfect.

Every HTML document should begin with the markup tag <HTML> and end with the markup tag </HTML>. The start tag <HTML> tells the browser that the document is an HTML-formatted document. The end tag </HTML>

marks the end of the document and is always the last item in any HTML document. Every HTML document should also have a header and a body.

1. The header

The header immediately follows the <HTML> start tag. The HEAD element contains information about the current document, such as its title, keywords that may be useful to search engines, and other data not considered displayable "content." Even if they don't display it, Web browsers do not generally render elements that appear in the HEAD as content. They may make information in the HEAD available through other mechanisms. The most commonly used header tag is the <TITLE> tag. Every HTML document must have a TITLE element in the HEAD section.

Though the other elements of the HEAD section are not required, some authors may specify ***metadata*** (data about data, which is generally not displayed on the page) in a variety of ways by using META tags within the HEAD section.

This META element can be used to identify other informatin about or properties of a document (e.g., author, expiration date, a list of key words, language) and even assign values to those properties. This is done by creating ***attributes*** for the META element, for example, <meta name="author" content="OBS">. A common use for the META element is to specify key words that a search engine may use to improve the quality of search results.

2. The body

Following the header comes the main document section: *the body*. The body contains the text and objects for display. This content may be presented in a variety of ways. For example, for visual browsers, you can think of the body as a canvas where the content appears: text, images, colors, graphics, etc. For audio Web browsers, the same content may be spoken. Like the header, the body has a start tag <BODY> and an end tag </BODY>.

Inside the BODY tags you may find things like normal paragraphs of text which are tagged as starting with <P> and ending with </P>, and between the paragraphs you may put different levels of text heads. (There are six of these heads, <H1> through <H6>, and they can occur in any order.) Lists can appear in a variety of different styles as either Ordered Lists <OL> (1, 2, 3 . . . A, B, C . . . I, II, III) or Unordered Lists <UL>, featuring a bullet next to each list item. Other text elements that you might find within the BODY are:

- Tables (<TABLE>) to organize complicated layouts
- Images (<IMG>) to insert graphics into the page
- Line breaks (<BR>) to add spaces

- Anchors (<A>) to link to other elements within the same page or on the Web

Again, HTML markup does not feature all of the display-oriented complexities of a word processor like Microsoft Word, but on the other hand, its power lies in its capability to hyperlink, to integrate into one linear document other remote documents or ideas.

3. HTML character entities

Certain characters, such as the left angle bracket (<) and right angle bracket (>), are reserved by HTML to represent special functions such as the start and end of HTML elements, graphic characters, and so on. Additionally, there are many other font characters you may wish to include in a document that don't have a direct analog on the keyboard (like © and #). These are called *special characters*, and HTML represents them in two ways. One way is to use a named entity (e.g., © for ©); the other way is to use a numeric character reference (e.g., © for ©)

4. HTML editing tools

HTML editing software enables you to create documents in HTML format. Most editors have features akin to a word processor. The job of the HTML editor is to help you place HTML tags in your document.

Since HTML is a nonproprietary text-based format (it is not owned by any one company), it can be created and edited by a wide range of tools, from simple plain text editors such as Notepad or SimpleText to sophisticated authoring tools such as Macromedia Dreamweaver, HomeSite, or BBEdit. Text editors offer control and speed, but require knowledge of HTML in order to be used effectively. What You See Is What You Get (***WYSIWYG***) editors are usually easier to use for beginners because they operate like most common word processors.

(ii) WEB PROGRAMMING

No overview of HTML would be complete without mentioning Web programming. HTML documents in-and-of themselves are pretty static. Basically, they represent a one-way push of information from the Web server to the viewer. But, many situations require a two-way interaction of data between the browser and the Web server. This interaction is where Web programming comes into play. There are two kinds of programming that allow the user to interact with the Web server: server-side programming and client-side programming.

Server-side programming is also referred to as CGI programming. The acronym stands for Common Gateway Interface. This is a standard way to pass data between HTML pages and programs that are running on the Web server. For example, say that you had a form on your HTML page and you wanted to e-mail the results to someone. HTML is not capable of performing this action. But, you could have a program (written in a programming language like Perl, Java, or C) that resides on the Web server that is capable of handling this task. The HTML page would submit the data to the program via CGI. The program would process the request, send the e-mail message, and then return a response back to the Web browser.

Other server-side programming includes Active Server Pages (ASP), Hypertext Preprocessor (PHP), or Java Server Pages (JSP). These pages are HTML pages that contain scripts (small embedded programs) that are processed by the Web server before they are sent to the user. A common use of these pages is to connect to a database and fill-in data "on-the-fly." For example, an author could build an Active Server Page to display a company's phone directory. The document would contain standard HTML tags for the top and the bottom of this page. But, in the center of the page (where the phone directory information will appear) there is a script that connects to a database and retrieves all of records. The script could then format and display the records for the browser and display them in the page as standard HTML.

Client-side programming uses the local browsing machine to interpret and execute the code embedded in the delivered HTML page. Whether the called for application is Javascript, Java applets, Flash, or other language-type applications, the server is not responsible for the processing—it has handed that off to the client machine. When a fast browser machine and a slower, less powerful browser machine ask for a server-side program to be run on a fast server, they both get a fast answer. However, if the same two machines had to execute the program as a client-side program, the faster machine would get the answer more quickly.

(iii) ACCESSIBILITY

Good HTML design means making content accessible to the maximum number of users. It's crucial to understand that people use the Web in very different ways. An HTML document should therefore present information in a way that people can access regardless of the hardware or software they are using, and what their connection speed is.

The W3C was created in October 1994 to "lead the World Wide Web to its full potential by developing common protocols that promote its evolution and ensure its interoperability." (http://www.w3.org/Consortium/). The WC3 develops technologies (specifications, guidelines, software, and tools) and serves as a forum for i Web users around the world. One of its primary goals is *universal access*, making the Web accessible to all, by "promoting technologies that take into account the vast differences in culture, education, ability, material resources, and physical limitations of Internet users on all continents."

Disabled Web users may experience difficulty using the Web. Because some people may not be able to read displayed text or see visuals or hear sounds, HTML pages can offer a text equivalent for all content, so that any browser can interpret a site's content and render it machine-readable, enabling the disabled user to access the information in the best way for him or her. For example, if your site uses images for your navigation bar, you should provide "alt tags" with text names or explanations for these images in order to make your content accessible to the maximum number of users. (The chapter **Accessibility** [7] discusses these issues in depth.)

By following the W3C's HTML guidelines, an author can make Web content more available to all users, whatever their browser or other Web-accessing agent (voice browser, mobile phone, automobile-based personal computer, etc.) or other constraints they may be operating under. Following these guidelines and providing alt tags may also help people find your information quicker by providing the search engines more of your machine-readable content on which to search.

(iv) FORMATTING AND STYLE

Well-designed HTML documents achieve their impact from the simplicity of design; they are intuitive, coherent, and flowing. The user should always know where he is. Generally, designs that seem simple and natural to the reader are often the result of intense efforts to make them seem this way. Like housework, when done properly, good HTML page design is invisible in the sense that it doesn't call attention to itself.

By using elements like paragraphs, tables, headings, font faces, colors, blank spaces, and images, the author can control the format and style of HTML pages. Content can be positioned on the page and attributes such as alignment, padding, boldness, outlining, or italics can be applied. (In fact, many Web pages overdo these things: especially when automatically generated from programs like word processors, HTML can get clogged with minutiae like elaborate use of fonts and fancy indenting that attempt to replicate a visual appearance that might not have been very good in the first place. Good HTML coding should not only produce a clear, clean page, it should do so with clean, well-structured tagging.)

A general rule is that the more complex the HTML document, the more likely that it will not enjoy universal access. Formatting and style are dependent on many things: the output device of the user, software versions, connection speeds, and user-configurable preferences. Unlike printed media, the author of an HTML document does not have explicit control of the display layout the viewer sees. In the HTML environment, "the reader rules." What the user sees depends as much on how her machine is configured as on the author's content tags.

1. CSS (Cascading Style Sheets)

"Cascading Style Sheets" (***CSS***) are a mechanism for adding style to multiple HTML documents. Instead of embedding display-related tags directly in the content, common display elements are aggregated into the stylesheet, which basically says "whenever you see an element tagged with this name, format it in this way." By using CSS, the author can control font faces, font sizes, font colors, line spacing and length, margins and indents, background images, colors, and other elements without tagging each and every one in every document of the site. CSS separates the *presentation* of the ultimedia productions.

2. XHTML

XHTML is an implementation of HTML 4 as an XML application. It is basically the same set of elements, designed to be used in the same ways, but expressed in the syntax prescribed by XML. (The next **section of this chapter** [3.3] discusses XML in depth.) This makes it more rigorous and able to be processed by XML tools. XHTML comes in three "flavors":

- *XHTML 1.0 Strict* does not include tags associated primarily with layout. It is intended to be used in a way that strictly focuses on structure, and it presumes that a corresponding CSS stylesheet will deal with any presentation issues.
- *XHTML 1.0 Transitional* permits some appearance-related tagging. It is designed to be used when it is important for the content to be viewable by older browsers that do not understand stylesheets.
- *XHTML 1.0 Frameset* is to be used when frames are being employed.

XHTML is a good example of how XML can be used to create vocabularies, or markup languages, for specific purposes. The purpose of XHTML is to provide the functionality of HTML—including HTML's tag set. But XML is much, much more than simply a reformulation of HTML.

3.3 XML: THE EXTENSIBLE MARKUP LANGUAGE

(i) OVERVIEW

XML has been—and continues to be—one of the most significant and successful developments of the digital era. It was created not to be a compromise between its two predecessor technologies, ***SGML*** and ***HTML***, but to be an advance beyond them. It is not simply a response to their limitations and, from some points of view, their failings ("failures" would be too strong a word); instead, XML builds on their strengths and their successes. Originally thought of as "SGML for the Web," XML is in many respects functionally equivalent to SGML. Although it omits some features of SGML, they are not essential ones for most applications, and some of XML's advances have been incorporated into the SGML standard. Most publishers who implemented SGML find the transition to XML to be an easy one. And XML in no way makes HTML obsolete; in fact, one of the most common uses of XML data is to transform it to HTML for Web delivery. Even after XML and its related technologies are fully implemented in browser technology, HTML will still be important as a simple and convenient Web-presentation tag set. However, there is no longer any question that XML is the foundation on which digital publishing will be built.

HTML was successful in no small part thanks to its simplicity; but this simplicity quickly became a limitation. The world needed a markup technology much more powerful than HTML in order to accommodate the wide range of content deliverable over the Web—and other purposes beyond simple delivery of content. HTML's simple set of tags mainly used for designing Web pages proved inadequate. Publishers, institutions, developers, scholars, and commercial entities needed to be able to tag their content in ways that were meaningful to them: journal publishers needed tags for articles and abstracts and affiliations; book publishers needed tags for chapters and authors and references; literary scholars needed tags for stanzas and dialog and scene directions; airlines needed tags for airports and departure and arrival times. Although linking was at the heart of HTML, it was soon evident that a more robust technology than HTML's simple anchor-to-target linking was needed: multiple-ended links to multiple documents were required, as well as bidirectional links, and links activated in many more ways than just "click here," and links that did more than just taking the user to a destination, and links that could be associated with any kind of element, not just an explicit anchor. As the Web became a more and more fundamental and dynamic environment for exchanging and managing information, for providing and receiving services, and for buying and selling products, a much more robust infrastructure was required than HTML could offer.

It might have seemed at first that SGML was the proverbial solution in search of a problem, and was ready-made to address the needs of this new digital world. In many ways it was. It is an international standard that provides a flexible, robust, nonproprietary technology for managing information of all sorts. Its principles and methods gave rise to HTML in the first place, and it has been widely used for managing and exchanging information in many industries, from pharmaceuticals to aerospace, from SEC filings to reference and journal publishing.

Ironically, it was both SGML's flexibility and its stability that kept it from being exactly the technology the Web was looking for. Because SGML could be implemented in so many different ways and offered so many options to its users, it was very difficult to build tools and software for: it required keeping track of too many alternatives, allowing for too many contingencies. Software developers needed it to be a bit more restrictive. (For example, tags in SGML are not case sensitive; a section can begin with the tag <SEC> and end with </sec>. XML requires the cases to match—so when XML sees a start tag for an element, it knows exactly what end tag to watch for. SGML does not, in fact, even require that every end tag be explicitly expressed; XML does. This rigor makes XML much easier to program for.) And the very lengthy, laborious international process required to change the published SGML standard—a virtue of SGML that makes it extremely stable—is an obstacle in the rapidly changing digital world. XML's ability to respond to new ideas and new developments is one of the key factors in its rapid evolution and wide acceptance. (See above for a more detailed recounting of this **history** [3.1.2.2].)

1. XML is a metalanguage

The most important thing to recognize about XML at the outset—and the thing that most sets it apart from HTML—is that it is not a set of tags, a "markup vocabulary"; rather, it is a way to *define and use* a set of tags, to invent and implement various markup vocabularies. It is not just a markup language, it's a ***metalanguage***: it's a way to *create* markup languages. It does not have any "words" of its own. Unlike HTML, in XML <Q> only means "in-line quotation" if you want it to; it could mean "question" (or "quotient" or anything else, whether it starts with Q or not).

XML provides a well-defined, broadly accepted syntax for creating markup schemes to address a wide variety of general or specific needs to fit various circumstances. It enables the development of tag sets focused on projects as small as a single book or journal (the book you are reading has one that applies specifically and only to *The Columbia Guide to Digital Publishing*), or whole collections or classes of books or journals (Wiley Interscience has one, Elsevier's Science Direct has another), or to achieve particular functionality (bibliographical information for a linking service like **CrossRef** [4.5.5.1], for example, or bookselling information with a standard like **ONIX** [4.4.2.3.2]), or even whole industries (the automotive industry has one, and aerospace, and pharmaceuticals—these actually all originated as SGML, also a metalanguage like

XML). XML has even become fundamental to how software itself is written and exchanged and implemented; Microsoft, for example, has made a major commitment to XML, as have an increasing number of developers.

Because XML is a widely accepted, formally defined, published, nonproprietary standard, it makes it possible for content tagged according to one of these schemes to be interpreted without any specific tools or software—it can be interpreted by any person or system that understands XML. In fact, unlike SGML, it does not even absolutely require a formal definition of the tag set; it is possible to create what is referred to as ***well-formed XML*** that behaves according to the syntax and structuring XML requires in a one-of-a-kind document. (More on **well-formed XML** [3.3.2.5.1] below.) Certain characters are restricted in their use, for example, < can only be used (and must be used) to start a tag. Elements must be nested properly: if a section of a book (beginning with <SEC>) contains a bulleted list (beginning with <BL>), the bulleted list has to end (</BL>) before the section does (</SEC>). These rules, and others like them, are really quite straightforward and simple; that's part of what makes XML so appealing. (A full definition of the XML standard, as published by the W3C, can be found at *http://www.w3.org/TR/2000/REC-xml-20001006*.)

2. XML is also a family of standards

Although strictly speaking, the acronym XML refers to the Extensible Markup Language itself, it is also used more generically to refer to a whole family of related standards that have developed around it. ***XSL***, for example—the **Extensible Stylesheet Language** [3.3.3.3]—is a companion standard developed as an advanced technology for defining stylesheets for XML documents. There are actually two parts to XSL: ***XSLT*** (**XSL Transformation** [3.3.4.4]) is used for transforming one XML document into another (perhaps to make it conform to a different definition), or even into a non-XML document; and ***XSL-FO*** (**XSL Formatting Objects** [3.3.3.3.2]) provides a language for specifying presentation. ***XPath***, the **XML Path Language** [3.3.5.2], is a technology for addressing the structure of an XML document; ***XPointer***, the **XML Pointing Language** [3.3.5.3], uses XPath to locate specific points in an XML document based on its structure and content; and ***XLink***, the **XML Linking Language** [3.3.5.1], provides many of the advanced linking capabilities that HTML lacks. This is not a complete list, by any means. One of the most dynamic things about the XML-based digital world is that new, related standards like these continue to be developed. When they have passed through the proper review and approval process, they are issued as recommendations by the ***W3C***.

3. XML is used for other standards

The examples in the previous paragraph are ones that are generally thought of as "XML standards," and they are published by the W3C. But one of the powerful aspects of XML—and one of the advantages of its wide acceptance—is that it is used to create a multitude of other standards for various purposes. One that is becoming commonly used in book publishing is ***OEBPS***, the **Open eBook Publication Structure** [11.6], an XML-based standard for tagging and organizing files to be used in electronic books. (The **Open eBook Forum** [11.2.1.3] is also working on related standards for e-book metadata and e-book rights.) An important XML implementation used in journal publishing (and being expanded to other types of publishing) is ***CrossRef***, an interpublisher linking service that uses XML for the bibliographic information defining the articles and other publications being linked to. Although it did not originate as an XML standard, ***ONIX***, the metadata standard for bookselling, is increasingly implemented as XML. Math and science publishers are beginning to use ***MathML***, an XML-based scheme for marking up mathematics. Newspaper publishers use ***NewsML***. ***SVG*** (Scalable Vector Graphics) is an XML-based language for describing graphics. ***ICE*** (Information and Content Exchange) is a standard largely used in syndication. ***SOAP*** (Simple Object Access Protocol) enables software to be accessed and implemented over the Web. The very proliferation of so many standards like these in so many industries is a testament to the power and pervasiveness of XML.

4. XML and SGML

The similarities between SGML and XML are far greater than their differences. In a real sense, XML can be thought of as a natural evolution of SGML prompted by the existence of the Web. For those publishers who had already made a commitment to SGML before XML was developed, the transition to XML is quite straightforward, and the SGML files they have archived can usually be converted easily to XML. SGML files tagged in a professional, consistent, well-disciplined way often observe many or all of the rules that XML requires (such as proper nesting of elements and using case consistently in tags), and many of the features of SGML that XML omits are ones that were rarely used anyhow.

Nevertheless, XML and SGML are, in fact, separate, different, and co-existing standards. SGML is an international standard governed by the ISO; it was officially adopted as ISO 8879, the Standard Generalized Markup Language, in 1986. XML is not an ISO standard; it was published, officially, as a recommendation of the W3C in 1998. Both SGML and XML continue to evolve. The W3C entertains and reviews proposals for modifications to XML and for the creation of XML-related recommendations like those mentioned above; although care is taken to keep the basic standard itself as stable as possible (having learned from the instability of the HTML world), the XML family of technologies continues to evolve rapidly. Because it is a much more cumbersome and formal process to change an official ISO standard (deliberately so: stability is one of the cardinal virtues of ISO standards), SGML does not change nearly as quickly as XML. However, two modifications—one known as Annex K and the other a Technical Corrigendum known as TC2—have helped keep the SGML standard more in phase with XML.

Some of the differences between SGML and XML have been mentioned above. XML requires tags to be case sensitive; SGML gives you the choice of making them case sensitive or not. Every start tag in XML must have a corresponding end tag, whereas SGML has a feature known as "omittag" that allows tags to be omitted or implied in certain circumstances. (When SGML was created, conciseness was an important design principle; much coding was done manually then, and storage was at a premium, so saving keystrokes was helpful.) XML requires elements to be nested properly, without overlapping (the "contained" element must end before its "container" element does), whereas SGML allows for the creation of very complex and open-ended structures, which makes it much harder for software to keep track of things. SGML has "inclusions" which are, in a sense, free-floating elements that can occur anywhere throughout a structure; XML (when it has a formal definition) requires that the definition specify everywhere any given element that can occur. In SGML, an empty element (one that has no end tag and thus contains no content, like <IMG> for image) can look just like a normal tag that applies to what follows it; in XML, an empty element must either be expressed as <TAG></TAG> or <TAG/>. XML also limits each document to a single root (top-level) element. There are a handful of other such rules where XML and SGML differ.

In general, XML tends to make things more restrictive and thus simpler, or at least clearer. SGML was created to be extremely flexible. In fact, SGML does not even require a particular character set, or particular delimiters, to be used. Although most SGML tags use the < and > delimiters that XML requires, it is possible to define the delimiters to be $ and % instead, or any other characters. (That means a processing system can't know that < means "here's a tag"; it has to be told, because $ might mean "here's a tag" and < might mean "less than." An XML processing system can trust that < always and only means "here's a tag.") SGML's flexibility is powerful, idealistic, and paradoxically an obstacle to its wide implementation in the real world. Although XML is still very flexible, it is more restrictive than SGML, and this has ironically led to much broader use. Sometimes rules make things easier.

5. XML and HTML

The differences between ***XML*** and ***HTML*** are far greater than the differences between XML and SGML. Whereas XML and SGML are really just different approaches to doing much the same things, XML and HTML are fundamentally different things altogether. HTML is a specific set of tags (a deliberately limited and simple set) designed to guide a Web browser in formatting the tagged content and to enable linking within or between Web sites. XML is not a set of tags at all, but a language designed for marking up content of all sorts (text, graphics, computer code, commercial information, intellectual information) in order to specify what the component parts of that content are, and to describe them. HTML is a *presentational* tag set: it is ideally the output of a process, designed for a specific way of viewing the given content. XML is, in its best use, a *source* markup, designed to be transformed into something else, to be archived and used in many different ways. In fact, HTML is a frequent output from an XML archive. XML retains the information about what the elements in the source content *are* and how they *relate;* HTML typically loses that information, focusing instead on what the content should *look like* in a given presentation.

If XML is a less formal standard than SGML, HTML is less formal still. In fact, when it was originally created it didn't even have a formal definition; because it was more a de facto standard, with no clear standardization process, it was modified frequently, especially as the browser developers added features to compete with each other. This early chaotic situation was reined in somewhat, and formal definitions of HTML were produced; the most formal of all, XHTML, is HTML 4 expressed as XML. (That's an interesting example of the flexibility of XML: although it is not at all HTML, HTML is one of the many—infinitely many—tag sets that can be defined in XML.) Even so, HTML was implemented in a very loose way by the browsers. They tolerated a lot of HTML code that, strictly speaking, was incorrect. On the one hand, that makes it easy for HTML coders (and is another reason for HTML's wide appeal); but on the other hand, it creates a permissive mess where a given file will display properly in one browser (or even one version of a given browser) but differently, or not at all, in another. XML was designed to have what is referred to as *draconian error handling*: by general agreement, if an XML tool (like a browser) encounters an incorrectly coded XML file, it should reject it, rather than trying to handle the error. This rigor—plus the fact that XML does not have to be complex or difficult—makes for a much more stable environment.

Does this mean XML will ultimately replace HTML? Probably not. Keep in mind that they are fundamentally different, and thus are used for completely different things. It is now technically possible to display an XML file directly in some Web browsers without first converting it to HTML; and this will increasingly be done as XML proliferates and as people become more accustomed to using stylesheets to govern display. But it will be useful, for some time to come, to transform an XML file into HTML so that it can be viewed in virtually any browser. (Although the book you are reading is marked up entirely in XML, users of the on-line version see HTML that has been generated automatically from the XML by a content management system, or CMS.) And HTML will always be useful for the simple, straightforward, one-display-only situations (like marketing material on the Web) that does not require the more sophisticated approach of XML.

(ii) USING XML FOR STRUCTURED MARKUP

1. Document analysis

For most publishers, the first step in implementing XML is ***document analysis***: selecting the kinds of content to be described, figuring out what elements of the content should be delineated, deciding what to name them, clarifying how they relate, recognizing and codifying variants of them, and determining what nontextual information about them might be useful. Sometimes, this can be as simple as the familiar process of writing up editorial guidelines or a design memo; for single-project definitions, the document analysis process may use those familiar tools as a starting point. But often, the document analysis is far more complicated—in fact, the document analysis process can be the most difficult, time-consuming, and expensive part of an XML implementation.

Document analysis is the foundation on which a formal ***Document Type Definition*** (DTD) or ***schema*** is built. But even when a publisher uses ***well-formed XML*** without a DTD or schema, document analysis is unavoidable. Whether it is done systematically or haphazardly, whether a prescriptive, formal definition is created up front or whether a set of tags evolves descriptively as content is created, some description of the component parts of a set of content must ultimately be developed. Although the informal, evolutionary approach may be tempting, most publishers find that they can't fully exploit the power of XML without the benefit of the kind of clear, explicit, and consistent definition of their content that a DTD or schema provides.

1. SCOPE

The most basic factor that affects the complexity of the document analysis process is the scope of the desired definition. Although it is possible—and can be powerful—to write a definition specific to a single title, most DTDs or schemas are created for classes of documents: groups of documents that share certain characteristics. Usually, that means they share a common structure. A medical publisher may need a definition for its journals; a reference publisher may need one for encyclopedias or dictionaries; a university press may develop one for a certain series of monographs. That way, the investment in the DTD or schema can be amortized over many publications, not just one. More important, the definition will be a tool that will help manage and develop a whole body of content in a coherent way.

Publishers are often tempted to broaden the scope of their definitions to encompass more than one class of documents. The medical publisher may publish not only journals, but textbooks and monographs and surgery atlases as well, and so may want to have a single, master "house DTD" that handles all these things. This is almost always a mistake. The structure of a journal is fundamentally different from that of a textbook or a monograph; elements that may appear similar are not even called by the same names. Journals have articles; each article often has many authors, each of whose affiliation must be clearly spelled out; articles may begin with an abstract and keywords and perhaps a publication history; most of the articles are structured exactly alike. Monographs and textbooks have chapters; the authors are not usually identified in the text itself; the chapters are composed of a huge number of possible elements (compared to the few permitted by a journal) which can often occur in any order, and few of those possible elements actually occur in any given chapter.

Developing a definition for either of these classes of documents—journal articles or monograph chapters, for example—can be quite straightforward, but developing a definition that accommodates both of them at once is problematic. The result is likely to be a large, unwieldy, permissive set of elements with very neutral, generic tags that are hard for human beings like editors, authors, and designers to deal with. Since it doesn't work to call an article a chapter or a chapter an article, they might both be called "documents"; the internal structure may be divided into sections and subsections, or into divisions that have numbers associated with them (e.g., <DIV2> may be subordinate to <DIV1>), or the internal structure may be "flat," running text with a variety of subheads and other elements embedded in it, with no real hierarchy enforced. Although each chapter in a book may start with a chapter number tagged <CN>, a DTD that attempts to manage journal articles as well cannot require that <CN> to be present. Generally speaking, definitions resulting from an overly broad scope turn out to be either complex and abstract or neutral and simplistic.

The solution is to develop either a suite of definitions or a definition with modular components. The medical publisher mentioned above may, in fact, wind up with a DTD or schema that encompasses the full range of its publications (sometimes called an ***archival DTD***); this may be the foundation for the organization of all its intellectual property in a **content management**

system [10] (***CMS***). That definition will necessarily be large and complex and abstract. However, it will likely be teamed with several specific-purpose definitions (sometimes called ***base DTDs***) that are designed for specific classes of publications. That way, the journal editor can have tags for article titles and abstracts and affiliations, whereas the monograph editor can have tags for chapter numbers and chapter titles. Each of those classes of documents can be defined appropriately for its unique structure and terminology.

Another advantage of this approach is that the definitions can be developed over time. That medical publisher might first invest in a journal DTD, to optimize simultaneous print and on-line publication where the payback is greatest; and even that DTD might be composed of modules or subordinate DTDs for main articles, book reviews, letters, and the other types of documents published in a journal. That publisher might later develop a DTD for monographs, and still later one for encyclopedias and one for surgery atlases; finally, when the need for a CMS becomes compelling, it might develop a master archival DTD to tie all those classes of publications together. Publishers who take the opposite approach, attempting to develop the master scheme at the outset, often invest a lot of time and money in something that turns out to be only marginally useful and which needs to be constantly revised when it encounters the real world of publishing real documents. However, it can also be a mistake to develop separate DTDs for separate divisions within a publishing house without adequate collaboration and coordination; the more terminology and modules those various "house" DTDs can share, the better. The scope of the document analysis is ultimately a very individual decision for each publisher, and a critically important one.

2. GRANULARITY

Another factor that influences the complexity of the document analysis process is ***granularity***—the level of detail to be tagged. This is where the demands of electronic publishing become most evident, because the electronic environment usually calls for more granular tagging than print publishing requires. In print, it is often sufficient to tag authors' names as <AU>, but in an electronic environment it is helpful to be able to distinguish surnames from first names and middle initials, suffixes like Jr. or III from degrees like Ph.D. or MSSW, nicknames like "Babe" Ruth and "Buzz" Aldrin from pseudonyms like Mark Twain and George Eliot. In print, a reference section may just begin with a single <REF> tag and the references themselves may be simply treated as paragraphs with a particular pattern of bold and italic and punctuation, but to be useful in the digital world, computers need to be able to distinguish lead authors and journal abbreviations and volumes and issues and dates of publication in each and every reference citation. All of those elements need to be tagged distinctly, resulting in highly granular tagging.

In their document analysis process, publishers need to make decisions about what level of granularity is necessary and practical for their content and modes of publication. It is also wise to consider at what stage of the editorial and production process it makes the most sense to do the more detailed tagging. In the book you are reading, the authors were asked to mark glossary terms and cross-references, and were provided with a simple mechanism (styles in Word) for doing so. This reduced the amount of such tagging the editors needed to do, and eliminated the need for the compositor to bother with it. (Programmatically generating such tags is not as simple as it seems. Cross-references may not be phrased exactly as the referenced article is titled; human intelligence—somebody reading and understanding the content—is needed to find them. Likewise, if all occurrences of terms in the glossary were highlighted, the text would be unduly clogged with them. Authors and editors, not keyboarders or coders or compositors, are in the best position to make these kinds of distinctions.) On the other hand, rich tagging of references is usually best left until late in the process, because the necessary coding is so dense that it obscures the reference for the author or the editor. In that case, scripts are often written that pick up on the typographic patterns in the finished references and generate the needed tags. (This scripted process must usually be reviewed and manually fixed by a person, because not all references will follow the scripted patterns precisely; and it depends on very rigorous editing of the references to conform to specific styles.) Some publishers elect not to tag references richly at all, because the way their content is used in the electronic environment does not require it.

3. FUNCTIONALITY

Ultimately, functionality is the determining factor in document analysis. If the resulting XML will be used primarily or only for print publication, it will likely be much simpler than if it needs to accommodate electronic publication as well. In print, no unit smaller than a whole book may be sold, or perhaps chapters and articles will need to be managed as units; in the electronic environment it may be important to provide users access to much smaller chunks of content. Likewise, the rich **linking** [3.3.5] and **metadata** [3.3.6] capabilities of the electronic environment are not usually meaningful in print.

However, it can be a mistake to focus too narrowly on the electronic environment (especially if limited to today's electronic environment), because that can result in a definition that is not adequate for print. On-line publishers today take for granted many compromises that cannot be tolerated in print. Sometimes, these are graphic issues (such as print needing information about page breaks or facing spreads that are meaningless on line, and using fonts or characters not yet available on the Web). It is often tempting for publishers to "dumb down" their tagging to the simple requirements and capabilities of ***HTML*** or ***basic OEB***, in the process sometimes losing the important distinctions provided by tags like <CN> or <AU> or <ABSTRACT>, which are not available in HTML.

It's also important to recognize that some definitions are not created for publication at all. Especially in the sciences and scholarship, XML schemas and DTDs may be created to enable and enhance the collaboration of practitioners. These specialists may organize the content and use terminology unique to their community. A microbiologist may not know or care that when a genus and species appears in text it's italic, and in one kind of subhead it's bold italic, and in another it's caps and small caps (whereas these distinctions are critical to a compositor); but the definition she uses may make numerous taxonomic distinctions that have little or no use in the publishing and production process. She may also think that it is obvious that the "E" in E. coli means Escherichia, and may not appreciate how difficult it can be to generate an apparently simple genus and species index. Although one of the great benefits of XML is the power to transform content tagged according to one definition to the tags required by another, there are cases where such a **transformation** [3.3.4] is not at all trivial.

4. THE POLITICS OF DOCUMENT ANALYSIS

One factor often overlooked in the process of document analysis is the need to consider all the interest groups who may need to participate. These groups often have conflicting interests. Publishers are used to balancing editorial needs with those of the design and production staff; in the print-only publishing of the past, many conflicts were finessed by the separation of the editorial and production processes. In the digital world it becomes a bigger problem when those two constituencies have their own unique terminologies and views of the content, because they're exchanging electronic files instead of just paper. Today, the electronic publishing department is a factor, too, bringing a whole new set of needs and issues to the table. The profusion of electronic modes of publication, from Web sites to e-books, compounds the problem. Even the marketing department now has an interest in how the electronic files are structured and coded. When the publisher wants to exchange or license content with aggregators or other publishers, still more issues emerge. Making sure all these constituencies are served by the ultimate definition without bogging down the document analysis process in complexity, speculation, and conflict can be one of the biggest challenges publishers face today.

2. Document Type Definitions (DTDs)

Once the document analysis process has resulted in a scheme for organizing the content (often referred to as the document model), that scheme needs to be formalized in a language that enables a computer to interpret it. When XML was created, it borrowed what SGML used for this purpose: the Document Type Definition (***DTD***). This is a language with a very specific vocabulary and syntax designed for rigorously specifying such definitions. DTDs are by far the most common way to formalize document models, and are the language most SGML- and XML-enabled tools currently require. (It is not, however, the only such language. The **XML Schema Language** [3.3.2.3.1], published as a recommendation by the W3C in 2001, has features not available in DTDs. ***RELAX NG***, now part of a draft international standard (ISO/IEC DIS 19757-2) also has features not available in DTDs and even goes beyond XML Schema in some ways: it can describe XML vocabularies that XML Schema cannot describe. Both XML Schema and RELAX NG use XML syntax, unlike DTDs. Schemas may eventually replace DTDs as the primary method for formally defining document models. But since schemas are not yet widely used or implemented in publishing-oriented software, publishers currently still need to understand and use DTDs.)

It's important to recognize that the word "type" in Document Type Definition does not refer to typography; DTDs define types of document. For a given class of documents, a DTD defines the component parts of those documents (**elements** [3.3.2.2.1]), provides ways to describe or differentiate variations of given elements (through **attributes** [3.3.2.1.3]), and enables the creation of modular units of code or separate information objects (like a graphic file or an external document) which can be referred to by name (**entities** [3.3.2.2.5]). These three things—elements, attributes, and entities—are the building blocks of DTDs.

1. ELEMENTS

The most recognizable component parts of a document are the ***elements***, because they usually correspond to the parts we are used to distinguishing typographically. In the book you're reading, for example, the chapter number is an element, as is the chapter title; the chapter author's name is an element and his or her affiliation is another element; the chapter introduction is not just indented text, it is a special element as well; each of the four levels of subheads are elements, and so are the various extracts, lists, and other items that are visually distinct on the printed page.

In XML, these elements are clearly distinguished by start tags and end tags; the end tag must be identical to the start tag except it is preceded by a slash. The beginning of this chapter might look like this in XML:

<CN>3</CN>
<CT>Markup: XML and Related Technologies</CT>
<AU>William E. Kasdorf</AU>
<AFF>President, Impressions Book and Journal Services, Inc.</AFF>
<INTRO> Markup enables the various parts and features of a given set of content to be distinguished and named . . . .</INTRO>
<H1>Overview</H1>
<H2>What is markup?</H2>
<TX>At the most basic level, markup can be thought of as the tags and codes embedded in a given set of content . . . .</TX>

Here's what the DTD for the first three elements of that simple structure might look like:

<!ELEMENT CN (#PCDATA) >
<!ELEMENT CT (#PCDATA) >
<!ELEMENT AU (#PCDATA) >

Translated into plain English, this means: "I declare an element named CN, which contains parsed character data; I declare an element named CT, which contains parsed character data; I declare an element named AU, which contains parsed character data." (A bit more elaborate and meaningful example is given below.)

The reason this example is so clear and simple is that the elements correspond exactly to the editorial and design components we are used to seeing, and their structure is completely flat: the elements do not overlap or nest one inside another. (In fact, this example uses exactly the same tags as the example of editorial type marking on a **paper manuscript** [3.1.1] at the beginning of this chapter.) This is perfectly legitimate XML; the tags above are the actual tags used in the base DTD for this book. (That base XML is viewable in the on-line version.)

2. ELEMENTS DELINEATE STRUCTURE

However, ***elements*** aren't always as obvious as those in the example above, or even visible at all. There can be *container elements* that are, in effect, wrappers that contain other elements. This book, for example, is really structured in a hierarchical manner: chapters contain sections which contain subsections, down to four levels. Subheads are properly considered part of the section or subsection they apply to, not separate unrelated elements placed between sections of text. Likewise, the affiliation could be considered part of an element called "author," which might also contain an element called "name"; we might want to distinguish between the author's role and the organization's name, and to know what the author's *last* name is. The text contains such things as cross-references (which are distinguished in the print version by being set in bold) and links to on-line examples (not visible at all in print). At the beginning of each section, there could be other “invisible” elements, such as keywords and index terms. Taking all this into account, the coding for the beginning of this chapter could look like this:

```
<CHAPTER id="c12345">
<TITLE>Markup: XML and Related Technologies</TITLE>
<AU><NAME><FMNM>William
   E.</FMNM><LNM>Kasdorf</LNM></NAME>
<AFF><ROLE>President</ROLE><ORG>Impressions Book and
   Journal Services, Inc.</ORG></AFF></AU>
<INTRO>Markup enables the various parts and features of a given set of
   content to be distinguished and named . . . .</INTRO>
<SECT level="1"><HEAD>Overview</HEAD>
<SECT level="2"><HEAD>What is markup?</HEAD>
<INDXENT>Markup<SUBENT>editorial</SUBENT></INDXENT>
<KW>markup</KW><KW>tags</KW><KW>codes</KW>
   <KW>coding</KW>
<TX>At the most basic level, markup can be thought of as the tags and
   codes embedded in a given set of content that delineate and describe
   the component parts of that content. An editor marks up a
   <LINKXMPL>paper manuscript</LINKXMPL> by labeling a chapter
   number “CN,” a chapter title “CT,” a first-level subhead “H1” or “A,” an
   extracted block quote “EX” or “BQ.” Traditionally, this markup has
   provided the instructions for a typesetter, who inserts a different set of
   markup (often <CROSSREF>proprietary markup</CROSSREF>)
   that controls the composition of that content in a particular format
   using a particular composition system . . . .</TX>
</SECT></SECT></CHAPTER>
```

This is more complicated than the previous example, but much more powerful. (The actual archival XML used for this book is even more complex than this example; it can be viewed in the on-line version.) Does that mean that this richer version is “better,” or the “right” way to define the elements? Not at all. It is a better way to tag the data for a content management system, but the previous simpler example is much better for an editor or designer or production person to work with. Forcing those people to work with the coding in the richer, more hierarchical form is likely doomed to failure; it is simply too hard for people to keep track of these complexities (unless they have special tools like XML-enabled software to make it easier for them). On the other hand, it would be a waste to archive the data in the simplistic form given in the first example; too much is missing that is useful in electronic publishing. This is why many XML implementations use more than one DTD: so that the structure and the tagging can be optimized for each environment, from simple styles-based environments like Word or QuarkXPress to powerful, highly automated environments like content management systems.

3. ATTRIBUTES

Attributes are the modifiers for elements. If elements are the nouns in an XML definition, attributes are the adjectives. They are an extremely useful tool. They can be used to identify instances of elements (*which* chapter?—<CHAPTER no="12">) and to describe elements (*what level* of subsection?—<SECT level="2">; *what kind* of list?—<LIST type="BL">). XML requires that attributes follow a very rigid syntax. They exist within start tags; they must be separated by a space from the element name (and from each other, if an element has more than one attribute); they must be named; the attribute name must immediately be followed by an equal sign, which must be immediately followed by the attribute value, which must be enclosed in straight quote marks.

Attributes are often used for ***metadata***. In the example above, the chapter element is given an identification number via an attribute: <CHAPTER id="c12345">. The ID actually used in this book uniquely identifies this chapter in the content management system, and allows the chapter to be used in another context (or even in another place in this work) without data needing to be changed. (Although the <CN>3</CN> was used in the writing and editing process, the more complex and abstract coding with the ID as an attribute is used by the content management system, because this particular batch of content may not always be Chapter 3. Those IDs are generated and managed by computers, not people.) All sections and subsections of this book actually have identification numbers like that, which enables the text to be revised and renumbered dynamically: the section you're reading was section 3.2.2.3 when it was written (the third sub-subsection of subsection two of section two of Chapter 3), but that number may change due to content revisions; its ID, however, will never change. Such unique IDs enable the use of ***DOI***s, **Digital Object Identifiers** [15.4.2].

Attributes are also commonly used to distinguish variations that may be meaningful in one context but not in another. (They are an important part of the way **stylesheets** [3.3.3] work, in HTML and SGML as well as in XML.) For example, an italicized phrase in a book might be simple emphasis, or a book title, or a genus and species, or a technical term. In a print presentation, these might all appear the same, in italics; but in an on-line version the book title might link to a reference and the technical term to a definition in a glossary.

(They might also appear in different colors.) If they were distinguished as different elements (which they could be), it would be necessary, in the print stylesheet, to define each one of them separately (even though the definition is always the same, simply italic). But by using an encoding like <EMPH type="title"> or <EMPH type="glossref">, the EMPH elements can all be simply italicized in print (and the attributes ignored) while the appropriate distinctions can be made in the on-line version—without changing the tagging in the file.

4. EMPTY ELEMENTS

Most ***elements*** are delineated by a pair of tags that mark the points in the content where the given element begins and ends (using the syntax <TAG> . . . </TAG>). However, there is a special kind of element that does not "contain" any of the document content: ***empty elements***. They occur either as a start–end pair with no content (<TAG></TAG>) or as a start tag with a slash at the end (<TAG/>). (The latter is an example of how XML is more explicit than SGML. SGML permits a normal start tag to simply be empty, e.g., <TAG>; this requires a processing system to know enough about that tag to realize that it does not in fact "code" what follows it, as a normal start tag would, and that the system should not be looking for a corresponding end tag.)

A common example of an empty element is an image, where the tag simply identifies an image that exists outside the document content. For example, <IMG id="Fig_5.3"/> would call for Figure 5.3 to appear (or be referenced) at that point in the content; there would be no end tag (</IMG>). Another common example, from HTML, is the <BR> command, which imposes a line break; in XML, this must be <BR/>. Empty elements are also often used as "storage places" for metadata, information about the content that does not actually appear in the content. For example, a biographical reference might want to record the birthplace and burial place for each person even if that information didn't appear in the article as such; this could be done with an empty element such as <METADATA birthplace="Boston, MA" buried="Arlington, VA"/>.

5. ENTITIES

Entities enable basically any chunk of digital content—text, code, image data—to be given a name and then be referred to by that name instead of being directly incorporated into the XML document itself. A graphic could be given the name "Fig_3.1"; a left double quotation mark could be given the name "ldquo"; a modular part of a DTD defining a group of emphasis options could be given the name "emph.grp." The entities to be used in valid documents must be defined in the DTD or schema; they are then called out in the document using the delimiters "&" and ";": "&Fig;_3.1;" would call out the graphic named above, and "“" would call out a left double quote. (The last example, called a parameter entity, is a special case—with the syntax %emph.grp;—because it occurs only within the DTD, not in a document.)

Entities are a surprisingly powerful feature of XML. They provide flexibility, enabling changes to be made once (in the entity definition) rather than every time that the given named chunk of data would otherwise appear in the content; and they are a vehicle to make things simple and intelligible that would otherwise be unwieldy or indecipherable to a human being.

Let's take the entity "&Fig;_3.1" as an example. The actual graphic file needing to be called out might be stored in a computer in a folder called Columbia Guide to Digital Publishing, in a subfolder called CGDP Examples, and it might have been named PaperMS.tif. To actually call up this graphic in the XML file without using an entity would require a "path name" that would look like this:

```
Bill_PowerBook:Columbia Guide to Digital Publishing:CGDP
Examples:PaperMS.tif
```

That's a very cumbersome name to have to embed in the XML. By defining an entity (with that cumbersome path name), that graphic can be called "&Fig;_3.1;" whenever it is needed in the XML document. Not only does that make it more convenient and intelligible, it makes it more flexible as well. The path name given above might have been correct when it was in the author's laptop; because the name isn't meaningful without a location (a computer needs to know where to find the file being referred to), that path name is different when the XML document is being used by the compositor or by the host of the on-line version. In fact, those two vendors wouldn't even use the same graphic file: the compositor would use a high-resolution .tif file, and the on-line host would use a lower resolution .jpeg file. If an actual graphic file name had been embedded in the XML every time this image was to appear, each of those instances would have to be found and changed when the file was handed off from the compositor to the on-line vendor or vice versa. Instead, because an entity was used, the vendor can simply place the desired path and file name in the definition of the entity, and the XML document itself can remain unaltered. In the digital world, as content is exchanged and reused in a variety of environments, entities provide a powerful adaptation mechanism.

Special characters are another common use of entities. XML is based on **Unicode** [3.3.3.4.1], a very large standard character encoding specification that can eventually accommodate over 65,000 characters by using two bytes to describe each character. Even this will not be enough for all the world's languages; UCS, the ISO's 32-bit Universal Character System, accommodates two billion. (Many XML implementations specify a subset of Unicode known as UTF-8, a variable-length encoding that is compatible with ASCII.) By adopting the Unicode standard, XML is able to unambiguously specify any of the 49,194 characters currently defined. This is done by assigning each unique character shape (called a ***glyph***) a number in a 16-bit system. The number for the left double quote, for example, is 8220. All XML processing systems know to interpret the entity "“" as a left double quote—it can only mean that. However, that sort of encoding is not very human readable. For that reason, it is common to define entities for such special characters (usually in a DTD) so that a more intelligible entity like "“" can be used. HTML uses a set of named and numbered entities known as ISO 8859/1, but this is an 8-bit encoding accommodating only 256 characters; and the ISO has published other useful standard lists for Latin and Greek characters, mathematics, and other purposes. Even when those common named entities are used in XML, they must be defined or declared; the only "built-in" encoding XML uses is Unicode. The exceptions are five named entities for special reserved characters in XML: < for "less than" (<), > for "greater than" (>), & for "ampersand" (&), ' for "apostrophe" ('), and " for "quote" (").

Parameter entities are a special kind of entity that can only be used in DTDs. They are useful in making component parts of a DTD modular in order to streamline both the writing and the revising of the DTD. For example, a DTD might want to allow three kinds of emphasis: italic, bold, and bold italic. Because one function of a DTD is to specify what things can occur within other things, it would be necessary to specify, for each element, whether it can contain these three kinds of emphasis. But by creating a parameter entity—called, perhaps, "%emph.grp;"—it is possible to simply specify where this named group can occur. The real benefit of this comes when it's necessary to change what the entity was created to define. It is a simple matter to add small caps to the emphasis options in the definition of the entity; wherever, throughout the DTD, %emph.grp; is referred to, it now includes small caps. Otherwise it would have been necessary to find and change every place this occurred. Such entities are a useful way to manage many commonly used or commonly invoked aspects of DTDs, like the kinds of lists permitted, or the kinds of notes, or the various elements associated with figures (figure number, figure legend, figure credit, etc.), or even the complete definition of a table. Experienced DTD writers use entities extensively to make their work not only more efficient but more intelligible and manageable.

6. DEFINING RULES AND PARSING

One of the key aspects that distinguishes the formal definitions provided by DTDs and schemas from simple generic tagging schemes is that they not only define elements and their attributes but can also provide rules to govern them. It is possible, for example, to specify that a level two section must be "contained in" a level one section, or that a list is not valid unless it has three or more items. It's possible to specify that a <CN> must be the first element in a chapter, and that it must immediately be followed by one and only one <CT>. The DTD can permit one or more <AU>s, but require that for each <AU> there must be one and only one <AFF>. Without such rules, the first subhead in a chapter might be a level two subhead, the chapter number might be missing, and an author might have two affiliations, but there wouldn't be anything technically "illegal" about the document.

A ***parser*** is a software program that reads a tagged document, analyzes it against the specified DTD or schema, and flags or reports any aspects of the document that violate the given document definition and rules. When a DTD simply defines the elements, the parser can do little more than report that it found the specified tags and that the document follows the rules specified by the XML standard. But when rules are added to the definition, the parser can check to see if they were followed. In the example mentioned above, it would point out that the <CN> element was missing, that there was no level one section preceding the level two, and that there were too many <AFF>s. This kind of processing can be extremely valuable, particularly when large volumes of data need to be checked for conformance to a definition.

Because of this, publishers are often initially tempted to write their DTDs very restrictively, to make the system enforce the rigor that's difficult to get from authors and editors. In some cases, this is appropriate and useful. But in other cases, too many rules unnecessarily burden the editorial and production process. Sometimes, it's okay for an <H2> to be the first subhead in a chapter. Once in a while, an editor needs to allow a list to have two items. Even if that author's affiliation is ultimately needed for publication, it is a problem if the authoring or editing or composition system does not permit you to proceed without it. These realizations sometimes inspire publishers to relax all the rules, or to undo each rule as soon as the need for an exception is encountered. This can result in DTDs so permissive that they become almost useless.

The best solution is not only to achieve the proper balance of restrictiveness and permissiveness, but to have the ability to change such things as needed in different situations. It may seem to contradict the whole principle of a DTD to allow it to be tweaked indiscriminately; but tweaking it judiciously is a very useful strategy. To manage documents in the authoring and editing stages (except for the kind of rigorously controlled environments typically found in the publication of technical documentation, where the authors and the editors are employees of the publisher and a constant model is in force), a permissive DTD is often useful; but the rules can be turned on later, when it's essential to confirm that everything is as it should be. That way, for example, the chapter can be edited even though the author's affiliation is missing, but it won't be transmitted to the compositor without it. Such manipulation of DTDs is common in real-world editing and production situations, where work must be able to proceed at some stages with flawed or fragmentary documents but must not be allowed to proceed beyond other stages without such problems being found and fixed.

As powerful as the parsing process is, it is important to recognize its limitations. First of all, a parser can only tell if the tags have been used *legally*, not if they have been used *properly*. If an <H2> follows an <H1> as the DTD requires, the parser will think it's fine; it will not know if that subhead actually should have been tagged as another <H1>. If the end tag for a <SUP> is mistyped as </SUB>, the error from the parser's point of view is not that there is no end tag for <SUP> (one might still be coming up, farther on), but that there is no start tag <SUB>. Plus, the reports many parsers provide can be quite cryptic, requiring some knowledge of XML and the DTD to be properly interpreted. Finally, the shocking truth is that not all parsers are alike; some will flag things that others will pass over. Parsers are very valuable tools, but they are only one part of an effective quality control process.

7. AN EXAMPLE OF A SIMPLE DTD

Let's look again at the beginning of this chapter as it might be tagged by a basic but effective DTD, and then look at the DTD itself. (The actual XML used for this book—both the base level XML derived from the authors' styled Word files and the archival XML as maintained in the content management system, are viewable in the on-line version. For purposes of illustration, the following example is richer than the former but not as complex as the latter.)

```
<CHAPTER id="c12345">
<TITLE>Markup: XML and Related Technologies</TITLE>
<AU><NAME>William E. Kasdorf</NAME>
<AFF><ROLE>President</ROLE><ORG>Impressions Book and
   Journal Services, Inc.</ORG></AFF></AU>
<INTRO>Markup enables the various parts and features of a given set of
   content to be defined and distinguished . . . .</INTRO>
<SECT level="1"><HEAD>Overview</HEAD>
<SECT level="2"><HEAD>What is markup?</HEAD>
<PARA>At the most basic level, markup can be thought of as the tags
   and codes embedded in a given set of content that delineate and
```

```
   describe the component parts of that content. An editor marks up a
   <LINKXMPL>paper manuscript</LINKXMPL> by labeling a chapter
   number "CN," a chapter title "CT," a first-level subhead "H1" or "A," an
   extracted block quote "EX" or "BQ." Traditionally, this markup has
   provided the instructions for a typesetter, who inserts a different set of
   markup (often<CROSSREF>proprietary markup</CROSSREF>) that
   controls the composition of that content in a particular format using a
   particular composition system . . . .</PARA>
</SECT></SECT></CHAPTER>
```

The DTD for the above might look like this:

```
<?xml version="1.0" encoding="utf-8"?>
<!ELEMENT CHAPTER (TITLE, AU+, INTRO, SECT+)>
<!ATTLIST CHAPTER
      id ID #REQUIRED>
<!ELEMENT TITLE (#PCDATA)>
<!ELEMENT AU (NAME, AFF)>
<!ELEMENT NAME (#PCDATA)>
<!ELEMENT AFF (ROLE, ORG)>
<!ELEMENT ROLE (#PCDATA)>
<!ELEMENT ORG (#PCDATA)>
<!ENTITY % emph.grp "IT | B | BI | CSC">
<!ELEMENT INTRO (#PCDATA | %emph.grp;)*>
<!ELEMENT SECT (HEAD, (PARA | SECT)+)>
<!ATTLIST SECT
      level (1 | 2 | 3 | 4) #REQUIRED>
<!ELEMENT HEAD (#PCDATA | IT)*>
<!ELEMENT PARA (#PCDATA | LINKXMPL | CROSSREF |
   %emph.grp;)*>
<!ELEMENT LINKXMPL (#PCDATA)>
<!ELEMENT CROSSREF (#PCDATA)>
<!ELEMENT IT (#PCDATA)>
<!ELEMENT B (#PCDATA)>
<!ELEMENT BI (#PCDATA)>
<!ELEMENT CSC (#PCDATA)>
```

Translated into plain English, here's what this DTD says:

- I am a Document Type Definition that conforms to version 1.0 of XML and uses the character encoding specified in UTF-8.
- I declare an element called CHAPTER that must have the attribute called id of the type ID (which must be a number) and which must

contain one and only one TITLE followed by one or more AUs followed by one and only one INTRO followed by one or more SECTs.

- I declare an element called TITLE that contains parsed character data.
- I declare an element called AU that contains one and only one NAME followed by one and only one AFF.
- I declare an element called NAME that contains parsed character data.
- I declare an element called AFF that contains one and only one ROLE followed by one and only one ORG.
- I declare an element called ROLE that contains parsed character data.
- I declare an element called ORG that contains parsed character data.
- I declare an entity called emph.grp that contains the elements IT, B, BI, and CSC.
- I declare an element called INTRO that contains parsed character data or anything in the entity called emph.grp.
- I declare an element called SECT that must have the attribute called "level" (which must be 1, 2, 3, or 4) and which must contain one and only one HEAD followed by one or more PARAs.
- I declare an element called HEAD that contains parsed character data or the element called IT.
- I declare an element called PARA that contains parsed character data or one or more LINKXMPLs or one or more CROSSREFs or anything in the entity called emph.grp.
- I declare an element called LINKXMPL that contains parsed character data.
- I declare an element called CROSSREF that contains parsed character data.
- I declare an element called IT that contains parsed character data.
- I declare an element called B that contains parsed character data.
- I declare an element called BI that contains parsed character data.
- I declare an element called CSC that contains parsed character data.

This DTD explicitly defines every element and what it must or may contain, every attribute that must or may be used, and every entity (just one, in this case). Note how much longer it took to say it in English: the DTD syntax was deliberately designed to be terse. The XML Schema language is written in XML itself. This same example will be given as **schemas** [3.3.2.4.3] below.

There are a few more interesting things to note in this example. Both the PARA and INTRO elements make use of the %emph.grp; parameter entity, which means they can include IT, B, BI, and CSC (until that entity is redefined), whereas only IT is permitted in a HEAD. Note also that the chapter identification number is explicitly defined as an ID number. This is an example of ***datatyping***, which is much more widely available in schemas—the successor to DTDs in the XML world.

3. The role of standard DTDs

With all the complexity involved in the preceding discussion, it's no wonder that publishers often say "isn't there some standard DTD I can use so I don't have to go to all that work?" The answer is "Yes, but not so fast." Yes, there are some excellent general purpose DTDs; they are the result of an untold amount of discussion and development over many years by many very smart people; and they are extremely valuable. Does this mean that a given publisher should just adopt one of them as is and say "hey, this will work well enough for me"?

Maybe, but probably not. Standard DTDs either tend to be very big and complex (and very generic) or very simplistic (and very generic). Although they can, in fact, be quite useful, they can also be overwhelming and yet insufficient for the particular publications and purposes you want to use them for. Remember that the fundamental point of a DTD is to define a class of documents. The difficulty in creating a general-purpose DTD is that it cannot be optimized for one publisher's specific documents, reflecting how that publisher wants to structure and name and use things, without being problematic or even unusable for most other publishers. The broader the community of publishers they attempt to serve, and the wider the variety of documents, the more generic these DTDs have to be. That makes them hard to use in day-to-day editorial and production work. Even if they do happen to fit the documents you plan to use them for, you still need to go to the effort of analyzing your documents and determining *how* to use them. In many cases, it's more work to adapt your editorial and production processes to a standard DTD than simply developing a custom (or "bespoke") DTD that does exactly what you want it to.

The big standard DTDs have two main uses. First of all, they often serve as the basis for publishers' own DTDs. They provide well-thought-out models that are sophisticated, time-tested, and usually thoroughly documented. Even if you can't use them without modification, they give you a tremendous head start. Second, they are important as a vehicle for interchange: even if neither party uses a standard DTD "off the shelf," the standard DTD offers a well-defined, public model that can serve both as a known target for the provider of the data and a known source for the recipient. (In this respect they are sometimes referred to as "interchange DTDs" or ***reference DTDs***.)

The stories of three such standard DTDs—ISO 12083, TEI (the Text Encoding Initiative), and MEP (the Model Editions Partnership)—are enlightening and instructive. There are many more; the best and most effective standard

DTDs tend to be developed for specific purposes within specific industries (automotive, aerospace, financial, pharmaceutical, etc.). Another widely used standard DTD, for example, is ***DocBook***, developed originally for technical and software documentation but increasingly used outside that sphere. And sometimes one aspect of a DTD developed for a particular community turns out to be quite useful outside that community. The DTD developed by the U.S. Department of Defense for procurement, the CALS model (the acronym stands for Computer-aided Acquisition and Logistics Support), has contributed one of the most widely used table models: the CALS table model is often incorporated in other DTDs.

1. ISO 12083: IT'S ALL ABOUT STRUCTURE

Arguably the granddaddy of the standard DTDs, ISO 12083 traces its history back to the very beginnings of the development of structured markup. It grew out of the Electronic Manuscript Project sponsored by the AAP in the 1980s, a pioneering attempt to develop coordinated, comprehensive, standard SGML models for books, serials, articles, and math. Eventually developed into an international standard reference model (having gone through the elaborate ISO adoption process described above, but largely authored and championed by Eric van Herwijnen), it was published as an ISO standard in 1993. Currently it is an SGML DTD, although efforts are underway to update it as XML.

ISO 12083 has found its widest use among scientific journal publishers. A study done by Inera for the Harvard University Libraries (their excellent white paper is available at http://www.diglib.org/preserve/hadtdfs.pdf) found that although most leading scientific journal DTDs are modeled on ISO 12083, none actually use it without modification. A paper entitled, "Should We Be Using ISO 12083?" (http://www.press.umich.edu/jep/03-04/hicks.html) came to the same conclusions from the point of view of a book publisher. While it is an excellent model on which to base a publisher-specific DTD, ISO 12083 generally proves to be too complicated and yet too generic to be used in its unaltered form, except as an interchange DTD.

One reason for this is that on the spectrum from rigorous structure to permissiveness and flexibility, ISO 12083 takes a firm position at the rigid end. It is a very idealistic DTD. It conceives of publications as boxes-within-boxes; its fundamental structure is one of nested subsections within sections, and it enforces this structure with the strictness of a schoolmarm. Having spent time in its class, one is simultaneously grateful for what has been learned and relieved to have graduated from it.

What gets in the way of editorial and production processes are not only the deep hierarchical structures of ISO 12083 (which can be handled well by sophisticated systems but are very problematic for styles-based environments like word processors and desktop publishing programs) but also the generic, context-sensitive naming of elements that is a logical consequence of its structure. Subheads, for example, are not tagged <H1>, <H2>, <H3>, etc.; instead, they are all tagged <TITLE>, as is the chapter title of a book. All of these take their meaning from the context in which they reside: a <TITLE> at the beginning of a chapter, before the first <SECTION>, must be a chapter title, whereas the <TITLE> that comes after a <SUBSECT3> but before a <SUBSECT4> is what an editor or typesetter would think of as an <H3>. This kind of abstraction drives editorial and production staff crazy. Especially when the structures are deep, it is very difficult to keep everything straight. Plus, it's rigid: if the chapter you're editing has what looks like an <H4> right after an <H2>, ISO 12083 makes it very difficult to accomplish that; you have to establish the proper hierarchy even if the intervening level three has nothing in it but the desired level four. If a list is embedded inside a paragraph, you can't just end the text above the list with an </P> and then start the text after the list with, perhaps, a tag like <P type= "no_indent">; ISO 12083 gets out its ruler, slaps your wrist, and says "no, I'm sorry, that's wrong; it's all the same paragraph, you can't end it until the whole paragraph with the list embedded in it is over."

But this very rigidity turns out to be useful for computer processing—which is what it was designed to facilitate in the first place. If you have a rigorously defined structure, and enforce it strictly, people may struggle or rebel, but computers smile and say "quite right; just so; thank you very much." This is what makes ISO 12083 such a good model for archival systems—especially systems that are designed to manage complicated assortments of content, keeping track of how all the pieces originally fit together but also making it possible to rearrange and recombine the pieces into other structures. It turns out to be very handy to have that generic label <TITLE> on every subhead; when a passage from one book, for example, which includes a second-level subhead, is quoted in another book, that title is no longer a second-level subhead; in its new context it is a subhead within an extract. If it carries the <TITLE> tag and is processed by a system powerful enough to handle context-sensitive tagging, nobody has to find that tag and change it to <EXTHEAD> or something of the sort.

The custodians of ISO 12083 are not unaware of these issues. The 1998 scope statement for the standard itself acknowledges that,

> "This International Standard presents a reference document type definition which facilitates the authoring, interchange, and archiving of a variety of publications. This document type definition is deliberately general. It is a reference document type definition which provides a set of building blocks for the structuring of books, articles, serials, and similar publications in print and electronic form. This

International Standard is intended to provide a document architecture to facilitate the creation of various application-specific document type definitions."
—*(http://www.xmlxperts.com/scope.htm)*

It's consistent with ISO 12083's strictness that although it acknowledges that most users will need to modify it, it contains strict rules about *how* it must be modified. Always the teacher.

2. TEI: A WEALTH OF OPTIONS

If ISO 12083 is the strict disciplinarian, TEI, the Text Encoding Initiative, is that favorite teacher who let you read *Ulysses* instead of *Middlemarch* or write a term paper comparing Wagner's operas and Marvel Comics—and grade yourself. TEI is all about diversity and freedom. It originated as a tool for literary scholarship, and unlike ISO 12083 it is mostly used in the humanities. TEI was launched in 1987 and is continuously developed and maintained by a consortium of four universities—Oxford, Brown, Bergen, and Virginia—and several other organizations; the current custodian of the standard is the Association for Computing and the Humanities at the University of Virginia. It originated as SGML but has been updated to XML.

The fundamental thing to understand about TEI is that it is essentially *descriptive* rather than *prescriptive*. It reflects the needs of its originators to describe virtually any document—a novel, a seventeenth-century economics treatise, a fragment of a medieval manuscript, a poem, scene from a play—in a way that is not only manageable by the computer but useful to the scholar. It is not as concerned, to the extent ISO 12083 is, with how a publication *ought* to be structured; its mission is to give scholars of any kind of document a way to describe how it *is* structured. In addition, it needs to provide ways to describe the appearance of elements whose structure may not be apparent, or where the appearance itself is something the scholar needs to record: a word crossed out in the manuscript, a notation inserted in the author's handwriting, another word obscured by a stain, a phrase printed in red.

The result is not, strictly speaking, a single DTD, but a huge collection of modular components with which to create DTDs. If the documents you are attempting to tag are dramatic works, TEI provides a well-thought-out model for how drama should be tagged; it knows about acts and scenes, dialog and stage directions, and names them as such. (In this respect, it is the polar opposite of ISO 12083's deliberate neutrality, with its generic naming.) Likewise, if there is poetry, TEI gives you appropriate tags useful to poetry. If there is marginalia, TEI gives you a way to tag it as such. If you care about what the highlighted phrases *are* in your documents (which ones are book titles, which are operas, which are foreign words), TEI gives you a way to distinguish them; but if, instead, you need to record the *appearance* of the highlighted phrases (italic vs. bold vs. small caps), TEI lets you do that. It is all about options. There are currently 500-some elements provided in 31 DTD fragments in the whole TEI scheme. Not only that, TEI is designed for customization: while it provides a formal method for assembling the various components into a new TEI-compliant DTD, it also allows unlimited use of new attribute values. That way, an expression like <div type= "peculiar"> would process properly as a TEI-compliant document even though TEI doesn't know what "peculiar" means.

This is not to say that TEI is not concerned about structure. True TEI documents begin with a root element, <TEI.2>, which is divided into two basic components, both required: <teiHeader> and <text>. The text can be structured a number of different ways. The most basic is to divide it into optional front matter, required body, and optional back matter, which is how you would structure a typical book. Because TEI publications are often composed of a collection of documents, the text element can be further subdivided so that instead of just one <body> section, they can have groups of subordinate <text> elements, each of which might have its own front matter, body, and back matter. Beyond that, an entire collection of publications can be defined as a *TEI corpus* comprising any number of <TEI.2> publications, each structured in the ways mentioned above. The header—an important part of any TEI publication—can contain a wealth of useful information, including bibliographic information, information about the sources, the revision history, and information about how the document was created and by whom. The body of the text can be organized hierarchically (<div0> containing <div1> containing <div2>, etc.), recursively (<div> inside <div> inside <div>, etc.), flat (a series of parallel <div> sections), or other ways; and those <div>s can be classified any way you want, using the "type" attribute. Again, it's the polar opposite of ISO 12083: total flexibility. That does not mean there is *no* structure; it just means that you can define the structure pretty much any way you want, and make it as permissive or restrictive as you want.

Part of the mission of TEI is not just to make such a wealth of options available, but also to provide guidelines for their use. These guidelines are officially published and maintained; the current version, known as P4, was approved by the TEI Board in 2002, and work on P5 is proceeding. Publishers can create DTDs that follow these guidelines and use only the approved component models (while fully exploiting the flexibility of those models), in which case their DTDs are TEI compliant and begin with the root element <TEI.2>; these are known as *views* of the TEI system. Or they can use the components in whatever way they want and need to, perhaps not necessarily following the guidelines in every respect (for example, incorporating only selected elements from a module rather than all the elements in a given module); such a DTD would still be recognized as TEI based but it would not, technically, be TEI compliant. Finally, because the richness in TEI can also be overwhelming, a single subset DTD called ***TEI Lite*** has been created (a "view" of TEI), which offers approximately 150 of the 500-some TEI elements. TEI Lite is both a useful basis for a publisher-specific DTD and a convenient interchange DTD for passing documents from one TEI-based system to another. (Thorough documentation and information about TEI is available at etext.lib.virginia.edu/TEI.html.)

3. MEP: STAGES OF ENRICHMENT

What is most interesting about ***MEP***, the Model Editions Partnership (http://www.mep.cla.sc.edu/mepinfo/mep-info.html), is that it is designed to accommodate the fact that not all the desired tagging can be accomplished by the same person or at the same stage of editing and production. Developed by a consortium of twelve editorial projects devoted to producing editions of historical documents, MEP is an excellent example of the use of TEI for a specific purpose. There are three MEP DTDs, all single-file (not a collection of modules, as TEI is) and designed not to be modified; they use TEI modules in the prescribed fashion to result in fully TEI-compliant DTDs.

Why three DTDs? Not for three different types of documents; all three DTDs are intended to apply to the same documents. Instead, they are designed for progressive enrichment of the tagging. They recognize that certain elements are evident in the printed documents MEP is designed to handle, certain elements take extra work, and some things require subject specialists. Instead of creating one master DTD that asks for all possible rich coding to be done, MEP published these three separate but related DTDs, providing for what they refer to as "gradual markup levels."

MEP Level One accommodates markup of blocks of text, font changes, and other aspects of a document that are readily apparent visually to anyone without knowledge or understanding of the content. Level One markup can reasonably be expected to be accomplished by a transcriber or a conversion service.

MEP Level Two adds hyperlinks for notes and cross-references. This level of markup cannot necessarily be done in the initial data capture phase because the things that need to be linked are often not typographically distinct. Some of these things can be done programmatically, but usually somebody needs to read through the content. That person needs a basic understanding of what to look for, but probably doesn't need to be a subject expert. Note that this level of coding, though not needed to reproduce the printed document, is considered a basic requirement for most electronic publications.

MEP Level Three adds markup for things that are not at all evident but that are intellectually important: things like names, dates, and places; bibliographic information; highlighted or emphasized phrases; editorial interventions; etc. These things typically need to be tagged by someone who has some knowledge of the content's subject matter—ideal work for grad students.

What is so refreshing about MEP is that it realizes not only that the ultimate, ideal tagging does not need to be done all at once, it probably *cannot* be done all at once. Publishers often don't appreciate how XML makes it possibly to gradually enrich their content. Taking this approach enables the right things to be done by the right people at the right time. Some things can be best done when the data is captured in the first place; some things can best be found and tagged by a copyeditor, who reads and understands the content; some things can best be done by a compositor, who very likely has more powerful technology and the ability to script and automate some processes that would otherwise have to be done by hand; and some things are best left for later. Whereas in the past, each of these participants in the process would use a different kind of file, often undoing and redoing each other's work, XML makes it possible for them all to build on each other's work.

4. Schemas

Schemas have actually been used in the database world for many years. In a general sense, the word "schema" refers to the spelled-out plan of a database. For a typical database, the schema might define what the various records are, and within each record, what each field is for. In the past, many of these were fixed fields, meaning certain numbers of characters were allotted to each field: for example, a schema might specify that the first nine digits of a "subscriber name" record are a Social Security number, the next fifteen are reserved for "last name," the next ten for "first name," the next one for "middle initial," and so forth. (Such schemas are responsible for the truncated names often seen on magazine address labels and the like.) Rigidity and compactness are important virtues in such a database, enabling fast, accurate, and simple processing. Schema languages were developed for various purposes that provided powerful information- and data-processing functionality.

Although SGML and XML can be used to define such databases, in the publishing world they are more commonly used to define, in effect, a text database. In that world, much greater flexibility is needed, for which XML's tagging is ideal. At first, the only "legal" way to describe an XML document model (in a sense, a schema) was with a DTD. But while XML was being embraced by the publishing world, it was also being embraced by the database world, and that world felt very restricted by the limitations of XML's DTDs.

That world was used to many of the more powerful features available in various database schema languages. Several languages—for example, DCD (Document Content Description), DDML (Document Definition Markup Language), XDR (also known as XML-Data), SOX (Schema for Object-oriented XML), and one reassuringly called RELAX (Regular Language description for XML)—were put forth as possible candidates as successors to the DTD. Meanwhile, the W3C was working on its own successor to the DTD, and in May 2001 issued ***XML Schema*** as a recommendation. The most important alternative to XML Schema is ***RELAX NG*** (RELAX Next Generation, a unification of the Japanese standard RELAX and James Clark's TREX), the successor to RELAX and now a draft international standard (ISO/IEC DIS 19757-2).

1. XML SCHEMA LANGUAGES

XML schema languages accommodate virtually all the functions of XML DTDs, but at the same time address many of the limitations of DTDs. The first and most obvious difference is that schemas are written in XML itself, not in a separate syntax as DTDs are. Although schemas are more verbose (the DTD syntax is deliberately terse)they are also more expressive and can describe some XML vocabularies that cannot be described with DTDs. (This doesn't mean they are *easy* to understand, though: it is possible to create very complex structures with XML schemas.) Even more significant, though, is that schemas do not need separate, specialized software: they can be "read" by any software that can read XML. This means that they can be written and edited with the same tools used to write and edit XML documents. They can even include their own documentation in XML—a big advantage. And because XML schema languages are generally namespace aware, it is much easier for schema authors to work with namespaces than for DTD authors.

XML schemas also offer much stronger ***inheritance mechanisms*** than DTDs do. Going far beyond entities (the functions of which can be accomplished with schemas, though entities as we know them in DTDs aren't formally retained), schemas enable the definitions of elements to depend on the status or values or definitions of other elements. These inheritance mechanisms are often spoken of as *parent–child* relationships. It's easiest to visualize this in presentational terms. If, for example, extracts (block quotes) inherit all the properties of body text but, in addition, they are indented on the left and right (extracts thus being children of the parent body text), then when the definition of body text is changed, the extracts correspondingly change. This is a commonly used mechanism in defining stylesheets; when used in schema definitions, it can be very convenient and powerful. For example, the affiliation element at the beginning of this chapter could inherit its "required" status from the author element. Thus by making the author element required or not, the affiliation would be required along with it.

A particular feature of XML Schema is that all elements can have default values. (In DTDs, only attributes can have default values.) This can save a lot of work and provide for better consistency. For example, a publisher's schema might provide for a metadata element called <publisher> and default to the name of the schema's owner. That way, the name would always be incorporated in exactly the same way (by default, rather than by having to be entered as content), and the content of that element would only need to be provided when a different publisher was being referred to.

2. DATATYPING

One of the most powerful features that XML schemas brings from the database world is ***datatyping***. This makes it possible to specify not just that an element contains data, but that it must contain a particular type of data: an integer, a date, an ID, a Boolean expression, a Uniform Resource Identifier (URI) reference, or any of a number of other types. Datatyping was available in a limited way through attributes in DTDs; but in schemas, it is possible to specify a data type for any element. Specifying that a given element is a date, for example, makes it possible to ensure that a given instance of that element is expressed correctly, in a specified form, and that it is a valid date in the first place. A parser can then find dates incorrectly expressed (a month and day missing the year, for example, or a day with the value 32), and can also find places where that element is used where it shouldn't be (tagging, by mistake, something that is not a date at all). Judicious use of datatyping can enable computers to help find certain kinds of mistakes much more easily than human proofreaders can.

3. TWO SCHEMA EXAMPLES

Here are two example schemas that model the same XML vocabulary as the DTD example that appears earlier in this chapter. The first example shows a RELAX NG schema while the second example shows an XML Schema. Both schemas are quite verbose so only some of the more interesting elements are shown.

4. RELAX NG

```
<?xml version="1.0" encoding="utf-8"?>
<grammar datatypeLibrary="http://www.w3.org/2001/XMLSchema-
   datatypes" xmlns="http://relaxng.org/ns/structure/1.0">
   <start>
        <choice>
```

```
            <ref name="CHAPTER"/>
        </choice>
    </start>
    <define name="CHAPTER">
        <element name="CHAPTER">
            <attribute name="id">
                <data type="ID"/>
            </attribute>
            <ref name="TITLE"/>
            <oneOrMore>
                <ref name="AU"/>
            </oneOrMore>
            <ref name="INTRO"/>
            <oneOrMore>
                <ref name="SECT"/>
            </oneOrMore>
        </element>
    </define>
  <define name="TITLE">
        <element name="TITLE">
            <text/>
        </element>
    </define>
    <define name="AU">
        <element name="AU">
            <ref name="NAME"/>
            <ref name="AFF"/>
        </element>
    </define>
. . .
    <define name="emph.grp">
        <choice>
            <ref name="IT"/>
            <ref name="B"/>
            <ref name="BI"/>
            <ref name="CSC"/>
        </choice>
    </define>
. . .
    <define name="SECT">
```

```
            <element name="SECT">
                <attribute name="level">
                    <choice>
                        <value>1</value>
                        <value>2</value>
                        <value>3</value>
                        <value>4</value>
                    </choice>
                </attribute>
                <ref name="HEAD"/>
                <oneOrMore>
                    <choice>
                        <ref name="PARA"/>
                        <ref name="SECT"/>
                    </choice>
                </oneOrMore>
            </element>
        </define>
...
        <define name="PARA">
            <element name="PARA">
                <zeroOrMore>
                    <choice>
                        <text/>
                        <ref name="LINKXMPL"/>
                        <ref name="CROSSREF"/>
                        <ref name="emph.grp"/>
                    </choice>
                </zeroOrMore>
            </element>
        </define>
...
</grammar>
```

5. XML SCHEMA

```
<?xml version="1.0" encoding="UTF-8"?>
<xs:schema xmlns:xs="http://www.w3.org/2001/XMLSchema"
    elementFormDefault="qualified" version="1.0">
    <xs:element name="CHAPTER">
        <xs:complexType>
            <xs:sequence>
```

```
        <xs:element ref="TITLE"/>
        <xs:element maxOccurs="unbounded" ref="AU"/>
        <xs:element ref="INTRO"/>
        <xs:element maxOccurs="unbounded" ref="SECT"/>
      </xs:sequence>
      <xs:attribute name="id" use="required" type="xs:ID"/>
    </xs:complexType>
  </xs:element>
  <xs:element name="TITLE">
    <xs:complexType mixed="true"/>
  </xs:element>
  <xs:element name="AU">
    <xs:complexType>
      <xs:sequence>
        <xs:element ref="NAME"/>
        <xs:element ref="AFF"/>
      </xs:sequence>
    </xs:complexType>
  </xs:element>
...
  <xs:group name="emph.grp">
    <xs:choice>
      <xs:element ref="IT"/>
      <xs:element ref="B"/>
      <xs:element ref="BI"/>
      <xs:element ref="CSC"/>
    </xs:choice>
  </xs:group>
...
  <xs:element name="SECT">
    <xs:complexType>
      <xs:sequence>
        <xs:element ref="HEAD"/>
        <xs:choice maxOccurs="unbounded">
          <xs:element ref="PARA"/>
          <xs:element ref="SECT"/>
        </xs:choice>
      </xs:sequence>
      <xs:attribute name="level" use="required">
        <xs:simpleType>
          <xs:restriction base="xs:token">
```

```
                        <xs:enumeration value="1"/>
                        <xs:enumeration value="2"/>
                        <xs:enumeration value="3"/>
                        <xs:enumeration value="4"/>
                    </xs:restriction>
                </xs:simpleType>
            </xs:attribute>
        </xs:complexType>
    </xs:element>
. . .
    <xs:element name="PARA">
        <xs:complexType mixed="true">
            <xs:choice minOccurs="0" maxOccurs="unbounded">
                <xs:element ref="LINKXMPL"/>
                <xs:element ref="CROSSREF"/>
                <xs:group ref="emph.grp"/>
            </xs:choice>
        </xs:complexType>
    </xs:element>
. . .
</xs:schema>
```

5. The document instance

Once the content belonging to a given class of documents has been analyzed and defined, it is ready to be tagged according to that definition. Each resulting tagged document is known as a ***document instance***. This is more than simply a piece of text with tags in it. In order to be considered ***valid XML*** or SGML, a document instance must be properly tagged and structured as defined by a particular DTD or schema that is specified in a ***DOCTYPE declaration*** at the top of the document. (A declaration for this chapter, for example, might be <!DOCTYPE chapter SYSTEM "CGDP.dtd">.)

Every tag used in the document must be defined, and it must be used according to the proper syntax: in XML, if there is a <DIV1> there must subsequently be an </DIV1>, and if a <DIV2> occurs between them then an </DIV2> must occur before the </DIV1>. (Thus the <DIV2> element is properly nested inside the <DIV1> element. An element is not allowed to start inside another element and end outside it.) Not only do those tags have to follow the rules (e.g., <DIV1> cannot end with </div1>), they also have to be declared in the DTD or schema: if the DTD or schema only allows for <DIV1>, <DIV2>, and <DIV3>, and a document has the tag <DIV4>, it will be invalid. If a document contains an element tagged <FN>, it might seem obvious that this is a footnote, but unless <FN> is declared in the specified DTD or schema, it is not allowed.

Although this rigor might seem restrictive and cumbersome, it is where XML gets much of its power. It ultimately makes things easier, because it enables computers to do some of the work. A parser can read the document instance, check it against the specified DTD or schema, and report the errors it finds. A human being might easily overlook that <DIV4>, because it's "obvious" what it means; but if processing or presentation systems don't know what to do with a <DIV4>, it creates problems if that tag slips through. Likewise, <FN> might mean "first name" instead of "footnote"; if the definition specifies that it can only occur within a name (between the tags <NAME> and </NAME>), then if it is used to tag a footnote, the parser will help catch the mistake.

A valid document instance must not only be properly tagged and structured, it must be complete. If the type of document a DTD defines is "book," and specifies that a book must include front matter, chapters, and back matter, then a single chapter (lacking front matter and back matter) won't be valid: a chapter is not a book. This is one of the most common reasons why, in the real world of publishing, it is almost never practical to have only one DTD or schema. The fundamental component parts like chapters, front matter, bibliographies, and indexes are often written as modules that are then called up by various DTDs in the appropriate situations. When a single chapter is being edited or composed, it's convenient to use a DTD that considers a chapter a whole document; but once all the chapters are finished and the final book is assembled, it is good to have a DTD for the whole book that makes sure such items as title page, TOC, and index are present.

1. WELL-FORMED VS. VALID XML

Although the clarity and discipline of a good document model, and documents properly tagged according to it, are very valuable, there are many situations where such rigor is not possible or practical. While SGML requires a DTD for every document, XML permits documents to be ***well formed*** without a DTD or schema. A well-formed XML document uses the proper syntax, as defined in the XML standard, and all its elements are nested properly. Technically, all XML documents are well formed, because if they don't follow those rules, they aren't considered legal XML. Thus a "valid XML" document, which is tagged according to a specific DTD or schema, is of course also well formed. But the term "well-formed XML" is usually used to refer to documents without DTDs or schemas.

It is extremely important to recognize the difference between well-formed XML and valid XML. Publishers are often assured that a given vendor, or a given application, or a given process, will provide "XML"; if they neglect to clarify what kind of XML they will get, they may be in for a big disappointment. To use an extreme, if ridiculous, example, a file beginning with the tag <BOOK> and ending with the tag </BOOK> and having nothing but plain ASCII text between those tags is, technically, well-formed XML. But it is also useless XML. So is a file where every element is simply tagged as a <P> or <PARA>. Most publishers need their documents to be tagged consistently according to some well-defined scheme. If one editor or compositor tags abstracts as <ABS> and another editor or compositor tags them as <ABSTR>, both can deliver perfectly legal, well-formed XML. But those files will not be compatible. Although it might be tempting to settle for well-formed XML, most publishers are much better served by valid XML tagged according to a DTD or schema that fits their particular needs.

This is not to say that all well-formed XML is worthless. Nothing could be further from the truth. It is extremely useful to be able to add new tags, for example, when unexpected elements occur. Although it may be appropriate to then modify a DTD or schema to account for them, it is often not possible or practical to do so at the time the new element is encountered. This often happens in the course of writing or editing or composition; well-formed XML provides an excellent mechanism to manage such a situation. If a book DTD didn't include a definition for recipes, it is very useful to be able to create such tags as <recipe>, <ingredient>, <amount>, <instructions>, and <step> and use them in a systematic way when a recipe is encountered. That will save a lot of subsequent retagging and reformatting work later. It also provides a good way to specify what should be done with these elements: a designer can be notified that there is a new element, called <recipe>, which includes ingredients, amounts, instructions, and steps; the designer can then specify what to do with those elements, and a production person can create a stylesheet to format them, all without requiring the file to be recoded. And of course those elements can be located easily—a big advantage when large documents, or large quantities of documents, are involved.

6. Namespaces

Sometimes, it is useful for a given XML document to use elements and attributes that have been created for other unrelated documents and defined in other DTDs. For example, there is a simple set of tags called the **Dublin Core** [3.3.6.3.1], developed in the library world, that is used to mark basic metadata like title, publisher, and language. Beyond the simple convenience of using these tags rather than having to invent new ones, it is extremely useful, when exchanging data with others, to use a commonly recognized set of tags like this. That way, one user can identify that particular set of tags by name, and another user can recognize them: for example, "this document uses Dublin Core tags." This is more than simply providing a set of tags; it associates a specific semantic meaning with those tags. The tag <dc:title> doesn't just mean "here's a special kind of title that I want to make sure you don't confuse with another kind of title (perhaps the tag <title>)," but rather "when I use the tag <dc:title> it means exactly what Dublin Core defines as a title." (The tag <title> could still be used in the document to mark other kinds of titles—chapter titles, subtitles, whatever the document model allowed them to be.)

The mechanism XML provides for doing this is called XML ***namespaces***. An element definition can include an xmlns attribute, which associates that element with a particular namespace, identified by a URI. Such an element name has two parts, separated by a colon: the *prefix*, which identifies the namespace, and a *local part*, the actual element name. Thus, in the Dublin Core example, the element <dc:title> specifies that the element is not just a title, but is a title as defined in the Dublin Core. The DTD or schema would need to contain the expression xmlns:dc="http://purl.org/dc/elements/1.1", the *namespace URI*, for Dublin Core, which serves the function of making those element names unique. This is what prevents collisions with other more localized use of similar tags, making it possible to use a tag like <title> which will not conflict with the tag <dc:title>. (Note that identifying the namespace URI doesn't imply any actual interaction with that location; the XML processor simply substitutes the URI in place of "dc" when processing, in order to make that name precise and unambiguous, but it doesn't actually attempt to access that location.)

Namespaces help XML to be more portable, more universal, and more modular. When there is a well-defined and well-known set of elements and attributes available publicly, it is often convenient to use them as part of a more specialized definition. Dublin Core is a useful example from the world of books, libraries, and metadata; even more commonly used namespaces are those for HTML or OeB-PS, the Open eBook Publication Structure. But it is also useful to create a new namespace, perhaps within the context of a given publishing house, which can then be used by reference in any number of DTDs and schemas.

(iii) DEFINING THE APPEARANCE OF XML DOCUMENTS

XML documents gain much of their flexibility and power by avoiding purely presentation-related tagging , thus enabling the appearance of the document to be adapted to each mode of presentation. A cross-reference might be typeset in small caps in print but be rendered in blue lowercase letters and underscored in an on-line version; a warning might be set in a special font and positioned in the margin of a print instructional manual, but on line it might be rendered in red and set in a box, or it might be made to blink in an e-book. It's much more useful for the source XML of the former to use the tag <cross-reference> rather than <smallcaps> and of the latter to tag <warning> rather than <span style= "padding: 10px 10px 10px 10px; background-color: rgb(255, 0, 0);">.

At some point, of course, presentation does need to be determined: we don't want to read the XML itself, we want to see it formatted in a useful way. When the content is to be read on paper, we need to typeset it; to view it on line, we need to tell a Web browser how to render it; to read it as an e-book, we need to adapt it to the features and limitations of a particular e-book technology. To do this, we may need to convert the source XML file to another kind of file (a composition file, an HTML file, an e-book file); or, if the appropriate technologies are available to us, we may be able to use a stylesheet to specify the desired appearance, thus using the source XML file directly rather than having to create an alternative file or files from it.

1. Converting to HTML for Web display

By far the most common way XML files are used today is for the creation of HTML files for Web presentation. Although recent versions of the leading Web browsers enable the direct display of XML through the use of stylesheets, it is still necessary or desirable in most cases to provide an HTML file to specify how the content should be presented in a browser.

This can be done in either static or dynamic ways. Frequently, the HTML files are created by a combination of **scripts** [3.3.4.2] and handwork from source XML files, resulting in a separate set of files. This is adequate when the source XML is stable and when the resulting HTML does not need to be adapted for various users (for example, a chapter of a book or a newspaper article in an archive). But when the content may need to change, or when the presentation may need to be customized, this static approach becomes problematic. With two or more versions of the content (a source XML file and one or more HTML files derived from it), the task of keeping those versions in synch is a burden and prone to error. A more dynamic approach is better, by which the HTML files are created on the fly as needed. Sometimes this is done by the same sorts of scripts used to create static HTML (although such scripts need to be 100 percent effective, requiring no manual intervention). A more convenient solution can be provided by a **content management system** [10.2] that is designed to automate the necessary conversion.

2. Cascading Style Sheets (CSS)

A more sophisticated method of specifying how a browser should present a document is with Cascading Style Sheets (***CSS***). A stylesheet is a separate file that contains presentation specifications for a document or a group of documents. It is a way to give names to groups of formatting instructions. A stylesheet can tell a browser to make elements tagged as <crossref> blue, or to put elements tagged as <warning> in a box and to color them red. It can specify fonts, sizes, spacing, and other presentational aspects, enabling such specifications to be left out of the document itself.

This has two complementary virtues: one stylesheet can apply to many documents, and many stylesheets can apply to a given document. A magazine publisher with an archive of hundreds or thousands of articles may wish to redesign how those articles are presented over the Web; through the use of stylesheets, those new specifications can be made in one updated file without requiring a single code to be altered in all those archived articles (if they were coded to enable the use of stylesheets in the first place and have tags where needed). For example, author names that were previously centered and bold at the beginnings of articles can be made flush right and italic, as long as the author names are all tagged properly; without a stylesheet, the "bold, centered" codes would have to be changed to "italic, flush right" codes wherever author names appear at the beginnings of articles—and *only* there (a messy task at best in a large archive). Likewise, a book publisher might want to publish a reference work in a variety of electronic media; one stylesheet could be used for Web presentation (utilizing the space and color available on desktop or laptop displays), another for Palm devices (perhaps monochrome and designed for the small screen), and others for various e-book formats. Stylesheets are one of the best ways to realize the benefits of presentation-neutral XML tagging.

Cascading Style Sheets were originally developed for HTML, not XML. To be useful in most HTML-oriented contexts they generally use the limited number of elements HTML makes available. This is accomplished through the use of **attributes** [3.3.2.2.3], whose use is permitted with only certain elements in HTML, such as <p> and <div>. For example, author names can be considered a special sort of <p> and tagged as <p class="author">. Then, a CSS can be provided that includes the following:

```
.author
{
text-align: right;
margin-top: 60px;
font-family: Palatino, Times New Roman, serif;
color: #663399;
font-size: 28pt;
font-weight: bold;
}
```

This instructs the browser to display <p>s of the class "author" as a separate block, set flush right 60 pixels from the top of the window, in 28-point bold Palatino if available (with Times New Roman as second choice, and, lacking that, in a serif font), in a particular shade of blue. Such style specifications can be provided for other elements in the document, not only making it much easier to tag those documents, but also making it much easier to change their format later. (The on-line version of this book includes an example of the CSS used to display that on-line version, using the opening of this chapter as sample text, as previous examples have done.)

3. XSL, the Extensible Stylesheet Language

Whereas CSS is a stylesheet language designed specifically for the Web and HTML, ***XSL***—the Extensible Stylesheet Language (first published as a Recommendation by the W3C in October 2001)—is much more powerful and versatile. It is designed not only to specify the presentation of XML documents, but to enable them to be transformed as well. Moreover, it is designed to accommodate both Web-based and print-based presentations.

Just as XML itself bridged the gap between the limitations of HTML and the complexities of SGML, XSL bridges the gap between CSS and ***DSSSL***, the Document Style Semantics and Specification Language. DSSSL is a very complex technology that is even beyond the scope of many who mastered SGML; it is typically used only by expert programmers. XSL is designed, like XML, to be more user friendly and to lend itself much more readily to the development of software tools. But just as XML builds on and complements HTML without replacing it, XSL should be thought of as a complementary technology to CSS, not a successor technology. In fact, one of the most common uses of XSL is to create HTML documents that work with CSS stylesheets for rendering documents in Web browsers. It's especially significant that this can be done automatically on a Web server. The underlying formatting models of CSS and XSL are designed to be compatible and interoperable.

1. XSLT AND XSL-FO

There are two distinct aspects to XSL: *transformation* and *formatting*. Transformation is done by a technology called ***XSLT*** (XSL Transformations, discussed at more length **below** [3.3.4.4]) and formatting is done by the use of XSL Formatting Objects (***XSL-FO***). Both of these functions (collectively referred to as XSL) are accomplished through stylesheets that are designed to be used with a particular class of XML documents. The underlying principle is that to apply a given presentational design to a set of XML documents, the documents first have to be restructured to correspond with the desired presentation, and then those restructured documents can be rendered as specified. The stylesheets give names to a particular set of features (formatting objects) and specify how they are intended to be presented. XSL-FO provides not just a language for specifying what these formatting objects should look like in a given mode of presentation, but a specific vocabulary—the names of the formatting objects themselves.

It's important to realize that the formatting instructions in XSL-FO are not "embedded" in the source XML documents—it's not a way to say, "this is a <CN>; make it 24-point Frutiger and center it at the top of a new page" or "even though the other <H2>s are bold, make this particular one bold italic." The formatting instructions only operate on ***formatting objects*** specified by XSL-FO. The elements labeled with the original "vocabulary" (the tags in the source document, whatever they may be, as defined in its specific DTD or schema—e.g., <CT> or <H2>) need to be transformed (usually, but not necessarily, with XSLT) into a separate, very specific vocabulary: the formatting objects as specified by XSL-FO. Sometimes, this results in a new file, now tagged as formatting objects, on which an XSL-FO stylesheet operates; other times, it is done on the fly without that intervening state being preserved as a file.

The power of XSL, and its main advance over CSS, is that it recognizes that an essential aspect of presenting a document in a certain way is to rearrange its parts—and even to omit parts or create new ones—to fit the desired presentation. (Another member of the XML family, ***XPath***, provides a way to express the structure of XML documents so that those relevant parts can be described and addressed; see the sections on **transformation** [3.3.4] and **linking** [3.3.5] below.) Imagine, for example, that a given XML document is to be published both as a chapter of a book and as an article in a magazine. When it is a chapter in a book, it has a chapter number; the author's name may appear after the chapter title, while the author's affiliation may appear in an "About the Authors" section in the back of the book. Illustration credits may appear in the front matter. When it is an article in a magazine, there is no chapter number; the author's name and affiliation may appear at the end of the article; and the illustration credits may run sideways in small type beside the illustrations. XSL (with XSLT and XPath) not only provides the ability to rearrange the parts appropriately (creating two "result" documents—the book chapter and the magazine article—from the single "source" XML document) but to leave some parts out and create others that don't exist in the source document (the chapter number in the book might be an example of such ***generated text***). Most important, this can all be done automatically, without manual intervention, leaving the original XML source document completely intact, able to be transformed again and again.

2. XSL-FO IS A SPECIFICATION LANGUAGE, NOT A FORMATTING ENGINE

When people first learn about XSL-FO, they often mistakenly think that it performs the formatting. Because XSL-FO gives you the ability to describe almost every last detail about how you want the pages to look, they imagine that you then just need to run it on an XML file and generate a PDF file beautifully formatted as specified. This omits a very important part of the process—the formatting engine. XSL, like XML, is a language, although, unlike XML, it does have a specific vocabulary (it is more like HTML in that regard). XSL is not *software*. In fact, also like XML, it is developed precisely to be software neutral, enabling anybody and everybody to develop software to work with it. So what is needed, to get from that XML file to that PDF file formatted as specified in that XSL-FO stylesheet, is a rendering engine that understands XSL-FO and processes XML files accordingly: software (whether in a browser or in a composition program) to interpret the XSL-FO specifications and render a result.

At this writing, this XSL functionality has been implemented in no commonly used composition programs and only the latest Web browsers (although several promising programs are in development, mostly for generating PostScript and PDF using XSL-FO). However, because of its power and flexibility, it will eventually become an important part of how documents are presented on line, in print, and in e-books.

4. Fonts and character encoding

Fonts and character encoding are an important and often overlooked aspect of presentation. Although the desktop publishing revolution of the 1980s put fonts into the hands of the masses (many students today have never touched a typewriter; the documents they produce on their PCs can have rich and exuberant, if sometimes misguided, typography), fonts and the characters they represent are generally taken for granted or misunderstood. They are our window onto the content; one idealistic view of typography argues that it is best when it is so transparent that it seems to disappear. Few appreciate how much work it takes not only to accomplish that typographic clarity, but just to avoid the destruction of a well-composed document when it is rendered without the proper fonts or characters, resulting in awkward spacing, unintended reflow, and the anomalies that can make accented characters appear as crescent moons.

It is important to understand the difference between a *character*, a *glyph*, a *font*, and a *character encoding*. The most abstract of these is the character itself. It is the basic granular unit of written language; each language uses a fixed collection of characters, called an alphabet, to spell words and construct sentences. The XSL specification refers to the formatting object "fo:character" as an "atomic unit" that the formatter maps to a glyph. Glyphs are the graphic shapes designed to represent characters visually. We distinguish a D from a C from an O because the D is flat on the left and round on the right, the C is round on the left and open on the right, and the O is round all around. Of course there are thousands of variations on how to render those basic shapes; the word *font* is often used to refer to a specific collection of glyphs in a particular design. The character A when represented by a glyph in the Times Roman font looks like this—A—but in Times Italic it looks like this—*A*—and in Arial it looks like this—A. The visual presentation is different in each font, but the underlying character is the same, a capital A. (Technically, a font also refers to that collection in a particular arrangement for a particular rendering technology. The Times Roman font for Windows is not the same as the Times Roman font for a Macintosh—they are not exactly the same collection of characters, and they are arranged differently. One can even still buy a font of Times Roman in handset metal type.) To make this even more interesting, some characters (in some fonts) look almost identical, but mean entirely different things: a reader is more likely to distinguish a 0 (zero) from an O (capital oh) or a 1 (one) from an l (lowercase el) by context than by shape; and a capital O is visually distinguished from a lowercase o not by shape but by relative size.

Computers do not tolerate the ambiguities that readers do. They need to be told unambiguously what each character is through a *character encoding*, a way of assigning a code to each character so that it is identified the same way by the system that originated it and the system that receives it. Groups of characters given certain character encodings are called *character sets*. The most common of these is ***ASCII*** (American Standard Code for Information Interchange), which allows for 128 different character encodings. That number is determined by the fact that when an ASCII character is represented in binary notation (the ones and zeros that computers use at their most basic level), it can use no more than seven digits. The character A in ASCII, when represented in ***binary notation***, is 1000001; when represented in ***decimal notation***, it is 65; when represented in ***hexadecimal notation***, it is 41. All three of these are the *same* character encoding, an A in 7-bit ASCII. (Note that this does not specify what that A should look like when represented visually; for that, a font needs to be specified, and the rendering system needs to know where to find the A in that font in order to display the desired glyph. If the font used has a crescent moon in the position where the rendering system expects to find an A, it will display a crescent moon.)

It may seem that 128 characters should be plenty, when we in the English-speaking world use an alphabet of 26 characters, but in fact it's woefully inadequate. First of all, note that a capital A and a lowercase a are different characters, requiring different character encodings. (TTY, the 6-bit encoding from the paper-tape era, had to use an extra "shift" character to distinguish caps from lowercase.) When numerals and punctuation marks are added, and a few spots are reserved for control characters like spaces and tabs and carriage returns (can those students innocent of typewriters really appreciate what a carriage return is?), 7-bit ASCII fills up. In fact, only 96 of the 128 positions are for characters; the other 32 are reserved for control characters. Although it is adequate for most English-language uses, the need to encode common foreign accents and printer's marks (like a bullet, •, or a trademark, ™, or a section mark, §, common in legal publishing) requires at least another binary digit. ***Extended ASCII*** is an 8-bit character set commonly used in computing today, which accommodates 256 possible encodings.

Not all systems, unfortunately, use that eighth bit exactly the same way. This accounts for some of the problems in converting files from Windows to Macintosh: although the basic 128 characters in 7-bit ASCII use the same encodings in extended ASCII, some of the additional characters are encoded differently in those two environments. To avoid this ambiguity, there is an international standard 8-bit encoding called ***ISO 8859***. However, those 256 characters are still not even close to enough for English-language publishing, not to mention non-Latin languages.

1. UNICODE

In order to accommodate not only the broad needs of English-language publishing, but the needs of many of the world's languages, from Japanese to Greek to Farsi to Urdu, XML is based on a vast character encoding system known as ***Unicode***. (Unicode is also central to much of the important software used today, from Java to Microsoft Word.) In the full Unicode system, there are 32,768 "planes," each of which accommodates 65,536 characters; the first of these is referred to as the Basic Multilingual Plane (***BMP***).

Although only a small portion of these available character encodings have yet been officially assigned, Unicode makes it possible to encode a huge number of characters unambiguously in XML. At the same time, it incorporates previously existing standards: the encodings of the 128 characters in 7-bit ASCII and the 256 in 8-bit extended ASCII (the ISO 8859 version) are identical in Unicode, enabling systems that can't handle 16- or 32-bit encodings to simply ignore the high-order bits and get by with a more limited character set. And because Unicode has such a vast capacity, additional encodings are periodically added to the standard. For example, a comprehensive character set for mathematics, called ***STIX*** (Scientific and Technical Information Exchange), is being incorporated into Unicode, with a corresponding font that enables most math characters that currently have to be displayed as graphics on the Web to use a true scalable font.

The encoding standard known as ***UCS-2*** uses two 8-bit bytes and thus accommodates 65,536 possible characters; a 32-bit version, known as ***UCS-4***, will accommodate over two billion. (UCS-2 does not have enough room for traditional Chinese, for example.) Because most of today's computers do not use bytes of 16 or 32 bits, there is an additional standard—integral to Unicode—known as ***UTF*** (UCS Transformational Format) that enables the use of Unicode while reducing the encoding size. (Otherwise, representing most of the commonly used characters in 16-bit UCS-2 encoding involves a lot of extra zeros: the A that is encoded as 1000001 in 7-bit ASCII and 01000001 in 8-bit extended ASCII is 0000000001000001 in 16-bit UCS-2. You can imagine what it is in 32-bit UCS-4.) UTF-8 uses as few bytes as necessary, up to four, to represent a character; UTF-16 provides access to fifteen more planes of Unicode than UTF-8. All true XML processors must support UTF-8 and UTF-16 encoding. These unambiguous character encodings are perfect for computers, but can be unintelligible to humans. For that reason, ***entities*** are often used in XML files to make it easier for human beings to work with them. XML can use decimal or hexadecimal numerical character references (which look and function like entities; in effect, they're a special kind of entity) natively, without declaring them in a DTD or schema. But since these are hardly more intelligible than binary (the decimal entity for A is A and the hexadecimal entity is A), entities like those in the ISO sets are often used for special characters (such as Á for Á). The catch is that such entities must be declared in a DTD or schema, making them off limits for simple well-formed XML, in which the decimal or hexadecimal numerical character references must be used.

(iv) TRANSFORMING XML DOCUMENTS

Even more than its ability to facilitate the presentation of one document in many ways, the most powerful virtue of XML is how it enables the effective and efficient transformation of one document into other documents—with different structures, different tags, different elements, and even different content. It is what most often justifies a publisher's investment in XML. When documents are created for a single purpose, used once, and discarded, there is little need to produce them in XML. But when a document created for one purpose needs to be used for another purpose, and then another, and then still another, publishers begin to realize the complexities and costs involved in **data conversion** [5]. XML's ability to reduce or eliminate those complexities and costs is the reason for its rapid acceptance.

Only a few years ago, publishers saw this as something they could postpone dealing with. Two developments—the rapid evolution of digital production technology and the rise of the World Wide Web—have made it a key issue for publishers of all sorts. Even setting aside the issues of digital publishing (as in on-line publishing, e-books, or CD-ROMs), digital production is almost universally (if not always effectively) implemented in publishing today. Writers write on computers, not typewriters; although some book and journal editors may still edit on paper, newspaper and magazine editors do not have that luxury; typesetters now no longer rekey most of what they typeset, and although they may print out pages for proofing, they furnish digital files from which the publications we read are printed. At each of these stages, electronic files are produced; today, they are mostly incompatible with each other, requiring a combination of data conversion and manual intervention in order to be used by their recipients. (This is not just about text: images are almost universally processed in digital form too, and they are increasingly created digitally in the first place.) When publishers discover that those "final" digital files for print are not the end of the process—now they need files for Web sites, and for reuse in other publications, and for licensing or syndicating to others, and for e-books—the argument for XML is unavoidable.

1. Manual conversion with text editors

In most editorial and production contexts today, files are converted from one form to another in manual and relatively laborious ways. Worse, the resulting files are usually created for a single, specific purpose. The editor needs to wrestle the author's word processing files into something her editing software can use; the typesetter needs to craft pages one way or another from the files the editorial department produced. Before SGML and XML came along, too little thought was given to optimizing the whole process. Even as XML is now more commonly being brought into the picture (often late in the process, after composition; increasingly, as part of the composition process; and sometimes as early as the editorial stage), the conversion of files from one form to another is still mostly done in only a semiautomated fashion. Sometimes, specialized conversion programs are used; often, this work is done using text editors such as BBEdit on the Macintosh and UltraEdit on Windows. These programs are often the favorites of people who spend their days converting files. They are simple, fast, straightforward, and have features that help expedite the process. For example, they can show element tags in one color, attributes in another, and links in still another, making the files much easier to work with. These text editors are also HTML friendly, providing convenient mechanisms for using HTML tags (although they are not parsers or validating editors). Much of the HTML published on the Web today is created with programs like these.

2. Scripting

To convert significant volumes of similarly tagged content, manual conversion becomes too time consuming and costly. ***Scripts*** are, in effect, sets of step-by-step instructions that make it possible to automate what an operator might do manually by scrolling through a file. Writing a script is more sophisticated than creating a ***macro***, which nonprogrammers can do in applications like Word and Excel, but less complicated than what software engineers do when they write programs in languages like Java or C++. For example, a script to change an XPress tagged numbered list from Quark into an HTML ordered list might have expressions to say, in effect, "read until you find an @NL_FIRST: tag; insert an <OL> tag; then replace the @NL_FIRST: tag with an <LI> tag; then keep reading (and incorporate that text, but throw away any returns) until you see another @ . . . : expression, and if it's an @NL_MIDDLE: tag, replace it with an </LI> tag and another <LI> tag" and so on until the Quark tags have been replaced by <LI> . . . </LI> tags around each list item and the list as a whole is enclosed in the proper <OL> . . . </OL> tags. This is an example of a simple conversion that can be completely automated by a script if the XPress document was properly styled (though they often aren't).

Scripting languages like ***Perl*** and ***Python*** have become essential tools for conversion in the publishing world because they have special capabilities for handling text and text-oriented tagging. Unlike numerical databases, which are often highly structured and can have strict size limitations for fields and records, text-oriented systems need to be able to deal with arbitrary and unique tagging embedded in text of indeterminate length. Languages such as Perl and Python make it possible to use expressions like "look for patterns of three integers enclosed in parens followed by three integers, a hyphen, and four more integers" (which could find phone numbers) or "look for patterns of a carriage return followed by a tab followed by a capital letter" which might be useful (but not infallible) in finding places to insert <p> codes. Perl and Python are popular not only because they are very useful, but also because they are free. They are examples of ***open source*** software that can simply be downloaded from the Internet and used without any cost or license. A similar (and more powerful) commercial scripting language specifically designed for text processing and commonly used for SGML and XML is Omnimark.

3. Validating editors

In some publishing environments—particularly those where the authoring process is strictly controlled, as in technical documentation departments—it's helpful for the writing and editing to be done with software that is specifically XML-aware. In book publishing, manuscripts are often acquired after they have already been written, when it's too late to require the author to use specific software and codes, the copyediting is often done by freelancers, and structure and coding may differ from book to book. Technical documentation publishers, on the other hand, often have a strict, well-defined structure and coding that must be used for all projects; the writing is usually done by in-house employees or under contract; and editing must be tightly integrated with authoring and production because the content is subject to constant change at any stage. In such an environment, "guided authoring and editing" tools can be very useful. (**Content management systems** [10.3] are an even more powerful solution.) Magazines and newspapers fall between these two extremes: although they often start with unstructured content, they benefit from the consistency offered by tightly integrated editorial and production systems.

Some validating editors are part of technical documentation systems like Adobe's Framemaker or ArborText's Epic; others are standalone software applications like Corel's XMetaL. What such applications have in common, and what distinguishes them from conventional word processors like Microsoft Word, is that they support XML functionality to a much higher degree. They typically enable the use of any arbitrary DTD or schema (rather than requiring a standard, generic one to be used) and then guide the user to structure and tag documents only in ways that conform to that DTD or schema. Whereas conventional parsing is usually done to a whole file after it is created, a validating editor in effect parses the content as it is being created. For example, a writer of an assembly manual might be required by the DTD to start with a list of parts in which each <part> must contain one and only one <quantity> followed by one and only one <partname> (and can contain only those elements). If she omits the <quantity> in a given <part>, or tries to code two separate <quantity>s, the system will alert her that it is invalid; moreover, it will not give her the option to insert a <warning> inside a <part>. If the editor of a book is using a validating editor with a DTD that requires subheads to be nested hierarchically, when he tries to insert a subhead into text where the preceding subhead is <H1>, the validating editor will only give him the option of inserting an <H2> or another <H1>; it will simply not give him the option of inserting an <H3> or <H4> there if the DTD requires these subhead levels to be used sequentially.

Beyond this ability to restrict the content to conform to a particular document model, validating editors usually also offer other convenient features that result from their ability to incorporate a DTD or schema. For example, they make it virtually impossible to omit the end tag for a given start tag; when that assembly manual writer inserts a "part," the validating editing software probably presents her with a cursor poised between <part> and </part> tags; and it may even present her with <part><quantity> | </quantity><partname></partname></part>. Such software also usually has a graphical user interface that makes it easy to see the coding structure and which enables multiple views of the content—turning the codes on or off, applying styles to the coded elements to make them more easily distinguishable, and revealing the underlying XML. (The on-line version of this book shows an example of what the beginning of this chapter looks like in Corel's XMetaL and ArborText's Epic.)

Although they offer clear advantages for structured authoring and editing, validating editors have not been widely implemented in publishing. This is partly due to the fact that XML has not yet permeated the publishing world to an extent that makes them necessary; and it is also partly due to their expense. Many publishers cannot yet justify the cost of supplying such software to all their authors or editors, whereas they can expect them all to use a common word processor like Microsoft Word. (It's likely that Word will eventually incorporate the features of validating editors, which will dramatically alter this situation, given Word's dominant position in the market.) However, it should be recognized that in many cases today, and in many stages of the publishing process, a validating editor can be more of a hindrance than a help. Authors do not want to be burdened with such restrictive tools; publishers have a hard enough job just getting decent word processing files from them. And much editing must be done to files that are invalid, or "not yet valid"; some validating editors are so oriented to the proper creation of a valid file that they are not very tolerant of invalid files. (As these tools evolve they will become more flexible in that regard.) So outside of highly structured environments like technical documentation publishing, it is more common for authoring and even editing to be done in word processors, creating files that still need conversion from stage to stage.

4. XSLT: XSL Transformations

Converting data—from one word processor to another, or to a composition system's tagging system, or to a database's particular structure, or to HTML for Web delivery—often does not involve XML. Instead, these conversions take documents with one proprietary set of codes and one particular structure and convert them to documents with a different set of codes and structure.

When new needs arise, new conversions typically have to be done. These can be laborious and expensive; sometimes, they're prohibitive, impeding the implementation of new technologies.

XML offers not just a better way to encode files to expedite the creation of alternate presentations or alternate versions of those files, it also offers a language with which to specify such transformations. ***XSLT***—XSL Transformations—is designed to facilitate transforming one XML document into other XML documents. (It can also be used to convert XML documents to non-XML documents; one of its most common uses is to create HTML documents from XML documents, but it can also be used to create XPress tagged documents for typesetting in Quark, for example.) XSLT is an essential part of the process of formatting XML documents with XSL (see the previous section on **XSL** [3.3.3.3]): it is used to create, from a source XML document, a new XML document that is structured to correspond with the XSL stylesheet and the formatting objects (XSL-FO) that it specifies. Although XSLT is primarily intended to be used as part of XSL, it can be an extremely useful way to specify how to transform an XML document for any purpose, not just for presentation. It could be used, for example, to transform an XML file of employee data to create files for an employee directory, business cards for the appropriate employees, the contact section of the company Web site, an emergency contact list, or even a vacation schedule (providing the necessary information is either present in the source XML file or can be generated from it). And just as XSL-FO needs software to interpret and process it (XSL-FO specifies the desired format, but it doesn't actually render the resulting presentation), XSLT processing software is required to interpret an XSLT stylesheet and produce the desired files from the source files. (Some of the most popular XSLT processors currently are Michael Kay's Saxon, the Apache XML group's Xalan, and Microsoft's MSXML.) One especially useful factor is that XSLT stylesheets are themselves XML documents and thus can be created, managed, and interpreted by XML-aware tools. Due to the verbosity of XSL, however, a specialized XSL editor or IDE (Integrated Development Environment) is a necessity when creating nontrivial stylesheets.

XSLT sees documents as *trees*, and its basic purpose is to transform a *source tree* into a *result tree*. XML documents always begin with a *root element*; think of this as the trunk from which the rest of the tree branches out. (This metaphor ignores the invisible part of the tree below the ground.) Whereas a DTD or a schema specifies how the branches and twigs and leaves are *supposed to* relate to each other in a particular *class* of XML documents, XSLT needs to be able to work with how those branches and twigs and leaves *actually do* relate to each other in a *specific* XML document. For example, a DTD might specify that the root element <book> must have three branches called <frontmat-

ter>, <body>, and <backmatter>; the <body> element must have one or more of branches called <chapter>; each <chapter> must have a branch called <CN> that contains text (think of the text as the ultimate leaf at the end of the line), plus a branch called <CT> that contains text, plus a branch called <chaptext> that must contain at least one <section>, which in turn can contain any number of <subsection>s, each of which must begin with a <title> and must contain one or more <para>s; and so forth. In a given XML document that conforms to this DTD, there might be twelve <chapter>s in the <body>; the first one might contain one <section> with three <subsection>s; the second one might contain two <section>s, the first of which contains five <subsection>s and the second of which contains four <subsection>s, the fourth of which in turn contains three <subsection>s of its own; and so forth. This is the actual tree for that particular XML document.

XSLT works with a companion technology called ***XPath*** that provides the language by which the actual structure of an XML document (or a portion of one) is described. It models an XML document as a tree of *nodes*—the points at which one element branches off from another. (See below for a more complete description of **XPath** [3.3.5.2].) XSLT specifies how to create a certain "result tree" from a given "source tree." To do this, it associates certain patterns in the source tree with *templates* that specify how to create that particular part of the result tree. These patterns can be thought of as pieces of a jigsaw puzzle, or as door keys, which have descriptions that fit what is found at some nodes but not at others. (The science minded can also think of this as the way that RNA is used to create proteins, by matching patterns of nucleotides with specific amino acids.) The XSLT processor moves through the source tree, node by node, testing out these patterns to see if any of them fit; when it finds one that fits, it then creates a portion of the result tree as instructed by the template that corresponds to that pattern.

Take, for example, the hypothetical XML file mentioned above that might be used both as a chapter in a book and as an article in a magazine. Using the stylesheet for the book, an XSLT processor might find the node at which <title> first occurs in the source tree (which is then called the *current node*); the corresponding template might change the element name to CT. Similarly, it might find and tag the author's name as <AU>, find the affiliation and ignore it, and so forth. Using the stylesheet for the magazine, on the other hand, the XSLT processor might (from the same source XML file) output the tags <article_title> and </article_title> around the title, put the author's name at the end of the article with the word "by" in front of it and tagged as <byline>, followed by the author's affiliation tagged as <authinfo>, and so forth. Thus these XSLT stylesheets would produce two very different result trees, one for the book chapter and one for the magazine article, with tags that don't occur in the source documents, with the elements rearranged appropriately for each use, and with new text generated as needed—all without an editor or production person having to intervene manually. And although the result files in this example are XML files, they could just as well be XPress-tagged files for Quark composition or HTML files for Web presentation.

This example makes it sound simpler than it is. XSLT is not just a method of following a linear path and substituting one string for another. Using XPath, it has the ability to describe the current node—the point in the document it's addressing at a given time—in a very context-aware way, looking backward and forward to discern parents and children of the current node, as well as ancestors and descendants, all within very complex structures, and to generate entirely different structures as a result. To give another simple example, this is what gives it the ability to treat the first <title> element it finds in that hypothetical XML file as a <CT> while treating a <title> element found in a <subsection2> as an <H2>. The pattern it is matching is not simply what it finds at a given point in the file (element names, attributes, entities, even specific text) but the context in which it finds it. It also recognizes that more than one pattern might match a given node, and has a protocol for resolving which template should be used in such a case. Despite its power and complexity, though, XSLT is a surprisingly accessible technology, and it is rapidly becoming part of the core toolset of publishing in the digital era.

(V) LINKING IN XML

In the fields where electronic publishing has had the biggest success so far in being preferred by its users over print—especially journal and reference publishing—the most frequently cited benefit is linking. Users of reference material often search through large amounts of generalized information for certain very specific information. Simple search mechanisms are inadequate to this task—they are imprecise, unpredictable, and often return far too many hits without providing any good way for the user to know which hits are most relevant, apart from simplistic and often misleading relevance rankings based on occurrences of specific words. These users need to be guided through the information in intelligent ways, with links that either guide them to more and more specific detail about the information they seek or, on the other hand, links that lead them to supporting background information and other relevant resources. Likewise, the reader of a journal article—particularly in a scholarly, scientific, or medical journal—needs to consult the other articles cited in the reference section at the end of that article; scholarship and science today are fundamentally cooperative activities. (In fact, this was what led to the creation of the Internet and the World Wide Web in the first place: researchers' need to exchange information about their research.) Linking such journals electronically has become not just an enhancement; it is a necessity. As electronic publishing becomes better established in other fields, linking will become a fundamental expectation in them as well. The reader of an e-book expects a link from a table of contents to the chapters listed; the user of a technical manual expects a link from a mention of a figure to the figure itself; a student expects a link from a glossary term in a textbook to the definition of that term. Providing these links is both the biggest opportunity for publishers to exploit in electronic products in the long term and the biggest obstacle to developing them in the short term.

The linking we have become accustomed to on the Web is one of the simplest methods possible: one-directional, anchor-to-target links. HTML requires that tags be embedded in the file to mark the spans of content that serve as the anchors of the links, resulting in the colored and underlined phrases we typically see in Web browsers. In addition to marking the beginnings and endings of these anchors, an explicit destination needs to be provided as an attribute of each anchor tag. Sometimes these destinations are another point in the same file (***internal links***), but often they are the URL (the address on the Web) of another Web page (***external links***). Clicking on the anchor simply takes the user to the destination. This is the fundamental purpose of HTML and the Web: central to both the HyperText Markup Language and its companion protocol HTTP (HyperText Transfer Protocol) is this concept of hypertext, a fluid interconnected network of information.

However, as the Web has evolved, it has become apparent that much more sophisticated linking technology is needed. It would be useful, for example, for links to work in both directions: clicking on either end would take the user to the other end. It would be useful to link to more than one target in more than one document from a single anchor. It would be useful to be able to specify other actions for links beyond simply jumping to a destination, and to activate the links in other ways than requiring a user to click on an anchor. It would be useful to include information about links—to name them or to describe what they are for, for example—and to store and manage information about the links outside the documents they apply to. It would be *very* useful not to have to embed anchors in documents at all, but to be able to link to or from any element that exists in a file (or even to locations within or across elements), and to be able to specify those locations in an efficient and systematic way. To address these needs, three related technologies have been developed as part of the XML family: **XLink** [3.3.5.1], **XPath** [3.3.5.2], and **XPointer** [3.3.5.3].

1. XLink: the XML Linking Language

Fundamentally, the purpose of linking is to explicitly describe the relationship between two information resources. Building on HTML's linking (and drawing on other important standards, particularly ***HyTime***, a standard developed for multimedia and hypermedia, and ***TEI***, the Text Encoding Initiative that is the foundation for much scholarly use of SGML), the XML Linking Language (***XLink***)—issued as a Recommendation by the W3C in July 2001—provides an XML syntax for describing not only one-directional links, but "multiheaded" links (links that point to more than one resource), for associating metadata with links, for specifying how links are actuated and how they behave, and for enabling links and the information about them to be maintained separately from the documents or resources they link. In addition, XLink makes it possible for any element in an XML document to be the anchor, or originating point, of a link, and—through XPath and XPointer—for any point or range in an XML file to be the target of a link. (Note that although XLink links always exist in XML documents, they can link to things other than XML documents—graphic files, for example.)

XLink defines a ***traversal*** as using or following a link, and an ***arc*** as information about that traversal, such as which direction it goes, how it behaves, and what actuates it. (Link behavior and actuation are discussed below.) There are three basic kinds of arcs: *outbound* like HTML's <A> anchor, which go from the local resource where the link appears to the remote resource or target; *inbound,* which go *to* the local resource *from* the remote resource (useful in retrieving a piece of information from an external resource and incorporating it into the local one, for example, to update a price in an advertisement from a product database); and *third party,* where both ends of the link are remote. Third-party arcs make it possible to separate the linking information (often in what are called ***linkbases***) from the documents being linked.

Instead of using a separate element (like the <A> element HTML uses), XLink uses attributes that can be added to any element in an XML document to make that element a link. There is a fixed set of ten attributes—type, href, role, arcrole, title, show, actuate, label, from, to—which are specified in the XLink **namespace** [3.3.2.6], http://www.w3.org/1999/xlink. This namespace must be declared in an XML document using XLink, and as "global attributes"—able to be applied to any element—these attributes must be preceded by the prefix xlink. Thus a link from a glossary term to a glossary might include the expressions, "xlink:href glossary.xml" to point to the glossary file and "xlink:title Glossary" to add the title "Glossary" to the link. (Actually, it would be better to point to the specific *term* in the glossary, not just the glossary file itself; that's where XPath and XPointer come in.)

These XLink attributes can either be applied one-by-one to individual elements in XML documents (whether those documents are valid to a particular DTD or simply well-formed XML) or the XLink attributes can be used in the DTD that defines a specific class of documents. Through the DTD, certain attributes can become default attributes, eliminating the need to specify them on every element to which they apply in every XML document in which they occur. For example, if all glossary terms in text are tagged as elements (e.g., <glossterm>term in text</glossterm>), all the functionality of linking them to the glossary (even popping up the title "Glossary" or "Definition" and finding the right term in the glossary via XPath or XPointer) can be defined once, where the element <glossterm> is defined in the DTD, so that the XLink attributes do not have to be applied every time a glossary term occurs in the text—and those attributes can be changed in that centralized way as well. The glossary terms thus not only become automatic link anchors (without <A> elements needed in the files) but their targets can be automatically specified as well. For publishers who have spent significant effort embedding IDs and other HTML linking apparatus into files, this will be an enormous benefit.

Two of these XLink attributes are particularly interesting: *show* and *actuate*. The show attribute has five possible values: new, replace, embed, other, none.

- The value "new" calls for a new window, frame, or presentation pane to be loaded. In the glossary example above, the glossary might open up in a new window in which the glossary would be presented when the user clicks on the glossary term. For a link that points to several resources, a window might pop up that would list the titles of those resources, so the user could select one.
- The value "replace" replaces the current window, frame, or pane with what is being linked to. This is how most links work in HTML, sending the user to the destination.
- The value "embed" replaces the *presentation* of what is being linked from with the *presentation* of what is being linked to. Typically, this would not be used for a whole document, but for something within a document, like an image or an updated price.
- The value "other" leaves it to separate markup to specify the behavior of the link.
- The value "none" not only specifies no behavior, it also indicates that no separate markup to specify the behavior exists.

The actuate attribute has four possible values: onLoad, onRequest, other, none. The value onLoad instructs the link to take effect as soon as the local resource is loaded. This is how the <IMG> element in HTML works: as soon as a browser opens a document, it locates the image files pointed to by the <IMG> tags and presents them, without the user having to take any action (other than waiting for those images to appear). XLink makes this behavior accessible to any element—for example, to automatically retrieve an updated price on loading any document with <price> elements that have been defined to do this. The value onRequest requires some action to be taken to actuate the link. Most often, this action is the user clicking on the starting resource of the link, but it could also be software-driven: for example, there could be a timed countdown before a link was activated. Like the show attribute values, other and none indicate whether or not there is separate markup specifying the actuation of the link.

Note that show and actuate allow the behavior of the link to be specified and controlled by the link itself, not by external technology like a browser. This enables these link behaviors to be specified within the XML documents themselves, in DTDs or schemas, or—even better—in a linkbase, where they can be modified and updated without requiring the XML documents being linked to be altered. Because our image of publishing is still print-centric, we tend to think of published documents as being "finished" when they are published, but in the digital era this is no longer necessarily the case. Not only can the published documents themselves change, their intellectual and technological environments continually change as well. Journal publishers are well aware of this already: a link from a reference to a cited journal article may be available today that was not available yesterday; keeping such links up to date is a monumental task unless it can be automated. But publishers of all sorts will come to find linking as the most fluid and dynamic aspect of their publishing enterprise. Publishers will want to enhance their documents with links that were not possible or practical when those documents were first published; they may want to link to resources that did not previously exist. The ability to link to and from documents without having to modify those documents (for example, without having to insert IDs or <A> anchors), to link to documents not owned by or under a publisher's control (which raises important rights issues), and to manage and even publish links separately from the documents they link are powerful benefits to publishers and their customers. XLink will soon become an indispensable technology for publishers of all sorts in the digital era.

2. XPath: the XML Path Language

An essential enabling technology underlying both XLink (in conjunction with XPointer) and XSLT is ***XPath***, the XML Path Language (published as a recommendation by the W3C in 1999). Both of those languages use XPath to address particular parts of actual XML documents based on their structure.

As mentioned above in the section on **XSLT** [3.3.4.4], XPath models an XML document as a tree of nodes—the points at which one element branches off from another. (XSLT uses this model to specify how to transform one tree into another tree; **XLink** [3.3.5.1] uses this model to specify locations within XML documents to or from which to link.) Rather than needing to know what the actual tags are in a specific document (though it *can* use those tags), XPath gets its power from being able to relate to the underlying structure of XML documents: for example, it can express which elements are parents or children of other elements. The tree model is not simply an arbitrary metaphor; it permits certain kinds of structures and not others. A tree starts with a root element; as elements branch off that root and then subsequent elements branch off those, each node has only one parent (and thus a particular set of ancestors, or parents of that parent), and its children are children of no other node (as are their descendants, the children of those children, descendants of no other node).

The most common expressions that XPath is used for are *location paths*, which specify, for a given context, the set of nodes (one or more) that conform to a certain pattern, the specified parents (and ancestors)—looking back toward the root element—and children (and descendants)—looking onward away from the root element—of that context. XPath can, however, use more than just these structural features in an expression. It can use numbers (giving it the ability to count) and Boolean expressions (like *and*, *or*, and *not*); it can also use element names, attribute names, and other aspects of the markup to express a particular location in an XML document. So, for example, XPath provides a way to express these useful things:

- "Any <emphasis> element with the attribute 'type="italic"' occurring inside an <H1> element" (so that if <H1> subheads are bold italic, such emphasized terms could be rendered as bold roman instead of italic, for example).
- "The first <BLOCKQUOTE> in each <article> that does not have the attribute 'type="bookreview"'" (so that XSLT, in transforming a file in which both block quotes and abstracts are tagged as <BLOCKQUOTE>, can find the first one in each article and change it to an <abstract>, except in the book reviews).
- "The <glossitem> whose <glossterm> is a string whose value is the same as the value of the string in the current <glossref>" (enabling XLink, from a term marked as a <glossref> in text, to locate the matching definition in the glossary).

Because XPath is based on the structure of a document, not its content, it can be used only to express locations in a document that are nodes of the document tree. But it is sometimes necessary to address not just nodes, but other locations within an XML document. To accomplish that, particularly for the purposes of linking, XPointer was developed.

3. XPointer: the XML Pointing Language

The newest member of this group of XML technologies, ***XPointer***, the XML Pointing Language, was designed primarily to provide the ability to link to almost any point or range in an XML document (or in their external parsed entities), whether it is a node on the document tree or not. In fact, the W3C XPointer Recommendation explicitly defines *point* as "a position in XML information" and *range* as "all the XML information between a pair of points." XPointer, which uses the term *location* to refer generically to a point, a range, or a node, has the ability to address any of these three types of locations. (XPath can address only nodes.) What an XPointer expression identifies in an XML document (which is called the *resource*) is referred to as a *subresource*; a subresource can be as small as a point itself or as large as any arbitrary range between two points, perhaps encompassing many nodes (a whole chapter, for example, or a range of text to be highlighted), or even a group of such things.

XPointer is designed specifically to be used within Uniform Resource Identifier (URI) references. To do this, it uses what are called *child sequences*, which it specifies by integers separated by slashes; each integer specifies which child of the current element should next be addressed (in "document order"). Thus "/3/1/2" specifies the second child of the first child of the third child of the current element. Beyond that, XPointer can also count characters in the text (and ignore any intervening markup), so that it is possible to point to locations with extremely fine granularity. This gives XPointer the ability to specify any arbitrary string of text (whereas XPath's "string-value" can only be the entire marked up content in an element). Such a range is not confined by the document's structure (where nodes on the tree occur); it is possible for a user to "drag" any span of content and for XPointer to describe the resulting range. (Note, by the way, that "document order" is not necessarily the same as "display order": if an Arabic term, which reads from right to left, is quoted in an English document, the document order is the "reading order," not simply the left-to-right sequence displayed on a screen.)

It's important to realize that what XPointers point to do not actually have to exist. This tolerance makes it practical to implement XPointer in the real world. If an XPointer processor cannot find the subresource specified by a particular XPointer, it will move on to the next XPointer rather than hanging up (and it may or may not give a message saying "subresource not found"). In fact, it is possible to express XPointers that provide multiple options, in effect saying "point to X, but if you don't find X, then try pointing to Y instead."

(vi) METADATA

Although it is valuable for XLink to be able to link documents, for XSLT to transform them, and for XSL-FO to specify their presentation based on both structural markup and the content itself, it can also be extremely useful to be able to link, transform, or style documents based on additional information that is neither markup nor the marked-up content. Such information *about* the content and its markup is known as ***metadata***.

Metadata can augment and extend the content or markup in many ways:

Identification. Perhaps the most common use of metadata, identification is often accomplished by inserting a simple, unique numerical ID as an attribute to an XML element. For example, a membership directory might need to distinguish between various Mary Smiths, so that when the name "Mary Smith" appears in the roster of the Rules Committee it links to the right person's contact information. The XML document might use her membership number like this: <member ID= "3982-98182">Mary Smith</member>. The membership number won't actually appear in the published information; it works behind the scenes as metadata to identify each member unambiguously.

Classification. It's often useful to sort information into specific categories. Mary Smith's organization might classify its members as to their status, what committees they serve on, and so forth. In such cases, there is often a fixed set of possible alternatives (membership status might be "new," "former," "active," or "retired"; there might be only six possible committees); using metadata, XML can ensure that only those alternatives are used, and that they are used properly. Thus an entry for Mary Smith might be expressed like this: <member ID="3982-98182" status="active" comm="Rules">Mary Smith</member>. Although the metadata for status and committee is not actually part of the marked-up content, XML can use it (through XSL and XSLT) so that a directory created from that XML document could omit the members whose status is "former" and insert the words "Rules Committee" in the proper place in Mary Smith's entry.

Description. Descriptive metadata is usually more open-ended and unstructured than classification metadata. Whereas the metadata for classification in the previous example is very disciplined (only certain terms are possible, and they must be stated in a specific way), it is also possible for metadata to capture *any* potentially useful information. For example, users of the membership directory might want to know what Mary Smith's interests and areas of expertise are. Her entry in the membership data might include expressions like "expertise="children's literature, picture books, Sendak, Burkert"" and "interests="painting, photography, scuba diving, chocolate"." Not only would it be impossible to decide in advance what all the interests and areas of expertise might be, it would be foolish to attempt to classify them, because that would limit what could be included. One of the great benefits of XML (over most proprietary formats) is its ability to provide "storage spaces" for all sorts of information, even information with no currently defined use.

Documentation. Metadata can capture not just information about the content itself, but also information about the process of developing and managing that content. It is often used to record when a given piece of content was acquired, when it was updated, who changed it, what it has been used for, where it was published, and so forth. Although publishers commonly keep such information in databases (or as notes in the margins of manuscripts and proofs), the power of XML is that this information can be stored right in the XML documents themselves, rather than in some external location. A journal publisher might want to track when a given article was submitted, when it was sent out for peer review, when it was accepted for publication; that information can be embedded as metadata in the journal article itself. A textbook publisher might want to keep track, for a given figure, of who it was acquired from, what permissions it has, how it was modified for publication, and what books it was used in. The organization publishing the membership directory above might want to know when Mary Smith became a member, when she became part of the Rules Committee, and how recently her interests and expertise have been updated. All of this information can be incorporated in the XML documents with metadata.

Although it can be very useful to store the metadata right in the XML documents, it can be just as useful to store it separately. It would be cumbersome and unmanageable for all the metadata in the examples above to be incorporated everywhere Mary Smith's name appears. As long as she is unambiguously identified (in this case, with the ID attribute), the other metadata can be maintained elsewhere. In fact, it is usually best to do that: it's much easier to maintain such information in a single place—often, in an entirely separate XML file or even a database from which the relevant information can be retrieved. Such a separate file can contain a wealth of information about Mary Smith, any portion of which might be useful in a given instance. Metadata also tends to grow over time, because new information is needed, new classifications become useful, more activity needs to be documented. Keeping a single well-maintained metadata file or database quickly becomes not just a convenience but a necessity.

1. RDF: the Resource Description Framework

Publishers need to use metadata to describe their information effectively, in whatever ways make the most sense for each particular set of information and for each particular use of that information. A book publisher, for example, might want to use metadata for information relevant to bookselling (hardcover vs. softcover edition, the size and weight of the book, the number of pages, even how many fit in a carton) but other metadata for editing (such as documenting the writers, editors, and illustrators and what they did when). A professional organization might want to use metadata for information about its members (e.g., status, year joined, committee participation, membership ID). However, a key purpose of metadata is not just to keep track of such information within a given organization, but to exchange it with other organizations or individual users. The book publisher needs to give the relevant bookselling information to bookstores and distributors; the membership organization needs to use the member metadata to communicate better with its members and others interested in the organization. This leads to an obvious problem: while a given organization needs the flexibility to define its metadata in whatever ways make the most sense to that organization, users outside the organization need to be able to find and interpret the metadata properly. How will a given bookseller know how to find the information about the weight of a given book (to calculate the shipping cost) without knowing each publisher's way of coding that metadata? How will an organization trading a mailing list know how to find the active members, or the members of certain committees, without knowing the other organization's way of coding that metadata?

In order to provide a foundation for such metadata interchange, the W3C developed RDF, the Resource Description Framework. This consists of a syntax (published as a Recommendation in 1999) and a schema (as of this writing, still a working draft). Any resource available on the Web (anything that can be identified by a URI, a document or a portion of a document) can be described by RDF. Just as XML doesn't prescribe a certain set of codes—it just governs *how to specify* a set of codes—RDF isn't a "universal metadata set" but rather a way to structure a given set of metadata. In RDF, each resource has a number of *properties*, and those properties have *values*. (Technically, properties are also resources, because they can then have properties themselves.) These are expressed in *statements,* which have a predicate (the property), a subject (the resource), and an object (another resource or a literal value).

Using this book as an example, the *resource* might be the Web site for the on-line version; one of the RDF *properties* of that resource is "title," which has the *value* "The Columbia Guide to Digital Publishing." Thus an RDF *statement* would say "this on-line book (the resource) has a title (a property of that resource) which is 'The Columbia Guide to Digital Publishing' (the object, the value of that property)." Another property of that resource is this chapter ("this book [resource] has a chapter [property] which is 'Chapter 3' [object, value] "). The chapter itself is also a resource, one property of which is *its* title, which has the value "Markup: XML and Related Technologies" (thus "this chapter [resource] has a title [property] which is 'Markup: XML and Related Technologies' [object, value]"). The Resource Description Framework doesn't specify what those properties must be or what their values are; it simply supplies a common syntax for structuring them. Specifying the set of properties for any given set of information is left to that information's particular schema, and the values of those properties are determined by the specific instances in which that schema is applied.

Particular collections of properties are identified by **namespaces** [3.3.2.6], which enables the use of standard sets of properties that various communities can define and share. (See below for examples of some that are used in publishing.) The **Dublin Core** [3.3.6.3.1], for example, defines a set of metadata important to the library and publishing communities (with properties like <dc:title>, <dc:contributor>, and <dc:subject>); **ONIX** [3.3.6.3.2] defines a set of metadata important to bookselling (with properties like <NumberOfPages>, <Weight>, <PackQuantity>). Because some properties can have a number of values—there are many <dc:contributor>s (authors) of this book, for example—RDF provides three different ways of organizing such groups. A <Bag> is a simple collection, the order of whose elements doesn't matter; in a Sequence (<Seq>) the order does matter; and <Alt> describes a collection whose elements can serve as Alternatives for one another (for example, something provided in three different languages). Collections of properties or values can be given unique names or IDs so that they can be described collectively, rather than individually.

2. XMP: the Extensible Metadata Platform

In the fall of 2001, Adobe Systems announced an important implementation of RDF, which enables XML metadata to be embedded in application files. Adobe published this Extensible Metadata Platform (called ***XMP***) as ***open-source*** software, making it freely available to developers. Whereas application files (the files used by proprietary application software like word processors, page layout programs, and graphics programs) are ***binary*** files that can only be interpreted by those programs, XMP makes it possible to embed XML metadata in them that can be read by any XML-aware application that implements XMP. The Extensible Metadata Platform can accommodate metadata defined by any arbitrary schema, as long as it is described in RDF syntax. Initially incorporated in Adobe's Acrobat, InDesign, and Illustrator products, XMP will eventually be incorporated in all of Adobe's products and many other publishing-oriented software programs as well. With this capability, publishers will be able to incorporate authoring and revision information into page layout files, creation and permission information in artwork files—in fact, any desired metadata, whether for identification, classification, description, or documentation. This metadata will be able to be shared with other XMP-enabled software and extracted from or embedded in XML documents themselves, thus dramatically streamlining the use and interchange of editorial, production, and publishing information.

3. Metadata vocabularies in publishing

Because an important use of metadata is to facilitate the interchange of information and content, many specialized metadata vocabularies have been developed and published as standards. In some cases, these vocabularies are published as **namespaces** [3.3.2.6] and serve mainly to provide a universally available set of tags that publishers can incorporate by reference into their XML documents. **Dublin Core** [3.3.6.3.1] is an example of a widely used metadata vocabulary that originated in the library community; it is used in the **Open eBook Publication Structure** [11.6] for metadata describing e-books and their component files. In other cases, metadata vocabularies have been developed for specific commercial purposes: **ONIX** [3.3.6.3.2], for example, is an available but optional set of metadata that facilitates the marketing and selling of books; **CrossRef** [3.3.6.3.3], on the other hand, requires certain metadata to be provided by any publisher who wants to participate in the CrossRef system. Each of these provides an example of how metadata is used in publishing in the digital era.

1. DUBLIN CORE

The Dublin Core Metadata Initiative (***DCMI***, http://www.dublincore.org) is an international, interdisciplinary organization (the first workshop of which was in Dublin, Ohio, in 1995) whose mission is to foster the development of metadata standards and specialized metadata vocabularies. Its most significant contribution so far (along with its influence on the development of **RDF** [3.3.6.1]) has been the Dublin Core Metadata Element Set (***DCMES***), a card-catalog-like set of "core properties" that are useful in describing information resources. Although Dublin Core is often seen as having a library orientation, the Dublin Core elements are designed to be relevant to information providers and users of all sorts; and although Dublin Core metadata is mainly used on the Web, it is designed to be useful to any medium, including print.

There are fifteen elements in the Dublin Core set. They are indeed basic, but they provide a very helpful way to eliminate the ambiguities often associated with common tag names. For example, in general use the tag <title> might refer to the title of a book, the title of a chapter in that book, the title of a section, or even the title of a person (e.g., <title>Queen</title> <name>Elizabeth</name>, <title>Dr.</title> <name>Caligari</name>). Dublin Core enables a publisher to stipulate that a certain use of "title" (specifically, as <dc:title>, meaning "title in the sense specified by the Dublin Core namespace") is used for the name by which a resource is formally known (in this case, perhaps, the title of the book—but not a file name or a URI or an ISBN, each of which might also identify that book). Another Dublin Core property, "identifier," is used for an ID such as a URI, a DOI, or an ISBN; "description" is available for an abstract, TOC, or even just a free-text description of the resource; and "subject" is generally used for a collection of keywords describing the resource. Likewise, Dublin Core provides an unambiguous way to specify the "publisher," the "creator" (perhaps an author, or an illustrator, or a composer—or perhaps an institution or an organization, which might, for example, be the *creator* of a volume of conference proceedings but not necessarily its *publisher*), and the name of "contributor"s (like the chapter authors of this book).

Because these core properties are so commonly applicable, the Dublin Core **namespace** [3.3.2.6] (xmlns:dc="http://purl.org/dc/elements/1.1") is one of the most widely used by publishers today. It is often used in combination with other more specialized metadata vocabularies. One of its most important applications in digital publishing is as the basis for the metadata used in the "package file" specified by the **Open eBook Publication Structure (OEBPS)** [11.6.6], which specifies all the documents and other files provided in an OeB publication. The entire set of Dublin Core metadata is incorporated in OEBPS, but it is augmented in two ways: there are some additional attributes, like the "role" attribute added to <dc:creator> and <dc:contributor> (enabling the specification of roles like author, editor, and illustrator) and the "event" attribute added to <dc:date> (so that different kinds of dates—of creation, of publication, of revision, and so forth—can be differentiated); and there is an additional <x-metadata> element that can be used for metadata not accommodated by Dublin Core (like price, for example).

2. ONIX

A rich metadata vocabulary designed primarily for bookselling, ONIX grew out of three separate but related initiatives. The first version of ONIX was developed in 1999 by the AAP (the Association of American Publishers) primarily to provide information on print books to Internet booksellers; ONIX Version 1 was published in January 2000. At the same time, in the United Kingdom, a group known as BIC (Book Industry Communication) expanded their BIC Basic data element set for book retailing. Internationally, EDItEUR had developed the EPICS Data Dictionary for product information for the bookselling trade. In 2001, these three initiatives led to the release of ONIX 2.0, which now accommodates both print and electronic books, sold conventionally or over the Web. It is a standard governed by an international steering group and maintained by EDItEUR.

ONIX provides an extremely large collection of elements that describe books in numerous ways. Designed both for XML and for non-XML databases, it specifies both plain English names (e.g., <NumberOfPages>) and concise tags (e.g., <b061>) for hundreds of possible metadata elements. These are organized into groups such as product numbers (e.g., <ISBN>, <DOI>, <UPC>, and <PublisherProductNo>), e-publication information (e.g., <EpubFormat>), title (with fifteen possible title tags) and authorship (twenty-one tags), "extents and other content" (e.g., <NumberOfPages> and <NumberOfIllustrations>), subject (twenty-five tags), audience (such as <USSchoolGrades> and <InterestAge>), publisher information (sixteen tags), publishing dates, rights information, dimensions (e.g., <Height>, <Width>, <Thickness>, <Weight>), related product information, supplier information (e.g., <MinimumOrderQuantity> and <DiscountPercent>), sales promotion information, and so forth. Although publishers may be reluctant to revamp their internal product and marketing databases to comply with ONIX, it is an extremely useful metadata vocabulary with which to communicate such information to others, and it is comprehensive enough so that almost any publisher's existing data can be mapped to it.

3. CROSSREF

Metadata is central to CrossRef (http://crossref.org), a cooperative reference linking service established by a group of international STM (scientific, technical, and medical) publishers to enable readers of journal articles and other publications to be able to link from the references in one publisher's articles to other publishers' cited publications. CrossRef was the first major use of the Digital Object Identifier (**DOI** [15.4.2]). When publishers join CrossRef (at fees based on their size), they submit *headers* consisting largely of metadata about the articles they want readers to be able to link to. The CrossRef service registers DOIs for these articles and maintains a "metadata database" that enables these articles to be identified. Participating publishers then submit properly tagged references contained in journal articles they are publishing, and CrossRef returns those references with the appropriate DOI for each one it finds in its database so that the publisher can embed that information as a link in the on-line publication. When on-line readers of the published journals click on a resulting linked reference, the CrossRef service takes them to a URI specified by the publisher of the publication cited in that reference. The function of that URI is entirely up to its publisher: it can provide access to the cited article, it can provide an abstract and ask for a password or other proof of a subscription for full text access, or it can offer a combination of those and any other viewing or purchase options. (Although dominated by STM journals, CrossRef has recently been expanded to accommodate conference proceedings and reference works as well.)

The CrossRef metadata for each registered article is specified by an XML DTD that has been recently updated to a schema. Certain elements are required, such as the journal title, its ISSN, publication year, volume and issue, first author, page numbers, DOI, and the URL to which published references citing that article should be directed. In addition, publishers may submit other metadata that may help users identify those articles. For example, in addition to listing the (required) first author, the publisher might also want to provide the other authors of a paper, and to distinguish their surnames, like this:

```
<author sequence = "first">
<given_name>Charles F.</given_name>
<surname>Goldfarb</surname>
</author>
<author sequence = "additional">
<given_name>Ed</given_name>
<surname>Mosher</surname>
</author>
<author sequence = "additional">
<given_name>Ray</given_name>
<surname>Lorie</surname>
</author>
```

Although that richness of tagging can be a burden on authoring and editing (until systems that make such tagging easy or automatic are more widely implemented), the accessibility gained by it can be of great value to the publisher and its readers. This is true of metadata in general: although it may seem to be a burden and a complication at first, in the long run it adds enormous value to publications in the digital era. (A more detailed discussion of **CrossRef** [4.5.5.1] and of **linking in general** [4.5] is provided in the chapter on organizing content.)

3.4 COMMUNICATION, COOPERATION, COLLABORATION

What is markup ultimately all about? Communication, cooperation, collaboration. It's about sharing information we have; it's about being able to get beyond the competitive obstacles that have impeded progress in the past; it's about working together in a meaningful and productive way.

In the past, when markup schemes were private and proprietary, they were a way of restricting communication, cooperation, and collaboration to a chosen few, to the members of a closed community. What is most exciting about markup in the digital era is how dramatically it has broken down the barriers that held us back in the past. The degree of collaboration today is truly unprecedented. Now, competitors work together to develop common solutions. With intelligent and conscientious markup using standards, we have the basis—particularly with the XML family of technologies—for extending this collaboration to future generations while getting immediate and concrete benefits from it today.

The author wishes to thank the electronic publishing staff at Impressions Book and Journal Services, especially David Nelson and David Niergarth, who taught him most of what he knows about markup languages and who provided invaluable advice in the writing of this chapter. Many thanks also to Laura Fillmore and her staff at Open Book Systems, the creator of the Guide's content management system, who contributed most of the content for the section on HTML.

BIBLIOGRAPHY

Adobe Systems Incorporated. "eXentsible Metadata Platform (XMP)." 2002. http://www.adobe.com:80/products/xmp/main.html

Bradley, Neil. *The XML Companion,* 3[d] ed. Harlow, England: Addison-Wesley, 2001. http://www.bradley.co.uk

Coombs, James S., Allen H. Renear, and Steven J. DeRose. "Markup Systems and the Future of Scholarly Text Porcessing." Communications of the Association for Computing Machinery 30 no. 11 (1987): 933–947. http://doi.acm.org/10.1145/32206.32209

Cover, Robin. "The Cover Pages: Online Resource for Markup Technologies." Oasis. 2002. http://www.oasis-open.org/cover/sgml-xml.html.

DeRose, Steven J., David Durand, Elli Mylonas, and Allan H. Renear. "What is Text, Really?" Reprinted with commentary in ACM Journal of Computer Documentation 21, no. 3 (August 1997). http://doi.acm.org/10.1145/264842.264843

Dodds, Leigh. "Eclectic: The XML-DEV weblog." http://weblogs.userland.com/eclectic/

Editeur. "ONIX Product Information Standards." 2002. http://www.editeur.org/

Flynn, Peter, ed. "The XML FAQ." http://www.ucc.ie/xml/faq.xml

Garshol, Lars Marius. *Definitive XML Application Development*. Upper Saddle River, N.J.: Prentice Hall PTR, 2000. http://www.phptr.com

Gillam, Richard. *Unicode Demystified: A Practical Programmer's Guide to the Encoding Standard*. Harlow, England: Addison-Wesley, 2002.

Ginsparg, Paul. "Creating a global knowledge network." Paper presented at the Second Joint ICSU Press - UNESCO Expert Conference on Electronic Publishing in Science, UNESCO HQ, Paris. February 20, 2001. http://arXiv.org/blurb/pg01unesco.html

Goldfarb, Charles F. "XML Times." 2002. http://www.xmltimes.com

Graham, Ian S., and Liam Quin. *XML Specification Guide*. New York: John Wiley & Sons, 1999. http://www.wiley.com/compbooks/graham-quin

Graham, Tony. *Unicode: A Primer*. Foster City, Calif.: M & T Books, 2000. http://www.mulberrytech.com/unicode/primer/

Harold, Elliotte Rusty, and W. Scott Means. *XML in a Nutshell,* 2[d] ed. O'Reilly, 2002.

Harold, Elliotte Rusty. "Cafe con Leche XML News and Resource." 2002. http://www.ibiblio.org/xml/

Kay, Michael. *XSLT Programmer's Reference, 2d ed.*. Birmingham, U.K.: Wrox Press, 2001. http://www.wrox.com

Kennedy, Dianne. "ISO 12083 Information." XMLXperts. http://www.xmlxperts.com/12083.htm

Mulberry Technologies. "XSL-List—Open Forum on XSL." http://www.mulberrytech.com/xsl/xsl-list/

Oasis Technical Committee. "RELAX NG." 2002. http://www.oasis-open.org/committees/relax-ng/

Open eBook Forum. "Open eBook Publication Structure Specification." 2002. http://www.openebook.org/oebps/index.htm

Ray, Erik T. *Learning XML*. Sebastopol, Calif.: O'Reilly Associates, Inc, 2001. http://oreilly.com/

Tennison, Jeni. *XSLT and XPath on the Edge*. New York: Hungry Minds/M & T Books, 2001. http://www.jenitennison.com

Text Encoding Initiative. *Web site*. TEI Consortium. 2002. http://www.tei-c.org/

Unicode Consortium, The. *The Unicode Standard, Version 3.0*. Reading, Mass.: Addison-Wesley, 2000. http://www.unicode.org

World Wide Web Consortium (W3C). "W3C Technical Reports and Publications." 2002. http://www.w3.org/TR/

XML.com. "XML from the Inside Out." O'Reilly. 2002. http://www.xml.com

XMLHack.com. "Developer news from the XML community." 2002. http://www.xmlhack.com

Organizing, Editing, & Linking Content

JOHN STRANGE
Group Production Director, Blackwell Publishing

The production and distribution of content are two of the most important functions carried out by publishers. Historically, these publishing functions had only to concern themselves with how to produce and distribute physical items: books, magazines, and journals printed on paper. However, since the mid-1990s publishers have recognized that in order to meet the demands of digital publishing, their publishing processes require radical rethinking. The traditional print requirements must continue to be fulfilled, but the additional demands of digital publishing must also be met. The content must be available electronically—usually on-line. It must be consistently produced to a high standard, available at the same time or ahead of print, and it must provide maximum functionality—which often means linking both internally and externally, and sometimes means including nonprint content. Of course, all of this must be achieved at minimum added cost to the publisher.

4.1 OVERVIEW: THE TRANSITION FROM TRADITIONAL TO DIGITAL PUBLISHING

Two distinct phases in the period of transition from a print-only to a parallel print and digital publishing world are beginning to become apparent.

In the first phase, digital publishing is treated as an adjunct to the traditional publishing process: something that happens after print. The content is produced as it always has been, and after the print requirements have been fulfilled, these "paper" documents are digitized—for example, as Portable Document Format (PDF) files, or are "back converted" into Extensible Markup Language (XML)—and are then processed for print distribution.

In the second, more "mature" phase of a transition to a digital publishing process, there is no such separation between the print version and the electronic version of the content. Electronic publication is just one part of an integrated production process that also includes—but is no longer centered around—print publication. This change requires a much more radical re-engineering of publishers' production processes. Electronic production methods must be introduced into production department workflows to ensure content is handled electronically from origination to distribution. The organization of the content then becomes of primary importance: it must fulfill the traditional needs of production (for example, proofing) and it must also meet the requirements to deliver both print and electronic versions of the content.

As well as necessitating far-reaching changes to production processes, the opportunities offered by publishing content digitally can also transform traditional publishing models.

4.2 STRUCTURING CONTENT

> XML makes it easy for a computer to generate data, read data, and ensure that the data structure is unambiguous.
>
> —XML in 10 points, *W3C Communications Team. http://www.w3.org/XML/1999/XML-in-10-points*

An integrated digital publishing process requires *structured* content. The earlier in the production process at which content is structured, the greater benefit there is for the publisher. XML, which is discussed in detail in the chapter on markup, is an international standard for marking up the semantic structure of documents and is an industry standard for structuring content.

(i) XML IN THE DIGITAL PRODUCTION PROCESS

Two main models illustrate the use of XML in production processes. These models correspond to the two phases in the transition from traditional to digital publishing described above in the **overview section** [4.1].

1. XML-out

The first model could be called ***XML-out***. In this model, the production process follows a traditional print-oriented workflow, with XML as the result of the composition process. The content being produced is delivered to a typesetter as word-processing documents or hard copy. The content is imported or keyed into a typesetting system and Postscript, PDF, film, or camera-ready copy (***CRC)*** output is created for the print product. A second output of structured content, usually in XML, is created by a ***back-conversion*** process run on the typesetting files. Many companies offer data conversion services to support this market, specializing in the conversion of typesetting files to structured XML content. The "Computer Software > Data Conversion" category of Yahoo! (http://www.yahoo.com) is a useful starting point for finding details of data conversion specialists.

This XML-out production model may actually make use of structured content before the XML is created. For example, the content delivered to the typesetter for pagination could be a structured Microsoft Word document where the document's structure is highlighted using paragraph and character styles. A common approach to getting structured word processing documents into typesetting systems is to transform them first into an intermediate structured format such as ***Rich Text Format*** (RTF, details at http://msdn.microsoft.com/library/en-us/dnrtfspec/html/rtfspec.asp?frame=true). However, word processing formats are not neutral standards and are not recommended for a "future-proofed" digital production process.

2. XML-in

The second model is an ***XML-in*** production route. In this model, the content is structured into XML as early as possible in the production process, putting XML into the production system from the start. In some industries with a limited base of content creators (for example, technical documentation), it may be possible to get authors to structure their content by providing them with appropriate software or templates. Comprehensive lists of XML editors can be found at http://www.xml.com/pub/pt/3 or http://www.xmlsoftware.com/editors/.

However, for most publishers, requiring authors to create content using an XML editor is not possible and the responsibility for structuring the content falls to the publisher. Usually, an author's job is to create content, not to mark it up in XML, and so the author should be allowed to use whichever word processing software he or she wishes to create the content. In order to convert these authored documents to XML, a software application that converts unstyled word processing files to a rich XML structure can be used. Some publishers have developed their own automated or semiautomated solutions that use the power of word processors' macro languages to assist in these transformations. *The Columbia Guide to Digital Publishing* was initially authored using Microsoft Word with custom templates that allowed authors and editors to use Word's Styles feature to mark up the text. A semicustom output routine was used to convert the content to XML, after which it was uploaded to an on-line content management system. (Examples of this process are provided in the on-line version of the Guide.)

Of the commercially available XML markup tools, some are effectively plug-in solutions to popular word processors. These are also listed at XML.com. Examples include eXtyles from Inera (http://www.inera.com), the Logictran XML converter (http://www.logictran.com/), and Tagless Editor (http://www.i4i.com). Word processing software vendors themselves are increasingly recognizing the need to support the manipulation and markup of structured content in addition to the conventional requirements of word processing software. Recent versions of Microsoft Word (from Microsoft Word 97) can parse and manipulate XML files via its Visual Basic for Applications programming language. This XML capability is achieved by installing the MSXML parser, which can be downloaded from http://www.microsoft.com/xml. Corel's WordPerfect 9 includes, according to its publicity, "advanced support for XML."

3. Benefits of XML-in vs. XML-out

There are many benefits of "XML-in" over an "XML-out" production process. If the XML file is created at an early stage in the production process, then this one file can become the source for both the print and the digital output. In the XML-out model, the XML produced by the back conversion needs to be checked closely for any errors that may have been produced by the conversion. This is usually a costly and time-consuming process, though it is useful for older content that needs to be digitized. In the "XML-in" model, the conventional proofing process acts as a check (but not a complete validation) of the integrity of the XML.

Also, the typesetting process (traditionally one of the most expensive parts of the production process) can be automated to a great degree if an XML-aware typesetting system is being used. The Buyer's Guide of XML.com (http://www.xml.com/pub/pt/12) provides a useful list of print production systems that support XML.

Another advantage of introducing XML markup early in the production process is that the on-line product can be created at a much earlier stage, if required. This allows, for example, an "***HTML proofing***" stage in the production process where the author can check the manuscript on-line after it has been copyedited. Corrections incorporated at this stage will reduce the cost of proof corrections when the content is typeset. An HTML proofing stage can also allow Web-based hyperlinks created in the article to be checked. In ***STM*** publishing it is now common for references cited in articles to be linked to on-line citation databases (see **reference linking** [4.5.5] below). The author checking the HTML proof has a chance to check any references that may not have matched due to errors in the citation details and correct these, thereby increasing the quality of both the print and on-line product.

(ii) CHOOSING A DTD

Perhaps the most important decision to make when deciding to use XML to structure content is deciding what ***Document Type Definition (DTD)*** to use. The DTD defines what elements can be identified in the marked-up document: it specifies the structure of the class of documents it defines. The DTD is also helpful in ensuring that the tags have been inserted correctly in the document by using a piece of software called a "***parser***." The parser takes the XML document and compares it with the definition of the elements in the DTD to ensure that no errors are present in the markup.

DTDs are actually part of the **Standard Generalized Markup Language** [3.1.2.2] (***SGML***), the precursor of XML. A new method of defining what elements are allowed in an XML document is being developed by the W3C: **XML Schema** [3.3.2.4]. The specification for XML Schema can be found at http://www.w3.org/XML/Schema along with excellent introductions to schemas and tools for working with them.

1. Bespoke (or Base) DTDs

There are two options when choosing a DTD. The first is to create a ***bespoke DTD*** or a ***base DTD***. This has some advantages: the DTD can be custom-made to fit the content, and the DTD can be updated or changed by its owner as required. Any introductory book on XML will include information about the technicalities of writing a DTD. The O'Reilly XML portal (http://xml.oreilly.com/) is a good starting point for finding XML-related books. XML.com also provides a list of XML-related books at http://www.xml.com/pub/pt/13. (The chapter on markup discusses the issues of **developing DTDs** [3.3.2] in depth.)

2. Standard DTDs

The second option is to use a standard DTD that has been created by a community of users, sometimes referred to as a ***reference DTD***. For example, the DocBook DTD (http://www.oasis-open.org/docbook/) is a popular DTD for marking up book content (it is primarily intended for technical manuals although in practice it is used to mark up a wide range of data). A good Web site for researching what public domain or standard DTDs are available for various subject areas is http://www.xml.com/pub/rg/DTD_Repositories.

The advantage of using a standard DTD is that there is often software available that can already process XML files marked up in that DTD. But there are disadvantages: there is no control over the development of the DTD—it cannot be customized to the content without diverging from the standard and potentially breaking workflows or software designed to process the content. The chapter on markup includes a discussion of two common standard DTDs, the **Text Encoding Initiative (TEI)** [3.3.2.3.2], and **ISO 12083** [3.3.2.3.1], the descendant of the Association of American Publishers (AAP) DTDs.

As part of a feasibility study for the establishment of an archive of digital journal content, a comparative study of various publishers' DTDs was carried out. Although the report is confined to DTDs for structuring journal material, its methodology and many of its findings are applicable to any type of content. It is recommended reading for anybody going through the process of either creating or choosing a DTD to mark up content. The report is available from: http://www.diglib.org/preserve/ejp.htm.

3. Granularity

"***Granularity***" is a term used to indicate the level of markup present in an XML file. For example, a bibliographic reference in a journal article could simply have start- and end-reference tags (low granularity) or every element in the reference could be identified—the authors, date, journal title, volume, and page number (high granularity).

One of the criteria to be considered when deciding what DTD to use is what level of granularity is required to mark up adequately the content and what level of granularity the DTD allows. Many DTDs have optional elements, which means that all possible tags don't necessarily need to be used (although they are supported where required).

The term, "functional granularity," signifies the pragmatic level of granularity in an XML file, and is based on the ultimate use to which the XML will be put. For example, some publishers of STM journals only mark up bibliographic references to journals in the XML versions of their journal articles. However, now that it is possible to link to proceedings and books as well as journals (for example via CrossRef), and an increasing number of those are available on-line, publishers will need to begin marking up references to those types of content as well, and consider whether it is worthwhile to go back and retag earlier material.

Functional granularity is also used in relation to the application of identifiers to content (e.g., should identifiers be assigned to subordinate elements of documents such as figures and tables as well as to the main document). For a discussion of functional granularity in relation to DOIs, see Section 9.2 of the DOI Handbook at http://www.doi.org/handbook_2000/application.html#9.2.

4.3 THE IMPACT OF DIGITAL PUBLISHING ON TRADITIONAL PUBLISHING MODELS

Academic journal publishing is an excellent illustration of two things. First, it shows how a transition to a digital publishing model requires publishers to organize and structure their content throughout their production processes. Second, it shows how digital publishing changes traditional publishing models.

(i) CASE STUDY: JOURNAL PUBLISHING IN THE DIGITAL WORLD

Digital publishing has been an integral part of the journal publishing program of STM publishers since the mid-1990s. In those few years, the possibilities that digital publishing offers have begun to change journal publishing profoundly.

1. Supplementary content

Digital publishing has caused the basic unit of the learned journal—the journal article—to change. Authors no longer restrict the content they submit for publication to what can appear in print: increasingly, authors include many types of "***supplementary content***" that can only be published electronically, such as sound files, data sets, and moving images. Occasionally the supplementary content is given as a link to an external Web site in the parent manuscript (this is especially true if the content is, for example, a large data set or database).

More often, supplementary content is supplied along with the parent manuscript and is hosted on-line along with the electronic version of the article. The print version of the article usually contains an explanatory paragraph stating what supplementary content is available and where it can be accessed. This can be problematic, as the location of the supplementary material will not always be known far enough in advance to include in the print publication. A solution to this problem is to assign the supplementary content a ***digital object identifier*** (see the chapter on **digital rights management** [15] for details on DOI). The DOI can then be cited in print and when the content goes on-line and the location is known, the DOI can be updated with the appropriate URL.

Electronic publication also means that information that could not economically be published in print can be included in the on-line version of the article with minimal additional cost. This information may include large tables and additional or color images. Occasionally, an image that has been printed in black and white will be published in color in the on-line version.

1. SUPPLEMENTARY CONTENT: RECOMMENDATIONS

- Ensure that the supplementary content is tracked along with the manuscript. Many publishers' tracking systems are set up to deal only with "primary" content.
- Ensure that the content can be included in peer review or other editorial processes (where necessary). Supplementary content often

follows nonstandard production routes that "short-circuit" the conventional production and editorial processes; this can lead to poor quality content.

- Ensure that the supplementary content is named in a consistent manner. The file names of the supplementary content should be based on the file-naming convention for the parent article to which the supplementary content is attached. This will make apparent during processing the relationship between the pieces of content.
- If the supplementary content is received as "native application" file formats (e.g., a Photoshop image) convert it into an appropriate neutral format for digital publication. If the content cannot be converted into a neutral format, the appropriate instructions for viewing the content must be provided where the supplementary content is published.
- Ensure that the supplementary content can be included in any **digital archive** [12] of the parent content. Digital archives may not be willing to accept native application files for digital content as they cannot be guaranteed to be future-proof.

2. "Disaggregation" of content

Digital publishing requires content to be organized, structured, and processed in logical units. A consequence of organizing content in this way is that once the content is originated and processed into these logical units, it can be published, repurposed, and transactions can be carried out (for example, on-line pay-per-view access rights can be purchased) at the appropriate level.

This kind of ***disaggregation*** is happening in the digital journal publishing world. The print "container" for content, the journal issue, is becoming less important than the on-line version. With print production, articles are gathered together and published periodically in journal issues. This is mainly for economic and pragmatic reasons: it would be impossible to publish and distribute each article separately in print.

However, these print restrictions do not apply on-line. Many journal publishers now have advanced digital publishing programs and are publishing individual articles electronically in advance of the print issue (this is generally referred to as "***article-based publishing***"). Because content is processed and uniquely identified at the article level, that content can be purchased on a per-article basis rather than a per-journal basis. This is an example of how flexible production processes and well-organized content can open or support new business models.

This publishing model has thrown up some interesting questions, such as how these articles—which aren't paginated into issues—can be cited by authors. Traditionally, journal articles are cited by referencing the journal name, its year of publication, volume, and page numbers. Many journal publishers are making use of ***DOIs*** to solve this problem. (See the section on **linking** [4.5] below.) The DOI can be included in references as an unambiguous way to cite the article. DOIs also solve the problem of linking to articles published in an article-based model. When the article is republished with pagination after the publication of the printed issue, the URL associated with the DOI is updated, and any DOI links to the preprint version of the article will automatically update to resolve to the paginated version of the article.

1. "DISAGGREGATION" OF CONTENT: RECOMMENDATIONS

- Examine your content and consider what units of information may be usefully disaggregated and published on-line as individual items.
- Ensure that identifiers (for example, DOIs) can be assigned at an appropriate level of granularity. For example, if you plan on publishing individual encyclopedia entries on-line with appropriate access control mechanisms, an identifier will need to be assigned to each entry.
- Ensure that the individual content units can be displayed digitally out of the context of the parent content. (For example, if a print-based publication is presented on-line as a PDF, how will items that begin and end half-way down the page be presented?)
- Ensure that it is possible to create links at the individual-item level, especially for interitem links (e.g., links between entries in an encyclopedia).
- Ensure that the on-line publishing system allows transactions such as access control to be carried out on the individual units.
- Ensure that it is possible to restrict searching mechanisms to the individual unit of content. (For example, "search only within this chapter" for on-line books.)
- Be realistic. Don't disaggregate for the sake of it. For example, there are few proven business and technical models for selling individual book chapters on-line.

Digital publishing also allows ***virtual journals*** and issues to be created by the publisher. These can be created by drawing together articles from different journals, along with nonjournal material. An example of a virtual journal is the *Signal Transduction Knowledge Environment* virtual journal at http://stke.sciencemag.org/literature/vj/.

4.4 INFORMATION ABOUT CONTENT: METADATA

(i) WHAT IS METADATA AND WHY IS IT IMPORTANT?

Metadata, according to the standard definition of the term, is "data about data." The entries in a library's card catalog and names in a telephone directory are real-life applications of metadata.

These examples illustrate two things about metadata. The first is that they show how important the applications of metadata can be, and by inference how important creating usable metadata is. The second is that they demonstrate probably the most visible use of metadata: finding things.

In the world of metadata, "finding things" is often referred to as ***resource discovery***. A resource is the thing to which the metadata is attached (for example, the book that the card catalog describes). Metadata enables many other functions that are integral to digital publishing such as production tracking, e-commerce, and **rights management** [15].

Another common term in metadata discussion is ***resource description***. This is simply another term for metadata. These terms are combined to form the name of a new standard for describing and sharing metadata: the Resource Description Framework (RDF). This will be discussed **later in this chapter** [4.4.3.1].

Using metadata to find a book or phone number is the last stage of a long process that has created the metadata. Before the card catalog was consulted or the phone book picked up, the metadata had to be defined, structured, exchanged, and interpreted.

(ii) DEFINING METADATA

In order to create the metadata that is attached to a resource, the parameters of the metadata must first be defined. Defining metadata means identifying the significant information relating to the resource being described. Of course, different users of metadata will have different ideas about what information might be significant, and what is considered significant depends on the eventual use to which the metadata will be put. This is where "***metadata vocabularies***" come in.

1. Metadata vocabularies

A metadata vocabulary is a defined set of metadata elements that are significant to a community of metadata users. For example, the ***Dublin Core Metadata Initiative*** (***DCMI***) has described a set of fifteen metadata elements that, in the words of the DCMI, provide "a semantic vocabulary for describing 'core' information properties, such as 'Description,' 'Creator,' and 'Date'" (http://dublincore.org/about/overview/).

2. "Core" metadata

There are many metadata vocabularies in existence to describe bibliographic data for documents, for example, the Library of Congress's ***Machine-Readable Cataloging (MARC)*** standard (http://www.loc.gov/marc/), the Text Encoding Initiative (***TEI***) header (http://www.tei-c.org/), as well as EDItEUR's ***Online Information Exchange (ONIX)*** standard.

Each of these vocabularies is aimed at different communities, and each contains metadata elements that are unique to that vocabulary. "Core" metadata can be considered to be the metadata elements that are common to different vocabularies. If each of the three metadata vocabularies was represented as a circle in a Venn diagram, the core metadata would be found in the intersection of the three circles. In the three examples above, each vocabulary includes metadata elements that contain information about the title of the document, its creation or publication data, and its author. These are core metadata elements.

3. Examples of metadata vocabularies

1. DCMI

The DCMI, launched in Dublin, Ohio in 1995, is "dedicated to promoting the widespread adoption of interoperable metadata standards and developing specialized metadata vocabularies for describing resources that enable more intelligent information discovery systems" (http://dublincore.org/about/overview/).

The initiative has defined a vocabulary of fifteen elements, the ***Dublin Core Metadata Element Set*** (DCMES), which describe the core metadata values that can be assigned to electronic (and physical) resources. The fifteen elements are: Title, Creator, Subject, Description, Publisher, Contributor, Date, Type, Format, Identifier, Source, Language, Relation, Coverage, and Rights. More detailed information on these elements and their meaning can be found in the chapter on **markup** [3.3.6.3.1] and at http://www.dublincore.org/documents/dces/.

Because of its simplicity, Dublin Core is an ideal metadata vocabulary to use when **exchanging metadata** [4.4.3.2].

2. ONIX

According to its Web site, "ONIX is the international standard for representing and communicating book industry product information in electronic form" (http://www.editeur.org/). The main use of ONIX is currently to encode supply chain metadata when this is being transmitted between publishers, wholesalers, and retailers. ONIX contains over 200 elements and unlike the DCMES, ONIX transactions must be encoded in XML markup. ONIX, too, is discussed in more detail in the markup chapter.

3. MARC

The MARC formats are "standards for the representation and communication of bibliographic and related information in machine-readable form" and include comprehensive listings of geographic areas, country names, special characters, etc.

(iii) STRUCTURING METADATA

Once a vocabulary of metadata elements has been identified, the metadata record must be created in the appropriate format. Some metadata vocabularies specify an encoding for markup; for example, ONIX specifies that XML must be used to mark up ONIX metadata records. MARC originally specified an ASCII record structure, but has now created an SGML/XML implementation. Dublin Core does not specify any encoding format: it can be represented in any encoding scheme, for example in HTML <meta> elements, or as a generic "field = value" form, depending on what usage is required.

An ideal method of encoding Dublin Core metadata records is as an ***RDF*** document.

1. Resource Description Framework (RDF)

Resource Description Framework (RDF), as its name implies, is a framework for describing and interchanging metadata (http://www.xml.com/pub/a/98/06/rdf.html). It is important to remember that RDF is purely a framework: it doesn't describe any metadata elements, just a framework for describing them. It is, in fact, the exact opposite of (and therefore an ideal fit with) the ***DCMES***. Dublin Core defines a metadata vocabulary, but no framework. RDF defines the framework, but no vocabulary.

Because it is encoded in XML, RDF is an ideal format for exchanging metadata. RDF can also be used to make data "self-describing" by embedding the RDF description within the data. Usually, RDF is considered for describing the contents of textual content. An interesting description of how RDF can be used to create self-describing images, "RDF for Self-describing Images," is at http://www.tasi.ac.uk/2000/09/rdfmeta/. RDF is also discussed in the chapter on **markup** [3.3.6.1].

2. Exchanging metadata

Because it uses XML, RDF is an ideal format in which to encode and exchange metadata messages. However, it is often necessary to convert one metadata vocabulary (e.g., Dublin Core) to another (for example, MARC).

Mappings between different metadata vocabularies are often referred to as "***crosswalks***." In practice, mapping one metadata vocabulary to another is no different from mapping one DTD to another, and because metadata vocabularies are more and more encoded in XML, mapping metadata vocabularies is actually a matter of creating a DTD-to-DTD conversion. One of the most useful collections of metadata mappings is "Mapping between Metadata Formats," from The UK Office for Library and Information Networking (http://www.ukoln.ac.uk/metadata/interoperability/).

(iv) THE SEMANTIC WEB

> The Semantic Web is a Web that includes documents, or portions of documents, describing explicit relationships between things and containing semantic information intended for automated processing by our machines.
> —*Web Architecture: Describing and Exchanging Data. http://www.w3.org/1999/04/WebData*

The Semantic Web is the ultimate application of organized content and metadata. In its current form, the main method of finding content on the Web is via search engines that use brute force to search through a huge amount of unstructured data (the search engine Google currently searches three billion documents http://www.google.com/press/pressrel/3billion.html). Despite the speed of the search engines, it is difficult to find content quickly and accurately on the Web.

Because the vast majority of content on the Web does not contain structured metadata, Web search engines cannot offer fielded searches, for example, the option to restrict searches to specific words in a document title or to search documents containing specific author names. This illustrates the difference between "machine-readable" data and "machine-understandable" data. Every document on the Web is machine-readable; that is, it is in a digital format that can be processed by computer applications. However, they are not machine-understandable: the computer applications processing the documents cannot identify the logical parts of documents and how documents may relate to each other.

True digital publishing is not simply a question of digitizing documents and distributing them on-line. It is about organizing content, ensuring it contains rich metadata, and establishing semantic links between pieces of content. By exploiting digital publishing technologies such as RDF and controlled metadata vocabularies to their full potential, the vision of the Semantic Web can be created.

> The World Wide Web was originally built for human consumption, and although everything on it is *machine-readable,* this data is not *machine-understandable* . . .

Resource Description Framework (RDF) is a foundation for processing metadata; it provides interoperability between applications that exchange machine-understandable information on the Web.

—*Resource Description Framework (RDF) Model and Syntax Specifiction. http://www.w3.org/TR/1999/REC-rdf-19990222/*

4.5 LINKING

Hyperlinks within documents and between documents are one of the main features of electronic publishing. They introduce an immediacy of use that departs from leafing through print pages or hunting for separate volumes. They also create opportunities to introduce a three-dimensional, or layered, approach to publishing so that an item can be viewed alongside the context to which it has been referred.

(i) INTRADOCUMENT LINKS

Intradocument links are links within documents to other parts of the same document. These can include links to figures, tables, headings, and references. The mechanisms for marking up these types of links in documents are well established. SGML and XML have the ID, IDREF, and IDREFS attribute types. To create links in an SGML or XML document, the following needs to happen. (Readers familiar with HTML will know these <A HREF> tags.) Potential targets must be identified as an XML element and given a unique ID number. A "validity constraint" on ID numbers in XML is that they must begin with a letter. A commonly used convention is to identify tables in a document as "t1," "t2," "t3," etc., or figures as "f1," "f2," "f3." For example, figures in an XML document may be tagged to look like this:

```
<figure id="f1"> . . . </figure>
<figure id="f2"> . . . </figure>
```

The sources of links must be identified as XML elements. The link element must have an attribute that is defined in the DTD as an IDREF or IDREFS type. If the attribute is defined as IDREF, it can only contain one link target. Attributes defined as IDREFS allow more than one link. Links to the example figures above could be encoded as:

```
See <link target="f1">Figure 1</link> above
See <link target="f1 f2">Figures 1 and 2</link> above
```

This is a generic solution for all links with a descriptive prefix in the ID value. Another generic option is to qualify the <link> tag with attributes (<link type="table">). Many publisher DTDs have specific citation elements for each object type, for example, "figref" and "tableref" for figure and table references. More detail on SGML/XML linking can be found in the chapter on **markup** [3.3.5].

1. Intradocument links: recommendations

- Ensure that the DTD being used is granular enough to tag potential target links (figures, tables, references, and headings) as XML elements in the document. The XML elements must also allow ID-type attributes, although the ID attribute can be optional.
- Ensure that the DTD includes an end tag for the text where the link is being made. Some DTDs only allow empty tags for links (e.g.: See<link target="f1 f2">Figures 1 and 2 above). This is not optimal because if the link is to be presented as hyperlinked text on a Web page in HTML, or eventually in XML, it can be difficult to calculate where to insert the end link tag.
- Ensure that the DTD defines the link element (i.e., the element that tags the source of a link) as IDREFS so that more than one target can be included in a link. If this is not the case, multiple links will be problematic to mark up. For example, the text "See Figures 1–3" would have to be marked up as: "See <link target="f1">Figures 1</link><link target="f2">-<link target="f3">3</link>." If multiple targets are allowed, the text can be marked up as: "See <link target="f1 f2 f3">Figures 1-3</link>."
- Where a range of targets in the text is given, ensure that each target is explicitly marked up. For example, the text " . . . as shown in recent studies [1, 3, 5, 7–10]" should be marked up as: " . . . as shown in recent studies <link target="b1 b3 b5 b7 b8 b9 b10">[1, 3, 5, 7-10]</link>." If each target isn't explicitly indentified, it would not be possible to, for example, create a pop-up window containing the relevant references to display to the user.
- Some presentations of links are better suited to print media than online. The use of superscript for Vancouver reference citations, for example, makes it difficult to read and click on them on screen. One option is to use an alternative convention when rendering the XML, for example, <link target="b1 b3">^{1, 3}</link> can be replaced with <link target="b1 b3">[1, 3]</link>. Reference citations can even be switched between the Vancouver and Harvard systems, for example, <link target="b1 b3">[1, 3]</link> can become <link target="b1 b3">(Smith 1990; Jones 1992)</link> to improve

legibility. Conversely, Harvard can be switched to Vancouver to reduce space in print.

(ii) INTERDOCUMENT LINKS

Interdocument links are links between documents. Examples of interdocument links are the following:

Links between chapters in a book ("as discussed in Chapter 10")
A link from one article to a figure appearing in another article ("shown in Chapter 10, Figure 1")
A letter and its reply
A published article and a commentary on the article or an erratum to the article

Interdocument links are much more difficult than intradocument links to encode. With intradocument links, the means of identifying the target is known (e.g., the target for any figure will be "f"-something). In general, all that can be encoded in the document is as much information as possible to enable the target to be found. The mechanics of creating the hyperlink from the source to the target will have to be left to an outside process.

One method of encoding interdocument links is to use an ID naming convention in addition to a file-naming convention. For example, if the naming convention for chapters in a book is "chapter_1.xml," "chapter_2.xml," etc., and the ID naming convention for figures is "f1," "f2," "f3," etc., then the text "shown in Chapter 10, Figure 1" could be encoded as shown in <interlink target="chapter_10.xml#f1">Chapter 10, Figure 1</interlink>.

If ***DOI***s are assigned to content at a granular enough level, then the link could simply be encoded with the DOI number as the link attribute value.

1. Interdocument links: recommendations

- If necessary use a file-naming and ID naming convention to specify the target of the links, although this kind of hard-coding of links has drawbacks—for example, any change to file names would break the links.
- Encode as much metadata into the link as possible. It may be possible to use an ***OpenURL*** type syntax (see **below** [4.5.5.3]) when specifying the targets of links. OpenURL is a *de facto* standard for wrapping metadata in URLs in order to make links.
- Consider assigning DOIs at a granular enough level to facilitate interdocument linking.

(iii) EXTRADOCUMENT LINKS

Extradocument links, or links to files or resources outside of a document, include URLs, ***FTP*** addresses, DOIs, and e-mail addresses. Ways to identify and create links for these are well established. The following descriptions are from WhatIs.com (http://whatis.techtarget.com/):

1. URL (Uniform Resource Locator)

A ***URL*** . . . is the address of a file (resource) accessible on the Internet. The type of resource depends on the Internet application protocol. Using the World Wide Web's protocol, the Hypertext Transfer Protocol (***HTTP***), the resource can be an ***HTML*** page, an image file, a program such as a common gateway interface application or Java applet, or any other file supported by HTTP. The URL contains the name of the protocol required to access the resource, a ***domain name*** that identifies a specific computer on the Internet, and a hierarchical description of a file location on the computer.
—*http://searchnetworking.techtarget.com/sDefinition/0,,sid7_gci213251,00.html*

2. FTP (File Transfer Protocol)

FTP, a standard Internet protocol, is the simplest way to exchange files between computers on the Internet. Like the Hypertext Transfer Protocol (HTTP), which transfers displayable Web pages and related files, and the Simple Mail Transfer Protocol (***SMTP***), which transfers e-mail, FTP is an application protocol that uses the Internet's ***TCP/IP*** protocols. FTP is commonly used to transfer Web-page files from their creator to the computer that acts as their server for everyone on the Internet. It's also commonly used to download programs and other files to your computer from other servers.
—*http://searchnetworking.techtarget.com/sDefinition/0,,sid7_gci213976,00.html*

3. DOI (Digital Object Identifier)

DOI . . . is a permanent identifier given to a Web file or other Internet document so that if its Internet address changes, users will be redirected to its new address. You submit a DOI to a centrally managed directory and then use the address of that directory plus the DOI instead of a regular Internet address. The DOI system was conceived by the Association of American Publishers in partnership with the Corporation for National Research Initiatives and is now administered by the International DOI Foundation. Essentially, the DOI system is a scheme for Web page redirection by a central manager.
—*http://whatis.techtarget.com/definition/0,,sid9_gci213897,00.html*

For a more thorough explanation of DOI, see the chapter on **digital rights management** [15].

4. E-mail (Electronic Mail)

> E-mail . . . is the exchange of computer-stored messages by telecommunications . . . E-mail messages are usually encoded in ***ASCII*** text. However, you can also send nontext files, such as graphic images and sound files, as attachments sent in binary streams. E-mail was one of the first uses of the Internet and is still the most popular use. A large percentage of the total traffic over the Internet is e-mail. E-mail can also be exchanged between on-line service provider users and in networks other than the Internet, both public and private.
> —*http://searchnetworking.techtarget.com/sDefinition/0,,sid7_gci212051,00.html*

(iv) EXTRADOCUMENT LINKS: RECOMMENDATIONS

- If URLs are cited in text, they should not be abbreviated. For example, www.yahoo.com should be corrected to http://www.yahoo.com.
- If DOIs are cited in the text, they should be prefixed by "doi:". For example, "doi:10.1046/j.14429993.2001.01130.x". There should be no space between "doi:" and the DOI number as "doi:" is a *de facto* ***namespace***.

(v) REFERENCE LINKING

Full (i.e., granular) markup of references allows authors and publishers greater control over their content and how it is referenced in electronic referral schemes. To enable publishers to add value to their on-line content, a number of mechanisms have been developed to enable direct access to the primary resource (e.g., CrossRef), linking to abstracted versions of article 'headers' (e.g., PubMed, ISI), or selective linking to one of several manifestations of the content (e.g., SFX, which uses the OpenURL standard).

1. CrossRef

"***Reference linking***" is the creation of links from references or citations in an on-line article to the items that the references cite. A sample reference and reference link is:

> Iwamoto, K., Fukuda, H. & Sugiyama, M. (2001) "Elimination of POR expression correlates with red leaf formation in Amaranthus tricolor." *The Plant Journal.* **27**, 275–284. [CrossRef: http://dx.doi.org/10.1046/j.1365-313X.2001.01082.x]

The above reference link is made via CrossRef, a collaborative reference-linking service that was launched in June 2000. The aim of CrossRef is to facilitate the creation of links from references in on-line journals to the cited article. Two years later, CrossRef's membership exceeded 153 member publishers, and the CrossRef database had grown to over 4.9 million articles from approximately 6,406 journals. The CrossRef database is projected to grow by over half a million articles each year.

While CrossRef was initially devoted to links between journal articles, its scope was expanded in 2002 when it began accepting metadata for other types of content such as books and conference proceedings, so that links to these types of content can be made.

1. HOW CROSSREF LINKING WORKS

To participate in CrossRef, each member publisher must assign a DOI to every article published on-line. All member publishers then submit the metadata of their published articles along with their DOIs to the central CrossRef database.

Once the metadata has been submitted, each member publisher can then query the references in their publications against CrossRef, which contains the metadata for all participating publishers. When a match is made between an entry in CrossRef and the reference being queried, a DOI is returned, and this can be used to create a link to the other publisher's article.

2. CROSSREF LINKING REQUIREMENTS

For a publisher to participate in CrossRef, they must organize and structure their content in two ways.

First, they must ensure that they capture the metadata associated with the articles they publish so that it can be submitted to CrossRef. The metadata requirements for CrossRef are quite standard. For example, for journal articles, the following metadata must be submitted: the article title, authors, journal title, the journal's print and electronic ISSN numbers, date of publication, volume, issue, and page numbers (where these are available).

Second, in order to create reference links, the publisher should mark up references in sufficient detail so that they can be queried against the reference database. (The application, which takes an incoming query and returns an identifier from the database, is commonly referred to as a "***reference resolver***.") Usually, the author names, journal title, year of publication, volume, and page numbers will be tagged in the XML version of the reference.

If every significant element in the reference is tagged with an XML tag, a query string can easily be made for the reference and queried against on-line bibliographic databases. It would be possible to mark only the start and end of the reference and leave the contents of the reference as untagged text. This untagged text could then be processed by a separate application to parse it into its logical parts and create the query string. Proponents of this approach argue that this avoids the expense of full XML markup. However, it is not a recommended long-term strategy. Not marking up the file itself means that every external process that accesses the files needs to have that intelligence built into it. Inevitably this leads to duplication of effort, extra cost, and possible problems with inconsistency. If the markup is present in the XML files, the applications that process them can be much more lightweight and it is easier to guarantee consistency.

3. HOW THE CROSSREF PROCESS WORKS

Once it has been identified, the significant information in each reference is converted to the appropriate query string for the database being linked to. For example, the following query string needs to be created in order to query the CrossRef database:

ISN | TTL | NAM | VID | IID | PID | YNO | TYP | KEY | DOI

where

ISN = ISSN
TTL = Journal title or abbreviation (if ISSN is not used this must be present)
NAM = First author name (may be left blank)
VID = Volume ID (or more commonly "number")
IID = Issue ID (or more commonly "number"—may be left blank)
PID = Page ID (or more commonly "number")
YNO = Year number
TYP = Resource type (may be left blank)
KEY = User supplied key
DOI = Digital Object Identifier

The CrossRef Resolver currently requires three mandatory fields (ISN and/or TTL, VID, PID) in order to ensure that only one identifier is returned. Please note that YNO is to be used in place of VID for unvolumed titles. Also note that at present the TTL field is assumed to be either a journal abbreviation or a full title.

A sample query to CrossRef from a journal article is:

| Australian Journal of Earth Sciences | Bourman | 46 | 4 | 523 | 1999 | | b5 |

The CrossRef database takes this information, deconstructs the query into its component parts, and runs a check across the contents of its database. If a match is found, the query is returned with the appropriate information filled in:

14400952,08120099 | Australian Journal of Earth Sciences | Bourman | 46 | 4 | 523 | 1999 | full_text | b5 | 10.1046/j.1440–0952.1999.00720.x

The last item in the response is the article's DOI number. This can then be used to construct a link to the article by appending it to the standard DOI URL stem, that is, http://dx.doi.org/10.1046/j.1440–0952.1999.00720.x.

Further information on the CrossRef reference resolver is available at http://www.crossref.org/.

2. Abstracting services

Prior to the availability of primary material on-line, content aggregators provided a mechanism for searching and rendering the abstracts of journal articles. These continue to provide a valuable research tool, as the metadata are often enhanced by additional classification terms (e.g., PubMed's MESH headings). The mechanism by which reference citations can resolve to these abstracts operates in a similar way to CrossRef.

Further information on the National Library of Medicine's PubMed service is available at http://www.ncbi.nlm.nih.gov/PubMed/citmatchlink.html.

3. OpenURL

Because there are often many possible ways to obtain a particular desired piece of content in a given environment, it is helpful to give the user a choice of options. This is often referred to as the "appropriate copy" problem: it's a problem if a user in, say, a university library, clicks on a link and is directed to a publisher's site where the requested article is offered for sale, without pointing out to that user that the requested article is already owned by that library and available for free by a different route.

OpenURL is defined as "an interoperability protocol that enables the context-sensitive resolution of service links for information objects" (http://edina.ed.ac.uk/projects/joinup/seminardocs/jennywalker.html). An information object is described by means of metadata and/or identifiers: it may be a citation in an abstract database (e.g., PubMed), the primary article (via CrossRef), or an entry for a book or journal in a library's catalog. An OpenURL is an actionable URL that transports metadata or identifiers for the object for which the OpenURL is provided.

OpenURLs rely upon separating the provision of linking services for a work from the description of the work. The reference link associated with content metadata should not be considered a part of the metadata, but rather as a service that builds on the metadata. This disconnection permits the provision of an overlay service component that is independent of the content itself. This can enable the delivery of a wide range of extended context-sensitive linking services. Within an OpenURL framework it is possible to create a consistent linking environment for users that stretches across many resources and is not tied to a single resource.

The specification of the OpenURL (as it is currently being implemented by a number of information providers), and other relevant material relating to the OpenURL can be found at: http://www.sfxit.com/OpenURL.html.

OpenURL currently supports the following identifiers:

doi : digital object identifier
pmid : PubMed identifier
bibcode : identifier used in Astrophysics Data System
oai : identifier used in the Open Archives Initiative

1. SFX: AN EXAMPLE OF AN OPEN LINKING SOLUTION

SFX is an open linking solution developed by Ex Libris. The SFX server is a commercial OpenURL-compliant service component that is locally managed by an institution (e.g., a library or publisher), which can define the relationships between different information resources to allow the user to take full advantage of their own systems, as well as to link to appropriate services. The SFX server offers a single point for the administration of linking services and for the collection of statistics.

More information about SFX is available at: http://www.sfxit.com.

2. DOI/CROSSREF AND OPENURL/SFX

The DOI, CrossRef, SFX, and OpenURL are complementary services that can work together. The current DOI/CrossRef model does not independently handle multiple resolution of DOIs. SFX and OpenURL are therefore working with CrossRef and DOI to solve the "appropriate copy" problem: where multiple legitimate copies of an article exist, there must be some mechanism supporting the selection of the most appropriate copy or copies for a particular user—typically that for which the user has access rights by virtue of their affiliation.

4.6 CONCLUSION

Much of this chapter has focused on digital production technologies in the context of journal publishing. However, the ideas and technologies discussed are in no way limited to that industry. Indeed, many of the technologies were initiated outside of the journal publishing world (some even outside of publishing) and have subsequently been adopted by journal publishers. Others, such as CrossRef started in journal publishing and are being expanded into other areas.

Regardless of the industry, some universal truths apply when approaching the challenges of digital publishing.

1. Stick to standards. The more standards-based the technologies you choose, the easier it will be to ensure interoperability between processes. Furthermore, it's more likely that your technologies will be future-proofed.
2. Understand your content. Perform document analysis on as wide a range of content as possible. It's much easier to plan your workflows around your content; it's much more difficult to force nonstandard content into an already-existing workflow.
3. Keep abreast of developments. The digital publishing world moves at a blistering pace, and technologies that promise to change the world one week often disappear without trace the next. The World Wide Web—particularly resources such as this guide—is invaluable as a means of keeping up-to-date.
4. Study existing implementations of the technologies or methods you plan to adopt. Who's already using the DTD? What does/doesn't it allow them to do? How can it be improved? It is usually prudent in digital publishing not to be on the bleeding edge—don't be a guinea pig for untried and untested technologies. Learn from others; avoid their mistakes and build on their successes.
5. When you're converting a traditional publishing process to a digital one, tough decisions will need to be taken. Workflows will change and staff and suppliers will need to adapt to these.
6. Recognize that more time spent planning the implementation of digital production processes makes the implementation more likely to succeed.

Content is the basis of publishing, whether print or electronic. If you spend time getting your content organized, getting your markup right, planning, and implementing production workflows, then developing digital publishing services to build on top of your content will be a much easier process than it otherwise might be!

Acknowledgments: Richard O'Beirne and Martin Clutterbuck contributed significantly to this chapter.

BIBLIOGRAPHY

Baca, Murtha, ed. *Introduction to Metadata, Version 2.0*. Getty Research Institute, 1998. http://www.getty.edu/research/institute/standards/intrometadata/

Connolly, Dan. "The XML Revolution." Nature. October 1, 1998. http://www.nature.com/nature/webmatters/xml/xml.html

Day, Michael. "Metadata: Mapping between Metadata Formats." U.K. Office for Library and Information Networking (UKOLN). 1996; updated May 2002. http://www.ukoln.ac.uk/metadata/interoperability/

DCMI. "Dublin Core Metadata Initiative (DCMI)." 2002. http://www.dublincore.org/

Digital Library Federation. "Andrew W. Mellon Foundation's e-Journal Archiving Program." Council on Library and Information Resources. 2002. http://www.diglib.org/preserve/ejp.htm

Editeur. "ONIX Product Information Standards." 2002. http://www.editeur.org/

Library of Congress. "MARC Standards." Network Development and MARC Standards Office. 2002. http://www.loc.gov/marc/

St. Pierre, Margaret, and William P. LaPlant, Jr. "Issues in Crosswalking Content Metadata Standards." National Information Standards Organization. 1998. http://www.niso.org/press/whitepapers/crsswalk.html

UKOLN. "Metadata." U.K. Office for Library and Information Networking. Maint Michael Day and Andy Powell. September 2002. http://www.ukoln.ac.uk/metadata/

Van Herwijnen, Eric. *Practical SGML*, 2[d] ed. Boston: Kluwer Academic Publishers, 1994. http://www.wkap.nl/prod/b/0–7923–9434–8

World Wide Web Consortium (W3C). "Metadata and Resource Description." 2001. http://www.w3.org/Metadata/

———. "Resource Description Framework." 2002. http://www.w3.org/RDF

5 Data Capture & Conversion

MARK GROSS
President, Data Conversion Laboratory
With contributions by John Shreeve and Michael Gross

This chapter discusses the ins and outs of converting and upgrading textual data and related information from all kinds of formats into markup languages for publishing purposes. While the issues and approaches apply to all markup languages, particular emphasis is given to the issues of converting documents into XML, SGML, and HTML. The chapter looks at the issues surrounding the capture of data from sources such as paper and microfilm, word processors, publishing systems, PDF, and ASCII—the main issue being the need to untangle content from structure.

5.1 OVERVIEW: ENTERING A WORLD OF STRUCTURE

If you're in the publishing world you've probably had some level of involvement with data conversion. Maybe, as an editor or writer, you have worked on print articles or books that have been converted into structured languages like Standard Generalized Markup Language (SGML) or Extensible Markup Language (XML) and have been republished on the Web, on CD-ROM, or in eBook format. As part of the process, you may have been asked by the company dealing with the conversion to supply your documents in a specific way. It might have been something as simple as making sure all your headings and subheadings were consistent, or to clearly define abstracts, bylines, and tables. Or you might have been given a style template to load into your word processing program.

Alternatively you might be a publisher interested in making your archives available electronically over the Web, and are involved in making the decisions that will make your materials as useful on the Web as they have been in print—and you need to understand the tradeoffs you are being asked to make.

You might not have got much deeper than this. But knowing that so many types of documents, from journals to technical manuals, are currently being converted into structured languages may well have led you to look further into the subject. The purpose of this chapter is to present the issues surrounding data conversion in a straightforward and easy to grasp manner.

TABLE 1. HOW VARIOUS FORMATS RATE FOR WHAT YOU WANT TO DO

	Data Format				
Primary Purpose	TIFF	PDF	HTML	XML	SGML
Distributing Page Images	Excellent	Excellent	Good	Good	Good
Re-Purposing	None	Limited	Limited	Excellent	Excellent
Searching	None	Limited	Good	Excellent	Excellent
Component Reuse	None	None	Limited	Excellent	Excellent
Enforce Standards	None	None	Limited	Excellent	Excellent
Data Interchange	None	None	Limited	Excellent	Excellent

(i) A STEP-BY-STEP APPROACH

1. Define aims

The first thing to ask when looking at a new data conversion project is how the converted material is to be used. This has a strong bearing on how the document will be converted and at what cost. For example, if the intent of the electronic publication is merely to provide an accurate image of the original printed pages, it would be sufficient to simply scan the document and turn it into an image-based Portable Document Format **(PDF)** [5.3.3.1] file (viewable with the free Adobe Acrobat Reader software). However, if the requirements of the e-publication are more complex—such as incorporating the materials as part of searchable databases, or making sections downloadable to new devices such as cell phones—a structured language like SGML or XML is probably indicated. The various decision categories are outlined in Table 1.

When it comes to cost, converting a document to SGML or XML is approximately ten times more expensive than simply scanning it and turning it into PDF. So making decisions on the aims of the project and your specific needs are the critical parts of the business case.

2. Determining the appropriate level of tagging

If conversion to XML or SGML is called for, the level at which information needs tagging must be determined. This, again, is dependent on what is going to be done with the document once it has been converted. If simple word searches are sufficient, there would be no need to identify and tag the various types of information in the document. But if the document being converted is a legal book and all the court cases listed in the book need to be easily identified and classified, then more complex tagging is required and every case would have to be appropriately tagged with the criteria you determine to be important.

With operations manuals, it might be useful to extract lists of tools and identify the steps of a procedure—in which case every mention of tool and machine parts would be tagged, and the various steps in a process would be identified.

And if the intention is to ultimately publish documents in different formats for different audiences, the tags for all the likely uses would need to be included. A word of caution—it is possible to get so compulsive about trying to identify all the possible tagging you might ever want that you design a project so complex it will be impossible to implement.

In short, converting to XML or SGML can be a very simple process of capturing text with very light tagging. Or it can be a very complex process involving the identification of many different elements of a document's content.

Much of the information that is tagged will be *explicit;* it will be clearly identifiable in the text or in the markup or styling in the original document. But some of the information that is tagged will be *implicit* and won't be mentioned in the text (or styled or tagged in the files). For example, the editor of an educational textbook might wish to identify the topic being covered in each section of a chapter, or identify the grade level of every question in the book. This information wouldn't be in the flow of text—the reader wouldn't see it. But having the information available would allow for automating the process of creating specialized versions of the book at a later date.

The great strength of modern **markup** [3] languages is they let you identify and tag as much or as little information as you want. But the more information you identify, the greater the costs. The golden rule is to identify how much of this tagging you will reasonably use in the foreseeable future, without building so much in that the complexity and costs sink the project. It's also helpful to realize that gradual enrichment is possible: you can start with a basic, functional level of tagging (including everything that's obvious or capable of being automated) and then add more later as it becomes practical or necessary to do so.

3. Analyze your data

Therefore it is critical that the first step is a detailed analysis of the document set to be converted—along with an understanding of the desired level of tagging. If SGML or XML is called for, then the results of this analysis will have been encapsulated into a Document Type Definition **(DTD)** [3.3.2.2] or **XML schema** [3.3.2.4] which defines the structure of the document. Often the task of analysis is outsourced to consultants. But as in any business, some consultants are good, some are not so good—and it is very difficult for the customer to distinguish one from the other. Consultants lacking real-world experience of SGML and XML may be very idealistic and tag nearly everything, which is impractical on a larger scale. Or they have a simplistic view of structured languages and are inclined not to think about the steps ahead, which can lead to difficulties in the long run. A skilled consultant, on the other hand, will not only carry out a realistic analysis, but will also convert sections of the document by hand and tag them appropriately. This gives a good idea of what the converted material will look like and ensures that it will work in the software environments it is going to be published in.

In any event, you need to stay involved to assure good results. You, as the owner of the data, know what's called for and need to continue to provide guidance to make sure your goals are fulfilled.

4. Data capture

Once the process and goals are defined, and a document is ready for conversion, there are four steps.

1. EXTRACTION OF TEXT

If the material is coming from an electronic source, the extracted text is expected to be 100 percent accurate. So, at the risk of oversimplifying, it is just a question of removing any formatting codes that get in the way, and also of retaining whatever formatting information can be used to infer the tagging and styling that will be done in later phases. If the source document is paper, the process is more involved. The document needs to be scanned and run through an optical character recognition (**OCR** [5.3.1.1.3]) engine. Once this is done, it is a question of checking through the text for errors, as OCR does not offer 100 percent accuracy. Alternatively, the material might be keyed and then proofed. The specifics of whether to use keying or OCR depends on characteristics of the materials; OCR is not always the cheapest way to go.

2. DETERMINING TEXT FLOW AND STRUCTURE

It is important to determine whether the text flows in a linear fashion, one paragraph following another, or whether it is structured in a different way. If there is a box in the top right-hand corner of a page, for example, how the text in that box should fit into the flow of information is examined. How columns flow and how blocks of text go around images must be considered.

3. OBTAINING NONTEXT OBJECTS

"Objects" can be pictures, photographs, line drawings, or chemical and mathematical formulas, or anything else that is not part of the flow of text. If all the photographs and other images are in a standard digital image format like ***JPEG***, ***GIF***, or ***TIFF*** they often can simply be extracted and, if need be, converted to another file format. If the source document is paper, then the image is scanned and a new image file is created. Mathematical or chemical formulas are treated in a similar way. A math formula, for instance, might be in a computer language like **TeX** [5.5.10], in which case that file format is either retained or the formula is converted to ***MathML*** or some other math description language. If keeping the ***TeX*** format proved problematical, the formula could alternately be converted into an image file.

4. ESTABLISHING RELATIONSHIPS BETWEEN TEXT AND OBJECTS

If the object is a picture, its position in and relationship to the flow of information needs to be worked out. This is straightforward if the reference to the picture is explicit—for example, "see figure 5." The picture would then usually be placed immediately after the paragraph in which it is first mentioned. (Sometimes images are grouped at the ends of the files or put in separate files.) Most formal books have explicit references like this. But in less formal books, a picture might simply relate to the topic being discussed and be placed in a box at a location defined by the art director, in which case a logical way to fit it into the flow of the text would have to be determined. One solution might be to define a rule that the best place for a picture of this type is after the first heading on a page or at the end of the chapter.

5. Creating your target format

Once you've captured as much of the source data as possible, you're ready to create your target format. The process may include reorganizing the information in a different order, inserting various codes, identifying text that doesn't belong, and deleting it—followed by a process of checking your work both electronically and through old-fashioned human effort. The conversion process can range from being an almost fully automated process to one that requires a high degree of human intervention. The key issues are how well you can define the transformation rules and deciding how much effort it is worth putting in to develop the necessary automation. Most conversion efforts are a combination of automation and human effort, and defining the right mix is the decision on which much depends.

6. Output

If your target format is a markup language such as XML or SGML, the document won't yet be ready for publishing as it consists of text and tags and lacks the niceties of a well-laid-out page. So it is necessary to provide formatting instructions. This involves creating the XML or SGML equivalent of a ***stylesheet*** (found in word processors and HTML editors). (See the chapter on markup for a discussion of **stylesheets** [3.3.3] and the chapter on composition and design for a discussion of **composition** [6.2] and **page layout** [6.10].)

Now that we've seen an overview, the rest of this chapter will provide more detailed information to help you get started.

5.2 UNTANGLING CONTENT FROM STRUCTURE

The first step in using modern markup languages is to consciously separate the content from structure.

(i) WHY IS IT IMPORTANT?

Separating content from structure and format is important because content is likely to remain relatively unchanged as it moves between the various types of media, while structure and format constantly need to be modified to suit the new medium. By separating the two, the content can quickly be adapted to different media and the translation process is made a good deal simpler than it would be otherwise. For example, in a print document, due to the limitations of paper, an "important concept" might be bolded and italicized, whereas the same content on a computer might be highlighted in bright colors in flashing reverse video. If the relevant text is coded with an "important concept" tag, the publishing system can "decide," based on the medium, how the display should be rendered. But if the text is coded with tags for bold-italic, as it would be in traditional publishing environments, the options would be severely limited. The text would look fine when sent to paper, but when prepared for a computer display, the publishing system would have no way of knowing that it needs to do anything other than use a bold italic font. In other words, there would be nothing to tell it that this particular text is an important concept and that on a computer screen it should be highlighted with bright colors in flashing reverse video.

Ideally, content prepared for the new digital age should not have any tagging that defines the look—only tagging that identifies what it is. While the philosophy of SGML and XML is focused on this concept, it is also the trend of most modern digital publishing.

The key benefits of untangling content from structure are:

- Modules of text do not change even while the structure and format change with the presentation medium.

- Presentation media can change over time to keep up with technology changes.
- Organization of text modules can change as the document is reused for different applications (extracts, collections of articles, technical documents reorganized for a different model or application, or updates).
- The author can focus on the text while the editor focuses on overall organization and style.
- The organization can own the collection of materials while the author controls the individual text modules.
- Even for a novel, which is not likely to get updated, the text can remain constant as it gets reworked for different presentation formats (hardcover, paperback, e-book, etc.).

(ii) IMPLICIT VS. EXPLICIT INFORMATION

Some structural ***identifiers*** are fairly obvious in source documents. Chapter headings and subheadings are a good example, particularly if they have been defined using style sheets in a word processor or HTML editor. They are referred to as *explicit* structures. But some structures are not always explicit. For example, "see figure 3" is explicit (provided there is only one figure 3), but "see figure above," "see illustration on next page," or "see figure later in this chapter," would be *implicit* and not so easy for a computer to figure out.

When converting an article written in a traditional format (word processor, HTML editor, etc.) it is necessary to isolate all the implicit elements and make them explicit. What needs to be explicit will vary according to the subject matter and purpose of the publication. With legal documents every case might need to be made explicit so lawyers can either refer to cases or produce a list of cases. And with journal articles all the references to other articles (external references) might need to be made explicit. These kinds of references would be in prose. But if the article needed to be discussed and referred to, the references would have to be put into a standard structured form so they could be used to search against an articles database. Some of the issues involved in tagging various kinds of publications are given in Table 2.

1. Identifying ambiguity

Automated conversion depends on being able to define rules that a computer can follow unambiguously. This definition is specific to your materials, and doing a careful job of this analysis is often the difference between success and failure. For example, the general rule might be that a section of text set in quotes is an article reference. But in your materials it might not actually be

TABLE 2. CONTENT TAGGING ISSUES AND CLASS OF PUBLICATIONS

Class of Publication	Types of Content To Be Tagged
Textbooks	Exercises, learning objectives, answers to questions, teacher's notes
Scholarly publications	Extensive bibliographic materials, Harvard style references, biographical notes and affiliations
Legal texts	Case and legal code citations, jurisdiction identification
Technical documents	Steps and procedures, tools and parts, illustrations of steps, lists of materials or parts
Software documentation	Calling specifications, interfaces, screen shots, illustration of input and output, lines of programming code
Historical and library documents	Dates, places and people, sources, archive locations
E-commerce	Catalog information, tables and information about products, ordering and billing information

referring to an article at all: it might be referring to a phrase or some other piece of information that happens to be in quotes in that article. The same is true of italics. A word or sentence might be emphasized in italics for a number of different reasons. It might be highlighting a book title, the name of a company, or an article; it might be a foreign word or technical term; or it might simply be emphasizing a point. The only way to truly understand the meaning is to read and *understand* the text. *Understanding* is not something computers do particularly well. Therefore human input is needed to provide context and to define the meaning of quotes, italics, and other elements, as they are used for these specific materials.

Depending on the purpose of a document, it might be necessary to identify certain items mentioned in the text. In a repair manual, for instance, you may wish to explicitly identify every mention of tools. This would allow users to automatically generate a list of tools needed for a specific repair procedure. In a legal text you may want to identify explicitly every mention of a case or a judge's name, so as to be able to produce case lists or other specialized reference aids. Again, the implicit information (references to tools) has to be made explicit in order to make practical use of it. This involves analyzing the different types of information in the document to work out how the process of conversion can be automated. Ideally rules can be defined and programmed into the conversion software to recognize specific information that needs identifying. Otherwise the material would have to be edited by hand, which is an expensive process. The better the rules definition process, the less editing by hand will be required.

When designing a conversion project it is necessary to decide which elements are worth marking up and which are not. Ideally everything that might possibly be needed in the future would be marked up. But there is a cost for resolving each level of ambiguity. So the usual practice is to settle on an appropriate balance of cost and benefits.

5.3 WHERE DOES YOUR DATA COME FROM?

(i) LEGACY CONTENT

Legacy data is material that has already been published and that now is to be republished for other purposes (and that, probably, was never intended for republication). It can be in nondigital formats (e.g., paper or microfilm) or in a digital format (i.e., produced using word processors or publishing systems).

1. Nondigital sources

1. PAPER AND MICROFILM

Paper documents may have been produced with a typewriter, word processor, publishing system, or with a pen. Or they might be photocopies of original documents. Paper has been the universal medium for nearly two millennia, and for good reason: it is universally readable without any special equipment. However, paper documents cannot be edited or formatted. The only way to make them electronic is to scan them or retype the text into a computer.

The same is true of documents on microfilm. (But microfilm needs to be enlarged to be viewed, as the image is much smaller than paper.) In terms of quality, so long as good technique was used to create it, microfilm matches paper. But because microfilm is a very high-contrast medium, and doesn't have gray scaling built in, pictures that depend on shading don't come out well. Many newspaper archives and research papers are only available on microfilm. (The paper was discarded when they were transferred to microfilm.)

Whether legacy materials are on paper or microfilm, the first step of the conversion process is to put them into digital format. If the quantity is small, the material can simply be retyped onto a computer and checked for errors by a proofreader. This is known as single-keying and proofing. But if the volume is large there are three ways to deal with it: key-entry processes; scanning and OCR; or a combination of these.

In the following sections, these options are examined in more detail.

2. KEY-ENTRY PROCESSES

Key entry is just typing the materials in. However, most key entry is done using some multipass process (such as double keying) in order to improve accuracy. ***Double keying*** involves two people independently typing the material into computers and producing two separate typescripts. Software programs are used to do a comparison of the two typescripts. Mismatches are highlighted for evaluation by an editor or proofreader, who then typically makes a choice to correct the file. These latter steps are necessary as human error is inevitable, however competent the typists. And note that there is still an opportunity for human error, because the final editor may make an incorrect choice or mistype something.

Where double keying is not considered sufficiently accurate, a triple-keying process can be employed. This involves three people typing up the same material independently. Another alternative to increase accuracy is to perform additional proofreading of the completed materials. Since keying and proofing are very labor-intensive processes, most large volume keying is done offshore (usually in India, the Philippines, or China), where labor costs are much lower.

The single-keying process (the first step of keying) achieves approximately 99 percent accuracy, although this varies widely with the materials and the proficiency of the operator. The double-keying process improves accuracy to between 99.95 and 99.995 percent. If greater accuracy is required, a combination of triple keying and proofreading is necessary. The standard today for most publishing projects is that material be provided at 99.995 percent accuracy. Lower rates of accuracy are only suitable for special applications like a search database or image-based PDF with text in the background. The exact meanings of those accuracy rates are as follows:

To put these numbers in perspective, a typical 6-in x 9-in trade book has 2,500 to 3,000 characters per page, and a typical 8.5-in x 11-in double-column journal has 6,500 to 7,500 characters per page. That means that 99.95 percent accuracy permits one or two errors on every book page and three or more on a journal page; 99.995 percent accuracy allows only a tenth as many, but that still means an error is permitted every seven or eight book pages and every three or four journal pages.

3. OCR

An alternative to keying is to scan documents and run them through an OCR engine. Invented during the late 1950s, ***OCR*** has long held a promise for replacing manual processes. Until recently, however, OCR hasn't offered a high enough level of accuracy unless it is performed using top quality input—meaning first generation documents printed in certain fonts that are good for machine interpretation. The initial accuracy of OCR was often 90 to 98 percent, depending on the materials; 96 percent accuracy means that four characters out of a hundred will be incorrect. In reading terms this means two characters in every line will be wrong. Proofreading and correcting material that starts at such a low accuracy is likely to be more expensive than double keying the material in the first place.

With OCR the computer analyzes patterns of dots and line patterns and figures out how they translate into alphabetical characters. This would be straightforward if everybody used the same font: the dots would either match up or they wouldn't. But people use a whole array of different fonts, making the process of identifying characters highly involved. The more sophisticated OCR algorithms, however, are able to identify the features of individual font sets. For example, they assess how many characters have loops and how many of those loops are closed.

OCR technology has improved significantly in recent years, enough, with some input, to produce 99.9 percent accuracy on the first run through. This has led some offshore facilities that traditionally used double keying to adopt OCR as the first step. Furthermore, it has reduced the cost of the manual process to the point where it might soon make economical sense to do the work in the more developed world.

The increasing speed of computers has made possible more sophisticated OCR heuristics. One approach used by the current generation of OCR engines is to use five or more different OCR engines to analyze the same text; the software then takes a poll. If a majority of the OCR engines agree on a character then that is the character that will be chosen. If not, the software identifies a character as ambiguous and flags it for further analysis. After analysis and correction, accuracy can reach 99.95 percent.

But even the best current OCR processes do not work well on older materials. OCR won't provide an acceptable degree of accuracy on degraded materials or materials created with unusual or very old typefaces, like those used on lead printing presses during the 19th or early 20th centuries. Without thorough proofreading, the level of accuracy would not be good enough for publishing purposes. Nor does OCR work well if the originals have been marked up for editing or other uses.

4. HOW MUCH ACCURACY DO YOU NEED?

In some circumstances, lower accuracy is acceptable. For searching of large databases in libraries and in litigation support applications, 98 percent accuracy, or less, could be good enough. Because the chances are low that an error will be in the one word being searched for, and there is usually significant redundancy among other similar words in the text, the chances of finding the right place are high enough. And since the cost differences are so significant (the 98 percent accuracy database could cost less than one-tenth as much as something more accurate), it could well make economically viable a database that could not otherwise be justified. In many applications relying on lower accuracy it is common to also retain images of the original pages to allow reference to accurate, before-conversion content.

As regards format and structure, when a document is processed using OCR there is no style information. All you get is the text and the look of the page. Titles, headings, tables, lists, and so on, are not formally coded as they would be in a word-processed document that has used stylesheets consistently. The newer OCR engines have a limited ability to infer what the different elements of a document should be. But the process is still far from perfect, which is why nearly all materials that come out of the OCR process need checking to ensure elements such as tables and cells have been correctly rendered. Most OCR engines provide "zoning" tools, which allow users to override the OCR software's default page layout decisions. On pages that contain any sort of complexity, you may find that prezoning the page before OCR yields noticeably better results.

2. Digital sources

Digital legacy documents have usually been produced in word processors, publishing systems, plain-text editors, or in text formatters. Unlike paper and microfilm documents (and disregarding computer error) the text retrieved from digital documents can be 100 percent accurate. The use of certain alphabetical characters, however, can be ambiguous. Hyphens, for example, have two applications and for conversion purposes they are dealt with in two ways: (1) they are removed when used to indicate a word division due to a line break; (2) they are retained when they're necessary for correct grammar or spelling. Style and structural elements can also prove an issue, depending on whether templates or stylesheets have been used consistently.

Let's take a more detailed look at the main issues surrounding documents from the various digital sources.

1. WORD PROCESSORS

Most authors create their documents with word processors. Word processors have evolved over the last 15 to 20 years into being sophisticated desktop publishing systems in their own right. Despite their power, people use them to varying degrees. Microsoft Word, for example, can simply be used as a word processor (albeit a very powerful one) to type up manuscripts. Or it can be used as a desktop publishing system to create fully formatted and illustrated newsletters and brochures. If the stylesheet function is configured, Word can also be used to create technical manuals with extensive hyperlinks and other navigational features. It can also be used to create fully functional Web sites. (Most of the content of this Guide—for both print and on-line publication—was originally created in that way.)

The text retrieved in the conversion process from a word processor will be completely accurate. And if an author has used the word processing features correctly, a good deal of the normally inferred information will be easily interpreted. For example, if an author used the table editor in Microsoft Word to create a table, then much of the information needed to create an XML table will be there. It will be clear where the rows and columns are and which cells are spanned. But if the author created a table using other features that merely make it look like a table, then retrieval of data will not be as straightforward. The author might have used the tab key to create a table, in which case it would look like a table on the page, but none of the table structure would be defined. Therefore the software set up to analyze the native code would have to visualize what the table should look like on the page by counting the number of tabs. This is not a perfect process. In the early days of word processors it was straightforward because everyone used the Courier typeface—a fixed-width font. But now, because all kinds of variable pitch fonts are in common use, the process has become highly complex.

Headings and subheadings can also pose problems. If an author has bolded and centered headings, the conversion software can easily be set up to correctly interpret such formatting instructions. But if documents that have been written by many different authors are being converted, and they've all formatted headings differently, you'd either have to set the software up for each individual paper (a highly laborious task) or make the software smarter to somehow guess the author's intent.

With legacy data it is a question of making the best of what you have. The fact is, when a document was written it was intended for a specific purpose, and no author or editor was likely to have considered its later being converted into a structured language. And it is usually not a practical solution to re-edit and clean up source documents to make them convert more easily.

2. PUBLISHING SYSTEMS

Publishing systems fall into four categories:

1. **Desktop publishing (DTP).** Until a few years ago, desktop publishing systems were mainly used to produce small periodicals, but now big magazine and book publishers use DTP systems such as QuarkXpress to produce their publications.
2. **High-end publishing systems.** These include applications such as Miles, Atex, 3B2, and XyVision, which are used by major publishers for large and fast turnaround of publications like newspapers, books (especially large or technical ones), and journals.
3. **Technical documentation systems.** These include software packages such as FrameMaker and RoboHelp, which are used to create technical manuals and other large documents that need standardized and highly structured formatting.
4. **SGML- and XML-based publishing systems.** The main applications are Arbortext Epic and FrameMaker (which now incorporates structured editing support in its base product). High-end systems such as XyVision, Miles, and 3B2 also offer this functionality. Output is in SGML or XML form, so it doesn't need additional conversion if it's staying in the original system. If it's to be used as input for another vendor's (or another type of) system, however, another conversion stage may be necessary.

Publishing systems have robust style and markup capabilities, and when used consistently and thoughtfully can theoretically provide much information to assist automated conversion. However, since most desktop publishing systems have no method to effectively enforce style rules, and the ***WYSIWYG*** interfaces and interactivity of modern desktop tools invite creativity, along with inconsistency and local formatting, there is no guarantee that the codes you're depending on always mean the same things.

People using higher-end publishing systems to create documents are more likely to use style and markup tools correctly, resulting in better consistency. More of the style information is therefore usable by the conversion process. This information should also be more consistent, because larger quantities of documents are coming from one source. But there are drawbacks with material from publishing systems. Some of their features can be customized to fit individual needs. This means that two composition houses and two compositors using exactly the same publishing system could well be using it in very different ways. Consequently the internal coding used to define structure and format might be quite different than expected, and the conversion process would have to be fine-tuned to accommodate those differences.

Each publishing system has its own issues. QuarkXpress, for example, is one of the most powerful and popular publishing systems available today, but until version 5, it didn't have an internal table editor. Quark makes use of tabs to simulate the appearance of a table, so when documents created in Quark enter a conversion process that requires a true table structure on output, the table structures need to be inferred from layout information. Third-party packages are available that let you create tables in Quark, but these too are not easily exportable.

See the chapter on composition and graphics for for more discussion of **publishing systems** [6.10].

3. TEXT FORMATTERS

Text formatters, such as TeX, troff, and IBM BookMaster, are text processing programs which take as input text files that contain specific page layout instructions and formatting codes interspersed within the text, and produce final page layout. Various codes dictate how text should be formatted: whether it should be bolded, underlined, or italicized, and so on. Text formatters work in a similar way to the now defunct WordStar word processor, and some large-scale publishing systems are text formatters (the coding is done on-line). The coding in text formatters is similar to raw HTML. If you view HTML in a text editor, for example, you see rows of formatting code juxtaposed with text. The same is true of text formatters. Because text formatters are not WYSIWYG, they can be more difficult for new users to master than more modern publishing systems.

Converting material created in text formatters tends to be straightforward because the coding is explicit, and usually used fairly consistently. The one major issue with text formatters is that they allow users to develop custom codes (also referred to as macros). If custom codes are used a lot you have to figure out what the codes mean and reverse engineer them. Text formatters often include "standard" macro sets built around the base code set, and conversion from a particular text formatter will usually involve customizing the conversion around the particular code set used in the source documents.

Text formatters are rarely used today. But some organizations still consider them to be the most efficient way to publish databases and directories.

3. XML and SGML source data

Material coming in as XML or SGML is presumably already highly tagged and, theoretically, should be easy to convert. And it is—so long as the DTD of the target document is similar in structure and level of detail to the source DTD. Usually, however, there will be some differences in structure or in level of detail, which could make converting XML and SGML documents a complex procedure.

The level of detail of a DTD is determined by how the converted document will be used. If a bibliographic reference at the end of a journal article merely had to be reproduced as text in the XML version, then the whole section could simply be tagged as a bibliographic reference, and that would be sufficient. But if the information in the bibliographic reference needed to be used at a finer level, for example, if elements like author names and journal titles and dates needed to link to a bibliographic database, then all the names of the journal articles referred to would need to be explicitly identified, as would the first and last names of the authors, names of publishers, and the dates of publication.

Identifying the component elements may be more difficult than it sounds. It is often difficult to tell from the look of a document which sections of text refer to titles of journals, authors' names, and so on. For example, it would be necessary to read the text to work out where a first name ends and a last name begins (names like Van Wyck pose difficulties in this respect). It is possible to automate much of this, but the rules are more complex than they appear at first glance and there needs to be a mechanism for human review to deal with the ambiguous cases and to do a sanity check.

Another common issue is that the target DTD might be more restrictive than the source DTD. The target DTD might stipulate that abstracts must always be at the front of journal articles. But the source DTD might not include instructions about abstracts—in which case, it would be necessary to come up with a way to reconcile this, and to work out what to do when you don't have an abstract. Alternatively, there might be an abstract but it is located in a different part of the article. This is a structural issue. Moving one abstract wouldn't be a major problem. But if a lot of elements have to be moved and from lots of different places (e.g., shifting end-of-chapter questions to the section they belong to) then a lot of work is involved.

The same is true of other types of documents. If a cookbook were being converted and the new cookbook had to have timing instructions placed in a specific field—but the timing instructions in the original were embedded in the text—it would be necessary to go through the text and tag all the timing instructions before beginning conversion.

Bibliographic entries are a good example of the kind of tagging that varies from one markup scheme to another. You may be converting from a source DTD that decomposes a bibliographic entry into all of its components (author, title, publication name, page number, etc.), to one where the DTD simply contains a tag for each entry, not the components. If punctuation and emphasis are removed from the source markup file, the software that you build to convert to the new DTD may actually need to work as a text formatter, in the sense that it needs to restore the original formatting that appeared in a printed version of a bibliographic entry. If you are going the other way (decomposing the appearance and punctuation into component pieces), you need to infer structure from appearance. In this case, you may not be able to fully automate the conversion process, since, although in theory you are already converting from structured, marked up copy, for these types of elements the conversion process will still need to deal with the same types of issues as when converting from paper or an unstructured publishing system.

These same sorts of issues could arise when converting documents that refer to legal case law (where, for example, case citations vary greatly from one markup scheme to another) and educational textbooks (where the decomposition of users' exercises, such as multiple-choice questions and answers, can vary greatly among various markup schemes). In both of these cases, you may find yourself breaking apart text or "gluing" it back together again.

(ii) PLANNING FOR FUTURE CONTENT

Most conversion activity today is related to material that already exists and was not really designed to be converted into someone's XML database. But what about materials that you know you're going to want to convert at a later date? Can you do something to make your job easier? Can you even reach that nirvana state, the "lights-out" conversion? The key factors are:

- **Consistency of your materials.** Are your materials sufficiently consistent to allow you to tightly define formatting rules for the future? Are your materials suitable for such tight constraints? Advertising copy, for example, is probably not suitable for this treatment, while cookbooks might be.
- **Control of your authors.** Can these rules be enforced for the people you depend on for new content? (If they're in-house authors you probably can, but if they're independent contributors and outside authors, you probably can't.)
- **Is it worth it?** Even if it is possible within your publishing environment to tightly script how your materials get produced, you'll have to consider the costs, tangible and intangible. Defining your needs in advance and building an infrastructure is a significant investment. Plus there are intangible future costs, which might include the training of new people. Before someone can contribute an article do they also need to become an XML expert? In this case, you would have to ask yourself whether it is efficient to require that knowledge contributors also worry about mechanical tagging requirements.

1. Word processors

The majority of documents are created in word processors, and when you have multiple outside authors you can often count on materials being submitted in one of several major word processor formats. From a conversion point of view, the downside of word processors is they don't have the enforcement procedures you need in XML. Authors can be provided with stylesheets to follow, but word processor stylesheets have several limitations compared to those found in a DTD. A DTD can dictate where and in what order all the formatting and text elements should be. It can also enforce these requirements by displaying error messages if the author fails to follow the rules laid out by the DTD. Stylesheets in a word processor do not do this. Authors can take them or leave them, or use them incorrectly. The stylesheet has no way of telling them they haven't correctly formatted a title or heading.

If authors follow the stylesheets given to them—and really do follow through—later conversion work will go smoothly. But stylesheets can easily be ignored, and it is human nature to do what is comfortable and not worry about the consequences down the line, especially if a deadline is looming!

2. Structured authoring environments

XML and SGML editing software packages, such as ArborText Epic, XMetaL, and Adobe FrameMaker, create structured authoring environments that can be set up to enforce the use of a DTD. This means that when an author writes his or her document the XML or SGML editor will give instructions as to what is required. A window will pop up saying an abstract, heading, or subheading is needed. XML and SGML editors will also constantly check that what the author has produced is structurally sound. None of this means the content is correct—that remains the author's responsibility.

Publishers that produce documents internally can control the writing environment. A newspaper or legal publisher whose writers work in-house could stipulate that the writers work in a set way. But the reality is, most publishers use authors that work outside, which makes it much harder to control the methods writers use to create documents.

If you were dealing with a captive talent pool it would be a simple matter to insist they use a word processor in a specific way (otherwise they would be without a job). But if the authors are Nobel Prize winning scientists, or world-renowned attorneys, they will work the way they want to—and you, of course, will go along with whatever it takes to bring those documents in. (A case in point: an authoring template was created for this Guide, but only about half of the authors—experts in the world of digital publishing!—used it. Those who did, loved it, acknowledging that it made the writing easier; but many others never tried. That template can be downloaded from the on-line version of this Guide.) Isaac Asimov, the master of science fiction, for example, didn't start considering a word processor until very close to the end of his career. It is even said that Radio Shack delivered computer equipment and people to help him with it, but he ignored them and never got around to using it. Obviously, no publisher was going to insist he work digitally. (It is also said that Asimov never had to recheck or retype anything he ever wrote, meaning, no whiteout. So having a word processor wouldn't have been much use to him. It would have just wasted his time as he waited for it to reboot.)

So how do you deal with new material? Unless you have very tight control over your authors, you need to lay down some basic guidelines that are easy to follow and do not demand much technical knowledge. You would also need to have a plan to deal with the material that is coming in.

3. Updating in the tagged language

Certain types of material in XML or SGML need to be constantly updated. Encyclopedias, almanacs, legal materials, and textbooks are prime examples. They need to be updated from edition to edition. The obvious way to do this is in a tagged language. If an XML database has been built with updating in mind, then tools are available to pull out sections of the text and update them. For this to work smoothly, authors need to be trained in working with structured languages. Currently this is only practical in organizations where all authors work within the system, or where an individual has been made responsible for checking materials before they go out for revisions and then carefully checking the materials before loading them back in. Even in organizations with tight internal control, it is not clear whether having authors working in tightly styled markup languages is the most effective use of their time.

4. Round-trip conversion

The alternative to training authors is *round-trip conversion*. This involves returning the XML or SGML to Microsoft Word (or other) format and sending it out to authors for revision. Although this sounds like the ideal solution, there are practical limitations. The major one is that since the word processor the author will be using will not have the constraints that a structured environment would impose, the authors could easily be damaging the XML coding. The following approach, used by Data Conversion Laboratory in a software application designed for legal publishing materials that continually needed to be updated, *partially* automated the process. As only small sections of a document needed to be updated, the SGML code was converted into WordPerfect (the word processor these authors were using) and the XML code was made invisible to the authors. When the authors sent their revisions back to the publishers, the software put the XML back where it belonged and displayed the changes for the editors to review. This method kept the XML code intact. A much simpler approach is to just reconvert the new articles as they come along. For most publications that rely on a constant stream of new materials this may be the right approach. However, if your publication is one in which the information is largely re-edited and recreated every year, providing some more robust process for outside authors may be worthwhile.

(iii) ISSUES SURROUNDING OTHER DATA SOURCES

As we've seen, incoming data is produced using many different tools, both electronic and manual. These tools generate data in various forms, each of which have inherent issues surrounding them when it comes to conversion.

1. PDF

Portable Document Format (***PDF***) is a print format and has not, typically, included any styling information. Unfortunately, people are often led to believe that PDF is a publishing format, and therefore it should be easy to convert PDF documents. In reality, PDF is more of a description of what the printed page looks like than a description of a document's original document structure. In fact, PDF is often referred to as "electronic paper," which is a pretty good name for it. It obviously has the formatting information to know that a certain line of type is 14-point Helvetica Bold and where that type is to appear on the page, but it doesn't know whether that line is a chapter title or a subhead, or what other lines go together with it to form a paragraph. Therefore, to do data conversion from PDF files you are forced to work out the meaning of styling and other elements solely from the look of the document.

There are additional conversion problems with PDF, the same ones as with print documents. Hyphens, for example, have two uses and are dealt with in two ways: a hard-hyphen joins two words together and is retained during conversion, whereas a soft-hyphen makes the page wrap in a uniform way and is removed. Sorting out these types of issues makes the conversion process more complex. A dictionary is often used to guess whether the hyphen belongs in the converted output, and it will guess wrong occasionally. In general, the kinds of things that are usually easy for a human to discern from a piece of paper, such as paragraph start and end, headers and footers, multicolumn text flows, complex tables, mathematical equations, paragraph headings, and footnotes, can be quite challenging for an automated tool. A PDF conversion tool has to be carefully tailored to the particular structures of the source PDF documents. And if the documents do not share a consistent appearance, the task becomes even more difficult.

Ideally, documents would be received in the form in which they were originally produced (e.g., word processor or publishing system) and not in PDF. That way, there would be some level of information to help automate the conversion. The further you get from the original document, the greater the information loss, which makes the conversion process more difficult and involved.

For the latest generation of PDF products, the preceding is no longer completely true. In Acrobat 5, Adobe introduced a concept called "tagged PDF," which allows software builders to enhance the PDF Writer module to output some level of structure information in the PDF document, so that it contains more than just page layout information. The latest version of Microsoft Word has some support for this, and other tool vendors have promised support for tagged PDF. Adobe would like to see this information added to as many software packages as possible, so that PDF documents can be more easily reflowed to fit the smaller screens of ***PDA***s, mobile phones, and other portable devices. As the support for a more structured PDF format grows, the task of converting PDF to other formats will become easier.

2. ASCII

ASCII documents are plain text documents that typically contain only those characters (characters from the standard ASCII character set) that can be typed from a standard computer keyboard, and as such, ASCII is the lowest common denominator among file formats. Most word processing and publishing systems include a way to "save as" ASCII text and import from ASCII. ASCII is most commonly seen in e-mails and in plain text newsletters or e-zines. ASCII is also found in legacy documents that were compiled over a decade ago, and files produced by text editing software are usually ASCII files. There is no styling or coding information at all—no bold, italics, underlining, table structures, or alignment information—just raw text. Material from ASCII sources is implicit. This means the material has to be either tagged by hand or run through software that can analyze what the tags should be by the look and location of the text.

In addition to the standard keyboard characters, which are mapped in ASCII to decimal values below 128, there are various flavors of what are typically referred to as extended ASCII character sets. In these extended ASCII sets, specific numeric values are used to represent certain nonkeyboard characters (such as the degree symbol and the cents sign). You will sometimes see various flavors of the "save as text" option in an authoring tool; this often allows you to specify the extended ASCII set to be used (e.g., Windows or MS-DOS). When you convert extended ASCII documents, you may need to account for the extended character mapping being used in order to properly perform the conversion.

Complex elements such as tables can be built using ASCII text, but it may need to be done manually. If a table is created in an ASCII document it is not a "real" table in the same way as one created in Word. The rows and columns are pieced together by measuring out spaces and lining up text manually, and sometimes making use of simple line draw characters from the keyboard (such as the underline and vertical bar). In order to turn handmade ASCII tables into material that can be used in an electronic publishing environment, all the appropriate information has to be inferred and inserted. Fortunately software is available that can do this. Products of this type count spaces and map out the "geography" of the page. The elements of this map can then be used as cues to identify tables and insert structural information.

Carriage returns (also called hard breaks) are also a problem in ASCII documents. They wrap the text at a set number of characters across the line (usually between 55 and 80) so it is easier to read. This means there is a carriage return after every line instead of after every paragraph, as is more usual. For conversion purposes all carriage returns that do not separate paragraphs need to be removed. This involves identifying where each paragraph ends, which is not easy when the last line of a paragraph stretches all the way to the right-hand margin. In that case, the only way to figure out where a paragraph ends is to read the document.

The fact is, unless explicit commands have been inserted into the text, as in the old XyWrite and troff languages, all information in ASCII documents is implicit and requires human input to decide what should become explicit. In some older proprietary word processing systems that did not contain powerful table editors, people would create "ASCII type" documents by using a mono spaced (or fixed width) font such as Courier typeface, where all of the characters, including lower- and upper-case letters and spaces, are the same width. This makes it easy to space over and create the look of tabular material. The same techniques need to be used when converting the inferred structures from these types of documents.

ASCII has historically been a popular interchange file format, but it is hoped that as XML continues to grow in popularity it will be used more frequently, as it allows for the interchange of not just the basic document text, but also representation of special characters, formatting, and structural information.

3. HTML

HTML is, technically, a very loose form of SGML, and as it is essentially a formatting code it includes few structural elements. Therefore, for conversion from HTML to be straightforward, styles such as the standard "heading 1," "heading 2," and "definition term" have to be used consistently. ***Cascading Style Sheets (CSS)***, a step up from standard HTML, brings HTML closer to SGML. Again, if used consistently, CSS can make the conversion process easier.

In practice, converting from HTML is often considerably more difficult than converting from more traditional publishing systems. This is because people want to give Web documents a sophisticated layout, and often the only way to do that within HTML is to align objects, such as navigational links, advertising, and text, or to simulate the look of multicolumn text, using HTML's fairly rich tabular structures. Of course, the documents will typically contain actual tables, often buried within these other "dummied up" tables (as HTML allows tables within tables). The result is that HTML documents are typically loaded with HTML tables that are not really tables in the publishing sense, and so the difficult part of a conversion from HTML is untangling the true tables from those that are being used to create a specific Web appearance. Like many other aspects of document conversion, if HTML documents are authored consistently, then performing legacy HTML conversion can be largely automated. But, unfortunately, consistency does not seem to occur very frequently in Web authored HTML documents, and so significant amounts of human intervention are often needed to aid in converting these documents to a more structured format.

5.4 THE CONVERSION PROCESS

Whether it is catalog assimilation for e-commerce or the conversion of scientific or technical documents, most large-scale document conversions fall victim to bad planning. This has unacceptable effects on schedule, quality, and costs. Therefore it is wise to have a definite plan. One of the most effective ways to do this is to divide the project life cycle into four phases:

1. Concept and planning
2. Proof of concept
3. Analysis, design, and engineering
4. Production

This four-phase plan ensures that potential problems are encountered and addressed early in the process. That way, the major issues involved in large-scale conversion are reliably dealt with and a project can be automated with greater accuracy.

(i) PHASE ONE: CONCEPT AND PLANNING

Although this is an important step, it doesn't have to be time consuming—not if you have thought everything through in detail. It may only take a few days (but is more likely to take several weeks).

What follows are the major elements of this phase.

1. Project concept

The first step is to clearly define the project and align people's expectations. At this point, the project concept is discussed at a high level, without getting bogged down in detail. Here are the critical questions to ask:

- What do you need to do and how quickly do you need to do it?
- Do you have in mind a particular technical approach?
- What are the goals and what are the success criteria?
- Which results are critical and which are nice to have?
- What is the expected budget? And what are the estimated costs?
- Where are the trade-offs in time, budget, and functionality?

The result of this analysis is a project concept document.

2. Materials evaluation

While a detailed inventory of materials would not usually be drawn up until the proof of concept phase, it is critical to get an early understanding of the project's scope. Design and implementation discussions on where best to focus resources will be based on this information. While the specific questions vary from project to project, typical questions are:

- How big is the project? (This needs to be quantified in terms you are used to thinking in—e.g., pages, books, journal issues, products.)
- What really needs to be converted? (Particularly for legacy materials, people often think in terms of "I need to convert it all." But in fact some materials might be obsolete, or not useful for other reasons, and may be left unconverted.)
- How much source variation is there? (Materials may have been produced in a multitude of electronic formats, on different operating systems, or by different typesetters. Some of it may be on paper, covered in dust, and stored in huge warehouses.)
- How much format variation is there? And how often has the layout format changed over the years? (Invariably, different authors choose different layouts. While it would be nice to have a strictly enforced template, if you are dealing with legacy data there will be a good deal of formatting inconsistency.)
- What are the special issues? (Tables, formulas, cross-referencing, and graphics are all areas that need special attention in the planning process.)

3. Rough-cut pricing estimate

Usually, there is not enough information available this early in the process to allow an accurate prediction of a project's overall production costs. There are simply too many variables that will not be finalized until well into phase two. However, it is possible (and useful) to start assembling rough-cut costing parameters. Rather than working with broad generalities, classify the material to be converted into categories, such as easy, medium, and difficult (or $2 pages, $5 pages, and $10 pages), and then estimate the volume of each. This approach will get you to a much closer estimate of the project's cost and also point to those areas where, if necessary, you can economize.

4. Project feasibility analysis

While the information collected so far is sketchy, it does offer an early opportunity to assess whether the project is still feasible. The following questions will need to be answered:

- If this is a million dollar project, does it still make good business sense to proceed?
- Is it possible to redefine the project's scope to reduce costs?
- Is there another way to do the project?
- Can certain elements be omitted to bring down cost? If so, does the project make sense at a reduced level?
- Most important, does it make sense to go on with phase two?

(ii) PHASE TWO: PROOF OF CONCEPT

The purpose of the proof of concept phase is to test, on a limited scale, the approach you have planned. It is an opportunity to examine the areas that were identified as being particularly risky, and to test on a small scale the hypothesis developed in phase one. The results of phase two will provide a more detailed plan that includes the following:

- Fleshed out functional requirements
- Preliminary software development
- A converted sample set
- More finely tuned cost projections

Depending on the size of the project, this phase usually takes three to ten weeks. It is well worth establishing a project timeline for this phase to ensure everything is accomplished on schedule.

The key stages and deliverables are described below.

1. Project initiation (week one)

Some kind of "kick-off" meeting is always a good idea. One of the main purposes of this meeting is to make sure that everyone on the team has the same understanding of the project concept. The team will likely include a project manager, domain expert, data analyst, programmer, and a senior editor. The project initiation is also where the detailed task plan is created and reviewed. The task plan helps ensure that everyone understands their role and responsibilities as a member of the team.

1. DEFINING THE SAMPLE SET

Important questions need to be answered in order to define the proof of concept. These include:

- What is to be proven?
- How big should the sample be? What is typical of the work to be done? What proportion of the material is typical?
- Which elements are known technology and therefore don't need to be part of this exercise?
- Which elements are risky or unknown and need special focus?

While there may be a tendency to try to do everything at once, or to do the easy parts first, the real purpose of this exercise is to focus on a small data set, and on the risky and unknown areas. Failure to identify where the project's critical challenges are could cause delays later, as these challenges tend to show up at the worst possible time.

The best way to avoid this is to focus on ten pages of difficult graphic references or complex tables, rather than hundreds of pages of straightforward or repetitive text. And if there are twenty major variations of material, don't try to analyze them all. Instead, pick the two or three that are most representative of the issues. On the other hand, don't fall into the trap of focusing only on the worst case—that will needlessly scare you—and lead you to assume that the project is much more difficult and expensive than it really need be. Having good information is the best defense.

2. Inventory of materials (middle of week one to week seven)

You need to have a good idea of the number of documents to be converted and the variability of them. The reason for this is that each type of material will likely require its own programming and conversion process. And while building software to help automate much of the conversion makes sense, you don't want to invest a lot of programming time automating for just a few pages of difficult material that can perhaps more efficiently be done by hand. While we like automation, it's not always the best solution.

3. Developing decision-making guidelines (week two to beginning of week three)

This is the heart of the proof of concept phase. The extent to which you can develop rules and guidelines for transforming your source materials into properly tagged data will be the most important determinant of the final cost of a project. Therefore, it needs to be handled with great care.

The domain expert and the data analyst will work closely together here to build a functional set of rules, endeavoring to generalize those rules and condense them into as small a set as possible.

4. Conversion specification document (week three to middle of week four)

It is helpful at this stage to formalize the various guidelines you've outlined into a single document. The *conversion specification document* will become a primary repository of project information. It will be continually consulted and reviewed by the end user, the domain expert, the analyst, and the programmer. The document expands the previously established guidelines into a set of rules that can be programmed for. It also identifies areas that are ambiguous and difficult to define; these areas will then need to be reviewed by the domain expert. The conversion specification document typically circulates among the various parties involved and becomes the central discussion document until issues are resolved. It is also the document that defines the programming efforts.

5. Proof of concept software and sample set conversion (week four to middle of week seven)

While most successful conversion projects combine automation with manual effort, programming should be done sparingly at this stage. There simply isn't time during the proof of concept to program for everything you might like. In addition, there will be a tendency to program for the easy things first. But the best way forward is to select a few complex elements that people doubt can be converted in an automated manner, then devise and test various programming approaches for those. This learning process will prove invaluable when you move on to phase three. For the rest of this phase, however, it is best to follow the conversion specification manually, rather than investing heavily in writing and testing programs.

The result of this phase will be a good sense of what can or should be automated, and what will need to be done manually, as well as some idea of the amount of time things will take.

6. Future phase planning and pricing (middle of week seven to week eight)

If everything has gone smoothly so far, you will now be able to more closely estimate the project's costs and schedule. As more materials are tested and converted in the next phase, these estimates will be refined. This phase is also the checkpoint at which to determine whether the project still makes sense. (This checkpoint lets you make a go/no-go decision based on the outcome of the proof of conversion.) The following questions are worth asking:

- Are the costs still in line with budget?
- Were we able to prove the concept that we came up with in the first phase?
- Are we getting the quality we expected?
- Was our original time estimate doable?

Deciding whether the project is feasible or not is a question of figuring out what the proof of concept has yielded.

(iii) PHASE THREE: ANALYSIS, DESIGN, AND ENGINEERING

Phase three is primarily a matter of refining the various deliverables done on the conversion sample for the fuller set of materials. You build on what was done during the proof of concept and expand the analysis, design, and engineering components. Additionally, you go back and program for all the things you did not have time for (or did not need to prove) during the proof of concept. Programming for gradual ramp up and full volume production processing will also be done at this point.

A typical timeline for this phase is shown in Table 3.

Key to phase three is planning for production, and the following sections highlight several key components of planning: process planning, quality planning, and production ramp up.

1. Production process planning

Integrating the various elements of the conversion process is too often an afterthought—which can be an expensive mistake. The most mundane things, such as agreeing upon file-name conventions and basic data trafficking procedures, are too often not properly planned in advance. Typically, a large conversion effort consists of between 30 and 50 independent steps requiring multiple skills, and often multiple vendors. There are also time dependencies that need to be integrated in order to ensure a smooth production flow.

In planning the production process, there are a number of important logistical considerations:

- How many pages a week can each step in the process handle?
- Can you keep up with reviewing and inspecting converted materials in the time frame they're being delivered?
- Technical questions will arise; will there be a dedicated point of contact between the conversion house and client?
- How will the materials be transported back and forth?

TABLE 3. PROJECT TIMELINE: ANALYSIS, DESIGN, AND ENGINEERING PHASE

Enhance and optimize software	Weeks 1 and 2
Knowledge transfer	Week 1
Modify decision-making guidelines	Middle of week 1 to week 2
Determine production sample	Middle of week 1 to middle of week 2
Refine conversion software	Weeks 3 to 5
Write specifications and convert sample	Weeks 3 to 5
Production planning	Weeks 4 to 6
Production engineering	Weeks 6 and 7
Production testing	Weeks 6 to 8

Another important question to ask is: how much time will it take?

Even with an ongoing production facility that handles thousands of pages a day, two to six weeks will still be needed for the integration to take place. Therefore it is wise to start early in phase three. And if you're going to be building a process from scratch, you should allow three to six months.

2. Production quality planning

While many of the standard quality-control processes apply to conversion projects, there is a significant difference. While a cookie factory can select its inputs, using only the choicest chocolate chips and finest flour, the conversion factory will typically need to deal with whatever comes. You can't really control your inputs very well. No matter how well you select your samples and trial materials, you are unlikely to test every significant variation. Many authors will have written the documents over a long period of time and at several locations. Plus many different editing packages will have been used on a variety of operating systems. So, like the people who created them, the documents will have personalities. And, like people, their behavior may not always be exemplary.

Ensuring quality control in this environment means building feedback loops at each step of the process. These checkpoints are designed to report when things are not meeting expectations—and provide guidelines, rather than rules, to the people inspecting the results. Information needs to flow back and forth easily in order to allow refinement of this process. You will also need to collect statistics so you can tell how much sampling will be needed as the process improves.

3. Production ramp up

Caution is crucial at this stage. The best approach is to plan for a few weeks of low-volume production through the initial production process. This helps identify any weaknesses in the process.

The entire production team needs to be aware that the purpose of the first weeks of production is to provide feedback in order to help engineer a smoother process. This is not yet the time to put dozens of people to work, but rather a time to assign a select few individuals who are capable of figuring out where improvements can be made.

(iv) PHASE FOUR: PRODUCTION

If you've done your job right in the preceding phases, then everything should be working smoothly now. But bear in mind that it is important to monitor results during the production process to make sure quality and productivity stay where they are expected to be.

Let's look at the various stages involved in the production process.

1. Full-volume production

Even after the production ramp-up stage, it is not necessarily prudent to plan for full production volumes immediately. It is best to gradually increase volumes, thereby allowing ample time for people to be trained and to come fully up to speed. Because you cannot totally control your inputs, it is likely that new issues may surface, even after production starts in earnest. It is critical for your feedback loops to be reporting on unexpected outcomes so that you continually refine and improve the process.

2. Production process control

A method to track production through the various phases will be needed. For smaller projects, Excel spreadsheets may be sufficient. But for larger projects, something more sophisticated will be required. At a minimum you need to know where in the process each batch of materials is, how long a batch is taking to go through, and how much material is awaiting each phase.

3. Materials trafficking

It is very rare that you have everything that needs conversion ready, in one pile, at the beginning of a project. More likely, materials will be readied gradually as the project progresses. In order to avoid slowdowns later in the process, someone needs to be in charge of trafficking the materials, making sure these are ready and complete, and forwarding them appropriately.

4. Process involvement feedback

When a project first goes into production, some elements will not be perfect. There will be room for improvement. Therefore you will need a method to formally collect information on exceptions and on what is not working properly. The method will need to be flexible, as different parts of the process will report exceptions at different times.

5. Packaging and delivery

This might seem elementary, but the finished materials have to be delivered to the right person. Clearly documenting what the materials are, how they are organized, and what is to be done with them can eliminate a lot of confusion and potential mishandling on the part of the recipient. This is also a convenient point to do some final quality checking and to document any specific procedures for the person you are delivering to.

6. Exception handling mechanisms

You will also need to allow for exception reporting—and deliver exception reports to the end user along with the completed data. Some documents, because of variations and inconsistencies, will inevitably need special handling by the recipient. It is wise to have a mechanism more sophisticated than yellow sticky notes.

(v) WHERE DO YOU GO FROM HERE?

1. The six keys to successful conversion

There has been a lot to absorb in this section. If you only take six things from what you have read, take the following:

1. *Don't just do it.* Figure out exactly what you want to accomplish before you start planning, then plan it before you do it.
2. *Project management and quality assurance are key issues.* To ensure that the project proceeds properly and on time, you'll need a dedicated team. Don't think of this as a part-time job; your critical team members need to be dedicated to the project.

3. *Communications are key.* The domain expert, the technical expert, and management all need to be on the same page.
4. *Select your sample set carefully.* It's better to pick 200 pages that are truly representative of the key issues than 5,000 pages on a hit or miss basis.
5. *Don't underestimate the value of a well-crafted production process.* Work through the details of the production process before you ramp up to volume processing.
6. *You'll need to be sure that it's working.* Build feedback loops into every step to monitor, control, and continually improve the production process.

5.5 ANALYSIS ISSUES

This section provides a brief discussion of some key items that should be on your analysis checklist.

(i) TEXT AND CHARACTERS

Although converting text characters is usually not considered to be the major issue in document conversion, there are some pitfalls. When users publish to paper, they sometimes take shortcuts that allow the document to print properly, but are not logically correct. For instance, documents can sometimes contain hard hyphens (instead of conditional hyphens) at the end of a line or a page. These are problematic when converted to a newer electronic format, as the conversion software has no definitive way to know whether the hyphen should remain. Even "normal text" can sometimes be problematic—certain tools produce ligatures for certain character combinations (e.g., "fi" and "fl"), which appear in the source document as a reference to a special font and character (which actually produces the ligature). In those cases, it will be necessary to deal specially with the font and character information in the source document to convert even basic text.

1. Fonts, special character encoding, Unicode

Depending on the target publishing format, issues related to fonts and special characters may or may not be a problem. For instance, if the source system used a particular set of fonts and the target publishing environment continues to use the same set of fonts, this will not be an issue. If the documents are being converted to structured markup, on the other hand, then nonkeyboard characters are typically converted to ISO-standard SGML and XML character sets—which can prove challenging. This is because in order to publish a specific special character in a modern publishing tool, you can simply use any available font (or even have one custom produced) and select from that font set. Part of the conversion effort involves examining the fonts being used, to determine if they are being used for their appearance (as is typically the case) or for certain special characters that are required. This could mean a significant analysis effort, examining the source document's fonts. Luckily, standard special characters are available in base character sets as well as the symbol font, so when only those characters are used, the mapping might have already been done.

The issue of converting specific symbol fonts should be made easier in the future by the use of ***Unicode***. Unicode is an attempt to put all types of special characters and foreign alphabets into one standard grouping so that all documents would, for instance, use the same representation of a dagger ("†"), a Greek Beta("β"), or a copyright symbol ("©"). Gone would be the need to determine special character mappings.

Another issue related to the conversion of fonts is that of using fonts for emphasis. Emphasis (e.g., bold, italic, bold and italic) usually needs to be maintained in the target document. Typically, a user turns emphasis on and off inside of a document directly, and that information is maintained in the document structure. In some cases, however, the user may select an "emphasized" version of a font, rather than simply turning emphasis on within a font. For instance, if the base font is Helvetica, he or she may select the Helvetica Bold font for emphasis. In such a case, it is important to note during the conversion analysis that font changes may actually mean changes in emphasis. And sometimes, those emphasized words and phrases are italicized or bolded because they have certain meanings—for example, book titles, genus and species, case citations—which may warrant special tagging that only someone understanding the content can determine.

2. Accents and diacritics

Some publishing systems support diacritic and other accent marks for any character. This often leads to situations where there is no equivalent character available in the target system (either in a new font or an ISO character entity). Either new characters need to be composed, or in some situations where this is not possible (or practical), these composite characters may need to be rendered as graphics. As more systems are based on Unicode (as current versions of Word are), and as XML becomes more pervasive, this problem will be reduced.

3. Non-Latin alphabets

Converting non-Latin alphabets has historically been a difficult task. This is because different publishing tools have had different ways of representing this information. On top of this, many foreign alphabets contain thousands of unique characters. Again, the use of Unicode will (hopefully) make conversion of these foreign character sets simpler.

(ii) TAGGING OF PARAGRAPHS AND HEADS

Although identifying paragraphs and heading levels is usually the easy part of a conversion, some questions need to be asked:

- Are paragraphs and heads tagged properly or do you have to guess from their appearance?
- Is the scheme consistent from article-to-article or chapter-to-chapter?
- What is the procedure when a head level is skipped?
- What is the procedure when different chapters have different levels of granularity?

(iii) CROSS-REFERENCES AND LINKING

One of the most useful aspects of document conversion is adding cross-reference linking. This is because modern publishing systems can turn these references into hyperlinks, thereby allowing users to quickly and automatically navigate a document. In typical documents that were produced for paper-only publishing, these potential links are usually done manually and therefore part of the task in a conversion effort is to add proper linking information.

Since cross-references typically follow a pattern, you can expect to be able to automatically convert most cross-references through software. However, some will not be caught, so a manual review will be necessary. For example, "see Table 3" or "see Figures 4 to 6" or even "see Figures 3, 4, and 5" can likely be converted to proper links via software, but "see Figures 3, 4, and the last part of 5" is not so simple. Although a human being may have an easy time knowing that "5" is a figure number, that's not the case for software. For example, the phrase "see Chapter 3 in handbook" may incorrectly result in a link to Chapter 3 of this publication, *not* the handbook (as was intended by the author).

There are also phrases that can be used in paper-based publishing, such as "see bottom of page" or "see below," that are best removed from an electronic repurposable version of a document. Concepts like a "page" or "above" and "below" do not necessarily apply in the same way. Again, some of these patterns can be caught in software, while others need to get caught the old-fashioned way—by reading the document.

(iv) LISTS

Structured documents often require that lists, both numbered and unnumbered, be tagged as such. Numbered (or lettered) lists are usually easier to identify, because of the sequential nature of what typically appears in the legacy documents. Unnumbered lists, particularly those that do not contain a leading character such as a bullet or a dash, are harder to differentiate and often require human intervention. In addition, authors often use multiple columns and tabbing to make a list occupy less space on paper, and these are the sorts of lists that need to be unwound for structured markup. But they are not always easy to recognize (e.g., as a list, not a table) and untangle (the list may be meant to be read down each column, or across each row and then down, which affects the true order of the list).

Another common challenge in technical repair manuals is that the markup for these types of manuals often requires differentiation between "lists" and "steps," where steps are defined as a sequence of sequential actions that need to be taken. For example, a list of tools needed, such as (1) hammer, (2) screwdriver, (3) pliers, etc., is not the same as a series of steps, such as (1) Remove the locking screw; (2) Open the compartment door; (3) Check the battery. Keywords can often be used to identify lists that need to be turned into steps, but the converted output needs to be checked carefully for errors.

(v) TABLES

Accurate table conversion is one of the most critical, complex, and laborious aspects of a document conversion. A proper representation of a table will include, among other properties, proper cell and row identification, vertical and horizontal alignment, separators, spanning, and differentiation of header and body rows. As with most other aspects of document conversion, what will exist in the source document can vary widely from project to project.

If the source document format contained table-editing facilities, and the document creators used the feature properly, then the conversion is often a matter of converting all of the attributes of the source documents into equivalent attributes of the target format. However, many documents were originally created in systems where full table-editing facilities did not exist (or where the users didn't know how to use them). Tabular information would typically have been formatted using tabs, lines, and spaces. In cases like that the conversion software needs to "guess" the structure of the table (or even what is in fact meant to be a table), making use of visible clues, such as the placement of lines, and the layout of the text. As tables can be very complex, and sometimes even a human being may have trouble determining the intent of the author in terms of what constitutes columns and rows, the act of guessing will typically not produce accurate results—and a manual effort will be necessary to correct errors. Even determining that something is in fact a table is not always easy, and it is sometimes necessary to have a premarkup stage for tables (and perhaps the number of columns in the table) to assist conversion software in performing the task of decomposing a table structure.

And because, as mentioned previously, some modern digital publishing systems do not contain built-in table-editing facilities, many documents that have been published recently contain tables simulated with lines and tabs, and will need to go through the process of inferring document structure. In addition, even when using publishing systems that contain full table-editing capabilities, authors often use tabs (either because of lack of expertise in the publishing software or because they're simply doing a table "quick and dirty"), and so this same process will be required.

(vi) GRAPHICS

Published documents include two basic types of graphics. One type is typically referred to as ***raster***, and contains representations of each of the "dots" (also referred to as pixels) that comprise the graphic. (These are also sometimes referred to as "bit maps.") Scanners and digital cameras produce raster graphics, and photo editing and picture cleanup software such as Adobe Photoshop and Corel Photo-Paint use raster graphics. The other type is usually referred to as ***vector***, and contains information about the individual "objects" that comprise a drawing. A drawing of an automobile, for example, would be represented in a vector graphic as a grouping of information about the lines, curves, text, colors, and shadings that comprise the drawing. Drawing and illustration programs such as Adobe IllustratorAutoCAD, and CorelDRAW are examples of programs that manipulate these vector drawings.

The chapter on composition and graphics discusses these **graphics formats** [6.8] in some depth. Since the two ways of representing a graphic are so different, the conversion issues involved are also quite different.

1. Raster

Many formats exist to represent a raster graphic, among them ***TIFF***, ***PCX***, ***GIF***, and ***JPEG***. Since a raster graphic essentially represents an image as a series of dots, converting a raster graphic from one format to another is a straightforward process—you can use any of a number of conversion programs. However, the image conversion may not simply involve a format translation; it may also involve changing the dimensions of the image, as well as the number of colors and color model used in the image. Raster conversions use different ***algorithms*** that have been invented to perform these tasks, and they can dramatically affect the resulting converted image. It is therefore important to test conversions to determine what best suits the particular needs of a project.

It is also important to understand that some raster image formats are known as "lossless," as they accurately represent every dot in the image. ***TIFF*** and ***PCX***, for example, are lossless formats, and you could convert an image back and forth between the two formats without any loss of image quality. Other image formats are known as "lossy," and do not represent every pixel in the source graphic. Rather, they use various methods to represent transitions of parts of the graphic. The ***JPEG*** format is the best known of these lossy formats. It is a format that works very well on photographs, in that it compresses a large amount of graphic information into a small amount of file space. However, with these lossy formats, each conversion of a graphic loses some of the quality of the original image. So care should be taken in using them, and in doing multiple conversions.

2. Vector

Since vector graphics contain the image, not as a series of dots, but as a series of objects that represent the image, and different sets of objects are likely to be used by different software packages, conversion from one vector format to another is very difficult. There are many aspects to a vector drawing, and if any one of them is not converted properly, the converted graphic will not be correct (think, for instance, of a map that contains thousands of lines and text; if some of the text is not placed in exactly the right location on the map, the result will be useless).

Each of the popular drawing tools typically uses its own file format, so converting vector graphics often becomes necessary as part of a document conversion. Many of these drawing programs have import filters that will convert other vector formats into their own. Third-party vector conversion filters can also be used for converting vector images. However, because of the complexity of vector conversion, the converted images will not necessarily be perfect and may require significant cleanup (or it may be easier to redraw an image). If you will not be editing an image, it may be best to use a rasterized or ***Encapsulated PostScript (EPS)*** version of the image in the target documents. Then, only when a particular drawing needs to be modified will cleanup be a necessary step.

(vii) INDEXES

Full-text search is an important way to get around electronic documents, but it is still useful to have the equivalent of a traditional printed book index. These tend to incorporate the editor's knowledge of the materials and point a user most directly to the sought-after information. The conversion problem is that indexes usually refer to page numbers that will not necessarily exist in the electronic product.

True, some publishing packages have provisions for supplying index information, so that a paper index can be autogenerated. In these cases, the conversion is typically straightforward since the index information points to an exact location, rather than providing a page number.

However, in most cases, the index will be converted from the information contained within a typical paper index, wherein the key term is followed by a series of page numbers (or ranges of page numbers). Converting this form of index to an electronic one involves some significant challenges, since the pages referred to in the paper index are an artifact of the original paper layout of the publication, and not necessarily relevant in a more modern repurposable document. Ideally, in an electronic index (as in the one created for this Guide), the user could click on an index entry and be taken to the exact location in the document that the indexer intended. This can present a significant challenge if the original index simply contains a page number, not a specific location. Text matching software can be used to try to locate the correct location of as many index terms as possible, but a significant percentage of entries will require manual intervention to determine an exact location—which, for a large index, can be costly. Often, the index term does not appear in the text at all, or in the same form.

Another (less costly) possibility might be to retain original page break information in the converted document, which would allow the user to click on an index term and be taken to the beginning of a specific page. This may be a problem, however, because a physical page may contain more than one "logical unit." For example, in an encyclopedia a page may contain several distinct articles. Taking a user to the top of a page may not be effective—the top of the page may be a completely different article than what the author intended. In such an instance, a compromise might be to provide index links to the top of an appropriate logical unit (e.g., an article or section). If that is acceptable, it will only be necessary to resolve those index entries that refer to pages that contain more than one logical unit.

(viii) BIBLIOGRAPHIC INFORMATION

Scholarly publications and textbooks are typically heavily loaded with bibliographic information. Conversion to a structured environment often involves decomposition of bibliographic entries into their individual logical components, such as article title, author, publisher, and date. (Having these components coded enables electronic systems to "recognize" the cited work, often providing a link to it.) When performing an electronic conversion, depending on the consistency of the source bibliographic information, many of these entries will be readily convertible using software. Journal references, for instance, are normally consistent and can be decomposed in this way. However, other types of references, such as to conference proceedings and books, are often done in a much looser format and decomposing them requires a fairly high degree of manual intervention.

Another difficult area is references to bibliographic entries. A typical article can contain hundreds of these. They are usually created using numeric ***identifiers*** (with a number typically superscripted or put into brackets), or with what are dubbed "Harvard" references, which place the names of authors and the year of publication in parentheses. Both types of references can be automated to a certain extent. But like other instances of information inference, they require manual review and repair.

(ix) FOOTNOTES

Modern publishing systems represent footnotes and endnotes in a logical way, which makes the conversion process straightforward. However, many documents contain footnotes created with "brute force" (for example, a superscripted 1) and these would ideally be converted to a proper link to the footnote. Again, this can be accomplished using software, but requires manual review because of potential errors (for example, if you convert all superscripted 2s to a footnote reference to footnote number 2, you may turn the superscripted 2 of $E=MC^2$ into a reference to footnote 2).

(x) MATH

Math and equations can be represented in many ways, and publishing tools have their own way of dealing with them. Some even come with an equation-editing tool. As with vector graphics, rendering of equations is a complex procedure. Tools do exist that convert equations from one format to another. But the results are rarely perfect and a significant amount of time is usually spent cleaning up complex mathematical equations. Common solutions for dealing with math in XML include incorporating the original math that was created using a specialized language like TeX, converting the equations to the ***MathML*** XML mathematics markup language, or simply incorporating the math as graphic elements within the XML.

5.6 SUMMING UP

Conversion professionals frequently get asked: "So once I get through all this, that's it—I'm done—right?" The answer is, "probably not." The bar has been steadily rising ever since Gutenberg invented the printing press, and it's likely that the world has not yet run out of new and creative ideas for using and delivering information. It's likely that the really interesting things we'll be doing five years from now have not been thought of yet. Which means that the data structures to support them may not have been thought of either.

So where does that leave you?

The fact that you're considering a conversion effort probably means that at some level you see benefits—reduced costs, new customers, faster throughput, and so on. The classic cost-benefit analysis should tell you how soon you'll see the benefits.

But the decision to go ahead is then complicated by the following factors:

- The long-term value of your investment. Will XML be made obsolete by something else? The answer to that is—maybe. A lot of "ultimate" solutions get replaced over time. Even so, it's unlikely that something new will be radically different. XML is an end point (although possibly only a temporary end point) in the separation of content from structure. The process is likely to be refined, but so long as your materials are properly structured, future conversion efforts to new or refined languages will be much easier.
- The cost of not doing anything. Can you really afford to wait? Moving your data into a more flexible structured format gives you new opportunities and new ways of distributing your content. What's the cost of not having that capability?
- What if it doesn't work? That's a real concern. You need to figure out how far ahead of the technology curve you want to be. Unless you have some very specific and unusual problems to solve, you should be able to find proven technologies that can limit risks to just a few areas. Of course, you should always have a plan B.

None of this is cut and dried, you say. Wouldn't it make more sense to wait until everything settles out? Probably not. There's just too much to lose by not keeping up. But you should tread carefully. We're currently living in a pivotal time in business. So you need to research and consult the good advisors (ask around to find these) to help you make the right decision. Once you are sure and have decided to take the plunge, converting to XML or other structured computer language will, in the long run, bring rewards on many levels.

Composition, Design, & Graphics

THAD MCILROY
President, Arcadia House
With contributions by Frank Romano, Professor, Rochester Institute of Technology

Publishing in the digital era, to an overwhelming degree, still means publishing in print. More often than not what is published electronically today first started as print. While much of the energy in digital publishing has shifted to the electronic conveyance and display of information, the bulk of the economic activity still centers on print-based publishing. Electronic publishing is the future of the industry, but print publishing pays today's bills. Today's digital tools, technologies, and techniques are as often used in print as in electronic publishing. Mastering print publishing demands knowledge of a broad range of processes and technologies surrounding composition, design, and graphics. Print publishing has reached the intersection of 500 years of analog craft and a new era in digital computer graphics. Publishing practitioners require an appreciation of both. This chapter is a broad overview of the processes and technologies that comprise the practice of print publishing in the era of digital publishing. We focus on the digital technologies that are moving the process forward into the future, and the traditional craft-based skills still important in the digital era that optimize quality in everyday work.

6.1 OVERVIEW

When desktop publishing was launched into the world in 1984 it contained the shock of the new, and we thought we were witnessing a revolution. It was only later, when things settled down a little, that we could see that all we had achieved was the digitization of analog processes. We were still doing the same things for the same reasons, but with different tools; nothing had really changed.

Printing has always been about trickery, and it still is. We go to great lengths to make continuous tone photographs into apparently random dot patterns, so that ink can be adhered onto paper in a way that fools the eye into seeing something that isn't really there. Color is itself an illusion, light reflected off printed surfaces in such a way that the eye and the brain perceive color. In electronic publishing, the processes are different but the point's the same: to make the medium disappear; to help the viewer see the image and the color, not the mechanism behind them.

In typography, the trick is to make the type invisible. The apex of the typographers' achievement is putting words on paper or on a screen in such a way that the reader won't even think about the process of reading them. They won't *see* the type.

But desktop publishing has clearly changed the process of publishing. Back in 1984 publishing processes were analog—done not on a computer, but mostly by hand. Portions of the process were digital—some of the typesetting and the color reproduction—but the most important work involved craftspeople making judgments based on years of working experience.

The impact of the desktop publishing revolution was to greatly increase the level of digitization in the graphic arts industries, while at the same time making the digital tools simpler and more affordable. The goal of digitization is always the reduction of process time and cost and this can only be achieved by making the process less complex and more automatic. Today publishing enjoys a degree of digitization that was unthinkable two decades ago, and works at higher speeds and lower costs than ever before. But digitization has not yet made publishing totally automatic, or freed it from the judgment of skilled craftspeople.

The traditional skills of the graphic arts technician, based on a fine appreciation of image reproduction, are now supplemented by the skills of the digital technician, familiar with the arcana of software, operating systems, and computer graphics. While a few parts of the publishing process have been "deskilled" and rendered automatic by software, at the same time, the details of digitization place enormous new demands on the publishing practitioner. To be a skilled production technician today is probably more demanding than it ever was.

This chapter reviews the science and craft involved in reproducing images, particularly on paper. We recognize that in today's cross-media world, ink on paper may be just one instance of an image or a document, and not even necessarily the most important one. But print remains a unique and compelling medium. We believe that mastering the complexities of image reproduction on paper will be important to publishers for many years to come.

6.2 TEXT, GRAPHICS, AND PAGE LAYOUT: THE THREE ELEMENTS OF A PAGE

When a reader looks at a page in a book or magazine he can easily see words and images. But he doesn't make the kinds of linear distinctions required of electronic publishers. For publishers every page is composed of text and/or graphics, each positioned by the designer in a geometrically pleasing arrangement.

On the computer the data that represents a page derives from each of these elements: ***text***, ***graphics***, and ***page layout geometry***. Pages are built in a page layout file, in which the text and graphics are positioned. The text is usually flowed into the page from a word processing program. Graphics are also brought directly into the page from files created in drawing or photo software.

To discuss graphics we have to look at all three of these elements. We have to understand them individually, and then see how they merge into the final publishing data.

6.3 DESIGN VS. PRODUCTION

One of the by-products of the digital publishing revolution has been a blurring of the distinction between the role of design and the role of production. Before the advent of digital production these roles were kept quite distinct. Designers worked with pen and paper to create the broad outlines of a page design. Typographic specifications were rendered by hand. Type was set by dedicated firms with sophisticated typesetting devices, proofread in ***galleys***, corrected, reset, and then pasted up by hand from galleys on to the finished page. ***Halftone images*** were photographed with special cameras, then stripped into the final page either in positive or negative form.

Typesetting was a specialized trade, as was "stripping," with its associated skills of ***trapping*** and page ***imposition***.

Desktop publishing brought all of these capabilities to desktop computers. Most designers today have taken on at least the role of the typesetter and the stripper, and they sometimes handle trapping and imposition as well. The roles of design and production are now intersecting and overlapping. The debate continues as to whether certain tasks are best left to the printer, and designers have differing viewpoints. We will play a neutral role in this chapter and describe all of the tasks that are involved in page production, leaving it to the reader to decide where the lines should be drawn.

6.4 THREE KEY TECHNOLOGIES

Along with the three elements of the page, there are three key technologies that when launched in the mid-1980s enabled the current practice of digitized publishing. It's impossible to imagine publishing today without them.

The first is the Macintosh personal computer. There were popular personal computers before the Macintosh, but the Macintosh was the first popular what-you-see-is-what-you-get (***WYSIWYG***) computer. For the first time designers and publishers could preview their work on an affordable home computer. By introducing desktop publishing on the Macintosh, Apple Computer created a loyal group of users that after nearly two decades would still rather fight than switch. The Macintosh remains the electronic publishing standard, controlling as much as 90 percent of the professional graphics production market.

The second technology was the laser printer. Having a fast, high-quality, and (relatively) inexpensive proofing device was essential to reassuring users that what they saw on the screen really would be what they got in print.

The third technology was ***PostScript***, a page description language designed specifically for the output of high-quality graphics from a desktop computer.

6.5 POSTSCRIPT: THE LANGUAGE OF PRINT PUBLISHING

In 1982 Charles Geschke and John Warnock left Xerox PARC (the Palo Alto Research Center) and cofounded Adobe Systems. Their original plan was to build a dedicated publishing workstation. This hardware would have required a ***page description language (PDL)***, they realized nearly as an afterthought, a *postscript* to the hardware system. They developed PostScript for that purpose, building on the work they had done on Xerox's PDL, Interpress.

Apple Computer was an early investor in Adobe, and company president Steve Jobs convinced Warnock and Geschke to create a version of PostScript for the Apple LaserWriter, released in 1985. Aldus released PageMaker page makeup software the same year, and desktop publishing took off. Around the same time Linotype licensed PostScript as an option for its Linotronic series of typesetters, giving PostScript an opportunity to prove itself for professional high-end graphics.

It's hard now to appreciate the original impact of desktop publishing on the graphic arts market. In 1985 the market was controlled by a range of vendors offering proprietary typesetting and color scanning systems. Complete page layout was not yet common—most pages were assembled by hand. Each of the available systems spoke a separate language, and used file formats unique to that system.

PostScript changed digital imaging in several important respects:

1. PostScript describes text, graphics, *and* entire pages, where most computer graphics languages of that period described just text, graphics, *or* page geometry.

2. PostScript is device-independent, designed to work with a wide range of output devices, at any resolution. Any manufacturer could license PostScript and build an interpreter to drive an output device. The output from each device would appear essentially identical, except for any unique characteristics of that device.
3. Adobe made the specifications of the PostScript language publicly available and encouraged software companies to support it.
4. From the earliest days of PostScript, Adobe recognized the value of fine typography. It licensed high-quality typefaces from the best foundries and built technology supporting quality typography into PostScript as well as the software and operating systems that supported it.

(i) COMPETITION

PostScript is not the only page description language available. IBM uses Advanced Function Presentation (***AFP***) in many of its large-scale printing systems; Hewlett-Packard uses Printer Control Language (***PCL***,also known as HP-PCL) in many of its printers; Xerox still supports Interpress in some of its office printers; and there are others. But PostScript drives nearly all of the professional graphics market. (Interestingly, Warnock and Geschke both worked on the Interpress project at Xerox PARC, and cite Xerox's failure to commercialize the product as their main reason for leaving Xerox to found Adobe Systems.)

Adobe Systems is not the only company offering PostScript. By making the PostScript specifications public Adobe was able to build a huge market for PostScript, but it also created competition, from companies such as Oak Technology and Peerless Systems. While Adobe remains the keeper of the PostScript standard, PostScript revenues are an ever-decreasing part of its business.

(ii) TECHNICAL ASPECTS

PostScript is a programming language with powerful graphics, text, and image capabilities. It utilizes a series of operators, dictionaries, arrays, stacks, paths, a coordinate system, and more to describe bitmap and vector images and text and page layouts.

PostScript is a text-based language. There are no pictures to see when you examine PostScript data. Bitmaps and vectors are converted into text coding along with font information, object location, color characteristics, page size, and so on.

PostScript is a device-independent language—independent of any one particular output device, and functioning similarly on all that support it.

When you create a page in QuarkXPress or Adobe PageMaker, you are interfacing with the program as displayed on the screen. Underlying what you see is what you get, and that is PostScript code. When you click "print," it is the PostScript code that is sent to the printer or imagesetter, not a QuarkXPress file.

After the PostScript has been generated it can be saved for later processing, but usually the code proceeds directly to the raster image processor (***RIP***). The RIP first translates the PostScript code into an intermediate format called the display list. The display list contains a simplified description of the page, specified as a series of objects. Instead of using points or inches, all objects in the display list are positioned in device pixels. When the display list is completed, the RIP creates a bitmap of the page and sends it to the output device. ***Screen angles***, ***screening algorithms***, ***trapping***, ***separations***, and many other functions can be embedded within PostScript and control various options upon output.

Depending on the configuration of the printing system, a RIP can be a physical chip residing inside of a laser or inkjet printer. It can also be a separate and proprietary piece of hardware connected to the printer or a software RIP running on a desktop computer.

(iii) POSTSCRIPT VERSIONS

The first version of the PostScript language was just called "PostScript." "Level 1" was added later to differentiate it when the Level 2 upgrade was announced (1990). In 1998, Adobe upgraded the language to PostScript 3 (not "Level 3"). In the past some users faced compatibility issues around the different versions of PostScript—for example, a file containing PostScript 3 data would fail to pass a Level 2 RIP. The issue is muted today, perhaps until the introduction of PostScript 4.

(iv) TYPE IN POSTSCRIPT

A key innovation of PostScript is its ability to control high-quality type. We consider this below in the broader context of **typography** [6.7] in digital publishing.

6.6 PDF — ADOBE'S PORTABLE DOCUMENT FORMAT

PostScript is a powerful programming language for text and graphics, but it has real drawbacks in digital publishing. The language itself is too complex for the average user to program or to edit. There is no standard way to view a PostScript file on a computer. Adobe tried to address this problem with a PostScript variant called Display PostScript, but it never caught on with most computer manufacturers or software developers. In searching for ways to make PostScript more accessible and predictable, Adobe developed PDF, the Portable Document Format.

The Adobe ***PDF*** is a file format for representing documents independently of the software, hardware, and operating system used to create them and also independently of the output device on which they're to be displayed or printed. PDFs are created and viewed using Adobe's ***Acrobat*** software (as well as other third-party software).

PDF and PostScript share the same underlying imaging model. Like PostScript, PDF is a page description language: a language for describing the graphical appearance of pages with respect to an imaging model. A document can be converted easily between PDF and the PostScript language; the two representations will produce the same output when printed. PDF is in some respects an alternate version of the PostScript file format.

There are important differences, though. While PostScript includes a general-purpose programming language framework not present in PDF, PDF has a plethora of user-accessible features not available in PostScript, such as the ability to annotate, alter, and navigate. And whereas a PostScript file has to be interpreted as a whole (because information required on page five may be embedded in page one—fonts, for example), a PDF file is "page independent" because any component page can be interpreted by itself without reference to other parts of the file. PDF is also used in many nonprint contexts, such as viewing pages over the Web or in e-books.

While application programs like QuarkXPress could theoretically describe any page as a full-resolution pixel array, the resulting file would be bulky and device-dependent. A high-level imaging model like PDF or PostScript enables applications to describe the appearance of pages containing text, colors, graphical shapes, and sampled images in terms of abstract graphical elements (called "objects") rather than directly in terms of device pixels. Compact Adobe PDF files are smaller than their source files, and can be downloaded a page at a time for fast display on the Web.

In addition to describing the static appearance of pages, a PDF document can contain interactive elements that are available only in an electronic representation of the file. PDF supports annotations of many kinds: text notes, hypertext links, markup, file attachments, sounds, and movies. A document can define its own user interface; keyboard and mouse input can trigger actions that are specified by PDF objects (so that an element on a page can be turned into a link or a button, for example). A PDF file can also contain interactive form fields to be filled in by the user, and can import the values of these fields from or export them to other applications.

It is also possible to embed structural tagging (such as XML) inside a PDF file, generally based on the styles used to create the pages in certain application programs. This is useful for marking the different elements on a page in order to handle them differently in different display contexts. Tagged PDF became especially important when Adobe gave PDF pages the ability to "reflow." Keep in mind that since PDF is a page-oriented technology, it doesn't reflow text *between* pages, as a page layout program does, but it can reflow text *within* a page. This is especially useful for viewing PDF pages on small screens like PDAs. (In effect, the pages become taller and thinner.) The ability to embed structural markup in the PDF enables elements like text paragraphs to reflow to fit the smaller screen while keeping such things as subheads from reflowing too.

Adobe PDF files can be published and distributed anywhere: in print, attached to e-mail, on corporate servers, posted on Web sites, or on CD-ROM. Adobe's free ***Acrobat Reader*** software is easy to download from the Adobe Web site. More than 300 million copies have been distributed worldwide.

Adobe PDF is fast becoming the workflow standard in the graphic arts industry. It also plays an increasing role in financial services, regulated industries, and government.

PDF's role in print publishing presents a fascinating anomaly. Originally designed purely as an electronic format (intended mainly to enable office workers to exchange memos and letters and spreadsheets between unrelated computers), it found some of its first and biggest adherents among print publishers attracted to its compactness, integrity, and relative reliability. As HTML use exploded on the Web, PDF suddenly seemed too tightly controlled and a tad overweight in the free-form world of (loosely) structured text tagging. But with each new release of the software more and more of PDF's inherent strengths shone through, and adoption expanded. By version 4 of Acrobat, PDF had reached a kind of critical mass.

Ironically PDF's huge success as an electronic document format is clearly related to its familiarity and comfort for a generation raised on print documents. Rob Enderle, a Research Fellow at Giga Information Group, called PDF the perfect "tweener format"—appealing to publishers in between the all-paper generation and the upcoming all- (or mostly all-) electronic generation. PDF files can offer most of the attributes of paper documents—page structure, elaborate graphics, and meticulous design—along with a host of extra features that can only work electronically.

Different features appeal to different users and markets. Some people like PDF as a presentation format—it's interactive, and you can incorporate bullet text along with moving images and sound. Some favor its collaboration features—documents can be restructured, annotated, and edited as they pass among a workgroup. Since the implementation of Section 508 legislation, Adobe is pushing PDF as a key platform for document accessibility (see the chapter on **accessibility** [7.2.1.4]). PDF is also a leading forms application supporting digital signatures, a key feature advancing the electronic document revolution. One of the leading e-book formats—the Adobe Acrobat eBook—is also PDF-based; its appeal is that the e-book pages and the print pages can look absolutely identical (although they don't have to).

PDF workflows in the graphic arts are explained in the section titled **PDF and prepress workflows** [6.12.11] below.

6.7 TYPOGRAPHY

Typography is the arrangement of letters and spaces on a surface, whether it's on paper or on a monitor, to communicate information and facilitate understanding. Typographers look at letters and their shapes and forms and color when combined into words and pages and documents, and think about their history and their future. Typesetters are tradespeople who set type for publication. While typography has remained a viable profession in the age of digital publishing, the task of typesetting now falls often upon the designer and the publisher.

Type today is still based on early typefaces, which were in turn modeled after calligraphic lettering in manuscripts, and much of the terminology we use in the digital era traces back to type's early history. Print began as chunks of metal, when Johannes Gutenberg invented movable type. The pieces of type were kept in large cases with compartments for each letter, called typecases. The lower part of the typecase held the lowercase letters, while the upper part held the capital letters (in the upper case). Letters, or symbols could be selected and placed next to each other in a type stick or composing stick, and a thin piece of lead was placed on top as a line spacer when the line was complete. The lines were then transferred to a larger type tray called a chase, and this was repeated until a complete page was assembled, made up of thousands of pieces of metal.

Points were used to measure the length of each metal chunk of type. For example, a 72-point H, in metal type, is a character cast on a metal block, and the block's top surface or typeface is exactly 72 points (one inch) in height. The actual character when printed will usually be smaller than the overall size of the metal, which is necessary because of the ascenders and descenders. In order for the type to line up squarely, each character must be cast onto the metal blocks, which are large enough to allow the ascenders and descenders to project above and below the baseline. In the end, all the characters end up being the same height, which determines the point size of the typeface.

In the 19th century inventors set about finding a way to create a machine that would set type automatically. Many machines were created with the intention to replace hand typesetting—the first was by Dr. William Church, in 1822. None were built well enough to stand up to commercial work until 1886 with the invention of the Linotype by Ottmar Mergenthaler. The basis of the Linotype was to set a single line at one time.

In 1887, the Monotype was invented by Tolbert Lanston. This machine was made of two parts, a keyboard and a caster. Each letter was cast separately, and justified (spaced) manually. When a key was tapped, it perforated a paper ribbon with a coded pattern of holes. Once the ribbon was punched, it was placed on the caster and compressed air was passed through the holes to position a case containing matrices over a mold. The combinations of punched holes positioned the case to cast a specific letter, and to adjust the mold width to suit the unit width of the character. Each character was cast, and delivered into a tray. (This was in fact a digital process. Those punched holes are the ancestors of the ones and zeros in the coding we use today.)

Over time, metal type faded away and methods for creating type on film—photographic typesetting—became possible. Photographic typesetting first used outlines of typefaces in different styles and sizes—an analog technique. Later, type for digital output was stored as bitmaps (sets of dots) or vectors (mathematical descriptions of the outlines) for each typeface and point size.

Some designers have more typefaces installed on a single computer today than even existed 20 years ago. Quantity doesn't imply quality, however, and there's an awful lot of junk type floating around on computers and available for free on the Internet.

The word "font" as it's currently used is a bit of a misnomer, though the current usage seems to have taken hold over the prior definition. While most people think it describes an entire typeface, it doesn't.

A typeface is a family of fonts, with all of the italic, bold, and other variants, and in the past, different sizes. "Typeface" is still correct, though now we don't concern ourselves with sizes because these can now be calculated on the fly on nearly any computer. Typefaces range from simple ones like Hermann Zapf's Palatino typeface, which is typically installed with just four fonts (roman, italic, bold, and bold italic), to some that have dozens of different fonts for anything from sophisticated typography to foreign-language work.

(i) POSTSCRIPT

In the early 1980s, Adobe Systems developed a way to describe typographic images as vectors, or outlines expressed mathematically. This gave type an elasticity that allowed more sizes and variations to be created from the same electronic definition. At the same time Adobe created PostScript, a page description language, and a RIP to instruct a marking engine how to image the described pages (see the PostScript section above, under **technical aspects** [6.5.2]). The ability to describe and render pages in PostScript with vector-based fonts is fundamental to today's graphic arts technology.

Type 1 fonts are defined within the PostScript program and are the original file format used for type output on PostScript printers. The PostScript language was later extended to provide support for the ***TrueType*** and ***OpenType*** font standards. Any new Adobe PostScript language device made today supports all three font standards.

1. Type 1 fonts

PostScript Type 1 is a worldwide standard for digital type fonts (International Organization for Standardization outline font standard, ISO 9541). Hundreds of companies around the world have designed and released more than 30,000 fonts in the Type 1 format.

PostScript Type 1 fonts are compressed since they require only one file to create all sizes of a single type style. To display these fonts the computer uses an outline description, a bitmapped (screen) font of the typeface, and (usually) Adobe Type Manager (ATM). The outline file contains information required to render the typeface, and the information is encrypted. PostScript Type 1 fonts use Bézier mathematics to describe the shape of the curve. This type of math uses fewer control points to extrapolate the outline of the letters.

Electronic "***hints***" maintain the look of type when printing below 600 dots per inch (dpi) and in type below 14 point. Hints include making sure all the letters line up, creating visually accurate curves and strokes, and adjusting overall quality. A hint may shift a letter so that it fits in with the other letters that are near it.

2. TrueType

Apple began developing what was to become ***TrueType*** in late 1987. At that time there were many competing font scaling technologies, and several would have been suitable for the Macintosh. In 1989 Apple and Microsoft announced their strategic alliance against Adobe, where Apple would develop the font system and Microsoft would create the printing engine. Apple released TrueType in March 1991. Microsoft introduced TrueType into Windows 3.1 in early 1992. Working with Monotype, they developed a core set of fonts that included TrueType versions of Times New Roman, Arial, and Courier.

On the Macintosh, TrueType fonts are made up of the SFNT resource and a FOND resource. These two resources are combined into one file and contain all the data required to create the characters. These were originally designed to work on non-PostScript printers, and to work on PostScript printers as well.

When looking on the Macintosh at a list of fonts, the TrueType fonts do not have a number for point size after them. These fonts must be stored in the fonts folder on the Macintosh, unless a software font manager is being used. On the PC, TrueType fonts have the file extension ".ttf". All TrueType fonts are located in the fonts folder, although if a font management program is used, they can be stored in a folder outside the font folder.

One of the most important things about fonts is to make certain that when you install them there is not another font with the same name. It does not matter if it is a different format, such as a PostScript font. If a TrueType and a PostScript font are installed on the system with the same name, it can cause problems for the user.

3. Multiple Master fonts

Adobe introduced ***Multiple Master*** fonts in 1991. These enable users to create additional fonts from two or more master designs within a single typeface family. Multiple Master fonts are totally elastic—they can be stretched horizontally and vertically and their strokes can be made relatively thicker or thinner (bolder or lighter) to create typographic variations. With the application Font Creator for the Macintosh, which is provided with each Multiple Master font, a custom font can be stored in the system folder or in a folder outside the system folder. In Windows, the ability to use Multiple Master fonts is built into Adobe Type Manager. The user has the ability to adjust a maximum of four attributes—weight, width, optical size, and style. Not all fonts allow a user to have control of all four attributes, though.

In 1999, Adobe stopped making new Type 1 and Multiple Master fonts.

4. OpenType

OpenType is the latest standard for digital type fonts, developed jointly by Adobe and Microsoft. OpenType is a collaborative attempt to end the font wars, unifying the competing formats of TrueType and Type 1 fonts (including Multiple Masters). OpenType supersedes Microsoft's TrueType Open extensions to the TrueType format. OpenType fonts can contain either PostScript or TrueType outlines in a common wrapper. An OpenType font is a single file, which can be used on both Macintosh and Windows platforms without conversion. OpenType fonts have many advantages over previous font formats because they contain more ***glyphs***, support more languages (OpenType uses the **Unicode** [3.3.3.4.1] standard for character encoding), and support rich typographic features such as small caps, old style figures, and ligatures—all in a single font.

While Adobe's standard OpenType character set numbers 246 glyphs, including the new Euro currency symbol, the specification affords a possible 65,000 glyphs. Adobe Caslon Pro Italic, as an example, contains 674 glyphs.

As of this writing OpenType remains more promise than practice. The technology is in place, waiting for the users.

(ii) MANAGING FONTS

Adobe's Type 1 fonts introduced the concept that there should be at least two computer files for a printable font: one used to display the font on a monitor (the ***screen font***), and one used for output (the ***printer font***). (There could also be an additional file for advanced typographic control.) Newer font technologies, TrueType and OpenType, dispense with the multiple-file approach and simplify font handling.

1. Screen fonts

Type 1 screen fonts are used for computer screen display, and contain the bitmaps used to display the font. Screen fonts sometimes look fine at the resolution of the screen (72 dpi on most CRT monitors), but are of too low a resolution to be sent to a high-quality output device. In almost all cases, printer fonts are used to send vector-based outlines to the printer.

2. Printer fonts

Printer fonts can be downloaded to the printer, downloaded onto a hard disk, or stored in read-only memory (ROM) on a computer. Some fonts are used more often, and in some environments it could save time to have them already residing in the ROM of the printer. Fonts can be manually downloaded to the printer, and by doing this it allows them to stay there until the printer is turned off or reset. In the long run, this can help save time because in a single day a font may be downloaded a few dozen times; it only has to be downloaded once each day if done manually.

3. Adobe Type Manager and other font management software

Adobe Type Manager (***ATM***) is a program that improves screen display by imaging fonts directly from their Type 1 PostScript language font files to screen bitmaps. This includes TrueType as well as Adobe-standard Type 1 fonts. It allows a user to print PostScript fonts to a non-PostScript printer. Without this program it is not possible to scale fonts on the screen. ATM also lets you remove your fonts (Type 1, TrueType, or bitmaps) from the System Folder's Fonts folder and store them on any hard disk. You can then use ATM to activate suitcases or sets (groups of fonts used together) as needed.

Fonts that are used all the time should be placed into a folder that will be activated all the time. Fonts that are used a little less frequently should be placed in a separate folder and only be enabled when needed. Fonts can be classified in a variety of ways, from the job they are for, to the type family or vendor.

Fonts load into system memory only when they're activated, so if you've got a large font collection, you can reduce an application's RAM requirements significantly by activating only those fonts you need for a particular project. ATM Deluxe also resolves problems with corrupted or conflicting fonts.

PostScript font support is built directly into Windows 2000 and beyond, and ATM is not required for basic font installation and rendering. (You must, however, install ATM on Windows 2000 and beyond if you use Adobe's Multiple Master typefaces and want to create custom font instances.) ATM is required for previous versions of Windows, including Windows 95, 98, and NT 4.0. (A free version of ATM, called ATM Light, is available from Adobe.)

Extensis Suitcase is another font management program that opens "suitcases" or groups of typefaces when needed, keeping others closed when not is use. Suitcase lets users load fonts from any drive, local or remote, and it also allows the user to see the typefaces on the screen exactly the way they will print. Extensis Suitcase is the workflow standard for font handling, rivaled only by DiamondSoft's Font Reserve.

(iii) FONT TROUBLESHOOTING

Fonts are still a problem area in graphic arts production. Here are some of the common font issues:

1. Characters are okay on the screen, but don't print correctly

- You're probably using a Postscript Type 1 font. The screen font is OK, but there is a problem with the printer font. Make sure that you installed both files.
- If you're using a TrueType font, the file may be corrupted. Re-install it from the original disk.

2. Characters are italicized or bold on screen, but not when printed

- "Slanting" a normal font is not recommended. First, a true italic is different from a slanted version: most typefaces have italics drawn very differently. It is the same for bold versions: bolding a font will make it regularly thicker, when real bold versions are generally more thick horizontally than vertically. Always use the true italic and bold fonts, rather than styling the roman font with the attributes on your styling toolbar.

3. Characters are bitmapped on screen (i.e., they are not drawn smoothly, but with big squares)

- You're probably using a PostScript font and there is a problem with the screen font. Make sure you installed it with the printer file. On old Macintosh system versions, the two files must be in the same folder to work properly. (This does not occur if you're using ATM, which calculates the screen font size using the PostScript file.)
- If you're using a TrueType font, the file may be corrupted. Re-install it from the original disk.
- If characters are bitmapped at large point sizes, ATM requires more memory so it can smooth out the characters. Increase the amount of memory allocated to the character cache size on the ATM control panel. If you can't do this, or if memory is still not sufficient, reduce the number of fonts currently loaded.

4. When you select a font, another one appears — or it appears, but with odd spacings or leadings

- This is an example of font conflicts, which are slowly becoming extinct. What is called a font conflict is in fact a font ID conflict. Each font has two kinds of IDs: its name, and an integer value, its ID number. Until recently, most programs were identifying fonts with their integer value. If you have two fonts that have the same ID (two public domain fonts, for example, for which their authors haven't asked Apple for a personal number), the software is confused about the appropriate font to use.

5. Text is printed in Courier instead of the PostScript font on your screen

- When the system can't find the file of the font you're using, perhaps because the file has inadvertently been renamed, it is replaced with the default font—Courier. The best thing to do is to install a new copy of the original font. Also, when you do not have the printer font—just the screen font—PostScript sets the default font (Courier). This is known as "silent substitution" because it happens with no alert to warn you that it is happening.

(iv) FONT EMBEDDING

The font data used in a job will be required when submitting jobs to a printer for output and for many other electronic uses as well. This can be handled in two ways: either by sending along the original fonts with the job, or by embedding the required font data in the output files (in PostScript or PDF). The problem is that most font copyrights do not permit the user to send along original fonts. Many do not even permit embedding.

All fonts produced by Adobe Systems can be embedded in PDF files, as well as other types of files. However, the end user license agreement for fonts from other foundries may not allow embedding, even though Adobe Acrobat may be technically able to embed either the entire font or a subset of that font. To determine whether a given font can legally be embedded in a PDF document or other file, you should contact the original foundry that created the font software.

1. Identifying the foundry

The easiest way to determine the creator of a font is to refer to "read me" files or documentation that accompany the font at purchase. If you do not have this documentation, there are a number of options for getting the font foundry information from the font itself, or from related data files. Here are some common ways of getting the font creator information.

1. USE ATM DELUXE'S SAMPLE WINDOW

If you have ATM Deluxe, use the sample sheet function to obtain font creator information. Microsoft Windows users can access this function either from within ATM or by double-clicking on the font file directly.

2. VIEW THE AFM FILE

If the font came with an Adobe Font Metrics (***AFM***) file, you can open this file in a text editor or word processor. There is usually a copyright notice near the beginning of the AFM file that will have the name of the foundry or font creator.

3. USE THE GET INFO COMMAND (MACINTOSH ONLY)

Select the font's screen suitcase or the printer font file. Then choose Get Info from the system File menu (Command + I). Any associated copyright or vendor information will display in the Get Info window.

4. USE THE TRUETYPE SAMPLE SHEET (WINDOWS ONLY)

Double click on the font; an OS- or ATM-provided sample sheet will be displayed. The font vendor will be listed near the top of the sample sheet. This works for TrueType fonts only, unless you have Windows 2000 or later, or have installed ATM.

5. USE THE MICROSOFT FONT PROPERTIES EXTENSION (WINDOWS ONLY)

Download the Microsoft Font Properties extension (http://www.microsoft.com/typography/property/property.htm), which provides comprehensive information about TrueType and OpenType fonts. Install the font properties extension, right click on the font, and choose Properties. Check the Embedding tab for embedding information, and the Names and Links tabs for information on how to contact the vendor.

2. Contacting a foundry

When you've determined which foundry created the font, but are still uncertain if you have permission to embed the font, you should contact the foundry. If contact information is not included in the identifying information specified above, try Microsoft's directory of type foundries (http://www.microsoft.com/typography/links/default.asp) or try searching on the Web for more information.

(v) CONTROLLING TYPE

The digital era has transferred much of the responsibility for typesetting from trained and experienced professionals to anyone who has access to digital tools. This is a brief overview of type control. It highlights some of the key issues faced when creating and formatting text on digital publishing systems. The bibliography contains additional in-depth resources on typography.

1. Typefaces

Type families refer to all the stylistic variations of a single typeface, usually referenced by one common name. A typical type family has four members:

- plain (or roman)
- bold
- italic
- bold italic

Type families can be more extensive. Helvetica, for example, includes light, regular, bold, condensed, extended, and combinations of all of those and more. Some type families have expert collections that can double the number of available characters, including ornaments, small caps, old-style figures, display, and swash characters. Note that although these characters can be represented in print, many of them cannot presently be rendered properly in electronic contexts like the Web.

The variety of family members enables you to achieve the typographic look you want and allows for a good deal of design flexibility. For example, it is often necessary to make a given amount of type fit into a predetermined amount of space on the page. When space is an issue, a condensed or extended version of a typeface can be a real lifesaver.

2. Measuring type

Pica was originally a type size, roughly equal to a 12-point setting. Today, it is the basic measurement of type. There are 6 picas in one inch.

In the desktop environment:

1 point = 0.01388 inch
12 points = 1 pica (0.166 inch)
72 points = 1 inch

Point size is more than the vertical distance of the overall typeface design, from the top of the tallest character to the bottom of the longest character. It is a fixed number and a face may use all or some of that space. Often, because some faces have very long ascenders and descenders, these typefaces look smaller than others, with short ascenders and descenders when both are printed at the same point size. (The visual size of a typeface is mostly an effect of its *x-height,* or the height of a lowercase x, though x-height is rarely used as an actual measurement.)

3. Spacing

Spacing is the amount of empty space that exists between words, letters, and lines. Spacing provides a means to avoid overlapping shapes and letters in order to improve readability as well as legibility. A basic rule of spacing is that if you notice the spacing, there is too much. Common types of spaces are the *em, en,* and *thin* spaces. The en space is one half of the em space and the thin space is either one-quarter or one-third of the em. The em is the square of the point size, so it has no value unless the point size is defined.

1. OPTICAL SPACING

It is difficult to have consistent spacing in typography because of optical illusions that are caused by the shapes of characters and the proximity of letter shapes. The combined appearance of the spacing between letters is called optical volume. Characters have some basic characteristics that they share with other characters. For example, the letters f, i, j, r, t, and l all are made up of narrow, upright strokes. Built-in kerning options usually take care of the optical volume problems, which is very important for display type—type over 14 points.

In other words, for spacing to look even and consistent in typography, it must be inconsistent. Optical spacing cannot be achieved by numbers alone. You must use your eye and develop a sense as to what is acceptable or not.

2. LETTERSPACING

Letterspacing is the addition or subtraction of space between letters. Word space values are usually also adjusted. Letterspacing is best used to modify headings, and should be applied with caution since too much spacing makes copy difficult to read. Some programs automatically add letterspacing when the text is justified (making all the lines the same length). This directly affects readability by controlling word shapes. Text that is all capitalized or placed in small caps may seem too tight, requiring additional letterspace.

3. KERNING

Kerning is the selective addition or subtraction of space between individual pairs of letters and between words. It is used as an optical adjustment function to make larger type look more visually consistent. Kerning moves a character into the preceding character's block. This can be applied to two letters, or to a whole word at once. When applying kerning to a whole word, do not select the last letter, or the space between words will also be affected.

Automatic kerning in some applications is the default, which may not be acceptable to the designer. Some programs can hold up to 200 character pairs that can be predetermined. Some programs contain kerning tables. Computers can now be set to remember kerning pairs and kern automatically. Kerning will therefore be consistent throughout the document. Since every font is a little different, a pair that requires kerning in one font may not have to be kerned in another font, or may need a different amount of kerning.

The top 20 kerning pairs that are most annoying and should be corrected when typesetting are: Yo, We, To, Tr, Ta, Wo, Tu, Tw, Ya, Te, P., Ty, Wa, yo, we, T., Y., TA, PA, and WA.

4. TRACKING

Tracking is the subtraction of space between a group of letters and is applied to all the letters using the same value. The higher the number placed in the dialog box, the tighter the track. When setting large display type, tracking may have to be adjusted. Actually, for display type, kerning is best. For text, tracking is usually best. Tracking affects the overall letterspacing in text. Some programs have automatic tracking options that can add or remove small increments of space between the characters.

5. LEADING

The term *leading* comes from the days of metal type when strips of lead were used to separate lines of characters. The thickness of the metal determined the spacing between the lines of type. Once metal type faded out of use, leading had to be measured in other ways. With digital type technology, leading is measured from baseline to baseline. Leading is always expressed in points: 10/12 means 10-point type with 12 points of leading (baseline-to-baseline).

Solid leading indicates that the type block will be set without any extra white space between the lines. An example is type set 12/12. With solid leading, the descender from the top line could touch the ascender from the bottom line, depending on the design of the type. This can be hard for readers' eyes to follow as they move across a line.

Leading is determined by type size, type measure, type style, and letter case. Type size is a fixed distance and the typeface design may use a lot of that distance or only some of that distance. Typefaces that are small on body—that is, they use less of the distance—have some degree of leading built in. Most applications provide an auto leading feature, where the amount is a percentage of the type size, usually 20 percent.

When the length of a line is increased or decreased, leading may have to be adjusted, too. When the measure of a line is increased, there is a longer path back to the beginning of the next line, so the white space may have to be increased to allow the reader to get there easier. Attributes of type may also influence leading. Since leading deals with the ascenders and descenders of characters, words set in all caps will affect the leading (because there are no descenders).

6. LINE LENGTH

Line length is, of course, the length of a line of type, usually measured in picas and sometimes expressed in the number of characters in an average line. For best readability, the formula to figure out the maximum ideal line length is the point size of the font times two (expressed in number of characters). The length of the lowercase alphabet in picas times 1.5 is also used. Wider faces look best with wider line lengths, and condensed faces look best with narrow line lengths. For wide pages, instead of wide line lengths, double or multiple columns of smaller lengths should be used. Multiple narrow columns are preferable to single, wide columns.

A line should have 55 to 60 characters or 9 to 10 words for optimum readability. Also, as a line's length increases, the size of paragraph indentions should increase too.

4. Type (point) size

Point size refers to the imaginary box that surrounds a character and extends from the ascender line to the descender line. The characters may fall anywhere within the box and vary in size, which explains why some typefaces appear smaller or larger than others. When categorizing type, the terms *display* and *text* are used most often. Display type is anything 14 points and over, while text type is below 14 points. Display type is used for headlines and subheads, and text is for text copy.

These are just generalizations and not rigid ranges. Perception of type size is influenced by the proportions of the typeface itself. The x height and counter size (counters are the enclosed spaces within letter shapes like the lowercase e or a) are easier to compare than the actual type size. Open counters can make a type size look larger than it really is. Type size should also be chosen so that the reader can move through the text easily. If the reader begins reading and comes across a sudden change, it will disturb the pace.

5. Alignment

Alignment is the vertical or horizontal relationship of elements on the page. All typefaces and size variations align on a horizontal reference called the *baseline.* This baseline allows type to line up when fonts and typefaces are mixed.

The baseline maintains horizontal alignment. Vertical alignment is maintained on an imaginary vertical line on the left margin. Optical alignment involves using some visual reference point. An example of this would be centering instead of lining up on the left-hand-side of a page. With optical alignment, characters that have curves or angles may have to fall slightly above or below the baseline. There are four alignment styles: *flush left, flush right, centered,* and *justified.*

Flush left alignment places the left side of the type along a common left edge. Since the type lines are different lengths, in "ragged right" formats the right side will not line up, thus it will be "ragged." This style is more informal and contemporary than justified.

Justified alignment places the beginning and end of each type line along the same line on both the left and right sides, so that every type line is the same length. The software places excess white space between words (and sometimes letters). This style is more formal and creates an authoritative impression.

Force justified applies to the last line of a paragraph, when it aligns to both the left and right margins. If the line is short, white space will be added to stretch out the line. This will usually add too much white space—there are very few applications for force-justified paragraphs.

Centered alignment places the midpoint of each line of type along a single midline. The type block is symmetrical with both edges, which are both ragged. This is used primarily for headings and pull quotes.

Flush right alignment positions the right side of each line of type along a single right edge. The left edge of the type block is ragged. This is used for special headings or captions in multicolumn formats. It's hard to read, so be careful using it.

Choosing the appropriate alignment is important. Justified text seems to give a formal feeling to the reader, whereas ragged text is a bit more informal. With justified alignment, the word spacing can become a problem, especially for short line lengths (where there can be too few words, so that adjusting the spacing between the words becomes excessive), which is why ragged left is used more often. Flush right and centered alignments are generally not used for body text, unless setting poetry, headlines, subheads, or captions.

6. Fixed spacing

Fixed spaces are spaces that are a certain proportion of the type size they are used in and that are not adjusted when lines of type are justified. The most common widths are the em, the en, the width of the numerals 1 through 10, and the dollar sign. If using spaces of a certain number of points, remember that the em is as wide as the point size. (An em is a square formed by the value of the point size. An en space is half of an em space, and a thin space is either one-quarter or one-third of an em.) If you need 3 picas of horizontal space, set three ems in 12-point type (1 pica = 12 points).

7. Hyphenation and justification

Hyphenation breaks words at the end of lines according to rules (called "hyphenation algorithms," which, for example, permit the suffix "ing" to be separated) or according to a list of words and the places they can be broken as stored in a dictionary. Hyphenation affects letterspacing and word spacing in justified text. Line-end hyphenation is suitable for text material, but not for headlines, subheads, and most display type.

In most applications the user can set preferences that control the number of hyphens in a row, and the hyphenation zone, which will control the lining up of the ends of lines. The following are some common rules that generally apply to hyphenation:

- No more than three hyphens should be used in a row.
- A word should have a minimum of two letters before the hyphen and a minimum of three letters on the next line.

- Hyphenate where there seems to be a logical break and so that the word is not confusing to read.
- Always hyphenate a compound word between the two words. An example is the word dragonfly. The hyphen should go between the words dragon and fly.

There are also rules about where to avoid hyphenation. These are:

- Words with six letters or less.
- One-syllable words.
- Instances where a syllable of fewer than two characters will be carried over.
- Words with two syllables pronounced as one.
- Quantities, figures, amounts, etc.
- Abbreviations.
- Immediately after numbering or a reference.
- Next to or after an abbreviated title.

8. Word spacing

Word spacing is the spacing between words. Unjustified word spaces are fixed, expressed in units. Word spacing must always be larger than letter-spacing and can be varied to adjust line length without affecting readability. Word spacing should be kept thin so that the text appears to the reader to flow smoothly. Word spaces are usually defined within certain ranges—minimum, optimum, and maximum—and in many cases can be tailored by users to their own taste.

The minimum word space is the smallest value, below which the space will not go. Having a minimum value reduces the likelihood that a line would be set completely tight (i.e., with no discernable word space). The maximum is the widest value allowed; usually this is the threshold point where automatic letterspacing might be employed. The optimum is the value that gives good, even spacing in most instances. This value is a percentage of the standard word space.

Without good hyphenation, word spacing in justified lines can be quite erratic and inconsistent. Thus many designers opt for ragged right and eliminate the problem altogether.

(vi) SPECIAL TYPOGRAPHIC SITUATIONS

1. Symbols

Symbols, signs, and ornaments appear in typefaces and are not letters. These also include marks representing words, monetary symbols, mathematical symbols, and flourishes. Some are designed to match a font, while others may be included in a separate symbol or *pi font*.

Pi fonts are collections of special characters. The name pi originally came from handset metal type, where pi referred to one style of type mistakenly put in the storage drawer of another style. When setting type, a composer may have run across a letter that did not match the face being used. This "orphan" would then be thrown into a box of pi type, called a hell box, to be sorted out later or sent back to the type foundry for credit when reordering a new font. Pi was also a form of type that had collapsed or spilled, and was usually attributed to the printer's devil: the apprentice.

On the Macintosh computer the Symbol font and Zapf Dingbats are the most commonly used pi fonts (Windows calls them Symbol and Wingdings).

2. Equations and math

Math currently presents special problems—and possibilities—in the digital era. It has always been difficult to typeset mathematics; in many ways, digital technology has made it far easier. Characters and fonts that used to be difficult or impossible to obtain are now readily available. It is even easy now to create special characters, with a program like Macromedia Fontographer, or to modify existing characters for special purposes. And the programs used to typeset mathematics continue to get better and better. Design Science MathType is becoming increasingly common, not just because it makes it relatively easy to set math even in a desktop environment (requiring no special knowledge of the mathematics), but also because MathType can create files for one format (usually for print) and save them in other formats (e.g., TeX or MathML).

It is the representation of math on-line that is still a problem. Today's browsers cannot represent many characters required for complex math. The solution is usually to use graphics instead of fonts—an inelegant solution, because the graphics don't scale or align properly when the surrounding text is resized or reflowed in the browser. **MathML** [3.3.1.3]—the Math Markup Language—promises to be a solution to this, but at this writing there are no commonly used implementations of MathML that enable it to be displayed easily. As this technology is implemented in future generations of browsers, the ability to represent math well on-line will improve. In the meantime, a vector graphic format, SVG, which eliminates the scaling and alignment problems associated with other graphic formats, will increasingly be used to display math properly. And finally, the STIX project (http://www.stixfonts.org/) is soon to release a very large font of math characters, encoded in Unicode, which will be copyrighted but available for free, designed for both print and on-line use.

3. Accents

Accents are marks placed over, under, or through a character as a guide to pronunciation. In non-English languages, accents represent certain sounds. Until recently, the letter and the accent mark were separate, and accented characters were formed by combining the two. This was accomplished by placing the proper accent mark (which has zero width) below, above, or through the letter. This is a significant problem for sophisticated markup and future electronic uses because the resulting file then actually has two character codes in it, one for the unaccented character and another for the accent (plus, very likely, some arbitrary spacing adjustments). Instead, the actual proper accented character should be used; this can be done even in common desktop environments, as long as the proper fonts are available. The increasing use of **Unicode** [3.3.3.4.1], the universal character encoding on which XML is based, removes the ambiguities formerly associated with accented characters and enables them to be specified accurately and unambiguously.

4. Quotes

Quotation marks were originally commas, and in the 1600s looked like the present French quotation marks (« »). English printers refused to use the French form and inverted the comma at the beginning of quoted material and used apostrophes at the close. In French and Spanish small angle marks on the lower part of the type body are used for quotations. In German, two primes are used.

Opening and closing punctuation marks indicate verbal statements or emphasize certain words. In American typography, double quotes are normally used, and single quotes are used within a double quotation; in the United Kingdom, the reverse is true. For good display typography, use quotes one size smaller than the text.

Most people who do not have any typographic skills do not know the difference between quotes and prime marks. A single prime mark is used to show feet or minutes, and a double prime mark is used to show inches or seconds. The prime marks are usually found in the Symbol font. One identifier of a good typographer is the use of curly quotes in typographic work. Curly quotes or *smart quotes* (sometimes called *typographers' quotes*) can be turned on in some applications like Microsoft Word or QuarkXPress to automatically apply the correct punctuation.

When creating a file that will be used on both the Macintosh and PC, it is necessary to choose a font that is available to both platforms. Choosing a prime mark from a font like Windows Symbol, which is not available for the Macintosh, causes problems because the Macintosh will substitute a different character for the prime mark.

5. Dashes

The main types of dashes used in typography are hyphens, en dashes, and em dashes.

1. HYPHEN

Hyphens break words on syllables at the ends of lines to allow even spacing in justification; they are also used in compound or connected words or phrases. One of the first signs of typographic experience is the proper use of hyphens. When determining whether a hyphen should be used or not, the following rules must be followed:

- Always use a hyphen when breaking a word at the end of a line.
- Always use a hyphen when connecting two or more words to create a compound phrase.
- Never use any spaces before a hyphen.
- Use spaces after a hyphen only in cases like the following: thirty- and fifty-year-olds.

2. EN DASH

En dashes are used to indicate ranges of numbers, where the words "to" or "through" are represented, such as "pages 1–9" or "January 13–19."

An en dash is also used to connect two nouns of equal weight, as in "East–West." Spacing around the en dash should be closed, so that there is no spacing on either side. The en dash is one-half the width of the em dash and is longer than a hyphen.

3. EM DASH

An em is the square of the current point size; an em dash is a long dash that size. Em dashes may be open with a space on either side or closed, with no space. What's most important is to be consistent.

It is a sign of typographic inexperience to use, instead of an em dash, a pair of hyphens (--) or a hyphen with spaces around it (-). Improper use of dashes is common on the Web, where the spaces often disappear and the dashes can't be distinguished from hyphens.

6. Ligatures

Ligatures are two or more characters designed as a single unit. Gutenberg's font had many ligatures (over 150) in order to simulate handwriting and to achieve even word spacing in his justified columns. Most current ligatures in English have to do with the letter f, since the top of the f creates a visual gap between it and the next character. When that character collides with the f (as do an l or an i), a ligature combining the two characters solves the problem. In foundry type the f actually extended beyond its metal body. Without the ligature, the typographer would have to cut off the dot of the letter i to make room for the overlap of the f. The most common ligatures are fi, fl, ff, ffl, and ffi. Some typefaces are designed not to require ligatures.

Although ligatures are a mark of fine typography, they present a problem for digital files. Some high-end composition systems automatically substitute ligatures so the underlying files still have separate characters for the component parts—an f and an i, for example. But in many cases, when a ligature is used, the underlying file has the code for a single character in a specific position on a special font—for example, the fi ligature. When those files are used for other purposes, special care must be taken to convert the ligatures back into their component letters. Ligatures also subvert searching: when a single ligature character exists in the file instead of the component letters, a search will not find the word if it is looking for the word spelled with the individual letters: the word "find," for example, might look like "5nd" if the fi ligature was in the 5 position on its special font.

7. Rules

A rule is just another name for a line. Rules are used to outline, underline, decorate, or add emphasis. Most software allows you to set rules to specific widths and thicknesses. The thinnest rule is called a *hairline* rule. Traditionally this was about a quarter-point thick. Some electronic publishing software defines a hairline as the smallest available unit of measurement. On the screen, that is a pixel, which is visible and may look okay; and even on a laser output, a line of toner will be drawn. But on a high-resolution device, a single pixel is too small to be visible and hairline rules disappear. Only a high-resolution proof can properly show the weight of most rules; what you see on the screen and on a laser proof are often misleading.

8. Ellipsis

Ellipsis dots indicate that something is missing, or conversation has stopped. These show that the author is purposely leaving out a word or words when quoting someone, and may also express a pause in thought. Ellipses are usually set with nonbreaking spaces between periods. That way, the spaces will adjust for justification, and the underlying file can be represented without the special ellipsis character. A common problem in unprofessionally produced files is that the ellipses are set with no spaces, resulting in dots that appear too close together, or with normal spaces, which permit them to break incorrectly at the end of a line.

9. Small caps

Most of the characters we read are at the x height. Small caps match the x height of a particular type and size, and are slightly expanded. Some programs create small caps by shrinking and stretching full caps, but true small caps are only found in expert typefaces. Depending on the typeface, additional letter-spacing may have to be added if the characters look too crowded or tight. Text that is all caps should be done in small caps, as well as abbreviations of awards, decorations, honors, titles, etc., following a person's name.

Small capitals are useful for section headings or chapter titles, to accent important words or phrases in midsentence, or at the beginning of a paragraph for a lead-in. True small caps are one sign of a truly professional typesetting job. However, care must be taken when the files are used for other purposes. Most true small caps are typed as lowercase letters, which allows them to be combined properly with full caps. When only small caps are used (with no full caps, as in some subheads or cross references), the underlying file will not know where the true capital letters have to be.

6.8 GRAPHIC TYPES AND FILE FORMATS

As computerization and digitization began to flourish in the graphic arts, in the absence of available standards, each vendor had to invent digital data formats. Most created specialized proprietary file definitions that were usually incompatible with the competition. Over time the larger vendors learned that proprietary file formats helped them to maintain their dominant positions in the marketplace. The second-tier competitors pushed for standard formats as a way to gain acceptance for their systems.

The introduction of Macintosh, IBM-compatible, and Unix (and later, Windows) computers created standard hardware platforms for the graphic arts industry. Standard hardware platforms running standard operating systems led to relatively inexpensive and widely used software, creating a basis for the development of a series of interchangeable file formats.

Most of the monochrome typesetting and page composition systems (and their file formats) have been retired. Some proprietary color systems, known as color electronic prepress systems (***CEPS***), are still in use, but most have been replaced by desktop prepress systems. Data in some of their file formats is still used, although it's rarely a production issue. Of the leading vendors of the CEPS era—Crosfield (from England), Hell (from Germany), Scitex (from Israel), and Screen (from Japan)—only Screen still operates as an independent company. In April of 2002, Rudolph Hell, the founder of the scanner manufacturer that bore his name, died at the age of 100, and Heidelberg, the current owner of Hell patents and trade names, announced soon after that it was discontinuing the manufacture of all scanners and most imagesetters.

The wide range of graphic file formats in use today is in part a legacy of these competing systems, but also an indication of the range of specialized functions comprising design, prepress, and printing processes.

(i) GRAPHIC TYPES VS. FILE FORMATS

Text, graphics, and pages are stored, translated, and conveyed in a number of formats. It's important to understand the difference between a file format (such as GIF or EPS) and the types of graphics (such as bitmap and vector) that applications produce, in order to appropriately save graphic data. There are literally thousands of different file formats, but only a handful of graphic types.

(ii) GRAPHIC TYPES

Most discussions of computer graphics refer to two graphic file types: ***bitmap*** (or ***raster***) and ***vector***. While it's true that most graphics are formed from raster or vector images, the real work of digital publishing involves a far wider range of graphic types.

There are eight:

- *Bitmap* files (also called raster files) specify images as matrices of pixels, such as in photographic images.
- *Vector* files contain images specified as mathematical equations. They are typically used to store line art and computer-aided design (CAD) information.
- *Fonts* are defined in a vector graphic format, along with "hints" for rendering the type in small point sizes or at low resolution. Font files are not printed, but the data they contain is used to render type in other graphic files.
- *Pages* are specified with a fixed geometric dimension (such as 8½ x 11 in), and may contain text (type) and any other kind of raster or vector graphic.
- *Animations* are collections of raster data to be displayed in a sequence.
- *Multidimensional graphics* are collections of objects (data and the code that manipulates it) that can be rendered in a variety of perspectives (usually three dimensional).
- *Video* graphics (moving images) are collections of two-dimensional rasters rendered in quick succession.
- *Multimedia* graphics are capable of storing two- and three-dimensional graphics, along with video and audio data.

Web graphics could possibly be considered as the ninth type of graphic. Some file formats can be rendered only via Web browsers, but their content is always one of the eight graphic types above. Web graphics are unique in their ability to interact with databases in real time, and to generate graphics on the fly based on user interaction.

Print publishing clearly focuses on the first four types of graphics: rasters, vectors, fonts, and pages. But as publishing becomes a cross-media enterprise, designers have to understand a range of nonprint graphic types. This section focuses on print graphics. See the chapter **Multimedia Publishing** [9] for a discussion of the others.

1. Bitmaps

The most basic type of computer graphic is the ***bitmap***. It is essentially a grid made from many tiny black-and-white or colored tiles (a *raster*). The tiles are called pixels, or picture elements. Lines are built up as rows of adjoining pixels, whether black-and-white, gray, or colored. The optical illusion of colors that are not present is achieved by ***dithering***, or mixing tiles of nearby colors or shades of gray. Dithering looks at the colors or grays in one row of tiles and the colors or grays in an adjacent row and then averages the two rows to create a third row in between them.

Black-and-white bitmaps require only one bit of data to describe each pixel—zero or one, on or off. A single bit per pixel does not provide enough information to specify a color or shade of gray. Images containing 256 grays (grayscale images) require 8 bits per pixel, and photographic-quality, full-color images require 24 bits per pixel to specify any of 16.7 million colors.

Bitmaps have a fixed grid and can produce unsightly results when an area of the bitmap is moved, enlarged, or rotated. Any change to a bitmapped image can become jagged and distorted.

Bitmaps print at their fixed resolution. Low-resolution bitmaps print at low resolution, even on high-resolution output devices. A 300-dot-per-inch (dpi) image printed on a 1,200-dpi printer betrays its low resolution.

Bitmaps are used primarily for pictures and scanned images. In paint programs (such as Painter, now a Corel product) pixels can be manipulated to achieve artistic effects that resemble those of traditional color painting. Image processing software (such as Adobe Photoshop) is used primarily to enhance scanned images for output, although its broad range of features and filters make it suitable for digital painting also.

2. Vector graphics

Vector-graphic images are typically produced by drawing programs. The images are composed of mathematically described lines (vectors), indicating direction and length (magnitude). They are often referred to as ***object-oriented graphics***.

Images described as vector graphics can be enlarged, rotated, reshaped, and refilled, and the software will redraw them with no loss of quality. These objects can be managed as if each item were drawn on a separate transparent sheet. The advantages of object-oriented artwork extend to the printing phase as well. Instead of dictating to the printer where each pixel should be, the program mathematically describes the object and lets the printer render the image at the highest possible resolution.

Thus, unlike bitmaps, object-oriented graphics are ***resolution-independent***. Object-oriented images printed on a 2,540-dpi imagesetter look far finer than the same image printed on a 600-dpi laser printer. Object-oriented graphics are the natural choice for illustrations, line art, display type, and business graphics. Object-oriented images have smooth curves, grayscale shadings, and tints.

3. Fonts

Fonts are often overlooked as a relevant graphic type, but are fundamental to both print and electronic publishing. Many problems with graphics files are related to fonts, precisely because they are so easily taken for granted that people neglect to think about them the same way they think about their image files or their text files. Fonts are covered in detail **above** [6.7].

4. Pages

Few discussions of computer graphics consider the page as a separate *type* of graphic, as pages are really just collections of rasters and vectors. Even fonts on a page are typically described as vectors. But it's important for designers to recognize page graphics as a separate type, because they contain information about the appearance of a page (trim size, bleed, trapping, imposition, etc.) that while technically speaking are vector data, are very specific to this type of graphic.

(iii) FILE FORMATS

In a computer, a ***file format*** is a unique method to organize a set of data. Software that uses the data in a file must be able to recognize and access data in a prescribed fashion. On the Macintosh the file format is ordinarily not visible in the file name, but can be accessed by using the Get Information command. On Windows and Unix computers, file formats are generally indicated as part of a file's name by a file name extension (suffix). The extension is separated by a period from the file name and contains three (and sometimes two or four) letters that identify the format, such as *filename.bmp* or *file-*

name.jpg (the Webopedia lists 2,700 file name suffixes; see http://webopedia.internet.com/quick_ref/fileextensionsfull.html).

Most of the thousands of different file formats are not used for graphics. The definitive work on the graphic file formats, the *Encyclopedia of Graphics File Formats,* by James D. Murray and William van Ryper (last published in 1996, now sadly out of print), described 100 file formats. Most designers and publishers use only a dozen or fewer common formats. Most of these are discussed below.

1. Types of file formats

The following are the most common types of file formats:

- *Text* formats describe either plain (***ASCII***) or formatted text documents. The most common are plain text (.txt) and Microsoft Word (.doc).
- *Raster* or bitmap formats describe rasters and bitmaps. The most common are (relatively) simple bitmap formats, like ***GIF*** or ***TIFF***, or compressed bitmaps, like ***JPEG*** (although GIF and TIFF can be compressed too). PCX is an extremely popular bitmap format on the PC, but has largely been supplanted for professional use by TIFF and JPEG.
- *Vector* formats describe vector graphics. PICT and PICT2 have been common on the Macintosh. EPS is the most common vector format today. Scalable vector graphics (SVG) is an XML-based vector format that is becoming increasingly important for Web graphics.
- A *metafile* format encodes a file that contains multiple types of data, although generally metafile formats contain just rasters and vectors. PICT2 and EPS are both metafile formats (both can contain both raster and vector data), though they're most often associated with vector graphics.
- The most common *font* formats are PostScript Type 1, TrueType, and OpenType. Traditionally font files are handled differently on Macintosh and Windows computers (see **Typography** [6.7] above), although OpenType is beginning to address these problems.
- *Page* formats are generally proprietary file formats, unique to each page layout program. For example, Adobe PageMaker, QuarkXPress, and Adobe InDesign each have widely used proprietary file formats that cannot easily be translated into any other format. PDF exists in part as an attempt to create an industry-standard format for pages.
- *Page description languages* (PDLs) describe the layout of a printed page of graphics and text in a form that can be understood by a raster image

processor. Adobe's PostScript is the most common PDL in the graphic arts, and renders data into .ps files that are generally unreadable by humans, but easily understood by printing devices.

- Special *page production formats* (JDF, TIFF/IT, DCS, and OPI) are used in print production for specialized purposes, such as job control, imposition, or low-resolution image substitution. JDF files impact graphics, but are not graphic file formats per se, and are described in a **separate section** [6.12.13.2].

Conversion between most different graphics file formats is not difficult (provided the target format supports the kind of data you're transferring). Most imaging applications (e.g., Photoshop), can import and export images in many different formats. (The Open As command in Photoshop offers two dozen different formats.) Page publishing programs such as QuarkXPress can import most common graphics file formats and save them to a similar range. Dedicated software, such as DeBabelizer Pro (www.equilibrium.com), can convert difficult files from obscure sources.

The greater challenge these days is choosing the best file format for specific production situations. The best format is one that handles all of the required data in the most efficient manner possible. For example, GIF is not usually appropriate for print graphics. JPEG is great for scanned images, but can lead to image degradation. Saving files in the native QuarkXPress format might limit their reusability in other production situations. This subject is examined in more detail in the discussion of specific file formats below.

(iv) FILE COMPRESSION

While disk storage continues to drop dramatically in cost per megabyte, rapid file transmission remains a challenge for large image files. File ***compression*** is still the norm rather than the exception. File compression technology also offers the option of archive creation—moving multiple files into a single compressed archive—which brings the workflow advantage of having all required output files in a single data file.

File compression techniques fall broadly into two categories, lossless and lossy. ***Lossless*** is as it sounds—no data is lost upon compression. ***Lossy*** might better be called "lossfull"—lossy compression leads to data loss, which can be unacceptable in print production.

Compression works by minimizing or eliminating redundancy in a file. If, for example, a bitmap image contained 100,000 blue pixels exactly the same color in a 500 x 200-pixel matrix, compression software could express the image as just "500x200xSKYBLUE" rather than as 100,000 individual pixels all containing the same blue pixel value. The image would shrink from about

300 kilobytes to less than 10 kilobytes. But when the file is opened, the software will restore all of the original pixels in the exact same order. This is lossless compression.

If the same image contained a bunch of red pixels scattered randomly throughout, compression would be a challenge. The formula describing the location of the red pixels could be nearly as data intensive as the original image. To maximize compression, the formula might have to approximate the location of the red pixels. When the image is reopened, the pixels will have shifted location, though the overall visual impression will remain similar. This is lossy compression. The higher the compression ratio, the greater the data loss. In images with similar tone values, this does not create a problem. In images with lots of tones and colors, lossy compression tends to visibly degrade the image.

1. Compression software

The StuffIt ***.sit*** lossless compression format is the compression standard for Macintosh computers. Files that are compressed losslessly on a Windows PC are usually compressed with WinZip ***.zip*** compression (which is built into the latest versions of the Windows OS).

JPEG is the industry-standard lossy file compression method for raster image files. Technically it is a standard for file compression, not a data format, but in day-to-day use, files appear as JPEG format (.jpg on Windows, JPEG on the Mac).

(v) CROSS-PLATFORM FILE ISSUES

The native file system used by Mac OS 9 and earlier versions includes a provision for each file to contain information about a file type and a creator code (of the application that created the file). ***File types*** and ***creator codes*** are four-character text strings embedded within the file. Through the use of type and creator codes, the Finder determines which application(s) can open a particular file.

This works just fine on the Macintosh, but to send and receive Windows files this information has to be translated by the software transferring this file. Macintosh files often end up unreadable on Windows machines, and vice versa.

The specifications for file names are dependent on the operating system used and the disk format that the file is saved on. The Macintosh has generally offered more freedom than Windows in file name lengths and in the characters used. While the latest versions of Windows allow for long file names, most special characters are still impermissible. Moving files between computer platforms is not automatic, and still requires care.

1. File format specifics

1. TIFF

The Tag Image File Format (***TIFF***) is a versatile bitmap standard. TIFF is a commonly used format for storing bitmapped images at various resolutions, gray levels, and colors. It does not store object-oriented images.

TIFF was originally developed by Aldus Corporation (since purchased by Adobe), and released into the public domain. A TIFF file contains a directory and a series of tags that specify certain types of data. This format is widely used for the transfer of all types of black-and-white and color scanned bitmapped images. TIFF files can also be compressed.

A useful feature of TIFF is the ability to decompose an image by tiles rather than scan lines. This permits much more efficient access to very large imagery that has been compressed (since one does not have to decompress an entire scan line).

TIFF has been sometimes criticized for its flexibility, in particular that the standard allowed too many different format variations. The latest version of the TIFF specification, 6.0, appears to have addressed most of the potential problems from the user's perspective. Nevertheless, the professional publishing community decided to tighten it further with TIFF/IT.

2. TIFF/IT

Tag Image File Format for Image Technology (***TIFF/IT***) is an ANSI standard (ANSI IT8.8) that builds on the Aldus 6.0 version of TIFF and carries forward the work done on Digital Data Exchange Standards (DDES) and Intercompany File Exchange Network (IFEN). TIFF/IT provides an independent transport mechanism for raster images and integrates high-end and desktop publishing formats. In practice, TIFF/IT should make it easier to exchange data between high-end and desktop environments.

The variation between TIFF implementations has led to the belief that valid TIFF files are often unreadable when transferred between different applications; the TIFF/IT standard is intended to address those variations. TIFF/IT can also simplify direct-to-plate and direct-to-press operations by providing a stable raster format. This is desirable for the following reasons:

- In computer-to-plate and computer-to-press environments it is costly to have a PostScript error occur late in the process. A stable raster file can be passed to a recorder with less chance for error.
- Imposition, trapping, color correction, and adjustments for press conditions can often be handled more easily with a raster file.

- It's generally easier to estimate the output time of a raster file based on its size. When PostScript vectors are "RIPped," even though the file size may be small, the job still may take a long time to output.

TIFF/IT has gained some momentum in the graphic arts industry, particularly among magazine publishers, but **PDF-X** [6.12.11.5] has begun to steal its thunder.

3. JPEG

JPEG (pronounced "jay-peg") is technically not a file format, but a method of compressing bitmap images. JPEG stands for Joint Photographic Experts Group, the original name of the committee that wrote the standard. JPEG is a popular file format for photographs or other continuous tone images, for print and the Web. The JPEG format supports CMYK, RGB, and grayscale **color spaces** [6.9.2]; it only works on continuous tone images. JPEG takes advantage of known limitations of the human eye, for example, the fact that small color changes are perceived less accurately than small changes in brightness.

The big advantage of this file is the compression that the format allows. It uses a lossy compression scheme that will discard data to compress the file by a factor of 10:1 or more. Image quality depends on the amount of compression applied. High image quality uses low compression and vice versa. JPEG implementations allow the user the choice of how much compression to apply to the file. At the higher levels, there is noticeable image degradation.

Repeated compression, decompression, and recompression of JPEG files increases the level of image degradation.

A new version of the JPEG specification, called JPEG 2000, has recently been published as an international standard (http://www.jpeg.org/JPEG2000.html). JPEG 2000 uses compression techniques based on wavelet technology, allowing for smaller files of higher quality than with the older JPEG format.

4. PICT

PICT is Apple's original file format for use with the QuickDraw graphics language. Many people think of PICT, and its more sophisticated sibling, PICT2, as vector formats. They are in fact metafile formats—able to hold both vector and raster data.

PICT is not an acronym and it is the oldest generic file format on the Macintosh. It is based on QuickDraw, the Mac's then native graphics language. It has been the Mac OS internal file format of choice when transferring (cutting and pasting) from one application to another.

PICT2 is an extension of the PICT format, and it has two subtypes: a 16.7 million-color version, commonly called 24-bit PICT2, and the more prevalent 8-bit PICT2, which holds 256 colors. PICT2 sets no limits on the resolution of bitmaps except those imposed by the application.

PICT2 is usually a better choice for presentations, in which the final image is viewed on screen (for multimedia) or as a slide, than it is for publishing. It is readily imported but poorly supported by publishing applications.

PICT is used by many screen capture programs for screen shots.

5. EPS

The most common vector format is Encapsulated PostScript (***EPS***). The EPS file format is a subset of PostScript. EPS files include a single image or a group of images, and optionally include a device- and platform-dependent preview. While they can contain bitmapped or vector information, the format is most commonly used for vector data.

If it contains vector-only information, the illustration can be scaled to any particular size with no degradation of image quality, and in most cases cannot be ungrouped, refilled, or recolored. EPS supports monochrome, grayscale, and color images. EPS files do not usually include fonts except in cases where a vector or page layout program has saved an EPS file with the fonts embedded. (These needed fonts are sometimes overlooked when files containing EPS graphics are transmitted to printers, a common problem that preflighting is designed to catch.)

EPS files can optionally contain a bitmapped image preview, intended so that systems that can't render PostScript directly can at least display a crude representation of what the graphic will look like. There are three preview formats: Mac (PICT), IBM (TIFF), and a platform-independent preview called ***EPSI***.

The primary image description in an EPS file is most commonly written in ASCII, which uses mathematical expressions to define the necessary shapes and curves and positions. ***Binary EPS*** is similar to the ASCII version, containing both a bitmapped preview image and the actual graphic. Instead of being a text-based description, the printable graphic is stored as a stream of numbers that represent the pixel attributes. Binary EPS is voluminous but well suited for outputting bit-mapped color images for four-color separation. A binary EPS color bitmap uses about half the disk space of its ASCII EPS counterpart. Many programs have a specific save option for binary EPS.

6. POSTSCRIPT

A PostScript file is a purely text-based description of a page. Instead of using pixels (as in bitmaps) or mathematical expressions (as in vector graphics), it is a programming language that describes, in ASCII text, the shapes, lines, spaces, positions, fonts, colors, and other features of a page. In most applications you can create a PostScript file from the Print dialog box. You can open this file with any word processor or text editor and modify it (if you know the PostScript programming language). Postscript is discussed more extensively **above** [6.5]. (An example of the PostScript code for a page in this book is provided in the on-line version.)

When you click the Print command for any job, the page is converted to PostScript code and sent to the printer's RIP or PostScript interpreter. You can save the page or document as a PostScript file—the same one that would have been sent to the printer—for later printing. You do not need the originating program to print a saved PostScript file. The PostScript file can be fed directly to a PostScript printer with a PostScript download utility. Unfortunately there is no preview image, and the graphic essentially loses its editability. A saved PostScript file includes all type and graphic information, and can also be converted to a PDF file.

7. PDF

PDF files are "distilled" from PostScript files using Adobe Acrobat Distiller software (or similar third-party software).

In a RIP, three functions ordinarily occur before a page is imaged: the PostScript is interpreted; a display list is written; then a halftone dot is generated according to the imaging device's recorder attributes. PDF distillation essentially performs the first two functions: interpreting the PostScript (where 90 percent of RIPping problems occur) and creating the (equivalent of the) display list. A PDF file is then reinterpreted back into a PostScript format data stream for output. (Because the file has been partially processed via PDF, the final output stage is generally faster than it would have been for the originating PostScript file.)

PDF and its PDF-X variants are discussed in greater detail **below** [6.12.11].

2. Special graphics formats

1. OPI

The Open Prepress Interface (***OPI***) is an extension to PostScript that automatically replaces low-resolution placeholder images (***FPO***—For Position Only) with high-resolution images. OPI is the solution to a problem: As high-resolution images are imported into a document, the size of the document increases nearly geometrically. Moving large files back and forth from design to production locations slows the process. Why not scan the images and save the high-resolution version at the printing or prepress location and create a low-resolution version that can be used for page makeup? Enter OPI.

The low-resolution file is easy to handle and allows the page to be assembled with all elements in position. When the final file is sent to printout, an OPI server replaces the low-resolution images with the high-resolution images. The only problem is that the images must remain essentially as they are; they can be cropped, resized and rotated, but the individual pixels cannot be manipulated. The images also cannot be renamed or moved to a different server without revising the OPI file as well.

2. DCS

OPI works with TIFF images. Desktop Color Separation (DCS) is a file format developed by Quark that creates four-color separations by saving images as a set of EPS files. It is used to exchange color data between image editing and page layout programs.

The basic specification, which Quark made freely available to other developers, includes five linked EPS files: the C (cyan), M (magenta), Y (yellow), and K (black) files of the separated image and a composite master file that allows users to print low-resolution composite files on a color printer. This standard also is called ***five-file EPS*** or ***EPS5***.

DCS files are generally faster for the designer to work with than OPI TIFF; OPI TIFF files generally are faster to output.

(vi) IMAGING AND HALFTONES

Professional graphic arts practice demands an understanding of a set of theories surrounding ***halftoning***, a process developed to allow printing devices to mimic the continuous tone appearance of drawings and paintings (and later, photographs). The technical details of halftoning represent a complex world, unlike any other. Understanding halftone reproduction involves appreciating a series of unique imaging concepts.

1. Continuous tone

The first concept is tone—***continuous tone***. While type is most often black against a white background, most paintings and photographs have a large range of color tones or gray levels between their lightest and darkest areas. Because the tonal gradation is generally gradual and continuous, rather than in sudden tone shifts, a painting or a photographic original is referred to as *continuous tone* (or ***contone***).

The challenge in printing a continuous tone image is rendering the many shades of gray (or other colors). In theory perhaps a press could have been invented that used dozens of tones of ink, from white to black and bright red to dark blue, but this would not have been practical or economical. Instead, halftoning emerged in the 19th century as a means of reproducing the appearance of continuous tone artwork.

Print is essentially a bilevel or binary process. There's either ink or no ink present in a given area of the substrate (which is generally paper). There is no easy means of modulating the visual strength of an ink in a defined small area. So an image has to be divided into numerous smaller areas, where ink will either be printed or the sheet left blank. If the areas are small enough, the eye is fooled into perceiving graduated tones.

Huge graphic art cameras were used in the old mechanical methods of making printing plates, along with filters and sheets of film. To create a halftone image, printers placed an actual screen with holes—like a window screen (but much smaller)—in front of high-contrast film. Using a large light, they exposed the film with the screen and a transparent version of the original art placed between the film and the light. The physical halftone screen was designed with a specified number of lines (of holes) per inch (***lpi***). The resulting dot size depended on the brightness of the light through the transparency: the more light that came through a given hole, the bigger the dot would be. The array of variously sized dots reproduced the image in negative form; the light areas of the artwork became the dark area of the film. Then, when the film negative was used to expose a printing plate, its dark spots created light spots on the plate.

Most offset printing uses screens of 150 to 175 lpi. A *coarse screen* is used for newspaper printing, usually ranging from 85 to 110 lpi. This creates bigger dots further apart, which makes it easier to keep the dots distinct on rough, absorbent newsprint.

2. Dots, spots, samples, and pixels

The second challenge in understanding halftoning is clarifying the key concepts that define it: spots, dots, samples, and pixels. The distinctions between these four terms can seem obtuse to the novice. The confusion compounds because the four terms are often interchanged. (See the on-line version of this book for examples.)

A ***spot*** is the smallest addressable image unit on an output imaging device. For example, most desktop laser printers can image at 600 ***spots per inch (spi)***. This is almost always marketed as "600 dots per inch" or 600 dpi. CRT computer monitors are typically 72 spots per inch (although newer LCD monitors feature higher resolutions). High-resolution output devices, such as imagesetters and platesetters, commonly address 2,000 to 3,000 spots per inch.

A ***dot*** is a matrix formed from spots. The dots form a halftone pattern. Each dot is formed from a cell defined as a matrix of device spots. For example, a dot representing a 50 percent tone might be made from an 8 x 8 array of 64 spots, 32 of which are black and 32 of which are white. The more spots per dot, the more shades of gray can be represented (see grayscale below).

A ***sample*** is the measure of a scanner's sensitivity or resolution. A so-called 600 x 1,200-dpi scanner can record 600 vertical image samples and 1,200 horizontal samples in each inch of an image.

A ***pixel*** is a two-dimensional point typically found in a digital contone image. It is the smallest addressable point in that digital image. Unlike a spot, a pixel has depth—typically up to eight bits. It is the combination of these bits that determines the relative brightness and color of the pixel. Most imaging systems can display 256 discrete shades in a single pixel, or 28 shades of gray ranging from black to white.

The power inherent in this simple notion is that by combining three pixels and assigning their 256 gray shades to red, green, and blue, millions of colors can be produced on an RGB display.

Digital contone image resolution, whether ***grayscale*** or ***RGB***, is expressed in terms of ***pixels per inch (ppi)*** (not dots per inch). Digital contones usually range from 72 ppi to about 300 ppi. Lower-resolution images are suitable for monitor display only, while higher-resolution images are required for printing.

When a digital contone is converted to a halftone, pixel values are interpreted and halftone dots are created to simulate the relative tone present in the original image.

Purely bitmapped or bilevel images, such as line art, scanned type, dithered bitmaps, and rasterized type, are not halftones. A bit in these images is either on or off, and corresponds directly to a device spot. Very high-resolution bitmaps are used to drive most graphic arts imaging devices; where a bit is on in the image is where a spot will be created on the medium used in the device.

Scanners record pixels of digital image data, but the resolution of the scanner is better referred to as its sampling rate.

When a halftone is created in a RIP, it is a bitmap of device spots. RIPs take as input contone images, vector artwork and type, and bitmaps, and generate a bitmap, which can also include a halftone, as output used to drive an imaging device.

3. Halftone variables

The appearance of halftoning is influenced by three factors: the screen ruling, the screen angle, and the shape of the halftone dot.

1. SCREEN RULING

A ***screen ruling*** is the frequency of a row of dots in a halftoned image, usually expressed as lines per inch (lpi). A higher screen ruling gives a smoother appearance, and better detail and sharpness. As the ruling gets higher, the image becomes visually more like the original contone image.

A high screen ruling isn't always better, and the choice of a ruling is tied to a particular printing process. Higher rulings are subject to midtone detail loss and significant dot gain, where the halftone dots become larger through a number of factors. In some cases larger dots in darker areas of an image can completely plug up, creating a solid. This is why each printing process has a practical limit for a screen ruling.

Newspaper printing makes this easy to understand, because the paper is of low quality, is very absorbent, and is usually printed at very high speeds with loose tolerances. Most newspapers use a screen ruling of between 65 and 100 lpi; any higher and the images are likely to turn to blobs. On the other extreme, jobs printed on expensive, coated, very smooth paper using a newer printing press with very tight tolerances can reliably use a screen ruling of 200 lpi, because this type of job is much less vulnerable to dot gain and image plugging. Typical commercial print jobs are run at screen rulings from 133 to 175 lpi, with 150 lpi being most common. Magazine printing typically uses 133 lpi.

Digital printing systems [8.4], such as those made by Heidelberg and Xerox, employ sophisticated multilevel dot generation techniques to create an appearance of high screen rulings with limited resolution. These machines are able to vary not only the size of the dot, but also the density of the dot, giving the appearance of multiple levels of gray despite their low resolution.

2. SCREEN ANGLES

Halftones are created as lines of dots. These are usually turned at different angles, called ***screen angles***, during production to further minimize the appearance of a halftone pattern. The simplest screen angle is 45 degrees. This angle produces the least apparent halftone, because the rows of dots line up with the edges of right-angled images. In black-and-white printing, or any printing that uses a single ink, the screen angle is almost always 45 degrees.

When multiple colors are printed, the darkest ink usually is imaged at 45 degrees, then the next darkest ink is imaged at 75 degrees, and so forth. Ideally all the inks are angled 30 degrees apart. Multiple inks can't have the same angles, or use angles other than those 30 degrees apart from each other; otherwise objectionable ***moiré*** (interference) patterns appear.

In **four-color process** [6.9.2.2] printing, black ink uses a 45-degree angle, magenta uses 75 degrees, cyan uses 15 degrees, and yellow is kept at 0 degrees (same as 90 degrees). It's not possible to print four inks with all four screen angles 30 degrees apart, so yellow is left alone because it is the lightest process ink and is the least likely to cause objectionable patterns.

The four-process ink angles, when printed, produce a pattern called a rosette, where the halftone dots of each screen form a circular pattern around a single dot that's an overprint of all four inks. Other rosette patterns are possible, though the *dot-centered* rosette is the most common. As the dots of each ink get larger or smaller, color is altered in the rosette. Rosettes also overlap to some degree.

Moiré can appear even when the angles are correct, but the appearance can be mitigated by altering each ink's screen ruling by a few lines per inch, or by increasing the overall screen ruling of all four inks. Moiré and its elimination was one of the driving forces behind the development of **FM screening** [6.8.6.5].

3. DOT SHAPES

Round dots were most commonly used before the advent of digital halftone imaging because there wasn't a simple means available to change the shape of halftone dots. Digital imaging devices can produce multiple dot shapes, and now the elliptical dot is most common.

Round dots, despite their name, tend to appear square as the dot size approaches the 50 percent point, and this can cause an abrupt increase in tonal values because the corners of the dots begin to touch. Elliptical dots don't exhibit this behavior. In general, dot shape is predetermined in a device's RIP and there's rarely a reason to alter the shape.

4. Dot gain

All printing processes exhibit ***dot gain***, or more correctly, tone value increase, to varying extents. This includes desktop inkjets, laser printers, digital presses, and any conventional printing press. Certain printing processes exhibit far more dot gain than others; for example, newspaper printing has much higher dot gain than high-quality sheetfed lithography on smooth coated paper. Dot gain is caused by a number of factors: paper quality and absorbency, printing plate exposure method, printing process, printing press conditions, and optical effects.

Most papers will absorb printing inks to some extent, especially if the ink is not set or cured immediately after impression. Absorbed ink can spread, and this is what causes dots to get larger. The degree of absorption depends on the porosity of the paper, the type of ink, the printing process, and the impression pressure. Hard, smooth, coated papers exhibit very little absorption, while soft, uncoated, porous papers like newsprint or brown kraft absorb ink very rapidly.

Dot gain is easily understood: when a halftone dot is supposed to be, for example, 40 percent in a digital image and on imagesetter film, but it prints at 60 percent, then it's said to exhibit 20 percent dot gain, the difference between 40 and 60 percent.

Dot gain is most apparent in tonal ranges from 35 to 75 percent, simply because slight dot size changes aren't as noticeable in the other areas—the dots are too small or large for any minor change in size to make a visible difference. The 50 percent area is especially prone to visible gain because it is at this dot size where the dots will begin to overlap, and any increase in size will be immediately apparent.

Some dot gain is caused when plates are made, especially when made from film. Modern computer-to-plate direct exposure with a laser reduces dot gain because each dot is imaged directly without film, and because laser light is extremely focused and does not scatter like ordinary light.

The printing process also affects dot gain. All printing processes use pressure to apply ink to paper. This pressure alone is enough to cause dots to spread, and each process has its own extra gain characteristics.

1. DOT GAIN COMPENSATION

Once the dot gain characteristics of a press or process are known, it's a simple matter to plug these values into a compensation curve. While it's best to perform a test, various standards have emerged for specific printing processes that specify a target dot gain within a range of densities.

A common standard is the ***Specifications for Web Offset Printing (SWOP)*** which specifies that images prepared to meet this specification exhibit a compensation for dot gain in all four printing inks.

Some often-encountered dot gain percentages include:

- Coated sheetfed lithography at 150 lpi: 15 percent
- Uncoated sheetfed offset lithography at 133 lpi: 20 percent
- Coated web offset lithography at 133 lpi: 22 percent
- Newsprint web offset lithography at 100 lpi: 30 percent

Generally dot gain compensation occurs during the conversion of an RGB image to the CMYK color space when using an application like Photoshop. Most often, all tones in an image are adjusted equally; but more sophisticated dot gain compensation techniques adjust for the varying amounts of dot gain at various tonal ranges. Many high-end scanners offer a dot gain adjustment feature when scanning to CMYK, though it's becoming more common to scan images in the native RGB color space of a scanner and monitor.

An important issue in the digital age, when images are used more than once—printed by more than one method (sheetfed and web, or sheetfed and digital) or published in more than one mode (including electronically)—is that the dot gain compensation that was correct for the first use of the digital image file (usually offset printing on paper) is not necessarily appropriate for the others. It is important to archive images with no compensation, so that the proper compensation can be applied each time an image is used.

5. AM vs. FM screening

Conventional halftone screening is called ***amplitude modulation (AM) screening***. Amplitude means size and AM screening breaks up an image into halftone dots of varying sizes to simulate the original image in print. ***Frequency modulated (FM) screening*** (also called ***stochastic screening***) keeps spots the same size and varies the frequency, or number, of spots and the location of those spots to simulate the original image. In FM screening, the concepts of screen angle and screen ruling no longer apply. The spots are randomly placed, and there is no direction (no screen angle) to the spots.

The concept behind stochastic screening is that dots placed randomly will not cause moiré patterns. FM screening software applies advanced algorithms to determine the optimum placement of dots, simulating random placement and avoiding visual artifacts.

A significant advantage of FM screening is the elimination of screen angles, which in turn eliminates any potential for moiré. FM screening can also improve the appearance of continuous tones in a screened image by eliminating the regular, periodic appearance of halftone dots. Fine details are more likely to remain fine in an FM-screened image. Disadvantages of FM screening include increased dot gain in images prepared for conventional halftoning, and a grainy appearance, especially in areas of flat tints.

The FM process has been slow to catch on since its introduction in the mid-1990s, although it shows promise in improving lower-quality flexographic printing, and is used with some regularity in high-end fashion magazines and catalogs due to its high levels of image sharpness and detail.

FM screening is perfect for high-quality color work. Some printers who offer waterless printing use FM screening because of the lower dot gain associated with that process. Waterless printing's lower dot gain counteracts any FM dot gain.

An FM screening method is usually used in inkjet printing as these processes usually aren't capable of generating conventional halftones with their relatively limited resolution and corresponding lack of gray levels.

FM screening is also useful when printing so-called "HiFi" color process work&mdash≥e **below** [6.9.2.3]. These six-plus color systems print more than four process colors; the additional inks must share screen angles with two of the four process inks, typically cyan and magenta, making moiré an inherent problem. FM screening, however, eliminates this problem.

6. Duotones

While a grayscale image appears with up to 256 gray levels on a computer monitor, an offset printing press has a far more limited range. The quality can be improved by increasing the tonal range with additional inks. Duotones, tritones, and quadtones are created using two, three, or four inks. Designers often spec a duotone; tritones and quadtones are used far less frequently.

Duotones are usually printed using black ink and one other color. The black ink ordinarily renders the shadow detail while a lighter color of ink (sometimes a gray) is used in the midtone and highlight areas. Depending on the color of the second ink, the duotone may alter the overall color of a halftone, rather than just adding to the tonal range of the grayscale.

6.9 COLOR

(i) THINKING ABOUT COLOR

An incredible range of radiant energies exists in nature, comprising the *electromagnetic spectrum*. The relatively tiny portion of this vast energy spectrum that we can see is called *light*—essentially the rainbow colors. Color is a psychological sensation caused by light energy entering the human eye. Color is a human experience.

In 1666 Sir Isaac Newton used a triangular glass prism to recreate the rainbow colors in his laboratory from a ray of sunlight entering his window. The rainbow consists of three major bands of color that we call red, green, and blue. This experiment was an important step in the development of color science.

Other color bands like yellow and orange also are visible, but these are narrow, and are only very small fractions of these three major bands. The key related fact here is that our eyes contain three kinds of vision cells (called *cone* cells) which happen to be sensitive to red, green, and blue light. Various mixtures of red, green, and blue light stimulate the corresponding cells in our eyes, and we then experience color.

The appearance of a color cannot yet be perfectly "measured" or "specified" with any instrument. (Human "instruments" are still the best.) Neither can a color nor the appearance of a color be *perfectly* reproduced by any means. But good color reproduction is still attainable. Only perfection eludes us. Printers have been dealing effectively with these limitations for years. Excellent color reproductions are made by using sound technical methods, a delicate balance of art and science, careful craftsmanship, process control techniques, and experience. It is neither easy nor simple to accomplish it, but nonetheless, it can be done. It usually means great cooperation and communication with all of the key members of the production team—from designer to printer.

1. Additive and subtractive color

Understanding *additive* and *subtractive* color is important to color reproduction. It also explains the basic difference between working with colored light (for instance, a rainbow or a computer monitor) and working with inks or paint on paper or canvas.

Additive color theory corresponds well with how the human eye perceives color. Start with colored light. If three different beams of light—red, green, and blue—are projected onto a white surface, where the three colors overlap humans perceive white. Where green and red lights overlap, yellow appears. Green and blue overlapping lights create cyan. Finally, where blue and red overlap the color magenta appears. Thus, three *primary* colors can be added together in various amounts to make many visible colors. This is the *additive* theory.

The same principle is true on computer monitors. If all of the tiny red, green, and blue pixels are turned on at once, it creates a white screen. In the same manner, various adjustments of the amounts of the three primary pixel lights added together will produce the millions of colors available on your monitor. This again describes the additive color principle.

Subtractive color begins with white light. The white light usually comes from a white surface such as paper. Paper is white because its surface reflects the *additive* combination of the red, green, and blue light to our eyes. The light comes from some white light source (for instance a lamp or the sun). To create subtractive colors, we use three primary *colorants* (that is, inks, paints, or dyes): cyan, magenta, and yellow. These colorants act like colored glass—they only allow certain specific colors to pass through to our eyes. Each colorant absorbs about one-third of the white visible light spectrum and transmits the other two thirds. Cyan ink, for example, absorbs red light. Magenta ink absorbs green light. The difference is that this light is produced by *subtracting* the colors that are not needed from the white light coming from the paper or canvas.

For any specific matching color, whether reproduced via additive or subtractive principles, a similar mixture of red, green, and blue light goes into the eye, stimulates the cone cells, and creates the same sensation.

(ii) COLOR SYSTEMS AND COLOR GAMUTS

A *color gamut* is a defined specific range of colors. It's been estimated that humans can see about 10,000,000 different and distinct colors. These millions of colors define the largest gamut possible. Other types of electromagnetic radiation—for example, X-rays, ultraviolet, and infrared light—are "out of gamut" for humans, and are not thought of as "colors." A ***gamut*** then is simply the total collection of possible colors that a given color reproduction system can describe. Since color depends on human vision, the human vision system has the largest gamut of all. (The on-line version of this book provides a diagram of several common color gamuts.)

1. Color in scanners and monitors: RGB

The RGB color system—based on the fundamental red, green, and blue of additive color—is used in all digital imaging, for scanning, processing, and displaying color information. In the computer, RGB digital color data is often coded using eight bits to represent the relative amounts of each primary. Thus with eight bits for each of the three primaries (RGB), it becomes *24-bit color.* Each primary has a decimal value in the range of 0 to 255. This type of image data is sometimes referred to as *RGB data.* It has the advantage that it is compatible with color computer monitors and televisions. It does not, however, represent the entire color gamut perceivable by the human eye, and not all monitors can properly display all the colors that RGB data can specify.

2. Printing color: CMYK and spot color

Printing presses print color in two principal ways. One is with **process color** [6.9.2.2.1], which uses four separate, transparent inks—the main subtractive colors cyan, magenta, and yellow, plus black (***CMYK***)—to produce all other colors. Each ink is printed using a separate printing plate. The plates print a layer of tiny dots and the overlapping dots create an illusion of various colors.

The other type of color used in printing is **spot color** [6.9.2.2.3], which means one specific ink for each color in a design. Spot colors are typically used in jobs that do not have full color images, but where highlight color is required.

1. PROCESS COLOR

Process color is the method of using four specific transparent ink colors to simulate full-color images. These four inks are cyan, magenta, yellow, and black, thus the name *CMYK printing.* (K is used for the black ink so that the letter B is not mistaken for blue and because the black plate is the *key* plate for registration.) Varying amounts of these inks are combined to create many different colors. This is how full-color images are produced. For example, combining yellow and cyan produces green. Combining magenta and yellow produces red. Cyan and magenta combined together create blue.

Process color is subtractive. This means that when equal levels of cyan, magenta, and yellow are combined they should create black. So why does process color require black ink? All inks absorb some extra light that they theoretically should let pass. They also do the opposite: they let some colors of light pass that theoretically should be absorbed. This results in “unwanted” color, which is one reason a perfect black can't be made from C, M, and Y. Black ink is used with C, M, and Y to compensate for this phenomenon. It's also used to boost the density of dark areas without resorting to larger total amounts of ink, which can cause printing problems: it would retard drying and cost more.

2. DEFINING PROCESS COLORS

Process colors are created by specifying how much of each of the four printing inks, CMYK, should be used. This is determined by percentages. For example, a purple color can be created with 65 percent cyan, 75 percent magenta, 0 percent yellow, and 0 percent black.

A solid black uses 100 percent black and 0 percent of cyan, magenta, and yellow. This is written as 0:0:0:100. The percentages are always written in the order of C, M, Y, and then K. To get a richer black, around 40 percent of cyan, 30 percent magenta, and 30 percent yellow are added to 90 to 100 percent black ink.

Most designers won't memorize the exact percentages of CMYK used to create a specific color. To address this problem, designers use a process commercial color guide or color matching swatches from a company such as Pantone, Trumatch, or Focoltone. These guides specify the CMYK percentages required to create most colors and provide a sample color swatch on coated or uncoated paper.

3. SPOT COLORS

Spot colors, often referred to as custom, Pantone, or solid colors, are created on press by using a single ink rather than creating that color with a combination of cyan, magenta, yellow, and black inks.

Spot colors are made by the off-press mixing of certain combinations of inks. In the past, it was difficult to get the exact combination each time, so spot colors were not always consistent. In 1963, Lawrence Herbert found a solution to this problem. He invented the ***Pantone Matching System (PMS)***. This system identifies each spot color with a specific Pantone color name and/or number and provides the exact ink formula to consistently achieve that color. The system is used by all commercial printers, so the same color can be reused at any facility. Designers refer to PMS colors: for example, PMS 641 is a rich blue, while PMS 605 is a yellow. The Pantone Matching System identifies each spot color with a name or number and provides the ink formula.

The ***Trumatch*** and ***Focoltone*** systems are often confused with Pantone. These systems also offer color swatches, but the colors are always defined by process color ink combinations, not by special inks. Designers use them to specify solid colors in designs that are to be printed with process inks. Adding to the confusion, Pantone also offers the ***Pantone Process Guide***, which also offers process color swatches, and the ***Pantone Solid to Process Guide***, which shows the closest process color matches to the standard Pantone system colors. Although many Pantone colors can be successfully simulated, the majority cannot due to the limitations of four-color process as compared to using premixed inks.

The ***DIC Color System Guide*** and ***Toyo Color Finder*** are two other systems for matching spot colors. DIC and Toyo are mostly used in Japan. Also the ANPA-COLOR systems show process conversions for Pantone colors when used in newspaper advertising.

Most color-matching systems also offer libraries for use with design software. The color you choose generally appears differently on a computer monitor than it does when it is printed. Printed color guides or swatches should be used for specification rather than the color shown on a monitor.

Designers often encounter problems in their use of spot colors. The problems usually relate to the overuse of these colors, or to carelessly combining process and spot colors.

4. USING SPOT COLORS

Probably the most common use of spot colors is matching a specific color in a company product or logo. Process inks can create yellow, but have difficulty matching the Kodak company yellow exactly.

Spot colors are also good for creating special color effects. Metallic inks such as silver and gold cannot be effectively simulated using process inks. Fluorescent colors cannot be created using process inks either. They use inks that have special chemicals added to them. Both metallic and fluorescent colors are best reproduced with spot colors.

5. VARNISH

A varnish is a printed coat of shellac or plastic, therefore it cannot be printed using process inks. It is not actually a color, but is designated as a separate spot color. Varnishes are often used to draw attention to a particular area of a design. Used, for example, on a photograph in a page design, the photograph appears to be very shiny compared to the rest of the page.

3. High-fidelity color

The ability of the four-color process to reproduce RGB colors is limited. Many times the resulting colors are not what customers expect. Most of these times, the hue is correct but the saturation or the brightness is not satisfactory. Here is when ***High-fidelity color*** comes into play. High-fidelity color is the reproduction of images using more than four colors to achieve better results than the four-color process.

In 1987, in an effort to expand the color gamut, Harold Kruppers introduced ***Color-Atlas***, a seven-color process designed to use red, green, and blue along with cyan, magenta, yellow, and black. This method allowed the use of traditional halftone screening because it never takes more than three inks to produce a single color.

In 1992, Mills Davis and Don Carli established the ***HiFi Color Project*** with the sponsorship of several industry vendors. Advances in separation software, increases in RIP and computer speed, the introduction of **stochastic screening** [6.8.6.5], and the evolution of **waterless printing** [6.13.1.3] promoted the interest in the HiFi Project.

HiFi color is applicable to projects that require critical and accurate color. Potential markets for high-fidelity color are catalogs, annual reports, high-quality books, packaging, maps, posters, and greeting cards.

Different high-fidelity color systems are available in software today.

Pantone took advantage of the fact that in the United States there are more six-color presses than seven- or eight-color presses, and came out with a HiFi six-color process. Pantone's ***Hexachrome*** process has a significant advantage over the other processes because it uses a six-color ink set of CMY plus orange, green, and black to achieve a larger gamut and increase the color saturation. It also has the most separation options.

4. Four-color transitions

Getting color to print involves four transitions, or stages: getting the image into the computer; manipulating the image inside the computer; creating useful proofs; and getting the job printed. Each area deals in a defined color space, and has special requirements and limitations. Getting from one area to the next involves a transition of data, and that transition is usually where color is affected. The four stages are as follows:

1. Importing the image. Most images are imported into the computer via scanner or digital camera. This work is handled in the RGB color space.
2. Manipulating color within the computer. Images are usually still in RGB, though they might be converted to CMYK at this point.
3. Proofing. This can only be done in CMYK, when proofing for final printed output.
4. Printing. This occurs when the file is sent to a commercial printer, who will output the final high-end version. This too is a CMYK process.

(iii) COLOR REPRODUCTION IN PRINT

There are six important criteria to achieve good color reproduction in print:

- gray balance
- tone reproduction
- tone compression
- color correction
- image sharpness and detail
- memory colors

1. Gray balance

Gray balance is the ability to reproduce the neutral gray of an area in the original image as a perfect neutral gray. This means that there has to be a proper balance of C, M, and Y in the **color separation** [6.9.2.2.1]. This is an important issue in the reproduction of color, because gray balance has a direct relationship to color reproduction. When proper gray balance is not achieved in the separation, while the grays don't reproduce faithfully, a cast of the color that is disproportionate to the gray balance will be seen. While these problems can be seen in the neutral areas, the same will be translated in the other areas of the image where there are hues also. It's critical to correct for gray balance first before venturing into any color correction.

2. Tone reproduction

Tones are the various levels of gray that can be seen between a pitch black and a pure white in a monochrome image. In a color image they are the various shades of CMYK that make up the different levels of the image. In addition to achieving an exact match of colors, reproducing these tones is a challenge to the printer. To achieve a good tone reproduction, there has to be a correct rendering of contrasts.

Contrast is the number of tones that can be found in a reproduced piece, be it on a photographic paper, film, plate, or a printed sheet. This is determined by the number of tones that can be found between the highlight and the midtone areas. A human eye detects the various tones found in this region better than the tones that are between midtone and shadow areas.

3. Tone compression

Another inherent problem in the printing process is the inability of the printing process to produce a density range that matches an original. A typical color transparency has a density range of 3.0, which far exceeds the capability of the printing process. In order to reproduce the original as closely as possible in the printing process, "tone compression" reallocates the range of image densities to what can be reproduced on a specific press.

4. Color correction

The term *color correction* is loosely used today for any change in color in a digital image. But ***color correction*** is specifically designed to address anomalies in the pigments of the process inks, usually termed ***hue error***. Since the inks are contaminated, a cyan is not a pure cyan by itself. It has also a small percentage of magenta and yellow. This is applicable for the other two colors as well (though it's much less in yellow). The excess of unwanted color that each of the process colors carries is the contamination, and this has to be addressed in reproduction. Correcting for these hue errors in the ink during the color separation process is properly called *color correction.*

5. Selective color correction

When only a particular color in the image needs to be altered, then selective color correction is done. If cyan is the contaminated ink, the areas of the image showing the sky can be increased or decreased in a particular hue, without affecting other hues. However, if there is an object in another part of the image with a similar hue, it also will be affected. Almost all of the modern desktop publishing image manipulation software programs have the ability to do something called fine field color correction, applying a color change to a particular hue in a particular object.

6. Image sharpness

A very noticeable aspect of high-quality color printing is the sharpness in the reproduction. If the details that are in the original are not reproduced accurately, then the job may not be accepted by the client. Image sharpness improvements compensate for scanning problems and press-specific reproduction challenges. Digital image modification software, such as Photoshop, is able to detect transitions between tonal areas and slightly darken the pixels on the darker side while slightly lightening the pixels on the lighter side, providing a clearer "edge" between the tones. This effect is called ***sharpening***. When used skillfully, it can improve an image, but when used to an extreme, it can distort the image.

7. Memory colors

The last key aspect of color reproduction is *memory colors.* These are the colors that come to mind when you think of a specific subject. Each person knows what color a sky should look like, and the color of skin. These are the colors that one's memory recalls from its directory, based on past experiences.

Even when a color separation may not be an exact match of the original, the areas of the image that contain common memory colors have to be treated with extra care.

(iv) PROOFING

A proof is a copy of a work in progress, made to reveal errors or flaws, predict results on press, and record how a printing job is intended to appear when finished.

The term describes a broad range of purposes, processes, and technologies. The four main purposes of proofing are:

- to get feedback from a work in progress in order to revise it and correct errors
- to show a client the likely outcome of a printed piece
- to provide direction to a printing press operator
- to serve as a (quasi-) legal contract between a publisher and a printer

The two main processes for creating proofs are analog and digital.

- *Analog* refers to conventional proofs created by exposing film onto photosensitive substrates.
- Digital proofs cover a wide spectrum of technologies, from computer monitors and laser printers to high-end color digital proofing systems.

The specific technologies used for proofing are many and varied.

Analog proofing technologies can be broken into two broad categories: monochrome and color.

- Bluelines and Velox are monochrome proofs created by exposing film onto photosensitive papers, usually to record type and image placement and page order.
- Color analog proof technologies, including DuPont's Cromalin and Kodak's Matchprint, are used (decreasingly) to preview the likely color reproduction of film separations.

As more and more print is driven directly by ***computer-to-plate*** (***CTP***) imaging, digital proofing is fast becoming the norm. The challenge for the designer and publisher is figuring out which technologies to employ at each stage of the design and production process, to maximize quality and minimize cost. Understanding the practical applications and the limitations of each one of these technologies is very important for selecting the optimal proofing device.

But most important in choosing any proofing technology is understanding what the proof has to show and the purpose for which it is being offered.

Black-and-white laser printers are more than adequate for proofing type and general page layouts. But even an expensive color printer may not provide enough detail to satisfy a press operator charged with ensuring the best printed result. Many production problems arise because the proof contains insufficient or inaccurate information about the actual content of a digital file. Mostly this is inaccurate information about color.

1. Preproofs and contract proofs

A simpler way of thinking about proofing purposes is to distinguish between ***preproofs*** and ***contract proofs***. Preproofs are used during the design stage and early in the production process, to give feedback on how the job is progressing in terms of type, page layout, and the placement of graphics. Contract proofs are used to judge critical color and to serve as instructions to the press operator and as a contract with the printer. Contract proofs require prints that exhibit accurate color and, in some cases, true halftone dots and screen angles.

The technologies associated with preproofs are monitors, laser printers, electrostatic printers, and desktop inkjets. The technologies that are often used as contract proofs are dye sublimation printers, continuous tone inkjets, and digital halftone devices.

The main uses of preproofs are to judge the effect of an overall color design, to check the placement of design elements, to observe text flow, to check color breaks for spot colors, and to provide reference in design composition. In contrast, contract proofs are used to judge the color reproduction quality, check registration, and determine precise image sizing.

2. Remote proofing

If a project is to be printed at various locations or if the design has to be evaluated by a client at more than one location, the same job may have to be proofed at multiple sites. The results will be the same as long as the different machines are calibrated to the same standards required by the prepress provider or the printer. A remote proofing approach is used not only for midrange and high-end proofers but also for low-end devices. This strategy avoids the costs and turnaround times associated with using couriers to ship proofs by hand.

Remote proofing is becoming a significant aspect of the digital publishing workflow, particularly at the preproofing stages. Color monitors are not always color-accurate, but their quality is sufficiently high to accurately represent design intention and page layout. PDF files are often used for remote color proofing, both to monitors and to locally printed output. The Internet has enabled a new generation of remote proofing workflows, well represented by the vendor RealTimeImage (www.realtimeproof.com). Remote proofing can be particularly easy for text-oriented black-and-white book and publication work, for which color fidelity is not an issue.

3. Printing conditions

Printing conditions refer to the characteristics of the press and consumables that will be used for the final production. Characteristics such as dot gain, substrates (the material being printed on, e.g., paper or cloth), and ink should be taken into account during the proofing process. Contract proofs are controlled by calibration software that compensates for dot gain and substrate and ink characteristics. Most digital printers can use different kinds of stocks, which allow them to simulate real substrate conditions.

4. Disadvantages of digital proofing

Although the printing industry is now moving toward the implementation of computer-to-plate technology with offset lithography, many printers still use imagesetters and film to make their printing plates. If a digital contract proof is being used by one of these printers, special care must be given to the film, to avoid mishandling, scratches, or fingerprints that could alter its quality or performance, since the proof being reviewed would not have been made directly from that film, as a conventional proof would be.

The ***RIP*** and its software determine the shape of the dots and the screening characteristics that produce the final film halftone screens on the imagesetters. Unless proofing is done with the same RIP, it is very probable that a digital proofer's RIP will produce different screen patterns than the ones produced by the imagesetter's. This can cause color inconsistencies and image fidelity differences between proof and printed piece. Inconsistency problems can occur even if the proofing system produces halftones, due to differences in screening patterns. Sophisticated software is available to adjust differences in color or image accuracy and match the final press sheet.

Digital workflows depend on digital files. If a file is altered during production, unintentionally or intentionally, the color, design element space, and graphic characteristics data are very likely to cause problems. Similarly, if file data is modified after a digital proof is done, the following proof or film results will differ from the first proof. Therefore, special attention must be given to the manipulation of these files, to keep track of all the changes that are made.

5. Acceptance of digital contract proofs

Digital proofs are facing the same acceptance problems that conventional methods (e.g., Cromalin) faced when they were introduced. These proofing systems were accepted very gradually at first, but today are almost industry standards. With new digital workflows and the introduction of CTP technology, the need for digital proofs is growing in almost every segment of the printing industry. However, adaptation to this technology is slowed by the human nature of printers. Proofing is so critical to a job's success, and the risk of a misleading proof is so great, that people are slow to trust a new method.

6. Viewing conditions

The light source under which proofs or printed sheets are observed has an enormous impact on their appearance. Proper light and a proper surrounding environment are needed to judge contract proofs and, in some cases, preproofs. The use of consistent light sources throughout the entire graphic arts process contributes to color accuracy and quality and avoids confusion during the creative and production processes.

The use of different sources of light can affect the appearance of a colored object. For example, a blue object will appear to be a deeper blue and greener under conventional fluorescent light due to the lamp's excess blue and cyan emission. ANSI calls for a 5000K light source for viewing artwork, proofs, and press sheets. A 5000K light source emulates what the human eye perceives as a sunny, bright day. All objects exposed under these conditions are neutrally exposed, which is very helpful for detecting image inaccuracies.

1. THE VIEWING BOOTH

A viewing booth consists of a 5000K equivalent light source placed inside a booth painted a neutral gray. The environment, or the surrounding space where the booth is located, also has an important influence on viewing conditions. Its light should be lower than the booth light, and it should also be gray. The reason for this is that any colored object inside the room will reflect some light over the objects being observed, altering their color characteristics.

7. The human factor

Opinions about image quality always differ from person to person. Different people may have different opinions about the appearance of color. Standard viewing conditions were created to narrow those differences. In the end, a good proof is one that the client approves, containing colors that can be imaged successfully on press.

(v) COLOR MANAGEMENT SYSTEMS

The concept of a standard ***color management system*** (CMS) dates back only to the late 1980s. After several slow and false starts, color management is demonstrably working. The many hardware and software vendors with a stake in a standardized approach to managing color have joined in the International Color Consortium (ICC) and have agreed on a single format for color profiles. There's now a general awareness of color management throughout the graphic arts industry.

Despite these developments, color management is employed only by a minority of designers and publishers. It may be because CMSs are still relatively complex to understand and to implement. There's a big gulf between the broad conception of a CMS, and the detailed reality of its implementation. There are also strongly differing opinions about exactly how to use existing color management standards.

1. What are color management systems?

Perhaps the largest confusion surrounding color management stems from early vendors' claims that it made good color reproduction *automatic.* Once implemented, color management does make color reproduction *predictable* and *repeatable,* no small feat. But good color still requires great skill on the part of the technician. It's not automatic.

The easiest way to get a handle on color management is to understand the three core concepts that underlie it.

1. CHARACTERIZATION

The first is characterization. A color management system uses software to describe the characteristics and performance of color imaging hardware, both input and output devices. These software descriptions are stored as profiles for each imaging device.

The ***ICC profile*** standard, combined with the availability of new, inexpensive spectrophotometers for color measurement, has spurred the development of profiling tools that free the user from reliance on device vendors for output profiles. Users can profile the unique characteristics of their specific devices, and not rely on generalized profiles from the manufacturer. This technology also allows commercial printers to create accurate profiles for specific ink-and-paper combinations on a particular press, running at optimum ink densities.

2. CALIBRATION

The second core requirement of a CMS is calibration. Monitors, printers, and scanners shift, over time, in how they capture or render color. Calibration corrects these drifting values. For color management to succeed, the profiled device must be calibrated so that its current operation will match (as closely as possible) the ideal described in the profile. If a color imaging device goes so far out of alignment that even careful calibration is unable to restore its color profile, the user must create a new profile that more accurately describes the current operation of the device.

3. TRANSFORMATION

The third pillar of color management is transformation, converting color data from one device to another. The transformation of color data, performed by the color transformation engine or color matching method (***CMM***, initials that are also sometimes used to mean *color management module*), is the complex heart of a color management system. The color data is invariably moving from one device-*dependent* (i.e., device-specific) color description to another, and so it has to be transformed through a device-*independent* color space, always one of the CIE variants, CIE XYZ or CIE LAB (see **below** [6.9.5.2]). This introduces a degree of conceptual complexity to color management that sidetracks many a user.

2. Device-independent color

The Commission Internationale de l'Eclairage (CIE, in English the International Commission on Illumination) created a standard color space in 1931 called CIE XYZ. In 1976 this was refined and named CIE L*a*b* (or CIE LAB, often referred to as simply LAB). The CIE attempted to define all color visible to an average human viewer (called the Standard Observer) in terms of three axes.

The vertical axis is lightness, or luminance, or L*. One end of the L* axis is white, the other is black, with a range from 1 to 100. The second axis is a*, encompassing green (–128) at one end and red (+127) at the other. The total number of values between red and green is 255, which is the maximum number of gray values in an eight-bit system. Red and green are opposites on the hue wheel in the LAB model. The b* axis is for blue and yellow, also opposites on the hue wheel, also ranging from –128 (blue) to +127 (yellow). In between those three values are, theoretically, all the values of color visible to humans (divided into units expressible in eight bits).

Behind the scenes in color management, when a color is converted from RGB to CMYK, the RGB values are converted first into LAB values. Then from the LAB values, the CMYK percentages are assigned.

3. Implementing color management

Apple and Microsoft both support color management in their operating systems, which allows software vendors to support color management without having to create custom implementations. Apple offers ***ColorSync***; Microsoft calls its system ***ICM***, for Integrated Color Management. Both of these systems support the ICC standard profile format.

To make color management work, *all* of the system hardware must be calibrated and characterized. This is done with software and test targets, and involves separate processes for input devices (scanners and digital cameras), monitors, and output devices (desktop printers, proofers, offset presses, etc.). Color profiles are then employed in different ways in publishing software like Photoshop and QuarkXPress. All of this involves a level of complexity that appeals only to dedicated users. Larger publishing organizations will often call in a special consultant. A list of color management specialists is available through the Graphic Arts Technical Foundation (http://www.solutionsonsite.org/pages/services/ColorSync.html).

4. Monitors and color management

It's a cliché of color management that still holds true: just visit a store that sells twenty different television sets to see the biggest problem of color management. Color monitors are of such high quality today that it's easy to ignore the problem, but when you view two dozen TVs side-by-side, the degree of disparity is plain to see. For the average computer user the computer monitor is the standard output for images. Monitors are so good as to be dangerous. The colors look vibrant and lifelike, but rarely represent the colors you'll find on a printed sheet, let alone on another monitor down the hall. The key to success in implementing color management is to use high-quality monitors, recently calibrated, and viewed under controlled lighting conditions (away from direct lighting, and against a muted background).

5. Color management beyond print

With the growth of the Web for publishing and e-commerce, interest exploded in applying color management to the Web. It's certainly possible for Web publishers to control the color of published images; controlling the color on the myriad types of monitors used to view Web pages is another matter.

Color management vendors such as E-Color, Pantone, and Praxisoft offer solutions tailored to managing color on the Web. Some of this technology does not rely on users calibrating their monitors or working in controlled viewing conditions, but clearly the results are nowhere near the standards set by print-oriented color management systems. The latest generation of liquid crystal display (LCD) monitors feature a degree of automatic calibration and color management uncommon in the more prevalent (and less expensive) cathode ray tube (CRT) monitors still used by most publishers. The future promises an improvement in the general level of color fidelity for most computer users.

6.10 PAGE PRODUCTION

One of the most significant changes to the composition and prepress process in the digital era is that page production software, which was previously limited to the composition of lines and pages of type and was used almost exclusively by specialists, now offers the sophistication of full prepress functionality, from typesetting to page design and layout to the assembly of all graphic elements, and is used not only by compositors and other production professionals but by designers and publishers themselves—as well as by people with no professional training or experience at all. While there are still some programs (typically the high-end composition programs) still used only by professionals and others used almost exclusively by amateurs (such as the low-end programs developed for home and office users), many programs (QuarkXPress being the prime example) are used for an incredible range of work, from the simplest flyer to the most complex college textbook.

(i) DESKTOP PUBLISHING

In the days before desktop publishing, designers typically worked with pencil and paper, generating "tissues" and written specs; then typesetters set the text into "galleys" of type and compositors assembled pages manually from their constituent elements. The type, graphics, and geometric page elements (such as rules and frames) were pasted down onto art boards. These art boards were photographed onto negative film, and plates in turn were created.

The first phase of the desktop publishing revolution transferred all of these functions to the computer. In doing so it turned designers and publishers into prepress production technicians and forever altered the balance of power between document originators and printers.

1. QuarkXPress

During the late 1980s several vendors (including Quark, Aldus, Letraset, and Ventura) competed to offer the best page layout software. Quark emerged as the winner and QuarkXPress became the standard. As with other companies that have a dominant position in the marketplace (think Microsoft!), Quark is often viewed as high-handed and unsympathetic to its customers. It's accused of poor customer support, of taking too much time between upgrades, and of charging too much money for the upgrades when they're finally released. But the company keeps coming through with the features most requested by those who need them the most. QuarkXPress makes designers and publishers feel empowered to drive their own design and production.

Quark's position was also assured by its XTension capability—third-party software companies are able to supplement the core functionality of QuarkXPress, making the program far more powerful than it would be through the efforts of only one vendor. For example, Autopage provides batch-pagination functionality to what is otherwise a mostly manual page assembly process, and XTags provides more sophisticated tagging and processing than QuarkXPress's tags.

2. Adobe InDesign

Only in the last few years has a competitor emerged that looks like it may have a fighting chance to dislodge QuarkXPress from the throne. Adobe InDesign is extensible in a manner similar to QuarkXPress—in fact, a key aspect of its architecture is to be as modular and extensible as possible, arguably exceeding Quark in that respect—and has the added advantage of tight interoperability with Adobe's best-selling illustration and image editing software, Illustrator and Photoshop. Adobe currently markets three different page layout programs: PageMaker (a desktop publishing program it acquired from Aldus), targeted mainly at the office market; FrameMaker, designed for long documents like books and manuals (it has editorial and XML capabilities far beyond what desktop systems offer); and InDesign, targeted at graphic design and production professionals. When it first came out, InDesign was viewed more as a design tool than a production tool (it has many particularly sophisticated design features), but as it has evolved it has been embraced by an increasing number of production professionals, particularly in the newspaper and magazine markets. Nonetheless QuarkXPress appears to be so well entrenched in the publishing industry that it may remain the page layout standard for some years to come.

3. Supplementing desktop systems

Until recently, prepress shops and printers felt that they needed to supplement the functionality of desktop software with more sophisticated prepress systems. Companies like Scitex and Heidelberg offered expensive dedicated hardware and software packages that were the standard for most large prepress and printing firms. Two things have changed. Desktop hardware and software is now essentially as powerful as the dedicated systems, at a much lower per workstation cost. And the move towards PDF workflows has further migrated prepress functionality to the desktop. Today's high-end prepress systems are dedicated mainly to processing PDF files. The two leading systems, Creo's Prinergy and Agfa's ApogeeX, have become the standard systems for interpreting PDF files and outputting them, mainly directly to plate.

(ii) OTHER PAGE PRODUCTION SYSTEMS

Although desktop publishing software is used to produce the vast majority of print pages today, other systems are important, particularly in certain focused areas of publishing like books and journals. Much professional work in those markets is done on specialized high-end systems, some of which are evolving to utilize XML in ways far in advance of desktop systems. Most technical manuals and other documentation are produced on "tech doc" systems that typically straddle the functionality of desktop and high-end systems and also often incorporate sophisticated SGML or XML functionality. And in certain disciplines, the venerable but powerful public-domain TeX is commonly used, even by authors.

1. High-end composition systems

The heyday of high-end composition systems was the 1970s and 1980s, before desktop publishing came to dominate the market. Many of the systems from those days no longer exist, but several have adapted to the changes in technology and are still in use, particularly by experienced composition specialists who have the knowledge to take advantage of their sophisticated capabilities. The leading such systems are XyVision, Miles 33, Datalogics, and Penta (all of which are veterans from the 1980s), as well as Advent's 3B2, a newer system that emerged in the 1990s. Most scientific journals (particularly technical ones), many large encyclopedias and complex college textbooks, and much high-volume professional work like legal, tax, and accounting material is composed on such systems, although they are used for high-volume production of more straightforward work as well.

These systems are typically characterized by robust SGML and XML implementations, powerful batch pagination capabilities (often coupled with interactive pagination as well), and sophisticated typographic controls, including the ability to set complex tabular and mathematical material. To professionals, these capabilities are not only desirable but, in some situations, essential: for highly technical, large-volume applications, these systems can do things that are simply not possible or practical in the desktop publishing environment. (The best desktop tools can, with sufficient work, produce virtually any page the high-end systems can; what they typically lack is the automation needed to do complex, typographically sensitive work in high volume.)

However, there are many reasons why these high-end systems are not in wider use. The price of the software may seem to be the obvious obstacle: whereas desktop software can be purchased for a few hundred dollars, high-end systems cost thousands of dollars—sometimes many thousands. However, these systems' productivity often more than justifies the investment. The more serious issue is personnel rather than price. These systems often require significant expertise on the part of their operators; their sophistication makes them complex. Although they have all migrated to standard operating systems (most work in Unix or Windows environments), they often require an extensive infrastructure and expert systems management.

2. Tech doc systems

There is a class of page production systems that occupies something of a middle ground between desktop publishing systems and high-end systems.

Most of these systems were originally developed for the production of technical documentation, an environment often characterized by a high volume of uniformly structured material. Whereas commercial compositors usually have to be able to produce a huge variety of formats, documentation environments usually depend on standard templates that are used for most or all of the publications. Arbortext and Adobe's FrameMaker are the leading such systems. It is appropriate to consider TeX and Corel's Ventura in this context as well.

Whereas high-end systems can be, and are, used to produce any pages these tech doc systems produce (often with more sophisticated typographic controls), the tech doc systems have a number of advantages. In keeping with their middle-ground status, they are more expensive and complex than desktop publishing systems but less so than most high-end systems. Most importantly, they are often integrated with an editorial functionality, whereas desktop and high-end systems typically compose pages only after the editorial process is complete. Particularly when they are SGML- or XML-based—a core capability of Arbortext and an important one of FrameMaker—they enable not only the composition to be structured but the editing as well. These "structured editing" environments offer the capability of providing a user-friendly interface that guides writers and editors to the proper use of elements and tags. They usually offer multiple views, with or without tags, and even reveal the underlying XML tagging (for those who care to look). They can interpret the specifications in a Document Type Definition (DTD) or ***XML schema*** and can be programmed to allow users to insert only the tags permitted at a given point in the text. So, for example, if the user asks to insert a list, the system first checks to see if a list is permitted at that point in the text, and if so, presents the user with the cursor positioned between <LIST> and </LIST> tags, with an <LI> tag already generated. These editorial tags are also typically tied to the stylesheets that guide production of the typeset pages (or other forms of presentation). Although these systems can be difficult to implement when the published material is varied and the editing is done largely by freelancers, they work extremely well in highly structured environments with in-house editing.

3. Ventura

In the early days of desktop publishing, one of the leading programs was Ventura Publisher. Whereas QuarkXPress and Aldus Pagemaker were more often used on the Macintosh, Ventura was the leader on the PC, and was particularly suited for composition of longer documents. Lacking the capabilities of the high-end systems (and aiming for the desktop market rather than the professional market), and lacking the marketing muscle and wide acceptance of QuarkXPress and Pagemaker, Ventura dropped out of favor in the late 1990s. However, it was acquired by Corel, a Canadian company that has managed to offer some competition to other market leading programs (its illustration program, CorelDRAW, competes with Adobe's dominant Illustrator, and its word processor, WordPerfect, competes with Microsoft's dominant Word). In late 2002, Corel issued a new version of Ventura that has XML capabilities far exceeding those of its desktop competitors (Corel also owns a leading XML editing program, XMetaL, which it acquired from SoftQuad) while retaining its historic orientation to long-document production. Whether it will prevail in the marketplace remains to be seen, but at this writing Ventura once again seems worth paying attention to.

4. TeX

TeX (pronounced "tech," and technically, though not commonly, spelled with a subscript Epsilon and a chi: T_EX) is a fascinating program originally developed by Donald Knuth, a mathematician at Stanford, who became frustrated at how hard it was to get his papers typeset properly. In the late 1970s (well before the desktop revolution, and before Postscript) he created TeX along with a font technology known as Metafont and a specialized font family known as Computer Modern (and put them all in the public domain, well before open source was in vogue). TeX was designed specifically for mathematical composition—although it can be used for nonmathematical material as well. TeX is commonly used only in a very few disciplines (mathematics, engineering, and in some of the physical sciences such as physics and astronomy), but in some of these narrow areas it is almost universally used. Some composition services use TeX as their main composition engine. Thus TeX is unique in being used both as an original authoring tool and as a professional composition tool.

TeX "thinks" of a math equation as a mathematician does. Unlike most math composition programs, TeX builds equations based on the mathematical meaning of their components. It "understands" what an integral or a summation is, what a numerator and denominator are, what operands and variables are—and, to a great extent, formats them and positions them automatically based on the proper mathematical conventions. Moreover, TeX provides powerful macro writing capabilities, which its users often eagerly embrace, in order to create long cumbersome expressions with just a few keystrokes. Its hyphenation and pagination routines are also sophisticated, enabling it to recompose any or all lines within a paragraph to accommodate a correction or fix a page makeup problem. These features are what make TeX powerful to a knowledgeable user in a controlled environment, but they make TeX files particularly problematic to convert for other systems. Some standard macro packages have been developed for TeX (the most common of these is LaTex), but even when these are used in a rigorous and disciplined fashion they usually work best when the entire composition and production process is done with TeX or with a very TeX-aware system like Arbortext's.

6.11 IMAGE CAPTURE AND IMAGE PROCESSING

(i) SCANNING

A scanner takes a physical image—either a photograph, a 35-mm slide, a print, a transparency, or line art—and, using a light source, electronically converts that image into binary data that can be used to store the image on a computer.

Some publishers still choose to use outside services for scanning, but many publishers—especially magazine and newspaper publishers—do their scanning in house. The quality of scanners has risen dramatically in the last few years, while the prices have dropped to very affordable levels.

Scanners can be characterized two ways: by the types of originals they're capable of scanning or by their mechanical construction. In terms of types of originals, ***reflective scanners*** handle photographic prints and original artwork. ***Transparency scanners*** handle transparencies—film negatives and positives. ***Dual function scanners***, as the name implies, handle both reflective and transmissive (transparent) originals.

There also are three types of mechanical construction. ***Flatbed scanners*** hold reflective and/or transmissive originals on a glass plate parallel to the desk or table that holds the scanner. ***Drum scanners*** feature a cylinder around which the original reflective or transmissive artwork is held. The drum is rotated in front of the light source and the scanning heads. A transparency scanner is designed to hold small-format film negatives or positives.

There is a fourth type, a handheld scanner, but this isn't suited to quality image reproduction. A specialized reflective flatbed scanner, the ***document scanner***, is optimized for the high-speed reproduction-quality image capture of large quantities of documents.

1. High-end scanners

The first scanners used in the graphic arts industry were high-end drum scanners. Early drum scanners included both input and output units: an analyzing (scanning) unit, a color computer, a screening computer, and a recording unit (sometimes in a single device). Final separated film separations were then assembled manually into pages.

A decade ago the least expensive professional scanner was about $10,000; 20 years ago, closer to $100,000 (and higher). Today price is not an issue. For example, as of this writing, scanners with 48-bit color at a resolution of 600 x 1,200 dpi sell for under $100, and scanners with 2,400 x 4,800-dpi resolution only a few hundred dollars more.

Desktop scanners do not have the built-in automatic scanning controls that traditional high-end scanners have. The scanner typically comes with control software, and most scanners come with color editing and manipulation tools that install on the computer. Some use Adobe Photoshop with a plug-in for controlling the scanner.

2. Transparencies vs. reflective art

Novices often prefer to scan photographic prints rather than negatives because the print is easier to visually evaluate. But photographic negatives and positives contain a lot more image detail and tonal detail than prints, and are much preferred for high-quality image reproduction.

Density range or dynamic range is the measure of tonal detail in an original image. The scale ranges from zero density to four—clear film to black. The mathematics of dynamic range are complex but the indication is clear—photographic prints have a dynamic range less than two, while transparencies have a dynamic range of up to three and a half.

It's important to keep in mind the output quality intended for the scans. Scanning for reproduction on a computer monitor is far less demanding than scanning for print reproduction. Scanning for reproduction on newsprint is far less demanding than scanning for reproduction on a glossy coated stock. Scanning an image that will be significantly enlarged is more demanding than scanning for small images—large-size image reproduction can reveal a host of errors, whether in the original or in the scanning process.

While even inexpensive scanners today offer very high resolution, the low-end scanners are deficient in their sensitivity to dynamic range. Purists still prefer drum scanners for optimal quality.

(ii) DIGITAL CAMERAS

Even as scanners have become affordable and easy to use, digital cameras are claiming an ever-increasing portion of original image capture. As with scanners, digital cameras are available in professional models with professional model price tags, but in fact consumer digital cameras, available for under $500, offer sufficient tone and image detail to satisfy all but the most demanding professionals.

Digital photography offers numerous advantages over scanning. One or more workflow steps are eliminated, as is the cost of film and photographic prints. In many cases the quality of the final image reproduction is actually higher, as the intermediate steps of photographic printing, followed by scanning, are eliminated.

1. Resolution

Digital camera resolution is expressed as a whole image matrix—the total number of samples captured. Kodak states that a camera with 1 million pixels can image a 5 x 7-in photo-realistic print. The current "high end of the low end" digital camera models are 3.x-megapixel cameras, indicating roughly three million pixels of data. Because of the interpolation of the data required from the sensor and limitations of the optics, these cameras are capable of resolving about 1,100 lines per picture in height and about 1,450 lines in width.

The most expensive professional digital cameras offer about six million pixels (still short of the estimated twenty million pixels in 35-mm film).

2. Color depth

Another key specification for digital cameras is ***color depth***, sometimes referred to as ***pixel depth***, a number such as 24, 36, or 42. This number refers to the number of bits used to describe each pixel.

Today's scanners and digital cameras offer 36-bit (12 colors per pixel), 42-bit (14 colors per pixel), and 48-bit (16 colors per pixel) color. These extra bits aren't used to generate colors that are later imaged. They're used to improve the color in the image as it is processed down to its 24-bit final form. Bruce Fraser has done an excellent analysis of the advantages of editing so called "high-bit" files and notes that major global edits for tone and color stand much less chance of running into visible posterization and banding than the same edits to a file that started out with eight-bit channels (http://www.creativepro.com/story/feature/7627.html).

3. ISO values

Another photographic term that has made the transition to digital—although somewhat loosely—is the ***ISO value***. This value refers to film sensitivity, or film speed. Film comes in various levels of sensitivity to light, from what are called "slow" film speeds (ISO 25 to 64) to "fast" film speeds (ISO 1600 and beyond). Each doubling of the ISO number indicates a doubling in film speed, so each of these films is twice as fast as the next. In general, using fast film lets you shoot under a greater variety of lighting conditions, and fast film is occasionally used in low light situations. The drawback to fast film is that you tend to get a grainier image.

Like film, digital cameras have a range of different sensitivities, which camera vendors have a tried to make roughly analogous to the corresponding ISO values in the film world. In digital photography cameras can be adjusted to act as ISO 100, 200, or 400. Higher end cameras offer a higher range of ISOs.

(iii) CCDS

When the information from a digital camera is transferred to disk it is pixel-based information, but when the picture is taken, it is captured through samples. The same is true of a scanner. Inside both a digital camera and most desktop scanners is a CCD—a charged-coupled device. CCDs receive light that either bounces off reflective paper or through transparent film. Most desktop scanners and digital cameras these days have what are called ***trilinear arrays***, meaning that in one pass the information from the red, green, and blue channels is simultaneously recorded and stored digitally.

There are three bars on the CCD with slightly different colors on them. Those colors are the filters. The length of the CCD indicates how much information it is capable of sampling. It is an arduous and expensive process to manufacture CCDs, so the longer they are, the more expensive. That is the big reason for the price jumps in both digital cameras and scanners.

A white light passes over the scanner and the light is bounced to a mirror that bounces the light to the CCD. (The light from the scanner bounces off mirrors and through lenses in order to be focused on the CCD.) The red filter only sees the information in the cyan range, the green filter sees magenta information, and the blue filter sees the yellow.

Other scanner sensors use complementary metal-oxide semiconductors (***CMOS***) or photomultiplier tubes (***PMTs***). Early CMOS sensors offered poor image quality, and were used mostly in low-end digital cameras and flatbed scanners. The quality of CMOS sensors is fast improving, and they are now incorporated in some professional cameras. PMTs are used exclusively in drum scanners.

(iv) CHOOSING A SCAN RESOLUTION

There are different resolution requirements for different kinds of scanned images—continuous tone and line art.

1. Continuous tone images

Several factors impact the choice of scanner resolution for continuous tone images. These factors fall into three main areas: the type of original, the quality of the reproduction, and the size of the reproduction.

Continuous tone originals don't usually contain a lot of image detail that has to be carefully captured in a scan. However, some contone images will contain text or other small image detail that demands a higher-than-usual scan resolution.

The quality of reproduction is determined mainly by the line screen chosen. The higher the line screen, the more scan resolution required.

Most of the time, scanned originals are reproduced at a size similar to the original or slightly smaller. But if an original image is scanned to be printed as a poster or other oversized print then additional scan resolution is required.

A formula for determining optimal scan resolution is:

SR = OLS x M x SF

where

SR = Scanning resolution (the number of samples per inch needed in the final scan file)

OLS = Output line screen (the line screen that will be used in creating the printing plates; newspapers use as little as 85 lpi; some high-end annual reports or catalogs use 200 lpi; 150 is most common in offset printing)

M = Magnification factor (the percentage enlargement from the original; a 4 x 5-in photograph scanned to produce an 11 x 17-in poster requires a 340 percent magnification resulting in a magnification factor of 3.4)

SF = Scan factor (the amount of oversampling used to make sure there's sufficient data in the scan)

Scan factor generates a lot of disagreement among specialists, who argue passionately for various measures between one and two. A factor of two is a conservative measure, appropriate when the original is extremely detailed. Most scans can use a factor of 1.2; the eye won't detect a difference.

2. Scanning line art

Text requires very-high-resolution scanning to avoid jagged edges; so does line art. In order to output line art on an imagesetter it requires at least 800 samples per inch—and preferably over 1,000.

3. Scanning for the screen

Traditionally CRT computer monitors were limited to a resolution of 72 ppi. Scanning images for computer display involved a simple choice. Would the user want to magnify the image? If the answer was yes, a resolution of perhaps double (144 ppi) was called for. Otherwise 72 ppi was sufficient. LCD displays are manufactured today with a resolution as high as 200 ppi, so electronic publishing is starting to approach print in its demands for higher resolution. At the same time, bandwidth remains a major factor for the Web publisher and encourages the smallest possible file size. JPEG compression offers the best compromise—high-resolution images can be posted to the Web with modest file sizes.

4. RGB vs. CMYK

All scanners and digital cameras capture images in RGB mode. All computer monitors display images in RGB mode. Nearly all printing is done in CMYK mode. So when is it appropriate to convert an RGB image into CMYK? Many graphic arts professionals are more comfortable doing image processing in CMYK mode. However, the increasing need for images to be reusable both for electronic and print publishing suggests that RGB is the more appropriate mode. Converting images back and forth from RGB to CMYK does lead to some loss of color detail, but the larger problem is that an early conversion to CMYK may lead to unnecessary workflow steps. The most efficient workflow for cross-media publishing is to maintain images in RGB format for as long as possible, converting them only to CMYK when their print destination is certain.

5. Image reuse and archiving

In traditional print publishing, images were scanned for a specific print purpose. The output size had already been specified, so the optimal scan resolution was matched to the intended output. The new workflow of electronic publishing seeks to maintain the maximum flexibility of image reuse. Future requirements can never be determined accurately in advance. Perhaps an image printed in a book on a quarter-page will be required to be reproduced full-size on the cover of the next edition. With storage costs continuously dropping, the most efficient scanning workflow captures and archives images at the highest possible resolution for maximum flexibility in the future.

6. Scanner tips

The combination of high-quality imaging devices and very good imaging software has made it possible for near amateurs to reproduce high-quality images. On the other hand, scanning and image correction for professional publishing is still a task that requires both knowledge and experience. It's beyond the scope of this chapter to cover all of the intricacies of scanning and image correction. But some basic tips can benefit both the amateur and the professional:

- Desktop scans may not offer enough quality for professional publication. When in doubt, turn to a professional scanning service.
- Place originals in the center of the scan bed, not at the edges. Most desktop scanners use a lens to focus the sample information onto the sensor. At the edges, some of the information is refracted.
- Clean the flatbed scanner glass with the proper cloth and cleaning fluid, usually purchased in a camera store. Ordinary glass cleaner is not

a good idea. Never use paper to clean the glass—it can create microscopic scratches on the glass.

- Blow dust off pictures and negatives with canned compressed air or a blower.
- Wear disposable cotton gloves when handling film, so that the oils in your fingertips won't damage the emulsion on the film.

(v) ADOBE PHOTOSHOP

QuarkXPress dominates the professional page layout market. Adobe Photoshop *is* the professional image editing market. There are no competitors. There are other programs that will do *some* of what Adobe Photoshop will do. There are a few programs that will do *most* of what Adobe Photoshop will do. But Adobe has focused so completely on the needs of designers and prepress professionals that it has succeeded in precluding any serious competition. At the same time the software has become the favorite also of professional photographers and of Web page designers.

Like QuarkXPress, Photoshop is extensible. Plug-ins, "actions," brushes, scripts, and styles greatly extend Photoshop's design and production capabilities. The software is also scriptable, so that repetitive functions can be automated (see http://share.studio.adobe.com/Default.asp).

Adobe also offers a slimmed down, simplified version of Photoshop, Adobe Photoshop Elements, designed specifically for photo hobbyists and amateur photographers. It offers a higher degree of automation, and a $99 suggested retail price (vs. $600 for the full version of Photoshop).

(vi) CLIP ART AND DIGITAL PHOTO LIBRARIES

Supplementing a designer's arsenal is a huge range of no-cost and low-cost clip art and digital photography. Nearly all of it is available on the Web. High-quality photographic images are available from stock services, although the cost of the best images remains high and carries numerous use restrictions.

Some photographic images are preseparated into CMYK, although most are offered as RGB. The better vendors color manage their images. (A good source of information on color production issues with these images is available at http://creative.gettyimages.com/source/services/color_resources.asp.)

6.12 WORKFLOW

Unlike other manufacturing assembly lines, graphic arts workflows do not follow a model production process. Each design studio, each publishing house, each production service, and each printing plant is different. Designers and publishers have integrated computers into their workflow. Content creators are now doing many of the tasks that used to be done by compositors, prepress houses, and printers. Printers and prepress services have lost control over file preparation for printing. And the method of digital file preparation determines the rest of the process. (Our focus here is on a prepress workflow for print; other sections of this book discuss creation of **on-line publications** [10] or **e-books** [11].)

(i) COMPONENT FILES

The beginning of a prepress workflow for high-end printing is to take a variety of component files—image files (raster files, typically generated by Photoshop), artwork files (generally vector files created in programs like Illustrator and FreeHand), and text files (usually originating as word processing files, most often Microsoft Word)—and assemble them into pages using page makeup software like the **desktop** [6.10.1], **tech doc** [6.10.2.2], or **high-end** [6.10.2.1] systems discussed above.

(ii) CONSOLIDATED FILES

Consolidated files are used to bring all of the component files, both raster and vector, into a single format—a container—that is accepted by an output processing system. The consolidated format has been PostScript, but PDF is now a key alternative. Font handling, color handling, resolution, target output device, and compression must be set up in advance in order to achieve an acceptable consolidated file.

In PostScript, altering the consolidated file after creation requires recreation from the original component files. PDF started the same way, but now there are many tools for editing PDFs.

(iii) EDITABILITY

The need to make changes to a job is inherent in a graphic arts workflow. Author's alterations, printer's errors, and Murphy's Law make editability an issue at every stage in the process. With automated production processes, it's vital to get the job right as far up front as possible and then have the ability to make changes at each step if necessary. However, in the digital age care must be taken to make sure the ultimate archive files incorporate all the changes that have been made along the way. If composition files are archived (or XML files derived from those composition files), and the printer makes changes to the PDFs at the printing stage, those changes will not be reflected in the archive unless special effort is taken. When possible, it's best to go back to the archived (or to-be-archived) file to make the change, and generate replacement PDFs, so there is no danger the archive does not match up to the finished product.

(iv) OBSTACLES TO WORKFLOW AUTOMATION

If technology helps us work faster, better, and more efficiently, why is it that technology is not always successful, particularly in graphic arts? The answer is, there are too many variables. This is a developing industry, and it lacks standardization.

The ultimate workflow would be one that is completely digital. Traditional print publishing has problems related to incompatible equipment and disconnected "islands of automation" created by new electronic publishing processes, as well as entirely new digital production bottlenecks.

Islands of automation are highly automated processes within the workflow that are not continuous with the other steps or processes that precede or follow in the workflow. For example, computer-to-plate technologies don't always feature reliable digital proofing. The benefits of having a filmless and time-effective platemaking process are diminished by the fact that some publishers require a film-based proof.

Bottlenecks occur when one of the processes in the workflow has less capacity than the demands placed on it. Each process is composed of many steps. Every step or production operation has a certain capacity, and the capacity of each of these operations is not the same. Some stations work faster than others, meaning that at some point some workstations will be idle while others will be overloaded. Islands of automation lead to very fast, highly automated processes linked to slower processes that will become system bottlenecks. The problem with bottlenecks is that they end up determining the capacity of the entire system.

(v) WORKFLOW AUTOMATION

Workflow automation combines simple and complex tasks that do not require manual intervention. However, in the graphic arts, there are probably as many exceptions as rules. Exceptions are those jobs that do not run easily through the workflow. Managing exceptions is extremely difficult. Exceptions are more expensive than managing regular standardized processes because they require operator expertise and intervention.

(vi) WORKFLOW DESIGN

When designing a workflow, it's necessary first to analyze the different steps that are encountered most frequently; then, to identify the individual processes to produce the desired results; and finally, to design a workflow, or a group of workflows, that can handle those steps in an efficient manner. Workflow design does not streamline each task in order to save time at that step in the process, but rather optimizes the entire process. The whole is the sum of its parts. The following are some of the typical tasks in a print production environment:

- Design
- Typesetting
- Scanning
- Image correction
- Page assembly
- Color management
- PDF file creation
- Proofing
- Correction
- Preflighting
- Trapping
- Imposition
- RIPping
- Plate output
- Printing
- Storage/archiving

Each one of these tasks has its own requirements. Workflows differ widely. Each one may combine tasks that are largely manual with others that are highly automated.

(vii) NETWORKING

To create a network is, in essence, to connect computers and other communications devices in a way that many users can share common resources.

Local area networks (LANs) connect hardware and software via communications channels within a close proximity. An example of a simple LAN is two computers linked with a telephone wire and connected to a printer. The network could be in a single floor, or several floors within the same building, or even a few buildings, but within close proximity. The connectivity is usually created using twisted copper wire or coaxial cable between these devices. In a slightly larger network, the network could consist of a few computers, a file server, shared hard drives, a laser printer, storage devices, a color printer, and possibly an imagesetter. Software runs the network and manages all the activities in the network. When used properly, LANs allow a number of users to share the cost of expensive hardware, software, and storage devices. See the **networking** [2.6] section of The Technical Infrastructure chapter for more detail.

1. Servers

Digital data has to be stored, managed, processed, and transferred to produce a job. Servers are necessary to network workstations and other hardware. Print and prepress servers perform four different functions: file, print, application, and database.

A *file server*'s function is to store a large number of digital files and share the data or some applications with other workstations on the network.

An *application server*'s function is to perform a certain task when files from the network are sent to a specific folder on the server. One of the most common shared applications is image trapping.

A *database server*'s function is to handle all file tracking functions.

The *print server*'s function is to spool all the printing files from the network to a central area until the printer is free. The spooler permits monitoring the printer and scheduling jobs for printing with the goal of allowing various workstations to use the same printer.

2. Open Prepress Interface (OPI) servers

Work with high-resolution images can be inefficient, especially when moving digital files over a network. High-resolution images have large amounts of data that cause bottlenecks in the prepress workflow. Although faster networks and better file compression techniques have improved transmission speeds, file size problems in data transmission have been compounded by the addition of supporting applications like trapping and imposition. An ***Open Prepress Interface (OPI)*** server is a prepress production tool that permits the use of low-resolution images to facilitate the workflow. These low-resolution images are derived from high-resolution ones but they are radically smaller, speeding up transmission over digital networks.

With OPI, high-resolution images are kept on a standard server while *for position only* (***FPO***) images are used in page layout programs. The result is a much smaller layout file that is very easy to transfer across a network. At the same time, on the main server, the full image is available for any direct operation like color correction or retouching. When the layout and the high-end image are complete, the layout is sent to an OPI server queue where the FPO is automatically replaced by the high-resolution image. Another benefit of the small size of the layout file produced with OPI is that these files open faster for other prepress production steps like imposition and image trapping.

3. DCS and OPI

Many OPI solutions also support Desktop Color Separation (***DCS***), an industry-standard convention for handling color separations created with desktop publishing programs. DCS originated with Quark as a way to manage color separation files. DCS works with **Encapsulated PostScript (EPS)** [6.8.5.1.5] files. In producing color separations, DCS-compliant programs generate a set of five EPS files. These five files include a main, or *composite* file, as well as a file for each color separation: cyan, magenta, yellow, and black. The composite file contains the names of the cyan, magenta, yellow, and black EPS files and the path name to their storage location; PostScript commands to print a non-separated version of the image; and a 72-dpi PICT version of the image for viewing on the screen.

In a typical DCS operation, the user places the composite image in the Quark file. When the user prints the job, Quark sends the color separations instead of the composite image. OPI systems that also support DCS enhance this operation by allowing the color separation files to be stored on the server, so Quark does not have to transmit these large files at print time. Quark sends only the callouts (which contain the pathname to the separation files), and the OPI-compliant imagesetter fetches those files accordingly.

PDF workflows are changing the nature of networks, servers, systems, and prepress. With scripts or plug-ins, many routine tasks can be automated. A script might take a QuarkXPress file, open it, distill it, open Acrobat, perform a function, save it, and then invoke server functions to trap the PDF, impose it based on the electronic work order, direct it to a proofer, and prioritize it to a print queue.

(viii) TRAPPING

Trapping is compensation—before printing—for the mechanical errors that result in misregistration of images on a printing press. Typically, trapping spreads (expands) or chokes (contracts) light colors in relation to darker colors so there aren't distracting white gaps if the colors don't register precisely.

Most imaging and page layout programs offer trapping features. Manual trapping is available in Macromedia FreeHand, QuarkXPress, and Adobe's Illustrator, InDesign, and Photoshop. Dedicated trapping programs such as ScenicSoft TrapWise interpret color data in the job file and automatically apply chokes and spreads. Automated trapping produces professional results more easily and with fewer pitfalls than manual trapping within application software. Most RIPs also have a trapping function, called in-RIP trapping, that is controlled by plug-in software available for the main imaging and page layout programs.

Proper trapping is rarely completely automatic; someone with an understanding of the process has to make decisions and use trapping software properly. The need for trapping can be overcome by designing a job that does not require trapping by either spacing out the colors, by only using colors that can be achieved by overprinting (where red and yellow make orange, for example), or by building common colors. (A useful tutorial is available at www.thelawlers.com/FTP/Trapping%20How-to.pdf.sit.)

High-end prepress systems all offer professional trapping functions, in most cases offering better results than are available in desktop systems. Most designers and publishers pass the responsibility for trapping to their prepress and print service providers.

(ix) TRIM, IMPOSITION, AND BINDING

Pages are not usually printed consecutively but into signatures. A ***signature*** is a large piece of paper that is folded and then bound and trimmed to make the pages of a book or other publication. *Imposition* is the arrangement of the pages on a large press sheet so that when that sheet is folded the pages read consecutively and are right side up. The specific imposition depends on the size of the press sheet and the size and number of pages, as well as on how the job will be folded and bound. The trim size is set to accommodate the requirements of imposition and binding.

Most of the work of trim, imposition, and binding is handled by the printer or prepress service provider. But the designer has to understand the basics, as certain elements impact the geometry of page layouts.

The essentials of imposition are described in a booklet published by Xerox and available at www.xerox-techsupport.com/dc2000/Documentation/EX2000%20v1.21/DBProAdd_ENG.pdf.

(x) PREFLIGHT

Traditionally in the graphic arts, designers and publishers submitted their artwork for printing pasted up on boards, called mechanicals. While cumbersome to produce, and tough to alter, they had the great advantage of being easily examined visually. A printer's customer service rep could look at a mechanical and move the job easily into production. Sales and estimating knew how to price the job. Scheduling knew how long the job would take. And the production department knew exactly what steps to follow to bring the print job to a successful completion.

The art board was a blueprint for the job, and it also contained all the job elements. As the art board moved through film and stripping, it became the "die" for the final printing plates.

By contrast, electronic files bear none of these attributes. To plan, estimate, and produce a printing job from digital files requires very different skills and knowledge than doing so from the traditional art board, skills that are not in the repertoire of conventional prepress staff. And, because electronic media is not immediately revealing of its content, it must be examined carefully by a digital imaging professional, to determine the complexity of the job in process. There are a host of potential problems associated with hardware and software, with file preparation, and with operator error.

A procedure has been developed to help prevent the worst of these problems from fouling up prepress production. This procedure is called ***preflight***. Preflighting refers to a structured series of tests that a page layout file and its associated files must pass before entering the imaging workflow. The purpose of preflighting is to add predictability to prepress and printing processes. Preflighting identifies problems, aids solutions, and improves scheduling.

Preflight can't prevent all of the potential problems associated with digital file output. But it can address the largest single problem area: files badly prepared by insufficiently trained operators. Until designers and production staff are more consistently trained, and until software and hardware stops going through so many revisions and changes, the best production processes must include this defensive procedure.

If, during production, an unexpected problem is encountered, this can throw the whole schedule off. Retrieving missing fonts or missing graphics files from a customer sometimes takes hours, or even days—and is certain to delay a production schedule. The more complex problems can also take hours to remedy. Spotting problems before a job goes into production ensures a manageable workflow.

Missing fonts and font substitution are probably the most frequently encountered problems in digital imaging. (With traditional mechanicals, font use was not a problem because all type was received as line art, ready to be photographed.) The second most frequent problem is missing or incorrectly prepared graphic files.

Other problems are tougher to detect, and tougher to remedy. These include analyzing files for halftone specifications, analyzing trapping requirements, and rebuilding blends and vignettes.

1. Common prepress file problems

Preflighting is designed to catch these most common prepress file problems:

- Fonts are substituted
- Spot colors are defined as RGB
- Spot colors are incorrectly defined as CMYK
- Traps have been modified or incorrectly set
- There is no bleed allowance
- Illustrations or graphics are not linked
- Blends are stair-stepped
- Screening has not been specified properly
- There is too much image compression.

Experienced designers and production staff will preflight their own work before submitting it to a service provider. But, although this step may be redundant, nearly all service providers will also preflight files before committing them to printing.

An ideal page layout or image design program would prevent a designer from making the kinds of mistakes that preflight catches. Some software has begun to use this kind of artificial intelligence. But many errors are subjective and job specific. Preflight is likely to continue to play an important role in production workflows for the foreseeable future.

Some software is available today to aid in the preflight process. Markzware FlightCheck is the most notable example, while Enfocus PitStop is widely used to preflight PDF files.

The PDF file format, of itself, serves to reduce many of the errors caught in preflight. More significantly, PDF lends itself to the kind of automated workflows where errors can be checked and corrected without operator intervention. Tools are becoming available that reduce the time and effort spent preflighting PDF files.

PDF AND PREPRESS WORKFLOWS

No discussion of graphic arts workflow is complete without examining PDF's increasingly dominant role. It is fast becoming the key underpinning for the way prepress and print is managed. **PDF** [6.6] is the present and future of workflow.

The key strengths of PDF as a file format play well in the world of prepress. It provides a single open format for different software to process. The apparent arbitrariness of PostScript output is eliminated, so PDF provides the foundation for a print production system that delivers consistent, predictable results. PDF files proof easily. Errors are significantly reduced.

PDF—the file format—has to be discussed separately from Adobe's Acrobat software. Acrobat is the leading application for creating PDF files, but other vendors offer software that can create PDF files (and some that can edit them, separate them, etc.). Bugs and shortcomings in Acrobat are not necessarily PDF problems, per se, and vice versa.

Adobe controls an estimated 95 percent of the market for PDF creation. The Acrobat software has three main elements. ***Acrobat Distiller*** is used to create PDFs from PostScript. ***Acrobat Reader*** is used to view and print PDF files (Reader is also offered by Adobe separately for free). Adobe Acrobat provides some editability for the text and graphics in PDF files, the ability to annotate them, and the ability to add multimedia elements, links, bookmarks, and other functionality.

There are hundreds of other developers offering software to create PDFs, or to enhance PDF workflows. Adobe offers a brief listing at www.adobe.com/products/plugins/acrobat/main.html. PlanetPDF has a more complete list at www.planetpdf.com/mainpage.asp?MenuID=193&WebPageID=612.

1. Acrobat and PDF versions

There are several versions both of the Acrobat software, and, more importantly, of the PDF format. The current version of Acrobat, Acrobat 5, can distill to PDF versions 1.2, 1.3, or 1.4.

Old PDF 1.0 and 1.1 documents (created mainly by Acrobat 1.0 and 2.1) should be handled with care. PDF 1.2 and above behaves far more consistently. In graphic arts production, new PDF files are best saved to the latest format. For wider distribution, it's preferable to use the 1.2 version to ensure compatibility with older versions of Acrobat and the Acrobat Reader.

2. PDF workflows

Why is the industry shifting from PostScript to PDF? There are three key reasons:

1. PDF IS (SOMEWHAT) BULLETPROOF

PDF can solve two huge headaches associated with conventional prepress workflows: missing fonts and graphics and bad PostScript. The nature of the format, and of the distillation process that creates PDF files, encourages the inclusion of all font and graphic data necessary for successful file output.

Bad PostScript is reduced (though not eliminated) because the distillation process simplifies the original PostScript data, converting it into PDF's far more predictable data style. Some of the font and graphic data that gets embedded into PDF files can still lead to RIP-choking misery, but users unanimously report PostScript normalization as a key PDF benefit.

2. PDF IS COMPACT

The graphic arts industry has long employed various compression techniques, from Photo CD to JPEG. Adobe's PDF specification encourages the use of JPEG compression (along with other compression techniques), which can dramatically shrink output files, while minimizing image degradation.

3. PDF IS EFFICIENT

PDF files are truly page independent—unlike PostScript, PDF files can be pulled apart a page at a time. Pages can be edited, repositioned, trapped, and imposed.

3. Establishing a good PDF workflow

Successful PDF workflows involve attention to detail. There are three key aspects to this:

1. PROBLEM ONE: GARBAGE IN, GARBAGE OUT

PDF is not a cure-all for every production problem. Garbage in, garbage out has two major ramifications. The first reflects how the file is constructed. The second concerns the PostScript that is generated.

Some analysts refer to PDF as if it will solve *all* preflight and production problems. It certainly *tackles* several of the most common preflight challenges, including missing fonts and graphics. Because PDF files are created from rendered PostScript files, many issues that could lead to problems in a RIP have already been preprocessed during the PDF file creation stage, and so are no longer preflight challenges. Still, many preflight issues must be separately addressed in a PDF workflow, including missing fonts and graphic elements, incorrect color specification, or trapping.

One frequently encountered preflight issue is files built to an incorrect trim size. For example, due to press configurations, some printers recommend an 8-3/8 x 10-7/8-inch trim rather than 8-1/2 x 11 inch. Acrobat and PDF, per se, will do nothing to tackle this problem.

Another challenge is graphics files defined in RGB rather than CMYK. Acrobat can address the problem, but it has to be carefully instructed to do so.

Some specialized software is made specifically for preflight in PDF files, including products from Markzware, Enfocus, and Callas.

2. PROBLEM TWO: FONTS STILL A HEADACHE

Adobe Systems is the inventor of PostScript, but Adobe's Acrobat Distiller can be unfriendly to fonts when creating PDF files for prepress output.

As mentioned above, the good news about Distiller's handling of fonts is that it can embed font data within a PDF document. This solves two problems. First, designers and publishers don't have to figure out which fonts they're supposed to send along with their job, and they can avoid the panicked last minute phone calls about missing fonts. Embedding fonts is an option in Acrobat Distiller, an option that's always recommended. This will include the font data in the PDF file.

The font problems occur when fonts are not embedded. This can happen for two reasons. Some font vendors, for copyright reasons, prohibit font embedding. Acrobat has a feature that supports this prohibition, and users cannot override it. The other reason is that Distiller allows users to subset the fonts and include only the specific characters used in a document (rather than every character in a typeface). This can lead to problems if the PDF has to be altered later to include a letter or symbol from the font that was not present in the original.

TrueType fonts embedded into PDFs can also lead to problems in that some PostScript RIPs still choke on them.

3. PROBLEM THREE: DISTILLER'S UGLY INTERFACE

Acrobat Distiller easily earns the "Incomprehensible Interface of the Decade" award. The Job Options in Distiller require something close to a master's degree to comprehend. There are default options for distilling files to e-book, print, press, or screen, but, as is the case with most default settings, tweaking is generally required. This leads the user to a far more challenging set of options, such as:

- Distill with prolog.ps/epilog.ps
- Preserve document information from DSC
- Preserve EPS information from DSC
- Preserve overprint settings
- Preserve level 2 copypage semantics
- Preserve, apply, or remove transfer functions

Additional less-than-obvious settings appear under Compression. These offer the user tremendous control over the degree of lossy or lossless compression applied to different parts of a page file. But choosing, for example, between "subsampling" and "bicubic downsampling" is far from intuitive.

Adobe offers a complete explanation of these options in the documentation for Acrobat or through Acrobat on-line support (www.adobe.com/support/products/acrobat.html), but these are time consuming and impractical for the average designer or publisher. The standard advice for users is to consult with their output service provider. The problem is that, with so many choices, each output service provider invariably has different preferences. As a result, it's difficult to create a true "PDF master" file that will be usable for the full range of future possible output choices.

4. High-end systems

There are two important systems used by larger printing and prepress companies to mass produce pages from PDF files: Creo's Prinergy and Agfa's ApogeeX. Each of these systems builds upon PDF's inherent strengths to provide highly efficient prepress workflows. High-volume users of PDF generally choose service providers supporting one or the other of these systems.

You can find information about Prinergy at http://www.creo.com/products/software_solutions/workflow/Prinergy/index.asp, and about

ApogeeX at http://graphics.agfa.com/product/CatProd_DisplayPublic.html?id=7391.

5. PDF/X

PDF/X is a file format specification based closely on PDF and designed specifically for file exchange in the graphic arts. It is also what's called an "application standard," in that it defines how compliant prepress software and systems should render PDF/X files.

1. PDF VS. PDF/X

It's easier to appreciate PDF/X not as a file standard that lets you do more than PDF can, but as one that lets you do less. Martin Bailey, a technical consultant who has been a key player in developing the PDF/X family of standards, writes, "The important point is that you can do a lot of things in PDF that are not appropriate for graphic arts use, and that can cause problems when outputting for high-quality reproduction." PDF/X limits the range of options in PDF to a specified subset.

While some control of PDF workflows is available through the job options preferences in Adobe Acrobat, this method is cumbersome and prone to errors. It also fails to address the increasing number of alternate applications that can create and process PDF files.

Unfortunately, compounding the complexity of this new file format is that it comes in three flavors. PDF/X-1 is a file format for *blind exchange,* where all technical information and content is held within one single file and nothing has to be supplied alongside it. PDF/X-2 is a format for more open exchanges. PDF/X-3 was developed for color-managed workflows.

PDF/X-2 is still under development. It will be a superset of PDF/X-3, and will allow device-independent color spaces, just like PDF/X-3.

The 2001 ISO standard defines both PDF/X-1:2001 and PDF/X-1a:2001, which prohibit OPI and the encryption of files. It's expected that many more tools will be available for handling PDF/X-1a files than PDF/X-1 because they are much easier to produce.

In order to comply with the standard, a PDF/X-1a file MUST have the following characteristics:

- Fonts are embedded
- Images are embedded
- Color elements are encoded as CMYK, spot, or Device N
- MediaBox and TrimBox or ArtBox are defined
- Trap is indicated as "on" or "off"
- Printing condition is characterized.

2. WHICH VERSION?

Martin Bailey recommends PDF/X-1a for ad delivery and catalog work in the United States. The commercial print and packaging markets will be best served by PDF/X-2. Work for output on digital presses is probably best sent as PDF/X-3.

3. TIFF/IT VS. PDF/X

As discussed **above** [6.8.5.1.2], TIFF/IT is a variant on the TIFF format, analogous to the type of variants now being created for PDF. The advantage of TIFF/IT is that it's well established (it was defined officially in 1998). TIFF/IT has been used for millions of pages (mainly for magazines) and it has a proven track record.

The big disadvantage is that it creates mainly bitmap files that cannot, for all practical purposes, be edited. It also creates huge files—an average of 35 megabytes for a four-color page.

PDF/X, by comparison, is lightweight and flexible (or at least the underlying PDF structure is). The architecture of PDF was designed to carry structural tagging and metadata, making it well suited to cross-media publishing. This additional data capacity makes PDF and its variants more powerful in managed workflows built on the principles of computer-integrated manufacturing (CIM).

The momentum behind PDF/X, combined with its versatility, suggests that it will largely replace TIFF/IT in the next few years.

6. For more on PDF

Consultant Stephan Jaeggi offers a series of four excellent small publications (in PDF format of course):

1. *Basics.* An introduction to PDF technology (intended for all readers).
2. *Management.* Economic and organizational aspects of PDF (for managers).
3. *Creation.* The creation of PDF documents (for advertising agencies, graphic artists, publishers, etc.).
4. *Production.* Processing (for prepress technicians).

The site is at www.prepress.ch/visionwork/english.html.

There are several PDF-specific Web sites. Try www.planetpdf.com and www.PDFZone.com.

For mail lists devoted to PDF support go to: www.adobe.com/support/forums/main.html and forum.planetpdf.com/scripts/wbpx.dll/~planetpdf-forum.

Adobe offers the Acrobat Expert Center at studio.adobe.com/expertcenter/acrobat/main.html (registration required).

Michael Jahn has a very good site at www.jahn.org.

DIGITAL ASSET MANAGEMENT (DAM)

1. What is digital archiving?

At first glance, digital archiving seems so simple—just storing digital files for later reuse. But in the last decade digital archiving has become much more elaborate, and now encompasses a range of services that go far beyond keeping a bunch of files backed up on disk.

As with so much in digital technology, the challenge of defining digital archiving stems from a lack of agreement even on the basic terminology. The term *digital archiving* refers to a range of digital storage services, although print and prepress service providers use a host of other terms, including image management, ***DAM***, digital content management, digital library management, asset services, and media management. Compounding the confusion, each term has a slightly different meaning for each user. So there are no established standards, either for the nature of archiving services, or the nomenclature.

While there is no consensus on what to call it, most agree that there's more to archiving than just storing files on disks. A publication from Gistics called *Media Asset Management: ASK How Guide,* defines media asset management as, "the systematic organization of digital media files enabling an authorized individual to quickly find, retrieve (or physically locate), and/or route an item to an authorized or designated person or into an automated work process."

In the predigital age of the graphic arts, image archiving involved storing film (and occasionally plates) along with the original transparencies and other artwork that went into a publication. Service providers routinely stored film because the storage cost was usually lower than the cost of regenerating this material, and because storing film tended to tie a publisher into a service provider. Indeed the commercial printing industry adopted the anomalous trade practice that it deemed plate-ready film the physical property of the service provider, even though the publisher had usually paid for the cost of its manufacture, and the images contained within remained the copyrighted property of the publisher. (This is not the case in book and journal printing, where the publisher has normally been considered the owner of the film.)

In this analog age, the truly valuable archives were collections of original art—mostly photographs and drawings. The major qualifier of "archive value" was the ability of the copyright holder to lease the artwork to other publishers, or the necessity for a copyright holder to reuse the work for his own publications, in a format other than that contained on the film (or plates) held at the last printer or prepress service provider.

Digitization has changed the fundamental nature of the archiving process and its perceived value. The physical cost of saving a digital file is very low. It takes up next to no space. At its most basic level, the act of creating a digital archive means using the Save command and tossing a disk into a drawer. No wonder that there is little perceived value in the basic process.

As with most digital processes, the cost (and the value) is not in the technology, it's in the value added by skilled and knowledgeable workers. A file saved on a CD-ROM sitting in a desk drawer or a file cabinet may in theory be an archive but in this form it is neither secure nor readily accessible, and so provides little real value.

Digital media is perceived as stateless, that is, having no mass. It's just bits and bytes, floating through the ether. But digital archiving proves that digital media has substance as well as form. In the end, bits and bytes must be recorded on physical media, either magnetic or optical. If that media suffers physical damage, those bits and bytes cease to exist, no matter how rarefied the ether. So a fundamental principle of digital archiving is physical security. Security in turn has two value axes—degree of security and duration (i.e., how well is the data protected, and for how long?). This physical manifestation of the data is reflected also in the core hardware systems designed to enhance the mobility of the data. A good digital archive uses fast, secure storage, a robust server, and a robust network.

Once the archive is physically secure and readily accessible to all interested users, the truly tough challenge begins—creating a software interface to a digital archive so that graphic objects (text, images, multimedia objects) will be obviously available to everyone who can extend their value. Digital media is fundamentally mobile, while analog media is fundamentally static. The challenge of digital archiving systems is to enhance the inherent mobility of digital media, to make it easy for publishers to pull additional value from their digital assets. Mobility is enhanced mainly by ingenious software tools that help manage digital data, and by ingenious users finding new ways to extend the value of the data.

2. The dual value of digital data

The traditional view of the value of a digital archive is that maintaining images in digital form reduces the need to rescan images and recompose pages. The value is primarily in cost reduction.

The term *media assets,* with the emphasis on assets, represents a new view of digital archiving. Digital images have value in building a company's business, and the more frequently they're used, the more business they potentially generate. The uses can be more of the same, or the images can be repurposed into other media. Users want to be able to track images, but they also want the ability to repurpose images. This translates into efficiency both in terms of costs and in terms of process.

Fundamental to efficient graphic arts workflows is robust DAM, whether handled in house or by an outside service provider. It's also an essential step on the path to **content management** [10.4].

3. Media formats

Even the most basic DAM system has to confront two difficult challenges:

1. What format(s) should be used for archiving?
2. How can file integrity be assured?

As discussed in **above** [6.8.5.1.3], JPEG is now a common format for large bitmap images. It's chosen because it produces compact files, with compression ratios of 10 to 1 common. However, compression leads to image degradation. Image archives might be better held in an uncompressed TIFF format, but these images can be unwieldy for production. Designers and publishers face tough and important decisions on archive file formats.

The rise of PDF workflows raises questions about file integrity. Because PDF files are now editable, the expeditious method for making last-minute changes is within the PDF file itself. But if the PDF file is generated from a QuarkXPress file, in this case the *digital master,* how can we ensure that the last-minute changes will be properly recorded to the master? Successful DAM systems must be implemented in the context of the broader production workflow.

See the chapter on **archiving** [12] for an in-depth discussion of archiving in the context of digital publishing.

THE FUTURE OF PRINT WORKFLOWS

At this stage in the development of digitization of print workflows, the publishing industry continues to straddle the old craft-based process, with a degree of computer control and automation unthinkable two decades ago. PDF is fast assuming a role as the format that will underlie tomorrow's fully automated production process. A new set of data standards and workflow initiatives are now being built around PDF.

1. The Digital Smart Factory and CIM

In a May, 1998, speech to the Web Offset Association in Toronto, William Davis, Chairman and CEO of R.R. Donnelley, one of the largest printing companies in the world, said, "In this game manufacturing discipline will win. The craftsman who has to leave his thumbprint on every page will lose." He continued: "We are a decade behind in manufacturing best practices."

His comments reflected the modern challenge to the graphic arts. Traditionally the manufacture of print has been craft-oriented, from design to print. Designers made their reputations by creating unusual print pieces, with beautiful typography, tough-to-match colors, and unusual trim and bind requirements. Printers made their reputations by dealing under deadline with these extraordinary print demands.

The growth of alternative media and continuing cost pressures on print producers have forced a reexamination of the way that print is created. Over the last few years there has been ever-increasing interest in making the process more predictable, repeatable, and economical. These pressures have lead the industry to a search for improvements in the automation of print production, and toward computer integrated manufacturing.

Computer integrated manufacturing (***CIM***) is a term used to describe the complete automation of a manufacturing plant, with all processes functioning under computer control and with digital information tying them together.

Professor Frank Cost, of the Rochester Institute of Technology, a leading expert on process control of manufacturing in the graphic arts, said in a February, 2000, presentation at the Seybold Seminars in Boston that the goal of CIM is, "to effectively capture and store information available at any point in a process that is needed at any other point."

CIM seeks to automate the process where possible. "A lot of people talk about CIM as though the end goal is complete automation," Cost said. However, he added, "most processes cannot be completely automated. Automated steps are integrated with other steps that are not as automated." He concluded that, "Ultimately, we want to manufacture things faster, better, and cheaper—that's why we're doing all of this."

The concepts behind CIM have been heretical to an industry that grew up on unique designs and custom manufacturing, performed by artists and craftspeople. But a new generation of practitioners, schooled in digital imaging and computer technology, is beginning to realize that excellent print quality is still achievable within a more automated framework.

Different industry groups are approaching the automation challenge from different perspectives. Most of the work is going into standards development. One group, the Digital Smart Factory Forum (www.smartfactory.org; also see http://www.dnps.org), is trying to build a conceptual framework around applying the principles of CIM to the graphic arts. As they point out in a recent conference brochure for the 2000 Digital Smart Factory Conference in Orlando (http://www.recouncil.org/events/smfactory.pdf), "Over $9 billion of systemic cost found in the North American graphic communications industry . . . can be freed up by computer integrated manufacturing [CIM], networked production, and supply chain management techniques. Changes brought on by desktop publishing and CTP (computer-to-plate) pale in comparison."

But most of the energy that is moving the industry forward is coming from the standards groups, most prominently those involved in developing the Job Definition Format (JDF), PrintTalk, and PPML standards.

2. JDF

JDF is an open, extensible, XML-based print workflow specification that carries a print job from creation to completion. The JDF specification extends the job ticket concept by linking together the upstream authoring, production, and management with the downstream manufacturing and delivery. A JDF job ticket begins with the product intent and ends with the processing specifics. The ability to capture product intent makes it possible to describe the end product without having to specify the details, providing publishers with greater flexibility and control.

Originally developed by Adobe Systems, Agfa, Heidelberg, and MAN Roland, JDF is governed by CIP4 (http://www.cip4.org), an international operating standards body, based in Germany. The antecedents of JDF are first of all CIP3 (the acronym means International Cooperation for Integration of Prepress, Press, and Postpress), which in the late 1990s developed the Print Production Format (PPF), a file format used for ink key presetting, folding, and trimming. At the same time Adobe was building into PDF a format subset called Portable Job Ticket Format (PJTF), designed to control PDF output.

JDF is designed to streamline information exchange between different applications and systems. JDF allows the integration of varied products from diverse vendors into seamless workflow solutions.

It has several key features:

- The ability to carry a print job from genesis through completion. This includes a detailed description of the creative, prepress, press, postpress, and delivery processes.
- The ability to bridge the communication gap between production and management information services (MIS). This ability enables instantaneous job and device tracking as well as detailed pre- and post-calculation for scheduling and costing of jobs.
- The ability to bridge the gap between the designer's and publisher's view of the product and the downstream manufacturing process.

JDF facilitates job costing and job monitoring with full production transparency. For job costing, both planned and actual production times and operating data are reported to MIS. JDF tracks what materials have been consumed at various production steps; it also supports job quotes and ordering via Internet-based solutions and e-business applications.

JDF is a vendor-independent standard. It is highly extensible. Features of XML (http://www.w3.org/TR/REC-xml-names) have been chosen to allow easy extension of the specification to support processes and devices not anticipated in the current version of the specification.

The Job Messaging Format (***JMF***), is a subset of JDF that handles communications with equipment on the shop floor. It facilitates real-time communication among print MIS systems, computerized workflow control systems, and prepress, press, and post-press equipment. These may include major equipment, such as platesetters, or subsystems, such as in-line color measurement devices. JMF can be used to establish a queue, discover the capabilities of a JDF-enabled device, determine the status of a device (e.g., whether it's currently RIPing or idle), and so on.

3. PrintTalk

PrintTalk (http://www.printtalk.org) is an organization formed, as stated on its Web site, "by print management systems and e-commerce companies to define a 'best practice' common and open communications interface between their products." The ***PrintTalk*** format is an XML standard that provides a single format for printers to collaboratively communicate business transactions and print specifications with their buyers and among themselves.

PrintTalk uses the JDF and Commerce Extensible Markup Language (cXML). The group's work has been recognized as an implementation of the JDF standard, and is embedded within JDF. By incorporating PrintTalk, the JDF intent list has been enhanced to provide a richer descriptive capability. While JDF describes the piece to be printed, PrintTalk specifies the external communication of business processes between printer and buyer.

The initial release of PrintTalk contains support for request for quote, quote, change order, and purchase order. Followup versions are planned to provide specifications for order confirmation, order status request, order status, and invoice. The PrintTalk consortium says it plans to continue to work with CIP4 on further JDF enhancements, but will at the same time continue to develop the PrintTalk business objects independently.

4. PPML

PPML is the Personalized Print Markup Language. Developed by the members of PODi (Print on Demand Initiative, http://www.podi.org), it is an XML-based print language designed to make it faster to print documents that have reusable content, specifically for digital printing. Proprietary technologies have to some extent provided this ability in the past, but PPML is the first industry standard approach. The first implementation defined by PODi uses JDF.

PPML 2.0 has support for digitally formatted print job tickets, better support for different workflows, and it defines a method of reliably moving PPML jobs from system to system.

The PPML 2.0 architecture includes generic printer control, so that jobs that specify advanced printer features such as duplexing, finishing, and paper selection can be created without knowing what machine will print them. Any PPML-compliant printer with the appropriate features will accept the same print file, no matter what software created it and what printer does the output.

Software that conforms to these PPML 2.0 rules will create jobs that pack and unpack identically and run smoothly on different systems, even between Mac, PC, and Unix/Linux platforms.

A related new feature is support for checksums—the ability to ensure that a print job uses exactly the desired version of a graphic or other job component. Using this feature, document producers will be able to transmit partial jobs to a print shop in advance, as each part becomes available, knowing that the final print run will contain exactly the desired content.

5. Other initiatives

Other initiatives in development across the publishing industry, some focused more on document creation, others on document production, are Information Content Exchange (***ICE***) and Publishing Requirements for Industry Standards Metadata (***PRISM***). The primary group behind these initiatives is IDEAlliance (International Digital Enterprise Alliance, http://www.idealliance.org). It is a nonprofit organization dedicated to advancing "user-driven, cross-industry solutions for all publishing and content-related processes by developing standards, fostering business alliances, and identifying best practices." Founded in 1966 as the Graphic Communications Association (GCA) it has fostered the development and adoption of standards such as GRACoL, ICE, JIFFI, Mail.dat, papiNet, PRISM, PROSE XML, SPACE XML, SGML, and XML.

6. Process control

Process control is an essential aspect of workflow improvement. Like workflow, the term is vague and often applied loosely. *Process control* is defined as the modifying, altering, or redesigning of a production work method to deliver greater value. This is done with the collection and analysis of data, hence *statistical process control* (***SPC***): the application of statistical methods to analyze data and study and monitor process capability and performance.

The printing industry continues to struggle with a means to control the entire production process, for the reasons discussed above. Still, most larger printers have continuous quality improvement programs in place. Many have achieved ISO 9002 certification. (ISO 9002 is a quality assurance model made up of nineteen sets of quality system requirements. It applies to organizations that produce, install, and service products.)

Companies that achieve ISO 9002 certification must meet certain requirements, including:

- Have an established policy on quality and a quality procedure manual.
- Have an officer designated for ensuring and maintaining quality standards.
- Have regular reviews of quality. Audits are to be done both in house and by an external independent body.
- Have policies on various other issues including and not limited to staff training and development.
- Maintain a list of approved suppliers.
- Have all written procedures stated simply, unambiguously, and understandably.

7. On-press color control

Part of the challenge for CIM and its data standards is finding equipment that can react to the data being transmitted. Much of the installed printing and binding equipment is from a predigital generation. It's slowly changing, as equipment is retrofitted, and a new generation installed. A key development in this area is on-press color control systems.

When a printing press has a digitally controlled ink system it can be equipped with a closed-loop color control system. Densitometers and/or spectrophotometers scan a color bar on the sheet. The data is analyzed and used to control the ink settings. Color characteristics are matched to targets in a closed loop. Solid ink density, dot gain, print contrast, trapping, and up to thirty other variables can be read.

By adjusting the press automatically, make-ready time and materials can be reduced by 30 percent (or more), color accuracy can be improved, and overall waste lowered. Additional benefits are achieved when the data is collected throughout a press run or compared between press runs for statistical process control.

Many new presses are being shipped with built-in closed loop color control systems. Recently constructed presses with digital ink controls are candidates for retrofitting with these color systems.

PRINT BUYING ON THE WEB

The great dot-com bubble that ended abruptly in early 2000 impacted the printing industry as surely as it did most other businesses. Millions of dollars were poured into new business ventures that planned to take control of the way that print was purchased and produced. The bubble has now burst and many of the best financed start-ups have disappeared. Sifting through the rubble, the question that remains is what impact the Internet and the Web will have on print production in the next few years, and how long it will take before the bulk of print production is Internet-enabled.

Eliot Harper's Dot Com Watch (http://members.whattheythink.com/home/basicdotcomwatch.cfm) lists 286 print-oriented Web sites, including 58 that have "ceased trading." They range from companies that supply paper and other supplies, to more ambitious firms that can mediate an entire production workflow. A CAP Ventures report classified the print dot-coms in several different ways. One broad category is "commodity versus customized." *Commodity* refers to low-ticket items that are ordered repeatedly and with minimal effort, such as office stationery, forms, and business cards. *Customized* refers to jobs containing unique content, which tend to be ordered once and not repeated.

Tighter classification definitions include these categories:

- Digital customer link. These are traditional print service providers who have developed or acquired an Internet interface with the primary intent of supporting their existing relationships with print services buyers.
- Project management. These vendors offer third-party solutions to print service providers with the intent of improving their internal work processes or the print procurement and management processes of the printer's customers. In many cases, these solutions are offered primarily to the print service provider, not the print buyer directly.
- Tools providers. Their products facilitate the various stages of the procurement process, for example, to spec jobs, obtain bids, submit and track jobs, and facilitate collaboration. Those that focus mainly on procurement-related tasks are categorized as buy-side e-procurement. Facilitators provide a solution that enables the print procurement process, but does not participate in the process once it is initiated.
- Publishing. This group divides into those solutions that mainly cater to independent authors and those that primarily serve publishers.

Seybold Reports independently classifies print dot-coms into four categories:

- Storefronts. Sites that provide the same functions as a traditional graphic arts distributor or equipment dealer.
- RFQ sites. Sites that let a print buyer frame the specifications for a job, then post the job for open bidding.
- Workflow managers. Sites that let the print buyer shepherd the job through the design, bidding, and production processes.
- Services. Sites that sell only information of one sort or another.

The challenge in using the Internet as a networked intermediary for print production is the chasm between commodity and custom manufacturing. The bulk of commercial printing does not fall into the category of straightforward repeatable work. The bulk of commercial printing is one-off jobs: brochures, spec sheets, and other forms of collateral, which are anything but a commodity.

Print is still custom manufacturing. Over time, workflow management, PDF workflows, color management, and process control together can move print out of a custom manufacturing mode. But most print is just not sufficiently automated to move to the network.

Print buyers have very personal relationships with their printers. While they have literally thousands of firms to choose from, most work with just two or three. Print buyers, if pressed, will admit that many different printers could potentially satisfy their requirements, but they'll swear adamantly that they'd rather fight than switch. It's clear that the relationships they've built, and the clear communications they've established, are an essential part of getting the high-quality print work they require.

International Paper's publication *Via Basics: Estimating* explains the process both of choosing the right printer and of receiving accurate estimates from the chosen printer. The booklet is explicit about the intricacies of choosing the right printer. "One of the basic misconceptions about commercial printing is that every printer has the same skill level," the booklet states. "There are many variables that distinguish printers, not the least of which is their mix of equipment and the creativity inherent in the printing process. . . . Knowing your printer's capabilities, processes and specialties can make all the difference to a successful project and a fairly priced print job." *Via Basics: Estimating* recommends to print buyers that they take a plant tour at prospective print suppliers, and that they examine print samples and get to know the best sales reps.

This advice reflects the beliefs of most print buyers. While pundits often state that print has become a manufacturing commodity, the buyers of print believe that it is anything but. They see each printing company as distinct, a compendium of equipment, processes, personnel, and practices. For the average print buyer, this is not a commodity to be purchased over the Web.

Several of the dot-com vendors portray their Web-enabled software and services as workflow systems, rather than print buying systems. They seek to use the Web to simplify job submission and job tracking between print buyers and their chosen printers. They swear that they're not seeking to disrupt existing buying relationships, but only to make those arrangements more efficient through the use of Web technologies.

The Web will eventually become a vehicle by which most printing is purchased, scheduled, monitored, proofed, and invoiced. But too many opportunists moved too quickly into an immature space, and created havoc from which the industry is only now beginning to recover.

6.13 PRINTING PROCESSES

A printing process is the method used by a particular type of equipment to transfer an image to a substrate (the material being printed on, such as paper). This implies that a printing system will have an intermediary step, a medium that carries the image before reproduction can proceed. The mechanics of printing systems vary in order to cater to specific applications. For a long time the printing industry recognized five major processes:

- Relief printing (letterpress, flexography)
- Planographic printing (offset lithography)
- Recess printing (gravure/intaglio)
- Stencil printing (screen)
- Digital printing (toner and inkjet)

Having a basic understanding of the differences between these printing process will enable you to better prepare files that capitalize on their strong points and accommodate their limitations.

(i) OFFSET PRINTING

Offset is the method of transferring an image from the plate to the substrate through an intermediate rubber blanket. The lithographic process operates with three basic cylinders, all heavy and made of metal: the plate cylinder, the blanket cylinder, and the impression cylinder.

- The plate cylinder is wound with the printing plate, which is the carrier of the image that is to be printed.
- The blanket cylinder is wound with a rubber blanket. The image is transferred from the plate to the blanket, and then to the paper (or other substrate), when the substrate is passed between the blanket and the impression cylinder. The blanket is resilient, to compensate for the

unevenness of the substrate. Thus even poor quality stock can be used in offset printing.

- The impression cylinder is just a bare cylinder that applies pressure to impress the image from blanket to the substrate. Pressure between the impression cylinder and blanket cylinder is adjusted for stocks of different thickness.

The image areas accept ink and transfer them to the blanket. The orientation of the image on the plate is readable. When transferred to the blanket it becomes unreadable, because it's a mirror image. In the next revolution, the image is transferred to the paper that travels between the blanket and the impression cylinder and is once again readable. The image is first offset from the plate to the blanket and then offset from the blanket to the paper. For this reason, lithography is also called *offset printing*.

1. Types of offset presses

There are two ways in which paper can be fed to an offset printing press: either in sheet form or roll form. Presses that feed cut sheet paper are called sheet-fed presses and the presses that feed paper from rolls are called web-fed presses. Presses that can print on both sides of sheet or roll paper at once are called perfecting presses.

Most of today's presses are capable of printing many colors using multiple sets, or units, of plate, blanket, and impression cylinder. Multicolor presses exist in two-, four-, five-, six, eight-, and even ten-color configurations.

The plate used in lithography has a flat surface and is called planographic. There is no physical or mechanical separation between image and nonimage areas. The plate material can be paper, plastic, or metal.

2. Inking system

The purpose of the inking system is to apply an accurately measured or metered amount of ink to the plate. Each process requires a special type of ink and method to apply it to the image carrier. Some inks are thick (like a heavy paste) and others are fluid. Some systems continuously bathe or immerse a roller or cylinder; others intermittently supply a limited and metered amount of ink.

If the ink is a thick paste, then it can be distributed by a series of soft rubber rollers. Fluid inks require miniature wells or cups to transfer the ink. These wells can be part of the image carrier itself or a special type of inking roller.

3. Waterless offset

Waterless plates were developed by Toray Industries of Japan in 1973. Image areas are in recess from the nonimage areas. Waterless offset avoids problems associated with ink–water balance and paper expansion due to moisture content.

Aluminum is the base material for the plate, and the plate is not anodized, as are conventional offset plates. A light-sensitive photopolymer coating is given to the aluminum base. The waterless plates are made from either positives or negatives, depending on the plate type used. These plates are capable of producing very high screen frequencies, in the region of 200 to 300 lpi with negative working plates and 400 to 600 lpi with positive working plates.

(ii) LETTERPRESS

There are two kinds of relief printing: letterpress printing and flexography. Relief printing uses raised image areas for printing, and pressure to imprint the image or text onto a substrate. The raised parts of the printing plates are the areas that both receive ink and come into contact with the surface being printed. The images are also reversed on the printing plate, known as "wrong reading," so that when they come into contact with the paper the image is printed opposite that of the plate, so the image becomes "right reading" when printed.

Letterpress printing is one of the earliest forms of printing, long predating Gutenberg's invention of movable type. (Printing was invented centuries earlier in the Orient. The Chinese and Koreans carved whole pages of text out of wood and printed on rice paper.) Gutenberg cast type in metal and set the letters into lines of text on flat surfaces. Ink was then applied to the surface with rollers and a piece of paper was pressed down onto it. Because of the pressure involved in letterpress printing you can actually feel a slight indent on the printed letters.

For a long time letterpress was the most popular form of printing. It is still what many people envision when they think of printing. Letterpress is no longer used in commercial printing except for special tasks such as numbering tickets; however, it is still used in some very small print houses for newspapers or, for aesthetic reasons, to produce books by hand.

(iii) FLEXOGRAPHY

While all the major forms of printing can be employed in package printing, flexography is by far the dominant process. Flexographic printing (often called "flexo") is used for most packaging because it can print on a wide range of substrates—from plastics to heavy cardboard—and can be used for both short and medium print runs.

Generally speaking, flexo is much tougher to work with than either offset or gravure because dot gain and misregistration are greater. Through the 1960s and into the 1970s, flexography had a terrible reputation as a low-quality printing method that was used only if nothing else would work. Colors were dull, and registration was all over the map. The latest flexo presses easily rival offset's quality, though a lot of old presses still in use tend to perpetuate flexo's reputation for low quality.

In the same way that web offset has SWOP (to increase quality control across the industry), flexography now has its own set of standards, called Flexographic Image Reproduction Specifications and Tolerances (***FIRST***).

The most important feature of the flexographic printing process is that it uses flexible printing plates made from rubber or photopolymers. Because they're flexible, they can print on uneven surfaces. Offset, with its flat metal plates, can only apply ink on smooth papers; the smoother the paper, the better the image.

Flexo presses work easily with water-based inks, rather than the oil-based inks common in offset lithography. Because of contamination concerns in food packaging, water-based inks are often required. They're also far more environmentally friendly.

Flexographic substrates are classified in three categories:

- Paper and paperboard. These include corrugated boards, solid bleached sulfate and recycled paperboard (folding cartons), coated papers (labels and gift wrapping), and uncoated sheet fed (paperback books).
- Polymer films. These are polyethylene (dry cleaner bags, candy wrappers), polypropylene (snack food packages, candy wrappers), and polyvinyl chloride (wall coverings).
- Multilayer or laminations. These are metallized papers (gift wrapping) and metallized films (snack food bags).

Most of the design challenges for flexographic printing revolve around the dot size and dot gain characteristics of flexo plates. Small type tends to spread and blur, particularly serif faces. In halftone imaging, highlight detail is tough to hold. Flexo tends to work with coarser screens than offset or gravure, rarely going above 150 lines. Registration is another challenge in flexographic printing. Because of the range of flexible substrates used, tolerances are much wider than in offset printing.

(iv) GRAVURE

In simple terms, gravure is printing using a cylinder with holes in it. Gravure, or rotogravure, is industrial *intaglio* printing. Intaglio printing involves transferring an image from a sunken surface (as opposed to relief printing, which prints from a raised surface). The image to be printed is etched or engraved below the surface of the image carrier, or gravure cylinder.

The gravure printing process uses an ink fountain, a gravure/image cylinder, an impression cylinder, and a doctor blade.

The gravure cylinder is etched or engraved with a pattern of tiny cells or holes. The cells are what hold the ink and put the image on the paper or other substrate. The cells are etched or engraved at varying depths and widths to produce the different tones in an image. The deep cells hold more ink and produce the darker, or shadow, areas of the image. The shallow cells hold smaller amounts of ink and produce the lighter, or highlight, areas of an image.

The gravure cylinder is partially submerged in an ink fountain and is rotated to pick up ink in the engraved cells. A doctor blade then scrapes against the surface of the gravure cylinder to remove any ink on the nonimage area.

The substrate is passed between the gravure cylinder and the impression cylinder and the ink that remains in the cells is then transferred to the substrate from the pressure created by the two cylinders. The printed paper then moves through a drying unit to fix the ink to the paper.

The gravure printing process has many advantages. One advantage is the size and speed of gravure presses. Gravure presses are the largest and fastest-running presses today. Presses range in width from under 12 inches to 265 inches (6.7 meters or roughly 22 feet). This allows for printing on various substrates, including sheet vinyl for floor covering.

Gravure press speeds are extremely fast and are limited mainly by the substrate used. Publication presses typically operate at a speed of 3,000 feet per minute. Depending on the product being printed, packaging presses usually run at half the speed of publication presses. Gravure has the highest continuous operating speeds of any commercial press type.

Another advantage to gravure printing is the image carrier, or the gravure cylinder. The majority of gravure cylinders are made with steel as the base material. This is then coated with copper to give the cylinder engravability, stability, and reproducibility. Copper can easily be engraved and the image remains stable, even under high nip pressure (the pressure created between the gravure cylinder and the impression cylinder). Copper can also be removed from the cylinder and replaced so that the cylinder can be engraved or etched and used again. In addition to the copper coating, the cylinder can be coated with chrome to allow for longer press runs.

The gravure cylinder, because it is a gapless cylinder, has an advantage compared to the image carriers of other printing processes. A gapless cylinder allows the image to go completely around the cylinder (unlike lithography, for example). Lithography plates take up only a portion of the cylinder because space is required to fasten the plate to the cylinder, and there is a gap where nothing is being printed as the cylinder rotates. The gapless gravure cylinder allows continuous printing and results in a minimal amount of unprinted space. This reduces paper waste and saves money. The ability of the gapless cylinder to achieve a continuous print, or pattern, makes gravure ideal for printing items such as wallpaper and textiles. The gapless cylinder also allows for many different image layout options, including random and nested images.

Gravure inks are another advantage of this printing process. Because the image carrier, or gravure cylinder, is resistant to virtually all chemicals, inks can be formulated to print on any substrate. Gravure inks are also fast drying, allowing for faster print-run times. They also have little show through, which occurs when ink printed on one side of the paper or substrate can be seen through the paper on the other side, making the use of thinner substrates more of a possibility. In addition, gravure inks do not rub off the finished product. Also, because the ink is transferred directly to the substrate from the gravure cylinder there is precise color control throughout the press run.

Gravure printing is also known for its ability to print high-quality images, as well as its ability to achieve intense color with one pass through the press. The engraved cells of varying widths and depths give gravure an extended tonal range, allowing very light highlight dots (at 5 percent) to the densest solid blacks. This results in quality often unmatched by other printing processes.

Ink density is also consistent throughout the process and the engraved cylinder can lay down varying ink film thicknesses, or densities, when necessary. The engraving of the cylinder controls color as well, allowing millions of impressions to be produced without color variation. This makes gravure a good choice for printing work in which exact color matches are critical (such as catalogs that feature product colors).

1. Uses of gravure

Gravure is used for nearly 20 percent of all printing done in the United States, typically for three types of printing. The first is packaging printing, including bags, boxes, labels, folding cartons, and gift wrap. Gravure is also used for publication printing. This includes catalogs, magazines, newspaper supplements, and mass mailing advertisements. Magazines with a large subscription base (anything over one or two million copies), often choose to print on a gravure press. The third area gravure is used for is product printing. Product printing is the printing of materials such as vinyl, wallpaper, floor coverings, and textiles.

2. Disadvantages of gravure

The main disadvantage of gravure is its prepress cost, which is the highest of any of the printing processes. Engraving or etching the gravure cylinder is expensive, as is the cylinder itself, in comparison to the plates used in other printing processes. Gravure is more appropriate for long print runs (typically in the millions). It is not economically feasible to produce gravure cylinders for short runs.

(v) SCREEN PRINTING

Screen printing is a type of printing in which a fine fabric or metal mesh is stretched over a frame. Ink is pushed through the screen onto a substrate, using a rubber squeegee.

A photopolymer coating is applied to the mesh after it has been stretched across the frame. A film positive is placed on the photopolymer and is then exposed to harden the photopolymer in areas that will not print (the nonimage areas). The unexposed photopolymer, which is the image area, is washed away to create the open areas of the stencil. The screen is then pressed against a substrate and ink is forced through the open areas of the stencil to create the image.

Screen printing is the only printing process that is not restricted to flat substrates. Screen printing can be used to print on practically any flat or three-dimensional surface, including paper, plastic, or metal. It is typically used for signage, printed circuit boards, plastic containers, and printed garments.

(vi) DIGITAL PRINTING

Any printing device that images directly from a computer to print could be considered digital. Usually digital printers do not contain pigment-based inks; they contain dyes, toner, or, electrographic inks. (See the chapter on **digital printing** [8] for a more in-depth discussion of this topic.)

Most digital presses use technology that originated in the humble copy machine. Lasers are used to write the image, and electricity and toner then affix the image to the substrate. Each image printed is a new image, rather than being a duplicate reproduced from a master, as is the case with all the printing technologies discussed above. Printed jobs go directly from the computer, through the RIP, and begin printing. Some adjustments may have to be made to get the desired effect, but in theory, the first job printed is the final version. This means that the time, materials, and expense that the other printing processes require up front for setup (*makeready*) and proofing are much lower—in fact, they can be close to zero—for digital presses.

One of the main advantages of digital printing over other methods is customization. In digital printing, every print can contain new information derived from a computer database. *Variable data* is the buzzword used by the printing industry to describe the way digital presses handle new information for each page. Each page can contain different names, places, colors—anything that can be programmed into a database can be changed. This creates tremendous marketing opportunities. One of the obvious applications of this process is the production of the mailers from magazine and travel marketers that declare, "You, Jill Smith, have just won One Million Dollars!!" Another application of digital printing could be a brochure sent to a regional list of car owners offering the opportunity to custom design a car with choices of color, model, features, etc. If you reply, next comes a mailer showing the car you designed and information on how you can order it through a local dealer. Most direct mailings have a 1 to 2 percent response rate; the kind of mailer just outlined can generate up to a 40 percent response.

Another use for digital printers is to make just a few copies of a book. Increasingly, publishers are using this technology to allow them to offer books that were out of print or which have very low demand. The unit cost is higher than for a mass-produced book, but when you need an out-of-print book, price is not as important. While the price per page, or even per book, is higher than in lithography, digital printing saves the expense of carrying inventory. In addition, since lithography prints such large quantities, there is a risk that the information may become obsolete before it is all sold or distributed. Digital printing saves the expense of throwing away unused materials.

1. Large format inkjet

Most inkjet printers are desktop-sized and used for small office, home office, and consumer printing. The quality of their color output has risen dramatically the last few years, while costs have dropped substantially.

Large-format printers can be over 40 inches wide, and are usually fed from a web roll, so they make various lengths possible. These large, or wide inkjets have created a niche print market. There are many uses for them, including posters, banners, display units, and proofing.

Their resolution capabilities are comparable to desktop inkjets, usually 300 to 600 dpi. Inkjet printing forces colorants through nozzles onto the paper; most use dyes instead of pigments because the particles have to be water soluble. There are inkjet dyes that resist moisture and fading and are suitable for outdoor use. Many large-format printers contain six color units, the basic CMYK set plus a light tint of cyan and a light tint of magenta. This allows brighter, more detailed highlights, and less dot gain in the midtones. Inkjet printers render images in lines that run across the substrate. Banding can occur in large flat areas of color, so these should be designed with care.

Large format inkjet is ideal for creating unique banners, posters, and display booth panels. For short-run poster work, this is a better option than screen printing. Substrate choices are broad and include paper, cloth, canvas, backlit film, rigid board, Tyvek, and vinyl. The quality is very high.

6.14 WORKING WITH PRINTERS

If print was a commodity product, then any old PDF file could be submitted to any old printing company via the Web and a final product could be satisfactorily delivered a few days later. But as this chapter has shown, print is a custom manufacture, not a commodity. For this reason communication remains a vital element of successful print manufacturing. Working successfully with a printing company means ensuring that the ambiguous becomes explicit. The areas for discussion include equipment, capacity and workflow.

Here are some specific questions to ask your printer before submitting a job to them:

- What are the limitations of your press (e.g., minimum and maximum print area, how much space to leave for crop and registration marks, optimal linescreen, color capabilities, and adjustments for dot gain)?
- Do you use color management?
- Who handles trapping?
- Do you support [specific software or file format]? Which versions?
- What work do you handle in house, and what do you send out?

Most printers operate with a set of trade customs that specify roles and responsibilities. These should be reviewed prior to submitting a job.

The key to a successful print job is coordinating all parts of the workflow. With workflows distributed between designers, publishers, prepress services, and print shops, open communication is vital.

6.15 RESOURCES

Here are some useful resources on the Web:

(i) FILE FORMATS

- Stanford University Academic Computing Services' "Graphic File Formats at a Glance": http://acomp.stanford.edu/acpubs/Docs/graphic_file_formats
- A manual on graphic file formats: http://www.why-not.com/articles/formats.htm
- The Webopedia provides a full list of file format extensions: http://webopedia.internet.com/quick_ref/fileextensionsfull.html
- An even more extensive listing, with links to full data on each format: http://filext.com
- In-depth technical information on file formats: http://www.wotsit.org

(ii) IMAGING

- Probably the best on-line imaging tutorial is available from Adobe: http://www.adobe.com/support/techguides/printpublishing/scanning/psscanning.html
- Kodak Polychrome has some well-illustrated resources: http://www.kpgraphics.com/gen/prod_support/learning_ctr/index.html
- Kodak Polychrome Graphics. The Learning Center. 2002: http://www.kpgraphics.com/gen/prod_support/learning_ctr/index.html

(iii) UNDERSTANDING COLOR MANAGEMENT

- X-Rite publishes an excellent guide called *The Color Guide and Glossary,* available here: http://www.xrite.com/documents/mktg/L11–029.pdf. Even better, though more complex, is *The ColorShop Color Primer: An Introduction to the History of Color, Color Theory, and Color Measurement,* found at http://www.xrite.com/documents/mktg/ColorPrimer.pdf. X-Rite has a range of other semipromotional documents on color communication and imaging: http://www.xrite.com/helpdesk/document_main.asp.
- The ICC (International Color Consortium) offers some solid background information: http://www.color.org/info_profiles2.html.
- Apple has one of the most in-depth Web sites devoted to color management generally, and ColorSync specifically: http://www.apple.com/colorsync.
- Adobe has some good detail: http://www.adobe.com/support/techguides/color/main.html.
- Microsoft offers a solid introduction to color management, and specifics on color management in Windows: http://www.microsoft.com/hwdev/tech/color/icmwp.asp.
- Bruce Fraser and Brian Lawler are two of the best journalists covering color management. Links to many of Bruce's articles on color are available here: *http://www.creativepro.com/reviews/authsummary/40.html.* Brian offers many of his best articles on his own Web site: http://www.thelawlers.com/essays.html.

BIBLIOGRAPHY

Adobe Systems Incorporated. "Color and Color Management." 2000. http://www.adobe.com/support/techguides/color/main.html

———. "Introduction to Halftones and Scanning." 2000. http://www.adobe.com/support/techguides/printpublishing/scanning/psscanning.html

Bunting, Fred. *The ColorShop Color Primer: An Introduction to the History of Color, Color Theory, and Color Management*. Light Source Computer Images, Inc., 1998. http://www.xrite.com/documents/mktg/ColorPrimer.pdf

International Color Consortium. "Information on Profiles." Color.org. 2002. http://www.color.org/info_profiles2.html

Jaeggi, Stephan, and Bern Zipper. *Basics: An Introduction to PDF Technology*. Kiel: Heidelberger Druckmaschinen AG, 1999. http://www.prepress.ch/visionwork/english.html

———. *Creation: The Creation of PDF Documents*. Kiel: Heidelberger Druckmaschinen AG, 1999. http://www.prepress.ch/visionwork/english.html

———. *Management: Economic and Organizational Aspects of PDF*. Kiel: Heidelberger Druckmaschinen AG, 1999. http://www.prepress.ch/visionwork/english.html

———. *Production: Processing*. Kiel: Heidelberger Druckmaschinen AG, 1999. http://www.prepress.ch/visionwork/english.html

Kodak Polychrome Graphics. "The Learning Center." 2002. http://www.kpgraphics.com/gen/prod_support/learning_ctr/index.html

Lawler, Brian. "Index to the Brian Lawler Essays." Brian Lawler. 2002. http://www.thelawlers.com/essays.htm

Microsoft Corporation. "Color Management and Windows: An Introduction." December 2001. http://www.microsoft.com/hwdev/tech/color/icmwp.asp

Stanford University. "Graphic File Formats at a Glance." Academic Computing Publications. 1998. http://acomp.stanford.edu/acpubs/Docs/graphic_file_formats/

X-Rite, Incorporated. "The Color Guide and Glossary." 2002. http://www.xrite.com/documents/mktg/L11 029.pdf

7 Accessibility

FREDERICK BOWES, III
Electronic Publishing Associates

Digital publishing technologies offer publishers and other content providers a new dimension in shaping their publications. Well-constructed digital content can be configured to be used with a wide range of accessibility tools, including specialized software such as text-to-speech programs, designed to help people with disabilities gain access to published materials that would otherwise be unavailable to them. This has not been lost on disability advocates, who have driven recent federal and state legislation that puts increasing pressure on publishers to provide their products in formats accessible to people with a variety of disabilities. This chapter will inform the reader of key issues, problems, and opportunities in content accessibility and what publishers must do, operationally, to meet accessibility needs. It also contains strategic suggestions about factoring accessibility requirements into product and business plans.

7.1 OVERVIEW

The medium of print has always been a serious problem for people with disabilities, and as a result they continue to have great difficulty gaining access to the wealth of information and literature available to mainstream society. Effective, but limited, accommodations have been devised (e.g., Braille, books on tape, and captioned television), but the amount of information and literature distributed in these ways is small. The unfortunate consequence is that disabled persons are unable to participate fully in today's increasingly knowledge-based world, and as a result, rates of illiteracy and unemployment are shockingly high among disabled individuals, running as high as 50 percent among some groups. Underemployment of disabled people who experience print obstacles exacerbates the problem. Most of society, including publishers, views the situation as regrettable, but accepts it as a fact of life. By and large the problem is perceived to be a concern of the disabled community alone.

Two important elements of the social environment have begun to change rapidly: technology and the law. Digital publications offer new functionality that can be used by people with disabilities, meaning that the capability now exists to unlock print-bound knowledge. Meanwhile, through various pieces of legislation, for example, the Rehabilitation Act and the Individuals with Disabilities Education Act (***IDEA***), the federal government has mandated that access shall be provided for all disabled persons. Other national and state legislation is waiting in the wings that will have further direct and indirect effects on publishers of all types. This chapter is intended to introduce readers to issues of print accessibility and to suggest ways publishers can address them using digital technologies.

When used by publishing professionals, the term "accessibility" usually relates to whether the user may have permission to use a work ("May I have access to it?"), whether it is available ("Where can I get access to it?"), or even whether the subject matter is within the reader's intellectual grasp (*Ulysses* is considered not to be *accessible* to most fifth graders). In the context of this chapter, however, ***accessibility*** has a different meaning. It refers to barriers inherent in the *format* of a work that prevent a reader from gaining access to content available to readers without disabilities. Content in print form is inaccessible to blind people; videos (without captioning) have audio tracks that are inaccessible to the deaf; people with severe motor impairment cannot physically manipulate printed works; and print proves more than problematic for those with learning disabilities such as dyslexia.

(I) INACCESSIBILITY IS COSTLY IN THE INFORMATION AGE

1. Education and knowledge are essential tools in the 21st century

1. THE NEED FOR KNOWLEDGE WORKERS

Economic success in today's world is increasingly dependent on an individual's ability to perform as a productive knowledge worker. Rapidly evolving technologies are permeating all aspects of our lives, and people who do not learn new skills on a regular basis are destined to fall behind those who are able to keep up and who can leverage change so that they can advance in society.

Organizations of all types are having an increasingly difficult time finding and keeping workers who can master the latest productivity tools and learn other necessary new technologies. More and more, organizations are relying on the Internet and internal digital networks to provide information to their workers. Thus, to be an effective worker, the disabled individual must be able to acquire information from nonprint, that is, digital, sources. If that digital information is not accessible, people with disabilities, however otherwise talented, become less than effective participants in the workforce. Thus, information that is inaccessible creates real problems for disabled individuals and for the organizations deprived of their talents.

2. HIGH-STAKES TESTS IN SCHOOLS DEFINE MINIMUM COMPETENCE

Education reform measures are being implemented to assure that students reach a certain level of competence before they get the diplomas they need to progress to productive roles in society. New regulations stipulate that students with disabilities must pass the same high-stakes tests as students without disabilities. Inaccessible print curriculum materials and inaccessible (printed) high-stakes tests conspire to push students with disabilities off the ladder of basic success. If students cannot graduate from high school, they cannot move on to college or become productive employees. The cost to society as a whole and to each individual left behind over her or his lifetime is enormous, and all too frequently their problems are the result of inaccessible curriculum and performance assessments (tests).

3. LIFETIME LEARNING REQUIRES ACCESSIBILITY AT EVERY AGE

Much energy is going into addressing the curriculum and testing needs of children with disabilities, and the recent implementation of ***Section 508*** of the Rehabilitation Act (which requires all federal Web sites to meet specified accessibility criteria) has signaled the need to assure that the needs of adults with disabilities are also met (see http://www.section508.gov/index.cfm?FuseAction=Content&ID=3 and http://www.access-board.gov/sec508/508standards.htm). Like government agencies, many companies and organizations are migrating much of their previously printed information to digital formats for delivery over the Internet and intranets. With Web sites becoming most organizations' chief point of communication, the need is increasing for all people to be able to acquire and manage information in digital forms.

2. Economic costs resulting from content accessibility barriers

When individuals with disabilities are unable to participate fully in society there are a number of negative economic consequences.

1. LOST CONTRIBUTION OF POTENTIALLY PRODUCTIVE WORKERS

When individuals who could contribute valuable skills as members of the workforce are prevented from doing so because the education and information that they need is inaccessible to them, their contribution is lost. This can be especially problematic in tight labor markets when forces of supply and demand boost the cost of hard-to-find skilled human resources.

2. HIGHER COSTS OF UNEMPLOYMENT

When individuals are unable to keep up with training requirements and cannot progress as their jobs require, they are often laid off, and laid off workers result in unemployment costs. Workers who possess print disabilities, yet are otherwise capable, can keep up if they have access to materials in alternative formats, and they need not add to the unemployment problem.

3. LOWER PRODUCTIVITY FROM UNDER-SKILLED WORKERS

When workers are not trained to the maximum of their abilities, their diminished productivity represents an opportunity cost to the organizations that employ them. If organizations do not provide educational, training, and administrative resources that are accessible, they risk depriving themselves of the best that their disabled workers have to offer, and that results in lower productivity, which translates into higher than necessary costs.

4. ACCOMMODATIONS ARE EXPENSIVE

Schools and employers required to accommodate students and workers who have print disabilities find themselves locked into devising accommodations for individuals on a one-by-one basis. This becomes a costly, nonscalable burden that usually ties one teacher or helper to one individual at a time.

There are a variety of assistive technology and software tools that help people with disabilities deal with text material once it is in a suitable digital (i.e., nonprint) form. Some of these tools are inexpensive (e.g., basic screen readers), but the cost to convert the printed material can be expensive and time consuming. Additionally, the quality of the conversion is often an issue.

Thus there is a need for content developers and providers to supply digital versions of their works that are formatted to be effectively used by available assistive software and technologies. By so doing, they can release those working with the disabled to focus on the subject matter rather than having to expend their allotted time and energy in the costly task of converting print materials and making other accommodations. With properly prepared digital versions, teachers can concurrently support a larger number of students with disabilities. This could, potentially, reduce the steep per-person cost of accommodating individual students and others with disabilities.

3. Social cost of barriers

More than 11 percent of students in public schools are covered under the Individuals with Disabilities Education Act (***IDEA***). The IDEA mandates that local school districts must provide a free and appropriate public education (***FAPE***) in the least restrictive environment (***LRE***) to nearly six million students with disabilities.

Without digital curricular materials, schools are fighting an uphill battle, and the casualties are the children who, because they cannot keep up, drop out—especially from high school. Studies show that disabled students represent a disproportionate share of the nation's dropouts. Other studies document the likelihood that dropouts will experience greater than normal difficulty succeeding in society throughout their lifetimes.

Society incurs more than the economic cost of people not being able to get, hold, or progress in their jobs. People who cannot manage information in print form are generally limited in their ability to deal with the social infrastructure in which they live. From getting a driver's license, to completing a job application, to completing tax forms, the print-disabled person is at a real disadvantage. When it comes to participating in the political process—even at the most basic level of voting—they often find that important background materials are available only in print and thus are inaccessible to them. Without accessible information, the print-disabled person is likely to be a less informed member of society than one with no print disabilities.

People who are frustrated in their attempts to participate and yet see no way of improving their situation tend to be unhappy, unmotivated, and sometimes resentful and troublesome. People who are unable to participate simply because of inaccessible printed materials are likely to find themselves consigned to this disgruntled lot. By providing accessible textbooks for the millions of children with print disabilities, and by seeing that important everyday information is available in accessible digital form for those adults struggling to succeed despite their print disabilities, society can mitigate much frustration and eliminate demotivating forces at work for a great many of our citizens.

In summary, publishers and other producers of digital text will increasingly need to assure that their products are not only digital but also truly accessible. By doing so they will make it possible for students with disabilities to succeed in school and for adult citizens to manage the information aspect of everyday living and participate more fully in the workings of our information-intensive society.

(ii) THE CLIMATE IS CHANGING

1. Diversity is becoming law

Our society has increasingly pursued the benefits of enabling the inclusion of a wide diversity of citizenry in all aspects of life. In this context diversity embraces not only ethnic and cultural differences but also differences resulting from disabilities. While separating groups solely based on racial or ethnic differences (i.e., segregation) is no longer permitted, inclusion has not come so quickly to people with disabilities. Only recently has it become law that students with disabilities must be "mainstreamed," that is, taught in classrooms alongside their nondisabled peers. This is seen not only as a better learning environment for these students and a tactic that can reduce instances of ego-deflating isolation, but as a constructive step in fostering diversity.

2. Strong disability laws and regulations taking hold

Until recently there have been few laws that addressed the needs of people with disabilities except for the blind and visually impaired. (Braille laws go back to 1879; see http://www.aph.org/about/highlite.htm.) In the latter part of the 20th century, major legislation began to change the environment and empower disabled persons who'd previously been ignored.

Section 504 of the Rehabilitation Act of 1973 prohibits discrimination on the basis of disability and requires that accommodations be made for disabled students to eliminate barriers to participation in school activities.

In 1998 the Rehabilitation Act was amended by Section 508 to require that federal agencies' electronic and information technology be accessible to people with disabilities, including employees and members of the public. As of this writing, Section 508 standards do not yet specifically or directly apply to the private sector or to state agencies, but the bar has been set.

The Americans with Disabilities Act (***ADA***) of 1990 took effect in 1992 and made it illegal for private employers, state and local governments, employment agencies, and labor unions to discriminate against qualified individuals with disabilities in job application procedures, hiring, firing, advancement, compensation, job training, and other terms, conditions, and privileges of employment. Except where it would create an undue hardship, employers are now required to provide accommodations for their disabled workers.

The Individuals with Disabilities Education Act (IDEA), passed in 1997 and formerly known as the Education for All Handicapped Children Act of 1975, requires school districts to provide a free and appropriate education for all students—including those with disabilities. This law requires that the education establishment make every effort to supply students who are unable to benefit from standard print materials with necessary alternative materials and services.

In addition to 504, 508, ADA, and IDEA, there are significant state regulations already on the books and many more in the wings. States are free to implement the federal laws in their own ways, and California, New York, Texas, Florida, Georgia, and Kentucky all have laws requiring or strongly encouraging the provision of accessible versions of print materials to students. Officials and managers, under these new legal pressures to provide accommodations to people with disabilities, will begin turning to their suppliers to provide printed materials in accessible formats, and this will have consequences for publishers and other information providers and preparers.

3. Chafee amendment to the Copyright Act

In 1996 the Copyright Act was amended to permit "an authorized entity to reproduce or distribute copies or phonorecords of a previously published, nondramatic literary work . . . in specialized formats exclusively for use by blind or other persons with disabilities." Essentially this amendment established a limitation on the exclusive rights in copyrighted works, allowing "authorized entities" to convert printed works into digital text (a "specialized format") and distribute them to qualified individuals.

"Authorized entity" refers to "a nonprofit organization or a governmental agency that has as a primary mission to provide specialized services relating to training, education, or adaptive reading or information access needs of blind or other persons with disabilities" [Public Law 104–197 Sec.121 (c) (1)].

Under this legislation, authorized entities can make digital files of copyrighted works as provided by the law without having to go through the time-consuming (and sometimes expensive) process of obtaining the permission of the content owners. The end result is that digital copies of a publisher's printed work can be produced and distributed, albeit only as provided by the amendment, with no assurance of quality and with no knowledge of the publisher. The amendment is silent on business issues such as royalties and at what price, if any, the copy may be distributed. It does, however, expressly prohibit further reproduction or redistribution and requires that the copy include a copyright notice for the original work.

As legal pressures build on educators and administrators to comply with the requirement to provide timely accommodations to the print-disabled, they will be increasingly motivated to find ways to obtain copies of materials made under the Chafee amendment. Publishers concerned about how their works appear when converted to alternate formats and interested in knowing how their content is being used should consider making accessible digital versions available themselves. Converting print works into digital versions for people with disabilities on a one-by-one basis is costly and time consuming for authorized entities, and publishers may generate considerable good will with their customers by also supplying their works in an accessible digital format subject to license and contractual restrictions.

4. High-stakes student testing to validate competence is proliferating

As a nation we have become frustrated with a public education system that is costly yet turns out many young citizens who are not sufficiently equipped to take a responsible, productive place in society. This frustration has translated into increasingly proactive steps by federal and state governments to document student (and by implication, teacher) performance. Standardized tests that determine eligibility for advancement are increasingly seen as an essential part of the sea change that is needed.

In the same way that one must pass a standardized test to be deemed capable of driving a car, so students in an increasing number of states must pass a standardized ("high-stakes") test in order to get a high school diploma. Leaving aside whether the testing process itself is inaccessible, students regardless of disability must demonstrate mastery of a specified body of knowledge or not receive the high school diploma.

As parents pressure schools to see that their children pass high-stakes tests, school administrators out of necessity will gravitate toward a curriculum that is accessible to students with disabilities because these students must master the same content as their nondisabled peers. Publishers of curricular materials can anticipate that they will need to offer accessible versions of their textbooks to be competitive in this emerging environment.

(iii) CONFIGURABLE CONTENT CONQUERS MOST ACCESSIBILITY ISSUES EFFICIENTLY

In the print world, separate products must be produced to accommodate the needs of people with various types of disabilities. Large print, Braille, and audio editions are created for the visually impaired. People who have learning disabilities or who must deal with motor impairment have only these versions, which are not well suited to accommodate their needs, to work with.

With the arrival of digital technologies, new options are available to address a wide range of accessibility challenges. Documents containing not only content (text, images, etc.) but also formatting information can be packaged as digital files and delivered to software that can present a document in multiple ways depending on the formatting information it contains and the capabilities of the software. Thus, an HTML document can be displayed in a browser that is configured to show the content in a manner preferred by the user.

By embedding formatting information (i.e., tagging) in a digital document, the publisher of that document makes it possible for special software to present the content in ways that are accessible to the user. For example, a talking browser used by the blind to read Web pages to them can recognize the text following an <alt> tag in a document as alternative text that is to be "read" to describe a picture that the unsighted user would otherwise find inaccessible.

We will discuss issues related to making digital documents accessible further on in this chapter; suffice it to say that by producing a well-tagged digital version of a work, a publisher can, with a single digital document, respond to many needs that currently require multiple conversions or are wholly unmet for people with disabilities. For people with motor difficulties, an impressive variety of ingenious devices exists that enable people to interact with computers in ways that would not be possible with a printed book. People with learning disabilities, such as dyslexia, can use "***text-to-speech***" (***TTS***) software to read text to them as they follow along in the printed text at their own pace.

The major benefit that digital documents provide for addressing the needs of people with disabilities is that well-tagged text can be manipulated by specialized software that understands the tags and itself has been configured by the user to produce a specific accessible output. The same file could be read aloud at a fast pace by "reader" software for one person and read slowly for another without degradation in quality. That same file could also be used on a computer screen by a paraplegic who can manipulate a computer keyboard with a pointing or clicking device attached to her head.

When one well-tagged file serves multiple purposes, the cost of accommodating the needs of people with a variety of print disabilities can become manageable. While the focus of this chapter is on accessibility, it should be noted that tagged digital files, that is, configurable content, can generate even wider benefits.

In the same manner that sidewalk curb cuts designed for wheelchairs benefit travelers with rolling suitcases, and close-captioned television broadcasts created for the deaf are appreciated by hearing people in noisy waiting rooms, bars, and health clubs, so publications provided in digital form for accessibility reasons can also provide meaningful side benefits to the nondisabled population. For example, students for whom English is a second language would benefit if their textbooks could be read to them by software; the same will be true for adults who can understand spoken words yet are unable to read as they struggle with official information of various types.

(iv) DIGITAL TECHNOLOGIES NOW MAKE CONFIGURABLE CONTENT A PRACTICAL PARADIGM

In architecture there is a concept known as universal design, which in essence advocates that buildings and other structures be designed from the outset to accommodate people requiring special considerations and especially the disabled. Ramps, elevators, Braille enhanced signage, and handicapped-accessible rest rooms can all be "designed in" so that a wide range of visitors can be seamlessly included. In the print world, the paradigm of communicating information through fixed format media is inherently limited and therefore unsuited to universal design. To make printed information accessible requires special accommodations that are costly and often not responsive to time demands (it often takes months to get a Braille or audio version of a book produced).

The digital paradigm, on the other hand, is ideally suited to incorporating the cost-saving principles of universal design. By building content flow cues into documents and by embedding tags that enable software to navigate and present content according to user-configured options, the producer of a digital document creates a single universally designed version that can be configured to meet the needs of many.

The concept of universal design is being applied in innovative ways to learning activities (dubbed ***Universal Design for Learning*** or ***UDL***) by the Center for Applied Special Technology (***CAST***) (http://www.cast.org/udl/). CAST is focusing on how to employ universal design to produce fully accessible school curriculum materials that will meet the needs of a wide variety of students, including those with disabilities. A single digital text can be used by a variety of disabled students (depending on the available software) as well as by their nondisabled classmates.

1. XML affords a flexible, cost-effective solution

What makes it feasible for content producers to consider producing accessible digital documents is the increasingly widespread use of Extensible Markup Language (**XML** [3.3]) for content-management applications and Hypertext Markup Language (**HTML** [3.2]) for document distribution. Producers can tag the same files they use to produce printed products with special tags for accessibility (or other predefined purposes), and by using style sheets output them as needed into specified formats.

As explained in the chapter on **markup** [3.3.3.3], a master XML document can be transformed with a design-specific script or Extensible Style Language Transformation (XSLT) stylesheet to produce an HTML document that will have specific features and properties as defined by the script or XSLT stylesheet. Thus a single XML file could be output as an ASCII file for input to Braille software using one script or XSLT stylesheet, with another script or XSLT stylesheet to produce an accessible HTML file for Web distribution, and, using page layout software with Adobe Acrobat, output as an accessible PDF for printing or digital distribution.

The low incremental cost and the speed with which multiple variations can be produced digitally eliminates key obstacles, inherent with print, to meeting the needs of many people with disabilities.

(v) DIGITAL DOES NOT MEAN ACCESSIBLE

Just because a print document has been converted to digital form (e.g., via scanning) does not mean that it is necessarily sufficiently accessible for people with disabilities. There are currently three major categories of challenges that must be dealt with for digital versions before the accessibility problem will be fully addressed: the quantity and depth of the tagging or coding of the content (e.g., has alternate text been provided for all, or just selected, images?); the quality of the accessibility accommodations embedded in the content (e.g., how effective is the alternate text?); and the degree to which rights protection schemes render the digital content inaccessible (e.g., if the ability to copy text has been disabled, the document cannot be used with most assistive software).

1. Accessibility requires careful tagging

Tagging documents for accessibility is not dissimilar to tagging text files for composition, that is, codes are embedded in the text that enable the document to conform to a predetermined layout when presented. In the print composition process, text-editing software is used and codes (ideally XML) are embedded by the tagger according to design and markup rules established by the graphic designer. What primarily drives production cost and the speed of the markup and tagging effort is the complexity of the format of the finished document.

Since simple prose documents are essentially linear, and since there is likely to be little formatting apart from chapter headings, a minimal amount of tagging is required to make them accessible. Using XML makes such works highly configurable, and so the tagging task is generally not likely to be complicated or expensive. Estimating the work involved would be similar to estimating the cost of converting a manuscript for simple typesetting and composition.

Textbooks, magazines, economic reports, and the like involve more complex layouts and design features that permit multiple pathways through the content. The greater sophistication in appearance and in navigation (how the reader is expected to move between content elements) creates bigger markup challenges for producers of accessible digital versions. The person tagging a complex document (such as a high school science textbook) must know how the various elements should best be identified and sequenced in the digital file so as to enable electronic reading tools and other assistive software to correctly recognize and deal with them. Since there are many more content elements (footnotes, sidebars, tables, charts, etc.) in a textbook than a novel, marking up and tagging such works for conversion to accessible digital versions will be significantly more challenging, time consuming, and costly.

2. Tagging alone is not enough

Simply correctly identifying the content elements as to type and establishing the preferred content flow for the disabled user is not enough to make a work truly accessible. There is room for considerable variation in how different tagged elements are dealt with. Descriptive HTML tags such as <alt> and <longdesc> are only as good as the supplemental alternative content that they introduce. How tabular or math material is presented can be helpful or confusing depending on how conscientious the content preparer has been in providing cues and content for those not able to see the material. It is even more important for disabled users that tags and navigation aids in a digital document be used consistently than it is for the design of the print work to provide a consistent infrastructure for nondisabled readers.

1. DEPTH OF DETAIL

Providing alternate content for images introduces an important and often under-appreciated subjective element into the conversion process. Consider these two possibilities for alternate text for a picture in a book about race horses:

1. "Affirmed running in a large fenced-in field."
2. "Big brown horse named Affirmed, seen running in his favorite pasture in front of a sign reading Jonabell Farm, Lexington, Kentucky. Affirmed lived from 1995 to 2001, was the last Triple Crown winner, and sired seventy-eight stakes winners."

Technically, both descriptions meet the standard for accessibility, yet one clearly imparts more information than the other. The first example would be satisfactory if there were an accompanying caption containing the other information. Absent a caption, however, if detailed information were elsewhere on a page or even on another page, the editor might want to include this material for the benefit of the unsighted reader so that he or she could make the same kind of connection that the sighted reader might make using visual cues.

2. TABLES, CHARTS, AND GRAPHS

Authors of alternate content are particularly challenged when it comes to dealing with tables, charts, and graphs. The creator of <longdesc> text for a chart might say "Bar chart showing the distribution of the 417,049 votes cast for the three candidates. (1) Mr. Smith 175,321 or 42 percent; (2) Ms. Jones 168,432 or 40 percent; (3) Mr. Clancy 73,296 or 18 percent," or they might simply say, "Chart showing that Mr. Smith won 42 percent of the 417,049 votes cast, Ms. Jones 40 percent, and Mr. Clancy 18 percent."

3. EDITORIAL QUALITY OF ADDED CONTENT

The way alternate content is written can also cause the disabled reader to draw different information from an illustration than that gleaned by a sighted reader. For example, a writer producing alternate text for a picture of Norman

Rockwell's "The Problem We All Live With," a 1964 painting of Ruby Bridges, (http://www.guggenheim.org/exhibitions/rockwell/problem_lg.html) might say, "Picture of a little Afro-American girl with braids in a white dress carrying a schoolbook and ruler walking to school with two white men with arm bands in front of her and two behind her." Another might go further and mention, "She and the federal marshals are walking right to left past a wall upon which the racial epithet 'nigger' has been scrawled and which has been splattered by a hurled tomato that now lies on the ground." The additional text almost certainly conveys the information that the original author intended to communicate, but omitted. Both, however, meet strict accessibility guidelines simply by being there.

Being sure that disabled readers are able to get the critical subjective points of charts, tables, diagrams, pictures, and other illustrations through well-written and properly edited alternative text may be a compelling reason for a publisher to provide authorized accessible versions of its books, periodicals, manuals, and other publications. Certainly the editor and publisher of a school textbook that is the basis for important testing will want to be sure that the alternate text in digital versions contains content of sufficient quality to assure that the disabled student can extract the same significant information from an illustration as a sighted student.

3. Security versus accessibility

There are other issues associated with making digital versions available that are largely related to copyright and the use of digital rights management (***DRM***) technologies. DRM technologies are starting to be used by electronic publishers and other content owners to "lock" the content of digital documents before distributing them so as to protect against misuse and redistribution.

The difficulty is that locked content cannot be used by the software tools that make it accessible to people with specific disabilities. For the benefits of accessible digital text to be realized, the text must, currently, be selectable (i.e., it can be copied and subsequently pasted) by the user so that it can be input into the wide variety of available specialized software applications such as screen readers that address the needs of people with specific disabilities. The problem for publishers is that if the content can be selected and copied, it can be redistributed, and it therefore is no longer secured. Encrypted content that can be read only by a specific piece of equipment or a specific piece of software is by design unavailable to all other assistive software. Thus, publishers who secure their content before making it available render it essentially useless for users with disabilities.

This problem is widely recognized. It poses very real challenges for publishers whose customers operate in an increasingly aggressive legal climate and are required by law to provide accessible copyrighted works to disabled individuals. A number of organizations such as the ***Web Accessibility Initiative*** (***WAI***) of the World Wide Web Consortium (W3C) (www.w3.org/wai) and the Open eBook Forum (OeBF) are working to find a solution by standardizing file formats. A number of ad hoc working groups are wrestling with the problem, but to date no viable vision of a solution has been articulated.

The assistive technology field, that is, the developers of specialized software that aids people with specific disabilities, is small and badly fragmented, and is unlikely to offer a coherent solution. By means of special plug-ins and other symbiotic software tools, producers of mainstream software products, such as Adobe, are able to address the problem somewhat effectively within their restricted software environments. In this situation, publishers could elect to produce and distribute an accessible edition that could be individually designed and secured for only those secure environments, but people with disabilities would then have no alternative but to set aside their accessibility software of choice and acquire specified tools that can make use of the work in question and provide the accessibility features they need. Publishers would have to produce multiple editions, one for each of the vendor-specific controlled environments.

As of this writing, no scalable solutions that can reasonably address this problem exist or are on the horizon. So long as the software tools preferred by people with disabilities do not have the ability to receive protected content, to use it within the rules of a specified protection scheme, and to preserve it so that redistribution is not possible, people with disabilities will find publishers highly unlikely to produce and provide accessible versions.

For now, the only solution to the secured content problem for those required to accommodate individuals with disabilities is to have the print version digitized, that is, scanned or rekeyed and then tagged under the provisions of the Chafee amendment—generally an unattractive alternative because it is usually costly, time consuming, and vulnerable to quality control issues.

7.2 A CLOSER LOOK

Now that we have a sense of the general issues involving accessibility, let's take a look at some of the specifics. When it comes to tackling significant challenges, understanding the issues is only the first step. The closer we get to developing solutions to complex problems, the quicker we renew our appreciation for the familiar saying, "the devil is in the details." When it comes to accessibility and digital publishing this is especially true. In the next sections we will discuss specifics about what constitutes accessible formats and look at the formats that are currently in use.

(i) WHAT ARE "ACCESSIBLE" OR "ALTERNATE" FORMATS?

1. The laws are ambiguous

As is often the case with laws enacted to remedy complex problems, legislation relating to the accessibility of published materials is clear in its intent but short on specifics. Terms such as "disabled" and even "print-disabled" are not explicitly defined. At times legislation refers to earlier laws that are also not specific and that use terms whose generally understood definitions have changed over the years.

1. CHAFEE AMENDMENT

To illustrate, the 1996 ***Chafee amendment*** to the Copyright Act (http://www.loc.gov/nls/reference/factsheets/copyright.html) was enacted to provide a specific exemption from copyright to allow an authorized entity to create specialized formats of nondramatic literary works in a timely manner for "blind or other persons with disabilities." According to the amendment, "'blind or other persons with disabilities' means individuals who are eligible or who may qualify in accordance with the Act entitled 'An Act to provide books for the adult blind,' approved March 3, 1931 (2 U.S.C. 35a; 46 Stat. 1487) to receive books and other publications produced in specialized formats." The 1931 wording simply states that the law applies to "adult blind residents of the United States." In 1966 the law was amended to include "blind and . . . other physically handicapped readers certified by competent authority as unable to read normal printed material as a result of physical limitations" (http://www.loc.gov/nls/pl89522.html). Current brain research leaves it unclear whether learning disabilities should be construed as the result of physical limitations.

2. INSTRUCTIONAL MATERIALS ACCESSIBILITY ACT MEANING OF "PRINT-DISABLED"

The proposed ***Instructional Materials Accessibility Act (IMAA)*** of 2002 (S.2246) introduced on April 24, 2002 (and at this writing working its way through the legislative process) limits to "blind and print-disabled" persons the authorization to use content provided from the proposed National Instructional Materials Access Center. Nowhere in the proposed legislation is the term "print-disabled" defined in any detail, and it is unclear what sort of students will benefit under the Act should it become law. It is worthy of note that of the six million students deemed disabled under IDEA and therefore entitled to receive accommodations, less than 2 percent are categorized as blind or low-vision. How many of the remaining 5.8 million would be considered print-disabled under this law is not known. The AAP has used the term "sight-disabled" (instead of print-disabled) in its publicity supporting the IMAA bill, and it remains unclear as to how the IMAA will affect students with dyslexia and other learning disabilities or even those who are deaf or have motor impairments.

In federal and state legislation, when the terms "accessible content," "alternate formats," and the like are used, it is in the context of addressing the needs of the "disabled." Without a clear definition of "disabled" it is difficult to define exactly what accommodations will be necessary to make an electronic file accessible for the person in question and therefore to determine what would constitute a suitable alternative format.

2. Sections 504 and 508 of the Rehabilitation Act cover all disabilities

While the Chafee amendment and the IMAA have been driven primarily by the needs of visually impaired schoolchildren, the Rehabilitation Act is broader in scope and is aimed at meeting the needs of disabled adults as well. As a result, Sections 504 and 508 of the Rehabilitation Act require a more inclusive interpretation of disability than just the needs of visually impaired students.

1. DIFFERENT REQUIREMENTS FOR DIFFERENT DISABILITIES

Different disabilities create different requirements for media to be accessible. People with blindness and low-vision disabilities need accommodation with images, tables, and page navigation. The hearing impaired need help with soundtracks, multimedia objects, audio prompts, etc. People with motor impairments need digital files that the software supporting their special equipment can faithfully represent and correctly manipulate. People with dyslexia and/or other learning disabilities need digital files as content for text-to-speech and other specialized software.

For example, should a video clip in a multimedia document always be required to accommodate the needs of the deaf by incorporating a transcript of any spoken content and include descriptions of sounds in the clip? Should the title and composer's name be provided in <alt> text for any background music? How about the performer's name? Without clear definitions, these sorts of questions illustrate that any determination of accessibility is subjective at best. While there is legal history to guide actions regarding such things as physical accessibility, for example, handicapped parking access and ramps in lieu of stairs, there is no legal history when it comes to content accessibility.

2. FORMAL QUALITATIVE STANDARDS FOR ACCOMMODATIONS ARE NOT IN PLACE

Given that Sections 504 and 508 relate to all disabilities, the challenge of providing suitable print alternatives could be daunting if unique versions were required for each disability. The matter is made more complicated when issues such as the quality of individual accommodations are factored in. A blind person would have a right under the law to challenge the accessibility of a digital work if there were no alternate text for illustrations; but what if alternate text were present but it inadequately described the subject? To illustrate, "Figure 4. Table: Number of books sold by state" doesn't give the disabled reader the same access to the values in specific data cells (e.g., New York = 27,345 books) as a nondisabled person would have. Similarly, embedding additional tagged text in a file doesn't result in accessibility if the description is limited or cryptic.

3. What can we conclude about accessible alternate formats?

In some ways, attempting to come up with a clear-cut definition of *in*accessible content is analogous to trying to define obscenity. With apologies to Justice Potter Stewart, depending on one's disability you "know it when you see it." As a rule, when laws and regulations don't provide adequate definition and direction, standards and guidelines evolve on their own. They attract popular support, they become widely adhered to, and in some cases receive formal recognition (e.g., standards from NISO and ANSI). Often such standards eventually get incorporated into laws and regulations.

1. THE IMAA'S PROPOSED "NATIONAL STANDARD FORMAT" FOR SCHOOL MATERIALS

It is likely that this pattern will apply to some degree with alternative formats, because the proposed IMAA is a vehicle for this to happen. It requires that publishers submit their content to the IMAA-created national repository in a "national standard format." It also establishes a protocol for creating the "national standard" and calls for a consensus of nominated affected parties to establish the definition. The American Foundation for the Blind has a summary of the legislation at www.afb.org/info_document_view.asp?documentid&=1704. The testimony of Pat Schroeder, President and CEO of the Association of American Publishers, supporting the IMAA, contains an enlightening discussion of the issues (including file formats) and can be found at www.publishers.org/press/test062802.htm.

It is anticipated that the national standard format that emerges via the IMAA will be XML based, and, since the IMAA is largely being driven by the needs of the blind and low-vision community, many expect it to closely resemble the recently adopted ANSI/NISO Z39.86–2002 standard, "Specifications for the ***Digital Talking Book***" (http://www.niso.org/standards/standard_detail.cfm?std_id=710) that was developed by an international consortium, known as ***DAISY*** (Digital Accessible Information SYstem), that focuses on the needs of the visually challenged (http://www.daisy.org/about_us/default.asp). Whether the IMAA's national standard format will ultimately reflect the needs of students with other disabilities is unclear because the meaning of "print-disabled" within the scope of the IMAA itself is not clear.

So far the school textbook market has been unable to express its needs and requirements to publishers in a consistent enough manner such that they can be addressed cost-effectively. Those needs must, nevertheless, be addressed, and the IMAA holds the greatest promise to date for introducing order into an otherwise chaotic situation.

As federal and state legislatures pass laws aimed at leveling the playing field for the disabled, and as regulators interpret the imprecise language of the laws, publishers must maintain as much flexibility as possible in their approach to providing files in digital formats, remembering that the IMAA, if and when it becomes law, will only apply to school materials, while the challenge of providing accessibility to content cuts across the entire population.

2. NEEDS OF BRAILLE MAKERS NOT LIKELY TO GO AWAY

The IMAA is supposed to supercede state laws requiring electronic files, but some members of the Braille lobby are not necessarily willing to concede that their states will drop their own long-standing programs in favor of a national solution, especially since those programs serve more than just the needs of school students. Publishers, on the other hand, would not welcome a situation where a mandatory national standard format and infrastructure is put in place, yet they also must continue to deliver files in other formats for various states. Whether the IMAA in final form will in fact supercede state laws and free publishers from having to deliver multiple formats appears at this writing not to be fully resolved, and it remains to be seen if the IMAA will eliminate the current Babel of formats resulting from many incompatible and idiosyncratic state Braille laws.

3. NO STANDARDS FOR NON-K–12 PUBLISHERS

Outside the K–12 market, no equivalent legislation is in the works. Whether the IMAA solution for the school publishing segment will provide a model for postsecondary, scholarly, professional, and other publishing markets will bear watching. For now, publishers must make their own determinations and be responsive where required in the manner requested by the school, teacher, or end user.

4. What about Adobe's PDF?

Adobe's Portable Document Format (***PDF***) can provide an attractive alternative to a print format in that it reproduces a page on a computer screen exactly as it appears on paper—in full color and with graphics in position. Adobe's ***Acrobat Reader*** and ***eBook Reader*** are free software that can present PDF files and make them more manageable to some with disabilities. (By offering magnification, for example. For those with motor impairments, Acrobat Reader allows users to "turn pages" and otherwise navigate through a work that they could not manage were it in printed form.)

1. PROTECTED TEXT MAKES PDF NOT ACCESSIBLE

Much of this functionality is similar to what eBook technologies offer. A PDF formatted work is generally deemed inaccessible, however, because the technology used does not permit text to be extracted from the document for use with assistive software such as text-to-speech tools. Many people with disabilities find that Acrobat Reader and eBook Reader are insufficient for their specialized needs, and they choose to use a wide range of assistive technology solutions. For these people, there is a significant need to be able to export PDF content into an interim format for import into their specialized assistive resources.

2. SECTION 508 HAS DRIVEN ADOBE TO ADDRESS ACCESSIBILITY NEEDS

Because PDF has become widely used by government, corporations, and other entities producing large numbers of widely circulated documents (e.g., tax forms), the recent implementation of Section 508 of the Rehabilitation Act requiring that all government technology applications be accessible to people with disabilities (http://www.usdoj.gov/crt/508/508law.html) has created a major imperative for Adobe to deal effectively with PDF accessibility. Adobe has made recent strides in addressing this issue as evidenced by a number of changes incorporated into Acrobat 5.0. Readers are invited to examine this information at http://www.adobe.com/products/acrobat/access_wp1.html and http://www.adobe.com/products/acrobat/access_faq.html#2.

3. SECURE PDF REMAINS A PROBLEM

While Adobe is making progress in facilitating accessibility to the content in PDF documents, an additional problem remains when document security is factored into the mix. Acrobat 5.0 allows authors to "secure" documents so that the intellectual property they contain can be distributed and used only under controls set by the author or publisher. If Adobe allowed the text to be exported for use with accessibility software, the security would be compromised. Publishers should familiarize themselves with the information provided by Adobe on this subject in question 10 in the FAQ (see link above). Whether a PDF can be accessible is now more a function of whether the author or publisher has "locked up" the text using the security system and not so much an issue with Acrobat PDF technology.

5. What alternative formats are actually being used today?

In terms of the kinds of files they specify, existing state laws requiring publishers to produce files that can be used to make Braille differ.

1. TEXT FORMATS

According to Pat Schroeder's IMAA testimony, currently any of up to six formats could be required of a schoolbook publisher (i.e., HTML, SGML, ICADD22, Microsoft Word, RTF, and ASCII). Information is hard to come by for other markets, but anecdotal evidence indicates that the needs for alternate formats for college students and adults with disabilities are being met in much the same manner as those of school students.

2. UNSTRUCTURED ASCII IS MOST COMMON FOR PRINT WORKS

ASCII is the format most often specified for the production of Braille, as it is a lowest-common-denominator format for the many mom-and-pop Braille making operations. A complete list of state Braille requirements can be found at http://www.afb.org/info_document_view.asp?documentid=360.

The files that textbook publishers are required to supply for use by those producing Braille and for use with specialized assistive technologies generally have no accompanying graphics, and as a result publishers have no rights issues involving artists and photographers when they supply these files. Some publisher-supplied files omit text from sidebars, from "balloons," and other content elements of a highly designed book. Formatting for emphasis (boldface, italics, etc.), is often lost as well.

Digital files can easily be widely circulated, and publishers have ongoing concerns that when they provide their valuable content in digital formats, they are running a risk of these files being misappropriated, thus putting their revenues in jeopardy. Because unstructured ASCII files have been essentially stripped of all formatting information, they are considered "low-value" files by many publishers and therefore seen as not carrying the same risk of piracy as would files that could be used to create a reasonable facsimile of the original printed work (e.g., PDF and HTML). Decades of providing ASCII without mishap supports this perception.

3. HTML COMING ON STRONG FOR ELECTRONIC WORKS

With the rise of the World Wide Web and the migration of the Web browser paradigm to PC and network interfaces, HTML has burst on the scene as an important format. Because of the importance of the Web to people of all ages worldwide, the W3C (http://www.w3.org/) has established the ***Web Accessibility Initiative*** (***WAI***) to be sure that the Web's resources are as available as possible to people with disabilities. (http://www.w3.org/WAI/).

4. W3C/WAI GUIDELINES BECOMING A *DE FACTO* STANDARD

In its document, ***Web Content Accessibility Guidelines*** (http://www.w3.org/TR/WAI-WEBCONTENT/) the WAI explains how to make Web content accessible to people with disabilities. The WAI guidelines are the closest thing we have today to describing in detail what should constitute a truly accessible document. These guidelines are helpful not only for content delivered over the Web, but also for any content that will be delivered through an HTML browser interface on a local or enterprise-wide network. The guidelines are incorporated in a Web-based software tool called ***Bobby*** that examines Web pages and produces a report identifying and describing anything on the page that does not conform to the WAI guidelines (http://bobby.watchfire.com/bobby/html/en/index.jsp).

(ii) SO WHERE ARE WE NOW?

1. Many assistive technologies; all require digital content

To recapitulate, there are a variety of assistive technologies that are suited to the needs of people with various types of disabilities. These technologies provide functionality such as text-to-speech, configurable display options (e.g., magnification, changing text, and background colors), and navigational features that enable physically challenged users to manipulate the text by means of special devices that compensate for their motor deficiencies. For the most part all of these require content in a digital form that they can manipulate and deliver in a manner suited to the needs of the individual user.

2. Scanner generated ASCII is the dominant file form

Because publishers do not supply electronic files for this purpose, content generally must be scanned from printed works and massaged to make it ready for use. As described in the chapter on **data conversion** [5.3], page scanners can convert printed text to unformatted digital text using optical character recognition (OCR; see the **OCR** [5.3.1.1.3] section of the data conversion chapter) technology. It should be noted that while OCR conversion technology is powerful it is by no means perfect, and those doing scanning are advised to provide for a quality-control and file-cleanup process as part of the conversion.

Scanners deliver OCR text files that are essentially devoid of structure, tags, or anything but the words themselves. This lowest-common-denominator kind of file is in what is usually referred to as ASCII, and is currently the mainstay of technology-based solutions for people with disabilities.

3. Braille users are unlikely to be moved

For the blind and people with low vision, Braille has a strong base of supporters who are opposed to text-to-speech and even audio solutions. Their requirements are addressed by numerous laws and long-standing federal programs including operation of the American Printing House for the Blind (http://www.aph.org/), founded in Kentucky in 1859 and funded federally since 1879, and the National Library Service of the Library of Congress (http://www.loc.gov/nls/) established by an act of Congress in 1931. Though obtaining Braille in a timely manner is difficult, Braille advocates are committed to improving the Braille system rather than replacing it. So long as this is true, there will continue to be a strong demand for the basic ASCII text files that Braille producers require.

4. Publishers can anticipate increased demand for electronic files

As people realize how much can be done with good electronic files to make content accessible for people with disabilities, and as the pressures to deal with nonprint information over the Web build, publishers will need to recognize that digital publishing strategies must factor in the need to deal effectively with accessibility of future, current, and backlist publications.

(iii) WHAT IS INVOLVED IN MAKING A DIGITAL WORK FULLY ACCESSIBLE?

Creating a fully accessible work is a combination of science and art. At one level are specific steps that must be taken and others that may need to be avoided if a work is to pass technical muster. The art lies not in whether something is done but in how it is done. The presence of an <alt> tag may meet the requirement that a graphic have alternate text, but it does not measure how well the description does its job. Let's look at what goes into making digital works accessible.

1. Accessibility is a matter of degree

The steps needed to make a document accessible depend on how accessible one wants to make it. The National Center on Accessing the General Curriculum (***NCAC***), a collaborative effort between the U.S. Department of Education's Office of Special Education Programs and the Center for Applied Special Technology (CAST), has developed a useful way to consider levels of accessibility (see http://ulc.cast.org/about_ratings.htm).

At one end of CAST's continuum is unformatted text (essentially untagged text without images or any layout information). At the other end is the fully tagged XML document that is not only richly accessible but also includes embedded learning supports (e.g., in-line comprehension questions that can be helpful for some with learning disabilities) that can be displayed using special software (or selectively filtered by a script or XSLT stylesheet). Enriching documents is not within the scope of this chapter, but it is useful to realize that a fully accessible, XML-tagged digital work can provide a base to which considerable learning value can be added relatively easily using additional special purpose tags.

2. Steps to making a document accessible

Making a document accessible involves several steps:

1. Producing a digitally processable version of the content (text, images, etc.)
2. Producing navigation pathways through the content (links, table of contents, sidebars, etc.)
3. Producing text equivalents for images (<alt> and <longdesc> tags)
4. Producing text equivalents for tabular materials, graphs, and charts
5. Producing text equivalents for multimedia elements (captioning, transcripts, etc.)
6. Quality control checks including review of text equivalents for editorial quality

For detailed information concerning making digital works accessible, the reader is referred to the rich resources section of the Web Accessibility Initiative (WAI) Web site at http://www.w3.org/WAI/. Of specific interest will be the guidelines, checklists, and techniques pages. The American Council of the Blind provides another comprehensive Web resource called *A Guide to Making Documents Accessible for People Who Are Blind or Visually Impaired* (http://www.acb.org/accessible-formats.html).

3. Degree of accessibility desired drives costs

Those engaged in creating accessible digital versions of printed materials will soon find that they need to establish internal production guidelines to define the level of effort that they are prepared to put into the task. Costs can build quickly in the editorial and production process of creating good quality alternative text for pictures, and especially tables, charts, and graphs. Costs can also mount if extensive linking and navigation capabilities are added. As a general rule, the further along a document is on CAST's accessibility continuum, the more cost was incurred to get it there.

(iv) SOME KEY PROBLEMS IN DEALING WITH ACCESSIBILITY TODAY

As digital delivery—and sometimes, exclusively digital delivery—of more and more content is expected, several problems related to accessibility have risen in significance. Seven of these are described below, ranging from the difficulty in obtaining accessible materials in a timely manner to legal and business issues.

1. Much of the Internet is not accessible

Despite outstanding efforts by the W3C's Web Accessibility Initiative, most Web sites are not accessible. More and more printed information is moving to the Web for distribution, and people with disabilities encounter barriers to that information whenever they deal with a Web site that is not accessible. As Web designers strive to create imaginative and effective Web sites, often they employ techniques such as frames and Flash, that, while making Web pages effective and memorable for the nondisabled, render the pages inaccessible to many disabled users.

2. Braille infrastructure is not responsive enough

Under the current well-established system, Braille works are typically produced on a to-order basis. This means that production of a Braille edition does not begin until it has been formally ordered. The process of producing Braille is time-consuming and very labor intensive even with the benefit of special software. That students too often get their Braille editions long after their classes have moved on to the next book is a long-standing and knotty problem. Without getting into all the whys and wherefores, suffice it to say that this is the problem that has brought publishers and the blind community together and resulted in the proposed IMAA legislation. The problem could be mitigated if non-Braille alternatives were deemed acceptable to disability advocates, but the Braille approach is well entrenched and solutions to the Braille timeliness issue must be found.

3. Digital Rights Management is in conflict with accessibility needs

Publishers are reluctant to provide electronic files for a number of reasons. One of them is a fear of misappropriation of intellectual property. If electronic files are secured with DRM technology, then the content cannot be exported to the assistive technology tools and software that people with disabilities need in order to get access to the subject matter. At present the only way to secure content and provide the necessary functionality is for the assistive technology to be able itself to interact directly with the DRM system. Current eBook initiatives are building elements of assistive technology (e.g., text-to-speech, magnification, use of color) into the eBook readers so that text would not need to be exported from the secure environment provided by the eBook reader software. While this seems to be a positive approach, it is limited at best in that only those who are contractually (because they've passed the DRM authorization requirement) and physically able to use the particular reader will benefit, and the degree to which their needs will be met will only be as good as the assistive tools embedded within the eBook reader. Users of other technology and those who do not meet the DRM requirement would still find the work inaccessible due to its security.

4. Legacy and backlist works can be expensive to convert

Many publishers have only recently begun to realize that they should be systematic about archiving and documenting the electronic files used to produce their products. Most do not have usable electronic files for their previously printed works. Often files cannot be located, and when they are, it is not uncommon to find that last-minute changes were made in production and the original files were not updated. Sometimes the files are in old versions of software that cannot be processed, and in almost every case they will be in a format that would not be optimum for archiving (e.g., Quark as opposed to XML). If files are not in good shape, they may need to be created from scratch by using a conversion service. One advantage of converting is that the new files could be created in a desirable archive format (e.g., XML or SGML), making subsequent reuses straightforward and cost effective.

5. Embedded rights

In most cases publishers have negotiated rights to use illustrations, photos, and even quotations in their published works, and unless the permissions agreement is very recent, it is unlikely that the publisher has the right to use that material in anything but the original printed edition. Considering the number of such items that might be found in a typical illustrated book, a publisher has a large renegotiation task if it wishes to start making electronic versions available. It may be that if the electronic files are only used in situations where the Chafee amendment applies, the waiver that supercedes the copyright holder's rights would also apply to the other rights holders. The cost and hassle of resolving the rights issues for content embedded within the publisher's work is a significant disincentive for many publishers who might otherwise consider providing electronic files. One option publishers can entertain is removing the questionable items and inserting a message such as, "image has been omitted pending resolution of copyright." The publisher should consider using the <alt text> or <longdesc> tags to provide text content that could mitigate the impact of the exclusion.

6. User unfamiliarity

The notion that a printed work might be available in a useful electronic form is something that is not widely appreciated simply because so few accessible works are available. Currently most people, even teachers, do not expect there to be digital versions of print products (especially books). In time, if eBooks do catch on in general society, this may change, but as of this writing there has been insignificant demand for electronic files other than for Brailling, and there is no effective infrastructure that would help users locate and learn how to use them. Not only are students and parents unaware of the options, their teachers are also often equally in the dark. With no apparent demand, publishers have little or no incentive to produce accessible electronic versions of their print products. This is likely to change, however, as the impact becomes more widespread of Section 508, the IMAA (if enacted), and the rapidly growing number of state laws.

7. Lack of business models

To date, publishers have not seen a market demand, and so logically they have not brought accessible electronic versions of their works to market. Because there are incremental production costs involved and no market direction to indicate what format would attract a sufficient number of customers, publishers have been unable to gauge the economic consequences of marketing accessible format versions of their works. For now, absent any assurance of cost recovery or prospect for profit, publishers are largely content to limit their activity to whatever they are required to do by law (more than half the states have laws requiring publishers to provide Braille ready files of textbooks).

Audio books have proven that if publishers see a way to repackage their content and make sufficient money at it, they are likely to do so. If and when a model is established that would support publishing accessible electronic versions, we can anticipate that products would likely come to market—provided, of course, that content security issues are also effectively dealt with.

8. Chafee confusion

Schools are required to accommodate students with disabilities, which includes obtaining accessible versions of textbooks. Schools cannot charge for these materials. But in most cases schools cannot purchase and receive them in a timely fashion anyway, because there is nothing for them to purchase, so they are left to fend for themselves.

Schools use scanning and assistive technologies as the best available alternative. Relying on the copyright waiver in the Chafee amendment, schools do not pay royalties or even request permission from publishers. Staff labor and the cost of acquiring scanners and the assistive technology are not usually linked to any particular piece of accessible content. As a result, schools believe that they are getting what they need at no cost. Publishers believe that marketing accessible versions of their products may be difficult if schools believe that, since they can make copies "for free" under Chafee, the accessible electronic format should be provided by publishers at no charge.

(v) WHAT ARE CURRENT DRIVERS FOR CHANGE?

There are several forces at work that can be considered potential drivers of change.

1. Stronger laws

The impact of Section 508 is starting to ripple through society, and publishers are beginning to realize that their institutional and corporate customers who deal with the federal government are going to require accessible content in order to be compliant. When cases begin to appear in court it is likely that most information producers will begin to take action.

The reauthorization of the Individuals with Disabilities Education Act (IDEA) and the much anticipated IMAA create additional pressure on schools. They must, by law, accommodate their disabled students. To meet this need, states are putting pressure on publishers for accessible versions, by passing laws that order schools to give preference in purchasing to titles that have them. Under Georgia's, law publishers must supply an "electronic format version" or be left off the adoption schedule.

California in 1999 passed legislation requiring that publishers selling to the state's postsecondary institutions supply "instructional materials in an unencrypted electronic form . . . [that] maintain their structural integrity, as defined, be compatible with commonly used Braille translation and speech synthesis software, and include corrections and revisions as may be necessary" (http://www.htctu.fhda.edu/AB422.html). Clearly the education market is becoming more aggressive and publishers will need to respond.

2. The Internet

The steadily increasing necessity for people in all parts of society to be able to navigate and plumb the Web is a powerful force for change. For professional and personal reasons, it has become imperative that people with disabilities be able to participate as fully as possible. The work of the W3C/WAI is continuing and with the empowering force of Section 508 as a motivator, consumers of electronic information who have disabilities are increasingly expecting to find accessible content and not encounter barriers.

3. XML technologies

XML technologies are evolving at a rapid rate and creating new options for publishers to cost-effectively produce multiple variations of a document from one carefully crafted and richly tagged "master" file. Publishers can create a heavily tagged XML document and then use a suite of ***XSLT*** scripts or other software to deliver their content in a variety of formats. A single properly crafted XML file could be exported as accessible HTML, as tagged PDF, as ASCII, or as other formats with minimal incremental cost once the first of each type has been accounted for. XML provides publishers with a workable paradigm for being responsive to various format needs on a timely and cost-effective basis. This capability should enable publishers to reduce the hassle and cost of providing quality accessible electronic formats.

Publishers currently creating their products using technologies other than XML may want to consider whether the emerging requirement to produce multiple accessible formats in addition to and concurrently with their core print editions provides a sufficient incentive to move to an XML approach.

4. Digital Rights Management

DRM technology is progressing steadily, but there may never be a solution to the challenge of protecting content and still enabling its export into a wide range of assistive technology tools. It is likely, however, that solutions will be devised that allow secure content to be presented using specific assistive software features built into a secure DRM environment. Early versions of this approach are emerging from such eBook development efforts as the Microsoft Reader Text-to-Speech (TTS) Package 1.0 (http://www.microsoft.com/reader/info/tts.asp) and the text-to-speech option in Acrobat eBook Reader 2.2 (http://www.adobe.com/products/ebookreader/pdfs/acrebookreader22.pdf).

While many people with disabilities will be able to benefit from this software-specific approach (and therefore it should be encouraged), nevertheless many others will still need to use special assistive technology and will require content in an electronic format that their technology of choice can manipulate. For them, publishers locking content in a single DRM environment creates an intractable situation.

5. High-stakes testing

The recent shift in education policy to requiring that students pass standardized tests in order to be promoted or graduate has already begun to highlight the plight of disabled students. These students must pass the same tests as their nondisabled peers, and they are faring much, much worse. It is anticipated that as pressures on the schools grow to bring up the success rate of these students, the demand for accessible electronic versions will grow rapidly as teachers look for ways to assure that their students are participating fully in the curriculum.

(vi) STRATEGIC CONSIDERATIONS RELATING TO ALTERNATIVE FORMATS

There are a number of business considerations for publishers relating to meeting the need for accessible versions of their works. Some of them have already been described earlier in this chapter, such as content security, embedded rights, file conversions, editorial and production costs, the absence of definitive standards, and the lack of good business models. Others are discussed below.

1. Alternate formats as products for sale

Publishers for the most part are not required to provide their titles in alternate formats except in the textbook market, where a few states have enacted legislation that will require or "encourage" them to do so. To the extent that there currently are pressures on publishers to deliver electronic files, it is generally only to facilitate the production of Braille. Section 508 in adult markets and high-stakes testing in the school market are strong forces that are likely to increase those pressures significantly.

It would seem that publishers could produce accessible digital versions that met WAI guidelines, which schools could purchase with funds from special education or instructional materials budgets. For schools now using materials prepared in-house, the cost of a purchased accessible version would be justified; it makes better use of teacher time, eliminates the need for equipment such as scanners, and the student gets a much higher-quality product in terms of converted text and in value-added content such as image descriptions and navigational aids. Schools concerned about testing results might also want to acquire alternate format versions directly from publishers for use with ESL and other technically nondisabled students who, nevertheless, are doing poorly on standardized tests due to reading and learning difficulties.

Publishers would need to work through DRM and pricing issues as well as how the digital version would be positioned for marketing purposes relative to the print. For example, could this be a special edition of the text sold as a stand-alone product? Or could it be something the publisher provides as part of a marketing package based on the number of print books sold?

Many models could be considered. The important thing is that if publishers decide to offer their works in alternate formats in response to legal and market demands, they should then consider enhancing those files with more than the minimum functionality required for accessibility, by making them attractive digital products that would be deemed worthy of being paid for.

2. Backlist conversions

State and district adoption cycles usually last several years—typically four to eight years. Therefore, even if a publisher modifies its current production processes to produce alternate formats efficiently, there will also be a need to create alternate format versions of backlist titles. Schools will need to provide alternate formats for students for books that are well into the adoption cycle, say five to six years or more.

Publishers may endear themselves to schools and presumably stimulate sales of print publications if they make an accessible alternate format available. Laws in several states require school buyers to give preference to titles with alternate formats. Security of the publisher's content remains an issue, but publishers may find that so long as the alternate format version can be distributed on a controlled basis (i.e., only to qualified students with disabilities), it makes good public relations to allow schools to acquire an alternate version directly from them. Schools are between a rock and a hard place. They should be quite willing to pay for an alternate accessible format delivered in a timely manner when compared to the cost of the teacher time and technology resources necessary to create a digital version that will serve a very small percentage of their students.

3. Competitive considerations

It is reasonable to assume that publishers will produce alternate format versions either because the law requires it or when their customers demand it. Markets being what they are, once one major publisher starts making one or more alternate formats available, others are likely to follow suit—especially if the pioneer gets incremental business as a result of their efforts. Different business models will very likely develop for the alternate format versions, depending on individual publishers' strategies. Eventually the market will respond to one model better than the others and that one will likely prevail.

Once competition begins with respect to the provision of alternate format editions, it is also reasonable to assume that publishers will want their accessible editions to be well received in the marketplace lest there be a negative halo cast on their meat-and-potatoes print product. They will likely begin to differentiate their offerings by paying special attention to the quality of the alternative text that is provided and the way the navigation works for the user. They may choose to provide teachers with assistance in understanding how to use the electronic version with their students for better results. Publishers may start to go an "extra mile" and add value to the digital version so as to make it more desirable than those from their competitors.

When a publisher begins to add value to converted digital files, costs start to accrue. Adding well-thought-out text descriptions of pictures, tables, and graphs should enhance the quality of the learning opportunity, meaning additional value for the customer and user, yet because of the cost, the publisher will need to plan carefully how much value it can afford to add. Certainly a high-profile, high-value-added effort to meet accessibility needs will reflect positively on the publisher with decision makers.

(vii) STRATEGIC PERSPECTIVES

As publishers look at the accessibility situation, they can consider a number of approaches based on their own sense of urgency. Contributing factors are likely to include the legal and social pressures in their market sector, their positioning within their market, their technology strategy, their cost structure, the nature of the content they publish, and their overall attitude toward innovation. It may make sense for publishers to consider one strategy for new products where they can address accessibility issues within the normal editorial and production process, and another for the more costly challenge of backlist and legacy works.

1. Minimalist approach

The minimalist strategy could be summarized as "Do what you have to do and no more." A publisher following this route would create a text-only ASCII file and have it at the ready for whenever there is a request for it. There would be little tagging, no alternate text, nothing more than the very minimum that is needed to comply with state Braille laws and adoption requirements. In terms of functionality, such files are roughly equivalent to the results of scanning a print version, but coming directly from the publisher, they would almost certainly be of higher quality, and available far more quickly. In CAST's continuum, mentioned earlier, the publisher would be providing unformatted text.

To date, providing files as required by Braille laws has been the total strategy of almost all publishers, due in part to the uncertainty about what exactly is expected of them should they provide other formats and because the risk-to-reward ratio that currently characterizes more aggressive approaches is not seen as favorable. While there tends to be no reward in the minimalist approach (in that no revenues accrue), it has the advantage that because there are no images involved, there also are no embedded rights issues. Also, these files are only made available under the terms of specific laws and regulations that generally have language prohibiting unauthorized redistribution.

The minimalist approach may, for the time being, continue to be the optimum strategy for nonschool publishers that are not yet under the same sort of legal and market pressures that school publishers face. Until there is a potential new revenue stream or a need to protect an existing one, publishers will likely choose to keep costs as low as possible and minimize risks as much as possible.

2. Pragmatic approach

This strategy could be summarized as, "Do what you have to do plus add whatever value can be securely distributed and supported by incremental income." In the pragmatic approach, a publisher would provide a digital version that would be more useful than the unformatted ASCII provided under the minimalist approach. In terms of CAST's continuum, the product would be called "formatted text."

A publisher might consider this alternate format as a product that should be paid for. It will contain incremental editorial and production value that makes it more valuable to the user than the minimum that would be required by law. It could contain images, layout, and navigation aids, for example, that would be missing from Braille-ready ASCII. Publishers will need to balance the cost of this added value against prospective revenues and/or cost budgets for the project.

In determining whether to offer a formatted text version, the publisher will also need to resolve issues related to embedded items for which it does not own the rights, for example, graphics and photos. The publisher also needs to decide, title by title, about the level of security it is comfortable with for each project and determine how it will want to structure the business model and configure the DRM implementation.

3. Leadership approach

This strategy could be summarized as, "Be proactive and position for maximum marketing value." In this approach the publisher overtly identifies with the needs of its customers and offers alternative format(s) and support in their use. Customers would come to know that a feature of choosing a particular publisher's print product would be the ready availability of that product in one or more alternate formats of good quality.

Instead of making a customer struggle with the problem of how to get an accessible version, this strategy would call for a sales message that lets the customer know how to get special editions and that they come with support resources. The publisher could offer multiple alternate formats that could be priced differently depending on the level of value added. The cost of doing this could be mitigated by having a single master XML file that has been well tagged and is available to quickly produce different levels of "accessibility editions" using various pre-established scripts or XSLT stylesheets.

4. Underlying considerations

Whether a publisher decides that the minimalist, pragmatist, leadership, or some other approach is most suitable, there are several considerations that publishers may want to ponder when determining what will work best for them. A few of these are:

1. IS OUTSOURCING AN OPTION?

Publishers will need to decide the degree to which they wish to control their alternate formats in terms of how they are positioned in the market, how they are designed and produced, how they are distributed, and how they are supported. Doing these things internally requires knowledge and skills that may not currently be present within a publisher's organization, and outsourcing all or parts of the accessibility solution may seem attractive. When it comes to audio, large print, and foreign language editions it is not uncommon for publishers to license their content to other specialty organizations rather than create and market the transformation products internally.

Ideally a publisher might be able to contract with a one-stop outsource organization to produce, distribute, and support alternate accessible formats of a publisher's printed products. At this writing, however, the author is not aware of any full-service organizations that produce, distribute, and support accessible alternate format editions on either a contract or license basis. As a result a publisher will most likely need to organize a combination of internal and external resources into a process that results in a hybrid solution.

2. TECHNICAL RESOURCES

Converting and editing files for accessibility requires skills that a publisher will need to have available when it starts to supply alternate formats. Ideally these requirements can and should be woven into the publisher's regular production processes so as to minimize incremental cost. For legacy work and for responding to individual customer requests, however, additional production and possibly editorial resources will be required. Publishers will need to develop them internally or establish a working relationship with an outside supplier or content licensee.

3. EDITORIAL RESOURCES

There are two areas where the quality of an accessible product is dependent on editorial resources. Earlier examples illustrated that well-authored alternative text and long descriptions are important aids to the sight-disabled reader's ability to grasp the content of graphical elements—pictures and charts, for example. The same applies to tables, formulas, and mathematical content. In addition, for complicated works, a knowledgeable person needs to be involved in decisions involving navigation paths as well as what content must be included and what might be left out. The publisher needs to develop expertise in creating the value-added content and in organizing that material for its most effective use.

4. LEGACY VS. CURRENT WORK

Alternate formats are not likely to be available for most published works in use now. Yet as we have seen, the demand for accessible versions can be expected to grow quickly thanks to Section 508, IDEA, and other federal and state legislation. Publishers are well advised to review their current portfolios and upcoming releases to decide what titles will need to be made available in alternate formats and to establish policies and protocols for creating, distributing, and supporting them either proactively or on an as requested basis.

5. HALO EFFECT

Publishers usually care very much about how they are viewed by their customers and other influencers in their markets. A publisher's reputation is often a key factor in a purchaser's decision to buy a product. Clearly a publisher should consider whether there is value in being perceived as sensitive to the needs of the disabled and supportive of those who work with them. In the education market, for example, in a state that "encourages" use of alternate formats, being seen as offering a solution to the customer's (i.e., the school's) need to support their students with disabilities could well influence a decision-maker's purchase of printed curricular materials. The same might be true of a publisher selling materials to institutions concerned with Sections 504 and 508 for use in training their staffs (e.g., nurses and office staff) where text-to-speech products might help with ESL issues.

Organizations that exhibit insensitivity to their customers' need for alternate formats may be perceived negatively. When people try to contact publishers to find out if an alternate format is available or if permission can be granted to scan a work, it is not uncommon for them to be unable to get a timely answer due to the organization's lack of policies. What answers they get are too often inconsistent, coming at different times from different people. Publishers should be sure not to frustrate customers needlessly simply because they either do not have clear-cut policies and protocols or have not communicated those policies and protocols effectively within their organizations.

6. BUSINESS MODELS

Print publishers considering providing alternate formats as products will have many new business issues to consider. For example, alternate electronic formats involve issues like security and end-user support that are not considerations for a print model. If DRM is used for security, there may be a number of new possibilities for pricing and restricting distribution for both content and functionality. This chapter is not about business models for secure electronic products, however, and suffice it to say that a publisher can formulate a variety of strategies based on the capabilities of the DRM system used that can be tailored to what would be deemed appropriate for a product serving the needs of those with disabilities.

7. USER SUPPORT

Printed publications do not come with user support, but electronic products usually have a support component that deals with both technical support and user training. Again, it is not this chapter's role to talk about user support per se, but simply to remind publishers that successful electronic products usually offer some degree of technical troubleshooting and user help systems. The quality of a product and the organization behind it are often judged by the quality of the support that accompanies it. Publishers who provide alternate formats that are more than simply copies of files will need to consider the quality of the support they provide specifically as it relates to how the disabled user can make best use of the alternate format product. This may be as simple as providing an accompanying tutorial and references to useful Web sites for more detailed information.

8. DRM SUPPORT

As mentioned earlier, publishers are unlikely to provide alternate formats unless they can secure the content. This generally means deploying a DRM system. DRM systems create ongoing support requirements that need to be factored into any analysis of providing secure alternate formats (e.g., an eBook or secure PDF). Administering the paperwork and licenses (renewals, etc.) will be a cost to be factored into decisions.

(viii) SUMMARY SUGGESTIONS

Given the rapidly changing nature of the accessibility issue, publishers may wish to consider the following suggestions:

1. Get organized about accessibility

While it is true that accessibility issues have not been a concern for most publishers, it is clear that the situation is beginning to change. As Section 508 takes hold and as other federal and state laws and regulations take effect, organizations of all types are being challenged to assure that people with disabilities have an equal chance to succeed. This means that the published information and knowledge provided to people with disabilities must be accessible. Publishers need to prepare for a future in which they will need to address their customers' need for alternate formats and accessible editions.

Publishers of all types should consider establishing a formal but flexible strategy for dealing with accessibility matters. The strategy should be based on a careful determination of their customers' needs; their own technical, editorial, and administrative resources; their marketing strategy; their preferred business models; and other factors.

Once the strategy has been established, operating protocols should be established for dealing with accessibility decisions in a timely manner, answering such questions as, what is to be done when a disabled customer asks for an alternate format; how many formats will be provided, and which ones; and whether to become active in promoting and opposing various accessibility-related legislative initiatives.

Once policies have been developed and protocols established, this information should be assembled into a reference document that can be made available throughout the organization to answer questions from customers, organization members, employees, or any other source. Finally, there should be internal "ownership" of accessibility matters. A person should be assigned oversight responsibility for shepherding the successful development and implementation of the protocols, for regular review and revision of the strategy, and for being the driver for any desired changes.

2. Get organized about content

Most publishers today understand the value of creating and maintaining electronic versions of their publications—it's old news in journal publishing. In many other areas, especially book publishing, locating a good electronic file corresponding exactly to a printed work is difficult if not impossible. In many cases the administrative files relating to embedded rights are also hard to find.

Publishers should, for all new publications, take steps to have permanent digital versions that are *exact* counterparts of printed works, and assure that all embedded rights are cataloged and that alternate text is composed in advance for those items, including credits as appropriate. With these things done in advance, a minimum amount of work will be required to produce future alternate formats in a timely manner.

For popular and recent legacy publications, publishers should consider investing in the creation of a clean electronic master file that exactly corresponds to the print work and contains value-added elements as desired. As in the case of new publications, publishers should take steps to resolve any and all embedded rights issues long before an alternate format is requested.

3. Get organized about technology

For a variety of reasons evident earlier in this chapter (and throughout this book), publishers should give serious consideration to creating a thoroughly coded and tagged XML master version of each publication that can be readily extracted into specific alternate formats (including accessible PDF). **XSLT technology** [3.3.4.4] is an effective means of producing multiple derivative documents from a single XML master, each with its own specific tagging and/or formatting.

Adopting this approach will require the organization to have ongoing access, either through its staff or a supplier, to XML and XSLT know-how. Further, it will require an organized approach to creating and maintaining the XML master files and to developing scripts or XSLT stylesheets or other transformation methods for accessible HTML, accessible PDF, ICADD22, ASCII, and so on.

4. Get organized about the market

Publishers should review their products and determine, for at least their most popular works, how they will respond to requests for alternate formats, especially for text for Brailling. Prompt decisions and clear explanations will reflect far more favorably on the organization than indecisive answers that are slow in coming.

It would make sense also to determine those titles that might warrant a proactive approach, that is, creating, before the market asks for them, secure accessible versions to support the marketing of the print programs. A textbook publisher might decide to create a well-tagged accessible HTML version of a book that is on the adoption list in a state where regulations require school districts to give preference to titles with alternate formats. A publisher of professional education and training materials might decide for strategic reasons to see that all of their products would include being available in alternate formats that meet Section 508 accessibility requirements.

7.3 CLOSING SUMMARY

Digital technologies have created the means to solve a problem that has existed for centuries—giving people with disabilities access to information and knowledge that have heretofore been unavailable to them because they are unable to manage printed materials. Recognizing this opportunity, our society at the federal and state levels has begun to actively address the knowledge needs of disabled people, both adults and children, by passing laws mandating the provision of electronic versions of printed materials.

These laws have for the most part not applied directly to publishers (except in their role as employers), but they do apply to many of those who buy publishers' products in quantity, such as schools and corporations. Not having resources, know-how, or often even the legal right to create alternate formats, these important customers logically will turn to publishers for the accessible products they must have. State education departments are already putting on pressure, and because of Section 508 it is likely that the postsecondary, library, and corporate markets will follow suit.

It is still very early to predict how publishers will most successfully deal with this changing situation. This chapter has highlighted a number of issues that arise for publishers as they endeavor to chart their course; some of them have no easy resolution at this time. Perhaps the most thorny concerns are the following:

1. Unauthorized redistribution of proprietary content contained in electronic copies.
2. How to provide meaningful accessibility in products secured with DRM technologies.
3. Embedded rights in legacy materials.
4. Whether accessible versions of publishers' products will be economically viable.

As the market for accessible content continues to develop, publishers should adopt a strategy that embraces as much flexibility as possible. Since the laws are fuzzy in their definitions and the market itself is unsure of exactly what it needs, it is difficult for publishers to make intelligent decisions. In this kind of environment, the best thing publishers can do is to make a disciplined, conscientious effort to develop flexible policies and a pragmatic, coherent operating strategy for dealing with the immediate needs of their customers for accessible knowledge resources. No matter whether a publisher's market segment is school districts, university libraries, corporate training providers, or professional databases, it will be affected, and having strategic guidelines for serving those needs will increase the likelihood that the publisher will be successful as the market evolves.

Digital technologies have given society the chance to overcome the accessibility barriers that have kept many disabled people from reaching their potential. The cost to society, their employers, their personal earning power, their ability to participate in society, and their self-esteem has been great. Over the next few years, publishers and other information producers will have increasingly effective software tools, which will allow them to design and deliver information and knowledge in electronic formats that, using principles of universal design, can cost-effectively serve the needs of all people, including those with disabilities. It will be an evolutionary process, and publishers are encouraged to begin factoring accessibility needs into their strategies and plans.

7.4 RESOURCES AND DOCUMENTS

(i) LEGISLATION — FEDERAL

This list contains links to actual legislation, clarifying summaries, and other related materials. Items are listed in chronological order.

- *A Guide to Disability Rights Laws: Americans with Disabilities Act (ADA).* (http://www.usdoj.gov/crt/ada/cguide.htm#anchor62335) A summary page published by the U.S. Department of Justice, Civil Rights Division, Disability Rights Section, with links to brief descriptions of the provisions of the major pieces of disability-related federal legislation. It also contains specific citations for each piece of legislation.
- *The History of the American Printing House for the Blind: A Chronology.* (http://www.aph.org/about/highlite.htm) A brief chronology of federal legal activity relating to the needs of the blind prior to 1931 put together by the American Printing House for the Blind.
- *NLS: That All May Read: Laws and Regulations.* (http://www.loc.gov/nls/laws.html) A listing of laws (with links) relating to provision of library service to blind and physically handicapped persons including the enabling legislation creating the NLS on the National Library Service for the Blind and Physically Handicapped (NLS), Library of Congress Web site.
- *Rehabilitation Act 1973.* (http://www.dot.gov/ost/docr/regulations/library/REHABACT.HTM) The provisions of the act are now found in Title 29 of the U.S. Code, but this is the complete text of Public Law 93–112 (93rd Congress, September 26, 1973) as originally written, which is generally easier to follow than the Code. Section 504 as originally written is the last section.
- *Rehabilitation Act of 1973 — Section 504.* (http://ericec.org/sect504.html) From the ERIC Clearinghouse on Disabilities and Gifted Education Web site, this contains the full text of Section 504 as amended through 1998.
- *Americans with Disabilities Act of 1990.* (http://www.usdoj.gov/crt/ada/pubs/ada.txt) This contains the full text of the ADA.

- *Americans with Disabilities Act ADA Home Page.* (http://www.usdoj.gov/crt/ada/adahom1.htm) This U.S. Department of Justice Web site is a complete resource of ADA-related information provided by the Department of Justice.
- *NLS Factsheets: Copyright Law Amendment, 1996 PL 104–197.* (http://www.loc.gov/nls/reference/factsheets/copyright.html) This site provides the language of the Chafee Amendment (1996) to the Copyright Law as well as much historical and other reference information including an excellent FAQ.
- *IDEA '97: The Individuals with disabilities Education Act Amendments of 1997.* (http://www.ed.gov/offices/OSERS/Policy/IDEA/) This site maintained by the OSERS branch of the Department of Education contains a wealth of information about IDEA. The text of the law can be found by following the link titled "The Law."
- *Rehabilitation Act Amendments (Section 508) Section 508 of the Rehabilitation Act of 1973, as amended 29 U.S.C. § 794 (d).* (http://www.access-board.gov/about/Rehab%20Act%20Amend-508.htm) This site has the full text of section 508 and also links to a good FAQ (list of frequently asked questions) relating to many aspects of Section 508
- *Instructional Materials Accessibility Act of 2002 (S.2246).* (http://www.theorator.com/bills107/s2246.html) and (http://www.congress.org/congressorg/issues/bills/?billnum = S.2246&congress = 107) The first link gives the language of the bill (proposed April 24, 2002 as Senate Bill 2246) as first introduced. The second is a site that will be tracking its progress.
- *Instructional Materials Accessibility Act Section-by-Section Analysis.* (http://www.afb.org/info_document_view.asp?documentid = 1704) This American Foundation for the Blind Web page contains a good section by section summary of the IMAA as it was prepared for submission.

(ii) LEGISLATION — STATES

This list contains links to actual legislation, clarifying summaries and other related materials. This list is a small sample of what is happening in various states and is not intended to be a comprehensive list. Many other states have legislation relating to the provision of accessible materials for students with disabilities, especially those requiring Braille.

- *California Education Code Section 67302- Bill Number: AB 422 Chaptered 9/15/99.* (http://www.htctu.fhda.edu/AB422.html) This links to a Web site maintained by the High Tech Center Training Unit of the California

Community Colleges that contains the text of the 1999 law that requires publishers offering materials for adoption in the state to furnish to state universities and community colleges, at no cost, unencrypted electronic files of their products for reproduction and distribution by state to students with disabilities.

- *Georgia Dept. of Education Rule 160–4-4-.10 Textbook/Instructional Materials Selection and Recommendation (effective 9/12/2002).* (http://www.doe.k12.ga.us/legalservices/160–4-4-.10.pdf) This links to the text of the Georgia rule regarding provision of instructional materials which says, in Section 3(k) entitled Minimum Requirements for Publishers, "The publisher of a textbook recommended by the State Board of Education shall provide an electronic version of such textbook."
- *Amendment to Section 200.2 of the Regulations of the Commissioner Implementing Chapter 377 of the Laws of 2001 Plans to Provide Instructional Materials in Alternative Formats for Students with Disabilities.* (http://unix32.nysed.gov:9280/specialed/publications/policy/alterformat502.htm) New York state passed a law requiring that "each board of education (BOE) and each Board of Cooperative Educational Services (BOCES) must establish a plan to ensure that every student with a disability who needs his or her instructional materials in an alternative format will receive those materials at the same time that they are available to non-disabled students." This links to a memorandum to school officials containing implementation information and an excellent FAQ explaining issues and offering suggestions for addressing them. It also has links to the legislation itself.

(iii) STANDARDS

These references relate to various standards efforts related to accessibility.

- *Section 508 of the Rehabilitation Act: Electronic and Information Technology Accessibility Standards.* (http://www.access-board.gov/508.htm) A site of the Access Board containing links to and information about the standards against which Section 508 compliance is to be measured.
- *Checklist of Checkpoints for Web Content Accessibility Guidelines 1.0.* (http://www.w3.org/TR/WCAG/full-checklist.html) This W3C site "provides a list of all checkpoints from the Web Content Accessibility Guidelines 1.0, organized by concept, as a checklist for Web content developers. Please refer to the Guidelines document for introductory

information, information about related documents, a glossary of terms, and more."

- *Requirements for WCAG 2.0: W3C Working Draft 26 April 2002.* (http://www.w3.org/TR/wcag2-req/) "This is a W3C Working Draft produced . . . to outline the requirements for Web Content Accessibility Guidelines 2.0. The Working Group encourages feedback about these requirements as well as participation in the development of the revision by people who have experience trying to create Web content that conforms to WCAG 1.0." Readers may wish to contact this group and contribute feedback.
- *Specifications for the Digital Talking Book—ANSI/NISO Z39.86 2002.* (http://www.niso.org/standards/resources/Z39–86–2002.html) This links to the standard in HTML format on the NISO site. Those interested in the DAISY Consortium and the standards it developed which are the antecedents of the DTB can be found at http://www.daisy.org/publications/specifications.asp.

(iv) MAKING ACCESSIBLE DOCUMENTS

- *A Guide to Making Documents Accessible to People Who Are Blind or Visually Impaired.* (http://www.acb.org/accessible-formats.html) This is an exceptionally comprehensive document and makes an excellent practical reference for those needing to produce accessible documents for the blind or visually impaired.
- *WAI Resources.* (http://www.w3.org/WAI/Resources/) This W3C Web Accessibility Initiative site contains a wealth of resources for those involved in making web pages accessible. The sections include: quick tips, FAQ, checklists, techniques, training, evaluation and repair tools, et al.

(v) OTHER RESOURCES

- *Dyslexia and computers.* (http://www.fmls.nu/sprakaloss/olsondyslexiandcompeng.htm) An article by Professor Richard Olson that provides research-based background on how computers can effectively provide remediation to students with dyslexia, one of the most common learning disabilities.
- *Accessibility of Information in Electronic Textbooks For Students Who Are Blind or Visually Impaired.* (http://www.tsbvi.edu/textbooks/textbook.htm) A report by the Texas Education Agency to the 75th Texas Legislature that comprehensively presents information about the specific needs of blind or visually impaired students. This is an excellent re-

source for detailed information about what must be done to make books accessible for this disability group.

- *Accessible Textbooks Clearinghouse.* (http://www.tsbvi.edu/textbooks/) A Web page containing a wealth of links related to producing accessible textbooks. They range from information about the *Texas Text Exchange to Accessibility and VRML*, from *Digital Talking Book Production Process to Delivering Accessible Library Services in a Distance Learning Environment.*
- "Chapter 3: Why We Need Flexible Instructional Media" in *Teaching Every Student in the Digital Age: Universal Design for Learning* by David H. Rose and Anne Meyer. (http://www.cast.org/teachingeverystudent/ideas/tes/chapter3.cfm) To borrow from the text itself, this chapter describes "how the qualities of various instructional media (text, speech, images, and digital media) affect their accessibility to students and see why flexibility in media is the key to providing instruction that reaches more students, more effectively" The authors are Co-Executive Directors of CAST, Inc., the Center for Applied Special Technology, a nonprofit education research organization doing pioneering work in the use of computers to improve learning for all students and especially those with disabilities.
- *Assistive Technology for Children with Learning Difficulties.* (http://www.frostig.org/pdf/ATguide.pdf) This guide, created by the Frostig Center under grant from the Schwab Foundation for Learning and written primarily for parents, "Describes the various types of assistive technology and how to select an appropriate technology. It provides the reader with a basic understanding of the how and why of various technologies and shows what can be done with digital content that is "aware" of the capabilities and functions of assistive technologies.

BIBLIOGRAPHY

"Accessible Textbooks Clearinghouse." Texas School for the Blind and Visually Impaired. 2002. http://www.tsbvi.edu/textbooks/

American Foundation for the Blind. "Instructional Materials Accessibility Act Section-by-Section Analysis." American Foundation for the Blind. 2001. http://www.afb.org/info_document_view.asp?documentid=1704

California Education Code Section 673029. High Tech Center Training Unit of the California Community Colleges., http://www.htctu.fhda.edu/AB422.html

Frostig Center, The. *Assistive Technology for Children with Learning Difficulties*. Pasadena: Schwab Foundation for Learning, 2002. http://www.frostig.org/pdf/ATguide.pdf

History of the American Printing House for the Blind, The: A Chronology. American Printing House for the Blind., 2001.. http://www.aph.org/about/highlite.htm

National Information Standards Organization. *Specifications for the Digital Talking Book (ANSI/NISO Z39.86–2002)*. Bethesda: National Information Standards Organization, 2002. http://www.niso.org/standards/resources/Z39-86-2002.html

National Library Service. *NLS Factsheets: Copyright Law Amendment, 1996 PL 104-197*. U.S. Library of Congress, 2001. http://www.loc.gov/nls/reference/factsheets/copyright.html

———. *NLS: That All May Read. Laws and Regulations*. U.S. Library of Congress, 2001. http://www.loc.gov/nls/laws.html

Public Law 101-336. Americans with Disabilities Act of 1990. http://www.usdoj.gov/crt/ada/pubs/ada.txt

Rehabilitation Act Amendments, Section 508 of the Rehabilitation Act of 1973, as Amended (29 USC 794(d)). The Access Board, http://www.access-board.gov/about/Rehab%20Act%20Amend-508.htm

Rehabilitation Act of 1973 (29 USC 701 et seq.). http://www.dot.gov/ost/docr/regulations/library/REHABACT.HTM

Rose, David H., and Anne Meyer. *Teaching Every Student in the Digital Age: Universal Design for Learning*. Alexandria, Va: Association for Supervision and Curriculum Development, 2002. http://www.cast.org/teachingeverystudent/ideas/tes/chapter3.cfm

Section 504 of the Rehabilitation Act of 1973, as Amended through 1998. The ERIC Clearinghouse on Disabilities and Gifted Education., 1998. http://ericec.org/sect504.html

Sutton, Jennifer. *A Guide to Making Documents Accessible to People Who Are Blind or Viusally Impaired*. Washington, D.C.: American Council of the Blind, 2002. http://www.acb.org/accessible-formats.html

U.S. Department of Education. "IDEA '97: The Individuals with Disabilities Education Act Amendments of 1997." Office of Special Education and Rehabilitative Services. 2002. http://www.ed.gov/offices/OSERS/Policy/IDEA/

U.S. Department of Justice. "ADA Home Page—Information and Technical Assistance on The Americans with Disabilities Act." U.S. Department of Justice. 2002. http://www.usdoj.gov/crt/ada/adahom1.htm

———. "Americans with Disabilities Act (ADA)." U.S. Department of Justice, Civil Rights Division, Disability Rights Section. 2001. http://www.usdoj.gov/crt/ada/

8 Digital Printing

GEORGE ALEXANDER
Executive Editor, the Seybold Report

The technology that is used to print books digitally has been evolving rapidly. Initially, sheetfed monochrome laser printers were the only technology available. But today, high-speed roll-fed devices are often used, full color is becoming more economical, and other printing technologies (such as inkjet) are coming into use. This chapter describes the available printing and binding options and some of the new publishing options they create.

8.1 OVERVIEW

The digital printing of books is a tantalizing concept. One can imagine walking into a neighborhood bookstore (or perhaps a neighborhood copy shop) and ordering virtually any book ever published. Within five minutes, the book could printed, bound, and in your hands. For publishers, there is the possibility of never having overstocks to dispose of. For educators, the technology can provide custom books for each class, or even for each student.

The technology to support these possibilities is not completely available yet (or if it is, the costs are still prohibitive for many applications). But the technology is getting very close, and costs are coming down rapidly. In this chapter, we will look at the digital printing technologies that are available today and some that are on the way. The associated input techniques and binding technologies are also discussed.

Increasingly, digital printing is taking work away from the traditional offset process. We will discuss the advantages and disadvantages of both approaches and list some of the applications for which digital printing is clearly superior. The shift from offset to digital printing also means changes in the where books are produced and how they are distributed. These, too, will be touched on.

8.2 DIGITAL PRINTING TECHNOLOGIES

The technology of digital printing has been evolving rapidly. It is not just the printing techniques themselves that are in flux, but also the associated technologies (such as those involved in scanning and binding). This section describes the technologies behind digital printing and some of the important related issues.

(i) INPUT: SCANNING, POSTSCRIPT, PDF, AND OTHER OPTIONS

Various methods and technologies are available to prepare material for digital printing. The most fundamental fact, however, is that digital printing is done directly from digital files. Content is either created in a digital format or it must somehow be converted from print to a digital format.

For the publishing industry, most files created in a digital format end up either in the ***PostScript*** language, or in its close cousin, the Portable Document Format (***PDF***). Both languages are the invention of Adobe Systems. Adobe, although it makes the specifications of these languages public, keeps tight control over the direction and details of both. Content that does not originate in digital form—that is, printed originals—must be digitized. Most often, this is done simply by scanning, which results in a bitmapped file, usually a TIFF.

The chapters on **data conversion** [5.3.1.1] and on **composition and graphics** [6.11.1] discuss the details of the processes of scanning and conversion by rekeying; for conversions, this section focuses on digital conversion rather than manual rekeying.

1. Scanning

Scanning—that is, making an image of a printed page rather than using ***OCR*** software to create a digital text file—is generally easy to accomplish, but it has a significant drawback. No matter how good the scanner, and how good the page being scanned, the image created via scanning is never quite as good as the same image created directly from the source data. Some degradation is inevitable in the image-then-scan sequence. For example, the pages are usually not precisely straight, since scanning is a mechanical process; the resulting images usually need ***deskewing***. Likewise, it is virtually impossible not to pick up specks of dust and other flaws in the image; this requires ***despeckling***. Finally, the pages usually need to be aligned into the position required by the new product, with uniform margins and with right- and left-hand pages being differentiated. In spite of great improvements in image-processing technology, these issues are still true. For that reason, scanning is now rarely used as an input method for digital printing. The big exception to this rule is reprinting books (and other documents) where no digital original is available—and this is the case for most reprinted books today.

The scanning process usually produces a bitmapped file known as a ***TIFF*** file. One-bit TIFFs are often used for text; they capture the image simply in terms of black or white pixels. Eight-bit TIFFs are more sophisticated: they are able to capture ***grayscale*** information (shades of gray) and thus are more appropriate when photographs appear in the originals. However, when text is scanned as 8-bit, it is often a bit blurry. The best results are accomplished by scanning at 8-bit and then downsampling the text areas to 1-bit (ideally, smoothing out the jagged edges of the type and despeckling the surrounding white areas) and leaving the image areas as 8-bit data.

2. PostScript and PDF

PostScript is a very general-purpose page-description language, and its incorporation into the first Apple LaserWriter was an important factor in the development of "desktop publishing" in the 1980s. The versatility of PostScript was important in its early success—it was much more flexible than the other languages used to drive printers in those days—but its very flexibility made it somewhat unpredictable. ***PDF***, which can be thought of as an efficient and predictable subset of PostScript, is gradually taking over PostScript's role as the normal file format for output to a digital printer.

Although other languages are used to drive office printers (notably Hewlett-Packard's ***PCL***) and to drive high-speed printers in data centers, PostScript and PDF are the norm for publishing applications. That doesn't mean, however, that all publishers provide their printers with PostScript or PDF files. Most are still providing native files from their layout package (e.g. QuarkXpress, Adobe InDesign, or Microsoft Publisher) and letting the printer produce the final PostScript or PDF file. This gives the printer more flexibility in fixing errors and avoiding production problems. New dialects of PDF (such as PDF/X-1a and PDF/3), along with the appropriate software support, promise to make it easier for publishers to supply files that will be suitable for printing. The chapter on **composition and graphics** [6.12.11.5] discusses these technologies in more detail.

It should also be noted that it is possible for PostScript or PDF files to consist mainly or only of bitmapped data (usually TIFFs), since the ability to incorporate TIFF images is an important feature of both of these technologies. This can be the cause of great confusion. Generally, when PostScript or PDF files are being referred to, it is assumed that they are text-based files that were generated from a digital page-makeup process; such files are editable and searchable, and use fonts and vector data to conform to the resolution of whatever output device is being used. If, on the other hand, they are simply scanned data captured as TIFFs and then enclosed in PostScript or PDF "wrappers," the data they contain is not editable or searchable and will not adapt; their resolution is dependent on how much data was captured in those original scans. Especially when PDF files are being provided to or received from a new source, it is important for all parties to be aware whether the underlying data is true text-and-vector data or bitmapped image data, or both.

(ii) IMAGING TECHNOLOGIES FOR DIGITAL PRINTING

The majority of digital printing is done with toner-based devices, but a growing amount is being accomplished in other ways. Each approach, and there are many, has a specific set of advantages and disadvantages.

1. Laser printers and other toner-based printers

The most common kind of toner-based printing device is the laser printer. A laser beam bounces off a spinning mirror and sweeps across a charged photoconductive drum or belt, which is discharged wherever the laser light touches it. Charged toner particles adhere to the drum or belt where it was exposed. The toner is then transferred to the paper (sometimes via an intermediate drum or belt). Once on the paper, the toner is fused (melted in place), usually by a hot roller. The most common production-speed monochrome laser printers are made by Xerox, Canon, and Ricoh. (Specific printers are discussed in the section on **available printing systems** [8.4] below.)

A color machine works on the same principles as a monochrome one, except that there are four different toners (cyan, yellow, magenta, and black). There are often four different lasers and four different drums (or belts) as well, but sometimes these components are used in common for the four toners.

The same sort of device can be built with an array of light-emitting diodes (***LED***s) instead of a laser and a spinning mirror. Heidelberg and Oce use this technology in their monochrome devices. And it is not even necessary to have a light source or a photosensitive drum. One supplier (Oce) has a color printer that uses a drum whose surface is encircled by fine electrical channels. The channels are rapidly and precisely charged and discharged as the drum turns, to attract charged toner to the appropriate spots. Another supplier (Delphax) uses a special charge-plate with tiny holes to deliver packets of electrons to charge a rotating drum in its electron-beam approach. Yet another (Nipson) uses magnetic toner and a steel drum with a special surface that can be magnetized via a special writing head. This technology is not suitable for color printing, since the toner has to be magnetic and magnetic materials of the appropriate colors are not available.

The quality possible with toner-based printing is limited by the resolution of the printer, which is usually stated in dots per inch (dpi). To reproduce photographs adequately, a toner-based printer must generally have a resolution of at least 600 dpi. This level of resolution is required because toner is a "binary" material—it is either present or not, and if it is present, it is at full strength (solid black). To give the appearance of various levels of gray (in a monochrome device) or shades of color (in a color device), the toner must be applied in "halftone dots" of varying size. If a printer's resolution is much below 600 dpi, the halftone dots are objectionably large. Simliarly, artifacts called "jaggies" are visible in the diagonal edges of text and line art when it is printed on machines with a resolution below 600 dpi. The appearance of both halftones and line art improves detectably as the resolution increases to about 1,000 dpi, but higher resolution than that has little visual effect.

To be useful for book printing, a printer must be resonably fast. A ten-page-per-minute printer could be used to print a 300-page book, but it would take half an hour. In most applications, that would be much too slow. Most book printing is done on machines that print upwards of 100 pages per minute (ppm). Sheetfed printers are available that run up to 180 ppm and roll-fed ones can go well over 1,000 ppm. (Details on the available machines are given **below** [8.4].) The fastest machines are not toner-based, but rather inkjet printers.

Even the fastest of all the digital machines can only match the speed of a moderately slow offset book press. But what digital printing gives up in speed, it compensates for in other advantages, such as flexibility, cost-effectiveness in short runs, and simplified binding processes.

2. Inkjet

Inkjet printing is an entirely different approach to digital printing. Tiny droplets of ink are squirted directly onto the paper from a printhead containing hundreds or thousands of nozzles, each under electronic control.

Most inkjet printing is done using ***drop-on-demand*** technology. Droplets are forced out of each nozzle as they are needed, either by heat (thermal drop-on-demand) or pressure (piezo-electric drop-on-demand). So far, though, the machines using drop-on-demand technology are just not fast enough for most publishing applications, though they are quickly becoming the standard way to produce color proofs. For really fast printing, ***continuous-inkjet*** technology is required. In this technology, all the nozzles in the printhead emit a continuous stream of droplets, but most are electrostaticly deflected back into a gutter and recirculated. Only the undeflected droplets continue on to the paper.

The pioneer in the use of continuous-inkjet systems for publishing is Scitex Digital Printing. Initially, the company supplied partial-page systems for applications like addressing and the printing of variable-text letters, but in recent years they have expanded into full-page systems. Their roll-fed monochrome (Versamark) and color (Business Color Press) systems are not only the first inkjet systems to be used for publishing, they are also the fastest available digital devices of any kind, capable of printing 500 to 1,000 feet per minute—

the equivalent of several thousand pages per minute. Drop-on-demand systems have yet to come near these speeds, though there is much promising development work in this area.

The resolution of the Scitex inkjet machines is just 300 dpi—low, relative to almost any toner-based machine used for book printing. The image quality of the printed result is limited by the resolution. The same will probably be true of other high-speed inkjet machines being readied for the market. But most inkjet technologies have an advantage that toner-based printing does not. Inkjet devices can have variable droplet size (or droplets that consist of variable numbers of sub-droplets) and this allows a certain amount of variation in shades of color or gray without resorting to hafltone dots. By exploiting this "grayscale" capability, inkjet vendors can produce output whose quality (especially where images are concerned) matches that produced by higher-resolution devices. So far, however, no devices that exploit this technique and that would be suitable for book printing are commercially available.

3. Elcography

Finally, there is another unique technology which is not related to either toner-based or inkjet printing. It is called "elcography," and the first elcographic press is being delivered to the first customer as this is written. A distinguishing feature of elcography is that it can print 8-bit greyscale data, reflecting the photographic background of its creators. The technique was invented by the Canadian company Elcorsy, and it is described in more detail in the section on **roll-fed printing** [8.4.2].

(iii) OTHER FACTORS AFFECTING CHOICES IN DIGITAL PRINTING

Although imaging technologies are a key factor in digital printing, other technology issues can play an important role when deciding what system to buy or use. These include costs, speed, flexibility, appearance issues, and binding issues.

1. Cost

Though capital costs are important in digital printing (color devices can range from the hundreds of thousands of dollars into the millions), it is running costs that tend to dominate discussions of the use of digital printing. It is not hard to see why: in many markets, digital printing is competing with offset, and offset's cost per full-color page (once the job is on the press and running) is only a penny or two per letter-size image. Throughout the 1990s, the cost of running a digital press generally exceeded $0.25 per page (and of course the ultimate customer had to be charged substantially more than that if the transaction was to be profitable for the printer). This meant that digital printing was confined to two small niches: very short runs (usually less than 500)—where offset's higher setup costs come into play—and variable-data printing. Now, with the latest generation of digital devices, page costs have come down substantially. The vendors say they will be in the under-ten-cents range for a letter-sized full-color page. If so, digital printing will be competitive at 2,000 copies—not yet the heart of the offset market, but a substantial inroad all the same.

Monochrome digital printing is already competitive with offset in most markets and, in fact, has almost completely eliminated offset in some. Sheetfed monochrome devices—notably the Xerox DocuTech family—displaced much of the low page-count work previously done on offset duplicators; and the high-speed monochrome machines from IBM, Oce, and others are starting to have a similar effect on short-run book printing.

2. Speed

For some applications, speed is important. A speed of 120 ppm sounds impressive, but if you are printing 600-page books on a printer that speed, it can only produce twelve copies per hour. At that rate, a run of 2,500 books would take well over a week, running three shifts and seven days. Only roll-fed printers have the speed necessary for book production in substantial volume. On the other hand, inexpensive sheetfed machines open up interesting new opportunities for very short runs and for printing individual books on demand.

3. Flexibility

Substrate flexibility—what materials can be printed on, and in what form—is an issue with some kinds of digital printing. Not every kind of paper will work in every machine. Some papers do badly with certain toners or certain fusing processes. Some tend to jam in specific machines. Many companies involved in digital printing rely on a qualification process, carried out by their printer and paper suppliers, to make sure that the papers they select will work in their machines. In general, newer machines are more flexible in terms of dealing with surface textures and paper weights than previous models. One supplier, Nipson, has found a niche in monochrome printing on hard-to-image substrates. The combination of its unique magnetographic technology and its low-heat "flash-fusing" approach mean that it can handle a wide variety of plastics and other materials.

Substrate flexibility also means the ability to run a mix of substrates, either in a single job or in successive jobs. Vendors have been adding extra feed trays to their machines, either as standard equipment or as options, in an effort to provide more of this kind of flexibility. This is one area where sheetfed machines have the upper hand. Roll-fed devices cannot mix paper stocks in a job, and it takes several minutes to switch them from one type of paper to another, whereas the same switch is instantaneous for a sheetfed machine with multiple input hoppers.

4. Appearance

The appearance of the printed page can be a very important issue in some applications, and of little significance in others. For a decade, digital-press vendors have been striving to match the appearance of offset-printed pages, since the failure to do so has been a stumbling block in their sales efforts. The current top-of-the-line machines from HP/Indigo, Xerox, and Nexpress do a good job in this respect. Among the problems that have been overcome are: toner sheen (the overly shiny appearance of heavy concentrations of toner), streaking, surface oil (remaining on the paper from the fuser rollers), ***halftone*** quality problems, and ***color gamut*** limitations. Some or all of these appearance problems are still to be found in lower-priced devices. In addition, software issues can contribute to appearance issues such as color problems, image resolution problems, and problems with fonts. These, however, can all be fixed with the right software and expertise (the chapter on composition and graphics discusses using **color** [6.9], **image resolution** [6.11], and **fonts** [6.7] in more detail).

5. Binding

Finally, digital printing requires different binding equipment than does offset. There is no market where this is more obvious than the book market. Offset book printing is done on large presses that produce signatures of eight, sixteen, or thirty-two pages. These have to be folded, gathered (collated), and then bound. Digital book printing is done one, two, or three pages at a time, and they are delivered in sequence from the machine, so no collation is required. Traditional binding equipment handles many hundreds of books per hour. It is unlikely that the binding process for a digital printer, even a very fast roll-fed one, would ever need to exceed one hundred books per hour. And for a sheetfed machine, the number would be a fraction of that. The traditional bookbinding equipment is simply inappropriate.

Suppliers of binding equipment are belatedly responding to this need, especially in the key perfect-bound (softcover) area. There are expensive machines (several hundred thousand dollars) designed to handle the output of the roll-fed printers and the fastest sheetfed ones, and inexpensive ($15,000 and less) manual machines designed to handle book-on-demand binding from slower sheetfed devices. For the moment, though, there are no machines in the great gap between.

8.3 USES OF DIGITAL PRINTING

(i) DIGITAL PRINTING VS. OFFSET PRINTING

Most books and journals are printed via the offset process. (Although other traditional printing processes, including letterpress, gravure, and flexography can also be used, this happens only rarely. See the chapter on **composition and graphics** [6.13] for a discussion of these processes.) For some book printing, digital printing (which includes toner-based processes, ink-jet printing, and other processes that do not involve making a plate or other master) is starting to be an important competitor to offset. Important suppliers of toner-based machines for book printing include Xerox, Heidelberg, HP/Indigo, Oce, Xeikon, and IBM. At present there is only one significant supplier of ink-jet printing equipment suitable for books, Scitex Digital Printing, but others are preparing to enter this field.

To understand the developing competition between offset and digital printing, it is useful to consider the main characteristics that distinguish them today: quality, speed, flexibility, cost, and operational factors.

1. Quality

Though both toner and inkjet printing have historically been unable to match offset quality, that has recently changed. Now, the best of the toner-based "digital presses" can match the quality of most commercial offset work. Some low-speed inkjet devices are also capable of offset-quality printing, but for now they are far too slow to be used for book and journal printing and are used mostly for proofing.

2. Speed

Toner-based machines cannot, in general, match the speed of an offset press running continuously. But an offset press doing short runs spends more time during job-to-job changeover than it does actually printing, and in that situation a toner-based device can be as fast or faster. The high-speed inkjet printers from Scitex Digital Printing are much faster than the toner-based machines, and they can compete directly on speed (although not yet on quality) with offset presses.

3. Flexibility

Each approach offers specific kinds of flexibility. Offset printing currently offers more flexibility in terms of papers, inks (including spot colors and varnish), and binding options. Digital printing, of course, offers the flexibility of completely changing each page from one impression to the next.

4. Cost

Offset has a higher cost for starting up a job, because plates must be prepared and some paper is wasted during the initial run-up to the first good sheet. The binding process that goes with offset (print in signatures, fold, gather, bind, and trim) can also be more expensive than the binding process for digital printing, where large signatures and gathering are not required. But, at present, the cost per page of the actual printing is lower for offset, and this is the dominant cost in long runs. So short runs are more economical with digital printing, and longer ones are more economical with offset. The crossover point between the two methods is somewhere between 200 copies and 5,000 copies, depending on the exact equipment being compared.

5. Operational factors

Generally speaking, offset printing requires a highly-trained operator and a production (factory-like) working environment. The quality obtained from an offset press often depends on the skill of the operator. Digital printing tends to place less demands on the operator and to produce more uniform results. It can usually be done in an office-like environment. One implication of these differences is that highly-efficient, "lean" manufacturing of print is more likely to be accomplished with digital devices, given devices of comparable speed.

(ii) PRINTING ON DEMAND

The phrase "printing on demand" (***POD***) is used in various ways, but we will choose the most restrictive meaning: the printing of a document in response to the requirement of a specific end user. This definition makes clear the difference between POD and "short runs" (see separate discussion in the section on **short runs** [8.3.3]). Examples of POD would include the production of a manual for a bulldozer at the time when the bulldozer itself is produced, and the in-store printing of a book for a waiting customer. Printing on demand is one of two types of printing (the other is variable-data printing) that digital printing can address but conventional printing, which is restricted to producing multiple copies of the same document, cannot.

Most printing that is done in the office and the home could be classified as printing on demand. Items are printed as the need arises, and only the quantity that can be immediately used is produced—often just one copy.

But successful examples of printing on demand as a business are hard to find. The reason for this is not technical. The technology for printing on demand is exactly the same as it is for short runs: if you can print a run of fifity copies, you can print a run of one. Rather, the non-printing costs surrounding printing on demand (selling, processing the order, delivering the document, and billing) tend to make the whole process uneconomic. A particular printer may be able to produce a single copy of a paperback book at a cost of five dollars, for example, but if it costs the printer an additional five dollars to process the order and do the billing, the prospects of a profitable POD business are slim. And it is hard to fit a sales force paid on commission, which is often the case in the printing industry, into a print-on-demand model.

1. Books on demand: making it work

Because of the business issues discussed above, successful ***POD*** operations generally need to be highly automated and paid for in an efficient transaction.

On-demand production of individual books in the bookstore, if it ever becomes a commercial reality, would be an example. Here, the transaction would be handled by a clerk who is already handling many other sales, so the transaction costs would be low. As of late 2002, there is only one actual case of a book production device being installed in a bookstore—the machine is made by the Instabook Corporation, and the bookstore is Book Express in Cambridge, Ontario, Canada). Several companies are developing similar devices, and they should appear on the market over the next few years.

The engineering challenge of creating a self-contained book-production machine is formidable, but a greater obstacle may turn out to be setting up the infrastructure that allows such a machine to have access to all the books it might be called upon to print, while still guaranteeing the publisher a suitable commission and no loss of control over the intellectual property. This problem, like the analogous problem for e-books, is far from being solved. The case of Book Express is instructive: the Instabook machine seems to be working fine, but there very few books are produced on it because of the limited number of titles available.

In a few cases, print-on-demand book production has reached relatively large scale. The best example is Lightning Source, a subsidiary of the book distributor Ingram. Lightning Source has developed a very efficient system for producing books digitally. The work produced is a combination of true on-demand printing (one or two copies) and short runs. By mid-2002, the company had produced over three million books and had over 100,000 titles in its system.

(iii) SHORT-RUN PRINTING

Once the print run is underway, digital printing costs more per page than offset printing. The cost difference is very high (but declining every year) for color pages. It is small but still significant for black-and-white pages. This economic fact means that digital printing can be justified only in selected niches where other factors make up for the high cost per page.

Some costs are incurred in offset printing before the first good sheet comes off the press. Two such cost areas, the cost associated with platemaking and the cost associated with the wasted sheets used in getting the press "up to color," are avoided entirely in digital printing. A digital device needs no plate and switches instantly from one job to the next. Normally, neither paper nor time is wasted during the switch. This means that if the print run is short, the overall cost for printing a job digitally can be less than offset even though the cost per page is higher with digital printing.

For jobs involving fewer than 200 copies of a document, digital printing is almost always less expensive than offset. Depending on exactly what kinds of presses are being compared, digital printing can sometimes be competitive up to 1,000 copies or more. And sometimes factors apart from the printing itself (for example, the avoidance of signature gathering when printing documents with high page counts) can help justify digital printing, making it economical at still higher quantities.

1. Applications for short-run printing

Short-run digital printing has found application in a number of book-publishing niches, including:

1. COURSE PACKS AND CUSTOM TEXTBOOKS

These are materials selected by a professor for a specific course, and produced in the quantity required for the enrollment in that course.

2. ADVANCE COPIES AND REVIEW COPIES

These are copies of a book produced ahead of the primary (offset) print run and used for promotion. Publishers want their books to be reviewed to coincide with their availability in bookstores, and they want the sales force to have advance copies to obtain bookstore orders. In the past, these needs for early copies have been satisfied, if at all, with "bound galleys" produced on high-speed copiers. Digital printing provides a better solution.

3. BACKLIST BOOKS

If a book has slow but steady sales of a few dozen to a few hundred copies per year, the publisher will be reluctant to tie up capital in an offset print run that will take years to sell out. But short runs of twenty to fifty books make sense in this situation, even though the cost per book is comparatively high.

4. SMALL PUBLISHERS AND SELF-PUBLISHERS

For many small book publishers, and most self-publishers, a very short initial print run, using digital printing, is a wise choice. If the book sells in sufficient quantity, a switch to longer offset print runs can be made.

2. The success of short-run digital printing

In the twenty-year history of digital printing, by far the majority of the work produced has been in the short run category. The reasons for this are organizational rather than technical: short-run printing doesn't require new approaches to purchasing, sales, and job management (as POD does), and it doesn't require new skill sets and new ways of relating to the customer (as variable-data printing does). For printers (and their customers) who move from offset printing into short-run digital printing, the relationship and procedures can remain essentially unchanged.

With each passing year, new digital printing equipment is introduced that features higher speed and lower cost per page. This causes digital printing to become ever more competitive with offset. The longest economical short run will get longer and longer. Eventually (probably within a decade or two) there will be no difference in per-page costs, and digital printing will take over most of the work that is currently produced using offset presses. At that point, there will no longer be a reason to distinguish short runs from other press runs.

(iv) PERSONALIZED AND CUSTOM DOCUMENTS

Custom and personalized documents are an area of special strength for digital printing. Custom documents are those created for a small group of readers; personalized documents are each unique. It is practical to produce custom documents via offset printing for an audience of at least a few hundred, but smaller print runs call for digital printing. And of course, personalized documents (with a run length of one) require digital printing.

The actual printing of custom documents tends to be less important than the creation of the document content, which is where most of the costs tend to lie. There have been relatively few examples of successful business opportunities based on the production of custom books. The most notable one is custom college textbooks. Several publishers, beginning with McGraw-Hill's pioneering Primis project, established repositories of content in various fields of study. Professors get to select the content they want for their classes and have it produced as a custom book. The technology to do this has been around for almost two decades, and there are several successful examples, but this type of custom publishing is still not wide-spread. It turns out that establishing the repository (and especially, obtaining permissions and setting up royalty arrangements for all the content items) is the most difficult aspect. Another fairly common application of custom publishing is in creating spin-off products from a database. For example, the technique has been used to create industry-specific subsets of a catalog for a company to hand out at a specialized trade show.

Personalized printing is occasionally used for books. Sometimes, each copy of a custom-published textbook is imprinted with the student's name, which is a trivial example of personalization. Personalized children's books, with the use of the child's name and other information (e.g. the name of a pet, or the child's street), are common. Sometimes even the child's photo is scanned and used in illustrations throughout the book.

(v) THE ROLE OF THE WEB

Much has been made of the Web as a potential competitor to print publishing. But the Web is a key enabler for certain kinds of printing. As is noted in the discussion of **printing on demand** [8.3.2], the transaction costs for books printed on demand are a key factor in making the process profitable. Books ordered over the Web can have a very low transaction cost, since the customer does all the work of specifying the book, the delivery address, the payment option, and so on. Similarly, custom and personalized book production operations are much more likely to be profitable if the books are ordered via the Web.

The Web can also be helpful in streamlining the process leading up to the publication of a book. A notable example of this is the large number of book production services that have sprung up to serve the small publisher and self-publisher. These companies tend to use the Web for almost all of their interactions with customers, including bidding and contracts as well as the receipt of the finished manuscript and illustrations.

8.4 AVAILABLE PRINTING SYSTEMS

(i) SHEETFED PRINTERS

The most common digital printing devices print on individual sheets of paper. They aren't as fast as roll-fed devices (which are covered **below** [8.4.2]), but they are more flexible (since it is easy to switch paper stocks and sizes) and usually less expensive. The first digital printing devices to be commercialized were monochrome laser printers, in the late 1970s. Not until the 1990s did digital printing in color really become practical.

1. Monochrome sheetfed printing

In 1976, the first of two high-speed digital printing machines was introduced. The two were notably similar in their basic laser-printing functionality, but very different in their implementation. What's more, the segments of the digital printing market that were pioneered by each machine would remain separate for decades. Only now, two-and-a-half decades later, are they finally merging to form a truly mass market.

1. IBM 3800

First to arrive was the IBM 3800. Its speed was astonishing for the time: 215 ppm. However, the 3800 made little impact on the publishing industry, for a variety of reasons—two of the major ones being insufficient resolution at 240 dpi and woefully inadequate fonts. The 3800, though, was not intended for publishing in the first place. It was intended to replace line printers attached to mainframe computers, a niche it filled quite well. At the time it appeared, all printed output in the mainframe environment was generated on mechanical impact printers—chain printers, train printers, flying-drum printers, and others of that ilk. They were noisy, inflexible, and often unreliable. During the machine's thirteen-year lifetime, IBM sold over 8,000 3800s. These trailblazing machines revolutionized the data center, and their offspring (right down to the HP LaserJet) revolutionized the office.

2. XEROX 9700

The other pioneering laser printer to appear in the 70s was the Xerox 9700, introduced in 1977. Unlike the IBM printer, the 9700 was not originally intended as a replacement for any particular machine. It printed 120 ppm at 300 dpi, and it could use any fonts that could be loaded into its memory (from 8KB to 32KB of bitmap memory, enough for 4 to 12 fonts at 10 point). One drawback was that a separate font was needed for each different size, and larger sizes took up more memory. Fonts could be downloaded along with the job to be printed.

The 9700 and its successors (down to the Apple LaserWriter) revolutionized document printing and publishing. Just as the IBM 3800 gave rise to an entire industry of laser printing for mainframe (and eventually office) output, the Xerox 9700 initiated an industry of laser printing for documents and publishing. (To this day, in the high-speed printing market, the convergence of the two segments is still not quite complete.)

Like all machines of its time (and most others for a decade to come), the 9700 was basically a text-only machine. The only graphics it could handle were small logos and crude line art assembled from special "fonts." These were limitations imposed by the technology of the day, in particular, the high cost of random-access memory (RAM). The 9700 was ideal for textual documents of high value and variable content, and it turned out that the insurance industry was its natural home. It could print out single copies of custom policies, replacing a pick-and-assemble manual process.

But the 9700 and the machines that followed it were too limited and required too much computer infrastructure to be used for ordinary publishing applications.

3. POSTSCRIPT AND DOCUTECH

Until the arrival of ***PostScript*** laser printers on the market in 1985, each brand of laser printer had its own interface language or "page description language," and software to drive laser printers was complex and expensive. PostScript would eventually put an end to the proliferation of proprietary languages, but it took years before computer performance increased to the point that driving a high-speed printer with PostScript was practical.

In 1990, Xerox announced the ***DocuTech***, the machine that dominated publishing applications of monochrome digital printing throughout the 1990s. This 120 ppm digital printer was initially marketed as a very sophisticated copier, but Xerox soon introduced a PostScript capability for it and it was increasingly used as a high-speed digital printer rather than a copier. With the DocuTech, Xerox began to displace large amounts of monochrome offset printing. It introduced new models in various speed ranges, culminating with the DocuTech 6180 at 180 ppm. It is still the fastest sheetfed digital printer capable of duplex (two-sided) printing.

The Xerox DocuTech didn't have much competition, though Kodak (first on its own and later in partnership with Heidelberg) did offer a 110 ppm device. The higher-speed DocuTech models were without competition until the 150 ppm Heidelberg Digimaster 9150 and the 155 ppm Oce VarioPrint 5160 were finally introduced in the fall of 2002.

4. THE MARKET TODAY

Xerox continues to dominate the high-speed monochrome sheetfed market. Apart from Heidelberg (whose machines are also sold by Canon, IBM, Ikon, and Danka), there are a number of vendors (led by Canon and Ricoh) with laser printers at 100 ppm and below, all looking for an opportunity to take some of the remaining monochrome business from offset printing (or from Xerox and Heidelberg). Some of these machines are very aggressively priced, and it is clear that both the initial investment and the cost per page of high-speed digital printing will decline sharply.

The DocuTech and the machines that compete with it owe a lot to copier technology. They all use photosensitive drums or belts, and they use either a laser or LEDs to create the image to be printed. Most of the manufacturers (Heidelberg being the major exception) are very active in the copier market as well.

There is one monochrome sheetfed machine worthy of mention that is outside the mainstream markets: the Delphax Imaggia. This is a specialized machine for check printing. It is actually faster than any other sheetfed printer, but it prints only on one side. It is capable of printing with magnetic ink (a requirement for checks) and it can handle an extremely wide range of paper weights. It uses Delphax' unique imaging technology, called electron-beam imaging.

2. Color sheetfed printing

The earliest color digital printers were basically color copiers with a computer interface. Their low speeds and modest quality, combined with a relatively high cost per page, meant that they could not be used for any "publishing" applications except early-stage proofing. In 1993, two companies—Indigo and Xeikon—began to change this. Xeikon's machine was roll-fed and is discussed **below** [8.4.2]. Indigo's E-Print 1000 was a 17 ppm printer using liquid toner (the company called it "Electro-ink"). From the start, it produced quality that could compete for many offset jobs.

During the course of the 1990s, copier companies gradually expanded the market for office color printing. Canon in particular found a corporate market for its CLC series of copier-based machines which are fast (up to 50 ppm) but which do not produce images whose quality can match Indigo's. The Canon machines are widely used in corporate and quick-print environments.

Xerox, too, offered copier-based printing to the corporate market. But with its introduction of the DocuColor series in the late 1990s, it began to focus more seriously on high-quality publishing markets in which it would be competing with Indigo. It took a further step in this direction with its iGen3 printer, a machine designed specifically to compete with offset printing. It was shown as a prototype at Drupa, the major international printing trade show, in 2000, and officially announced the following year. As of the end of 2002, volume production of this 100 ppm machine is just getting started.

In parallel with Xerox' development of the iGen3, Heidelberg and Kodak were also working on a machine to address offset markets, the NexPress 2100. It was first shown at Drupa 2000, and shipments of this 70 ppm machine began in 2001.

Meanwhile, Indigo had not been sitting still. It had made speed and quality improvements and had introduced a roll-fed model and a machine designed for printing on flexible plastic. But the biggest milestone for Indigo came in the fall of 2001, when it was purchased by Hewlett-Packard. This provided new financial and marketing resources, and it held the promise of streamlined, low-cost manufacturing in the future.

Thus, by the fall of 2001, the basic structure of the sheetfed digital printing market of today was in place. HP Indigo, Heidelberg, and Xerox are competing with each other for a share of the market that has traditionally been held by offset printing. These three vendors have deep pockets, broad market access, and expensive machines with very high image quality. Then comes a second group of companies, dominated by the copier vendors Canon, Sharp, Konica,

Oce, and Minolta, among others. They are focused on the corporate market and the lower-quality segments of the offset market.

These are all toner-based machines. (So far, no sheetfed inkjet machines are fast enough to compete for production work, although they are widely used for low-volume tasks such as proofing and book-cover printing.) Almost all of them use a photosensitive drum or belt, with a laser or LED array to create the image. The exception to this is the Oce CPS700, which uses circular electrodes embedded in its imaging drum to attract toner. This machine, which is also unusual in utilizing seven different colors of toner, produces excellent images. But its market has been limited so far by its relatively low speed (25 ppm) and high price.

(ii) ROLL-FED DIGITAL PRINTING

For really fast printing, a roll-fed (or "web," to use the traditional printing term) machine is needed. Paper-handling difficulties put an upper limit on how fast a sheetfed printer can be. So far, no sheetfed machine has been able to print faster than 180 letter-size pages per minute. But roll-fed machines can go much faster. Some of them print at speeds of 750 or 1,000 feet per minute which (depending on the maximum width of the roll) can be the equivalent of over 2,000 letter-size pages per minute.

But the use of paper in rolls has its disadvantages as well. Only one kind of paper can be loaded at a time (sheetfed machines can have as many kinds as there are paper drawers), and changing paper generally requires heavy equipment and several minutes of downtime. Once the new roll is loaded, though, the machine will be able to run for hours without attention.

Roll-fed machines, especially the fastest ones, present special data-processing challenges. These days, most publishing-oriented pages are printed from ***PostScript*** or ***PDF*** files. But it can take a second or two for a fast processor to take each PostScript or PDF page and "rasterize" it—break it down into the individual dots that the printer will ultimately image. Photographs, in particular, require a lot of processing power. If the processing takes, say, a second per page, but the printer is capable of printing ten or more pages per second, then the rasterizing process becomes a major bottleneck. The speed of transfer of data from the host computer to the imaging part of the printer can also be a bottleneck.

Various solutions have been devised to help with this—multiple processors working in parallel, parallelism in the transfer of data, rasterization and compression of images ahead of time, and so on. The use of simpler languages than PostScript and PDF can also help. Xerox Metacode, IBM AFP/IPDS, and Hewlett-Packard PCL are all much faster to rasterize than PostScript and PDF (although they are far less flexible), and so they are still widely used, especially in non-publishing applications (e.g., statement printing). This problem will gradually solve itself, since the processing speed of the average computer chip is increasing faster than the printing speed of the fastest printers. Eventually, the chips will be fast enough to keep up without difficulty.

While sheetfed printers have a lot in common with copiers, and are frequently based on copier designs, roll-fed machines are much more diverse. They use a variety of printing technologies that are not found among the sheetfed machines.

1. Monochrome machines

Most roll-fed printers installed so far are monochrome machines. They have been used for many years in statement printing (e.g., phone bills, credit card statements, brokerage account reports). But centralized statement printing is not a growth market, and all the companies that supply roll-fed machines have been seeking out additional markets. In recent years, a lot of emphasis has been placed on short-run printing of books. Other important markets have included personalized direct mail and printing of numbered or personalized documents (such as tickets and credit cards).

1. IBM

For many years, IBM has been active in this market. At one time, it was a dominant force in data-center printing. In recent years, IBM's Printing Systems division has focused increasingly on sales where printing is only one part of a solution that also involves consulting, software development, and integration. This has often meant that IBM has chosen not to bid on projects where the focus was the straightforward purchase of a printer. IBM's latest roll-fed system, the 4100, prints at up to 762 ppm and is a good fit for book printing.

2. OCE

IBM's narrow focus has opened up some opportunities for Oce (formerly Siemens), which originally made its mark selling IBM-compatible printers in the mainframe environment. It now sells roll-fed machines into a variety of applications, including book printing, and has become the leading vendor of roll-fed printers. Oce's VarioStream products run at up to 1,273 ppm and are used in a number of book-on-demand production facilities.

3. XEROX

Xerox, though it concentrates on sheetfed machines, also offers roll-fed ones. It offered machines built by Delphax (see **below** [8.4.2.1.5]), of which it was part owner, then switched to machines built by a Japanese subcontractor when Delphax was bought by Check Technology. The Xerox CFD models print at up to 1000 ppm.

IBM, Oce, and Xerox all offer roll-fed machines that use the traditional approach of creating the image on a light-sensitive drum or belt with a laser or LED array. But other roll-fed machines use more unusual technologies.

4. NIPSON AND MAGNETOGRAPHIC PRINTING

Nipson, a monochrome specialist, uses a unique technology called "magnetography" in its printers. A writing head, analogous to the head of a disk drive, creates magnetic spots on the surface of steel drum. Toner containing iron particles sticks to the magnetized spots, forming the image. The toner is then transferred to paper. Nipson's fastest machine, the Varypress, prints at 1,616 ppm. Nipson's main specialty is printing on all sorts of substrates (such as plastic credit cards and heat-sensitive materials) that other printers have difficulty with. But it is also active in direct mail printing and, in recent years, has begun paying more attention to book printing, especially text-only books. Nipson's magnetographic technology is unsuitable for color printing, since the materials that would be needed to make toners that have both the necessary magnetic characteristics and the required colors do not exist.

5. DELPHAX AND ELECTRON-BEAM IMAGING

Delphax was originally a joint venture of Xerox and two other companies, and then became a Xerox subsidiary. It was sold to Check Technologies in December 2001. Its printers utilize a unique electron-beam imaging technology. An alternating current knocks electrons loose from the air in tiny holes in the print head. The electrons are deposited on the surface of the nearby imaging drum or belt, and the resulting negative charge attracts toner. The technology is fast, simple, and rugged. Delphax has incorporated it into a sheetfed check printer (the Imaggia, mentioned **earlier** [8.4.1.1.4]) and a line of roll-fed devices, the fastest of which prints at 1300 ppm. The machine would be suitable for book printing. All the Delphax models are monochrome, but the company has begun development on a full-color machine for introduction in 2005.

6. SCITEX DIGITAL PRINTING AND VERSAMARK

The fastest of the monochrome printers is the Versamark press from Scitex Digital Printing. This is a high-speed inkjet machine (up to 750 feet per minute, or over 2,000 pages per minute). Its key features are its speed and low cost per page. Its print quality is limited, but its other features make it well suited to the production of materials where the highest quality is not an issue. And a new generation of printhead technology, shown in prototype form in the fall of 2002, will close part of the gap in image quality between this technology and the toner-based machines.

7. ELCORSY ELCO 400

A newcomer, just reaching the first customer site as this is written, is the Elcorsy Elco 400. This machine also features high speed (400 feet per second, or about 870 letter-size pages per minute) and low cost per page. The novel technology used in this machine is called "electro-coagulation." A special fluid, containing a pigment and a polymer, is passed between a rotating metal drum and an array of electrodes that is very close to the drum's surface. Whenever one of the electrodes is turned on, a spot of pigment is deposited on the drum. As the drum turns, it comes into contact with paper and the pigment is transferred. The technique should be capable of quite good quality. Early samples showed streaking problems, but these seem to have been fixed by a redesign of the imaging head. A special attribute of this technology is that it is able to print ***grayscale*** (8-bit) images, thus achieving high image quality compared to other digital printers. The machine's initial installations will be monochrome (or monochrome with spot color), although the technology is suitable for color printing as well.

2. Color machines

Two of the vendors of monochrome roll-fed systems (Scitex Digital Printing and Elcorsy) also have (or, in Elcorsy's case, plan to have) color machines. The Scitex Business Color Press is the speed champion, at 500 feet per minute. Elcorsy's competing product, when available, will run at 400 feet per minute. Both are far faster than the toner-based competition. The image quality of the Scitex product is significantly inferior to most toner-based printing, but may still be suitable for some books. The Elcorsy device is expected to have good image quality, and the prototype machine is promising, but the image quality issue will only be completely resolved by production use at customer sites.

Meanwhile, toner-based roll-fed color machines are available from Xeikon and HP Indigo. Xeikon started out in 1993 with a roll-fed color printer and, after dabbling briefly with a sheetfed model, has decided to remain a roll-fed specialist. Its two main products are the DCP 500D and the DCP 320D, which accept maximum paper widths of 20 inches and 12.6 inches, respectively. They each use eight imaging stations (four on each side of the paper) to print both sides simultaneously at up to 130 ppm. In digital book-printing operations, the Xeikon printers (which are also sold under the IBM and MAN Roland names) are often used for printing color covers and jackets.

HP Indigo initially offered only sheetfed printers, but has added the roll-fed w3200 model that prints 133 ppm. Among the roll-fed printers, it is clearly the leader in image quality.

For now, these are the only vendors active in color roll-fed printing for publishing applications. But others will probably enter the market. Several inkjet specialists have shown interest, and one of them, Aprion, showed a mockup of a self-contained book-on-demand printing system at a trade show in 2000. Another inkjet vendor, Dotrix, is actually selling a fast roll-fed machine that could in principle be adapted for publishing use. But so far, the company is marketing it as a machine for printing labels, plastic cards, packaging, wall coverings, and other non-publishing applications.

(iii) CLUSTER APPROACHES

It is possible to use several relatively slow printers, working simultaneously, to duplicate the throughput of a single fast machine. There are several reasons why this approach is attractive. You can start small (with one or two printers) and build capacity incrementally as required. You have a measure of redundancy, so the failure of a single printer does not stop the whole production operation. You may be able to save money, both on your initial investment and on your running costs, because of what might be called a "dis-economy of scale" in the printer market. For example, the price of a 120-ppm printer is more than the cost of four 30-ppm printers, and the cost per page is often higher on the faster printer as well.

One vendor in particular, T/R Systems, has specialized in cluster systems and has sold many of them. Some have been used in book printing. But interest in cluster systems has declined in recent years. One reason is that both the initial investment and the cost per page of fast printers has been declining, making the economics of clustering less attractive. But a more important reason is the new class of enterprise printer-management software that has become available. This software monitors printer use and printer failures throughout an enterprise, routing jobs to an alternative printer in case of machine failure, splitting large jobs among multiple machines, and handling internal accounting and billing. It provides most of the features of cluster printing as a subset, so there are fewer potential customers for software that is restricted to cluster printing. In addition to these enterprise-wide packages, many of the printer vendors now offer print-management software of their own that includes clustering features.

8.5 SALES CHANNELS FOR DIGITAL BOOK PRINTING

As digital printing becomes a common approach to book production, it is changing the business practices of the book-printing industry. Existing book printers find they have to make adjustments to allow for more frequent, but shorter, print runs. And many companies that were not previously involved in book printing are joining the competition. The new digital technologies have changed the market at two levels: they have led to a dramatic drop in the cost of the equipment required to become a book printer (it can now be done for a cost of under $20,000 if you are producing only a few dozen copies a day), and the minimum length of a print run has also dropped (in some cases, to a single copy).

(i) BOOK AND JOURNAL MANUFACTURERS

Many existing book and journal printers are embracing the digital technology. Typically, they do not offer a true "book-on-demand" service. Rather, they focus on short-run printing of from fifty to five hundred copies. Short print runs can often be handled within their existing production and job-tracking processes, and the adjustments to their sales and billing processes can be kept to a minimum. They can sell digital printing as an additional service to their existing book-publisher customers (who can still be expected to buy offset printing when the runs are longer).

(ii) BOOK WHOLESALERS AND DISTRIBUTORS

In some cases, book distributors and wholesalers are in a good position to implement digital book-on-demand services. They have to keep books in stock to supply their bookstore customers, so they know when a book goes out of print. They also know when there is demand for a book that is no longer available. So they are in a good position to sell publishers a service that would allow small numbers (or single copies) of slow-moving books to be produced in response to market demands. The most aggressive efforts in this direction to date have been Ingram's Lightning Source operation (based on IBM equipment) in the U.S. and Libri's similar service (based on Xerox equipment) in Germany. Both are set up to print single copies efficiently, though they also offer short runs.

(iii) VANITY PRESSES AND SELF-PUBLISHING SERVICES

Vanity presses (publishers who are paid by authors to produce their books) have been around for centuries. But the traditional book-printing technology has not been a good match for the very short runs that self-published authors often require. Vanity presses have therefore embraced digital technology, and today digital printing is often used for the books they produce. In addition, dozens of book-production services for self-publishers have sprung up in recent years, based on the availability of digital printing. These services—which are often indistinguishable from vanity presses, except that they generally do not offer case binding or offset printing—conduct most of their business over the Web. They not only offer book production, but also order-taking (again, via the Web) and fulfillment. In some cases, they also offer editorial or marketing help to the would-be author—all for a fee, of course.

(iv) COPY SHOPS

As copy shops have gradually switched from using analog copiers to digital ones that can double as printers, they have begun to be capable of printing books in small quantities. Since they are already geared to handling small transactions, no significant change to the business model is required. But they may have to invest in equipment for binding and trimming the books. They often turn to relatively inexpensive desktop book-binding systems (such as those made by Powis Parker and sold for under $5,000). These manual systems are easy to learn to use, are capable of producing high-quality books, and are suitable for low-volume production.

(v) DIGITAL PRINTING IN THE BOOKSTORE

Many of the production-related problems of the publishing industry would be solved if books were produced to order, in the bookstore. In recent years, several companies have worked on building suitable machines for this environment and one of them (Instabook) has actually placed a machine in a bookstore. Several other companies have made prototypes. It is resonable to assume that the technical problems associated with in-store book production will soon be (or have already been) solved. But another set of problems has not been solved: the problems associated with getting the digital files from all the publishers out to the bookstores (with suitable protection against illegal copying) and making appropriate royalty arrangements. These may prove to be the issues which hold up in-store book printing for years to come.

9 Multimedia Publishing

FLORIAN BRODY
President and CEO, Brody Inc.

Since the format of the book evolved from the continuous scroll to the page-oriented folio, no change in the practice of publishing texts has had such an impact on the way we perceive and use a book as electronic publishing. This paradigm shift changes the way text is perceived in time and space and the integration of text, video, and audio into a multimedia product is a logical step in an electronic medium. Yet it is not the technology that undergoes the biggest change, but the role of the publisher, who has to re-emerge as the agent of a new medium, still in *statu nascendi*. In the first phase of multimedia, everybody seemed to be empowered by the new tools and technologies to become a multimedia producer. Most multimedia publications do not live up to the promise of an interactive and integrated experience, but remain an exploration into technologies without a clear goal. It is the publisher who needs to act as the integrator of multiple media types, multiple experts, and multiple industries in order to do his job—to turn an idea into a product and make it public. This chapter gives an overview of the different technologies, standards, and business issues to be considered when extending electronic publishing into multimedia.

9.1 OVERVIEW

Multimedia is one of the core elements of electronic publishing. It provides the broad and varied communication channel expected from a digital medium and takes full advantage of the opportunities to convey a message. Developing content for a multimedia publication is a much more complex process than creating a digital replica of a printed publication. It involves multiple processes that go beyond the domain of a print publisher and encompass video and audio production. Not only the technology but also the rules of different industries need to be aligned to guarantee a successful product.

The traditional role of a publisher has been limited to the printed document but, much as Bodoni took on the execution and control of all steps in the book production process to ensure maximum quality of his books, the publisher has the unique chance today to enter a new medium and excel in the core competency of his profession—to transform the creative content of his authors, turn it into a product, and make it public.

"New media" and "interactive multimedia" have been in and out of fashion in digital publishing since the late 1980s. Considered by some as the be-all, end-all of electronic publishing and by others an unnecessary resource hog, multimedia has often become more a technology showcase than the multidimensional extension of the message. New media is only "new" until it becomes mainstream and *multi*media as a term indicates that the different media types are still poorly integrated. Once video, audio, and other media types are an integrated part of digital publishing, it will no longer be called multimedia. Something else will be multimedia.

This chapter explores the opportunities, benefits, and challenges of multimedia for the stakeholders in electronic publishing. It will be up to the authors, editors, and publishers if the integration of multiple media types in an interactive digital environment changes the way we read and explore content on digital screens. Paper publishing, like digital publishing, combines text with images. Books are published with a CD-ROM in the back, fashion magazines have ads with perfume samples, and URLs offer a direct link to Web sites with extensions to the editorial or advertising content.

These additional dimensions require careful planning of the narrative and a deep understanding of the media-relevant rules. By integrating multiple media types into a digital publication beyond text and still images, you add a time axis, multiple output channels (monitors, speakers) and you cross the boundaries of production domains, a step rarely understood by traditional publishing houses.

For the purpose of this chapter, multimedia publishing is understood as text-based documents with audio and video data, both off-line and on-line. The focus of this chapter is Web sites, e-books, electronic periodicals, and products that integrate digital and conventional media within the domain expertise of the publisher.

9.2 WHAT IS MULTIMEDIA?

(i) A BRIEF DEFINITION

> Multimedia. Main Entry: mul·ti·me·dia; Function: adjective. Date: 1962 : using, involving, or encompassing several media <a multimedia approach to learning>
> —Webster's Collegiate Dictionary. *http://www.m-w.com*

Multimedia is the integration of different media types into one presentation on a personal computer (PC). The term is most commonly used in reference to PC-based publishing products that combine text, audio, video, animation, and graphics.

For the purpose of this publication, ***interactive multimedia*** refers to the augmentation and integration of different media types into a text document. The deciding parameter is if the user is a reader and the content is read rather than viewed or explored in a game-like fashion. Most TV news shows or shopping channels provide video, audio, and animation combined with graphics and text on the screen. But TV is more or less actively watched, not read (see also **on-line multimedia** [9.3.4] below).

The integration of text, audio, video, and other media types into a new form will take digital publishing from a state where it imitates the old form on paper to a new information medium that is no longer considered "multi" but the form of choice to read a content-rich publication.

9.3 DECIDING ON MULTIMEDIA

The decision to use a certain publishing form needs to be guided by the requirements of the target audience and the content. The author, the editor, and the publisher of a book decide on the format, the use of images in the text or in a separate section, possibly on different paper. Do the images need to be printed in color on coated stock? Does a diagram or map have to be printed and bound in as a special foldout to be usable? Will the book include a CD-ROM and how will it be affixed? Will the CD-ROM need a seal to be broken as a sign that the user accepts the End User License Agreement (***EULA***)? These decisions are driven by the need to communicate the message but also by technical and financial limitations. Similar considerations need to be applied to multimedia. All rules and common sense applied in conventional publishing when considering images in the text, in a separate section of the book, or as a self-contained entity that may be attached to the book (such as a map in a travel guide) also apply to multimedia. In addition, the publisher has to closely look at the direct and indirect economic impact and benefit of extending into the multimedia domain.

(i) DECISION CRITERIA

In order to assess if a publishing project merits the use of digital multimedia, the stakeholders need to clearly identify the benefits. The author, editor, and publisher need to answer these questions:

- Will the addition of sound and/or video contribute to the communication of the core message?

- Can the target audience be expected to have the necessary hardware and software?
- Are the production and/or licensing costs within the budgetary limitations and the production time frame?

Unless this is the first multimedia project, the publisher will have aggregated certain expertise in house and should have access to experts for the design and the technical development. The availability of these resources will be critical in creating a successful multimedia product.

These and other aspects that are specific to the project will drive the decision to augment a text with other media types. See below for an in-depth discussion of the implications of different media types in the production process as well as the perception of the product.

Multimedia is also always the augmentation of a medium, in this case text. A typical presentation of business news on TV over lunch with over 50 percent of the screen covered with text, running ticker tapes, animated headlines, and only a small window with a talking head (often viewed in an office cafeteria with the sound turned off) is not considered multimedia—it misses interactivity and it is percerceived as a single medium. The presentation is fully integrated and perceived as one medium, if a jumbled one. In multimedia, when text is augmented by audio or video, it is clear that text dominates and audio and video are supplementary. This arrangement is most often used by publishers. Video augmented by text falls into the domain of video production and follows different rules.

1. Will the addition of sound and/or video contribute to the communication of the core message?

Depending on the text document, its objective and target audience, it may be beneficial to enrich the experience, provide better understanding of the content or communicate new ideas that are difficult to convey by text only. The same scrutiny used to select tables, graphs, images, or photographs for printed books needs to be applied to the addition of video, audio, or other multimedia elements.

Will the multimedia addition distract and make the reading overly complicated? Video and audio are time-based media types and require the reader to halt the flow of reading to experience the presentation.

In a travel guide, a QuickTime VR (***QTVR***) video of a resort is a great addition; a video showing people walking on the beach without further explanation will disappoint the reader, as she cannot gain additional knowledge about the location. An interactive map that allows the reader to locate the QTVR video clips in the environment is a valuable reference tool.

Similarly, a sound bite of local music will certainly be of more value to the user than a talking head of a tourist manager, repeating what is printed in the text. In a language guide, audio annotations can be extremely valuable if they are created considering how they will be used. Will the guide be used in a formal or informal learning environment? Will it be used while in a foreign country? Consider going the next step: rather than adding sound bites of single words or phrases, develop an environment where the reader can follow the spoken word in the printed text. The sound bytes are no longer an add-on but an integrated element of the learning experience. Now add a feature to allow the reader to record her own voice and compare the intonation. The addition of video, audio, or other elements to the text should always be well integrated and serve the message of the book.

2. Can the target audience be expected to have the necessary hardware and software?

Audio and video require additional resources from the hardware used to consume them. Video requires video cards with the necessary ***video RAM***, processing power, and ***color depth*** and monitors with a minimum resolution and refresh rate. The bigger the video image and the more frames per second (fps), the more resources will be needed.

You can safely assume that the average computer acquired over the last three years supports video output and audio input and output if properly configured and few or no other programs are running. Resource sharing can be tricky; if your application needs all the video RAM it can get, you need to alert the reader to free up the necessary resources. Today's computer monitors are quite usable for video representation but the sound output through a PC speaker is less than satisfactory. Additional speakers and as necessary a microphone should be recommended.

If you produce a multimedia-enhanced book for a high-end audience (e.g., a professional music or video guide), it makes sense to inform the prospective reader as to the hardware requirements for the consumption of the book. In the case of a music encyclopedia this may include a ***MIDI*** interface and specific instruments. A language course may require a headset–microphone combination to listen and record in parallel.

In all cases, the minimum requirements for multimedia in a digital publication should be clearly marked together with processor speed, screen size, and operating systems supported.

3. Are the production and/or licensing costs within the budgetary limitations and the production time frame?

Books and magazines are published with budgets of a different magnitude than movies. Whether you license movie and sound clips or plan to produce them yourself, plan the cost into the overall budget and schedule the production time. Consider the time and effort for negotiations with licensing partners, and the team effort when creating, editing, and testing multimedia additions to your product. As more multimedia elements get added, the size of the publication grows significantly, which has an impact on distribution costs.

A goal-directed approach that clearly identifies which elements are needed to accomplish the objectives of the publication provides the foundation for weighing the cost/benefit relations between multiple options.

The concept of the "quotation" as it is known in print publishing is not understood in a similar way in the video and music industry and what is considered fair use varies widely. See The Legal Framework chapter for more detail on **fair use** [13.1.7].

(ii) EXPANDING THE MEDIUM — THE BENEFIT FOR THE PUBLISHER

Traditional publishers need to clearly understand the benefits for their company before committing to adding multimedia to their field of competencies. The conversion of printed books into e-books can be accomplished relatively easily with available tools, and the distribution can be left to companies specializing in this area. Adding multimedia requires significantly different expertise both for the publishing team and the authors.

A publisher specializing in self-help and how-to books will have a different objective when developing a series of multimedia books than a trade publisher with an extensive backlist that waits to be converted into digital format.

(iii) SOME BACKGROUND ON MULTIMEDIA

Over the years, the term "multimedia" has been used to refer to a multitude of different solutions—and this in multiple ways. Common to these solutions is that the different elements are typically poorly integrated, initially not intended to be connected, yet they offer a significant augmentation in the informational bandwidth of the final product.

In the 1960s the term multimedia was used for presentation with multiple slide projectors connected to a control device that would be driven by a sound track with control information, directing which slide to change at a given moment. In the 1980s Apple started to use the term for the then new integration of video and sound into computer presentations. The CD-ROM became the storage and transfer medium of choice and in the early 1990s a wide variety of products with multiple multimedia features became available for different markets. Because of the complexity of the required hardware and software and the lack of a clear objective for the product, few of them were a commercial success.

1. A pioneering product: Beethoven's 9th Symphony

A groundbreaking product was the CD-ROM "Beethoven's 9th Symphony" produced by the Voyager Company in 1988; it defined a new style of educational narrative that was not possible before. The Macintosh computer at that time had a 9-inch black-and-white screen, 1 megabyte of RAM, and could not process music in an adequate form. The author, Robert Winter (at the time chair of the music department at UCLA), was looking for a way to create interactive music appreciation classes. Rather than adding a booklet to the music CD with comments like "now play track 4 from minute 2," Voyager created a set of commands that would allow ***HyperCard***, an early program developed by Apple Computer for hyperlinking text and multimedia content, to exactly control the music CD in a CD-ROM drive to play a piece in time increments down to 1/75th of a second. In an early version the product shipped with an unmodified audio CD and a HyperCard stack on a diskette. The current version integrates the Hypercard stack with the music on one CD.

Now in its second decade, it is still available at http://voyager.learntech.com/ and is a good example of how to use multiple media types to tell a story in a highly effective form with very limited resources.

(iv) ON-LINE MULTIMEDIA

The World Wide Web has enabled Internet access through its graphic user interface (***GUI***) for everybody, and as access speed has become faster over the last few years, multimedia has become an integral part of many sites. Technologies used include animated GIF files, Flash, video, and audio, as well as interactive solutions created both on static Web sites and as fully dynamic database-driven implementations. In fact, the on-line version of this Guide is an example of on-line multimedia.

Both audio and video over the Web are still limited in their quality due to bandwidth and processing power limitations. Streaming technology allows the delivery of large files as well as the continuous streaming of audio or video data that does not accumulate on the user's computer and thus cannot be copied and redistributed.

Electronic publishing solutions can benefit from on-line deployment both in the initial distribution as well as in providing access to video and audio content on demand as needed. Advertisers in a multimedia rich electronic magazine may be interested in providing current video content in exchange for some demographic information. This Guide is continually enriched by new examples added to the on-line version (as well as updates to the text content).

The MSNBC site at http://www.msnbc.com/ is an excellent example of how on-line multimedia can convey a message in much denser form than TV, because it can be directly compared to the live TV channels. The site integrates text, graphics, interactive maps, and videos in multiple bandwidths to cater to different connection speeds.

The difference between MSNBC on TV and MSNBC.com is not only the balance between video, audio, and text but also the ability of the user to actively control the time axis of the presentation and the selection of the content.

(v) MULTIMEDIA IN DIGITAL PUBLISHING TODAY

Electronic books and digital magazines are currently very limited in their ability to include multimedia content. The Adobe eBook Reader and the Microsoft Reader both allow links to external files but do not provide any form of multimedia integration. Night Kitchen with its TK3 product provides complete integration of video and audio but is limited in its ability to integrate with on-line content.

In 2002, several companies [NewsStand (http://www.newsstand.com), Zinio (http://www.zinio.com), Olive Software (http://www.olivesoftware.com), qMags (http://www.qmags.com)] launched solutions to distribute digital replicas of magazines. No full multimedia integration is yet available. Zinio provides a 3-D page-turning animation to enhance the reading experience and hyperlinks to Web sites, and Olive Software allows links to external media files.

As digital publishing gains new interest through the Microsoft Tablet PC effort and more powerful PDAs, electronic publications will expand into the multimedia domain.

(vi) LESS IS MORE: THE POWER OF TEXT

> Alice was beginning to get very tired of sitting by her sister on the bank, and of having nothing to do: once or twice she had peeped into the book her sister was reading, but it had no pictures or conversations in it, "and what is the use of a book," thought Alice "without pictures or conversation?"
>
> —*Lewis Carroll,* Alice's Adventures in Wonderland

The power of the written word lies in the specific way the information is conveyed. Children with limited reading abilities enjoy picture books and augmented books with touch-and-feel elements. The Tenniel illustrations in *Alice's Adventures in Wonderland* represent the perfect balance between providing a visual clue while not undermining the richness of the imagination. Endless attempts have been made to create picture books, playbooks, and multimedia versions of *Alice;* none of them has added much to its magic world.

Multimedia, like desktop publishing, is a powerful tool that needs to be used with a deep understanding of the narrative and the qualities of the different media types. The well-known phenomenon that readers vastly prefer the book to the expensively produced blockbuster movie holds equally true when directly integrating the printed word with video.

A college text on physics with interactive animations or a self-help book with a voice that guides through exercises is vastly superior to "just" the paper version. There is good reason why Kafka did not allow his publisher any depiction of Gregor Samsa and only Nabokov, being a lepidopterist, dared to create a drawing in his literary studies on *The Metamorphosis.*

(vii) RISKS AND THREATS OF MULTIMEDIA

The biggest risk in the implementation of multimedia is falling for a nice bells-and-whistles solution that does not contribute to the overall message of the publication. Often a clear indicator of add-on multimedia that is disconnected from the content is a video or flash animation on a Web site with a button for "skip intro." If the piece introduces relevant information, then why skip? If it does not add to the experience or the information, why have it there in the first place?

Every new medium has a lead-in phase where it is more a technical attraction than a content medium. The time it takes to fully comprehend a new medium varies but can rarely be accelerated by technology. The organizational infrastructures need to be established. As a medium, it took film over 20 years to make the step from a county fair attraction to a respected medium and ultimately an art form.

9.4 MULTIMEDIA EXPERIENCE

> Trying to explain interactive media to someone who has never experienced it is like trying to explain sex to a six year old. You have to experience it before you can truly understand it.
>
> —*Bob Stein*

Whether the author creates a multimedia publication from the ground up or adds multimedia to an existing publication, the ultimate goal has to be to provide a reading experience that is both satisfying to the reader and conveys the intended message. To accomplish this it is necessary that the author has an understanding of the media qualities of the video and audio elements similar to her understanding of the written word and the images she uses in her work. Depending on the type of work, video and audio can be very present, or ***Flash*** animations can become the guiding thread through the work, as long as the mesmerizing qualities of the sound and the moving images are subordinate to the message.

For some projects it may be sufficient to rely on the media experience of the author; for others it will be necessary to hire an experienced crew. In all cases it will be beneficial to provide the editor with access to professional support when managing and reviewing the project. In addition to a typographer, an illustrator, and a book designer, the project may need a sound engineer and a video editor to ensure that the experience is adequate and according to the quality level of the publishing house.

9.5 THE BUSINESS OF MULTIMEDIA

Expanding a publishing house into the domain of multimedia can become a very interesting proposition if the organization is ready to embrace the necessary change that includes a revision of the concept of "publishing." The need to engage experts in a variety of fields, including audio, video, project management, and media rights, changes the identity of the team and will have a lasting impact on all aspects of the company. The organizational philosophy and the inside and outside perception of the publishing house will change with the new line of products.

The publisher in the role of a mediator, as the one to "make public" the message of the author, is to become the central figure in the development of the next medium as multimedia becomes a new medium in itself.

To accomplish this, it will be necessary to develop new business models radically different from the film and TV industry as well as from the paper publishing industry. These changes will be more radical and more influential in our understanding of reading than the technical inventions.

9.6 MULTIMEDIA TECHNOLOGY

At the core of every multimedia product stand the authoring and delivery technologies necessary to create and consume the product. Integrating video and audio into an electronic text has become reasonably easy with new authoring tools. Reading the electronic publication is almost transparent and seamless on new computers. In addition, on-line solutions need server technology that manages the media data in an adequate way for streaming or download.

Here is a brief overview that explains the critical aspects of the different steps. Literature for all steps of the technical and artistic development is widely available; see the bibliography at the end of the chapter for print and on-line resources pertinent to the discussion below.

(i) DELIVERY PLATFORMS

The type of media used depends on the application as well as the delivery system. While books on paper as well as a TV show will be consumed in a relatively well-defined form, a digital publication with multimedia is extremely dependent on the hardware and software used.

If the author/producer has control over the delivery, then many more degrees of freedom are available for the definition of the product than when the limitations are given by the lowest common denominator of a standard ***Windows*** or ***Macintosh*** PC. Screen resolution, sound cards, and processing power vary widely, and it is often hard to predict how a given multimedia product will be perceived by the reader.

The wide variety of hardware and software combinations also requires that the author/producer cater to a range of setups that in turn can limit the creative possibilities. The power and speed of a CPU, as well as the video card used, can significantly change how a multimedia product is experienced. A large screen of 19 inches or above provides a different experience than a 15-inch screen. This difference is not only in size, as experienced with a smaller or larger TV set; the additional screen real estate can be used to show several windows in parallel.

When defining the minimum requirements for a given multimedia publication, the producer has to balance the technical minimum to accomplish the creative and informational needs of the product with the anticipated equipment of the target audience. An electronic publication on advanced 3-D animation targets an audience that most likely has fast machines and big screens. A language-training program for secondary schools that is also used in public libraries will have to restrict itself to a minimum configuration available in those environments.

PDAs and wireless phones are fast becoming delivery platforms for multimedia-enhanced publications and increasingly provide the necessary software to integrate video into text. ***TabletPC***s with touch-screen interaction are based on proprietary operating systems or Windows XP with TabletPC extensions and create a different user experience than standard PCs.

Electronic publications in a well-defined environment or for a closed target audience can be built for specific hardware and software environments. Professional or training applications can take full advantage of their hardware and software environment, with dedicated input and output devices and the usage setting. Adaptability to a wide variety of hardware and software platforms may be an advantage in the consumer market but can severely limit the functionality of a solution.

(ii) MULTIMEDIA TYPES

Media types considered for multimedia can be categorized by their data channel or by their way of interaction. Our senses define possible data channels where visual and acoustic information are the primary sources for directed information. Modern PCs provide the necessary hardware for audio and video output. Audio input is often supported and video input is available on higher-end machines with ***Firewire*** connection.

You can accomplish 3-D imaging either through mapping images into panoramas and ***QTVR*** movies, which can be navigated by the user, or as stereoscopic images that require the user to wear a device for image channel separation. The latter can be accomplished through glasses with polarizing or colored lenses or a wearable monitor setup with two small monitors. Tracking devices that can be handheld or mounted on the body provide 3-D navigation. While mostly used in virtual reality environments, 3-D tracking devices are very useful when navigating topological information.

Video and audio are the two media types most often used in the extension of digital publications, but tactile or olfactory extensions are equally possible. Tactile multimedia can serve artistic purposes, provide added experiences in a game environment, or provide an input/output channel for physically challenged users (e.g., by making it possible to "feel" when the mouse reaches the edge of a window or a button by feeding back increased resistance to the mouse). Spatial tracers can be used for positioning in a 3-D space in stereoscopic and virtual environment solutions.

(iii) MEDIA FORMATS

Digital audio and video come in a wide variety of formats, some developed for a specific purpose, many evolving from each other over time. Video and audio information needs to be compressed to be transmitted effectively, and most compression methods lead to a loss in quality. To effectively decide on the most appropriate format, it is necessary to evaluate the delivery chain and the limitations imposed by the available source material and the project resources.

Check for:

- Quality and type of original material available
- Processing steps affecting the quality
- Will the material be used sequentially or with random access?
- How many platforms need to be supported, and what are they?

- Quality required at final consumption (e.g., video resolution, video frame rate, sound quality, stereo?)

Video and audio can be kept locally (downloaded or delivered with the e-book) or streamed from a server. The decision depends on the availability of an on-line connection. Table 1 compares these approaches.

The requirement of an on-line connection can be used for a multitude of additional multimedia purposes. In addition to being a powerful content protection, material can be updated in a timely fashion. In an interactive training course, the system can add the most recent video clips or data for an interactive presentation. The obvious disadvantage of any on-line connection or "tethered" solution is the need to provide network access.

1. Video formats

Currently almost 100 different video formats are in use in some form. Every format has certain advantages and should be used for a specific purpose. For most applications, three technologies will have to be considered: ***QuickTime*** (QT), ***Real Media,*** and ***Microsoft Media Technology***. QuickTime supports the widest range of video encoding and file formats and is a very good choice for standalone solutions, e-books, kiosks, and presentation environments. It seamlessly integrates into the context and can be used with or without control interface. Real Media focuses exclusively on the delivery of video and audio media across the Internet or Intranet. It can work with or without a dedicated media server. Windows Media is Microsoft's solution and is tightly integrated into the Windows environment. Both Real and Microsoft Media are well suited to deliver streaming media, with Real aiming at becoming a content provider too. Which solution to choose depends more on the specifics of the product and how the different server solutions can support it than on the player front end. All three are available on Windows and Macintosh environments and support a multitude of video formats. For products that require a very wide acceptance, it may be beneficial to offer material in multiple formats to reduce the need to install a specific player.

2. Integration of video

Video occupies the same physical space as the printed word and still images and thus needs to be balanced in the layout of the page. Depending on the content and context of the page, video can be displayed within the page or in a separate window floating above the page. Whenever the surrounding text needs to be reviewed while the video is running, direct embedding is preferred. Showing the video in a separate frame relieves some space limitations as the window can cover parts of the text. A floating window can also take

TABLE 1. STREAMING VS. STORING MEDIA

Real-time streaming	Video/audio content streamed in real time from server. Bandwidth matched with viewer's connection. Best for continuous streaming, e.g., news, movies.	Needs Internet connection to view	Can be updated continuously	Effective copy protection
Progressive streaming/ progressive download	Media can be watched while being downloaded as soon as buffer is full. No special server or protocol needed. Good for short movies.	Hard-drive (HD) resident (downloaded)	Dynamic, needs new download	Needs digital rights management (DRM) for protection
Downloaded	File needs to be downloaded before it can be viewed.	HD resident (downloaded)	Static	Needs DRM for protection

advantage of a bigger monitor and run visually outside the electronic publication. The reference in the publication can be a hyperlink in text or symbolic form, a key frame of the video in the size of the video to be shown, or a smaller key frame that opens the video in a separate window.

Depending on the importance of the video content and the intended effect, full-screen video is becoming a very attractive solution. Faster hardware and better video compression make it possible to show video full screen on a computer monitor. This changes the paradigm from PC to TV and creates a new dimension in multimedia.

DVD is a very good video source with which to integrate full-screen or near full-screen video into an electronic publication. The control of the video can easily be accomplished through simple commands and does not require complex authoring. Especially when integrating video material into an existing text, creating a DVD that is used in parallel to a text opens multiple channels of delivery, since the DVD can also be used on a TV set with a paper version of the text. Currently there is no simple way to provide digital text on a laptop and control a video that runs on a TV set. Such two-screen solutions were common in the days of early PCs connected to Laserdisc players but are currently rarely used. PDAs that can communicate with a TV set via infrared or ***Bluetooth*** may open new opportunities for advanced platforms.

3. Audio formats

Audio has significantly different qualities than video. First and foremost, it does not compete with the printed word in the visual real estate. Audio can be triggered by hyperlinks in textual or symbolic form or by an interaction like page turning or zoom. Because the sound channel of PCs is often turned off, it is necessary to alert the user that audio information is available.

The best-known format today for music is ***MP3***, a part of the MPEG-1 standard developed by the ***ISO***. As with other ***lossy*** compression algorithms, MP3 reduces the amount of information available and thus the quality of the reproduction. The file's size is in direct proportion to the music quality: bigger files with higher sampling rates deliver better music. Within a reproduction environment of a PC or a portable MP3 player, this quality difference from an audio CD is negligible compared to the gain in space and flexibility. MP3 is widely used to digitize (***rip***) music from all sources and play it on small portable MP3 players as well as on MP3 software on a PC. Windows Media, Real Player, and QuickTime provide audio only along with video. Newer algorithms, like the proprietary Microsoft compression inside of Media Player 9, promise both smaller files and better quality music. The Real Media technology is most widely used for streaming on-line distribution of music and the differences from its competitors lie on the production side rather than the player. Real also positions itself as a media distributor similar to a cable operator. These differences come into play when setting up larger-scale streaming media servers.

With the wide acceptance of MP3 as a music distribution format and the availability of software to easily convert any audio source into MP3, rights protection has become a major concern of the music industry.

4. Media players

Most audio and video formats require specific player software. Here are some options and sources. This list of software is neither representative nor comprehensive and is not an endorsement of any certain product.

1. WINDOWS MEDIA

- Mac and Win: Windows Media Player http://www.microsoft.com/windows/windowsmedia/download/

2. REAL AUDIO/VIDEO

- Mac and Win: Real One Player http://www.real.com

3. QUICKTIME

- Mac and Win: QuickTime http://www.apple.com/quicktime

4. MP3

- Windows: Musicmatch http://www.musicmatch.com/
- Macintosh: iTunes under OS X http://www.apple.com/itunes/download/index.html

All players are free and offer upgraded or premium features for a fee but none of these are required for playback in an e-book environment.

Nielsen/NetRatings evaluated media player distribution and found that in August 2001, RealNetwork was first in media format use at work (28.8 million people) and at home (15.5 million). Windows Media had 13 million consumers at home and 8.8 million at work, and QuickTime had 8.2 million consumers at home and 5.3 million at work (News.com 2001).

(iv) AUTHORING TOOLS AND THEIR MULTIMEDIA CAPABILITIES

Multimedia integration into textual documents is dependent on the electronic publishing software used. Considering the objective of the project and the balance between text and multimedia, the producer needs to decide between the integration of multimedia elements in an electronic publication and the creation of an interactive solution that integrates text.

Flash is often the environment of choice for on-line solutions, and Macromedia Director is the development platform for complex applications that require a high degree of programming. There are few alternatives to Director: iShell from Tribeworks (http://www.tribeworks.com) provides similar functionality and has an easier learning curve but is limited in its features. Microsoft Powerpoint can be used for very simple presentations and can include audio and video. While Apple's Hypercard is still available, though no longer up-to-date, Revolution, a Scottish Company (http://www.runrev.com), has released a product with the same name that inherited from Hypercard the concept of organizing information similar to a card stack Adobe's LiveMotion 2.0 is a very powerful authoring environment for Flash animations and Adobe positions it as a complement to Flash. (Both Flash and Director are discussed **below** [9.6.6.1].) Adobe Atmosphere is a professional development environment for 3-D worlds on the Web. It allows the creation of realistic, immersive environments with a new approach to interaction and information representation and management. The development of complex multimedia solutions, which requires a script similar to a video production, is beyond the scope of this chapter. Selected literature concerning interactive multimedia production can be found in the bibliography.

(v) MULTIMEDIA IN E-BOOKS

The two major e-book software products, the Adobe eBook Reader and the Microsoft Reader, have extremely limited multimedia support. Both offer hyperlink capabilities to Web sites in Internet Explorer. Multimedia content can then be used in the browser window. Adobe Acrobat also has hyperlink capabilities and audio files can be embedded into the Acrobat file. QuickTime and other video files need to be linked and provided as separate files. Due to the extendibility of Acrobat, it is possible to write code to make a browser window appear on a page to make it look quasi embedded. The only e-book software with full multimedia integration is Night Kitchen's TK3 (http://www.nightkitchen.com). TK3 (for Toolkit #3) is based on the original Expanded Books Project at the Voyager Company, 1990–1991 (the author of this chapter co-invented the Expanded Books together with Bob Stein). While not widely distributed, TK3 offers the author and editor extensive control over the integration of multimedia content. TK3 has very limited Web integration and uses a proprietary file format.

(vi) MULTIMEDIA AUTHORING SOFTWARE

A wide variety of software is available for authoring of audio and video data. The technology used will depend on the input format, the quality required, and the form of delivery. Most products support a wide variety of formats but never all formats. QuickTime currently supports over twenty-four video and thirteen audio formats (http://www.apple.com/quicktime/products/qt/specifications.html) and is a good choice if you want to support only one type of player.

Audio and video authoring will require additional hardware and software. After you set the level of quality and professionalism for your product, the necessary process can be implemented and executed. Audio may need Musical Instrument Digital Interface (***MIDI***, a protocol designed to control musical instruments rather than transmitting sound information) interfaces, professional studio and mixing equipment, and high-end microphones or can be sufficiently produced with good audio sources on your PC.

As for video, the quality needs to be driven by the expected result and all elements of the production chain should be on a similar level.

1. Macromedia Flash and Director Shockwave

Flash and ***Director*** are proprietary technologies developed by Macromedia (http://www.macromedia.com) for on-line and off-line animation and interactive application development.

Flash is especially useful for small multimedia extensions of written text. It provides a self-contained solution that can be created and maintained in an easy way. The newest version, Flash FX, can also include streamed audio and video. Director together with the Shockwave player provide many more possibilities but require knowledge of the ***Lingo*** programming language (a programming language specifically developed for multimedia authoring in Director) and are more suited for complex solutions.

Flash allows the integration of audio data in MP3 format both from local files and streaming. Short videos of up to two minutes can be integrated as well. The video ***CODEC*** (the encoding and decoding software used for digital audio and video) used creates very small video files, and together with the vector-based animation used by Flash, the multimedia additions to your publication are very small.

Typical applications can be advertising in a periodical environment where a full video would be too expensive or too complex to produce. Whenever video footage or sound need to be integrated beyond just being played in a linear fashion, Flash comes in very handy as an interactive environment. The Flash player is required but can be downloaded for free. You can distribute the Flash player on line or on CD-ROM with your publication but you need to agree to the Macromedia licensing agreement, which can be found on their Web site.

If you have Flash or Shockwave files available, you can in most cases integrate them with a reference to an outside object. Depending on the digital publishing environment and additional programming, you can either play the Flash or Shockwave content in a separate window or directly integrate it into the page.

Fully interactive magazines—where text is subordinate to animation, video, and sound—are best developed in Macromedia Director, the de facto standard for multimedia development. It is a complex authoring tool specifically for the development of interactive multimedia and includes 2-D and 3-D animation as well as the ability to stream media in Real Media or QuickTime. Its Lingo programming language manages the different media elements and the interaction on a timeline that shows all "actors" at a given state. Such developments are at the crossroads of publishing and interactive multimedia development and require extensive interactive media, video, audio, and programming expertise. One of the inherent complexities of electronic publishing is the blurred line between text-driven e-books and interactive solutions.

(vii) INTEGRATION AND USER CONTROL

Integrating multiple media types requires a clear user interaction and a well-defined set of controls. The multimedia controls can be implicit, explicit as part of the product interface, or explicit as part of the text document. The decision on how to best implement the control elements will depend on the content, the target audience, and the objective of the publication. Control elements in the user interaction area of the program keep the text free of clutter and unchanged (in the case of legacy documents). A major disadvantage is that the control of more than one element on a screen leads to confusion. The use of an e-book engine significantly limits the use of custom control elements. Adobe Acrobat enables the use of extensions; the Adobe eBook Reader and the Microsoft Reader have no way to add control features to the interface.

Controls for audio and video elements directly on a page can consume significant space and create an overloaded look, but this has the advantage that the user can clearly see where she can find audio and video elements and how to control them.

Implicit control is accomplished by marking text or images as being "hot" and clickable. This requires the user to explore the area, but with a clear markup this should be easy to accomplish. In many cases, a combined approach using a small icon to indicate a move, an animation, or an audio piece that then triggers the start of the piece and the display of a control area is best. Page turning, answering questions in a textbook, or other interactions can also be used to trigger a multimedia piece. In children's books, the multimedia pieces are often hidden and left for the young reader to explore.

In addition to a static user control, multimedia content can also be offered in a random or event-triggered form. A multimedia marketing documentation for a sailboat can show different video clips randomly and a training manual for a lawn mower can show the same text with a different animation of how to service the blade depending on the specific model selected.

Audio and video may be offered in multiple sizes and qualities. This can be of interest to accommodate different hardware environments or different reading situations where some reading situations demand an integrated video or a full-screen video but where others could not handle these features.

1. Control conventions

The control of time-based media is in most cases modeled after the layout of the buttons on a VCR. While this is not the best way to control digital content, it has become a de facto standard. In addition to the arrow-shaped control buttons, a "shuttle control" that shows a pointer on a time axis allows random access to the content and gives the user a sense of location in the piece.

(viii) HYPERLINKS AND NONLINEAR TEXTS

Electronic texts have an inherently different form of linearity than paper-based texts. A conventional book can be flipped through much faster than an electronic version and you have a better sense of the spatial distribution of the content. Random access is much better in an electronic book where search and browse functions can provide access to information no paper book can offer with a conventional index.

Hyperlinks connect different parts of the text as well as multimedia elements. General aspects of **hyperlinking and hypertext** [4.5] are discussed in the Organizing, Editing, and Linking Content chapter. Multimedia elements can be linked with hyperlinks to play within the publication, in a separate window that automatically opens up, or in a separate application.

(ix) STANDARDIZATION

Multimedia publications depend on a wide variety of standards in the audio and video area. The Moving Pictures Expert Group (***MPEG***) has established a series of standards for compressed digital video and audio, which has become the foundation for many media formats used today. Table 2 outlines several of these standards. In addition, companies have developed proprietary formats for which they claim better compression and better sound and image quality.

With 10 seconds of NTSC TV using 300 megabytes of disc space, it is obvious that video and audio need to be compressed both to fit on storage media and to be transmitted on line. These compression methods are ***lossy***, meaning that some image and sound information that is not relevant to the presentation is lost in the compression process.

MPEG-1 and its superset MPEG-2 were developed specifically for the purpose of standardizing compression. MP3, which became a household name with the rise and fall of Napster, is part of MPEG-1; it stands for MPEG-1–Layer 3.

Data rates, data formats, and compression methods are the most important parameters, but new standards also address media integration and media metadata. These parameters are of special interest to publishers as they define the way media types are integrated into a publication.

Currently no standards exist for the user interface and the media control. When appropriate, the control button interface for a VCR is used on screen.

MPEG-4 is the successor to MPEG-1 and MPEG-2, technologies behind the MP3 audio explosion. Like its predecessors, MPEG-4 comprises audio and video technologies that condense large digital files into smaller ones that can be easily transferred via the Web.

Both Apple QuickTime and Real Networks endorse MPEG-4, with Microsoft including some MPEG-4 elements into their Media Player. Microsoft is promoting their proprietary format, claiming better quality and higher compression, with files being typically half the size of MPEG-4 at a similar quality level.

Table 2 gives an overview of some of the standards currently used.

The integration of multimedia elements into electronic publications is being defined in MPEG-21. The ***W3C*** has also established an extension to XML, the Synchronized Multimedia Integration Language (***SMIL***, pronounced "smile"). The recommendation for SMIL 2.0 was issued by the W3C in June 2001. Tim Berners-Lee, the founder of the Web and director of the W3C, states that it "enables authors to bring rich content to the Web in a format that is easily written and reused. SMIL 2.0 avoids the limitations of traditional television and lowers the bandwidth requirements for delivering multimedia content over the Internet" (Berners-Lee, 2001).

SMIL 2.0 is an XML application that allows the author to create engaging multimedia experiences for the Web and incorporate a wide range of data (audio, video, or text), which may be locally or remotely stored. With SMIL it is possible for the first time to synchronize multiple media types in a standardized way. This capability is especially valuable for a publisher expanding content with multimedia.

Comprehensive information on XML can be found in the chapter on **markup** [3.3].

TABLE 2. AUDIO AND VIDEO COMPRESSION STANDARDS

MPEG-1	Video CD and MP3—Coding of moving pictures and associated audio for digital storage media at up to about 1.5 megabits per second.
MPEG-2	Digital television set-top boxes, DVD—Generic coding of moving pictures and associated audio information.
MPEG-4	Multimedia for the fixed and mobile Web—Enabling the integration of the production, distribution, and content access paradigms of the three fields.
MPEG-7	Description and search of audio and visual content—"Multimedia Content Description Interface,"—"multimedia content data that supports some degree of interpretation of the information's meaning, which can be passed onto, or accessed by, a device or a computer code." (Martínez, 2002)
MPEG-21	Multimedia Framework (under development since 2000)—"Open framework for multimedia delivery and consumption, with both the content creator and content consumer as focal points. This open framework provides content creators and service providers with equal opportunities in the MPEG-21 enabled open market. This will also be to the benefit of the content consumer providing them access to a large variety of content in an interoperable manner." (Bormans, 2002)

9.7 RIGHTS ISSUES

Whenever you use any material that was not originally created by you for the very publication you are producing, you need to closely look into **copyright** [13.1.3] and **usage rights** [13.1.6] issues. Using multiple media types creates additional issues, because video and audio are managed under other regulations than text. These differences are both dependent on the media format and on the industry.

What could be considered fair use when it comes to quoting from a book may require payment of a license fee when the quote is from a movie. In addition, the movie, TV, and film industries are operating with completely different budgets than a book publisher. The different industries also apply usage rights models that are specific to their needs.

(i) USAGE RIGHTS MODEL

The rights for a text may be limited to a geographic region or a certain edition but are rarely limited by time. Film, on the contrary, employs a usage rights model that includes different types of rights depending on what you use the film for; geographic limitations and rights may expire after a certain period. These limitations may severely impact the multimedia integration of video clips.

When producing a multimedia electronic publication, consider the limitations imposed by different media types. These limitations may be in geography, the life cycle of the product, or the combination of different elements as much as in the technological limitations. In addition, you may find that certain organizations or industry segments have not yet embraced multiple media usage of their content and, with a lack of licensing standards, may not be ready to allow you to use their content.

(ii) INTEGRATION OF MULTIPLE MEDIA MEANS MULTIPLE INDUSTRIES

A film studio not yet ready to provide footage for an e-book may charge you the same rates for a 15-second 240 x 160-pixel clip that they would charge a national TV network (after all, you plan to sell the book everywhere in the United States, don't you?), which may be beyond your budget, especially as you would not be satisfied with a one-time usage limitation.

With these issues at hand you don't want to even think about international licensing or a reprint at a later time.

You will find that music rights may include stipulations as to who can appear close to whom: an e-book, *Conductors of Beethoven's Symphonies in the Late 20th Century,* may prove to be a real challenge for your production manager, as the music industry has strict regulations regarding proximity, so you may find yourself unable to present the *7th Symphony* conducted by Maestro X after the *6th Symphony* conducted by Maestro Y.

(iii) DIGITAL RIGHTS MANAGEMENT

The topic of ***DRM*** is covered extensively in the chapter on **digital rights management** [15]. Multimedia projects are particularly complex in this regard, due to the need to protect different media types and the need to adhere to different regulations. Some issues specific to multimedia are discussed below.

1. EULA — the End-User License Agreement

If your electronic publication contains executable code of a commercial software product, additional rules and limitations apply. Software products typically can only be used once the user has accepted the End-User License Agreement (***EULA***) that limits the usage rights of the end user and the liability of the software supplier. The text of a EULA can easily extend over several pages and significantly impact what the reader of the book can do with the software.

2. Production issues

Multiple media types require an exponentially more complex production process than conventional publications, both on a technical and a content level. The legal implications are equally complex and require close observation to ensure that the multimedia e-book will become a success. When integrating any executable code, ensure that the EULA is accepted. Music and video may require you to display additional copyright notices and warnings regarding the copying of the content.

Even the technologically trivial solution of adding a CD-ROM in the back of a book can quickly become a lending librarian's nightmare; and a password for on-line content within a book makes the management of lending rights even more complicated.

Ensure that the different usage scenarios of the target audience of your publications can be served with the solution you create. This includes the use in libraries, lending, resale, as well as the need to upgrade to newer versions for time-critical material, use in classrooms or under inclement conditions.

In addition, consider implications of the Americans with Disabilities Act (***ADA***), ***Section 508***, and other legislation designed to foster access to people with various disabilities when creating publications that need to be accessible to everybody. Multimedia extensions can make content available to users with disabilities and there may be significant advantages in including Braille-enabled features or text-to-voice in an electronic publication. The chapter on **accessibility** [7] discusses these issues in depth.

9.8 CONCLUSION

Multimedia is clearly the pointer into the future of digital publishing. It shows the potential of a new and exciting form of expression, and as it becomes more and more accepted, multimedia will melt into the new medium, which will go beyond the electronic book and create a new medium for a cultural memory.

I would like to thank Sarah Anastasia, Rebecca and Moishe for their support and contributions and Bob Stein for his inspirations in working with me in multimedia and electronic publishing for the past 14 years.

BIBLIOGRAPHY

Bormans, Jan, and Keith Hill, eds. "MPEG-21 Overview v.4." International Standards Organisation. 2002. http://mpeg/telecomitalialab.com/standards/mpeg-21/mpeg-21.htm

Bringhurst, Robert. *Elements of Typographical Style*. Vancouver: Hartley & Marks, 1992.

Brody, Florian. "Interaction Design: State of the Art and Future Developments." In *Multimedia Graphics: The Best of Global Hyperdesign,* edited by Willem Velthoven and Jorinde Seijdel. Chronicle Books, 1996.

———. "The Medium is the Memory." In *Digital Dialectics: New Essays on New Media,* edited by Peter Lunenfeld. MIT Press, 1999.

Cooper, Alan. *The Inmates are Running the Asylum: Why High Tech Products Drive Us Crazy and How to Restore the Sanity*. Indianapolis: Sams Publishing, 1999.

Gross, Phil, and Michael Gross. *Macromedia Director 8.5 Shockwave Studio for 3D: Training from the Source*. Berkeley: Macromedia Press, 2001.

Laurel, Brenda, ed. *The Art of Human-Computer Interface Design*. Reading, Mass.: Addiosn-Wesley Longman, 1990.

Levy, David M. *Scrolling Forward: Making Sense of Documents in the Digital Age*. New York: Arcade, 1990.

Mariano, Gwendolyn. "Tech giants push MPEG-4 standard." CNET News.com. October 4, 2001. http://news.com.com/2100-1023-273966.htm

Martínez, José M., ed. "MPEG-7 Overview (version 8)." International Organisation for Standardisation. 2002. http://mpeg.telecomitalialab.com/standards/mpeg-7/mpeg-7.htm

Packer, Randall, and Ken Jordan. *Multimedia: From Wagner to Virtual Reality*. New York: W.W. Norton, 2001. http://www.artmuseum.net/w2vr/

Pine, B. Joseph II, and James H. Gillmore. *The Experience Economy: Work is Theatre and Every Business a Stage*. Boston: Harvard Business School Press, 1999.

Powell, Thomas A. *Web Design: The Complete Reference*. Berkeley: McGraw-Hill Osborne, 2000.

Reinhardt, Robert, and Snow Dowd. *Flash MX Bible*. Indianapolis: John Wiley & Sons, 2002.

Rosenzweig, Gary. *Special Edition Using Macromedia Director 8.5*. Indianapolis: Que, 2001.

Vaughan, Tay. *Multimedia: Making It Work, 5th Edition*. McGraw-Hill Osborne Media, 2001.

Watrall, Ethan, and Norbert Herber. *Flash MX Savvy*. Alemeda: Sybex, 2002.

World Wide Web Consortium (W3C). "Synchronized Multimedia Integration Language (SMIL 2.0)." August 2001. http://www.w3.org/TR/smil20/

———. "World Wide Web Consortium Issues SMIL 2.0 as a W3C Recommendation." August 2001. http://www.w3.org/2001/08/smil2-pressrelease

10 Content Management & Web Publishing

BILL TRIPPE
President, New Millennium Publishing

MARK WALTER
Consultant, Seybold Consulting Group

This chapter tackles two subjects—the process of publishing on the Web, and the technology called *content management* that has emerged to address Web publishing. Publishers who have moved to the Web have found it brings all the challenges of print publishing—and some new challenges that are unique to the Web. Content management technology has grown to meet these challenges, but has also brought with it technical complexity that is new for some publishers. This chapter outlines the technical issues regarding content management, and gives the readers a framework for understanding how content management technology can help their publishing processes.

10.1 INTRODUCTION TO CONTENT MANAGEMENT

Most publishers' Web sites today have moved far beyond the simple presentation of static pages with marketing information—the so-called *brochureware* of the early Web. They are complex and ever-changing collections of information and images that serve a variety of purposes. They aren't used just for marketing publications (though that's a key function); they've become integral to how those publications are actually sold and delivered, and in an increasing number of cases how they are created as well. They need to integrate with publishers' internal systems (systems for managing subscriptions, for example) and relate to those of suppliers and customers as well (perhaps sending a customer for a book to Amazon.com, if the publisher chooses not to sell directly). A variety of people create or modify them. The result is an ever-increasing amount of interrelated content that needs to be kept up to date. It can't just be maintained; it needs to be *managed.*

(i) WHAT IS CONTENT MANAGEMENT?

It seems that everyone knows what content management is and yet nobody knows what it does. Content Management Systems (***CMS***s) have been sought by Web site managers as a "holy grail" solution to all their problems. But here's the catch: you already do content management. A CMS is merely a tool that you implement to support your internal workflow process that results in publishing a Web site or application.

Content management should be looked at as a process rather than a solution to Web publishing problems. CMSs should be selected on the basis of their compatibility with your organization's workflow. Pull out your project plans, lists of roles, procedures, and schedules before you even start looking at technology. Once you have established a clear idea of workflow, you need to begin analyzing what you want from a CMS, determine how that will dovetail with your workflow processes, and identify the type(s) of technology that your organization can support.

At the most basic level, manual creation and updating of pages on a Web site is a content management system. This works best when the number of contributors, changes, and visitors is small. The basic tasks of publishing content to the Web (formatting content, designing layout, making updates) increase exponentially as you add contributors. As a Web site grows, an increasing number of the contributors are not technical enough to edit an HTML page, and yet those with the technical expertise are still expected to live up to the high standards of instantaneous response and on-the-fly updates.

(ii) WHY CONTENT MANAGEMENT SYSTEMS ARE NEEDED

Prior to the advent of Web-based publishing, readers knew what to expect from each medium—the radio or television, versus the daily newspaper, for example, versus a news magazine, versus a book on the same subject. The radio and television could provide breaking, though often abbreviated, news; the same story in the daily newspaper would have aged since the evening before, but would likely have more depth and perspective on the event. The story in the weekly news magazine would have aged even more, but would compensate for this by going into even greater depth, and offering even more perspective. And the book, of course, would be the most considered, detailed treatment of the subject, going so far as to cite, by reference, primary sources such as government reports and secondary sources such as other books and articles on the subject—though it couldn't be expected to be as current.

The Web has changed all that. Depending on your topic of interest, you are likely to find everything from breaking news to multimedia to primary sources to book excerpts to whole books in electronic format. (You may also find all kinds of misinformation, amateurish treatment of material, and propaganda from all corners of the political spectrum.) You will also likely find duplicated material and out of date material, and a bewildering array of primary, secondary, and tertiary sources, compilations, recompilations, links, and clearinghouses. It's not merely a Tower of Babel, it is a vast metropolis of Towers of Babel—some still standing, some merely apparitions of a tower that once stood.

Pity the publisher who wants to make sense of all this, to bring order into this chaos. Publishers are faced with at least two forces that will only deepen this problem. First, the Web has not just *raised* the expectations of readers and consumers of media; it has created a whole *new set* of expectations that—simply by virtue of being on the Web—information will be continuously updated, comprehensive, and richly linked to all related information and ideas. Publishers of any kind of information on the Web need to make several first-order decisions of how much material they are publishing, how frequently it will be updated, and how integrated or linked their material will be with other materials on the Web.

Second, the Web has created an opportunity for a kind of *instantaneous publishing and syndication,* where new material is somehow available everywhere at once. Even in a relatively small Web site, many materials are interlinked. The home page for a publication links to articles inside. In turn, these articles have headlines and teasers that may appear on the home page, on a news summary page, and elsewhere on the Web site. These same headlines and teasers may then be syndicated out to other, related Web sites and over e-mail to remote readers. On a larger scale, of course—news services, financial reporting services—such syndication is happening on a grand scale. The result is a need for automatic publishing where content and links are delivered, updated, and maintained in several places at once.

These two forces—reader expectations and instantaneous updates and access—have combined to complicate the process of publishing on the Web for all but the smallest of publications or organizations. In response to these forces, publishers of all types have turned to content management technology. For larger enterprises, with multiple contributors and larger volumes of content, the need for technology is even greater.

1. Increasing complexity while maintaining consistency

Organizations that have done any publishing on the Web, even on the smallest scale, know the devil is in the details. This is true of all publishing of course; quality comes from careful attention to detail at every stage—research, writing, editing, page production, art research and rendering—all the way through distribution. Quality publishing on the Web means all of these things, and then dealing with the unique variables of the Web as a presentation medium. These include:

1. LACK OF CONTROL OVER PRECISE RENDERING

Publishers of printed materials have a high degree of control over the precise look of final pages. Review and quality control are maintained often right through to the point of printing and binding. The Web presents a fundamentally different process, where content is, in effect, often broadcast in raw form, and pages are rendered on different computers using different operating systems and different rendering software. This is particularly true of HTML pages; even when stylesheet languages such as **Cascading Style Sheets** [3.2.4.1] (***CSS***) are employed, the rendering computer may swap in different fonts, and the size and settings of the computer monitor may result in a different layout and even different colors being used. More recently, smaller, handheld devices such as personal digital assistants (PDAs) have become popular tools for connecting to the Internet. As a result, publishers who feel there is a reading audience using these devices (especially publishers who may want users to "look up" information on their site, even if extended reading of their publications isn't a prospect) need to deliver a modified version of their content appropriate for the smaller, less powerful devices.

2. LINKING

By its very nature, content on the Web is linked. These links need to be created and maintained. Even on a relatively small Web site, links expire and need to be updated.

3. A DIFFERENT READING EXPERIENCE

Publishers of print materials serve an audience with, by and large, well-understood and predictable reading habits. College textbooks, for example, are typically read in logical units such as chapters, and conscientious students highlight relevant sections and make marginal notes. On the Web, reading is not yet as well understood and predictable, so publishers are faced with accommodating many modes. Some users may want to print materials out for reading, in which case a publisher may want to make this both possible and straightforward. At the same time, other users may want to read the material on the screen, in which case a publisher will need to pay attention to how the material is organized into logical units that also can be read comfortably on the screen.

4. NAVIGATION

Print materials have implicit and explicit navigational features. These include the physical features of the printed piece itself, such as the number and dimensions of pages. Readers are directed by the logical ordering and organization of materials (into chapters, sections, and subsections), and by the detailed typographical features that support the organization—headings, page numbers, and the like. In print materials, experienced readers typically know how to utilize finding aids such as indexes and tables of contents. Web publishers have had to adopt the navigational features of print that work on the Web, and then develop some additional ones. Thus, some Web publishers rely on fairly traditional page layout, front-to-back navigation of longer materials broken into pages, and tables of contents. Early on, Web publishers enhanced navigation with more sophisticated tables of contents that expand to reveal deeper levels of structure, and automatic linking from the table of contents to individual pages. Because of the bulk of material on the overall Web, and even on individual Web sites, Web publishers and users have come to rely heavily on search engines. These search engines try, with varying success, to direct readers to the materials they are interested in. Typically, Web sites will employ a mix of these navigational features in recognition of the needs and habits of different readers as well as the inherent limitations of some of the features.

5. PERSONALIZATION

Web publishers have attempted, so far with very limited success, to *personalize* Web materials to the needs of their readers. There are two kinds of personalization. *Explicit personalization* is where the Web site publisher explicitly asks a reader to state preferences and interests, and then tries to shape the presentation of the material to the reader. The site http://my.yahoo.com is a popular example of explicit personalization. A user can log in to my.yahoo.com and personalize the home page to show, from among other things, news headlines, sport headlines, and local weather, as well as special interest topics in health, personal finance, and shopping. *Implicit personalization* is where the Web site publisher tries to determine the reader's interests based on past actions—such as pages visited, searches undertaken, and perhaps even purchases made. The site http://www.amazon.com is a good example of implicit personalization. While www.amazon.com does, in fact, use certain explicit aspects of personalization—a log in prior to making purchases, for example—it is also continuously personalizing each page based on books and other products you have purchased, browsed, or searched on.

6. INFORMATION ARCHITECTURE

The term ***information architecture*** has emerged to describe the intellectual and creative disciplines behind making on-line material more useful and readable. It encompasses many of the Web-specific issues we have listed so far—linking, navigation, personalization—along with more traditional disciplines such as graphic design, indexing, and editing.

7. INTERACTIVITY

Because of the computational power behind Web sites, users have come to expect elements of feedback and interactivity to go along with the content they are consuming. That is, contemporary Web readers assume *they can do something* in response to the material they are reading. This includes relatively simple and obvious features, such as, "mail this article to a friend," but it extends to include features such as message boards where readers can comment on the material and interact with other readers, polls where people can record their opinion on a topic, and related tools such as newsletters and e-mail alerts, where breaking and relevant news is delivered to the reader's in box.

8. OTHER MEDIA

The Web is increasingly a platform for multiple media presentation, especially as more homes and businesses are wired with *broadband* connections to the Web. As a result, snippets of audio, video, and animation are fairly common on the Web, some smaller Web sites are tailored to consumers with broadband connections (e.g., music sites and a video news clip site such as http://www.thefeedroom.com), and some sites offer "broadband" versions of the site that include more multimedia elements. The sports site http://www.espn.com is a good example of this; the broadband edition features numerous audio clips and video replays from recent games.

9. COBRANDING AND SYNDICATION

As part of the *instantaneous publishing and syndication* problem described above, where materials can appear simultaneously in more than one setting, the Web has created a low-cost and relatively automatic channel for publishers to syndicate their content. Prior to the Web, syndication was largely the province of large, dedicated organizations such as United Press International. With the low-cost communication provided by the Internet, and the low-cost publishing available through HTML, publishers of any size and scale can syndicate via the Web. There are some practical challenges to syndication via the Web; one of them is the practice of *cobranding*. Cobranding is something of a catch-all term used to describe the various relationships two companies may enter into as a means to share content. For example, a newsletter publisher of specialized investing information—let's call them Smithfield Press—may syndicate their content to several sites. Site A may publish the content and prominently brand the content as coming from Smithfield Press, but Site B, by prior arrangement with Smithfield, doesn't prominently brand the content, instead including it in its Web pages with a small, unobtrusive link to the Smithfield Press site. Cobranding assumes these kinds of relationships and many more, putting the publisher in the position of potentially having to create its content so that it can easily—ideally automatically—be syndicated and cobranded in a variety of ways.

All of these issues combine to make the process of Web publishing more complex, and increase the need for automation, especially on larger sites. When these issues of publishing complexity are combined with issues of volume and scale, the result is a challenging mix of editorial, production, design, and technical issues that has ushered in the new software industry of content management.

2. Volume of content and contributors

The Pope is Catholic, and the Web has a lot of pages. One measure of the size of the Web is to look at how many pages are being searched by http://www.google.com, certainly among the most popular search engines on the Web. At the time this chapter was written, Google claimed to be searching almost 2.5 *trillion* pages. The Web search engine CompletePlanet (http://www.completeplanet.com) estimates that the largest Web sites include the National Climatic Data Center, with over 41 billion Web pages, and NASA's Earth Observing System Data Gateway, with over 25 billion pages. Among commercial publishers and clearinghouses of published information, CompletePlanet estimates that LexisNexis has over 2.6 billion pages available over the Web, Westlaw over 500 million pages, and Dun and Bradstreet over 75 million pages.

These are the largest of course, but it is not unusual for a commercial Web site, or the site for a large organization, to number in the tens of thousands of pages. As organizations put more and more routine correspondence and documentation on the Internet, individual sites are growing exponentially. Moreover, there is little or no reason to remove content unless it is out of date or duplicative, so the amount of historical and archival information is growing.

Given this growth of content, Web publishers face important practical questions. How can all this content be efficiently kept up to date? In the best situation, how can the content be improved on, and expanded, over time? The answer to these questions is not, "A page at a time," but through systematic processes and the use of content management technology that allows updates and edits to be made in a central location and propagated across all of the pages. Think of the corporation that redesigns its corporate logo, and in the process needs to stop using and instead reprint all of its letterhead, envelopes, and other literature. A similar process needs to happen on a Web site, and ideally, this happens in a more centralized, rational way. Instead of seeking out and changing the logo in the thousands of pages it appears on, wouldn't it make much more sense to change it in one place, or a few places, and then "publish" that change all over the Web site? This is a simple example of what content management technology and systematic processes can do to help automate Web publishing.

In addition to the volume of content, the number of contributors to a Web site also drives the requirements for automation. As more users contribute to a site, their editorial changes and new contributions must be collected, (often) reviewed, and then published. Such a process assumes either highly detailed workflow, or the contributions of specialized editorial, design, production, and technical personnel, or both—or the systematic use of technology and processes that will make such processes automatic and routine. Content management technology fills this need by using tools such as forms-style interfaces that capture content in a structured format so that it can then be managed in formats such as relational databases and Extensible Markup Language (XML). It also can be used to route content through a review process, and give the reviewer the ability to automatically publish the updated or new content to the live Web site, or reroute it back to the author for more changes, and so on.

Just as the volume of content on the Web is growing, the number of people contributing to Web sites is also growing. This is true in commercial publishing applications and also in businesses, educational institutions, and other organizations where documentation, product information, and other materials are managed on the Web. The early days of the Web were characterized by a single, skilled user—the Webmaster—ultimately being responsible for the alchemy that got all content into HTML. However, more recent Web publishing conventions have pushed the creation and maintenance of content back onto the individual contributor—the writer and editor in commercial publishing situations, and the subject matter expert, often referred to as the business user or the knowledge worker, in organizational settings. As a result, content management technology increasingly emphasizes ease of use, and the latest products give these users familiar tools to interact with—allowing them, for example, to use the same word processor they use in their daily work when they are also interacting with the CMS.

3. Static vs. dynamic pages

As we have mentioned, the publisher of a Web site needs to make many first-order decisions about the kind of Web site being created. This includes things like scope of content and depth, as well as how often material will be updated. In terms of the way the site is managed, publishers also need to consider whether the HTML pages themselves will be *static* or *dynamic*. ***Static Web pages*** can be thought of as residing *whole cloth* on the Web site, with each reader, in effect, viewing the same copy of the same material. ***Dynamic Web pages*** are more accurately called *dynamically served Web pages,* where the elements of the page are stored in systems such as relational databases, and the software collects, organizes, and publishes the pages on the fly.

1. CGI, ASP, AND JSP

Early Web sites relied on a heavy-handed process known as ***CGI*** programming to generate dynamic Web pages. CGI stands for Common Gateway Interface, which was one of the first mechanisms that programmers used to generate content and run programs through Web pages. For example, early popular CGI programs would do things like print the current date and time when the page was generated, create a form for users to enter information, and display a counter of how many people had visited a certain page.

CGI programs were written—and are written and still used—to do much more complicated things with Web pages, but CGI programming proved to have inherent limitations, especially as traffic on the Internet grew. Each time a CGI program was run, it would create a new process on the server; for a high-traffic Web site, this would result in very inefficient processing. As a result, CGI programming has lost ground to mechanisms such as ***Active Server Pages*** (ASP) from Microsoft and ***Java Server Pages*** (JSP) from Sun. Both ASP and JSP are more efficient and, for the most part, easier to create, and allow developers to freely mix HTML, scripts, and other programs that could perform discrete, specialized functions, such as querying a database and displaying the results.

2. STATIC OR DYNAMIC? BOTH

In the early days of the Web, the question of static vs. dynamic was thought of in black and white terms, but the reality of contemporary Web sites is more complex. Indeed, pages are often a mix of both static and dynamic elements. A financial Web site, for example, might have a static page—an archived news story in a page layout—together with a piece of code that collects and displays the current stock quote for the companies mentioned in the article. Many sites generate their Web pages dynamically to a location on the Web server, where they then reside as "static" pages, ready to be served to readers. Overall, Web pages are composed of many elements, and the distinction between static and dynamic is less obvious.

Still, "content management" as a term and a technology has its roots in the very question of page serving. The first commercial CMSs boasted dynamic page serving as a key feature, and many second-generation Web sites were built on the basis of dynamic serving of pages directly from a CMS. More recently, other technologies have taken on the tasks associated with page serving, leaving content management technology more focused on the creation, maintenance, and enhancement of content through its life cycle.

3. THE THREE PHASES OF CONTENT MANAGEMENT

A distinction, then, between the three phases of content management is useful. Content is first created or captured, then managed, and finally distributed or delivered. Portal software and application servers now often handle *delivery* tasks in larger sites. ***Portal software*** has many definitions, but can accurately be thought of as the software that controls the presentation of content and applications to the end user. Think of http://my.yahoo.com again; it is a portal to the content and applications that a given user wants ready access to—breaking news, weather, popular searches, and chosen applications. ***Application servers*** are the intelligent engines behind the scene that manage the performance and interplay of all these applications running in one environment; an application server can be used, for example, to integrate portal software, content management software, and other key applications.

- At this writing, the portal software market is dominated by vendors such as Plumtree, IBM, and Sun, with many other companies accounting for small percentages of market share.
- The application server market has two clear market leaders with products from IBM (Websphere) and BEA (Weblogic), but Oracle, Sun, Microsoft, and others also offer application server software.

4. PERSONALIZATION

In addition to portals and application servers, content management technology has yielded another area of page serving to a specialized technology, and that is personalization. There are software vendors that offer specialized personalization tools, but recent market pressures have sent them scurrying to have their products appeal to a broader, ***customer relationship management*** (CRM) market; these include Net Perceptions and Edify. Significantly, vendors that produce application servers now include personalization components in their product offerings, and some application server vendors—such as Art Technology Group—try to differentiate themselves by the strength of their personalization tools.

10.2 TYPES OF CONTENT MANAGEMENT SYSTEMS

The term *content management* emerged in the late 1990s with the rise of systems to manage the process of collaborative authoring for large Web sites. These systems stored content objects in a database and managed the authoring and publishing processes associated with producing and maintaining Web sites. Because a Web site is a hypertext corpus, not a single document, and because the objects being managed by these systems were typically pieces of a Web page, not necessarily self-contained documents, vendors of these systems (Vignette, FutureTense, and Interwoven, for example) used "content management" as a way to differentiate themselves from the "document management" systems that preceded them. Where ***document management systems*** manage files that are self-contained documents, ***CMS***s manage files that are pieces of documents, or, in the case of Web CMSs, pieces of Web pages.

By the year 2000, Web content management had become such a popular software category that document management vendors (most notably Documentum and FileNet) added Web-specific capabilities to their products and changed their labels from document management to content management. By 2002, document management, as an industry term and software category, had been largely subsumed by content management, which had spread from its Web roots into other media, most notably print.

During 2002 and 2003, the scope of content management has (and will) spread farther, overlapping and enveloping digital asset management and collaboration systems. Digital asset management (***DAM***) systems, which also rose to prominence during the 1990s, are systems for archiving materials that a publisher considers valuable enough to treat as intellectual assets. For example, the artwork drawn for a book might be re-used in marketing and sales materials, both by the publisher and its distribution partners. By archiving and cataloging the artwork, the publisher is able to retrieve the original piece and save the expense of re-creating the artwork each time it's needed. DAM systems excel at indexing and cataloging media assets—particularly illustrations, photos, audio, and video, none of which were handled especially well by the first generation of Web CMSs. DAM systems feature extensive search tools and sport user interfaces that show thumbnails of assets that meet category or search criteria. However, as the Web content management software market grows more competitive, an increasing number of vendors are adding DAM capabilities, blurring the distinctions between the editorial- and production-oriented content management tools and the asset-centric DAM systems.

Today, the different types of CMSs can be classified along several axes. One axis is the type of media they favor: Web, print, CD-ROM, video, or a combination of media. A second axis is their price and scale—which ranges from Microsoft FrontPage (an $800 departmental software package) at the low end to systems that may cost more than $1 million to buy and install, on the high end. A third axis is the type of publication that the system serves. Newspapers are different from encyclopedias, and some systems are designed specifically with certain publishing genres in mind.

(i) WEB-CENTRIC CONTENT MANAGEMENT SYSTEMS

The most common type of CMS is one that is Web-centric, meaning it was designed specifically to support collaborative publishing of Web sites. Typically, these systems have no notion of printed documents and limited support for arbitrary XML documents, and so do not serve well as repositories for cross-media publishing.

There are dozens of commercial Web CMSs available and even a handful of open-source ones (where the source code is made freely available). The easiest way to categorize them is by the scale of operation they serve.

1. Departmental

Low-end systems—those that typically cost under $10,000—are designed for a single small Web site created by one to a handful of contributors. Two of the more popular systems—Adobe GoLive and Microsoft FrontPage—are sold in the box with the HTML editing tool of the same name.

With a departmental system, expect to find predefined templates designed for specific scenarios. You will have complete freedom in designing the look of your Web pages, but often you'll be limited in how much automation can be accomplished and how much you can customize the look or functionality of the product. Low-end products rarely have configurable workflow-automation modules or metadata schemas; they often are restricted to lower-priced databases (e.g., Microsoft Access) or run-time version of a database. They frequently lack published programming interfaces.

2. Midrange systems

Midrange systems, designed to support a large single site or several departmental sites, typically cost in the range of $20,000 to $100,000 for the software. They are more likely to support a mid-range database (e.g., Microsoft SQL Server); they'll usually have at least one browser-based interface for contributors; and they should allow at least some user-defined metadata fields.

The numbers of features and amount of flexibility varies in this segment. In general, products favor fixed functionality over the "toolkit" approach. Over time, a product may shift up or down from one segment to the next. Microsoft's Content Management System, for example, began as an inexpensive departmental system and gradually evolved to one that competed with much more expensive enterprise-level systems.

3. Enterprise-level CMSs

Today all CMSs that are intended for large organizations contain features specifically tailored to Web publishing. However, systems carrying the "enterprise" mantle in content management emphasize integration with industrial-strength components, especially databases and application servers, many of which might be supplied by other companies. They'll have an application programming interface (***API***) that programmers can use to connect the system with other systems in the organization. Enterprise-level systems must be flexible and easy to configure and integrate, because the intent is for them to serve as a foundation for many unique content management implementations within a single organization. As such, they are evaluated as much for what a developer might be able to make them do, as for what they do out of the box.

Though integration with other systems is important, high-end Web CMSs also offer a large array of their own features. Typically, they'll offer several authoring options, including forms-based templates, HTML editing tools, word processors, and even XML editors. They will allow Web pages to be broken down into components, with each component having its own style and content rules. They'll separate the content from the container style, so that designers can work on page layouts at the same time that writers work on content. Authors and designers will be able to preview their changes before publishing them. They'll feature sophisticated version control with which you can not only track the history of a single content object but also roll back a site to its state when published at a particular point in time. They'll allow you to define your own roles and tasks and set up automated routing and notification based on triggers, such as completion of a task. They'll have built-in full-text and field searching, and often will have tools to help set up and capture metadata. For all of these things there will be a set of functions that are standard with the system but which can be customized, by the vendor, one of its resellers or the customer.

For expensive systems (meaning those that average over $100,000 per installation), feature options may also include digital asset management, syndication, statistical reporting, and personalization. Leading vendors in this category include Documentum, Interwoven, Stellent, and Vignette.

(ii) XML-BASED CONTENT MANAGEMENT SYSTEMS

Several ***CMS*** products were built from the start on the assumption that text documents would be marked up with XML instead of HTML. In contrast with Web-centric and genre-specific systems, the XML-based systems are *not* specific to one medium or genre; their purpose is to support cross-media publishing. These systems (e.g., XyEnterprise Content@, Empolis SigmaLink) are typically employed in reference publishing applications, where there is a deep hierarchy to the element tree and a need to publish the content in multiple media, usually print or CD-ROM as well as on-line. The XML-based systems are characterized by SGML/XML-specific features, such as tools for automatically decomposing long documents into components that are managed as separate objects in the database. The user interface of the CMS presents editorial and production staff with one or more views of these objects in the database; typically a repository view (cabinet/folder structure) and user-definable publication views. The system usually has facilities for building publications, automatically re-assembling component pieces into linear documents for print or converting them into a hypertext corpus for a Web site. These systems also feature integration with leading XML editors and pagination tools.

Although XML-based CMSs are characterized by their knowledge of XML markup and cross-media publishing applications, they have much in common with other types of CMSs. They have library services, integrated search tools, workflow modules, and can manage graphics and other data types as well as text in their databases. They might have options for print production (in the case of XyEnterprise, for example) or knowledge management (Empolis). They tend to be fairly expensive to install ($75,000 to $500,000 or more for many installations), in part because the shift to true XML-based publishing usually requires enlisting the aid of vendors for services such as document analysis, data conversion, integration with authoring tools, and assistance with re-engineering the publishing workflow.

(iii) GENRE-SPECIFIC CONTENT MANAGEMENT SYSTEMS

The term *content management systems* came into vogue in the late 1990s, but systems for collaborative publishing have been around since the 1970s. For example, in the newspaper industry, a dozen or so vendors sell what are commonly called *editorial systems.* They are content management systems designed specifically to meet the needs of a newsroom full of journalists and editors. Similarly, the Quark Publishing System (QPS) is tailor-made to magazines. Systems like these that are tailored to specific publishing genres share much in common with those for Web publishing, including their use of standard database technology to track pieces of content and their status. Where they differ is in their support for the peculiarities of a specific type of publication.

1. Newspaper systems

Newspaper editorial systems are CMSs designed specifically for producing daily newspapers. Because a newspaper has such tight deadlines and layout constraints, newspaper editorial systems are characterized by a tight interface between the editing and layout tools. Typically, the editing tool interacts with the page composition tool in a way that shows writers and editors the exact line breaks that will appear when the article is published. The tools indicate to the author the number of lines that a story is too long or too short (over- and underset), so that editors working within the editing tool can edit articles to precisely fit an assigned layout area on the page. Because these systems hold the page geometry and stories separately in their database, they enable the newsroom staff to work simultaneously on multiple stories that will end up on the same page—an important consideration because the front pages of newspaper sections (almost always containing hand-picked photos and the opening portions of many stories) are usually the last pages in the section to close.

Because there are so many daily newspapers around the globe, and because their needs are quite similar, newspaper editorial systems come in a range of shapes and sizes, from relatively inexpensive, easy-to-install systems for weekly community papers, to expensive, heavily customized solutions delivered to top national or international dailies.

2. Magazine systems

Like newspapers, magazines are driven by their layouts. In fact, most magazines are much more free-form in their layouts than newspapers. Headlines frequently receive special treatment. Art directors work with creative staff to create unique illustrations or typographic effects. As a result, a system aimed at the magazine market must have seamless integration with a page makeup tool that is intuitive enough for designers to understand without sacrificing the control inherent in professional products. For the past 10 years, the most successful magazine system has been the Quark Publishing System (QPS), which is tightly integrated with XPress, the popular page makeup program also developed and sold by Quark. As a rule, magazines have less need for automation than newspapers (because of their longer lead times, less news to copy-fit on deadline), and they are not as uniform in their requirements as newspapers, which explains why there are so few other vendors making a living selling editorial systems to this segment of the publishing market.

3. Reference publishing systems

Certain types of print reference works, such as dictionaries, encyclopedias, or directories, are really collections of records rather than linear works. They are intended to be used as a resource by a reader seeking answers to a question rather than to be read from end to end for pleasure. When multiple people collaborate on such a work, they need to be able to work on multiple records without interfering with staff working on other records.

Because the on-line medium can deliver updates to a large work much faster and more economically than print, reference works are ideally suited to on-line delivery derived from the master database updated by the editorial staff. Yet this same database, if kept free of layout-specific markup, can be used to generate other products, including print books, CD-ROMs, and custom publications.

When you put these criteria together, you end up with a system that has native SGML or XML support and user interfaces tailored for working with individual records. The authoring and editing interfaces will be optimized for quick input and editing of records. There will be one or more intuitive tools for creating new publications by querying the database or selecting records by categories or even by hand. There will often be integration with Web and print delivery methods. Systems such as Vasont from Progressive Information Technologies fall into this category.

10.3 BENEFITS OF CONTENT MANAGEMENT SYSTEMS

Organizations implement systems to help with content management when the volume or complexity of the material or number of contributors become too large to effectively manage with the file system. The larger the number of files, the harder it is to keep track of them. The more contributors you have, the more likely you are to have bottlenecks, as key people in the process become overwhelmed with requests for assistance in updating pages. The database that underlies a CMS helps to organize the content, makes it easier to separate the content from the design of the Web site, and streamlines the publishing process by automating tasks.

(i) ORGANIZING FILES

A CMS stores content in a database. Regardless of whether it's a relational database or proprietary object store, the database affords certain benefits that typically make it easier to locate and manage objects inside it. First, for each type of content object you can create user-defined attributes (also called metadata or properties), in contrast with the file system, which records only the name of the file, its physical size, data type, and date that it was last modified. With the file system, no other metadata is possible, so users typically rely on the naming conventions of their file folders to organize their content. As the volume of pages on the site grows, the file system folders fill with pages, text files, graphics, and scripts, and it becomes harder and harder to keep track of all the pieces on the site.

In contrast, the database underlying a CMS tracks other properties—some defined by the CMS, others defined by the user—that help define and categorize the content. These properties might tell more about the status of the object (for example, "draft," "proofread," or "live"), might help classify material ("sports," "international," or "local" news), or might contain editorial or production information (such as the author of a story or the sections it appears in). The database can build indexes of these fields, which make it fast and easy to search for items that match certain criteria, such as all of the stories assigned to a certain editor who has just called in sick, or all of the pages that contain or reference a story that you're updating with new information.

The same content attributes that make it easier for editors or producers to sift through the content may also be used as selection criteria for readers. A portion of a page, for example, might embed a query that retrieves certain types of stories according to a reader's preference, or a query might automatically retrieve the ten most recently published stories.

Systems vary in their flexibility regarding user-defined fields. Most come with a predefined, default set of attributes, but because everyone's needs are unique, in general it's a good idea to look for a system that allows you to define your own properties for different types of content.

(ii) SEPARATE FORM FROM CONTENT

A key characteristic of Web CMSs is that they separate much of the content—text, graphics, and scripting—from the design of the HTML pages in which they are published. Designs are laid out in page templates, and pages are created, either in advance or dynamically ("on-the-fly") by pouring content from the database into the template. This separation of form from content was particularly important in the early days of the Web, because organizations kept changing their designs so often. Even today, though, publishers refresh the look of their Web sites much more frequently than the design of their printed periodicals. By separating the main content from the stylesheet, publishers can execute a redesign not only for new pages but also for previously published material, thereby keeping a site consistent in its branding and presentation. (By contrast, a redesign of a print publication affects only newly published material.) Knowing that you are likely to refresh the look of your Web site, a CMS helps lower the cost of implementing subsequent design changes.

Once you separate the content from the design, you can make it much easier for nontechnical staff to contribute to the Web publishing process. Using **input and editing templates** [10.4.5], nontechnical staff can write and edit material that the system lays out automatically and consistently. Freed from having to learn the intricacies of HTML, staff can focus on writing copy, whether it be press releases, product descriptions for the on-line catalog, or news stories. Using the database, these pieces of content can be labeled and assigned to sections and published into design templates that take care of properly formatting them on the page. The use of templates makes it easier for nontechnical staff to learn how to publish on the Web, which saves training costs, and it frees technical staff to work on technical problems, which reduces the overall cost of maintaining the site.

It's worth noting that although nontechnical staff may not have access to the design of the page templates, they still want to see how their material looks in the final layout prior to approving it for publication. Thus, a good

CMS provides staff with an in-context preview—one that shows the material being updated in the context of its final presentation. The best CMSs go one step farther and allow users to check out material for editing right from a browser view of the site—in other words, they can check out a story by pointing to the published result, and let the CMS take care of locating the story in the database.

High-end Web CMSs allow pages to be broken down into components, each of which can have its own attributes and styles. Because these components (layout regions) are objects in their own right, they can be added to or deleted from master page layouts independent of the other components of the master page, and they can be managed and revised independent of other portions of the Web site. The use of component objects has become a popular way to incorporate software applications on a site. For example, an automobile manufacturer might build an application called "dealer locator" that enables customers to enter their postal code and see what dealerships are in their neighborhood. By wrapping the content, software, and design of the "dealer locator" application into a component object, the system makes it easy for a designer creating a new site to simply select the "dealer locator" object and assign it to a layout component of a master page.

By separating form from content, and by managing the elements of a page at their component levels, a CMS also facilitates collaboration. Many people can be working on different pieces of content at the same time, even if those end up appearing as part of a single Web page. For example, the system may pull the headlines of the most recently published ten stories into a frame of the published page. The system can pull the headlines automatically from their respective stories and create the published list on the fly, rather than creating a static list that an editor has to manually update. By assigning roles and responsibilities, dividing up tasks, and using the system to allow many people to collaborate, the team can use a CMS to streamline the publishing process.

(iii) AUTOMATE MUNDANE TASKS

Many CMSs automate routine maintenance tasks associated with on-line publishing. Among these tasks are administration and backup, keeping track of different versions of files, and managing the links.

CMSs typically provide an administration module that technical staff use to set up and configure the system, but this module varies widely in its scope and feature set. At a basic level, it centralizes administration of users and groups, the security of the system and the access rights of the people who use it. It may provide routines that automatically create back-ups and archive copies of the Web site, and it can automate movement of files from a ***staging server*** to the live production site. (In Web publishing, a staging server is the computer that holds the final draft version of the Web site, where it is checked just before publishing on the "live" or ***production server***. If an analogy is drawn to print publishing, the staging server is the equivalent of page proofs.)

Version control refers to the use of a database to track different iterations of files. With a flat file system, each file in a directory must have a unique name, which means that new versions will overwrite old ones unless they are given new names. In contrast, a CMS, relying on the underlying database, can store and track multiple iterations of a single file. Whether it's to meet legal obligations, regulatory requirements, or internal quality-assurance directives, version control automates a tracking process that is extremely time consuming and error prone when done by hand.

Sophisticated systems go one step farther and allow an administrator to "roll back" a site to a previous state. This might mean showing the Web site as it looked at a specific point in time, as it appeared to a particular customer, or as it appeared with particular versions of the files in effect. Without such a database it would be extremely difficult (and expensive) to programmatically create an audit trail of revisions, particularly for a large site that changes frequently.

Another tedious task that CMSs alleviate is that of checking links. HTML prescribes hyperlinks as pointers to a specific file, optionally a specific anchor point in a file. When a Web site is composed of flat pages, any deletion or movement of a page can cause broken links. Most CMSs will check for broken links and warn you when moving or removing an item will cause links to break. More sophisticated systems will generate HTML hyperlinks dynamically from references to items in a database. During the publishing process, writers and editors can create internal links (links within the site) by pointing to objects in the database, and the CMS will take care of generating the proper URL. The system can also check links to outside Web sites, generating automatically a list of broken links that would otherwise take considerable time and effort to produce by manually checking each outside link by hand.

In summary, using the database to both authenticate users and to store and track content, CMSs formalize and decentralize the publishing process. They formalize it by imposing structure on the production workflow and the design of the site, and by enforcing predefined security under which contributors can change only the aspects of the site that they've been authorized to change. They decentralize it by enabling nontechnical staff to create, edit, approve, and publish material on the site without technical support. Like all editorial systems that are integrated with production, Web CMSs automate the publishing process by segregating tasks, routing material from one step to the next, and streamlining repetitive layout and makeup processes that tend to create bottlenecks in production.

(iv) MAKING IT EASIER TO INCREASE SOPHISTICATION

By organizing content into a database, and separating the content from its presentation, a CMS facilitates the extraction and manipulation of content, simplifies programmatic reformatting of the content for different contexts, and, therefore, creates a foundation for adding more sophistication to the operation of a Web site. For example, if a publisher wants to syndicate sets of stories to a secondary publisher, the database makes it easy to select stories of a certain type, and the CMS often has tools for loading these files onto an FTP site or for sending them as a package to the business partner.

As mentioned above, because the content is housed in the database separate from the page, the system can style it different ways, depending on the context or audience. Premium customers (e.g., subscribers) might be given a different navigation pane than guests, for example. Readers accessing the site from a mobile phone can be shown an abbreviated version formatted for a small screen. The materials cost of generating new renditions of on-line pages is extremely low compared to those of physical media (like paper or CD-ROMs), but a CMS puts into place the software infrastructure that eliminates the labor costs of manufacturing custom pages by hand.

In addition, the security and permission control of a CMS often provide very granular control over who has what type of access to different portions of a site. Business partners, distributors, or clients might be restricted to viewing or editing certain material, or shown specific versions of content based on their identity. For example, distributors and the public might be shown different pricing for the same items in the catalog. With a file system, separate pages would have to be built ahead of time for each version—one set of pages for the distributor and another for customers. With a CMS, the proper pricing can be pulled into the page dynamically as it's requested. Changes made to the pricing in the database will automatically be reflected in all pages that contain that item.

There are many directions in which a Web publisher might use the CMS as the basis for adding new features to a site. In mass-merchandizing e-commerce applications, the content may be personalized to each customer. For better retrieval, the publisher might apply a variety of indexing and search engines, as well as employ categorization software to help classify material according to an industry- or company-specific taxonomy of terms. To aggregate material from alternative data sources, such as business systems used elsewhere in the organization, one might use connectors supplied by the vendor or develop custom integrations using the vendor's application programming interfaces (APIs). All of these extensions build off the base technology of the CMS: its database, its publishing-specific features, and its programming interfaces to other computer systems.

10.4 ISSUES TO CONSIDER IN CONTENT MANAGEMENT

Users of content management technology might find themselves in the situation of Coleridge's Ancient Mariner. But instead of "water, water everywhere," these users might be found muttering, "software, software everywhere, and none of it terribly useful." There is a tendency in the use of software to emphasize features over practical use. Users are better served when the software is designed and implemented with the tasks and roles of the users clearly in mind. In the case of content management, it's important to remember that content management is a process, while a content management *system* is a tool that reflects your processes—ideally your best processes. With that in mind, let's look at some of the features of content management software, and how they align with how users might actually want to do their work.

(i) WORKFLOW

Workflow is a primary consideration in content management. The core of content management is the intellectual work of contributors, editors, reviewers, designers, and technical staff as content is created, managed, and published. Content management technology should then support and enable these processes, ideally making users more productive in their work, especially the core tasks of creating, updating, and improving upon content under management.

There are many approaches to workflow in content management, but most of them emphasize two things:

- Applying a process where content needs to be reviewed and approved before it can be published on the live Web site or otherwise distributed to a broader audience.
- Using a system of users, tasks, and roles to define workflow. Using such a system, content can then be routed for approval to certain users based upon a task they are scheduled to perform or a role they are performing.

Take a news gathering organization that wants to adopt content management technology for publishing to the Web. They may have ad hoc systems in place for material to be created in the field, edited at a news desk, and then reviewed by the editor in chief prior to being published. Content management technology could support this kind of workflow in a number of ways.

- To begin with, the editor in chief could be provided with an on-line form that would allow him or her to assign news stories to a given reporter in the field. That reporter could then be notified with an e-mail that assigns the story. (Alternatively, the editor in chief could have a mechanism to assign the story to a pool of writers, and the first one to accept it—for example, also through a form—could then begin working on the story.)

- After gathering the information and drafting the story, the reporter in the field could then use an on-line form to enter the story, or, alternatively, attach the word processing file they have been creating. When they feel the story is ready for editorial review, they could then submit the story electronically.
- The submitted story could then be routed to a copy desk. Again, as with the editor in chief assigning the story, the workflow could be designed to forward the story to a specific copy editor, or it could be designed to forward it to a pool of copy editors, and so forth. The submitted story could then be copyedited, and, depending on the preferences and working style of the organization, could then be sent back to the reporter for additional work, forwarded to the editor in chief for posting, or published directly by the copy editor if he or she has the right level of permissions.

Every organization's workflow differs. Some organizations are hierarchical and formal, with a series of reviews prior to publishing. Others are more ad hoc and informal. The workflow built into the CMS an organization chooses should be flexible enough to accommodate the kinds of workflow currently in use, and the kinds of workflow that would be an improvement for the organization. Finally, no workflow technology should be so rigid as to preclude workarounds—work shouldn't be frozen because a certain user has to perform a task and happens to be out that day, for example.

There can be subtleties to workflow, especially in larger organizations where the system of users, tasks, and roles can be complex. In a large editorial organization, a given user may perform different tasks on different projects, as well as different roles. For example, an editor may be a reviewer on one story with approval to publish it, but only be an extra set of eyes on another story, where a certain section editor ultimately must approve it for publishing. Another story might be routed with permissions set for any of several people to correct and change the text, while another one is only to be edited by certain personnel. Organizations that have more subtle and complex rules and assumptions in their workflow need to take some care to ensure that the CMS they are adopting can support such processes.

When organizations begin to look at their content management processes and the potential to bring technology to bear, they often confront issues of staffing—roles, responsibilities, how work is done now, and how it can be improved upon. Organizations have an opportunity to model how work is done, and then use technology to reinforce the best way the work can be done moving forward.

(ii) VIEWS OF THE REPOSITORY

Ultimately, content management is about creating content, keeping it up to date, and improving on it. To achieve this, content management technology must give contributors and reviewers ongoing, current, and easy access to the content under management. CMSs have many ways of storing content. Some use a relational database or other database technology, some use the existing file system, some have their own proprietary data stores, and some use a mixture of several of these. More recently, some systems have emerged to try to tie together several repositories into a single unified (sometimes called *federated*) view. Regardless of the details of the underlying approach, the systems must present the content to the contributor in some kind of human-comprehensible view.

- Most CMSs can present a kind of *vault* or *element* view, where all of the content elements in the repository are displayed in some kind of order. Our example news organization could display all stories as individual units, and then have them grouped by date, or by author, or by some kind of subject classification. The capabilities of the various CMSs will differ as to how sophisticated the views can be. Some organizations have enormous volumes of content and will want users to have more narrow views of the content. Some organizations will have complex subject taxonomies and will want the views to somehow support these. Other organizations will have sensitive or classified information that should only be viewed by certain personnel.
- Another useful view (in addition to this kind of element view) is a product view. Our example news organization might have compiled 200 stories into a collection for print. How could this product be stored, maintained, and retrieved as a product, while also maintaining the individual stories? This kind of reuse is at the heart of content management for some organizations, and is precisely where content management might have the biggest impact in cost savings and efficiency.
- Because of the size and complexity of some repositories, some organizations will want to essentially hide all the detail from the average contributor or reviewer. To that end, some CMSs offer highly personalized views, such as an "in-box" icon that only shows their

current work and perhaps some other content of interest or relevance. Others allow work to be routed through e-mail or through a browser interface that links the contributor directly to the content that he or she needs to work on.
- On the other end of the spectrum from the individual contributor, there are people who will require a view of all of the content. System and database administrators will need continuous access to all content in order to add new content, delete content, make bulk changes, and resolve problems with workflow.

Some organizations will require more than one of these views. Organizations that have more subtle and complex requirements for storage need to take some care to ensure that the CMS they are adopting can support such processes.

(iii) VERSION CONTROL AND LIBRARY SERVICES

If content is going to be properly managed, it must be, at minimum, securely stored during the time it is created and needs to be available for distribution. As with the other requirements we have been discussing, requirements for storage vary widely. Some Web sites are temporal, with little need for archival storage, while others exist precisely as archival sites—digital libraries, records archives, and the like.

As the Web has grown to include more and more routine documents, "content management" has expanded to include requirements for "document management." In document management, there is more of a detailed focus on the entire life cycle of a document, from the point of creation all the way through distribution. There may be reasons, for example, to maintain different versions of a document in addition to the final distributed one. There may be reasons to keep historical versions of important documents, to see how they changed over time. It may even be relevant to some organizations to know who changed what sections of a document, and when it was changed.

In addition to being able to maintain revision control over individual items, Web publishers may want to maintain revision control over Web pages, sections of a Web site, or even an entire Web site. There may be a situation where an important item that appears in many places on a Web site—a logo, for example, or a disclosure—needs to be updated on every page at once—or rolled back to a previous version. There may also be a situation where an entire site needs to be rolled back to a certain edition, or a snapshot be made of the site for archival purposes.

Mechanisms for both revision control and workflow typically work in concert with what some would call *library services*—the set of features in a system that include file locking, check in and check out, and reporting. These kinds of features prevent users from deleting or overwriting another's work, and give visibility into what content elements are used where.

Again, these requirements are going to vary greatly from one organization to the next, so organizations are going to need to look closely at their own requirements, and align them with the appropriate technology.

(iv) SCHEDULING: PUBLICATION AND KILL DATES

Many organizations have scheduling requirements for their Web content. A news organization may want to refresh headlines every hour. A company may want to publish a press release when the stock market opens—or closes. A retail Web site may want to launch a new home page with special items listed for sale.

There are also reasons to delete material at scheduled times. A site may have licensed material for temporary use, and is required to delete it by a certain date. A retail site may have a week-long promotion of items at reduced prices, and wants to be sure the sales prices are no longer posted after that week.

Content management technology can automate this kind of scheduling. While this is indeed a straightforward function, when properly used it can be very powerful, and it adds to the quality and control exercised over the content. Publishers can schedule automatic updates to sites—creating things like a daily, weekly, or hourly edition; sending automatic updates to readers with a keen interest in a topic; and refreshing the most popular areas of the site with new, relevant information to keep interest and traffic high.

(v) TEMPLATES AND STYLESHEETS

As we discussed above in the section on **static versus dynamic pages** [10.1.2.3], many Web pages are generated on the fly, or dynamically, and the text, graphics, and other elements are collected at the time the page is served to the reader. This overall approach to page serving is sometimes referred to as *template-based,* and the predominant approaches to creating dynamic Web pages—such as ASP and JSP—are sometimes referred to as template development environments.

In essence, templates were developed to deal with one of the fundamental problems encountered when CGI programs were used to produce dynamic pages. If a CGI program, written in a language such as Perl, were being used to produce a page, then the HTML encoding would typically be embedded in the Perl program. Because of this, even a minor stylistic change to the HTML would often require a Perl programmer to make the change. This put even basic page creation in the hands of programmers.

HTML-based templates essentially invert the approach, using HTML pages that then include links to programs and/or small snippets of programs for tasks such as database access and querying. The benefit of this approach is that it puts basic page creation into the hands of editorial, design, and production personnel. Programmers can then typically maintain their programs separately. The result is a nice separation of duties, where creative people can focus on creative tasks and technical people can focus on technical tasks.

If template-based approaches to page creation help separate the logic of the programs from the content of the page, HTML also had to come to grips with how it could better separate style from content. Early on, HTML pages were laden with low-level style commands and codes (e.g., changes in font size, color, and style, page dimensions, indents, spacing, and so on. If a publisher wanted to make consistent changes to the design of a site, they would be facing a blizzard of detailed coding to modify. What was needed, of course, was a stylesheet approach, analogous to what had been used in desktop publishing and phototypesetting before that. **Cascading Style Sheets** [3.2.4.1] (CSS) emerged in 1996 to help solve this problem. HTML pages can link to a CSS stylesheet that can then specify formatting based on the HTML tag. Thus, an <H1> HTML tag rendered with one stylesheet could be set at Helvetica 24 point, and the same <H1> tag rendered using a different stylesheet could be set as Times Roman 32 point, and so on.

HTML pages can still present the publisher with a hornet's nest of detail, and the process of maintaining them can be burdensome. But the publisher who makes effective use of templates and stylesheets can develop a leaner, more maintainable base of content. When a style needs to be modified, or a consistent change needs to be made across a site, the publisher will be in a much better position to do this efficiently, with higher quality, and a high degree of confidence.

(vi) TEXT-AUTHORING INTERFACES

There are four main types of tools that editorial staff employ for writing and updating copy in CMSs. Deciding which type is appropriate and selecting a product depends on the skill set and requirements of the authors. It's common for organizations to employ multiple tools for creating, editing, and revising content. Some types of content lend themselves to certain types of tools: HTML forms work well for updating metadata, directory listings, and other information typically stored as fields in a database; an HTML editor would be a better choice for creating page designs. In other cases, the choice may be one of desktop platform (Mac, PC, or Unix) or simply user preference. When shopping for authoring tools, bear in mind that the tool should always be evaluated by someone representing the target user group, preferably with your own material in hand for testing the product.

1. HTML forms

The simplest means of entering and updating content is the HTML form, which, in the context of a CMS, is also known as an input template. In this method, the administrator sets up a form that corresponds to a master definition of the article. The components of the article are separated into fields on the form; behind the scene, these fields are mapped to fields in the database.

There are advantages and disadvantages to this approach. One advantage is that forms impose a rigid structure, thereby guaranteeing that all articles will follow the prescribed template. Second, they remove the complexity of the database and underlying coding from authors. Third, they are easy for the system manager to administer. One disadvantage of HTML forms as an authoring interface is that they lack the text-processing tools of a full-fledged word processor.

2. HTML editors

The HTML files of a Web site are plain ASCII files that may be modified with any text editor. However, many people prefer HTML editors—tools specifically designed for the task. HTML editors typically color code the raw file, distinguishing markup from content to make the file easier to edit. They might contain a palette of tags, and show a rendered preview of what the page will look like in a browser. In the case of Microsoft or Netscape HTML editing tools, they use the browser itself as the rendering engine, so that what you see on the screen is an accurate rendition of what readers will see when the page is published.

In the case of departmental Web CMSs, such as Adobe GoLive or Microsoft FrontPage, the HTML editor may be included as part of the package. Systems designed for larger groups typically integrate with one or more third-party HTML editors, which are used to create designs for page templates.

3. Word processors

Because so many people are accustomed to writing documents with a word processor, vendors of CMSs go to considerable lengths to adapt leading word-processing programs (most often Microsoft Word) to Web authoring. These adaptations are an improvement over the manual method of writing the document in the word processor and then copying and pasting text into an HTML input template. They are also an improvement over the HTML export capability of Microsoft Word, which generates HTML code that rarely matches, and often conflicts, with the HTML created by the CMS.

Vendors tackle this problem in different ways. Some match paragraph and character styles in Microsoft Word to XML or HTML coding. Some add toolbars to Microsoft Word with which authors can select copy and apply tags that the CMS understands. Others read the underlying data file (RTF, in the case of Microsoft Word), and filter the file into HTML before loading it into the system. Regardless of the technical approach taken, the business objective is always the same: to make it easy for nontechnical business staff to create and revise content on the Web site. A given vendor's approach to solving this problem should be evaluated in light of that objective.

4. XML editors

If the text articles for a site are marked up in XML, then an XML editor might be called for. These are document editors, much like word processors, but whose native data format is XML and which offer XML-specific functions. These functions include a structural view of the document, prompts that suggest valid elements at the insertion point, and a ***parser*** for validating that the document, when saved, complies with the ***DTD***. The most popular XML editors, Arbortext's Epic, Corel's (formerly SoftQuad's) XMetaL, and Altova's XML Spy, all offer these features. Today they are most often deployed with an **XML-centric CMS** [10.2.2], but as **HTML-centric Web CMSs** [10.2.1] evolve to support XML, the use of XML text editors in Web publishing will become more common.

(vii) PERSONALIZATION

While most people think of My Yahoo! when they hear the word "personalization," this is one feature that has matured tremendously in the past several years and is increasingly a key feature in any good CMS. Personalization is commonly used to describe the ability of a system to permit front-end users to affect delivery of content. Users may seek to *customize* interface appearance by changing color schemes, font types or sizes, or sounds. Users may appreciate *personalized* greetings (e.g., "Welcome back, Jane!") or information presented in their preferred language(s) stored in a profile on the system. Personalization also permits users to *individualize* content streams based on preference, geography (e.g., zip code), and affinity, and to offer specific types of information by collecting *behavior-based* data ("Visitors who bought this book also bought this other book").

On the back end, personalization encompasses a whole new world of user management in collaborative workflow environments. Managers of a system can set permissions for content editing and asset management by role, IP address, log-in type, or other characteristics. For example, you may have a wide number of users who work from different locations—rather than requiring that they remember login names and passwords, you could automatically identify a user from the Human Resources department and correctly display the options for updating, editing, or deleting current job postings on your intranet or Web site.

The downside of personalization is that it increases the complexity of your Web site and may make it difficult to determine the success or efficacy of specific content. Providing high levels of personalization may be more than your users need or want. Carefully consider how people use your Web site and whether certain features are "nice to have" or "must have" before adding extra layers of technology and options for them to wade through.

(viii) SYNDICATION

As discussed earlier in this chapter, syndication is a common challenge on the Internet. Because of the lower cost of production and distribution, and the ubiquity of the Internet, publishers find many opportunities to syndicate their content. Moreover, because so much content is available for syndication, Web sites of all kinds include syndicated content—news feeds, special features, and the like. CMSs need to support both sides of this problem—help publishers syndicate content out, and help Web site developers collect and republish syndicated material.

A publisher with an active syndication program has a set of practical problems on their hands. For example, some large publishers have many internal and external Web sites and want to feed them syndicated material. But each Web site has a different template, causing publishers to craft different HTML versions for each template. Even in more automated environments, newly acquired content needs to be converted and loaded into the local databases, staged for delivery, and likely tweaked before being presented live.

Content management technologies have developed some practical solutions to the syndication problem so that it is less labor intensive. Protocols such as ***Information and Content Exchange (ICE)***, which creates an XML wrapper that helps servers facilitate the handoff of content packages, have emerged to help.

For organizations that are not engaged in commercial publishing and syndication per se, the underlying problem remains the same. They often need to deliver content to many different audiences, often in slightly different formats. This is best achieved with a repository of content in some kind of neutral format. It's no surprise that syndication solutions and protocols have landed on XML as a key piece of the solution.

10.5 EVALUATING A CONTENT MANGEMENT SYSTEM

Once a foundation has been laid that includes defining your organization's workflow and researching and understanding the features of a ***CMS*** that will be most beneficial, evaluation of a CMS is the one step that generates nearly as much heat and political discussion as apathy and confusion in an organization. On one hand, you may have to deal with hidden agendas, reluctance to move out of comfort zones, or personal preference: team members who have worked with a particular technology or commercial CMS will hotly defend those as "the best," or there may be those on your team who have friends who work for a commercial CMS vendor. Sometimes this results in an insufficient evaluation of products or time-consuming delays in dealing with differences of opinion.

On the other hand, the wide range of products—combined with a lack of technical expertise, time, or other factors—may result in over-investment in a single vendor. Vendor demonstrations are designed to convince the audience that the tool will meet all their needs, and it is important to avoid getting into a situation where you feel pressured or that you are being steered by a vendor. Somewhere in the middle, you'll hear a developer or IT director exclaim, "We can build that ourselves."

Establishing a framework for the evaluation of a CMS requires at least as much organization as mapping out your workflow and determining what features and functionality best suit your organization's on-line publishing process.

(i) FACTORS TO CONSIDER IN EVALUATING CONTENT MANAGEMENT SYSTEMS

When evaluating CMSs, be sure to address these issues:

- License costs
- Integration
- Implementation
- Documentation
- Training
- Service and support
- Availability of internal and external resources
- Maintainability
- Upgrades/updates

(ii) PROPRIETARY CMS DEVELOPMENT ISSUES

For several years after large-scale commercial CMSs began making their way to market, it was often the case that smaller companies that could not afford to spend $500K on a CMS found it much more cost effective to create their own CMS. In the late 1990s, Web project management and workflow conference sessions featured a split between speakers who had implemented full-scale CMSs and those who had created proprietary systems. Their stories inspired many attendees who returned to the office with their recommendations or for plans to fill a CMS market niche.

In recent years, the spurt of "do-it-yourself" (DIY) CMS activity has resulted in a wide range of mid-to-small scale CMSs as well as many industry-specific systems. A June 2002 Jupiter Research report predicts that homegrown CMSs will double by 2004 as a reaction to weak deployments, failed initiatives, and high-priced CMSs, but advises that one might, "consider a homegrown system if a content management initiative applies to a single Web property, the parent company has no desire to manage content across an organization, the number of contributors is fewer than twenty and the workflow is no more complicated than a few steps."

Embarking on a CMS development initiative is contra-indicated for non-software development companies with large Web sites, small development teams, and no experience in developing software. The pitfalls of such an initiative are many, but the biggest issues include team burnout, scalability, and integration. Unless your company is in the business of developing software, you may soon find it difficult to keep up with constant feature requests generated by external market forces or new technology.

There are exceptions, of course. One would be a situation in which the publisher has special requirements that lie outside of what commercial products offer, and a set of material that the publisher expects will demand a CMS for quite some time. The CMS developed for this book, for example, was custom made because the desired functionality was not readily available from content management vendors. For smaller companies or for organizations lacking crack development teams with time to spare, there is another alternative to the commercial CMS implementation: leasing an ASP solution.

1. Application service providers (ASP)

According to the not-for-profit advocacy group, ASP Industry Consortium (www.allaboutasp.org), an application service provider (***ASP***) is defined as a vendor that "deploys, hosts, and manages access to a packaged application to multiple parties from a centrally managed facility. The applications are delivered over networks on a subscription basis."

ASPs are used for a wide range of software applications, including CMSs. The ASP model has become very popular with small-to-medium size businesses. Its major advantages are lower entry cost, shorter deployment, and access to more robust networks with specialized technical support. This allows companies to focus on their primary business rather than diverting resources into expanding IT budgets, hiring developers, and developing a product that is outside of their core business model. Using an ASP works well for pilot programs, giving companies more than just a trial version or sandbox environment to test out software packages before making a long-term financial commitment.

While this model has many advantages, there are drawbacks that should be considered as well. Security is a major issue, both in terms of safety of your data and your investment. The stability of the ASP is a major consideration for companies who want to use an ASP for the long term—the consistency of your service may depend on the management and longevity of that vendor. Upgrades and feature enhancement are another area where ASPs sometimes fall short. Users may feel limited to standard packages with few add-ons, or saddled with feature enhancements that they don't want or need for their particular publishing model.

Selecting an ASP requires the additional steps of performing due diligence on the company, establishing or reviewing service level agreements, managing contracts, and licensing. Clearly there are trade-offs when using an ASP, but many small companies are finding that the benefits outweigh the disadvantages associated with giving up control of the software and servers. Recommending ASPs for CMSs is beyond the scope of this chapter, but names you may have heard include: Atomz, CrownPeak Technology, Clickability, and iUpload. Guidelines for evaluating ASP vendors are offered on the ASP Industry Consortium Web site (www.allaboutasp.org).

(iii) "YOUR MILEAGE MAY VARY" — OPTING FOR OPEN SOURCE

Open source CMS may be an option for your organization depending on what exactly you want to get out of a CMS, as much as what you are willing to put into it. Open source software is part of a developer driven initiative that results in wide variations in software quality, documentation, and support.

Open source describes software that complies with the criteria developed by a movement of developers who believe that software can evolve more quickly and be more useful when developers have the ability to access, modify, and redistribute the code. They are able to fix bugs, make patches, and add functionality. The criteria for open source software include free redistribution, access to source code, and permission to modify and distribute derived works (for a full description, visit the Open Source Web site, http://www.opensource.org).

The decision to use open source software often depends on company size and philosophy. Free licensing is a leading advantage for many small companies. Medium-to-large businesses may also consider vendor independence and control of infrastructure to be major factors. Again, philosophy plays a role in this decision. Many organizations support open source software as a matter of policy or as a reaction against costly licensing fees, preferring to absorb the cost of developing, managing, and maintaining open source or homegrown systems to maintain independence from larger software manufacturers.

There are many advantages to using an open source CMS. First and foremost is cost: licensing is free. With open source systems, you can pick a system that specifically meets your needs, or which you can modify to support your publishing model without being bogged down by excess features. By the nature of the movement, open source projects fix bugs faster and introduce new features at a faster rate than commercial systems. With open source products, you can spend a lot less time evaluating products because they are freely downloadable. Obtaining evaluation copies of commercial systems frequently requires many more steps and often such evaluation copies are not full featured. You can evaluate many more open source products in the time it takes to evaluate one commercial product, and may be able to perform a more thorough evaluation, because you will already have access to the source code.

1. Advantages of an open source CMS

- The user has access to the code and the freedom to modify it.
- The product is affected less by the corporate stability of the software manufacturer.
- The user may pilot a fully functional application.
- The open source community is very supportive when it comes to bug fixes, patches, and feature development.

2. Disadvantages of an open source CMS

- The documentation may be inadequate.
- Many systems lack complex functionality.
- Ongoing costs may equal or exceed those of commercial products.

The very nature of the open source movement means that products that aren't very good won't be around very long. Additionally, if you start with an open source product but run into serious problems, it is easier to abandon that product and switch to a different one. When an organization invests tens or hundreds of thousands of dollars on a commercial product, they feel compelled to make it work rather than admit they have made a bad purchase decision and chosen an unusable product.

Philosophy apart, cost, support, and control or input into development are major factors for selecting an open source system.

3. Cost

As with the evaluation of any system, an open source CMS needs to be looked at in terms of total cost of ownership. Clearly, cost is not always a simple calculation. While licensing is frequently used as an indicator of the cost of a system, it is not always the most expensive part of the project. As the CMS market continues to develop, license fees are increasingly negotiable with customization, implementation, support, training, and maintenance costs taking a larger proportion of the budget.

With open source CMS initiatives, the costs of adapting current systems so that they integrate smoothly with the open source system, writing documentation and support policies, finding and hiring trained staff to support the system, managing ongoing feature development, and user education should all be taken into consideration. Some companies may find that it is smarter and cheaper to go for a commercial product that includes updates, service, and support as part of a total package.

Keep in mind, however, that there is basically no relationship between the price of a software product and its quality. There are many well-known software applications that are very expensive to license, implement, and maintain but which continue to hold their place in the current software paradigm. On the other hand, there are many good software products with excellent documentation and (community) support that cost very little to maintain.

4. Control

For many companies, being able to access and modify the source is not a major benefit unless they are willing to pay developers to maintain and extend it indefinitely. Large companies with established, capable IT staff may seek open source alternatives because they plan to maintain and extend the system and view open source as a safer, more reliable route.

5. Support

For those organizations with strong IT staff, a major upside to choosing open source is that the open source community is very supportive. If you find a bug or run into a problem, there are people out there who can respond more quickly than commercial developers with patches and work arounds, with the fixed version available for download in equally short periods of time. Because of this extensive support network, open source products may have better support than their closed source counterparts.

Keep in mind that there are some fairly well-established open source companies making CMS, such as Red Hat, Covalent, and Zope Corporation. Many of the more established companies that offer open source CMSs offer extensive consulting services and can assist in the extensive process of collecting and documenting requirements, designing and implementing a system in cooperation with the in-house technical team. Such relationships provide in-house technical teams with education and orientation so that at the end of the deployment process, they can take on the continued management and development of the CMS independently.

Additionally, using an open source CMS eliminates your dependence on the company or developer for future improvements. Developing additional functionality or hiring an outside developer to assist you is not always an option with commercial CMSs. Finally, keep in mind your current as well as your future needs when selecting a CMS. In the current market, open source CMSs can work quite well for you if you are publishing a fairly uncomplicated Web site. However, if you need richer features, don't be afraid to look at a commercial CMS, even if just as an inspiration for developing functionality in an open source or homegrown CMS.

(iv) COMMERCIAL CONTENT MANAGEMENT SYSTEMS: ADDITIONAL FACTORS FOR CONSIDERATION

Were you ever influenced in your evaluation of any software suite by the quality or quantity of freebies handed out by the vendor at Seybold Seminars, COMDEX, or any other trade show? Of course not. Even so, be mindful of flash and sizzle marketing gimmicks in your evaluation of commercial ***CMS*** packages. At the risk of stating the obvious, not all CMSs are created equal. After the considerable work of defining workflow, requirements, and functionality is completed, one is still left like a babe in the woods to evaluate the dizzying and ever-growing array of commercial CMSs currently available on the market.

Many CMSs are specifically designed for very large enterprise applications and others for specific industry verticals. In recent years, the somewhat ironic increasing popularity of ROI has carried with it a new generation of CMSs designed with small- to medium-sized companies in mind. Following is a review of three major divisions to help pare down the wild and woolly beast that is the CMS market: first, price, size, and scale; second, underlying technology; and third, targeted industry vertical or market specialization.

1. Price, Size, Scale

The smartest shoppers compare not just prices, but total cost including licensing, customization, and implementation costs associated with a CMS.

Enterprise CMSs are large-scale packages intended for use across very large companies. The purchase generally includes a generous number of server, site, or user licenses. If you are running a large enterprise and budgeting at least $200K, you may be looking at products by companies such as Vignette, Documentum, Broadvision, Divine, and Interwoven.

1. UPPER-TIER CONTENT MANAGEMENT SYSTEMS

Upper-tier CMSs are more suitable for large departments and corporations, and you can expect licensing costs to start around $150K. Some names in this category include Stellent, Percussion, Microsoft CM Server, and Enigma.

2. MID-MARKET CONTENT MANAGEMENT SYSTEMS

These packages target medium-size companies or very large departments in even larger companies with development budgets in the sub-$100K range. As with any product, the lower you go on the price point, the more work is required on the customer end; you may have to do more integration with packages from companies such as Merant, RedDot, Obtree, Starbase, and Mediasurface.

3. LOW-PRICED CONTENT MANGEMENT SYSTEMS

CMSs are available at much lower price points for projects with simpler requirements. For those smaller organizations with less than $10K to spend, you may be researching products by companies such as Ektron, UserLand, and Infosquare.

2. Technology

Technology may be a major factor for certain implementations and could impact integration with other applications your company uses. Underlying technology is important in many other ways, including future scalability, responsiveness, and the ability of a system to handle high-load or high-traffic Web sites. Common technologies used for CMSs include: Active Server Pages, Cold Fusion, Java, Lotus Domino, PHP, Perl, Python, and Tcl.

3. Industry specialization

Industry specialization may be a crucial factor for your company. Some CMSs might be stronger at supporting your particular market vertical, whether it is a newspaper, reference database, or document- or book-length material. Investigate the vendor's customers and look for patterns—do you see client Web sites that look like what you want your Web site to eventually resemble? Does a particular vendor seem to have a large number of clients in your field?

Are they happy clients? Are the users of their Web sites happy with the operation of the Web site?

10.6 POST-IMPLEMENTATION ISSUES

A good project manager will take you far in the process of researching, evaluating, and implementing a CMS. However, to make life easier for everyone involved, take an active role in whatever incipient knowledge management initiative your organization may have by documenting all phases of CMS research and implementation for future reference by other departments. In the post-implementation review phase of any campaign or project, maintaining the product information, e-mails, software demos, and other information can also be helpful in developing processes, materials, and guidelines for staff training on your new CMS.

The authors gratefully acknowledge Jennifer Accettola, who assisted in the research and writing of this chapter.

BIBLIOGRAPHY

Addey, Dave, James Ellis, Phil Suh, and David Thiemecke. *Content Management Systems (Tools of the Trade)*. Birmingham, U.K.: Glasshaus, 2002.

Boiko, Bob. *Content Management Bible*. Hoboken: John Wiley & Sons, 2001.

Gilbane Report, The. "Content Management, XML, and e-Business News and Analysis." Bluebill Advisors. 2002. http://www.gilbane.com/

Neilsen, Jakob. *Designing Web Usability: The Practice of Simplicity*. Indianapolis: New Riders Publishing, 1999.

Seybold Report, The. "Analyzing Publishing Technologies." Seybold Publications. 2002. http://seyboldreports.com

Spicklemire, Steve, Kevin Friedly, Jerry Spicklemire, and Kim Brand, eds. *Zope: Web Application Development and Content Management*. Indianapolis: New Riders Publishing, 2001.

Electronic Books & the Open eBook Publication Structure

ALLEN RENEAR
University of Illinois, Urbana-Champaign

DOROTHEA SALO
University of Wisconsin, Madison

Electronic books, or *e-books,* will soon be a major part of electronic publishing. This chapter introduces the notion of electronic books, reviewing their history, the advantages they promise, and the difficulties in predicting the pace and nature of e-book development and adoption. It then analyzes some of the critical problems facing both individual publishers and the industry as a whole, drawing on our current understanding of fundamental principles and best practice in information processing and publishing. In the context of this analysis the Open eBook Forum Publication Structure, a widely used XML-based content format, is presented as a foundation for high-performance electronic publishing.

11.1 INTRODUCTION

Reading is becoming increasingly electronic, and electronic books, or ***e-books***, are a big part of this trend. The recent skepticism of trade and popular journalists notwithstanding, the evidence shows that electronic books are making steady inroads with the reading public, that the technological and commercial obstacles to adoption are rapidly diminishing, and that the much-touted advantages of electronic books are in fact every bit as significant as claimed. While opinions certainly vary widely on the exact schedule, most publishers believe that it is only a matter of time before e-books are a commercially important part of the publishing industry.

Nonetheless, becoming involved in electronic book publishing can be a daunting prospect for publishers. For one thing, current publishing technology and workflows, even if already computer-based, are typically not engineered to support electronic publishing in general, let alone e-book publishing in particular—in fact, these workflows are rarely based on sound principles of electronic publishing and document engineering. In particular, the prospect of trying to deliver content from a single data store not only through a variety of different delivery modalities (paper books, e-books, Internet Web sites, databases), but also into a variety of different electronic book reading systems (specific combinations of commercial hardware and software, often with distinctive data formats), looks particularly difficult and costly to publishers. Moreover, however rapidly they may be growing, e-book sales are still a very small portion of publishers' total revenue, and therefore investments in major process redesign are unlikely to be recovered in the next one to three years—all of which adds more uncertainty to deciding when, and how, to begin electronic book publishing.

Yet for many publishers, now may actually be the best time to begin to develop digital-product-oriented workflows and formats:

1. before further temporary fixes to obsolete production processes are made,
2. before even more legacy data (which will require expensive conversion) is created,
3. before more in-house staff are trained in obsolete techniques,
4. before more inappropriate partnerships are made, and unnecessary contracts are executed (with conversion providers, composition houses, and distributors, etc.),
5. while the cost of analysis and systems (re-)design is still fairly low, and
6. before any strategically important competition in the e-book arena has really begun.

As described in the chapter on **markup** [3], financially sustainable high-performance electronic publishing can only take place within a framework of standards for content, structure, and presentation; a framework that itself must be based on sound fundamental principles of information processing. Without such a foundation a variety of punishing limitations will prevent the development of the interoperability, functionality, and efficiency required for the commercial success of electronic products.

This is not only an issue for the success of individual publishers, but also for the general prospects for a thriving industry. Recognizing this, an organization of publishing industry participants has created the *Open eBook Publication Structure* (***OEBPS***), an XML-based content specification for electronic book content. This specification is now fairly widely used throughout the publishing industry as an interchange format for handheld electronic books, particularly in mass market and trade publishing. There is also a real possibility that the OEBPS could eventually become a standard integrating framework for a wider range of electronic publishing, including markets such as textbook and STM (scientific, technical, and medical), and even non-book-like delivery mechanisms such as the World Wide Web.

This chapter first introduces the notion of electronic books, reviewing its history and discussing some of the conceptual problems involved in thinking about what is or isn't an electronic book. It then reviews the advantages that e-books offer and discusses the difficulties in predicting the pace or nature of e-book development and adoption. This introduction concludes with an account of why, despite recent problems in getting the industry started, and despite the difficulties in predicting the near future, we can nevertheless be confident that electronic books will soon be a big part of our reading lives.

Next we analyze some of the specific critical problems facing both individual publishers and the industry as whole, problems that account for the difficulty in creating a flourishing e-book industry that delivers on the original promise of electronic books. The OEB Publication Structure is then presented as a carefully designed solution to these problems, one that not only reflects fundamental principles and best practice in information processing and publishing, but that also judiciously reconciles competing demands in a way that reflects the practical and business realities of electronic publishing. The chapter closes with a brief review of current e-book products and a guide to further reading.

First though, so that the forest does not get lost in the trees, we begin with a preliminary summary of the key features of the OEBPS.

11.2 OEBPS IN A NUTSHELL

This overview is designed to be useful to anyone with a general knowledge of electronic publishing issues and can be used, "standalone," to rapidly convey the fundamental nature of this specification. Everything mentioned here is discussed in greater detail (with references, acronym expansion, and descriptions of component standards) later in the chapter.

Note that in what follows "OEBPS" is for the most part used to refer to the OEBPS version 1.2, although we also make reference to some features of 2.0, now under development.

(i) BASIC DESCRIPTION OF OEBPS

1. What it is

OEBPS, the Open eBook Publication Structure, is "an XML-based specification for the content, structure, and presentation of handheld electronic books"; conformance to the OEBPS specification is defined both for e-book *content* (OEBPS "Publications" and "Documents") and for e-book *processors* (OEBPS "Reading Systems").

2. What it does

OEBPS enables publishers to create content in a single format that can then be rendered on a variety of reading devices.

3. Who developed it

OEBPS was developed, and continues to be maintained and improved, by a large inclusive group of publishing industry participants: publishers, software developers, hardware manufacturers, distributors, services providers, trade associations, public interest groups, and others. This group is now organized as the ***Open eBook Forum*** and membership is open to all interested organizations.

4. What it is for

The principal objective of the OEBPS is to contribute to the creation of a commercially and socially valuable electronic publishing industry by providing a common format for digital content.

From the perspective of the industry as a whole, having such a single common format will improve the interoperability and functionality of both content and reading software (increasing consumer confidence and satisfaction), lower overall development and processing costs, and support innovation and competitive differentiation—all things that are needed to develop a thriving industry.

From the perspective of the individual publisher there are similar immediate benefits in the interoperability and functionality of their products, opportunities for more efficient relationships with partners, and improvement in efficiency of production processes, particularly in the areas of integration with existing in-house workflows and for supporting multiple products and multiple delivery mechanisms. In fact, some publishers today are beginning to use OEBPS even though they have no immediate plans to publish e-books, because it is an effective way to organize and exchange digital content in general.

5. Why we need yet another specification

The practical development and use of electronic publishing content requires not just specialized individual standards (e.g., XML, CSS, Dublin Core), each based on sound principles of information processing, but it also requires an agreement on a coordinated selection, combination, and application of all these various relevant individual standards. OEBPS provides this framework: comprehensive, constrained, standards-based, and reflecting fundamental principles of information processing and publishing best practice.

6. What it is, in a little more detail

OEBPS specifies a coordinated application of established electronic publishing standards, most importantly **XML** [11.6.5.1], **CSS** [11.6.5.3], **XHTML** [11.6.5.2], **namespaces** [11.6.5.4], **MIME types** [11.6.5.5], **Dublin Core** [11.6.5.7], and **Unicode** [11.6.5.6]. In addition it also defines a packaging method (expressed in an XML Document Type Definition, or DTD) to ensure a consistent and complete organization of content and metadata, and a system to support alternative renderings when nonsupported types of data are included. Under development for OEBPS 2.0 are an **XPointer-based** [3.3.5.3] linking mechanism, an XPointer-based navigation system, modular support for arbitrary external metadata (in 2.0), and a number of further constraints necessary to ensure interoperability across devices with varying capabilities. In the selection and combination of these standards OEBPS was specifically designed to support innovation, functionality, and competitive differentiation, without sacrificing interoperability.

(ii) SOME VERY IMPORTANT FACTS ABOUT OEBPS

The following are aspects of OEBPS that are critical to understanding its role in the publishing production process and the current direction of its development.

1. Specialized XML vocabularies are encouraged

OEBPS is specifically designed not only to allow, but to encourage the use of specialized XML encoding vocabularies (tag sets). This enables consistency and continuity with in-house XML encoding, or with standardized domain-specific XML vocabularies (such as **TEI** [3.3.2.3.2], **DocBook** [3.3.2.3], or **ISO 12083** [3.3.2.3.1]), as well as allowing innovation and advanced functionality beyond what can be achieved with Extensible HyperText Markup Language (XHTML) markup—or any other prespecified general encoding vocabulary. To ensure that allowing specialized XML vocabularies doesn't reduce interoperability, OEBPS has two requirements: that style rules are specified for all XML elements other than those from the OEBPS ***Basic Document Vocabulary*** subset (see next item); and if alternative style rules are specified, at least one is from the OEBPS style language (basically a large subset of CSS2, with some additional constructs). Reading Systems must use these style rules when rendering specialized XML markup and all Reading Systems are required to process the OEBPS style language. These restrictions ensure that all OEBPS content can be presented by all OEBPS Reading Systems even if that content contains specialized XML vocabulary.

2. XHTML gets special consideration

In addition to allowing the use of any XML vocabulary (as long as style rules from the OEBPS ***Cascading Style Sheet*** (CSS), subset are provided), OEBPS identifies a large subset of ***XHTML*** 1.0 elements and attributes that may be used without style rules; OEBPS processors are required to render these, in the absence of style rules, according to the formatting semantics described in the XHTML 1.1 specification. This ensures that publishers who wish to can quickly and easily exploit existing HTML-based content, tools, and expertise. In addition, and most important, it allows the use of HTML elements—such as those for tables—that may be difficult to format correctly using CSS style rules alone.

3. OEBPS is used in several different ways

OEBPS is well suited for any of three different roles in the publishing process: a revisable archival format; an interchange format; and a native processing format. Probably the most popular commercial use of OEBPS at this time is as an interchange format: publishers convert their in-house formats into OEBPS, and then in turn convert OEBPS into the various proprietary e-book formats (e.g., Microsoft Reader's .lit, RCA eBook's .rb, or Palm's .pb, all discussed **below** [11.5.3.3.1]). This reduces (from *m* × *n* to *m + n*) the number of conversions necessary to provide content that exists in various development formats (*m*) to all available device formats (*n*). It also allows a single format that may be exchanged among content developers, publishers, composition houses, conversion specialists, content licensees, or other partners. Although use of OEBPS as an interchange format is the most common use, some publishers use OEBPS as their standard in-house (revisable) archival format, and, in addition, a number of Reading Devices process OEBPS directly.

4. Processing conformance targets *reading systems* not *reading devices*

As described above OEBPS content may be converted into another format before presentation to the human reader. To accommodate the full variety of such configurations the OEBPS, when it specifies processing conformance, takes as its subject the Reading System and not the Reading Device. OEBPS defines the ***Reading System*** as, "A combination of hardware and/or software that accepts OEBPS Publications and makes them available to readers." It defines the ***Reading Device*** as, "The physical platform (hardware and software) on which publications are rendered." The Reading System includes the Reading Device, and it may be identical with the Reading Device, but it may also extend beyond the Reading Device to include "processing and transformation of data at times prior to, or in locations distant from, its presentation to a human reader."

5. OEBPS does not *necessarily* compete with Adobe's PDF

Currently in the publishing industry there is a rough division between e-book strategies that are based on OEBPS and those based on Adobe **PDF** [11.5.3.2.2]. However, the preceding points should make it clear that this division, although an empirical fact at present, is not a necessary one. Just as OEBPS content is currently often converted to various proprietary binary formats before presentation on a handheld Reading Device, it might similarly be converted to Adobe PDF for presentation. In fact most general SGML/XML-based publishing (for instance, in STM journal publishing) does routinely produce Postscript or PDF from SGML/XML content as a natural product of the typesetting, or composition process; so it is unlikely that there are any decisive technological or practical obstacles to a similar strategy in e-book publishing. (Adobe Systems is an active member of the Open eBook Forum, an OeBF "Gold Sponsor," and holds a seat on the OeBF Board of Directors.)

6. Multimedia and active content is allowed, with conditions

Multimedia and "active" content, because of their variety, complexity, and processing demands, pose the greatest challenge to OEBPS's efforts to reconcile functionality and interoperability in the context of current hardware, software, and data formats. At present (in OEBPS version 1.2), a compromise mechanism of ***fallbacks*** is defined to allow the inclusion of multimedia and active content without undermining interoperability. It works like this:

1. Conformant OEBPS Publications are allowed to include multimedia/active content of any kind, but OEBPS Publications that do include such content must also specify a "fallback" to alternative content in a supported format (such as XML text, or a JPEG or PNG image).
2. OEBPS conformant Reading Systems *may* process and render multimedia/active content, but they are not *required* to—they are, however, required to process and present the alternative fallback content whenever they cannot process encountered multimedia/active content.

This strategy is a compromise. It does allow high-performance multimedia and active content e-books, and it does ensure a base level of interoperability for them; but it does not ensure the optimal level of interoperability because it does not guarantee that multimedia/active content will be rendered *as such* by *every* OEBPS reading system. Future versions of OEBPS will have improvements in this area.

7. OEBPS Publications can be easily created from XML documents

Producing OEBPS Publications from existing XML content can sometimes be an extremely simple process. For example, suppose that the content for an electronic book exists in several XML text documents that use an in-house XML vocabulary, and that there is a CSS stylesheet that specifies the correct formatting for this content and which does not use any of the CSS constructs that were excluded from the OEBPS subset. An ***OEBPS Publication*** would in this case simply consist of these XML documents, the file containing the CSS stylesheet, and an OEBPS Package file; although OEBPS does place several further constraints on XML documents, and doesn't support all of CSS2, it is still quite possible that no, or few, changes to either the XML files or the CSS file will be necessary to "convert" these files to OEBPS. A Package file must be supplied, but this file (itself an XML document defined by the OEBPS Package DTD) can be created simply by adding the following information to an existing blank Package template:

1. A unique identifier.
2. The title of the Publication.
3. The language of the Publication.
4. A list of the files that constitute the Publication, with their MIME media types (in this case that list would be the several XML content documents and the CSS stylesheet; the media types would be "text/x-oeb1-document" for the documents and "text/x-oeb1-css" for the CSS stylesheet).
5. A default order for presenting the XML documents.

Additional information is supported as optional, of course, but this is all that is typically required for a Publication that does not make use of unsupported media types or unsupported style rules. More complicated publications, such as those making use of style rules or media types not supported by OEBPS, are not significantly more complicated to organize as OEBPS Publications. For example, if a file consisting of content in an unsupported media type (e.g., a video clip) is referenced by a Publication, then a fallback file, containing an alternative version of that content in a supported media type (e.g., a JPEG image) must be also included; both files will be listed in the Package file, and the entry for the unsupported media type will indicate which file is to be used for its fallback. Similarly, if a stylesheet using unsupported advanced features of CSS is used, it must be correctly identified and a fallback stylesheet using only supported CSS must be included and correctly identified. Of course it may not always be easy to identify satisfying fallback content in supported media types, or to write a fallback CSS style rule to back up unsupported constructs, but the OEBPS format itself does not add any particular complexity to this process. In short, the production of OEBPS Publications is often a simple matter for publishers already creating SGML or XML content.

8. OEBPS 1.2 substantially improves formatting capability

OEBPS 1.2 responds to the highest priority request received from publishers after the first two years of experience with OEBPS versions 1.0 and 1.0.1: increased control over presentation. Toward this end OEBPS 1.2 provides a very substantially augmented set of CSS2 properties, values, and selectors. In addition it enlarges the OEBPS subset of XHTML elements and attributes (while removing deprecated elements and attributes), and improves ***namespace*** support.

9. OEBPS is widely used in the publishing Industry

OEBPS is already very widely used throughout the publishing industry and may be considered the "industry standard." This dominance is supported by the existence of conversion tools both for transforming various content development formats into OEBPS and for converting OEBPS into particular e-book device formats. Of course, not all e-book content production is based on OEBPS; some workflows move content directly from non-XML development formats into device formats.

10. OEBPS 2.0 will bring further improvements

OEBPS 2.0 will provide major improvements in several areas:

- *Metadata:* a mechanism for allowing OEBPS Publications to include metadata resources external to the package file;
- *Internationalization:* additional support for providing information about required glyph sets and writing systems;
- *Inter- and intra-document linking:* more powerful XPointer-based hypertext linking;
- *Navigation:* an extensive XPointer-based navigation mechanism external to the package file, allowing multilingual, graphical, and audio support as well as general high-function navigation (this navigation mechanism is already being used in the ***DAISY*** Consortium's ***Talking Book*** standard, ***NISO Z39.86***);
- *Accessibility:* the foregoing improvements (and those regarding navigation particularly) are wherever possible implemented in ways that improve the general ***accessibility*** of e-books to readers with perceptual disabilities.

11.3 ELECTRONIC BOOKS IN GENERAL

(i) E-BOOKS: BRIEF HISTORY AND FUTURE OF THE IDEA

Written language is of course fundamental to society as we know it, and imagined devices for enhanced reading have a history that long predates modern electronic computing. More modern references in imaginative literature and in twentieth-century science fiction further attest that technologically enhanced reading was a broadly compelling idea long before, and well apart from, its current appearance in connection with electronic digital computing.

The use of computers for reading is the central theme of the work of the three titans of modern computer-based communication: Vannevar Bush, Douglas Engelbart, and Ted Nelson—all of whom imagined and designed (and in the case of Engelbart and Nelson, actually built) influential systems for electronic reading. Later, the prescient *Network Nation* (Starr and Hiltz, 1978) also had electronic reading as the key benefit of "computer-based communication," describing many of the practices and features we now take for granted and providing a still-relevant analytic framework for comparing the advantages of oral, paper, and electronic interactions.

The earliest working systems for computer-based reading (e.g., Augment, FRESS), designed in the 1960s and 1970s (well in advance of both microcomputers and large scale computer-to-computer networking), were typically developed and optimized on (local) networked engineering workstations. Then, because networked workstations were so rare and expensive, such systems were deployed in production versions on mainframes accessible by remote terminals. Seminal work along these lines continued throughout the 1980s, developing both further seminal prototypes such as Notecards, Intermedia, and Microcosm. Eventually, in the mid-1980s to 1990s, commercial hypertext systems that promoted many of the features and technologies in hypertext and multimedia systems that we take for granted today were released; these included OWL's Guide, Apple's Hypercard, and EBT's DynaText.

Also in the late 1970s and 1980s, research attention turned to the possibility of distinctively *book-like* electronic reading on portable devices [Kaye and Goldberg 1977, Yankelovich et al. 1985].

In the early 1990s the revolution—the World Wide Web—occurred. Computer-based reading with hypertext links and access to vast amounts of material suddenly became widespread and compelling. Unfortunately, almost all of the research achievements of the preceding twenty years, amounting to a tremendous knowledge of best practice and fundamental principles, were ignored, and the Web was, and still is to some extent, a study in bad design. These failures ranged from linking functionality—one direction, untyped, point-to-point, embedded linking—to the underlying markup, which ignored the separation of presentation and content.

In the 1990s electronic books also moved out of the lab and into the marketplace, as actual hardware, reading systems, and content all began to proliferate, providing researchers with actual experience to reflect on and incorporate into their development efforts. Here again, it seemed as if the lessons of the 1960s to 1980s were more often ignored than exploited: early ***e-books*** were disappointing in their functionality. Of course, basic hardware and software limitations were equally to blame.

Today (2002) we take reading on-screen for granted, and it may be conjectured that in the developed world most reading (measured simply by the number of words read from one source or other) is probably already electronic. Book-like electronic reading in particular is a rapidly growing commercial phenomenon, with a wide variety of devices, software, and distribution systems, and a wide range of content genres.

(ii) TERMINOLOGY AND SCOPE: WHAT IS AN E-BOOK?

There are some obvious terminological issues here, and some conceptual ones as well.

First, the very notion of an "electronic book." Do we mean the hardware, the software, the digital content, or some particular combined selection from those three things? For the moment, because the ambiguity of the phrase "electronic book" (and the corresponding neologism ***e-book***) is actually useful and usually clear enough in context, we won't at this point settle on a particular sense. Later, when more clarity is needed, and after we have developed the conceptual framework needed to provide it, we will present terminology that attempts to more precisely match up words and concepts.

Apart from terminological uncertainty, one might also wonder just how "book-like" the content, the software, or the hardware must be to count as an electronic book. We seem to have a rough common understanding of what a characteristic scenario of e-book reading would be: say a high school student reading *Moby Dick* on a handheld device such as a PDA. The paradigm case is thus what reading researchers call "immersive" reading: the reader reads predominantly textual material in a predominantly linear manner (left to right, top to bottom), frequently losing oneself in the flow of the narrative.

This notion of e-book reading, an important one in general, has dominated much recent commercial thinking due largely to the attractiveness of business opportunities in mass market publishing (romance novels, "techno-thrillers," science-fiction and fantasies, horror, mysteries, popular novels, and the like). Here where reading seems to be largely immersive, the technological demands are modest (no hypertext or multimedia needed), and the revenue potential is probably rather greater than with reading for instruction or information.

But the boundaries of the e-book concept remain fuzzy, and the significance of this is more than academic.

Obviously e-book content need not be only fiction or other "aesthetic" reading. A textbook on history, or even physics, could be an e-book. And, almost as certainly, so could a mail-order catalog.

Can e-books contain multimedia or interactive content? Of course they can—and yet we wouldn't describe the appreciation of pure audio and video content (movies and music) lacking even auxiliary verbal content as "reading an e-book," even if the content were presented on a notebook computer, book size tablet, or PDA. What about a movie with just a little additional textual material, say links to persons and events, timelines, and so on.

What about art catalogs and financial data e-books? Can a desktop computer be (or be used as, or be used to read) an e-book? Can e-book content be served in real time over a network? How one draws these boundaries will have consequences for how we think about publishing products and strategies, but there is no advantage in ruling out possibilities by definition, so, again, we will leave these questions open until more precision is needed.

(iii) ADVANTAGES OF ELECTRONIC BOOKS

Electronic books can provide a number of advantages over paper books.

1. Capacity

A person cannot comfortably carry more than a dozen or so paper books, but hundreds or even thousands of books may be carried on digital e-book devices and on lightweight removable storage media.

2. Manufacturing

The mass production of multiple instances of paper books is an expensive and complicated process, but electronic books may be produced quickly and inexpensively, simply by copying digital files onto new physical media. And for this reason also electronic books need never be out of print.

3. Distribution

Distributing paper books requires physical transportation, warehousing, and shelving. Electronic books can be quickly and inexpensively distributed over the Internet. This is particularly important to regions that are distant from book manufacturing locations, or that don't have the local infrastructure for supporting face-to-face consumer transactions or for reliable and efficient transportation and warehousing.

4. Cost

The above advantages suggest that the total cost of e-books, to consumers, might become less than that of paper books. (On the other hand, many factors are in play in determining consumer pricing of e-books, ranging from the very substantial remaining costs such as acquisition and editing that are unaffected by digital electronic production, to the complex business dynamics in the publishing industry that resist any pricing changes that might result in lower net profit.)

5. Intelligent viewing

Computer-based presentation of text supports intelligent and customizable viewing. Outlining with expandable entries is the obvious and familiar example, but there are many other possibilities as well. For instance, advanced sections of a textbook, or sections of a manual that don't pertain to the product currently being repaired, can be hidden (perhaps marked with a clickable icon that expands the section in place), as can, in a play script, all parts except for those belonging to the actor holding the book. Colors, indentation, and font shifts can also be used selectively to systematically highlight features of current interest. Readers (as well as teachers, managers, or others) may specify these changes to suit their particular needs.

6. Intelligent navigation

Navigation can be similarly enhanced, allowing the reader to advance through a text in terms of natural logical units (sections, paragraphs, sentences, equations, problems, procedures, etc.) instead of arbitrary media-specific ones such as pages and columns.

7. Hypertext

Even though ***hypertext*** might be considered be a kind of navigation, or viewing, it is sufficiently powerful and compelling to deserve individual mention. All users of the Web are today familiar with following links from mentioned places, persons, bibliographic references, and the like. And within STM publishing the commonly used linking service **CrossRef** [4.5.5.1] has had a tremendous impact on how scientists use technical journals. The current state of hypertext functionality on the Web, and in most reading systems, remains very crude, but it is already extremely valuable to readers, and will in any case be undergoing rapid improvement over the next few years as **XLink** [3.3.5.1] and **XPointer** [3.3.5.3] technologies become widespread.

8. Retrieval

All contemporary electronic readers are familiar with, and highly value, the simple full text string searching available in word processors, Web browsers, and virtually all e-book reading systems. Pattern matching techniques such as "regular expressions" are sometimes available and can further improve retrieval, as can language specific processing such as identifying the morphological root word (e.g., minus indications of case or number), or matching against a thesaurus entry of semantically equivalent words. But most important, the underlying XML vocabulary can often be exploited, more or less as database fields, to improve retrieval precision, locating strings of characters only when marked as, for example, a *person, place, chemical, disease,* etc.; or only when within a *title, quotation, warning, poem,* etc.

9. Currency

Electronic books can be very easily updated. In fact one can imagine how, exploiting daily synchronization by wired or wireless networking, an e-book might be refreshed every single day, or even periodically throughout the day, to reflect changes in its subject matter: mistakes can be corrected, cautions added, statistics updated, new information included.

10. Multimedia

Electronic books can present audio and video content with a wide range of applications, from an instruction video in a manual, to pronunciation examples in a language textbook, to newsreels in a history textbook, to avant garde multimedia fiction. Although a great deal of the academic research on high-performance reading focuses on technical manuals and textbooks, the commercial possibilities in mass market and trade books are probably just as great: it may soon be hard to imagine that popular biographies of actors or musicians were ever simply text and still pictures. (See the chapter on **multimedia** [9] to get a sense of the possibilities.)

11. Interactivity and special processing

The availability of computer-based processing during the presentation of e-book content to human reader makes possible a wide variety of useful interactions. For instance, equations can be modified and re-evaluated by the reader, and charts, diagrams, and graphs can be "active," allowing the reader to change the data, coefficients, formulas, and axes, and see the consequences immediately. Exercises and tutorials can be presented and then automatically analyzed or graded, and the reader directed to the relevant remedial sections. A great deal of research is currently underway in this area, particularly for STM and educational publishing, as features of this sort have an enormous potential to provide unique valuable advantages.

12. Accessibility

Paper books present a huge problem for readers with perceptual disabilities. Electronic books, however, can easily make adjustments in type size, color scheme, and user interface. In addition, well-designed content can be easily adapted to high-function audio presentation, complete with cues for structure, hypertext, and other navigation possibilities. See the chapter **Accessibility** [7] for a discussion of these issues.

11.4 THINKING CLEARLY ABOUT E-BOOKS

(i) NAVIGATING THE HYPE

During the years 1999 and 2000 there was a flurry of commercial activity, and trade news, based on the expectation that a commercially significant e-book industry was imminent. There was a sense that the magic combination of improvements in hardware, software, standards, user interfaces, back-end workflow, connectivity, critical mass of content, publisher interest, consumer interest, rights management, etc., was finally here (or at least just around the corner) and that the combination would be explosive: e-books would replace paper books, society would benefit from improved functionality, and those companies in the vanguard of this change would benefit commercially.

To knowledgeable disinterested observers the predictions of the imminent success of the e-book seemed unlikely, given the state of the technology and the general complexities of the publishing industry. But because commitment to unlikely outcomes is at the heart of entrepreneurial success, it also seemed inappropriate for skeptics to do more than express caution and wish everyone the very best of luck. As investments increased, as new companies formed, and old companies launched new projects with greater and greater fanfare, there was increasingly more to lose in backing away from the earlier confident predictions—and so those predictions continued well past the point where it was obvious to almost everyone that they were unjustified. Finally, beginning in late 2001, with the same overwrought drama ("The Death of the Book!") with which the ambitious predictions had been made in the first place, trade journalists began to trumpet the failure of those expectations ("The Death of the *e-Book!*")

The truth is that these theatrics have little to do with the long-term trends in technology and everything to do with how entrepreneurial markets work, what raises investment funding, what promotes individual careers, and what draws attention to stories in the trade and popular press. And, of course, the generally optimistic mood of the mid-1990s had a role to play as well.

What remains true is that the basis for predicting a thriving e-book industry at some point in the near future remains as strong as ever. And, moreover, the empirical evidence, which corroborates that analytic basis, is equally clear: during the same period when the failure of the e-book was being opportunistically trumpeted by the trade journalists, actual e-book sales increased, while paper book sales remained flat or declined.

Making rational predictions about whether, when, or how e-books will emerge as commercially significant requires remaining relentlessly focused on the evidence—and cautious about any but the most well-supported, and least specific, predictions.

One must also avoid "red herrings"—things that are true, but irrelevant, and therefore misleading. Among the red herrings particularly disruptive to reasonable thinking about e-books are:

1. The replacement red herring

This is the claim that paper books and paper-based printing will (or will not) be completely replaced by electronic books. Paper books and paper-based printing will probably not "disappear" at any point in the foreseeable future—but that fact, never contested by any serious industry analyst, has *nothing* to do with whether or not electronic publishing will soon be important, and perhaps even more important, than print publishing, let alone with whether e-books in particular will be a commercial success, or how much of a success they will be.

2. The bed-beach-bath red herring

According to this red herring, as so aptly characterized by Tom Peters in an insightful article on e-books and libraries (Peters, 2001), no one will want to read an e-book in bed, in the bathtub, or at the beach. Whether this is so or not, and to what extent it is so, if it is, is irrelevant: bed, bath, and beach reading venues are commercially insignificant and therefore have little to do with the prospects of e-books. Commentators who smugly write that they cannot imagine taking an e-book to bed/bath/beach only advertise their ignorance of both actual reading behavior and the publishing industry—or their willingness to forego useful analysis in favor of an appealing but misleading image. (And, in any event, people do read e-books in bed, taking advantage of their light weight and unobstrusive backlighting.) The bed/bath/beach commentators may defensively claim that this is only intended as a playful allusion to the superior general aesthetics of paper book reading—but that claim itself might be called . . .

3. The lots-of-advantages red herring

According to this red herring, paper books have lasted as long as they have for good reason: they are intuitive to use, pleasant on the eyes, feel nice, don't need electricity, are fairly cheap, never crash, etc. Of course paper books have many advantages, and, indeed, many advantages over e-books—just as e-books have many advantages over paper books. The issue is not whether some technology has some advantages over another, but rather at what point, as technology and habits change, will the *weighing of competing advantages* begin to result in certain sorts of e-books being commercially important in certain publishing markets. Despite the many real advantages of paper-based reading and the many real disadvantages of electronic reading, most people in the developed world spend an enormous and increasing amount of time engaged in electronic reading.

(ii) WHY WE KNOW THAT ELECTRONIC BOOKS WILL HAPPEN

There is a broad general agreement among most publishers that electronic books will eventually be a commercially important publishing product. Reading is obviously becoming increasingly electronic (in fact, for many professionals in the developed world, it is mostly electronic) and publishers' data show that e-book sales, although still very small, are, unlike paper book sales, rapidly increasing. Most important, the specific advantages enumerated above remain as important as ever, and the technologies and infrastructure required to realize those advantages continue to mature and advance. While opinions may vary widely on the exact schedule at which e-books will become commercially important, what form they will take, what markets they will appear in first, or what structure the industry will take, few if any publishers doubt that it is only a matter of time before e-books are a significant part of our reading lives.

But since optimistic predictions about e-books have been wrong several times in the past, we might reasonably ask what, specifically, has changed to make this prediction reasonable now? Here are the most important changes:

1. Hardware improvements

Storage capacity, processing speed, size, weight, screen resolution, battery life, have all undergone enormous improvement in the last ten years, and they continue to improve. In some cases—storage capacity and processing speed for instance—the improvements are astonishing, literally orders of magnitude. General design, ergonomics, and aesthetics have also substantially improved. In the past, even right up until a year or so ago, many of these things were all cited as negatives; that soon will no longer be the case.

2. Software improvements

New carefully designed user interfaces, navigation techniques, information retrieval, annotation capabilities, special processing (e.g., multimedia, interactivity, dynamic diagrams, integrated reference tools) all provide attractive new functionality that is extremely important in the STM and education markets. Particularly important for competing in mass market and trade arenas are recent text rendering techniques that offer a reading experience nearly equal to print.

3. Ubiquity of reading devices

Today in the developed world the near ubiquity of laptops, cell phones, and PDAs, most of which are already used for reading of some sort, provide an already existing base of possible candidates as e-book reading devices. In addition there are growing numbers of tablet computers and specialized e-book devices.

4. Critical mass of content

Whereas until recently electronic delivery meant converting print material or typesetting files to new digital formats, text creation is now almost wholly digital from the start ("born digital"), and for the most part content is prepared with the anticipation of electronic as well as print delivery. As a result the most commercially important content, new content, is almost always already in electronic form and ready, or nearly ready, for digital delivery.

5. Data standards and interoperable tools

The increasing acceptance of SGML/XML element vocabularies for in-house archival formats as well as for interchange has substantially improved the interoperability and functionality of available content and stimulated the development of new software tools and applications for creating, managing, and delivering this content. (To be sure, much content is still created in low-function, noninteroperable desktop publishing and page description formats, but it is only a matter of time before these are either replaced by, or integrated with, SGML/XML-based systems.)

6. Culture of electronic reading

Due largely to the emergence of the World Wide Web and widespread e-mail use, the revolution in reading is not something that will happen—it is something that has mostly already happened, at least in the developed world. Obviously in the workplaces of the various professions and bureaucracies, reading and writing at the computer is the dominant form of work, as any tour through a modern office building will immediately reveal. Schools and universities do still account for much nonelectronic reading, but they are experiencing explosive growth in computer-based reading, as the typical college syllabus, on-line and filled with links to on-line reading assignments, demonstrates. Finally, the amount of time that all of us—adults, children, and teenagers—spend at the computer outside of work and school (surfing the Web, reading e-mail, shopping, listening to music, chatting, etc.) is also already very large and growing fast. So fast, in fact, that parents are now alarmed at the amount of time their children—or their spouses—spend at the computer. Today in 2002, unlike 1992, the special advantages to electronic reading (fast access to many resources, following hypertext links, retrieval by key word, phrase, or more sophisticated means, navigation, integration with other activities, multimedia, etc.) are familiar to, and valued by, almost everyone.

(iii) WHAT WE DON'T KNOW ABOUT *HOW* THEY WILL HAPPEN

However, while it now seems likely that electronic books will become commercially significant fairly soon, many things about just what this success will look like remain uncertain.

1. Form factor

What will be the most popular form factor—PDA-size, book-size, tablet-size devices? Will specialized devices fail to compete with the ubiquity, power, and familiarity of the laptop? Will the special advantages of tablet-sized readers overcome our reluctance to carry yet another device? Will the convenience of PDAs be more important than screen size and resolution? Will electronic paper offering lightweight or roll-out screens solve the size/readability dilemma? Perhaps different devices will be popular for different publishing markets—say tablet devices for magazines, laptops or notebooks for textbooks and STM, PDAs for mass markets? As is obvious from the profusions of different designs already in the market, there is little agreement amongst the experts on this.

2. Publishing markets

Where will we see commercially important e-book penetration first: mass market fiction? magazines? textbooks? technical documentation? STM publishing? business documents? reference works? Which markets will resist e-book penetration?

3. Industry structure

How will the current ecology of publishers, distributors, composition houses, content developers, software manufacturers, and hardware manufacturers change? Will publishers become distributors? Will distributors become publishers? Will in-house composition become popular again? Will conversion services become unnecessary . . . or more important than ever? Who will flourish? Who will be "disintermediated?"

4. Business models, intellectual property, digital rights management, and security

Will content be sold or licensed? If the latter, will it be pay-per-view, pay-per-month, or lifetime access? Transferrable or nontransferrable? Sold piece by piece or in large lots, to aggregators? What will be the infrastructure for digital rights management? Will content be encrypted and if so how? (See the chapter **Digital Rights Management** [15.2] for a discussion of these issues.)

11.5 THE FORMAT PROBLEM

(i) INTRODUCTION

In addition to the uncertainties described above, individual publishers and the industry as a whole face another family of problems, probably the most serious of all: a proliferation of competing noninteroperable and typically low-function content formats at every stage of the content development and delivery life cycle.

Content formats can be classified along different dimensions. The first and absolutely crucial distinction is between *logical* (or *structured)* formats and *presentational* formats; this distinction is the foundation for all sound reasoning about publishing strategies. In addition, reasoning about production strategies and, particularly, how to take advantage of existing electronic production processes for possible sources of digital content, also involves appreciating the characteristics of *binary* vs. *text* files, and *revisable* vs. *nonrevisable* files. We review these notions below. (For simplicity of exposition we allow ourselves to use the word "format"—and "file" and "content" as well—somewhat ambiguously; there are various fine distinctions to be drawn, but doing so is not necessary here and would complicate the discussion. Similarly we will also use "binary" and "text" in senses that, although conforming to common usage, are also not entirely precise and unambiguous.)

We then present a second independent categorization of formats based on whether they are typically found early or late in the e-book production process, and then, in the case of those found early in the e-book production process, we distinguish those found early or late in the *print* production process. These format categories, representing multiple dimensions, can help publishers new to e-book publishing sort out the immediate complexity that they are faced with when trying to align an e-book production project with already existing print production.

On the basis of this discussion we go on to consider some difficult challenges facing the individual e-book publisher, and the industry, with respect to content formats: coping with the sheer number of relevant formats, both for original content, and for final delivery; supporting functionality and innovation (or "competitive differentiation") without sacrificing interoperability; and leveraging current practices while simultaneously planning for future opportunities.

Next we sketch the general form of the solution to these challenges.

Then, in the following major section of this chapter we present a particular implementation of this solution: the Open eBook Publication Structure.

(ii) CATEGORIES OF FORMATS

1. Logical vs. presentational

The logical/presentational distinction is now widely recognized as fundamental to the design of workflow systems, to the choice of file formats, to the development of business strategies, and to sound reasoning about the publishing production process generally. This distinction is discussed at length in the chapter on **markup** [3.1.1] and some knowledge of the material presented there is assumed in the remainder of this chapter.

We will, however, reiterate several key observations:

1. THE LOGICAL APPROACH SEPARATES STRUCTURE FROM PRESENTATION

The heart of the logical approach to publishing is to organize the publishing process by identifying and describing what one might call the *logical* (or, alternatively, *structural*) components of the content (e.g., the title, author, chapters, sections, extracts, lists, technical terms, equations, citations, etc.) and then use rules to map presentational features (e.g., font size and style, lineation, pagination, horizontal and vertical spacing) to the logical component *types*—rather than associate processing with each individual component *instance.*

In the case of content being presented only in print form, or digital content primarily designed for traditional linear reading, often only the traditional "editorial" logical components are identified, as only those require typographic distinction. However, where the content is intended to support advanced functionality, many kinds of components (possibly including very fine-grained classification of domain-specific items: for instance, names of persons, places, and countries in a history book; or diseases, organisms, drugs, organs, anatomy, and treatments in a medical book) will be identified, regardless of whether they will be formatted distinctively, in order to support such things as information retrieval, navigation, linking, special processing, and the like. (In some cases publishing aimed at traditional print output also exploits fine-grained logical markup in order to manage integration of content from various sources, validation, indexing, and reuse.)

2. DESCRIPTIVE MARKUP IMPLEMENTS THE LOGICAL APPROACH

"Descriptive markup" is used to implement the logical approach. Descriptive markup identifies and often further characterizes instances of logical component types as those instances occur in content. Descriptive markup is contrasted with procedural markup, which indicates how something is to be formatted, not what it *is*.

3. SGML AND XML DEFINE DESCRIPTIVE MARKUP LANGUAGES

SGML and XML are "metalanguages" designed to support the creation of rigorous machine-readable definitions of descriptive markup languages and to minimize arbitrary variation among markup languages. XML is a simplified version of SGML, which is now widely used in publishing and information processing. Examples of SGML/XML markup languages are HTML/XHTML, TEI, DocBook, and ISO 12083. (Again, see the chapter on **markup** [3] for more information on SGML and XML and related standards.)

4. THE LOGICAL APPROACH YIELDS MANY ADVANTAGES FOR PUBLISHING

Publishing systems that are based on a logical approach to content generally provide vastly superior functionality, interoperability, efficiency, and cost effectiveness, compared to systems that are based on a purely presentational approach. It can be easily seen how this approach makes document creation and global changes in formatting simpler, but there are many other opportunities for improved functionality and interoperability as well. (See the chapter on **markup** [3] for both *why* this is so, and *how* it can be exploited.)

5. PRESENTATION FORMATS ARE STILL IMPORTANT

Although publishing systems based on the logical approach are superior in general, logical formats are not necessarily the right choice at every point in the publishing lifecycle—various presentational formats, derived from logical formats, may be superior at stages near final processing for presentation to a human reader.

6. COMPROMISE STRATEGIES MAY BE NECESSARY

In addition, the complexity of real-world publishing may require compromise solutions in any case. Conditions creating the need for compromise and decisions to choose suboptimal formats and production processes include: financial constraints; content in legacy formats; installed software; available expertise; difficulty changing production processes; hardware limitations; marketing timeframes, ROI timeframes, and business strategies; and the need for security and digital rights management. Nevertheless, it is the opinion of the authors of this chapter that resisting the development of production systems based on the logical approach (however qualified) typically results in unnecessary costs and loss of business opportunities.

2. Revisability and representation

We note again that in what follows we use terms like "format," "text," and "binary" in ways that, while conforming roughly to common usage, are not at all entirely precise or unambiguous. We try not to make existing confusions worse, but developing and using exact and fine-grained definitions here would complicate rather than improve the discussion. The on-line edition of this chapter includes examples that further clarify these terms.

1. REVISABLE VS. NONREVISABLE FORMATS

Revisable formats are intended to be easily edited to correct or revise content or formatting. Obviously word processing and page composition programs typically create revisable formats. Examples include native MS Word and QuarkXPress files (both "binary" files, see below) and LaTeX and SGML/XML files (both "text" files, see below).

Nonrevisable formats cannot be easily edited. Obviously nonrevisable formats tend to be output oriented. Examples include raster image files and device-specific typesetting files such as Linotron 202 data (binary files), and page description files such as Adobe PostScript (a text file) and PDF (a binary file).

2. TEXT VS. BINARY FORMATS

Text formats represent their data with a standard character encoding. An example is ASCII, which uses one byte per character; another is Unicode, which may use more than one byte per character. Although the use of the word "text" in this sense is common in information processing, it can be confusing: the term does not refer to the linguistic text of the document, nor is it to be contrasted with graphical or other media such as audio or video. "Text" in this sense simply means that the information represented—whether that information be formatting instructions, vector graphics, natural language prose, indexing locations, metadata, or hyperlinks—is represented using discrete symbols, such as those in the ASCII or Unicode standards, and is also encoded via a standard character encoding, such as that described in ASCII and Unicode. ASCII text files can be easily read by most general-purpose editors and Unicode text files by editors that process multiple-byte characters. Examples of text formats are SGML/XML, Microsoft's RTF, and Adobe's PostScript. Obviously text files vary very widely in their application and nature: some of them are revisable, some not; some are logical, others presentational.

Binary formats are formats that do not encode all their data in a standard character encoding such as ASCII or Unicode. Binary formats cannot be usefully viewed in a general purpose text editor and are often processible only by the creating application, software from a vendor's application suite, or specially created "black-box" conversion applications. Both the authoring software in common use for creating original content and the composition or page layout software most commonly used to lay out content for typesetting typically save their content in binary formats (e.g., native Microsoft Word files or native QuarkXPress files).

(iii) FORMATS UP- AND DOWNSTREAM IN E-BOOK PRODUCTION

It is natural to think of e-book production as a process that starts "upstream" with the original creation or identification of content, and then continues, "downstream," with the transformation of that content into various formats, including those that represent the page layout and rendering of the content.

The riverine metaphor is an oversimplification, of course. For one thing, there are iterative cycles of corrections and revisions that result in content flowing upstream as well as down—and the authors of this chapter would be the last to suggest downplaying this cycle: this information, and the techniques for creating and transmitting it, represent process knowledge that is fundamental to the effectiveness of an organization's workflow. Moreover, the propagation of corrections and revisions upstream, which is necessary in order to create the ideal "many-products-and-formats-from-a-single-source" production strategy described below, turns out to be a challenging process to manage efficiently.

We also note that most format categories can be found almost anywhere in the production process, or at least within a broad interval, so when we say that certain formats are found upstream, or downstream, we mean typically or for the most part.

Finally, and most important, we are taking the perspective of someone trying to align or integrate an e-book production with an already existing print production process; this means that formats that are *down*stream from the perspective of print production process may still be *up*stream from the perspective of e-book workflow. This perspective reflects the practical fact that the e-book publisher is typically not designing an ideal production process from the ground up and independently of any other constraints or activities, but is more likely making a connection with an already existing publishing workflow.

However, even if the production process is built from scratch to reflect current best practice, or an existing production process is restructured and rationalized, the metaphor still works. An ideal publishing production strategy, based on accommodating multiple content formats as inputs and then creating multiple delivery formats from a common interchange format (as described further below), still yields the topography of a river: one that has both tributaries and a delta.

In the section that follows, we organize our discussion of the various formats found in the production process in terms of where in the process they are most likely to be found.

Formats found upstream in the e-book production process and upstream in the print production process:

- Revisable binary formats and their derived revisable text formats
- Revisable text formats (general purpose)

Formats found upstream in the e-book production process and downstream in the print production process:

- Revisable binary formats and their derived revisable text formats
- Nonrevisable text and binary formats

Formats found downstream in the e-book production process:

- Nonrevisable binary formats
- Revisable text formats

1. Formats found upstream in the e-book production process and upstream in the print production process

1. REVISABLE BINARY FORMATS AND THEIR DERIVED REVISABLE TEXT FORMATS

There are a number of problems at the outset with using revisable binary files, such as those created by word processing or page composition software, as a source of digital content. Binary formats cannot usefully be edited with plain text editors. Most binary revisable files are in proprietary formats that have no public documentation and can usually only be used with a single software application or a suite of products from a single vendor. It is difficult to convert binary files into other formats unless this conversion has been anticipated and provided for by the software vendor.

Generally it is only possible to exploit binary formats if they can be converted into a *revisable text* format. However, the usefulness of the resulting text format will depend further on whether the original revisable binary format contained structural logical information, whether this structural information was preserved in the derived text format, and whether the revisable text format itself has a documented encoding that can be easily manipulated for further transformations.

Unfortunately, most text processors and page layout programs in common use fail to provide adequate support for the logical approach to text creation and publishing, and few create output in nonproprietary easy-to-transform representation schemes like SGML/XML. The text files produced by these programs are in a vendor-developed encoding system specifically associated with the original application (or a suite of the vendor's applications), and optimized for the support of interchange. A familiar example from general text processing is Microsoft's Rich Text Format (RTF). Although a text-based format (if publicly documented) is obviously easier to exploit than an undocumented binary format, these proprietary revisable text formats vary widely in their suitability as a source of content for e-book publishing. It may be possible to extract some structural information (if it is present) from vendor-specific text formats, but it will typically require expensive conversion based on ad hoc programming.

2. REVISABLE TEXT FORMATS (GENERAL PURPOSE)

Some revisable text formats may be described as "general purpose" in that they are not derived from a particular revisable binary format in order to support interchange. Well-known examples of a general purpose revisable text format in the area of education and STM publishing are TeX and its derivative LaTeX.

As always the critical factor in determining the suitability of revisable text format for e-book content is whether these formats include information about the logical structure. Content in markup systems where descriptive markup typically predominates, like LaTeX, IBM DCF/GML, and Scribe are usually very good candidates for converting into e-book formats either directly, or, better, through an SGML/XML interchange language. Only inspection and analysis will determine the actual extent to which structural information has been encoded. Even rigidly structured well-thought-out markup languages can be circumvented by careless or indifferent content developers.

A text-based revisable format that is particularly important to e-book publishing is, of course, ***SGML/XML***, and the various specific SGML/XML vocabularies such as TEI, DocBook, NewsML, XHTML, and the ISO 12083 derivatives common in STM journal publishing, as well as the many other local or in-house SGML/XML formats. As noted above, SGML/XML implements the "logical" or "structured" approach to publishing by providing a rigorous but flexible metalanguage for defining descriptive markup languages, reflecting throughout its design and philosophy publishing best practice and fundamental scientific principles of information organization. This provides all the advantages of functionality and interoperability described above, as well as improving ease of conversion (using transformation languages like XSLT instead of ad hoc programming) into a variety of other formats—usually at much less cost than the comparable transformations from vendor-specific formats. In addition, unlike the proprietary binary revisable formats and their derivative text formats, many SGML/XML vocabularies were often designed specifically to support electronic as well as print publishing. The identification of SGML/XML content upstream is valuable to the e-book publisher for several reasons, but primary among them is the possibility of creating downstream formats relatively easily. For the e-book publisher looking for sources of digital content, the discovery of material in a well-designed SGML/XML vocabulary, used with consistency, care, and discipline, is priceless.

Some of the word processing and page layout applications in common use can produce SGML/XML output, instead of, or as well as, both native binary files and text files in a vendor-specific encoding. This can be a promising source of content for the reasons noted above. Unfortunately—and this is a matter of considerable practical importance in the current publishing environment—not all SGML/XML content produced from common word processing and page layout software lives up to its promise. First, the structural information actually has to be created in the first place. If it is not there, whether because the software application does not provide the user with an effective environment for easily creating structured documents, or because the user did not use the software in a consistent disciplined way, then this information won't be present in the SGML/XML output either.

Publishers must beware of exaggerated claims by software manufacturers who will make it sound like creating useful SGML/XML output from their applications is just a matter of choosing SGML/XML from the "Save As" menu, regardless of how the content is actually prepared by the user. This makes as much sense as choosing "best-seller" from the menu and expecting to publish a best-seller. The result may be SGML/XML in appearance and even in syntax, but it will be little better than a typical presentation-oriented vendor-specific format unless the software application is specifically designed to support the logical approach and create well-structured documents, and the software is used in a consistent and disciplined way, with the intention of creating content in a structured logical format. For the same reason, e-book publishers must be cautious when obtaining SGML/XML content from other publishers or from conversion houses. Conforming to the syntactical conventions of SGML and XML is easy enough, but if the design or the execution is inadequate the cost and functionality benefits will not be achieved. Publishers new to electronic publishing should seek an independent analysis of the quality of the encoding they will receive before they make a major purchase or invest in conversion. Good professional analysis of SGML/XML content is inexpensive and easy to arrange.

2. Formats found upstream in the e-book production process and downstream in the print production process

1. REVISABLE BINARY FORMATS AND THEIR DERIVED REVISABLE TEXT FORMATS

In most commercial publishing, text creation and development takes place initially in word processing applications, and then the content is transferred to page composition programs for final page layout, although in some cases the same applications are used throughout the process, from creation to printing. In any event, downstream revisable binary formats have undergone final preparation of typography, graphics, indexing, lineation, and pagination and such. These formats often seem like attractive sources of content. For one thing, they are likely to contain more corrections, revisions, and other useful value-added improvements than the various earlier upstream revisable versions. In addition, they are often easier to obtain, as the typesetter is more likely to retain them than the publisher or compositor is to retain the original revisable files. (Although often it is discovered that a supposedly final typesetting tape doesn't match the printed book—because corrections were reset and added in pasteup or even in film at the printer.)

Unfortunately the transition from the development applications (like word processors and SGML/XML editors) to page layout applications often results in the systematic replacement of structural information, now presumably no longer needed, with formatting codes, and other specialized encoding intended only to support formatting, and not development, conversion, or any other use. The conversion of such formats (even if a text version is available) into other formats is almost never financially practical, and often not possible at all. These formats are typically highly specific to a particular application, and difficult to parse and transform. But most important, whatever structural information was available in the original revisable versions is now lost, having been replaced by application-specific processing codes. And it is this structural information that is needed for efficient creation of either new application-specific processing codes, or general-purpose interchange format. Regenerating structural information about the logical components of the document from application-specific processing codes, even when that information existed in the original revisable versions, is rarely financially feasible, even apart from the binary format and the undocumented, often ad hoc, syntax of the data: the relationships between codes and components are many-to-one (something can be bold or indented for many different reasons) and conditional on the now-missing original contexts. While it is true that information is added to content representation as it moves downstream, information is also removed, and by the time this representation reaches typesetting format much critical information is gone and cannot be recovered.

2. NONREVISABLE TEXT AND BINARY FORMATS

The downstream nonrevisable formats of particular interest to e-book publishers as sources of digital content are Adobe ***PostScript*** and Adobe ***PDF*** (Portable Document Format); the former is usually encountered in its text format, the later in a binary format. PostScript is a powerful programming language for creating typeset pages with vector graphics and high-quality fonts on all-points addressable devices such as laser printers. It was a key part of the emergence of desktop publishing in the mid-1980s, and today almost all word processing and page layout software creates PostScript output (a mixture of PostScript commands and data), which is processed by PostScript printers to produced formatted pages. Adobe PDF is a page description language closely related to PostScript. PDF can be produced directly from PostScript and is more suitable for electronic distribution.

PDF and PostScript are extremely attractive as possible sources of content as they are routinely created and archived by almost all publishers, are well-defined and publicly documented, and usually contain most corrections. Unfortunately, most PostScript and PDF files that you will encounter will contain little of the original structural information, even when that information existed in the original revisable formats, and the formatting information they do contain usually cannot be easily used to regenerate the missing structural information. Such files contain only the information needed to reproduce the *visual,* rather than *logical,* format of the page—the fonts, their sizes and position, colors and graphics, and so forth. (Although PostScript and PDF's nature as a page layout language makes it an unlikely source of revisable general-purpose digital content, PDF is itself a popular e-book format and can be easily and directly rendered by Adobe Acrobat or the Adobe Acrobat eBook Reader, as discussed below in the section on formats downstream in *e-book* publishing.)

However, although this is the typical situation today with most PostScript and PDF files one encounters, the current version of Adobe PDF has an extremely powerful capability ("tagged PDF") for including structural information such as that represented in the SGML/XML markup. If this feature becomes widely and fully supported by SGML/XML-based text processing and page layout software PDF files could in fact turn out to be an important source of revisable repurposable content.

3. Formats found downstream in the e-book production process

The vast number of publishing formats, many proprietary, rigid, and non-interoperable, poses a major problem for e-book publishers trying to design publishing strategies that are integrated with existing print-oriented workflows. But to make matters worse, entirely new content formats have been developed, and continue to be developed, specifically for the e-book devices themselves. Publishers of e-books must not only cope with diverse multiple formats as sources of digital content, they must produce a variety of different formats if they intend to make their e-books available on the many e-book reading devices already in existence.

1. NONREVISABLE BINARY FORMATS

These new formats include most prominently (following the usual practice of referring to them by their characteristic file extensions): ".lit," (for the Microsoft Reader), ".rb" (for the Gemstar eBook), ".pb" (for the Palm), and ".pdf" (for Adobe Acrobat eBook Reader). These are all nonrevisable binary file formats designed specifically for e-books and closely associated with specific software manufacturers. In addition to these well-known and widely used e-book formats, there are a number of others as well, and probably more under development.

Apart from the business strategies that motivate the development of any content standard, there are several other technological and commercial motivations that are frequently claimed for binary e-book formats:

- binary formats are faster and more compact
- binary formats can be a vehicle for delivering innovation and functionality that could not be supported by directly processing OEBPS XML content
- whether or not an innovation could be provided by directly processing OEBPS XML content, binary formats can help protect innovations and special functionality, providing competitive differentiation
- binary formats can more easily both secure content and provide digital rights management

2. REVISABLE TEXT FORMATS

Some Reading Devices can process and present HTML files and ASCII text files without markup. However, the revisable text device format that is important to e-book publishers is OEBPS itself. Some e-book reading software, such as the readers produced by ION Systems (eMonocle), Mobipocket, and GlobalMentor (Mentoract), process OEBPS, without conversion into any other format.

(iv) FORMAT-RELATED CHALLENGES

1. Functionality, innovation, and competitive differentiation vs. interoperability

In choosing a content format for publishing, two desiderata immediately present themselves as requirements, and just as immediately appear to be impossible to achieve simultaneously:

1. *Support for interoperability.* Content should be readable on multiple reading systems, and reading systems should be able to read many different kinds of content. Obviously this is valuable for business-to-business relationships in publishing, but it is even more critical for consumer confidence, and for making content as widely, and as reliably, available as possible. The experience of 1980s word processing—when most software created noninteroperable formats that couldn't be edited by software from other vendors, processed by third-party tools, or often even printed on arbitrary printers—must not be repeated in the e-book industry, where e-book interoperability is constantly compared to the nearly complete and transparent interoperability of paper books.
1. *Support for innovation.* Content developers and reading systems both should be able to provide new features, providing new value to customers, and "competitive differentiation" to businesses. The full realization of the promises of electronic reading will only be achieved over time, as advanced features prototyped in experimental systems are perfected and made commercially available. Format requirements must not prevent this diffusion of innovations.

But how can these two things be possible simultaneously? If in order to ensure interoperability a single e-book format is chosen as the industry standard, then that format will have a specific combination of capabilities. It will, for instance, support certain formatting features, certain media types, certain graphical features, a certain level of interactivity, and so on. Content that conforms to this format will be restricted to *only* these features; software that conforms will process these features, but possibly no others. Content providers who innovate beyond these features in their e-book content cannot be assured that their innovations will be processed appropriately and reading system developers cannot be assured that they can process this new content—unless there was an arranged agreement between the content innovator and the reading system developer. In these circumstances interoperability will quickly evaporate, and business strategies based on format and feature "wars" will further erode consumer and industry confidence, threatening the possibility of developing a thriving e-book industry.

2. Functionality vs. current reality

Real technological change always takes place in *medias res* and pretending that this is not so—pretending, that is, that we can develop plans to improve our current circumstance simply by figuring out what things would be like in an ideal world—rarely succeeds. Today the publishing industry possesses much content in various unpromising legacy formats, production systems unsuited for electronic publishing (unsuited, some would argue, even for efficient print publishing), staff with particular skills, certain financial vulnerabilities, and existing business strategies. Unless it had an enormous amount of capital, and could survive a lengthy period before the investment was recovered, a company that attempted to change everything at once and implement the ideal system would be unlikely to succeed commercially. This is a problem for individual companies, but it is also a problem for the industry: how can we accommodate, or even better, take advantage of, current practices, and at the same time prepare the industry to take best advantage of future opportunities?

3. The problems of format conversion

E-book publishers must decide what format(s) to choose for their e-books: HTML, XML, .lit, .rb, .pb, .wap, PDF, and so on. Each has advantages and disadvantages. But most disturbingly, each appears to limit the market to just those devices that use that format.

One solution to this problem is to settle on a single format, at least for delivery. But this is unpromising. For reasons of business strategy, differing technology commitments, and differing views about what approach would be best, it is unlikely that publishers and reading system manufacturers would agree on a single format. And even if they did, this would quite likely have a stultifying effect on progress and innovation in e-book functionality.

Another possible solution is to allow a thousand flowers to bloom, and assume that conversion software will be developed, as needed, to convert one format into another, at least insofar as such conversion is possible. But this solution too is problematic, as some simple combinatoric arithmetic will show. It would certainly be reassuring to have a conversion program that would convert every content format into every other format, but as can be easily deduced by the fundamental principle of counting, that would require ($n^2 - n$) conversion programs for n formats: for the seven formats mentioned above, forty-two individual conversion methods. This number grows rapidly as the number of formats grows.

Of course complete format interoperability, even if possible (and some conversions are not practical under any circumstances), is more than is required—we are only really concerned with converting certain common, and reasonably convertible, upstream formats into downstream formats. But although the combinatorics here are better, they are still prohibitive from the practical point of view. The number of conversion programs needed to convert every relevant upstream format into an e-book format is the number of input formats multiplied by the number of output formats. This function is not as threatening as the previous ones, but it still grows fast: for instance, if there are twenty upstream input formats and ten downstream e-book formats, there will be 200 required conversion applications, and each additional input format will require ten more conversion routines. To have a sense of what this really means in practice remember that formats are frequently updated, and each new version will typically require updating the relevant conversion applications as well.

(v) SOLVING THE FORMAT PROBLEM

These are the problems that the OeBF Open eBook Publication Structure was specifically designed to address. The basic idea is to define an interchange format that could mediate between publishers' formats and the various reading device formats. This would allow publishers to concentrate just on converting their in-house formats into the interchange format, perfecting this single conversion routine.

The single interchange format would then be the common coin of electronic publishing. The next step, converting from the interchange format into the final reading device format, could be performed by the reading system software or by distributors or by other partners. In any case the steps in the process are dramatically reduced in number: whereas the number of conversion routines necessary to convert publisher formats to device formats is inputs *multiplied* by outputs, the number needed for conversion mediated by an interchange format is inputs *added* to outputs.

Many of these input formats are proprietary and most are noninteroperable—that is, software that reads one format usually won't read any of the others. In addition, the nonrevisable formats are not only difficult to edit and update but for the most part difficult to adapt to different reading systems and delivery modalities. Almost all of these formats are specifically designed for supporting print publishing, and even when they nominally support electronic publishing, they are often inadequate for realizing the full range of functionality (as described above) anticipated for high-performance electronic reading. It is therefore difficult for publishers to get their content into a format appropriate for any sort of electronic publishing, and particularly difficult to get content into a format suitable for high-performance e-book reading. From the industry perspective, these problems mean that it will be hard to develop the critical mass of interoperable high-function content needed to create a thriving e-book industry.

Publishers are faced with worrisome questions: will a single proprietary device format eventually become dominant, and if so, which one? Or will there be a number of competing formats? Perhaps the number of formats will continue to increase, driven by efforts to innovate. From the publisher's perspective the situation is discouraging: the cost of converting their content to each possible e-book device is enormous and makes a commercially viable e-book venture look financially unpromising.

From the perspective of the industry as a whole the situation looks even worse. Even ignoring problems of individual idiosyncrasies, the number of qualitatively different conversion routines needed to convert every original content format into each device format is a geometric function that rises fast as new formats are added at both ends: the number of required routines is the number of input formats multiplied by the number of output formats.

Equally important is the perception of consumers: if consumers believe that buying a particular device will limit what they can read to books in a particular format, or that their purchased content will become out-of-date and unreadable when they buy new devices—obviously the consumer confidence needed to build an industry is not going to be there.

11.6 THE OEBF OPEN EBOOK PUBLICATION STRUCTURE

This section assumes a general knowledge of basic XML concepts (such as *DTD, document instance, validity, well-formedness, element, attribute, attribute value,* and *entity*) and some rough familiarity with the general nature and purpose of XML-related specifications such as XHTML and CSS. For more information on XML, and XML-related standards, see the chapter **Markup: XML and Related Technologies** [3].

(i) HISTORY

1. The development of OEBPS 1.0

The Open eBook Initiative was announced at the U.S. National Institute of Standards and Technology's first *Electronic Book* conference in October 1998. Following that conference, three companies (NuvoMedia, Microsoft, and SoftBook Press) that were manufacturing, or had plans to manufacture, e-book reading systems wrote a draft proposal to initiate an industry-wide discussion. In January 1999, at a meeting widely attended by publishing and software manufacturing representatives, the Open eBook Initiative was informally organized and an "Authoring Group" was formed and charged with the development of the specification. Victor McCrary, a NIST Technical Manager who had been encouraging and supporting the development of the OEB Initiative, became "Facilitator" of the Authoring Group.

Throughout the spring and early summer of 1999 the specification was substantially expanded and refined by the Authoring Group. In September the specification, now titled *The OEB Publication Structure 1.0* (OEBPS 1.0), was approved by the members of the OEB Initiative and released. For its work the OEBPS Authoring Group received a letter of commendation from the U.S. Department of Commerce.

2. The formation of the OeBF

In January 2000, the informal ***Open eBook Initiative*** became formally organized as the ***Open eBook Forum***, a nonprofit association of publishing industry stakeholders, with this stated goal:

> . . . to establish common specifications for electronic book systems, applications and products that will benefit creators of content, makers of reading systems and, most important, consumers, helping to catalyze the adoption of electronic books; to encourage the broad acceptance of these specifications on a worldwide basis among members of the Forum, related industries and the public; and to increase awareness and acceptance of the emerging electronic publishing industry.
> —*http://www.openebook.org/aboutOeBF.htm*

OeBF members include major publishers, hardware manufacturers, software manufacturers, distributors, service providers such as conversion and composition companies, key trade associations, public sector agencies, public interest organizations, and other related organizations including individual universities and libraries. It has broad support throughout the publishing and publishing software industry and strong collaborative relationships with key trade organizations, such as the American Association of Publishers and the American Library Association.

In addition to the Publication Structure Working Group (see below), the OeBF now has active working groups in the areas of Metadata and Identifiers and Digital Rights Management and Special Interest Groups in the areas of Business Development, Education, and Accessibility, and well as a systematic infrastructure for collecting and analyzing industry needs, and an architecture group (the Systems Working Group) for ensuring that the various technical products are coordinated and meet identified requirements.

3. Formation of the Publication Structure Working Group (PSWG)

In May of 2000 at the first formal meeting of the newly reorganized Open eBook Forum the charter of the OeBF's first Working Group, the ***Publication Structure Working Group (PSWG)***, was accepted by the OeBF membership and assigned the mission of "maintaining and advancing" the Publication Structure.

1. OFFICERS

The original officers of the PSWG, and their affiliation at the time, were, Chair: Allen Renear (University of Illinois, Urbana Champaign); Vice Chair:

Garth Conboy (Gemstar-TV Guide); Scribe: Dorothea Salo (Impressions Book and Journal Services); Maintenance Chair: Garret Wilson (GlobalMentor); Development Co-Chairs: Gene Golvchinsky (FX/PAL), Jerry Dunietz (Microsoft).

In the summer of 2001, Jon Noring became Maintenance Chair and in the spring of 2002, as work shifted from OEBPS 1.2 to OEBPS 2.0, Jerry Dunietz (Microsoft) became Vice Chair, Garret Wilson became a Development Co-Chair, and Dorothea Salo (then at the University of Wisconsin) stepped down as Scribe.

2. COMPOSITION AND CURRENT ACTIVITIES

The membership of the Publication Structure Working Group includes representatives of all major electronic publishing constituencies, including public interest groups and the major competing e-book software manufacturers, as can be seen from the contributor lists included in the standard. The PSWG carries out its work through weekly conference calls, e-mail discussion lists, and periodic face-to-face meetings. Membership in the PSWG is open to all members of OeBF, Principal and Associate, as well as to a limited number of "invited experts" and its records and minutes are available to OeBF members and to invited experts. Drafts of new OEBPS versions are widely circulated to the general public for comments prior to their submission to the OeBF—all comments, whether from OeBF members or others, receive written responses from the PSWG.

4. History of OEBPS releases and adoption

September 1999: OEBPS 1.0 is released.

Fall 2000: A year after its initial release, OEBPS is widely used in the publishing industry and has been incorporated into a number of software tools for creating device formats. An OEBPS conformance validator developed by the Brown University Scholarly Technology Group (STG) is made publicly available by STG and NuvoMedia.

Spring 2001: The OEBPS "package file" system for organizing publication content is adopted by the DAISY Consortium's Talking Book standard, now NISO Z39.86. For this collaboration OeBF and DAISY jointly received an award from the International Coalition of Access Engineers and Specialists, recognizing "significant innovative technical contributions to the access engineering profession."

June 2001: OeBF releases OEBPS 1.0.1, a "maintenance release" that corrected any errors or inconsistencies that had been reported during the first year and a half of use.

Spring 2002: Most commercial e-book publishing, other than that which goes directly from non-XML composition formats to PDF, is now based on OEBPS.

September 2002: OEBPS 1.2 is released, with improved support for formatting and presentation.

Fall 2002: Work continues on OEBPS 2.0, a major release with extensive new functionality, particularly in the areas of navigation and linking, internationalization, and metadata. Many of the new navigation and linking features, which are already completed, were developed in collaboration with members of the DAISY Consortium's Talking Book standard project and are similar to those of NISO Z39.86.

(ii) PURPOSE AND NATURE OF OEBPS

1. Official Purpose and Scope

The Open eBook Forum Publication Structure itself is perhaps best introduced by first considering its goals and objectives. The specification presents the official Purpose and Scope of OEBPS in section 1.1:

> In order for electronic-book technology to achieve widespread success in the marketplace, Reading Systems must have convenient access to a large number and variety of titles. The Open eBook Publication Structure (OEBPS) is a specification for representing the content of electronic books. Specifically:
> The specification is intended to give content providers (e.g., publishers, authors, and others who have content to be displayed) and tool providers minimal and common guidelines which ensure fidelity, accuracy, accessibility, and adequate presentation of electronic content over various electronic book platforms.
> The specification seeks to reflect established content format standards.
> The goal of this specification is to define a standard means of content description for use by purveyors of electronic books (publishers, agents, authors et al.) allowing such content to be provided to multiple Reading Systems.

2. Empirically identified objectives

The official goals articulated in section 1.1 are, at best, rather terse, particularly apart from the context and framework within which they were seen by the authors of the specification. We supplement them here with an expanded list obtained by generalizing from the observed activities of the working group.

Empirically speaking then, the following are the specific objectives that actually guided the decisions, priorities, and reasoning of the OEBPS working group.

1. SUPPORT CONSUMER CONFIDENCE IN PERFORMANCE AND INTEROPERABILITY OF DEVICES AND BOOKS

If consumers are not confident that the reading devices they are considering purchasing will reliably present the e-books they already have or will soon acquire, then consumers will not purchase those devices. And, similarly, if consumers are not confident that the e-books they are considering purchasing can be processed, and presented well, on their current devices, or on a device they might acquire later, they will be reluctant to purchase those e-books. The problem is the same in either case (purchasing e-books or purchasing reading devices), and failure to address it would be absolutely lethal to the development of an e-book industry. Consequently, supporting consumer confidence in both performance and interoperability was a high priority in the development of the specification.

However, it is important to recognize that it was not an OEBPS objective to ensure that a single representation of content (e.g., a data file) would itself be processible on any reading device. The objective was rather, as will be explained in detail later, to ensure that a single representation of content was processible by any OEBPS conformant *Reading System*—and therefore, ultimately, the content would be presentable on any Reading Device that was part of a conformant Reading System, yielding the functional interoperability described above.

Device-level interoperability is indeed desired by many members of the e-book community, and OEBPS was therefore designed to make device-level interoperability *possible*—itself a major achievement. But *requiring* device-to-device interoperability of data files is not consistent with the range of commercial e-book publishing strategies already underway. Fortunately, interoperability of content at the Reading *System* level can provide much, if not most, of the functional interoperability desired by consumers.

2. CREATE A CRITICAL MASS OF CONTENT

A successful e-book industry requires that a large amount of valuable content become available as fast, as easily, and as inexpensively as possible, and that the continuing production of e-books is financially sustainable. Consumers will not purchase e-books they are not interested in reading and they will not purchase e-book devices unless they believe that there is, and will continue to be, a large quantity of e-books.

3. LIMIT BURDEN ON CONTENT PROVIDERS

Content providers, such as publishers, must be able to create e-book content easily, whether by converting existing content to e-book formats or by the creation of new content. Therefore wherever possible the OEBPS makes it possible to exploit already existing content formats, production tools, and staff expertise, and, in general, to support simple manageable production strategies for e-book publishing.

4. SUPPORT CONTENT PROVIDER NEED FOR RELIABLE HIGH-QUALITY PERFORMANCE

Content providers require predictable high-quality reading system performance; they need to be assured of reading systems' rendering capabilities so that they can be confident that their books would be faithfully presented exactly as they are designed to be. The current situation on the Web, where browsers vary widely in their rendering behavior, is completely unacceptable in high-quality commercial publishing.

5. LIMIT BURDEN ON DEVELOPERS OF READING SOFTWARE

At the same time, the software companies developing electronic book reading systems need manageable processing requirements. Many current e-book devices still have significant limitations on processing speed, memory, screen size, resolution, and color, and the software engineering required to implement advanced formatting and browsing systems under those limitations is difficult. It is not currently possible, for instance, to completely implement CSS2 in a typical handheld reading device. In addition, functionality that may be possible from an engineering perspective may have prohibitive business consequences, such as cost or development time frame. A content format must therefore constrain processing and presentation requirements to those that can be reliably achieved in order to limit the engineering burden on software developers as well as provide predictable performance for content developers.

6. SUPPORT DISTINCTIVE NEW FUNCTIONALITY

Digital documents and computing resources provide extraordinary new possibilities for reading and writing: enhanced navigation, retrieval, annotation, updating and currency, multimedia and interaction, and so on. Moreover, these features are familiar to consumers from their experiences on the World Wide Web. E-books must, as soon as possible, deliver such new features in order to justify their claim to provide superior reading functionality. (But they must do so without diminishing interoperability or reliability, or placing excessive demands on software manufacturers.)

7. MAINTAIN EQUITABLE OPPORTUNITIES FOR COMPETITIVE DIFFERENTIATION

Chaotic competition based on proprietary formats would delay or prevent the development of e-books, reducing interoperability, consumer confidence, and, ultimately, functionality. But completely removing the opportunity for competitive development and innovation/differentiation would be equally damaging to the long-term social and commercial value of the e-book industry, discouraging new entrants and limiting innovation and functionality. The specification must therefore somehow support innovation and competitive differentiation without eroding functionality. In particular, competition must somehow be channeled into areas where it would benefit the industry, and society, the most, in the long run, and away from areas where it would be an obstacle to the development of social and commercial value.

8. POSITION INDUSTRY PRACTICES TO EVOLVE WITH EMERGING STANDARDS

Alignment with the trends and emerging standards in publishing, and in information processing in general, is, of course, critical. Even though efforts must be made to leverage existing practices and provide a content format that has immediate value, this format must be, as much as possible, consistent with emerging trends and standards, so that e-book publishing practices can evolve with publishing practices and standards in general.

9. PROVIDE AN AESTHETICALLY SATISFYING READING EXPERIENCE

Although many categories of books and documents benefit immediately from enhanced navigation, searching, annotation, and interaction, for others—such as mass market romance novels, techno-thrillers, and bestseller fiction—aesthetic satisfaction and the recreation of the traditional sense of being "lost in the book" is more important. In all cases, providing a satisfying reading experience, appropriate to the genre of text, is important for the success of e-books.

10. SUPPORT OTHER LANGUAGES AND WRITING SYSTEMS

Both the opportunities of the global marketplace and the moral requirement to ensure that all cultures have equitable access to the emerging world of electronic reading require that an e-book content format must support the world's languages and writing systems.

11. SUPPORT ACCESS BY READERS WITH DISABILITIES

People with perceptual disabilities must not be excluded from participating in the social and cultural world as that world becomes increasing electronic. Access to books by people with disabilities should not only not be impeded by an e-book content format, but that format should take advantage of the powerful resources of digital information and computer processing to improve and enhance that access, ensuring full participation in contemporary culture and society.

12. HAVE AN *IMMEDIATE* AND *DIRECT* IMPACT ON THE CREATION OF A FLOURISHING E-BOOK INDUSTRY

For a thriving electronic book industry to emerge, sound content standards need to be made available and updated in a timely fashion. If the needed standards are not available precisely when they are needed, at critical points in the development of the industry, then that development may be delayed or halted. Or, perhaps worst of all, it may proceed, but with suboptimal strategies that will prevent, perhaps indefinitely, the emergence of more functional and valuable technologies and products. And, in addition to timeliness, strategies for supporting the development of the industry also must avoid extensive dependencies on other projects or initiatives, and must not rely on long or complex chains of effect.

13. AN OVERARCHING SECONDARY GOAL: RECONCILE CONFLICTING PRIMARY GOALS

A glance at the goals listed above shows that many of them pull in different directions (e.g., high-function faithful rendering vs. manageable software requirements), and a number reflect the two fundamental opposed objectives mentioned earlier: interoperability vs. functionality and innovation; and exploiting current practices vs. preparing for future developments. The key challenge for OEBPS was to either develop innovative solutions that would reconcile these oppositions, and to make judicious decisions in weighing the tradeoffs of competing strategies. Understanding these conflicts will put many of the features of the OEBPS, both current and future, in perspective.

3. General nature of OEBPS: an application of already existing standards

One might reasonably ask why, when so many other standards already exist, is it necessary to develop yet another? The answer is important, and essential to understanding the fundamental nature of the OEBPS.

There do indeed already exist many information processing standards relevant to electronic publishing, for instance XML, XHTML, CSS, XLink/XPointer, XML Schema, RDF, Dublin Core, Unicode, image formats, sound and video formats, and so on. There are in fact hundreds of relevant standards, produced by large standards organizations such as IEEE, IETF, W3C, ISO, and NISO. These standards are typically powerful, detailed, expressive, carefully crafted, and based on sound principles of information processing. Each covers in great detail a very wide range of needs in its particular area, and, considered collectively, they together include all, or nearly all, aspects of electronic publishing.

However, to provide genuine practical solutions to the various problems described earlier in this chapter it is obviously not helpful to simply gesture toward the hundreds of existing relevant "vertical" standards, however complete and soundly developed they may be. What is necessary is that all players know exactly which standards are in fact being used, and moreover, they must agree on how much of each standard must be supported—for it is impossible to expect that software manufacturers working within specific hardware and processing constraints, as well as practical engineering demands, always implement all of a selected standard. Practical limitations, and the need for a high-level of predictable capability and behavior, require selection and further specific constraints.

Ironically it is precisely the features that make a specific standard a good one—expressive power, completeness, and flexibility—that can make specific standards difficult to use, without further constraint, in practical commercial contexts.

Consequently, the practical development and use of electronic publishing content requires not just the existence of specialized individual standards, however sound, but it also requires a specific detailed agreement on a coordinated and constrained application of a particular selection from the available relevant individual standards.

4. Summary: the purpose and nature of OEBPS

Reflecting on both the official statement of purpose and scope, and the empirically identified objectives, we would, in a sentence, summarize the purpose of OEBPS this way:

> The principal goal of the OEBPS is to contribute to the development of a commercially and socially valuable electronic publishing industry by providing a common format for digital content.

From the perspective of the industry as a whole, having such a single common format will, by improving the interoperability and functionality of both content and reading systems, increase consumer confidence and satisfaction, lower overall development and processing costs, and support innovation and competitive differentiation—all things that are needed to develop a thriving, socially valuable e-book industry.

From the perspective of the individual publisher, there are similar immediate benefits in interoperability, and in functionality of their products, opportunities for more efficient relationships with partners, and improvement in efficiency of production processes, particularly in the areas of integration with existing in-house workflows and for supporting multiple products and multiple delivery modalities.

The specific "empirically identified" objectives listed above amount to a statement of the various *functional requirements* that must, given the actual circumstances of contemporary electronic publishing, be met by the specification in order for it to achieve its goal.

In closing this discussion of nature and purpose we note that although OEBPS is rigorously based throughout on fundamental principles of information processing, and is carefully positioned to evolve with emerging trends and standards, it is also, in every aspect, and as a matter of philosophy, a *practical* solution to *current* problems in electronic publishing. Obviously this is the rationale behind OEBPS's basic nature as a comprehensive specification for applying existing standards. In addition, in all of its design decisions and in all weighing of tradeoffs and adjudication of competing desiderata, OEBPS always takes into account actual publishing practices, business realities, and current industry dynamics. In this way it is designed to provide an actual practical solution to the problems of e-book publishing, and not just the mere possibility of such a solution.

(iii) TERMINOLOGY

The various words in common use to describe the different parts and aspects of electronic publishing can easily be seen to be much too ambiguous and vague even for general conversation—consider, for instance, the various meanings of "e-book" mentioned earlier—let alone precise enough for use in a technical specification. Consequently OEBPS, like all technical specifications, begins with a carefully defined technical terminology. These definitions are in fact a good place to begin a general overview of the specific features of OEBPS, not only because the text of the specification makes constant essential use of these terms, but also because these terms, taken together, provide a useful initial orientation to OEBPS itself.

The following is the terminology defined in OEBPS 1.2 in the section "Definitions." In the specification itself the list is alphabetical, but we have rearranged the list here so that (with the exception of the last definition) like items are grouped together, contrasting items are adjacent, and the order has rough logic, progressing from general to particular and from data to presentation.

1. OEBPS Publication

OEBPS Definition: A collection of ***OEBPS Documents***, an ***OEBPS Package*** file, and other files, typically in a variety of media types, including structured text and graphics, that constitutes a cohesive unit for publication.

Comment: This is a fundamental concept in the specification. To summarize the OEBPS processing model: a *Publication* is processed by a *Reading System,* and the content then made available, on a *Reading Device,* to the human *Reader.* The terms Reading System, Reading Device, and Reader are explained below. OEBPS specifies conformance requirements for being a conformant OEBPS Publication, an OEBPS Document, and an OEBPS Reading System.

As described elsewhere the OEBPS Publication may be transformed into other formats before distribution to a Reading Device and so is not necessarily the format being distributed to consumers.

In so far as the OEBPS Publication is a representation of the intellectual content being published it might be considered, roughly, the "e-book," in the content sense, although if the OEBPS Publication is transformed into another format by the Reading System before being distributed to Reading Devices, then that derived format might perhaps also be reasonably called the "e-book." (We also note here that "e-book," like "book," is ambiguous between the physical book that may be bought, used, lost, etc., and the abstract edition or version of a work.)

2. OEBPS Package

OEBPS Definition: An XML file that describes an OEBPS Publication. It identifies all other files in the Publication and provides descriptive information about them.

Comment: The ***OEBPS Package*** identifies and organizes the parts of an OEBPS Publication, providing the information needed for a Reading System to process the Publication. The specific contents of this important OEBPS item are discussed in a **section devoted to it** [11.6.6].

3. OEBPS Document

OEBPS Definition: An XML document that conforms to this specification—generally containing textual content of an OEBPS Publication.

Comment: There are two kinds of ***OEBPS Documents***: Basic and Extended, as defined in the next two definitions. OEBPS defines conformance requirements for conformant OEBPS Documents.

4. Basic OEBPS Document

OEBPS Definition: An OEBPS Document that restricts itself to the markup constructs defined in this specification.

Comment: What this primarily amounts to is that Basic Documents use only the element names, attribute names, and attribute values of the Basic OEBPS Document Vocabulary, which is an XHTML subset. (In addition Basic Documents, like all OEBPS Documents, must meet the OEBPS Common Requirements and the OEBPS Common Document Requirements.) Basic Documents are discussed in more detail in the section on The Component Standards, below.

5. Extended OEBPS Document

OEBPS Definition: An OEBPS Document that uses markup constructs beyond those in this specification, but adheres to the extension mechanism defined herein.

Comment: An Extended OEBPS Document is an XML document that uses an XML vocabulary other than the Basic OEBPS Document Vocabulary—for instance TEI, DocBook, or an in-house XML vocabulary—or a document that mixes OEBPS Document Vocabulary with another, or several, other XML markup vocabularies. (Extended Documents, like all OEBPS Documents, must meet the OEBPS Common Requirements and the OEBPS Common Document Requirements.) Extended Documents are discussed in more detail in the section on The Component Standards, below.

6. OEBPS Core Media Type

OEBPS Definition: A MIME media type that all Reading Systems must support.

Comment: OEBPS specifies six ***Core Media Types***, two of which are defined in the specification and four of which are existing MIME Media Types. OEBPS Core Media Types are discussed in more detail in the section on The Component Standards, below.

7. Reading System

OEBPS Definition: A combination of hardware and/or software that accepts OEBPS Publications and makes them available to readers. Great variety is possible in the architecture of ***Reading Systems***. A Reading System may be implemented entirely on one device, or it may be split among several computers. In particular, a Reading Device that is a component of a Reading System need not directly accept OEBPS Publications, but all Reading Systems must do so. Reading Systems may include additional processing functions beyond the scope of this specification, such as compression, indexing, encryption, rights management, and distribution.

Comment: This concept, which is both extremely important and very easy to misunderstand, was carefully crafted to accommodate the full range of existing and possible e-book publishing strategies. A *Reading System* processes OEBPS *Publications* and presents them, on *Reading Devices,* to (human) *Readers*—but no assumptions at all are made about where or how this takes place. A Reading System can therefore include processing and transformation of content "at times prior to, or in locations distant from," its eventual presentation on the Reading Device. So in the case of a publishing process where, for instance, OEBPS is transformed by the publisher into a proprietary binary format (such as the e-book formats used by Microsoft, RCA, or Palm readers), and then that format is later distributed to Reading Devices where it can be rendered and presented for reading, the Reading System includes both the publisher's hardware and software, and the hardware and software that is the Reading Device; and it involves an intermediate transformation of content from OEBPS into a binary format. Of course Reading Systems need not be distributed in time and space, and they need not involve intermediate transformations—the entire Reading System may be contained on the Reading Device, and it may, or may not, process OEBPS Publications without transformation into an intermediate format. Reflection on likely network distribution strategies reveals that many variations are possible, and many of the differences amongst them will be invisible to the consumer. The concept of a Reading System is discussed in more detail in the section on The OEBPS Processing Model, below.

8. Reading Device

Definition: The physical platform (hardware and software) on which publications are rendered.

Comment: The OEBPS specification does not specify conformance requirements for ***Reading Devices***, which are only part of the Reading System. As described above, a Reading Device may, or may not, contain the entire Reading System. The concept of a Reading Device is discussed in more detail in the section on The OEBPS Processing Model, below.

9. Content Provider

Definition: A publisher, author, or other information provider who provides a publication to one or more Reading Systems in the form described in this specification.

Comment: Although this term typically suggests publishers, it is deliberately broad and may in different circumstances refer to authors, conversion service organizations, distributors, and others.

10. Reader

Definition: A person who reads a publication.

Comment: In the OEBPS specification, Reader always means a person. But be aware that elsewhere it is sometimes used to mean what OEBPS means by Reading Device or what OEBPS means by Reading System.

11. Deprecated

Definition: A feature that is permitted, but not recommended, by this specification. Such features may be removed in future revisions.

Comment: This definition is here in our list of OEBPS definitions for completeness; unlike the others it pertains not to the key features of the OEBPS framework, but rather is an obligatory definition of term important to the specification itself.

(iv) THE OEBPS PROCESSING MODEL

Although there is as of yet no formally defined OEBPS "processing model," the following informal characterization shows how the basic concepts of OEBPS processing fit together.

1. The specific intellectual content of a book or other publication is physically represented by an OEBPS Publication (a collection of files, organized by a Package file).
2. OEBPS Publications are processed by OEBPS *Reading Systems.*
3. An OEBPS Reading System includes a *Reading Device,* and the processing of an OEBPS Publication eventuates in the presentation of content, on the Reading Device, to a human *Reader.*
4. OEBPS specifies conformance standards for content (OEBPS Publications and their components), and for processing (OEBPS Reading Systems).

(v) THE COMPONENT STANDARDS

As emphasized above, OEBPS consists primarily of the coordinated applications of other standards. This section lists the most important standards applied by OEBPS and describes how they are used. In the process we will at the same time be presenting an overview of OEBPS itself.

1. XML

XML is a *metalanguage,* developed and maintained by the World Wide Web Consortium (W3C), for defining descriptive markup languages. For more information on XML see the chapter on **markup** [3.3].

XML is fundamental to OEBPS in two ways: OEBPS is a framework for organizing and supporting the delivery and presentation of XML content; and OEBPS implements this framework with an XML DTD (the Package DTD, discussed further below). In short, OEBPS is an XML framework for XML content.

Specific applications of XML in OEBPS include:

1. All OEBPS Reading Systems must be XML processors as defined in the XML 1.0 standard.

2. All OEBPS Documents must be "well-formed" XML documents. OEBPS Documents may also be, but need not be, "valid" XML documents, with respect to an XML DTD for their particular markup vocabulary. Although XML validity is not a requirement, the authors of this chapter recommend in the strongest possible terms that content providers ensure that their OEBPS Documents are in fact valid with respect to an XML DTD. (OEBPS Documents must also conform to the OEBPS Common Requirements, and Common Document Requirements; see OEBPS section 1.4 for these requirements).
3. OEBPS Extended Documents may use any XML vocabulary, such as TEI, DocBook, ISO 12083, XHTML, or a private XML vocabulary defined by the individual content provider. However, for all XML elements not in the OEBPS Basic Document Vocabulary, at least one style rule must be provided, and at least one of the style rules provided must be from the OEBPS style language. By not allowing the formatting of XML elements (other than those in the OEBPS Basic Document Vocabulary) to take place directly, without style rule mediation, and by requiring that at least one applicable style rule be from the OEBPS style language, OEBPS ensures a high level of interoperability even for unfamiliar XML elements—without reducing the opportunity for advanced functionality and innovation.
4. OEBPS Basic Documents use the OEBPS Document Vocabulary, a subset of XHTML 1.1 (OEBPS Documents that validate against the OEBPS Document Vocabulary DTD will also validate against the XHTML 1.1 DTD). Although validity is not a requirement for conformance, we strongly recommend, again, that OEBPS Basic Documents be valid as well as well formed.
5. The OEBPS Package File is a valid XML document. (The OEBPS Package vocabulary is defined in the OEBPS Package DTD, discussed further below.)
6. W3C specifications related to XML, such as namespaces, CSS, and XHTML, are used extensively in the current OEBPS specifications and future versions of OEBPS are expected to make use of other XML-related standards (e.g., XPointer).

We emphasize again that although OEBPS does not require that OEBPS Documents be "valid" (as defined in XML 1.0) with respect to an associated XML DTD (only "well-formedness" is required by OEBPS), it is strongly recommended that publishers ensure that all their OEBPS Documents are in fact valid. Publishers who create nonvalid documents will be far more likely to eventually encounter problems with interoperability, conversion, formatting, repurposing, and use of third-party tools. These problems will be expensive to resolve and will limit opportunities for new products and features. The lesser conformance level of "well-formedness" was included in XML in order to allow for the DTD-less processing common in casual Web publishing; this lower level of conformance is entirely inadequate for high-quality financially sustainable commercial publishing.

2. XHTML/Basic OEBPS Document Vocabulary

XHTML 1.1 is an XML document markup vocabulary, developed and maintained by the W3C, that corresponds roughly, in markup constructs and formatting semantics, to HTML 4.0, the SGML markup vocabulary widely used on the Web. For more information about **XHTML** [3.2.4.2] and **HTML** [3.2] see the chapter on markup.

OEBPS defines a subset of XHTML 1.1 and calls this the Basic OEBPS Document Vocabulary. All OEBPS Processors are required to recognize and process this XHTML subset, and content providers may use this subset without providing style rules for its elements. This allows content providers to easily exploit current XHTML content, tools, and expertise, and also to use XHTML constructs for document components, such as tables, that might be hard to format via CSS style rules. All Reading Systems are required to process the Basic OEBPS Document Vocabulary according to the relevant portions of the XHTML 1.1 specification.

OEBPS Documents that use only this XHTML subset are called Basic Documents. An OEBPS Document that uses any markup from outside this subset is an Extended Document.

The Basic OEBPS Document Vocabulary does not include all of the XHTML 1.1 elements, attributes, and attribute values. This is partly, as with the subsetting of CSS2 (see below), in order to minimize the burden on Reading System developers and reflect hardware and software limitations. But it is also in order to align the OEBPS Basic Document Vocabulary with the current direction of development in HTML, which is away from format-oriented markup and towards content- and structure-oriented markup. For the same reason any construct deprecated in XHTML 1.1 is either deprecated or omitted from the Basic vocabulary—these are, again, typically presentation-oriented elements and in most cases the OEBPS Style Language can provide the same formatting effects via a CSS style rule. This coordination with the direction of HTML development within the W3C improves interoperability and forwards compatibility.

Although only XML "well-formedness," and not "validity," is required of OEBPS Basic documents, we, again, very strongly recommend (as does the OEBPS Specification) that publishers ensure that their OEBPS Basic Documents are not just well formed, but are also *valid* with respect to the Basic OEBPS Document DTD.

3. CSS/OEBPS style language

The ***Cascading Style Sheets (CSS)*** standard, developed and maintained by the W3C, defines a mechanism for specifying the presentation of XML documents. For more information about CSS see the chapter on **markup** [3.3.2.6].

OEBPS defines a style language for use in OEBPS Publications that consists primarily of a large subset of constructs from CSS Level 2. Not all CSS2 properties are included in the OEBPS 1.2 style language: this is to minimize the development burden on Reading System developers and Reading Device manufacturers, who must, as described above, provide reliable performance on devices with limited resources. In addition to this CSS2 subset, the OEBPS style language also includes a few additional properties and values that provide special features that were urgently needed by book publishers—such as page layout, headers, and footers—but that were not available in CSS2.

In order to make advanced and innovative functionality possible, OEBPS Publications are allowed to use CSS2 style constructs that are not in the OEBPS style language, and may even use style constructs from other style languages. However, if they do use constructs from outside the OEBPS style language, they are required to also provide "fallback" style rules that *are* from the OEBPS style language. Allowing the use of style rules outside of the OEBPS style language supports functionality and innovation, while requiring that fallback style rules from the OEBPS style language be provided whenever style rules outside the OEBPS style language are used ensures a base level of interoperability for all OEBPS Documents—as all conformant OEBPS Reading Systems are required to support the OEBPS style language, regardless of whatever other style rules they support.

Style rules or stylesheets may be associated with an OEBPS Document in a number of different ways, with various restrictions on content and processing in order to ensure interoperability.

4. XML namespaces

The XML ***namespace*** standard, developed and maintained by the W3C, defines a technique for explicitly indicating which XML vocabulary an element or attribute name is from (supporting recognition and processing) and to avoid the ambiguity that would result if a document mixed XML vocabularies that contained different elements or attributes with the same names. For more information about namespaces see the chapter on **markup** [3.3.2.6].

With some restrictions, OEBPS Publications may use XML namespace prefixes and the declarations that connect namespaces to the URLs that uniquely identify a namespace. OEBPS Reading Systems are allowed to process these declarations and prefixes according to the namespace specification, although they are not required to do so. However, if an OEBPS Reading System is not "namespace aware" then it is required to process a namespace "qualified name," including the colon separator that delimits the prefix and "local part," as an element or attribute name. This in effect provides partial support for the appropriate handling of namespace prefixes in Documents and DTDs even by Reading Systems that do not do namespace processing *per se.* And it is what would be expected to happen under ordinary circumstances in any case: the string of characters representing the qualified name (i.e., the concatenation of prefix, colon, and local part) is simply recognized as a element or attribute name consisting of those characters, and is processed accordingly.

To maximize interoperability: no namespace other than the XHTML namespace can be declared a "default namespace" (non-XHTML namespaces must be declared by prefix binding only); and the XHTML namespace may *not* be declared by prefix binding, but may only be declared as a default namespace. These two restrictions, taken together, ensure that OEBPS Reading Systems that are not namespace processors can still reliably recognize all XHTML elements and attributes—by their canonical XHTML 1.1 names—whenever those elements and attributes are used in a document.

In summary, although OEBPS supports and constrains the use of namespaces, there is no general requirement that namespaces be used in OEBPS Publications, even for arbitrary XML vocabularies.

5. MIME media types

The MIME media typing system, developed and maintained by the IETF, is a technique for identifying content as to "media type" and a process for creating and registering new media types.

OEBPS defines a set of OEBPS Core Media Types that all conformant Reading System must support. OEBPS Publications may also include content with other media types (such as vector graphics, video, sound, scripted content, and so on), but for each resource of a media type that is not an OEBPS Core Media Type, OEBPS Publications must also include an alternative resource that *is* of an OEBPS Core Media Type. This restriction ensures that the use of innovative high-function content will not erode a baseline level of interoperability. However, the PSWG realizes that this may not be an entirely satisfactory solution for publishers wishing to produce books with multimedia or other special content. For more information on the OEBPS "fallback" strategy for media types see the section on fallbacks, below.

The OEBPS Core Media Types are given in Table 1.

TABLE 1. OEBPS CORE MEDIA TYPES

MIME Media Type	Type of Data	Where Defined
MIME Media Types defined in OEBPS 1.2		
text/x-oeb1-document	OEBPS Documents	OEBPS 1.2
text/x-oeb1-css	OEBPS CSS-subset stylesheets	OEBPS 1.2
MIME Media Types defined elsewhere		
image/jpeg	raster graphics	RFC 2046
image/png	raster graphics	RFC 2083
application/xml-dtd	XML DTDs	RFC 3023
application/xml-external-parsed-entity	XML "external parsed entity"	RFC 3023

6. Unicode, UTF-8, UTF-16

The ***Unicode*** standard specifies a large encoded character set (identical with ISO 10646 implementation level 3) for almost all of the world's languages and writing systems. UTF-8 and UTF-16 are techniques for representing Unicode encoding in specific bit sequences for physical transfer (UTF-8 includes the ASCII character set encoding as a subset). Unicode is widely used in the computer industry. For more information about character sets, Unicode, glyphs, and internationalization, see the chapter on **markup** [3.3.3.4.1].

To facilitate internationalization and support multilingual documents, OEBPS publications are allowed to use the entire Unicode character set in UTF-8 or UTF-16 encodings and all OEBPS Reading Systems are required to correctly parse these encodings. However, at this time OEBPS Reading Systems are not required to provide character glyphs (appropriate visual representations) for all Unicode characters.

Version 2.0 of OEBPS will probably provide further support for glyph set negotiation between Publication and Reading System.

7. Dublin Core

The ***Dublin Core*** is a simple metadata system for electronic resources. It was developed from within the library community and provides "card catalog-like" metadata to support searching and indexing. It is widely used. For more information about Dublin Core see the chapters on **markup** [3.3.6.3.1] and **organizing and linking** [4.4.2.3.1].

OEBPS requires three Dublin Core metadata elements (Identifier, Title, and Language), but allows and supports the full set of Dublin Core 1.1 elements and provides some additional attributes specifically needed by publishers. There is, however, no assumption that the Dublin Core metadata will be adequate for all purposes, or that only Dublin Core metadata should be provided with the OEBPS Publication. OEBPS also allows the inclusion of other publication-level metadata (either conforming to other existing standards, or arbitrary systems defined by the content provider).

Version 2.0 of the OEBPS will provide a mechanism for identifying and linking arbitrary external metadata resources to an OeBF Publication, including resources that provide metadata for parts of a publication or for aspects (fonts, DRM, etc.) of a Publication. In the requirements and planning documents for OEBPS 2.0 this support is referred to as "metadata modularization."

(vi) THE PACKAGE

Every OEBPS Publication contains exactly one OEBPS Package file, which specifies the OEBPS Documents, images, and other objects that make up the OEBPS Publication, along with fallbacks, metadata, and other information. The Package file, a valid XML document conforming to the OEBPS Package DTD, defines the OEBPS Publication.

1. Components of the Package

Following are descriptions of each of the component parts of the OEBPS Package. When reading the descriptions below the reader is encourage to refer to the **package file example** [11.6.6.2] that follows.

1. PACKAGE IDENTITY

A unique identifier for the Publication. An attribute value for the "unique-identifier" attribute on the Package's root element (<package>) points to the Dublin Core Identifier element (required) in the metadata section whose content is then considered the primary identifier for the Publication. An optional *scheme* attribute can be used to indicate the identifier system being used, such as ISBN, DOI, etc. (NB: The value of the "unique-identifier" attribute is not the unique-identifier, but rather identifies the Dublin Core Identifier element whose content is the unique identifier.) See the **identifier example** [11.6.6.2] in the package file example below.

2. METADATA

The ***metadata*** section contains a required Dublin Core metadata record (within a <dc-metadata> element) and may also contain an optional supplemental metadata record (within an <x-metadata> record). As mentioned earlier, all Dublin Core metadata elements are supported and three Dublin Core metadata elements—Identifier, Title, Language—are required. See the **metadata example** [11.6.6.2] below.

3. MANIFEST

This is a list of *all* files (documents, images, stylesheets, etc.) that make up the Publication and a declaration of their media types and fallbacks, if any. The Manifest also lists files that are fallbacks for other files or objects that have unsupported media types. The Manifest supports the identification, collection, and verification of all files in a publication (to support, for instance, downloading, reading into memory, or packaging in a physical transfer format). See the **manifest example** [11.6.6.2] below.

4. SPINE

The ***Spine*** is a default linear reading order for the Publication. Because the original, and still primary, purpose of OEBPS is to support book-like publications, a linear reading order (with constraints on the media types that may occur in it) is required in order to encourage a base level of common behavior across reading systems. Only OEBPS Documents may be listed in the Spine; other media types in the publication must be referenced from them—for instance, by using XHTML elements such as <object> and <a> from a file listed in the spine, or via a chain of files that begins in a file listed in the spine. Publications may, of course, have only a single file in the Spine. See the **spine example** [11.6.6.2] below.

5. TOURS

A rudimentary implementation of the "trails" functionality developed in the research hypertext systems of the 1970s and 1980s, the optional ***Tours*** are alternative reading sequences through a Publication. They may be used to support topical navigation, reader expertise levels, etc. As implemented in OEBPS 1.2, Tours have only a modest functionality; OEBPS 2.0 will have much expanded support for navigation of this sort. See the **tours example** [11.6.6.2] below.

6. GUIDE

The ***Guide*** is an optional list of files that contain fundamental structural components of the publication, such as table of contents, tables of plates or illustrations, foreword, bibliography, indexes, etc. Grouping these together and identifying them as to kind supports additional special processing. See the **guide example** [11.6.6.2] below.

2. Example of a Package file

```
<?xml version="1.0"?>
<!DOCTYPE package
 PUBLIC "+//ISBN 0-9673008-1-9//DTD OEB 1.2 Package//EN"
 http://openebook.org/dtds/oeb-1.2/oebpkg12.dtd
/>
<package
  unique-identifier="DA00042A"
  xmlns="http://openebook.org/namespaces/oeb-package/1.0/"/>
<!-- Metadata Section -->
  <metadata>
    <!-- Dublin Core Metadata Section -->
    <dc-metadata xmlns:dc="http://purl.org/dc/elements/1.1/">
      <dc:Title>Fish Food</dc:Title>
      <dc:Language>en</dc:Language>
      <dc:Identifier id="DA00042A"
       scheme="ISBN">123456789X</dc:Identifier>
      <dc:Creator
       role="aut" file-as="Eisner, Ariel"
       >Ariel Eisner
      </dc:Creator>
       [ Other Dublin Core elements as desired ]
      </dc-metadata>
    <!-- User Defined Metadata Section -->
    <x-metadata>
      <meta name="commissioning_editor" content="Bilbo" />
    </x-metadata>
  </metadata>
  <!-- Manifest -->
  <manifest>
  <!-- Stylesheets -- !>
    <!-- stylesheet with unsupported style constructs -- !>
      <item id="s01" href="fishbookstyles.css3"
       media-type="text/css" />
    <!-- stylesheet with supported style constructs -- !>
      <item id="s01" href="fishbookstyles.css3"
       media-type="text/x-oeb1-css" />
  <!-- Major structural components -- />
    <item id="intro" href="introduction.xml"
      media-type="text/x-oeb1-document" />
    <item id="c01" href="chap1-appetizers.xml"
```

```
    media-type="text/x-oeb1-document" />
  <item id="c02" href="chap2-starters.xml"
    media-type="text/x-oeb1-document" />
  <item id="c03" href="chap3-entrees.xml"
    media-type="text/x-oeb1-document" />
  <item id="c04" href="chap3-sidedishes.xml"
    media-type="text/x-oeb1-document" />
  <item id="toc" href="contents.xml"
    media-type="text/x-oeb1-document" />
<!-- other content, including media -->
    <!-- linked from each deep fry recipe -->
      <item id="w1" href="deepfrycaution.xml"
        media-type="text/x-oeb1-document" />
    <!-- linked from frontispiece and turbot recipe -->
        <item id="ap1" href="authorpicture.png"
          media-type="text/image/png" />
   <!-- example of short fallback chain . . . />
   <! -- unsupported media type; falls back to next item -->
   <item id="vv32" href="fishingclip.fli"
     media-type="video/x-fli" fallback="v19" />
   <! -- which is also unsupported, but with a fallback -->
   <item id="v19" href="fishingclip.mpeg"
     media-type="video/mpeg" fallback="p13" />
   <! -- the chain ends in an OEBPS supported media type -->
   <item id="p13" href="fishingpicture.png"
     type="image/png" />
</manifest>
<!-- Spine -->
<spine>
  <itemref idref="toc" />
  <itemref idref="intro"/>
  <itemref idref="c01" />
  <itemref idref="c02" />
  <itemref idref="c03" />
  <itemref idref="c04" />
  <itemref idref="c03" />
<spine>
<!-- Tours -->
<tours>
  <tour id="tour1" title="Salmon Dishes">
    <site title="Poached Salmon"
```

```
        href="entrees.xml#poached" />
      <site title="Salmon Cheeks in Bacon"
        href="appetizers.xml#salmoninbacon" />
      <site title="Broiled Salmon Steaks"
        href="entrees.xml#broiledsalmonsteaks" />
     [ and so on with more salmon recipes ]
  </tour>
    <tour id="tour2" title="Heart Healthy">
    <site title="Broiled Flounder" href ="entrees.xml#e6" />
    <site title="Poached Striped Bass" href="entrees.xml#e39" />
    <site title="Mixed Sushi" href="entrees.xml#e9" />
     [ and so on with more with more heart healthy recipes ]
  </tour>
    [ and so on with more tours of various kinds ]
  </tours>
<!-- Guide -->
  <guide>
    <reference type="toc" title="Table of Contents"
      href="toc.html" />
    <reference type="front_matter_table" title="Illustrations"
      href="toc.xml#illustrations" />
    <reference type="other.trails"
      title="Helping You Plan Your Meal"
      href="toc.xml#tours" />
  </guide>
</package>
```

(vii) TOWARD OEBPS 2.0

As of this writing, the OeBF Open eBook Publication Structure Working Group is now working on OEBPS 2.0. This version, like 1.2, responds directly to the highest priority needs expressed by the publishing community, based on their experiences with OEBPS 1.0.1.

OEBPS 2.0 will provide major improvements in several areas:

1. Metadata modularity

OEBPS 1.2 supports the full set of Dublin Core 1.1 metadata elements, along with other publisher-specific metadata. However, many publishers, distributors, and consumers (such as libraries, in particular) require ONIX, MARC, GILS, SCORM, or some other metadata standard that is more expressive and powerful for their particular purposes or in order to conform to the prevailing standard in a particular market or context of use. In addition, 1.2's requirement that metadata be included in the Package file is awkward and limiting in the production, distribution, and use of content. Responding to these needs, OEBPS 2.0 will provide a mechanism for allowing Publications to reference arbitrary metadata resources external to the Package file. This will allow Publications to make use of MARC, ONIX, SCORM, or any other metadata the Publisher wishes to use, to allow single metadata records to be shared by different Publications, and to allow the revision or addition of metadata without necessarily editing the Package file. Beginning with 2.0, responsibility for ongoing work in the area of OEBPS publishing metadata is now the responsibility of the OeBF Metadata and Identifiers Working Group.

This same modular mechanism will be used to provide better support for metadata in areas other than publishing, such as digital rights management, device profiling, internationalization and writing system support, and navigation.

2. Internationalization

There are powerful commercial and moral reasons to ensure that electronic publishing supports all of the world's languages and writing systems. China, for instance, may initially be a bigger market for e-books than the United States. OEBPS 1.2 allows the use of the entire set of Unicode characters, requiring that all Reading Systems accept both UTF-8 and UTF-16 encodings and parse Unicode correctly, as described above. But this is still not optimal for full internationalization, primarily because the requirement to recognize those encodings does not mean the Reading System (or its Reading Devices) can necessarily render all those characters. OEBPS 2.0 will have additional support in this area, including glyph resource specification (for the appearances of characters, particularly in non-Roman character sets) and improved writing system features, including additional writing direction control to accommodate languages that read from right to left. This support will use the metadata modularization mechanisms mentioned above, allowing improved flexibility in development, management, and sharing of internationalization resources such as glyph requirements.

3. Inter- and intra-publication linking

Hypertext linking is one of the most successful and valued features of electronic reading. OEBPS 1.2 supports the use of the XHTML "<a . . . >" element (in Extended as well as Basic Documents) providing basic familiar linking functionality. However, more powerful linking, such as that used in the research hypertext systems of the last 30 years, has long been requested by users; and, with the finalization of W3C **XLink** [3.3.5.1] and **XPointer** [3.3.5.3] standards, this advanced functionality will soon be appearing on the World Wide

Web. Readers will of course expect the same functionality, or better, from their e-books. OEBPS 2.0 therefore will include substantially improved high-function linking, based on XPointer, for both links internal to a Publication, and links to other Publications.

4. Navigation

Like hypertext linking, computer-supported navigation and browsing is also one of the most valued features of contemporary electronic reading. And, like hypertext linking, continued dramatic improvements in the area are expected to appear in Web browsers in the near future. OEBPS 2.0 will provide a powerful XPointer-based navigation mechanism external to the Package file, to support a variety of kinds of tables of contents, indexes, special views, and other sorts of navigation apparatus; it will also provide multilingual, graphical, and audio support as well. This system is fundamentally identical with that developed (with coordination with the PSWG) by the DAISY Consortium and released in the Talking Book standard (NISO Z39.86).

5. Packaging and compatibility

Currently the PSWG is discussing revisions in the Package file to improve modularity and more effectively support ongoing backward and forward compatibility.

11.7 IN CONCLUSION

Electronic books will happen, and they will be eventually a major part of our social and cultural lives. Given the potential advantages of e-books, current trends in technology, and current events in electronic publishing, there can be no doubt about this. However, just *when* e-books will emerge as a major commercial force is not yet clear; nor can we say for sure just what the e-book industry will be like: software, devices, content, market categories, distribution mechanisms, DRM, and the general structure of the industry are all very much still unsettled.

There are a few other things that we *can* be reasonably confident of.

One is that a flourishing industry, when it happens, will probably not be driven primarily by mass market content, but rather by content in the market categories that can make distinctive valuable use of the computational environment. This obviously means education and STM publishing, but also magazines and newspapers and certain sorts of trade content. Mass market fiction will be there, but the initial value, and the driving force behind development and adoption, will be in content that exploits the advanced features which have always been identified as providing the special value of electronic reading—and that are increasingly expected by a public for whom the World Wide Web is part of daily reading life. The nature of the future e-book is therefore best predicted not by reflecting on current e-books and imagining how they might be improved, but by reviewing the high-function experimental reading systems that have been developed in university and industry laboratories for the last thirty years, and by examining the current ambitious one-off efforts by contemporary entrepreneurs. The hard problem remains what it has always been, not designing high-performance reading systems that deliver distinctive value to the consumer, but the next step: how to create a sustainable industry that will support this level of functionality.

Which brings us to the second thing we can be sure of. Like the publishing industry in general, the electronic book industry will almost certainly be based on SGML/XML content and production processes. Only an SGML/XML approach (or one that embodies the same fundamental principles, regardless of the specific implementation) can support both the functionality and the interoperability that are needed to create a flourishing industry. SGML/XML systems are already in wide use. The next five to ten years will probably see the nearly complete conversion of existing production processes to ones based on SGML/XML.

What about OEBPS? Will it provide the general integrating format for all e-book publishing? We think so. SGML/XML-related standards alone cannot deliver the practical level of interoperability required for financially sustainable high-performance electronic publishing. There must be further agreement on the selection and application of these standards, and there must be agreement on specific techniques for allowing innovation without sacrificing interoperability. This is what OEBPS provides. Version 1.2 of OEBPS is already very widely used in e-book publishing, and, perhaps even more important, the publishing industry appears capable of evolving new versions of OEBPS to support emerging needs and directions.

11.8 SOME ADVICE FOR E-BOOK PUBLISHERS

Whether you are ready to leap immediately into the e-book fray, are considering your options, or are merely waiting until e-books become an established part of the publishing industry, you can and should act now to make your transition as smooth, efficient, and cost-effective as possible.

The first step is to learn the following.

(i) WHAT YOU MUST KNOW

- Learn about your current production workflow(s). What tools do your designers, editors, art staff, compositors, and indexers use? What electronic formats do they already produce (e.g., for delivery to the printer, or for promotional sample chapters on the Web)? Obtain and examine sample files if you can. If possible, talk to the people who actually do the work instead of their managers or supervisors.

- Learn about your current archiving procedures. What electronic files do you keep? If you outsource print production, what electronic files do your vendors return to you? Are those files binary or text? Are they revisable? Do they retain typographic quotes, structural information (such as styles or keymarking), layout, and design information? If there are last-minute corrections, are they made to the electronic files as well as the print plates?
- Learn all you can about e-book formats and production. The more you know, the better your decisions will be. Publishers draw on considerable background knowledge to make intelligent decisions about print production; making e-book-related decisions without analogous knowledge is dangerous.

(ii) WHAT YOU MUST DO

Once you understand where you are and where you are going, you can set workflow goals:

- Wherever possible your content should be created and stored in an SGML/XML format and your workflow and publishing strategies should be organized to take advantage of the opportunities offered by SGML/XML content. You may want to adopt an existing SGML/XML element vocabulary such as TEI or DocBook, or, if you have STM content you may want to consider a variation of one of the several widely used SGML/XML vocabularies for scientific journals. You may also prefer to develop your own SGML/XML DTD, as many publishers have. Although you can sometimes incur a small cost in lost interoperability when you invent your own SGML/XML vocabulary, as long as it is carefully designed, and, most important, consistently and correctly applied, you may not in fact lose any significant advantage—and, by having a system tuned precisely to your unique needs and opportunities you may benefit considerably in both efficiency or functionality. Although the initial investment in adopting an SGML/XML approach (whether an existing vocabulary or your own) may be greater than presentation-oriented approaches, production strategies based on SGML/XML can, all other things being equal, provide superior efficiency in process, and superior interoperability and functionality in products. That means that an SGML/XML workflow can actually produce your current products more economically and efficiently, quite apart from its benefit to future electronic products. Unfortunately, it is often the case that "all other things" are not equal and so you should . . .

- Respect the inherent difficulties and complexities of publishing and the accumulated wisdom of your current production process. In particular you must resist any reassuring claims that any software, or any general strategy (even SGML/XML) will easily and quickly solve your problems and immediately provide the full range of possible benefits. Although SGML/XML-based workflows have enormous advantages in the abstract, there are always difficulties in implementing XML workflows, especially in the current environment of inadequate tools and scarce general expertise. Don't be fooled by promises that this is simple. Proceed, but proceed with caution.
- Move as much of your production as possible toward a single workflow. The more consistent your workflow, the easier it is to obtain useful end products from it, and to institute consistent changes to increase its effectiveness. This does not necessarily mean investing in a gigantic end-to-end content management system, by the way; such systems are often inflexible, hindering more than they help. The goal is to extinguish unnecessary and confusing workflow variation, not to put your production methods in a straitjacket.
- Develop a house style guide for editing and composition, if you do not already have one. If you do have one, verify that it is being followed and that it does not need revision or augmentation to accommodate new directions. This guide should include keymarking abbreviations for editors and designers to use and for compositors to incorporate into stylesheets. Also, work out a scheme for canvassing production workers for needed changes to the style guide. No style guide should ever be considered so authoritative as to be beyond revision and no revision will be sustainable if it is not made in collaboration with the production team.
- Archive electronic files from your print-production process. When you move into e-books, it will cost you less to convert existing files than recreate them. Moreover, the larger your existing backlist of electronic files, the better the prices you will get from conversion vendors.
- Move your production methods away from binary, proprietary, and nonrevisable electronic formats toward text-based, open, and revisable formats. When this is not possible, try to salvage text-based and revisable files from the end of the process for archiving; for example,

request .rtf files rather than (or in addition to) Microsoft Word .doc files, and QuarkXPress tags or RoustaboutXT XML files rather than (or in addition to) Quark binaries.

- Beware, however, of asking for *lossy* electronic files merely because they are text-based. Badly exported HTML, for example, may (unnecessarily) lose important information such as typesetting styles, or typographic quotes and dashes. If you are unsure of the quality of electronic files you produce or receive, examine them yourself or have someone knowledgeable do it for you.
- Outsourcing conversion or composition is often a good idea, but you *must* maintain a thorough knowledge of the production process as well as recovering all products (especially intermediate files) and insisting on complete documentation of file formats, markup vocabularies, and conversions. Without this level of involvement and control, your costs will, eventually, soar far above what they need to be. And, in addition, opportunities for new products or innovation in functionality go unnoticed. Don't let your company be "deskilled."
- Ask for help if you need it! Find a knowledgeable consultant or trainer to explain your options and chart your progress. Hire in-house project management or production talent, or retrain existing employees. (A standards-aware Web developer should be able to move into OEBPS-based e-book production with relative ease.) Consider retaining a markup-savvy consultant to check the work your vendors are doing.
- Do not, however, offload all responsibility for developing workflows and schemas onto a consultant; what will you do when the consultant has finished the project and gone away, but no one in the company understands what was done?

11.9 FOR MORE INFORMATION

(i) THE OPEN EBOOK FORUM

The Open eBook Forum Web page is: http://www.openebook.org.

(ii) THE OPEN EBOOK PUBLICATION STRUCTURE

For more information about OEBPS see:

The Open eBook Publication Structure—Version 1.2. Open eBook Forum, 2002. http:// www.openebook.org/oebps/index.htm.

Salo, Dorothea. *OEBPS FAQ: Introduction to OEBPS-based eBooks.* http:// www.textartisan.com/oebfaq/.

(iii) CURRENT RESEARCH AND ANALYSIS: FUNCTIONALITY

A good recent account of new directions in e-book functionality:

Schilit, Bill N., Morgan N. Price, Gene Golovchinsky, Kei Tanaka, and Catherine C. Marshall. "As We May Read: The Reading Appliance Revolution." *IEEE Computer,* 32(1), January 1999, pp. 65–73.

A description of Microsoft's ClearType technology:

Betrisey, C., J. Blinn, B. Dresevic, B. Hill, G. Hitchcock, B. Keely, D. Mitchell, J. Platt, T. Whitted. *Displaced Filtering for Pattered Displays*. Proc. Society for Information Display Symposium. pp, 296-299. (2000).

A recent account of a project using "tagged PDF":

Hardy, Mathew, and David Brailsford. "Mapping and displaying structural transformations between XML and PDF." Proceedings *of the 2002 ACM Symposium on Document Engineering*. (McLean, Va., November 2002). ACM Press, *forthcoming*.

(iv) CURRENT RESEARCH AND ANALYSIS: USERS

Good accounts of recent research on e-book use:

Bell, Lori, Virgina McCoy, and Tom Peters. "E-books go to college." *Library Journal* 127 (8) (May 1, 2002): 44–46.

Bellaver, Richard F., and Jay Gillette. "The Usability of eBook Technology: Practical Issues of an Application of Electronic Textbooks In a Learning Environment." A report from Ball State University, available on-line at http://publish.bsu.edu/cics/ebook_final_result.asp.

Peters, Thomas A. "Gutterdämmerung (twilight of the gutter margins): E-books and Libraries." *Library Hi Tech,* 19(1) 2001.

Marshall, C.C. and C. Ruotolo. "Reading-in-the-Small: a study of reading on small form factor devices." *Proceedings of the Joint IEEE and ACM Conference on Digital Libraries (JCDL02),* Portland, Oregon, July 14–18, 2002.

Marshall, C.C., M.N. Price, G. Golovchinsky, and B.N. Schilit. "Designing e-books for legal research." *Proceedings of JCDL 2001* (Roanoke, VA, June 2001), ACM Press, 41–48.

(v) SGML/XML AND THE LOGICAL APPROACH

These two articles provide an overview of the engineering model underlying the logical approach to electronic publishing, which figured prominently in the analyses of the preceding chapter. For further information about XML and XML-related standards see the chapter on **markup** [3].

Coombs, James S., Allen H. Renear, and Steven J. DeRose. "Markup Systems and the Future of Scholarly Text Processing." *Communications of the Association for Computing Machinery.* 30(11) (1987): 933–47.

DeRose, Steven J., David Durand, Elli Mylonas, and Allen H. Renear. "What is Text, Really?" *Journal of Computing in Higher Education* 1(2) (1990) pp. 3–26. Reprinted with commentary in *ACM Journal of Computer Documentation* 21(3), August, 1997

(vi) BOOK-RELATED SGML/XML VOCABULARIES

We strongly advise new e-book publishers to consider choosing their element vocabulary from one of these two well-designed and widely used XML markup systems documented below, or to extend one of these systems.

The TEI: The TEI is one of the best designed and most widely used book-like XML vocabularies and there are many tools available to support its use. Although it may appear complicated at first, only the relevant portions need be used by any particular project; it is highly customizable and extensible. For simple publications, such as mass market fiction, TEI Lite, a popular TEI subset, may be appropriate. See: http://www.tei-c.org for more information. Sperberg-McQueen, C.M. and Burnard, L. (eds.) *TEI P4: Guidelines for Electronic Text Encoding and Interchange.* Text Encoding Initiative Consortium. XML Version: Oxford, Providence, Charlottesville, Bergen; 1990, 1993, 2002.

DocBook: DocBook is a general purpose document markup language, but particularly well-suited for technical documentation. See http://www.docbook.org/ for more information. Walsh, Norman and Leonard Muellner, *DocBook: The Definitive Guide,* O'Reilly 1999.

(vii) CLASSICS

For a sense of what the possibilities are, we strongly encourage reading the classics and studying the influential research systems. The early pioneering figures are Paul Otlet, Vannevar Bush, Douglas Engelbart, Ted Nelson, Andries van Dam. The advanced working systems, most of which were developed in the 1980s and many of which have functionality still not available even on the Web, include Augment, FRESS, Notecards, Intermedia, and Microcosm. An overview of the research as of 1987 is Conklin, Jeff. "Hypertext: an Introduction and Survey," *Computer* 20 (September 1987), 17–41.

These two articles inaugurated the recent phase of e-book research and development:

Kay, Alan, and Adele Goldberg. "Personal Dynamic Media" *IEEE Computer.* 10 (3), March 1977.

Yankelovich, Nicole, Noman Meyrowitz, and Andries Van Dam. "Reading and writing the electronic book." *IEEE Computer,* pp. 15–30, 18(1), October 1985.

(viii) WIDER ISSUES

Lynch, C. "The Battle to Define the Future of the Book in the Digital World." *First Monday: A Peer-Reviewed Journal on the Internet* 6, 6 (June 2001). http://www.firstmonday.dk/issues/issue6_6/lynch/index.html.

Although the authors have been involved in the development of the Open eBook Publication Structure, they write this article as individuals, and therefore the views presented here should not be considered in any way official with respect to the OeBF. In particular, no part of this chapter should be understood as authoritative with respect to the OEBPS specification itself. The text of that specification is the only authoritative expression of the intention of its authors and the OeBF. Finally, the authors emphasize that this presentation of the OEBPS is intended only as a general orientation to the OEBPS specification; in the interests of clarity, brevity, and value to the intended audience, it is not only incomplete but in several places presents a simplified version of the technical aspects of the specification. We would like to acknowledge the assistance of Gene Golovchinsky (FXPAL), Jon Noring, and Garret Wilson (GlobalMentor) in correcting parts of this chapter. The remaining mistakes are, of course, ours alone. Finally, we would like to commend the members of the OEB Authoring Group (1999–2000) and the OeBF Publication Structure Working Group (2000 to present) for their dedicated hard work toward the end of creating better tools for communication and culture.

12 Archiving

HEATHER MALLOY
Digital Archive Manager, John Wiley & Sons

Maintaining ownership of commercially viable digital assets is increasingly important. As digital files have become the de facto standard for use and reuse of products published both in print and electronic formats, libraries and publishers are working to create a viable way to store and preserve digital assets. Publishers have additional reasons for creating the process and infrastructure for storing their digital materials: the potential for reduced operating costs and increased profit margins associated with reusable content and the increased revenue derived from licensing, selling, or otherwise making available content that is centrally available. This chapter will focus on the issues facing publishers, but will also provide an overview of the wider issues involving archiving.

12.1 THE IMPORTANCE OF ARCHIVING

(i) COMMERCIAL NEEDS

The cost in both time and money to develop a digital archive is not trivial; however, as publishers have become increasingly interested in the reuse and cross distribution of digital assets, the question becomes not "should we archive?" but "can we afford not to?" While the promise of cross distribution and "make once, use endlessly" has not been realized as quickly as many had hoped (the modest revenues generated by e-Books being one example), there are proven and increasingly common ways of reusing and redistributing digital content.

Publishers own and sell their content—it is the core of their business. The fact that their content can be reused validates the need for managing and preserving their digital assets. The challenge is making the process economically viable over the long term by expediting the continued use of those files in an efficient way. The digital content must be easily and widely available to those who need to work with it, stored in a cost efficient way, while not limiting opportunities for reuse (for example, by storing only proprietary formats that require special software that may become unavailable or obsolete) or unnecessarily limiting access to files.

1. Ownership of assets

Publishers do not only hold an inventory of printed products, or CDs, or Web sites—the publishable content of these products is their main asset. Storing the physical assets past their useful life is wasteful and expensive. Creating a repository of digital assets not only makes it possible to create new products, it is a way to manage and safeguard the major assets of the company. This is especially important in an era when mergers, sales, and product partnerships provide an advantage to companies whose assets are readily available and accessible.

2. Reuse

Having files archived accessibly enables much more cost-effective reuse of them. Efficient storage of digital assets will increase productivity by minimizing the amount of time needed to retrieve files for reuse. To maximize the benefits of reuse, it is important to consider a number of initial and ongoing issues when deciding what will be archived.

- What is the primary or original use for the content?
- Are there additional current or potential uses for the content?
- Will the archive (or parts of it) be used only for internal purposes or will it also be available externally, as a commercially available product?
- How long will the content be archived?
- How quickly do the files need to be accessed?
- What will happen to the content after it is no longer needed commercially? How do you define content that is commercially viable?
- How has the process by which the content was created or modified been factored in to the eventual storage and reuse?
- Will the content be reused in its original form or in different formats?
- What are the security and rights implications of reusing digital content?

It is not easy to anticipate the possibilities of reuse, and certainly many future uses have not yet been thought of. However, the possibilities will grow and publishers who have planned for continuing access to their electronic files are in a much better position than those who are limited in their ability to repurpose their existing content. It is much more expensive and time consuming to digitize and convert print legacy content than to be able to start off with a clean digital copy, and indeed, having the content available digitally may spur the development of new products and uses (Reid, 2002).

1. DIRECT REVENUE

A publisher's digital files may be reused or repurposed in ways that maximize the revenue generated from a publication, including the following:

- Subsidiary rights licensing
- Print-on-demand products
- Electronic add-ons to print products
- Electronic versions of scholarly journals
- E-books
- Electronic-only products.

While all of these channels are commonly part of the business of publishing, a company that has control of the digital files used to create its publications has more flexibility to use existing content in multiple ways. For example, a print book can generate additional revenue when the content is licensed for foreign sales. The book might be available as a ***print-on-demand*** product when it is no longer practical for a publisher to manufacture, distribute, and warehouse large quantities of printed books. If it is an educational product, supplementary material might be repurposed from the existing file. The title may also be published as an e-book, containing the same material but available in a digital format. If the original files are created and archived in a way that allows easier conversion and repurposing, the resources needed to create these additional or alternative products are minimized (though not nonexistent). Additionally, a company that has organized, complete, and centrally accessible content may find it easier to create partnerships with companies that depend on or aggregate publisher content.

2. INDIRECT REVENUE

There are also nondirect ways in which the use of digital assets can support the sales of primary print and electronic products, such as:

- Supplying content for companion Web sites
- Supporting sales and marketing efforts
- Enhancing product information distribution
- Enabling faster publishing cycles.

Product content is an important part of these possibilities, but there are additional sources of information and content beyond the obvious published content that are of use in supporting the sale of the primary products. Cover images, marketing copy, and title metadata are all sources of support if they are easily available for use.

3. FUTURE USE

It is impossible to know all of the potential ways that archived digital files may be used in the future. However, digitizing legacy print content is time consuming and expensive. It is not only disappointing, but also potentially costly, to discover that a file or product has a possible new life as an electronic product or even as a reprint but that there are no digital files available. The cost of recreating the content may be more than the anticipated return.

(ii) LONG-TERM PRESERVATION AND ACCESS

Preserving and providing long-term access to digital information has been an issue of concern for libraries for years. While publishers have been involved to some extent in this process, especially with electronic journals, most such efforts have concentrated on the preservation of and access to library collections. Libraries have an understandable concern that publishers may remove or withhold access based on market or internal decisions—the publishers own the content. Plus, as commercial enterprises, many publishers are inherently less stable than libraries—they can go out of business.

However, there are reasons other than commercial ones that necessitate the preservation and conservation of digital content—including maintaining scholarly access, providing redundant access, and providing wider access than private ownership allows. While these may not seem like commercial needs in the strictest sense, maintaining a productive partnership with customers has obvious economic benefits, so it is in the publisher's interest, as well as the library's, to address these needs. Publishers who own the files bear some of the responsibility for preservation and access (Meyers and Beebe, *Archiving from a Publisher's Point of View,* 1999). This is especially important for products published only electronically.

12.2 OTHER CONCERNS FOR ARCHIVING

In the context of archiving, not all files are created equal. In addition to considering the types of products that should be archived, publishers must consider the file types and formats as well. This requires thinking about the workflow involved in creating a published product. In fact, consideration must be given not only to the way a publication's files are created in the first place, but also how they might be used to create other kinds of file sets for other products. For example, a file created or stored in a proprietary page layout program may have limited use when the content is needed for a completely different product.

(i) ARE COMMERCIAL NEEDS AND SCHOLARLY PRESERVATION MUTUALLY EXCLUSIVE?

If the publisher must be concerned with the commercial use of digital content, what about the more altruistic concerns of long-term preservation and access? How can a publisher balance several different priorities? One author has suggested that "preservation is a service of the future that cannot depend on financial rewards" (Arms, 1999), because it involves content that may or may not have sufficient value to publishers—the cost of maintaining the files may not be balanced out by their economic value, though their social and cultural/ historical value may be undiminished.

As something that has value and usefulness outside of its short-term purpose, a digital file may need to be preserved and remain accessible in forms other than that in which it was created. For format independence, an ***XML*** or text file is often the best, but when these are archived without the final published format, or without the means to create that format, the archive may not be acceptable, because the look and feel of the publication may be lost. If the publisher is maintaining the source or "official" version of the product as well as a content repository for repurposing, several different formats may need to be archived and maintained.

While from a commercial perspective, reusing content as a means to generate additional revenue may be a primary focus, publishers also have a responsibility to make sure that their electronic content continues to be accessible to users, especially in the case of electronic-only products. Long-term preservation and access and commercial reuse do not have to be mutually exclusive, though building an effective archive that serves both purposes does require thinking about the life cycle of the content, from the creation of the files and metadata to short-term storage for commercial use to preserving the content over the long term (Burke et al., 2001). Additionally, for publications that are electronic-only, there is an important connection between commerce and preservation—buyers are legitimately wary of purchasing electronic-only content if there is no assurance that it will be available indefinitely (Burke et al., 2001). Other concerns related to archiving electronic-only content include:

- **Versioning.** If a product is published in multiple versions or iterations or is continuously updated, which is the definitive product? Do multiple versions need to be archived, or do the differences between them need to be documented?
- **Links within the content.** How should they be maintained? Do links to outside sources need to be preserved?
- **Subscription management.** With paper subscription products, the subscriber has physical ownership of the publication. An electronic product may live on a server outside of the subscriber's control. What happens to back copies if the subscription ends? The same question applies if the publisher ceases production.
- **Format.** What constitutes the product: the content alone or the content in a specific layout or presentation?

- **Content.** A print publication contains more content than chapters or articles. Front matter, back matter, issue information, and other information also needs to be correctly archived—a task more complicated in an electronic framework, where parts of the publication may exist independently of the print publication framework.
- **Security implications.** Where is the balance between preserving digital content and providing access? How are permission issues related to reuse handled?
- **Metadata.** What kind of metadata is required by outside users of the material and how is that metadata maintained and accessed?
- **Costs.** Who will pay for the costs of archiving material, especially if it is not archived by the publisher?

These issues may seem to be outside of the scope of archiving, but they are intrinsically related, because one of the main purposes of a digital archive is to make new distribution routes and sales possible—especially of electronic products.

(ii) PUBLISHERS AND LIBRARIES COOPERATING

Standards such as the **OAIS Reference Model** [12.4.5.1.2] or the **Open Archives Initiative Protocol for metadata harvesting** [12.4.5.1.4] (see below) are helping to define methods and communications between data repositories. Additionally, libraries and publishers are working together on pilot projects to investigate the practical implementation of offsite, or library controlled, archives.

There are also concerns common to most archiving projects, commercial and library-based. Library archiving projects provide insight into the challenges and potential outcomes of large-scale archiving projects.

(iii) SHOULD EVERYTHING BE ARCHIVED?

In a white paper published by Sheridan Press, Barbara Meyers and Linda Beebe note that not everything needs to be archived. The ultimate decision will vary among publishers, but they suggest the following considerations:

> Does the work contribute to knowledge development? Will it continue to have intellectual value in the future? How has the audience responded to the totality of the work? Can archiving in electronic form add value to the existing work? Is there likely to be an audience for the work in another format? Are secondary or parallel products likely to meet audience needs? Is there potential for combining this work with another to create a more expansive and useful product?
> —*Meyers and Beebe,* Archiving from a Publisher's Point of View, *1999*

The last four issues are probably the most important for an archive devoted to commercial repurposing, and they should influence both the structure of the archive and the format of the content. An archive containing content for reuse should be structured in a way that facilitates that process, and the content it holds should be formatted in a way that is useful for purposes other than the original. The first two points do matter in that even though they may be unknowable at the beginning of the process, if it is decided that certain files should not be archived, they are lost to future development.

12.3 WHERE TO IMPLEMENT THE ARCHIVE

A digital content repository does not exist in a vacuum, but as an important part of a digital content management system. The archive acts as a staging area where content is stored and circulated back into the workflows of product creation and distribution, not as a dead end where files go to die once they've been published to paper. Deciding how and where to implement the archive is a complex decision, particularly when development might involve significant financial investment in advance of financial returns. Archiving is a classic "buy or build" dilemma for most publishers: whether to do the work in-house, turn it over to an outside vendor, or (most likely at first) partnering with others while retaining appropriate control and involvement.

(i) THIRD-PARTY VENDORS

Printers and typesetters have often played the role of commercial archivist for publishers. They work with the definitive files for a print publication, and they provide a convenient gateway for reprints and certain types of reuse. Several such vendors have launched archival storage services for publisher's digital files, often focusing on files in **PDF** [12.4.3.1.1] format. The advantage of this type of service is that a publisher does not have to develop the infrastructure or resources for archiving in-house, and if their modes of reuse depend on the types of files that happen to be stored at the vendor, or if most of the anticipated reuse options depend on maintaining the look and feel of the original print publications, this may be an acceptable option.

However, there are disadvantages. The files are outside of the publisher's immediate control and so are subject to their vendors' provisions for security, backup, and ready accessibility. The publisher will not have control of or, usually, even access to complete records. Files may be dispersed among several vendors, increasing the difficulty of tracking and maintaining quality. The format of the files stored by these services may be limited to the composition files (which can be in proprietary formats for which the publisher lacks the resources to manipulate the content) or print files (for example, PDF), which do a good job of maintaining the look and feel of the published print products but have limited opportunities for other types of reuse. There may be additional costs associated with retrieving and possibly converting the files, again limiting the options for reuse or cutting into the revenue that may be generated by those subsequent publications.

(ii) NONCOMMERCIAL REPOSITORIES

Another option is to place the files in the care of a noncommercial repository such as a library. This option may help alleviate concerns about long-term access to published content and relieves the publisher of some of the costs associated with the internal storage and management of internal files, but it is typically not an option for digital files that are used to create a print product. It is a more likely option for electronic journals. Several libraries, such as Yale and Harvard, are working with publishers to maintain archives of their e-journal content (http://www.diglib.org/preserve/ejp.htm).

An example of this type of project is JSTOR (http://www.jstor.org), a nonprofit organization that provides an electronic archive of back issues of journals, the time frame depending on a "moving wall" licensing agreement. In practice this means that a publisher might agree to license its journal content with a three-year moving wall, and that each year another year of the journal is archived, with a three-year time lag from the current volume year. The theory is that the integrity of and access to the content will be preserved while minimizing potential conflicts with revenue streams or other agreements.

However, as a stand-alone option, third-party archiving both takes away many of the options for reuse of the files for commercial purposes, and does not address reuse of current content, or commercially viable older content, and requires a publisher who pursues this option to create additional infrastructure for managing content internally and implementing standards for content and metadata exchange.

(iii) IN-HOUSE DIGITAL ARCHIVE

An in-house digital archive has many advantages for a publisher. Within a content-management framework, a repository for content is necessary if there is the intent to reuse the content beyond its original publication. It allows the flexibility to plan a workflow and content creation structure based on the repurposing of content and allows for fast access to the files. It also allows direct supervision of the publisher's content.

The disadvantages to taking on the responsibility of creating and maintaining an in-house archive include the costs of creating and maintaining the system, restructuring workflow, training users, and managing and maintaining the system. There are additional considerations if, in addition to acting as a repository for commercially usable content, the system is also acting as a definitive archive of published content.

(iv) COMBINING OPTIONS

None of the above options may be suitable, or immediately practical, taken alone. It is likely that a combination of approaches will be required, depending on the needs of the publishers and the content users. For example, a publisher may store current material in-house, transferring older files to a third-party offsite or noncommercial repository. A library may maintain electronic journals. In addition, a publisher's archiving strategy and mechanism may evolve over time. It may be necessary to utilize third-party resources initially, as in-house solutions are being developed. Even a rudimentary archive is better than no archive at all.

A related option is the development of a distributed archive, where the costs and concerns are spread among several entities. A distributed archive allows multiple locations and technology to be used in a way that allows scalability, redundancy, and the separation of content from the medium in which it is stored. There have been several projects based on this idea, mostly involving libraries or research institutions rather than publishers, however, the principle holds true for both—with publishers able to distribute their assets within their company and also among outside partners. An example of such a project is the Cedars distributed archive prototype (http://www.leeds.ac.uk/cedars/archive/archive.html), developed on the OAIS model.

12.4 TECHNOLOGY ISSUES

Archiving a digital file that is in an inaccessible format, or for which the software or hardware needed to read it is no longer available, is nothing but wasted time and effort. Additionally, the quality and structure of the file itself may affect its ability to serve as either a reusable digital asset or as a resource for long-term preservation.

(i) THE PROBLEM OF OBSOLESCENCE

The state of technology is constantly changing; many digital files become unreadable within a relatively short time after creation (Martin et al., 1999; Meyers and Beebe, Unsettled, 1999) or are left in such a state that they are significantly less useful than a hard copy.

This is an issue that is recognized as the main challenge in archiving, both for preservation-based library archives and publisher's internal archives.

The Task Force on Archiving of Digital Information (http://www.rlg.org/ArchTF/) set out a recommendation in 1996 for ensuring continued access, involving updating media and formats as more stable platforms are developed, and creating standards and protocols for storing and migrating data (Meyers and Beebe, Unsettled, 1999). The standard thinking is that there are two main options for dealing with technological obsolescence: migration and emulation.

1. Migration

Migration means shifting the digital files to current formats and standards as the original environment becomes obsolete, as well as replacing the storage medium as it becomes too old to safely store the data. There are significant and ongoing costs associated with this, both in equipment and in the human resources (whether done in-house or purchased from vendors) needed to facilitate the transfers. In addition, migration may be impossible for certain types of files if they are intrinsically associated with their format or medium (Martin and Coleman, 2002).

2. Emulation

Emulation requires mimicking the original environment on current software and hardware. It also means that the software used to create the original content must be preserved as well (National Library of Australia, N.D.). Emulation is commonly given as an option for preservation, but there is limited evidence that it is a viable preservation or archiving technique.

(ii) FORMAT VS. CONTENT

If the content is preserved for reasons other than reuse in other forms, the format of the product may be just as important as the content (Arms, 1999). For example, when a publisher wants to be able to reproduce the original print pages in various ways—reprinting on other presses, digital or on-demand printing, delivery over the Web—preserving the format of those pages is paramount. (That's what PDF is for.)

However, for commercial purposes, the widest scope for reuse lies in storing content in a way that is not dependent on a proprietary software programs and which enables it to be converted and reformatted with limited effort. Proprietary formats are still widely used by publishers whose main source of revenue is, in many cases, a print product, and do serve legitimate purposes for certain types of reuse. A publisher that intends to reuse its content has to, from the beginning, determine how the software and formats used to create its products will affect the way they are reused, including keeping proprietary file types and software accessible over time. As discussed in the **technology** [12.4] section, these files will need to be continually migrated and the software used to access it maintained. In practice, most publishers, especially those who need to publish to a print file, will want to store source content along with PDF (Kasdorf, 2000).

(iii) FORMATS

The format of the digital files is also a very important issue in digital archiving. Many types of file formats are employed in the creation of both print and electronic publications. A print book might have its text initially composed in a word processing program such as Microsoft Word or WordPerfect, the pages created in a page layout program such as Quark, and the printer files in Adobe Acrobat, as PDF. SGML and XML are also used to create files. Additionally, electronic products such as software and Web sites may be created in any number of proprietary formats. Libraries may also employ additional formatting of electronic files.

Most of the debate over digital format types for archiving has been between PDF and XML/SGML.

1. Sample of format types

1. PDF

Portable Document Format (***PDF***) is a cross-platform page format that preserves the look and feel of a document and allows additional formatting and manipulation, such as font embedding and linking, searching, and highlighting.

In addition to its formatting capabilities, PDF stores certain data elements within the file including font information; presentation elements and colors; and metadata such as author, title, subject, and keywords.

PDF is often used during the print production process for proofing (Kasdorf, 2002), printing, and for publishing to an electronic format where look and feel and accessibility are important. Therefore, for many publishers, the majority of the files that they are archiving may be PDF.

PDF may also be a reasonable option for digitizing paper files, though it is important to note that this usually involves scanning each page as an image before converting to PDF. The process preserves the format of the document, but without much of the flexibility that a text-based PDF has. In addition, the file sizes are often much larger since the PDF is actually made up of individual images of each page, and errors may be introduced due to inadequate character recognition in the scan (Ockerbloom, 2001).

The advantages of using PDF files in an archiving environment include:

- PDF maintains the look and feel when the format of the document is as important as the content.
- PDF is compatible with digital printing.

- Acrobat's widely available multiplatform reader allows users to access and share the files from most systems.
- Embedding metadata in PDF files allows easier access and exchange.
- PDF is easy to create.

The disadvantages of archiving PDF files include:

- PDF is of only limited use in conversion.
- PDF lacks intrinsic structure (a problem that can be minimized or eliminated by archiving of the source files or embedding tags in ***Tagged PDF*** when the mechanisms to do so become more available).
- PDF is not ideal for on-screen viewing, because the print pages are rarely legible without zooming.
- It is a proprietary format (though it is an open standard, meaning that non-Adobe tools are available).

Though PDF is a stable and widely used format, it could become obsolete. If PDF files are used for archiving, certain steps should be taken to maximize their usefulness and life span, such as archiving the source text (and graphics) from the PDF, quality checking any PDFs that are archived, and making plans for upgrading or converting obsolete files.

2. XML

XML is a markup language used, among other purposes, to define the structure of a document, though not necessarily the appearance. The biggest advantage to archiving XML files is that it provides great flexibility to reuse and repurpose the files. On its own, it is nonproprietary and so not dependent on any specific software to be readable.

A well-structured XML file may stand alone, but normally a Document Type Definition (DTD) is used to formally define the elements of the document (Kasdorf, 2002). Without the DTD, the document may be correct but it introduces the possibility of inconsistency and leads to more difficulty in exchanging or transforming the document.

A single DTD does not necessarily need to be used for all types of content—one option is using product-specific DTDs, such as a DTD for journal articles, and a different one for textbooks, for example. However, the more consistent the file, the easier it will be to reuse and repurpose the files later—the "wrapper" of the content may be less important in a reuse case. This, as well as the fact that XML is not platform and system specific, and requires no specific hardware and software—minimizing the possibility of losing files to obsolescence—is the main advantage of archiving content as XML (Kasdorf, 2002).

Disadvantages include the potential loss of formatting and visual information—though related technologies such as the **Extensible Stylesheet Language** [3.3.3.3] (XSL), that help define and preserve information about the look and feel, may help close this gap—the cost and time involved in developing and implementing DTDs, and making the necessary changes in working practices.

Overall, initiating the use of XML as an archival format is more beneficial than not, especially when alternative formats such as PDF and composition files are also archived. See the chapter on **markup** [3.3] for more detailed information on XML.

3. PAGE LAYOUT AND COMPOSITION PROGRAMS

Page layout software is commonly used in the creation of print products. Depending on the software, it usually allows the creation of a file that incorporates the look and structure of the print page. The program may be proprietary and not overly successful at separating the content from the format, limiting the use for digital conversion and storage.

There are valid reasons to archive composition files: when files are to be revised and republished in the same format, they will be easily editable with the same software used to create the original pages, and the format coding will not need to be redone for the unchanged portions. PDF files are not equivalently editable: if only PDFs are available, text files will need to be extracted from them and reprocessed, recomposed into pages again (unless the changes are so minor that line breaks and page makeup are not affected—just updating prices, for example).

There are enough problems with composition files, though, that archiving them alone, without text or PDF files to accompany them, is not acceptable in an archival system.

The main problems with proprietary composition files are losing access to the software that created them, not having supporting files (such as fonts or graphics), and perhaps even needing access to hardware that was used to create the files. Additionally, if the intent of archiving the files is to reuse them in multiple environments, saving the files in a way that limits this flexibility may result in costs in money, time, and effort. The chapter on **composition and graphics** [6.1] contains more information on such software.

4. GRAPHICS SOFTWARE

Many graphics formats are used in the creation of publishable products, and the format used depends on the type of product that is being created. When those graphics need to be used for new purposes or published in new environments, they may not be suitable. For example, images originally created for print publication are typically high-resolution files designed for offset printing, but the resulting file sizes are much too large to publish on-line. If down-sampled versions of the images are archived for on-line publication, they will probably not be suitable for subsequent print publication. And even if the high-resolution files used for the original print publication are kept, they may have been optimized for a particular printing environment (adjusting for the dot gain and tonal range associated with printing on uncoated paper on a web press, for example) and thus would not be appropriate for a different environment (from sheet fed printing on coated stock to digital printing on a Docutech).

Additionally, many graphics are created by proprietary software, burdened by the same issues as any proprietary files. Common graphics file formats include: ***GIF***, used mainly for Web-based products; ***JPEG***, another format used commonly in Web-based applications for photographs and more complicated images (Luna, 1999); ***TIFF*** is an industry standard and can accommodate large, complex, high-resolution images and is used commonly for print products. The chapter on compsosition and graphics covers **graphics formats** [6.8] and **processing** [6.11] in more detail.

5. OTHER SOFTWARE AND APPLICATIONS

As new publications become more dependent on multimedia enhancements, and as new types of electronic products are developed, an archive must be able to adapt to accommodate them. The number of potential formats and file types needing to be archived will grow, and each has its own issues. For example, if a software program licensed from a third party is included with a publication, the publisher may not own the rights to that software, nor the rights and permissions associated with reusing the content in other media. This is a common problem with images: particularly for previously published material being archived, publishers often find that they only received permission for the use of images in the original print publication and are prevented from using them on-line or in other forms. Additionally, many such files do not exist in an analog alternative, as the text in books does. A music file or digital movie is intrinsically tied to its electronic format.

(iv) STORAGE MEDIA

Storage media change frequently: microfilm, CD-ROMs, networked hard-drive storage, Web servers—the change in the technology of storing digital files is relentless. This means that not only must publishers keep up with the changes, there is also always a risk that a particular storage medium will become inaccessible when "better" technology comes along, or that in reality the medium will not live up to its promise (e.g., microfilm: see Baker, 2002). Any archiving or digital content management project must be planned with this in mind.

In addition, the requirements of the content will help determine the structure of its storage. For example, if a certain object is accessed frequently, off-line storage is inefficient. These issues become even more important when the definitive or source version of the content is electronic. If the source product is a print book or journal, in a worse case scenario the files can be recreated from the print product (assuming a copy still exists—see the chapter on **data capture and conversion** [5] for a discussion of this procedure). But for electronic-only content, migration from medium to medium may be the only option.

An additional reason for carefully considering the "container" for the archived content is that as it grows more important to have digital data available and usable, discrete archives will need to communicate with each other, and along with file format and metadata, the storage medium will affect interoperability and accessibility.

(v) METADATA

Metadata is important in any discussion of digital archiving in that the metadata describes the content and allows it to be easily accessed, retrieved, and perhaps navigated. The metadata associated with a digital file might contain nothing more than the title, author, and publication date of the publication it was originally created for, or it might be a source of rich and extensive descriptive information that enhances the use of the publication, defines the scope of the use of the products, facilitates the commercial transfer and distribution of the content or its publication in various forms, or acts as a resource on its own.

Numerous standards are being developed for the exchange and storage of metadata, many based on the needs of preservation of digital content. From a given publisher's perspective these standards may only address some of the relevant metadata issues, and may even conflict or overlap. There are additional issues, such as the need to balance the information currently held in the company's internal systems with the metadata needs of outside users—including libraries and similar organizations, and commercial customers as well, whose needs may be quite different. For a publisher creating a digital archive, this means gathering and supporting not only title and retrieval metadata, but also content metadata, descriptive metadata, and distribution metadata. This task is made harder by competing creation and preservation standards, by the different needs of commercial customers, by the lack of standardization or infrastructure within the company gathering the information, and by the differing needs and capabilities of those who must create or capture the metadata and those who receive the metadata. All of these needs may not be accommodated by the information historically gathered by the organization; in most cases, additional metadata must be identified and defined and the means to gather, store, and distribute it must be developed. Content creation is also affected by the need to gather acceptable metadata. Many file formats allow or require the embedding of metadata within the files; this will become more significant as the Extensible Metadata Platform (XMP, discussed in the chapter on **markup** [3.3.6.2]; also see http://www.adobe.com/products/xmp/main.html) becomes more widely adopted.

1. Overview of some relevant metadata and archiving standards

Below are a few of the relevant emerging metadata standards for publishers. These, and others, are discussed more extensively in the chapters on **markup** [3.3.6] and on **organizing, editing, and linking content** [4.4].

1. ONIX (ON-LINE INFORMATION EXCHANGE)

On-line Information Exchange (***ONIX***) (http://www.editeur.org/onix.html) is a standard developed to communicate book product metadata, such as bibliographic, marketing, and rights information. It is a very extensive and comprehensive set of metadata, useful for describing and selling both print books and electronic products. ONIX is designed to expedite transactions between publishers and book distributors and to reduce the need for creating external reports or customized data for each distributor.

2. OPEN ARCHIVAL INFORMATION SYSTEM REFERENCE MODEL

The Open Archival Information System (***OAIS***) reference model, another ISO standard (at this writing still in draft form) provides a structure for access and preservation. According to Brian Lavoie, an archive that conforms to OAIS standards enables users to:

> Negotiate and accept appropriate information from information producers; Obtain sufficient control of the information to ensure long-term preservation; Determine the scope of the Designated Community; Ensure the information is understandable by the Designated Community without the assistance of the information producers; Follow documented policies and procedures to ensure the information is preserved against reasonable contingencies, and to enable the information to be disseminated as authenticated copies of the original or as traceable to the original; Make the information available to the Designated Community.
>
> —*Meeting the challenges of digital preservation: The OAIS reference model*

3. DUBLIN CORE METADATA INITIATIVE

The ***Dublin Core*** initiative (http://www.dublincore.org) works to establish metadata standards for different businesses and organizations and has published the evolving Dublin Core metadata set. It takes a three-pronged approach with the development of the metadata standard, working in conjunction with other standards groups to develop the technical infrastructure, and education and dissemination of these ideas. The metadata standard consists of a group of fifteen basic elements, such as title and creator.

4. OPEN ARCHIVES INITIATIVE PROTOCOL FOR METADATA HARVESTING

The Open Archives Initiative (http://www.openarchives.org/) works for interoperability standards in the distribution of XML-based metadata. The protocol for metadata harvesting (***OAI-PMH***, available at http://www.openarchives.org/OAI/openarchivesprotocol.htm) defines a structure for this exchange and is based on the Dublin Core metadata set.

12.5 ISSUES IN DEVELOPMENT AND IMPLEMENTATION

(I) COST

The creation of a digital archive is not cheap, whether the repository is managed outside the company or from within. Development and design, implementation, training, and ongoing maintenance result in significant costs that may not show results immediately.

Most publishers do not have the resources in house to design and develop an archive system, especially in the context of a larger content management strategy, and must work with outside consultants to help articulate their needs. It is not just a matter of paying someone else to do the work. Within the company, staff at all levels need to be involved in defining the project scope and making sure that the resulting system fits their needs. This involvement includes getting buy-in from senior management, researching needs, identifying and implementing process changes, integrating the systems into existing systems, testing, and administering the system. Other costs associated with the system design depend on the scope of the archive, the types of access it will offer, and the type of files that will be archived and the amount of processing planned for archived files.

Once the system is developed it must be implemented (including modification of workflow and process integration), and users must be trained to use the system. Provisions also need to be made for the ongoing support and future migration of the system.

Each of these phases has associated costs. Depending on size and scope of the systems, the costs may vary by hundreds of thousands of dollars. Even if the content is eventually archived by a noncommercial organization, the cost to the publisher remains, as libraries and similar organizations are unwilling and unable carry the costs all by themselves.

(ii) QUALITY CONTROL

Managing the quality of the files is an essential task for ensuring that archived files are correct and accessible. There are several parts to confirming the quality of a file to be archived:

- Correctness of content
- Completeness of content
- Correctness of metadata
- Acceptability of format
- Ensuring accurate file transfers and manipulation
- Planning for ongoing migration
- Maintaining version control

The quality of the content depends on the way the files were created. Enforcing strict standards for file creation minimizes the problem of corrupt or unusable files, and allows certain checks on the files in a way that minimizes manual intervention and the attendant costs. For example, if strict file naming is specified, an automatic checking procedure can be established to confirm the correct file names.

Additionally, the files should be created in a way that allows as much cross-platform access (such as using standard file names and extensions) and backward compatibility as possible.

Creating metadata that conforms to standard and widely available norms will also increase the chance that the (correctly created) file will still be accessible through the archive system, and be available for ongoing use and reuse. Additionally, the metadata must be confirmed correct (for example, if it is created and stored as XML, it must validate against the DTD; the same holds true for all content created in this format) and match the submitted content.

The choice of formats is dictated by current needs (i.e., what is being produced—a print book, a Web site, etc.) as well as potential future use. Some of the most commonly available files, such as composition files, have limited reuse possibilities, and are more vulnerable to becoming obsolete, as new versions of the content creation programs are released or superseded.

Files in XML, as noted throughout this chapter and in other chapters, probably have the most flexibility—they can be read on any platform, without special software (minimizing the risk of obsolescence) and their structured format allows easier repurposing. PDF, combined with the XML files, allows the record of the format to be maintained, and while PDF is a proprietary format, it is used widely enough that there is less risk.

No matter what file formats are archived, they must be checked as far as possible for correctness, not only of content but also of creation. Content checking may be a combination of automated and manual checks, and the creation of the file may also be checked against rules. These checks may include checking header information, file resolution, linking and embedding of other files, embedded metadata, file size, etc.

Apart from the format and metadata choices there are other requirements for ensuring accurate data. Version control is important for archiving, since keeping track of the correct or "published" file becomes more difficult if the content is produced in multiple formats and for multiple audiences, and updated on different schedules. Additionally, there needs to be a determination of the depth of files archived for a certain project. For example, final, published files may be required, perhaps XML and PDF, which come with a certain assurance of accuracy. However, what if the manuscript files or initial, unedited files are needed? These types of files may not be as accurate.

(iii) WORKFLOW

Creating the infrastructure for digital archiving affects all interested parties, from publishing staff, to authors, to the consumers of the information. While implementing a new workflow may be difficult, it provides an opportunity to create a more efficient and content-neutral environment.

1. Publishers

The availability of digital content allows new flexibility in the way that it may be used by many publishing groups within the company, and may change the way the content is gathered and produced. For example, a legacy system may store certain metadata elements. But with the creation of a digital archive, content itself is now available to be redistributed in a wider area. With this new opportunity comes the need to store the files and metadata in a way that encourages this possibility. Many publishers now send sample chapters and other content and book title information to different content aggregators and distributors. The more the content is stored in a granular and standardized way, the easier it will be to generate information and content streams. The most important action may be in rethinking from the beginning how metadata and content are gathered and stored. Archiving digital content should not be an end-stage or final process, but part of an integrated workflow that begins with an understanding of the cycles of content use and reuse.

Publishers have an interest in archiving their digital files efficiently and effectively in order to exploit these assets with minimal use of additional resources. Additionally, publishers of digital-only content, or content in which the main format is electronic, have a responsibility to their customers to maintain access to the content in a usable format and on an acceptable platform. Creating a viable way to store and reuse information means restructuring the way content is conceived, created, stored, and distributed. This affects all areas of a company, from marketing to production to IT.

An expanded skill set is now needed to support archiving. While having content archived encourages efficiencies, certain groups have more responsibility. Production groups are major players in successfully creating a digital archive. They are often responsible for managing the creation and movement of the files through the system, and in the case of an archive they may be the main people responsible for making sure the content is correctly archived.

IT also has a large role to play in the development. Content management systems, including archive components, often straddle the line between IT departments and publishing units, and as the largest group of technological professionals, IT departments often must work to implement and integrate new content-based systems into the constellation of business systems that already exists.

Marketing, sales, subrights, content developers—these are the groups that are the main beneficiaries of new content systems. Once electronic content is easily available and accessible, these groups have the opportunity to take advantage of the content and expand their various efforts—a change in workflow that in itself may lead to more changes, as they realize the possibilities.

2. Service providers to publishers

The archiving of digital files affects vendors as well as publishers. A typesetter may need to restructure its workflow to accommodate the changing file creation needs of a publisher. For example, if a publisher's archiving standards necessitate certain file names or embedded metadata, the person or business that creates these files will need to adapt. This might mean more than simply adopting a naming scheme; it might require the component files to be structured differently.

The main ways that the implementation of an archiving system may affect the workflow of a vendor are file creation, versioning, metadata embedding, file naming, and delivery.

The way the files are created may change with the implementation of a digital archive. There is no longer room for individual operator preferences if the resulting digital files are to be consistent. For example, a composition file is made up of the text, images that may have been embedded, tables, and metadata. If the only use of the file is to go to the printer, it may not matter how the component parts are organized. In the past, it was acceptable that a file look consistent—how it got that way was less important. Today, consistency in creation results in more flexibility for reuse. But if the files and its parts are to be reused and repurposed, changes may need to be made in structure and consistency. Graphics and table components may need to be stored separately, rather than embedded. File naming may need to be changed to identify the objects once they are detached or separated from the files. The scope of the files may also need to change. More granularity is better than less, when the intention is to repurpose the files. For example, creating book files at the chapter level may not be enough—each object in a project may need to have its own structure, name, and metadata. Another change may be in transferring the files. If a publisher has an in-house digital archive populated by content created outside of the company, the means of transferring and identifying the data (both what it is and what version it is) become more important. These changes may increase the difficulty for vendors, who often work with many publishers, all of whom have their own standards, and that will have to be integrated with their own internal systems.

Additionally, archiving files for commercial reuse necessitates a higher quality of deliverables from a typesetter or printer. The digital files may act as a source or definitive document for many other primary or ancillary products, and so must be accurate. Moreover, what needs to be correct about them may not be apparent in the originally published product: proofread pages for print will not necessarily reveal whether links, metadata, and file names are correct.

3. Customers

The development of electronic products affects the way that customers such as libraries receive, store, and organize content. Files may be accessed electronically, but archived by the publisher. Different formats for library content may necessitate new licensing, cataloging, and record keeping, and for the librarian or other customer may require changed working practices and skills.

When the transfer of data is electronic rather than by truck, the impact for the customers may be based on changes in storage space (from shelves to hard drives), access, and control over content.

4. Authors

When the issue of reuse becomes important, the way the content is created may also be affected. The use of templates by authors as they create their publication is becoming increasingly common. One of the benefits of this is that it can make it easier to acquire the content, to edit and process the content, and to store and reuse the content. Knowing that content is centrally archived, in standard reusable and re-accessible formats, may also hold significant appeal to authors considering a work relationship with a publisher—making good archiving a way for publishers to attract the best authors.

(iv) CONTENT MANAGEMENT

An archive is not usually a stand-alone system, but is part of a larger content management strategy. The creation of content and its flow in and out of the archive usually depend on interrelated systems and working practices. With the possibilities of reuse, the archive is not the final resting place for "used" content, but a link in an ongoing process of creation and use. See the chapter on **content management** [10.4] for an extensive discussion of this.

(v) COPYRIGHT AND DRM

Security and permissions are huge issues for digital archiving. A digital file's possibilities for reuse are minimized if the permissions don't exist. Additionally the digitization of content allows more granular reuse, with the attendant permissions needs.

The outstanding problems surrounding the archiving and reuse of digital content include contractual issues, permissions tracking, format restrictions, and access.

It has only been in the past several years that publishers have actively pursued reuse and electronic permissions at the beginning of the publishing process. This is important because even if the electronic content exists, reuse is limited if the appropriate permissions have not been secured, not just at the title level, but also for individual components. A print title may have the appropriate permissions for electronic publishing, but certain images, tables, or quotes may not. This may eliminate certain types of reuse or necessitate lengthy research in tracking down permissions.

Once permissions have been secured, and a way to track them has been developed, they must be implemented within a framework of electronic access. One benefit of an archive is wider availability of digital files, and one disadvantage is the wider availability of the files. Wider access introduces a greater likelihood of misuse, inadvertent or not. The impression given is that if the file is available to me, I have permission to use it. As this is not usually the case, any archiving system should have a way not only to monitor or access possible restrictions and permissions, but a way to restrict access to unauthorized users.

12.6 CONCLUSION

Archiving digital content is a necessary part of any digital publishing strategy. It extends the benefits and efficiencies of a digital workflow, and will contain the primary assets of a company. There are many ways to implement a digital archive, but in all cases the following topics must act as a guide.

1. *Identifying content.* What type of content do you produce? Books? Journals? Software? Where are these files currently kept?
2. *Identifying need.* Do you plan to reuse these files? As reprints? For new products? For scholarly research?
3. *Other systems.* How will the archive fit in with your current title and business systems? With other content management systems? How does a digital archive fit into your content management strategy?
4. *Metadata.* How do you plan to catalog and retrieve your content? Will you create your own metadata definitions? Use an existing standard?
5. *Platforms and location.* Will the archive be supported in house? At a third party? What hardware and software will be used?
6. *Workflow and training.* How will the archive affect current working practices? Will new staff need to be hired? What kind of training will be involved?
7. *Costs.* What is your budget for this system? How will you fund ongoing development and maintenance?

12.7 RESOURCES

(i) ON-LINE REFERENCES

Adobe's XMP technology. http://www.adobe.com/products/xmp/main.html

ONIX information. http://www.editeur.org/onix.html

Digital Object Identifier. http://www.doi.org

Metadata Information Clearinghouse. http://www.metadatainformation.org

(ii) ORGANIZATIONS AND COMMITTEES

Open Archives Forum. http://www.oaforum.org/

Open Archives Initiative. http://www.openarchives.org/

Task Force on Organizing of Digital Information. http://www.rlg.org/ArchTF/

European Commission's Open Information Interchange. http://www.diffuse.org/oii/en/oii-home.html

International Council for Scientific and Technical Information. http://www.icsti.org/

Research Libraries Group. http://www.rlg.org/toc.html

Library of Congress National Digital Infrastructure and Preservation Program (NDIPP). http://www.digitalpreservation.gov/ndiipp

Cedars Project. http://www.leeds.ac.uk/cedars/

Andrew W. Mellon Foundation's journal archiving program. http://www.diglib.org/preserve/ejp.htm

Digital Library Federation. http://www.diglib.org/about.htm

JSTOR. http://www.jstor.org

BIBLIOGRAPHY

Arms, William, Y. "Preservation of Scientific Serials: Three current examples." Journal of Electronic Publishing 5 no. 2 (December 1999). http://www.press.umich.edu/jep/05-02/arms.html

Baker, Nicholson. *Double Fold: Libraries and the Assault on Paper*. New York: Vintage Books, 2002.

Beebe, Linda, and Barbara Meyers. "The Unsettled State of Archiving." Journal of Electronic Publishing 4, no. 4 (June 1999). http://www.press.umich.edu/jep/04-04/beebe.html

Burk, Alan, James Kerr, and Andy Pope. "Archiving and Text Fluidity / Version Control—The Credibility of Electronic Publishing." The Humanities and Social Sciences Federation of Canada. 2001. http://web.mala.bc.ca/hssfc/Final/Archiving.htm

Guthrie, Kevin M. "Archiving in the Digital Age: There's a Will, but Is There a Way?." Educause Review 36, no. 6 (2001): 56–65. http://www.educause.edu/ir/library/pdf/erm0164.pdf

Hicks, Tony. "Should We Be Using ISO 12083?." Journal of Electronic Publishing 3 no. 4 (June 1998). http://www.press.umich.edu/jep/03-04/hicks.html

Hodge, Gail. "Digital Archiving in theNew Millennium: Developing an Infrastructure." Sheridan Press. 2001. http://www.sheridanpress.com/PDF_docs/DigiArchiving.PDF

Kasdorf, Bill. "XML and PDF—Why We Need Both." Impressions Book and Journal Services. 2000. http://www.impressions.com/resources_pgs/SGML_pgs/XML_PDF.pdf

Lavoie, Brian. "Meeting the Challenges of Digital Preservation: The OAIS Reference Model." OCLC Newsletter 243 (January/February 2000).

Luna, Ben. "Demystifying Graphics File Formats." PC Update 18, no. 4 (May 2001). http://groups.melbpc.org.au/digimage/startingout2.htm

Martin, Julia, and David Coleman. "Change the Metaphor: The Archive As an Ecosystem." Journal of Electronic Publishing 7, no. 3 (April 2002). http://www.press.umich.edu/jep/07-03/martin.html

Myers, Barbara, and Linda Beebe. *Archiving from a Publisher's Point of View*. Sheridan Press, 1999. http://www.sheridanpress.com/PDF_docs/archiving.pdf

National Library of Australia. "Preserving Access to Digital Information (PADI): Emulation." http://www.nla.gov.au/padi/topics/19.html

Ockerbloom, John Mark. "Archiving and Preserving PDF Files." RLG DigiNews 5, no. 1 (February 2001). http://www.rlg.org/preserv/diginews/diginews5-1.html#feature2

Patrick, Michael J.. "Demystifying Digital Archiving: Demystifying File Formats." Foreword Magazine (September 2000). http://www.forewordmagazine.com/eword/September/0600demystify.asp

Reid, Calvin. "A Little DAB Will Do at Simon & Schuster." Publisher's Weekly (August 5, 2002).

Research Library Group. *RLG and OCLC. Trusted Digital Repositories: Attributes and Responsibilities*. Mountain View: RLG, Inc, 2002. http://www.rlg.org/longterm/repositories.pdf

Sidman, David, and Tom Davidson. "A Practical Guide to Automating the Digital Supply Chain with the Digital Object Indentifier (DOI)." Publishing Research Quarterly 17, no. 2 (Summer 2001): 22–23. http://www.contentdirections.com/materials/PRQ-CDIPracticalGuide.htm

Walsh, Norman. "What Is XML?" O'Reilly XML.com. October 1998. http://www.xml.com/pub/a/98/10/guide1.html#AEN58

13 The Legal Framework: Copyright & Trademark

WILLIAM S. STRONG
Partner, Kotin, Crabtree & Strong, LLP, Boston, Massachusetts; Author, The Copyright Book: A Practical Guide

The purpose of this chapter is to give a succinct overview of the various legal doctrines that apply to digital publishing and to make the concepts and basic rules as accessible as possible. This chapter does not substitute for legal advice on any specific matter that the reader may encounter; rather, it is intended to help the reader be more alert to legal issues that may arise, and be a more informed consumer of legal services. It does not, of course, purport to address all the legal issues that a publisher will encounter. Publishers are businesses, and must deal with all the laws that affect businesses of every kind. Nor does this chapter address some issues that are common to everyone who does business on the Internet, such as the laws of consumer privacy, e-commerce, and the like. The main focus is on copyright, as that creates the property that is the currency of publishing. This chapter will also deal with other intellectual property principles and with some other concerns, such as libel, that are uniquely central to publishing.

13.1 COPYRIGHT

(i) OVERVIEW

The title of this chapter was not chosen lightly. Many people outside the publishing and entertainment industries, and indeed not a few inside those industries, view copyright as something external, superimposed, like traffic laws. It is not. The law—and most especially ***copyright***—is the framework on which publishing is built.

As the word implies, copyright had its origins in a right limited to the making of reproductions—and this right was further limited to books. In fact, it started out in the early 1700s as a limited replacement for a rapidly eroding system of royally chartered printing monopolies. Since then copyright has grown, and continues to grow, because technology evolves, the marketplace changes, and the public's (or at least its legislatures') perceptions of fairness evolve and change with them.

1. What can be copyrighted

Copyright now encompasses a broad range of rights in a broad range of materials: written works, images in any medium whether two- or three-dimensional, musical works, motion pictures, sound recordings, computer programs, and so on. Any product of the human mind can be copyrighted so long as it meets a few basic criteria. See **criteria for copyrightability below** [13.1.2].

2. Copyright term

Copyright in the United States used to last no more than fifty-six years. Now it lasts far beyond the lives of the creators of copyrighted works. If a work is created by one or more individuals, the benchmark term is the life of the author (or the last of joint authors to die) plus seventy years. If the authors are anonymous, or publish under a pseudonym, the term is ninety-five years from first publication, or 120 years from creation, whichever expires first. (This can be converted to life-plus-seventy by disclosing the identity of the author in the records of the Copyright Office.) If the work is "made for hire," the term is ninety-five years from first publication, or 120 years from creation, whichever expires first. (Note: More complex rules apply to U.S. works created before 1978.) While the adoption of these rules has brought the United States more or less into harmony, going forward, with the laws of its European trading partners, there may be less to that harmony than meets the eye. For the next several decades, works of foreign origin published before 1978 may have dramatically longer copyright terms overseas than in the United States, depending on when they were published and when their authors died. An Internet publisher with a foreign presence or assets may thus be exposed to infringement actions abroad that could not be maintained against it in the United States.

3. Copyright is national and international

As the preceding paragraph suggests, copyright is both national and international. Technically speaking, each country determines the law of copyright within its own borders. However, almost all countries of the world are members of the ***Berne Convention*** and through that convention have harmonized their copyright laws to an extraordinary degree. Almost all countries now extend to the works of foreigners much the same protection as to works of their own citizens. The basic principles of copyright are thus essentially standard worldwide, although the enthusiasm with which the law is enforced varies substantially. But each country's copyright law has its own particular quirks. The law discussed here is that of the United States, unless otherwise noted.

(ii) CRITERIA FOR COPYRIGHTABILITY

To be eligible for copyright, a work must conform to the following rules.

1. Expression

The work must contain some concrete *expression* of ideas or information; ideas and information themselves are not copyrightable.

2. Originality

The work must be *original* with the *author.* The term "author" does not mean what it means in everyday speech. Ironically, its modern meaning in copyright is really an ancient, Latin-derived meaning: the person who causes a thing to come into being. Thus, a person who creates a copyrightable work (or that person's employer) is an "author" even if in everyday speech we might instead call him or her a painter, filmmaker, or composer. The term "original" also has a special meaning in copyright law. It does not mean "something never seen before," but rather "something that the author created without copying the work of someone else." In theory, two people could create identical works and, so long as neither copied from the other, each would be entitled to a copyright. Note that the copying need not be intentional. If the purported author copied from another source, even subconsciously, copyright will be denied.

3. Creativity

The work must contain a modicum of *creativity.* This requirement means less than meets the eye. The level of creativity required for copyright is extremely low. It has little in common with "creativity" as we use that term in ordinary speech. The U.S. Supreme Court, in the landmark case of *Feist Publications, Inc. v. Rural Telephone Service Co.* [111 S.Ct. 1282 (1991)], ruled (contrary to some lower courts) that telephone "white pages" cannot be copyrighted. However, subsequent cases have granted copyright to yellow page directories, compilations of auto resale prices, and other things that we would not usually think of as "creative." Where a database is concerned, or a compilation of smaller works such as an anthology, copyright lies in the author's "selection or arrangement" of the things included in the database or other compilation. There must be some faint glimmer of the author's own personal judgment, as opposed to the mere aggregation of facts on a commonplace grid. (The full implications of this have yet to be explored. For example, should copyright protect a customer list that owes its existence to the customers rather than any creativity on the part of the merchant?)

4. Variety of possible expressions

There must be more than a handful of ways of expressing the same idea or information. If there are not, the law holds that idea and expression are "merged." For example, there are not many ways to write up the rules of a card game, and copyright in any particular way of doing it will be severely limited to those phrases where the author had some true discretion—or copyright may be denied altogether, so as to avoid creating a monopoly in the underlying ideas.

5. Fixed in a medium

The work must be *fixed* in a *tangible medium of expression* for more than a transitory period of time. The phrase "tangible medium of expression" is all-encompassing; the law is medium-neutral. Where digital media are concerned, "fixation" requires only that the work be stored in such a manner that it can be retrieved. While you are typing a to-be-deathless work of prose on your computer, it is stored only in the computer's temporary memory and arguably not fixed. Once you save that work on your hard drive or a floppy disk, it is certainly fixed for copyright purposes.

6. Nontrivial quantity

The work must be more than trivial in quantity. Thus, copyright generally does not protect short phrases and slogans and the like.

7. More than purely functional

The work must be more than purely functional. Functional machines and devices, however creative and original, are protectible only by patent or trade secret rights, not by copyright. This distinction, once very clear, has been muddied by the application of copyright to computer software. In the early days of the digital revolution, the wise old men of copyright decided that since software begins as a written work it should be copyrighted, brushing aside the objection that the only value of software lies in its ability to perform functions. That decision is now embedded deep in the law, and courts are obliged, when dealing with software infringement cases, to try to distinguish within a program what portions are dictated by functional considerations and what portions are "expressive." This is no easy task.

In the context of publishing, denying copyright to functional elements means denying it to, for example, the layout of a book or the architecture of a Web site, no matter how original that layout or architecture may be. Graphic elements (such as illustrations) that can exist independent of the layout are protected, as is of course the text, but not the manner of their physical arrangement. In parts of Europe the law recognizes a limited right in page layout and typography, but U.S. law does not.

8. U.S. government works

Assuming a work meets these various criteria, it is protected by copyright, with only one exception: works of the U.S. government—that is, works created by government employees within the scope of their official duties—are not protected and are free for anyone to use.

9. Copyright is automatic

Furthermore, a work that copyright protects receives that protection automatically. The answer to the common question, "What do I have to do to copyright this article/ poem/photograph?" is, simply, "Nothing."

Before 1978, "nothing" would have been a very wrong answer. It is not in the purview of this chapter to go into the details of older copyright laws that are no longer in effect. Any electronic publisher who wishes to make use of materials published before March 1, 1989, should consult one of the already published sources on the technicalities of applicable law. However, because misinformation on the topic of, "What do I have to do to get a copyright?" is so widespread, a word should be said here about copyright notice and registration.

1. COPYRIGHT NOTICE

Copyright used to require adherence to certain formalities. The first and most important of these, for publishers, was the affixation of copyright notice. This notice—in the form "©1965 John Jones" or an acceptable variant—had to be placed on works when they were first published, and at all times thereafter, or the work would enter the public domain. (This was never true in most of the world, but applied in the United States until the U.S. joined the ***Berne Convention*** in March 1, 1989.) Exceptions, and opportunities to cure omission, were few. Since March of 1989, however, copyright notice has not been required. However, it is still advisable, both as a "no trespassing" sign and to avoid any possible defense of innocence (such as, "I looked for a copyright notice but I didn't find any so I assumed it was OK to copy") on the part of an infringer. In an electronic publication, the copyright notice should appear at least on the first screen that any user will see when calling up the work.

2. REGISTRATION

The other important formality was that of registration. Registration was not necessary for an unpublished work, unless one wanted to obtain federal copyright rather than relying on state (so-called "common law") copyright.

However, once a work was published, registration was critical to maintaining copyright. Before 1978, copyright in the United States consisted of an initial term of twenty-eight years, beginning with the date of first publication, and a renewal term that was, at first, twenty-eight years and was later lengthened. If a copyright was not registered, and the registration was not renewed in the twenty-eighth year following first publication, the work would go into the ***public domain*** when its first term expired. This was a common fate for works that had gone out of print; publishers had little incentive to renew copyright and authors, for the most part, were ignorant of the requirement. In 1992, renewal was made automatic. And for any work created or first published after 1978, it is not a relevant concept.

Registration in the United States Copyright Office, though no longer critical to the survival of a copyright, is still advisable. If effected in a timely manner it makes the owner eligible to recover attorneys' fees in any action against an infringer, and also to recover so-called "statutory damages" from the infringer. The details of this will be discussed below (see **copyright registration** [13.1.4]).

(iii) WHO IS THE COPYRIGHT OWNER?

Copyright belongs in the first instance to the author or joint authors of the work. However, the "author" for legal purposes is not necessarily the human being who actually created the work. There are certain circumstances under which copyright will be owned by the person or company for whom the creative individual worked. Works to which this applies are called "works made for hire" (or ***works for hire*** for short).

1. Works for hire

There are three basic types of work for hire.

1. WORKS BY REGULAR EMPLOYEES

Works created by regular employees within the scope of their employment. These are employees who receive a regular wage or salary from the company for which they create materials, and whose job description includes the production of those materials. (Things they create on their own time, in their own homes, on their own budget, belong to them individually.) Typical of such works are magazines and newspapers, which are created largely by the salaried writing staff, and databases (e.g., Lexis-Nexis) created by the staffs of the publishers. Materials created by freelance writers do not fall in this category.

2. WORKS BY SURROGATE EMPLOYEES

Works created under circumstances where the creative party is so subject to the direction and control of the hiring party that he or she is treated as almost a surrogate employee of the hiring party. For example, a person who is nominally a freelance software designer, and receives a 1099 from her client, but who works full time on the client's premises doing work assigned by the client's chief software engineer, may well be considered "for hire," but that person's twin brother who works part-time at home on the same projects may not. The determination of work for hire status is ad hoc and based on the gestalt of the situation, not by self-applying rules.

3. COMMISSIONED WORKS

Finally, there are a few types of works that can be treated as made for hire if they are specially ordered or commissioned, and if the hiring and creative parties agree in writing to treat them as works for hire. The specific types of work that are relevant to the publishing industry are:

- Contributions to a "collective work," that is, a work created by the selection and arrangement of separately copyrightable elements. For example, a person who writes a weekly column for a news Web site could agree that his or her columns would be works for hire.
- Translations.
- Supplementary works. The statute defines these as works "prepared for publication as a secondary adjunct to a work by another author for the purpose of introducing, concluding, illustrating, explaining, revising, commenting upon, or assisting in the use of the other work." Examples include forewords, afterwords, pictorial illustrations, maps, charts, tables, editorial notes, answer materials for tests, bibliographies, appendixes, and indexes.
- Compilations (a term that includes both collective works and databases). Thus, the editor of an on-line journal can agree that her editorial work in selecting and arranging the content of the journal will be work for hire.
- Instructional texts, a term defined to include *only* works that are intended for use in systematic teaching activities. In other words, text and curriculum materials can qualify as work for hire, but such things as "how to" books for the weekend carpenter and "Teach Yourself French at Home in 21 Days" do not qualify.
- Tests.
- Answer materials for tests.
- Atlases.

In order for a work of one of these types to be considered made for hire, the parties must agree in writing, preferably in advance of the work being done. The written instrument should specifically state that the material being commissioned will be "work made for hire" or "work for hire."

(iv) COPYRIGHT REGISTRATION

As mentioned above, it is advisable to register copyright in any published work. If the copyright is registered within three months following first publication, the copyright owner has two significant advantages if it becomes necessary to go after an infringer. The first of these is that the copyright owner is eligible, in the court's discretion, to recover its attorneys' fees in any infringement suit. The threat of having to pay the plaintiff's attorneys fees can be a major inducement to a defendant to settle a case quickly and on terms favorable to the publisher.

The second advantage is that the copyright owner can elect so-called "statutory damages" in lieu of actual damages. Statutory damages are discretionary with the judge or jury, and they can be as high as $150,000 per work. There is a punitive element to them, in addition to mere compensation. If real damages are small or difficult to determine, but the infringer's conduct is particularly egregious, statutory damages can prove a great benefit to the plaintiff.

Copyright registration, at $30 per work, is a small price to pay for such advantages. It is not only inexpensive but simple. Bear in mind, though, that registration of a collective work (such as an issue of a periodical) does not effect registration of contents not owned by whoever owns copyright in the collective work. If a contributor to an e-journal or other work has reserved copyright to him- or herself, it should be separately registered in order to obtain the benefits described above.

The forms and instructions for registering copyright are included in the online version of the Guide, and are also available on the Web at http://www.copyright.gov/forms/

(v) THE RIGHTS OF A COPYRIGHT OWNER

Copyright is often described as a "bundle of rights." The rights in the bundle are the following.

1. Copies

The right to "reproduce the work in copies." This right—and all other copyright rights—applies not only to the work as a whole but also to any part of the work that could stand on its own as copyrightable subject matter.

2. Derivative works

The right to create derivative works based upon the work. A ***derivative work*** is defined as one in which the original is "recast, transformed, or adapted." In a sense, this is a subset of the right of reproduction, because to be a derivative work a new work must reproduce something of the original. Within the world of publishing, the most common traditional derivative works are new editions, abridgements, and translations. Published works are often licensed outside the industry for derivative works such as motion pictures, where often nothing more than the plot (and often but little of that) survives the process of derivative creation.

Licensing of electronic rights in a print publication is not, *per se,* an exercise of the derivative work right. Digital files are considered by the law to be mere "copies" rather than derivative works. However, where a digital file of a work has been substantially altered—for example, enhanced by the addition of hyperlinks, or pared down by the removal of graphic illustrative material—it may well qualify as a derivative work.

3. Distribution

The right to distribute the work publicly. The right we refer to in common speech as the right of "publication" is an amalgam of the reproduction and distribution rights. Distribution in the digital context includes any transmission of electronic impulses that causes a copy to be made in the recipient's computer.

4. Public performance

The right to perform the work publicly. Within publishing, this is not a relevant right, but publishers often license the performance of their publications by such means as audiotapes, live stage performance, and motion pictures. Note that performance of a derivative work such as a motion picture is considered to "perform" that part of the original work that is embedded in the derivative.

5. Public display

The right to display the work publicly. This right used to be of little value, but it is crucial in the digital world. Whenever a reader is allowed to view a published work on-line, the right of public display is being exercised.

In the electronic context the rights of distribution and display become intertwined. If a user logs onto a publisher's Web site, views a work, and then downloads a copy of the work, has the publisher engaged in reproduction, distribution, display, or all three? In many cases this is merely a philosophical quibble, but it could be important if the publication and display rights were owned by different people. Logically, it seems that all those rights have been involved. Electronic publishers should therefore be sure to secure both the distribution and the display rights in their contracts with rights holders.

6. Importation

The owner of the distribution right within the United States also has the right to prevent importation into the United States. Although there have been no cases to date on "importation" via the Internet, it seems logical to assume that the right to prevent importation includes the right to prevent transmission into the United States, even where the transmitter has the right to use the work within the country where the transmission originates. If a digital copy is made outside the United States under circumstances that would make it an infringement if the copy were made within the United States, transmission into the United States is forbidden completely. If the copy is made with the copyright owner's permission, then its importation is permitted for personal use, for official governmental use, or, with limitations, for use by libraries and some other nonprofit charitable institutions.

(vi) DEALING IN RIGHTS: ASSIGNMENTS AND LICENSES

"Assignment" is the term most used by lawyers to denote a transaction in which the copyright owner transfers all or most of the copyright. ***License*** is the term generally used when the copyright owner grants one or more specific rights. "License" is the correct term when the grant is of a limited duration, although the term can just as properly be used when the arrangement is good for the entire term of copyright. The Copyright Act uses the broader term "transfer" to mean all transactions in which a copyright, or any exclusive right (however broad or narrow) under that copyright, is granted to one person by another.

As this discussion indicates, the various rights in the copyright bundle can be parceled out in any number of ways, and assigned or licensed separately or together. A typical book contract may start off with a requirement that the author assign "all right, title, and interest, including but not limited to copyright throughout the world for all terms of protection." During the course of negotiation, though, some rights—for example, electronic rights, non-English-language rights, rights outside North America, performance rights, first serial rights (i.e., the right to license magazine excerpts prior to the book launch)—may be carved out and reserved to the author.

The author or publisher may then license translation rights on a language- or country-specific basis. They may license electronic rights to a specialist Web publisher, performance rights to a Hollywood producer, and serial rights to a weekly magazine. Rights may also be licensed for quite different durations. Foreign language rights, for instance, are rarely licensed for more than ten years at a time, and electronic rights are often licensed for only two or three years at a time, whereas motion picture rights are generally licensed on a perpetual basis. In short, the only limitations on the ways that the bundle of rights can be divided up are the limitations of what the market will bear.

1. The importance of getting it clear, precise, and in writing

It is important when licensing rights to make very clear what rights are being licensed and for what periods of time. In dealing with electronic rights, this includes making clear whether specific identified technologies are involved, or whether the license is for "all electronic and other digital media now known or hereafter discovered" or "all media" or words to that effect. In licensing electronic rights one should also be careful to specify whether the licensee has the right to publish the work only in its entirety, or "in whole or in part," and whether the licensee may include the work in compilations such as databases. It is essential to say what the duration of the license will be; unless expressly stated otherwise, any license will be deemed to be good for the life of the copyright. It is also essential, if the license is to be exclusive, to say so in so many words. Any license that is not expressly identified as exclusive will be deemed to be nonexclusive.

1. TRANSFER OR SUBLICENSING

It is also important to specify whether any exclusive license may be transferred or sublicensed. The Ninth Circuit held in *Gardner v. Nike,* 279 F.3d 774 (9th Cir. 2002), that an exclusive license is *not* transferable unless the licensor has so agreed. The trial court held, and the Court of Appeals appears to have concurred, that an exclusive license may also not be *sublicensed* unless the contract so provides. These rulings are at odds with established industry practice, and copyright scholars believe them to be in error. Nonetheless, unless and until this case is reversed, or the clear trend of case law goes the other way, one must draft any license with a weather eye to the position the court took in *Gardner v. Nike.*

In practice, this means that in any license agreement, the licensee should insist on inserting in the agreement the following language, or words to similar effect: "This license is freely transferable and may be assigned or sublicensed at the discretion of the licensee." Assuming it consents, the licensor may nonetheless wish to condition its permission on the licensee's remaining responsible for all payments due to the licensor and all actions and omissions of its transferees and sublicensees.

2. THE *TASINI* CASE

A few words should be said here about the case of *New York Times Co. v. Tasini* [533 U.S. 483 (2001)]. In that case, several freelance writers sued several periodicals publishers for unauthorized electronic distribution of their articles.

The publishers relied on a provision of the Copyright Act that spells out the rights of a periodical publisher in a contribution to its publication, where there is no written agreement. That provision states that the publisher in such circumstances has the "privilege of reproducing and distributing the contribution as part of that particular collective work, any revision of that collective work, and any later collective work in the same series" [17 U.S.C. §201(c)]. The publishers argued that since they were including entire issues of their periodicals in electronic databases, they came within the protection of this statute. The Supreme Court did not agree, finding that inclusion in a larger database from which individual articles could be extracted one by one destroyed the integrity of the original collective works. Therefore the publishers had infringed the authors' copyright by including their articles in these databases. Surprisingly, despite the efforts of the dissenting justices, the Supreme Court made no distinction between the inclusion of a periodical in a database where many publishers' works are mingled and a database where multiple issues of a single periodical are collected.

In order to reach its result, the Supreme Court had to determine that upon being incorporated into an electronic database the original issues of *The New York Times* and other periodicals lost their identity as distinct collective works. However, the Court did not say that this same loss of identity would occur if an electronic version were made of a single collective work. *Tasini* does not mean that the electronic version of a *single* collective work is inherently different—in a copyright sense—from the original. Many other cases have held that an electronic version of a work is covered by the same copyright as the print version. However, the logic of the Supreme Court's opinion could lead in unexpected directions. (There is also the curious case of *Greenberg v. National Geographic Society* to contend with, which held, it seems, that the addition of image-retrieval software to an archival compilation creates a *new* work, not merely a revision of the older compilation [244 F.3d 1267 (11th Cir. 2001)].) The course of safety is to ensure, in any license governing a contribution to a periodical, that the licensee has the right to include the contribution in electronic versions as well as print, and in electronic databases.

Interestingly, the Supreme Court in *Tasini* did not address the issue of whether the publishers had acquired the display right in the articles concerned. Arguably, this would have been an alternative basis for ruling in favor of the authors. The databases at issue in the case were not merely "published" but also posted on-line, thus engaging in "public display" of the plaintiffs' articles. Nothing in Section 201(c) of the Copyright Act says that a periodical publisher acquires the right of public display. Again, prudent publishers will ensure that their license forms include that right.

The Supreme Court also did not address the narrower issue of whether whatever rights the publishers had acquired were sublicensable to parties such as Lexis-Nexis. As discussed **elsewhere in this chapter** [13.1.6.4], nonexclusive licenses are presumed to be neither assignable nor sublicensable, and this could have provided an alternative basis for a ruling in the authors' favor. But the Supreme Court was evidently interested in laying down a broader ruling.

3. THE *ROSETTA BOOKS* CASE

Another recent case is *Random House v. Rosetta Books* [150 F.Supp.2d 613 (S.D.N.Y. 2001, *aff'd,* 283 F.3d 490 (2d Cir. 2002)]. In that case Random House, whose author contracts gave it the exclusive right to publish certain works "in book form," argued that Rosetta's "e-books" infringed its rights. Rosetta, which promoted its products as electronic books, found itself in the ironic position of arguing that "book form" did not include electronic book form. The court, at least on a preliminary basis, sided with Rosetta.

4. THE IMPACT OF *TASINI* AND *ROSETTA*

It is doubtful that these cases will have much long-term impact on the publishing world. Publishers can easily protect themselves from the rule of *Tasini* by obtaining explicit licenses of electronic and database rights from their authors. Indeed, the publishers sued in *Tasini* now do exactly that. As for *Rosetta Books,* the contract language at issue there had been written in 1961, before anyone imagined publishing an electronic book. But *Tasini* is a cautionary tale of what can happen when parties fail to define the scope of a license clearly and in writing, and *Rosetta Books* is a cautionary tale of how narrowly courts can construe license language where new technologies come into being after a license has been written.

Tasini also indicates the risk that any electronic publisher takes on when licensing electronic rights from a print publisher. The *New York Times* and other print publisher defendants were sued for exercising rights that they had not in fact obtained from the authors. But the electronic database defendants were sued for publishing in good faith things they thought the *Times* et al. had the right to allow them to publish. Thus, the "warranties and indemnities" clause, in which the licensor warrants that it has the right to issue the license, and agrees to defend and indemnify the licensee if someone claims otherwise, is a critical part of any electronic rights license.

2. Language-specific licenses

In the print world, it has long been common to limit English-language rights geographically (e.g., to "North America" or "the United Kingdom" or "Commonwealth countries") in the licensing of books. (Journal articles are typically licensed with no geographical restrictions.) In CD-ROM publishing such divisions may still make sense, depending on the circumstances. But in Internet-based publishing, such divisions make no sense. Any license of rights for Internet-based publishing should be worldwide, at least with respect to any given language.

3. A few thoughts on licensing strategies

1. SHOULD THE AUTHOR OR PUBLISHER RETAIN ELECTRONIC RIGHTS?

When an author and a publisher are negotiating a book contract, should the author retain electronic rights or assign them to the publisher? Most large publishers now have some electronic publication capability; all of them want to control electronic rights if for no other reason than to prevent their use by someone else in competition with the print rights. Publishers usually prevail in this battle, sometimes conceding that if they do not exercise electronic rights within (say) three years those rights revert to the author. But the question of royalties is often fudged, since many are unwilling to predict what market-rate electronic royalties will be two or three years down the road. A common form of this fudge is to say that royalties will be negotiated when the rights are exploited, in light of then-existing industry practice.

Bear in mind that different considerations may apply to the right to license electronic uses of *parts* of a book rather than the book as a whole. A publisher should probably always have the right to license small-scale electronic uses of material from the book, as this is a fairly risk-free source of additional revenue.

2. WHAT ABOUT FOREIGN LANGUAGE E-RIGHTS?

The issue of foreign language e-rights is a subsidiary, in a sense, of the larger question of foreign rights. Book publishers are more willing to give up foreign language rights than other subsidiary rights, because few of them operate in more than one language and there is no real competition between editions in different languages. The party who is in the best position to find a licensee for foreign rights should have those rights. An individual author may be in a poor position to market and license foreign language e-rights, or indeed print rights. If the publisher believes it has the capability to license them, it should ask for those rights, and the author should seriously consider granting them. (The author must bear in mind that the publisher will then typically take from 20 to 50 percent of whatever revenue foreign language rights generate.)

3. WHAT IF THE BOOK IS INTENDED AS AN E-BOOK?

Publishing new content in e-book form is still so experimental that it is hard to say anything much about it. The author of this chapter represents one e-book company, and can say that that particular company insists on obtaining print rights as well as e-rights. The reasoning behind this is both to prevent being undermined by print publication and to preserve future options.

4. SCHOLARLY JOURNALS SHOULD KEEP ELECTRONIC AND PRINT RIGHTS TOGETHER

When a scholarly society is negotiating a journal contract, electronic rights normally go hand-in-hand with print rights. Journal publishers typically now make their journals available in electronic form as an additional service (often at no additional fee) to their subscribers. There are also journals that are published only in electronic form. In any case, no journal publisher will accept a separation of print and electronic rights, because for journals the competition between the two could be fatal.

5. PERSONAL POSTING OF JOURNAL ARTICLES

When a contributor is negotiating with a journal, should the author be able to retain the right to post his or her article on a personal or departmental Web page, or to circulate it in an electronic analog of the old-fashioned "preprint"? Practice on this varies widely, and there is no "best practice."

6. WORLD RIGHTS IN FOREIGN LANGUAGES

Should an electronic publisher ask for world rights in all languages? Or only in English, Spanish, or whatever its native language may be? So long as it secures exclusive worldwide e-rights in its own language, the answer to this question has no competitive implications. In other words, an American e-publisher can safely leave French language e-rights on the table without fear of meaningful competition.

7. ELECTRONIC RIGHTS IN FOREIGN LANGUAGES

When the original publisher is licensing out foreign language rights, should it license print and electronic rights separately or together? If the foreign publisher has both print and electronic capability, the rights should probably go together, giving the licensee the discretion of whether and when to go electronic. If the foreign publisher is exclusively a print publisher, it will want electronic rights for self-protection, but the licensor may be reluctant to, in effect, bury them in that manner. (As noted above, different considerations apply to the right to license electronic use of excerpts, rather than the work as a whole.)

If the foreign publisher is an electronic publisher, much will depend on calculating whether a Spanish electronic edition of the work, for example, may pre-empt the Spanish language market for the work, making it impossible for a Spanish print edition to flourish.

4. Nonexclusive licenses

The foregoing discussion has focused on exclusive licenses. A great deal of electronic publishing, however, is done under nonexclusive license. For example, services that aggregate scientific journals typically receive nonexclusive distribution licenses from the original journal publishers. Such licenses are nonexclusive for the obvious reason that the publisher is looking for additional sales that it cannot make on its own; it is not seeking to hand over distribution to someone else.

The publisher may of course agree, for additional remuneration, that it will not license the material to any service that competes with its licensee. Such an agreement does not in itself make the license exclusive. If the publisher has retained distribution rights that are not limited by geographic market or in some other way, then by definition the aggregator has not acquired exclusive rights. Rather, such an agreement gives the licensee a contractual right to prevent the publisher from doing a similar deal with any third party.

Nonexclusive licenses are also the vehicle for a great deal of content that appears on consumer-oriented Web sites. For example, a Web site featuring medical or business information may reuse material from newspapers, books, and other sources under nonexclusive license, often purchasing content through syndication services. The nonexclusive license is the preferred vehicle for secondary, follow-on uses of this type. Such uses are designed to extract further value from materials once they have fulfilled their main purpose.

Nonexclusive licenses are usually less expensive than exclusive licenses. They impose less duty of promotion on the licensee. They preserve the licensor's options to seek other revenue sources, and they avoid tying down the material in an unproven business.

Nonexclusive licenses are not transferable by the licensee unless the licensor expressly agrees otherwise. Like exclusive licenses, nonexclusive licenses are presumed to last for the life of the copyright unless the parties otherwise agree.

5. Permissions

A particular variant of the nonexclusive license is generally referred to in the publishing industry as a ***permission***. This is the sort of license that one publisher gives to another to use excerpts from a work. For example, publisher A may wish to use a photograph of Afghanistan from publisher B's news magazine in A's e-book on the war on terrorism. Or B may wish to quote a long passage from A's e-book in an article on the same topic. In the print environment, such permissions have been routinely granted, for a fee.

Requests for permission to reuse print materials in an on-line setting have caused a great deal of anxiety among print publishers. They are concerned, understandably, that granting such permission will cause them to lose control of their material altogether. This has been particularly true where illustrations are concerned. Loss of control over isolated passages from a text work will not do much damage, but if an entire photograph is digitized and put up on the Web, it is at risk of widespread unauthorized distribution and other reuse. Photographers are keenly aware of this; publishers seeking to produce electronic versions of their print works—especially journals and books—have often had to remove or replace illustrations before doing so, because they were unable to get electronic rights for those images.

As between electronic publishers, however, there should be no such impediment, for the material is already at risk and one more exposure will not materially impact its protection. The chapter **Digital Rights Management** [15] discusses the mechanisms for protecting and dealing in these rights in more depth.

(vii) FAIR USE

Permission is not always required for reuse of another's copyrighted material. As a matter of policy, the law allows ***fair use*** without regard to the copyright owner's approval or disapproval.

A very old doctrine in copyright law, fair use permits the reuse of copyrighted material in reasonable quantities for purposes that are culturally useful—or at least benign—and do not undermine the market or potential market for the work. Examples of such use include news reporting, criticism, scholarly commentary, scholarly quotation, and parody; but no exhaustive list of fair uses is possible. In determining whether a use is fair, courts look at the nature and purpose of the use, the nature of the original work, the magnitude of the use (both qualitatively and quantitatively), and the "effect of the use upon the potential market for or value of" the original work [17 U.S.C. §107]. Many publishers and authors would like there to be agreed-upon guidelines for fair use in the digital environment, such as those that were developed for classroom photocopying and educational use of off-air videotapes. None exist, however, and it is unlikely that any will in the foreseeable future.

Determinations of fair use are always necessarily ad hoc and dependent on the particular facts and equities of each situation. Fair use has the virtue of flexibility and the defect of unpredictability.

In the example given above (see **Permissions** [13.1.6.5]), it would not be fair use for A's e-book about the war on terrorism to use illustrations from B's news magazine without permission. The reason is that A is using the photograph to enhance, and enhance the value of, its book. If the photograph is worth a thousand words, then publisher A should not expect to get a thousand words for free. However, if the subject of A's book were not the war itself but how the news media covered the war, and it included the photograph for purposes of criticizing or commenting on the manner in which news photographers covered the war, that *would* be fair use. In the latter case, A's ability to criticize would be in jeopardy if we required permission. B should be careful, though, to present the image in a way that is consistent with the intent of the use. For example, its fair use defense will be strong if the photograph is reproduced smaller and at a poorer quality level than in the original, much weaker if the photograph occupies a full high-definition screen and thus begins to look like mere illustration or even the *raison d'etre* of the work.

1. Fair use in the digital era

Much has been written about fair use of this type and the reader interested in knowing more should consult the many available sources. For present purposes, though, it is important to make one point: there is no intrinsic reason why the fair use calculus should operate any differently in the traffic between print and electronic media, or between electronic media, than within the world of print. Some copyright owners may protest this; they may argue that electronic dissemination of the user's work will magnify the impact of the use on the market for the original by obviating the need of other would-be users to come to the original rights-holder for permission. That is not a spurious argument, but it is a misleading and dangerous one. It is misleading because what the fair use doctrine cares about when assessing market impact is whether the use will supplant the market for the original work, not whether it will, as an unintended by-product, enable scofflaws to avoid copyright fees. And the argument is dangerous because, taken to its logical conclusion, it could seriously undermine the role of fair use in our culture, and that would have disastrous consequences. No court has yet suggested that any such revisionism is called for, and we should hope none will.

It would also be wrong to deny fair use the chance to grow into areas where things are possible that never used to be. In 1976, when Congress last addressed fair use, no one could have imagined the sort of multimedia works that digital publishing allows. For example, imagine a work of musical scholarship that is "illustrated" with audio clips of certain jazz performers' work, or even video clips of their performances. It seems to this author that the general principles of fair use apply just as well here as they do in the print-only world.

1. CRITICISM

Criticism, in the strictest sense of that word—scholarly analysis of the music, or a review of a performance—can justify quite extensive use. Of course, because a sound bite has entertainment value that a few measures or bars of sheet music do not, one must be careful that the written criticism is the dominant element and that the musical excerpts are no longer than needed for the purpose.

2. ENTERTAINMENT

At the other end of the spectrum from "criticism" is entertainment. The electronic equivalent of a "coffee table book" ought not to be able to make free use of sound and video where the purpose is not to critique or educate but simply to entertain the reader.

3. ILLUSTRATION

Somewhere in between criticism and entertainment lies what may be called illustrative use. One would certainly have to observe narrower boundaries of use if publishing, say, a life of Duke Ellington, than if publishing a critical study of Ellington. In the print context, the author of a biography would normally seek permission to use photographs of his or her subject. By analogy, permission would normally be required for digital video or musical illustrations—but not in all cases.

There are in a sense two kinds of illustrative use. Note that we excuse critical uses because without them the critic could not make her point. In the same way, there are surely cases where an illustration is not a "mere" illustration—in which the author is simply enhancing the value of a text by including other peoples' work—but a piece of a puzzle without which the reader would be in the dark. For example, to convey the full meaning of Ellington's place in the evolution of jazz it could well be necessary to include music clips of his work and of the work of musicians before and after him. (In a sense, this is a blend of biography and criticism.) Some recent cases have upheld the right of a documentary filmmaker to use motion picture excerpts in a documentary about the studio that produced the motion pictures [e.g., *Hofheinz v. AMC Productions, Inc.*, 147 F. Supp. 2d 127 (E.D.N.Y. 2001)]. By analogy, the use of music clips in the Ellington biography would be fair use, so long as the clips did not exceed what was necessary for the purpose. (A publisher wishing to make use of entire pieces of music, or of longer segments than are justified by fair use, can obtain a MIDI license through the Harry Fox Agency at www.nmpa.org/hfa/midi.)

Or suppose, to give another example, someone is writing an opinion piece about the 2002 Olympic figure skating scandal. Would it not be a fair use to include video clips of portions of the Russian and Canadian programs, if the purpose is to bolster an argument that certain elements in those programs deserved to be scored a certain way? Even though the copyrighted works—the skating films—are not the object of the author's criticism, the use supports a critical debate. To put it more starkly, to require permission for a limited, disputational use of copyrightable material could stifle debate. Therefore the use should be considered fair.

4. APPROPRIATE QUANTITY AND QUALITY

The author and publisher should be careful to ensure, however, that the music or video clip—as with any portion taken from a copyrighted work, be it text or images—truly supports the scholarly purpose, by enriching or enabling the reader's understanding of the discussion to a degree that cannot be accomplished otherwise. Of course, that standard by itself could justify including the whole recording, which would be nearly impossible to defend in court. Hence the further limitation that the music or video clip should not exceed what is truly necessary to the author's purpose.

It is always a given in these things that the use must not be so extensive as to substitute for the original in the marketplace. On this topic, if an author wants to reduce his/her risk, one stratagem—at least where visual materials are concerned—is to use a quality level of image that does not pose a threat to the original. There is, of course, no similar fudge available where music is concerned.

5. PROMOTIONAL USES

In contrast to all of these uses are those that are primarily for promotion of the new work. Promotional uses are presumptively unfair. For example, even though an electronic book about Duke Ellington might lawfully use limited video or audio clips of Ellington interspersed in the text, it would not be fair use to use those same clips to advertise the book on the publisher's Web site. Nor would it be fair use to use them on the boot-up screen of the book, any more than to use a copyrighted picture of Ellington on the cover of the print edition of the book. All such uses should be paid for.

Yet even this generality is subject to qualification. It might well be fair use to include on the boot-up screen or Web-site promotion a reproduction of an image if that image were the target of the new work's criticism. For example, a publisher might be entitled to use an image of Barbie in advertising a feminist work attacking America's doll culture. The publisher would want its design to convey clearly to the viewer that the image was the object of criticism, thus avoiding the impression that the book is taking a free ride on the popularity of the Barbie brand. This example illustrates, rather starkly, the point made above, that fair use determinations often depend on the gestalt of the use and on the perception of the viewer.

6. OTHER USES

Off to one side of the criticism-narrative-entertainment continuum are uses, enabled by the Web, that the courts are beginning to grapple with, and for which analogies from the print world are less useful. One such was at issue in a case in the U.S. Court of Appeals for the Ninth Circuit, *Kelly v. Arriba Soft,* 280 F.3d 934 (9th Cir. 2002). The plaintiff was a photographer who posted some of his work on his Web site for advertising purposes. The defendant's ditto.com service used Web crawlers to find images on the Internet and cached "thumbnail' versions of them on its servers. A user would initiate a search for images of a particular subject, and in response would be shown thumbnail reproductions of whatever the search turned up. If the user wanted to see any particular image in greater detail, the service would then provide a "framing link" to the full image at the source. Over thirty of Kelly's photographs were used in this manner.

The Ninth Circuit held that the thumbnail reproductions were fair use as they were not in competition with Kelly and could not be said to impinge on his market. It held, however, that the framing of full-screen images was *not* a fair use. It found that the user's demand for Kelly's image might be satisfied in this manner, and moreover, that Kelly suffered additional commercial harm because the link avoided Kelly's home page, thus depriving Kelly of the marketing benefit to his other images. The court also stated that this unauthorized access heightened the risk to Kelly that he would lose control of the digital versions of his images. The court held that the framing infringed Kelly's exclusive right to display his images publicly.

The outcome in this case is understandable but somewhat worrisome, as it makes the use of framing and hyperlinks more dangerous than had been thought. Unless this decision is reversed, or rejected by other courts, a prudent publisher will be careful in how it uses links, especially framing links, to add value to the content of what it publishes. At the very least, one should be wary of framing links to Web sites like Kelly's that exist primarily to promote the products of the Web-site owner, or that are vehicles for third-party advertising. (A framing link omits the advertising, and thus impinges on the economic benefit of the Web-site owner.) Framing links to Web sites that are primarily informational in character are safer, though not free of risk. The publisher wishing to provide framing links should try hard to put itself in the Web-site owner's position, and not do to others what it would not wish done to itself.

Framing has trademark implications as well as copyright implications. A publisher that uses framing in composing a work should be careful that the visual result does not risk confusing the reader as to the source or sponsorship of the framed material. In other words, framed material should be clearly credited so that no reasonable reader would assume that there is any sponsorship or approval or other relationship between the framer and the framed.

Finally, one development—it may be too early to call it a trend—that deserves mention is the movement on the part of some Web-site owners to establish linking policies. (Publishers should consider this option themselves.) A linking policy stipulates the kinds of links that are acceptable to the owner and the kinds that are not. It is also too early to say if such policies are legally binding, even if supported by "click-through" licenses.

(viii) PROTECTING COPYRIGHTS AGAINST INFRINGEMENT

Anyone who owns any exclusive right under copyright may sue to enjoin (i.e., to obtain a court order prohibiting) future infringement, and to be compensated for infringement that has already occurred. Compensation can be in the form of actual damages—the dollar value of the injury inflicted on the right holder—or a surrender by the infringer of the profits gathered from the infringement; in effect, the plaintiff may choose the larger of these two sums. In lieu of either of these, the copyright owner may ask for statutory damages (discussed **above** [13.1.4]), which are set in the discretion of the judge or jury. In addition, as noted earlier, a publisher that has registered its copyright before the infringement occurs, or within three months after publication, is eligible in the court's discretion to recover its attorneys' fees.

Any U.S. copyright owner must have registered the work as a prerequisite to bringing suit. Non-U.S. copyright owners can sue without having registered.

1. Copy prevention and encryption

The law gives electronic publishers three other techniques for protecting their property against infringement. The first is the right to prevent the unlocking or decryption of any work that the publisher has chosen to protect with such technological measures as copy prevention or encryption. The ***Digital Millennium Copyright Act*** (***DMCA***), enacted in late 1998, makes it unlawful (a) to "manufacture, import, offer to the public, provide, or otherwise traffic in" any technology that is designed or produced "primarily" to circumvent encryption or other protective technology, and (b) to market any otherwise lawful technology as a circumvention device. It is also unlawful to use any anticircumvention technology to gain unauthorized access to an encrypted work—although not to reproduce a work to which one has lawful access. Affected copyright owners are entitled to sue those who violate this law.

This part of the DMCA has proved highly controversial. A few high-profile cases have punished very visible scofflaws, such as a young man who cracked the code that encrypts DVDs and who spread his discovery to all via the Internet. These cases have rallied the forces of "free information" to oppose copyright owners, so far in vain, but the battle is ongoing. A disinterested observer might discern fanaticism on both sides of the issue, and might also be forgiven the thought that copyright owners have gotten too much of a good thing. The real question, though, may not be whether the law is constitutional but whether it has any chance of achieving its objectives. The cases have shut down one or two public martyrs, but do not appear to have suppressed generally the *samizdat* whereby decryption devices are made and circulated.

1. NONFUNCTIONAL PROTECTION MECHANISMS

Only two classes of works are excluded from the protection of these anticircumvention rules. The only one of these that is relevant to publishers is works whose technological protections malfunction or have become damaged or obsolete. This is not a large exception. The issue of which classes of works, if any, should be outside the DMCA's protection is scheduled for reappraisal by the Register of Copyrights in 2004.

2. OTHER EXCEPTIONS

Some persons, too, are exempt from this law: libraries and similar institutions seeking to gain access to works "solely in order to make a good faith determination of whether to acquire a copy"; persons engaged in encryption research and security testing; and a few others not relevant here. Also, circumvention aimed solely at functions that collect information on the user is permissible, unless the function already allows the user to opt out of such data collection.

3. FAIR USE IN THE CONTEXT OF ENCRYPTION

An open question is whether there is room for fair use in this tightly regimented system of rules. To put it another way: is it fair use to engage in unauthorized decryption, etc., if the end use to be made of the decrypted work is fair? The statute finesses this point, and it will be left to the courts to work it out.

2. Closing infringing Web sites

The second tool given to copyright owners in the DMCA is the right to demand that an Internet service provider (ISP) take down any site that is involved in infringement. This is done by means of a notice to the designated agent of the ISP, following certain statutory formalities laid out in Section 512 of the Copyright Act [17 U.S.C.§512]. The ISP must "expeditiously" remove or disable access to the offending site and notify the owner of the site that it has done so. If the owner objects, elaborate dispute-resolution rules come into play. If the ISP does not have a designated agent for receiving such notices, or fails to comply with the procedures required by law upon receipt of the notice, then the ISP can itself be regarded as an infringer and vulnerable to suit.

3. Protecting copyright management information

The third tool is the right to protect one's "copyright management information." For publishers, the relevant copyright management information is that which identifies the work, the author, the copyright owner, any terms and conditions for use of the work, and any URLs of or links to sites where such information can be found. (When using other publishers' works, publishers should likewise be careful not to remove any such information without permission. When using performance works—e.g., motion pictures and recordings of musical performances—they should be careful not to remove the name of the performer without permission, as that too counts as copyright management information. For audiovisual works such as motion pictures, the names of the writers and directors are also protected.) The theory—for which there is no empirical evidence—behind protection of this information is that, when present on a work, it tends to discourage unauthorized copying.

Under this provision of the law, publishers can prevent the intentional removal or alteration of copyright management information, the knowing provision of false copyright management information with intent to conceal infringement, and the knowing distribution or importation of works on which copyright information has been removed or altered. Publishers can also seek damages for any violation of these rules, in addition to damages for actual infringement; statutory damages for violation are not less than $2,500 per work.

Is it permissible to remove copyright management information when making a fair use of a work? The law does not say so explicitly, although it says that removal is allowed when permitted "by law." The law of course includes Section 107 of the Copyright Act, the fair use section. Although that section itself says nothing about copyright management information, as a matter of common sense it would be gross overreaching to require that when making a fair use of someone else's material one must include all the copyright management information attached to the original.

4. Hacking

The fourth tool given to electronic publishers is the Computer Fraud and Abuse Act [18 U.S.C. §1030]. This statute, enacted to deal with malicious computer hacking, gives anyone who posts password-protected content on-line the right to sue anyone who "intentionally accesses a computer without authorization or exceeds authorized access, and thereby obtains . . . information. . . . " The damages available under this act are limited, however. Its major deterrent effect may be the threat of criminal prosecution.

13.2 TRADEMARK LAW

Trademark law affects publishing as it affects every other business. A publisher's name and imprints are its "brands" and should be protected in the same manner as any other company's brands.

Trademarks, unlike copyrights, are based not on creativity or originality but on consumer perception. They may begin with the inspiration of a business owner, but they owe their life to the customers of that business. Trademark protection is based ultimately on use of the mark in commerce, and from the public's identification of the mark with a particular company.

What makes a good trademark? There are of course many ingredients, and choosing a strong brand always involves a bit of inexplicable magic. But from the legal standpoint, there are a few rules that one should follow.

(i) THE STRENGTH OF THE MARK

Trademark law—as distinct from the world of sellers and consumers—assesses the strength of a mark on a spectrum ranging from "fanciful" to "arbitrary" to "descriptive." A fanciful mark is one such as "Kodak" that has no inherent meaning; an arbitrary mark is one such as "Apple" that has no inherent meaning as applied to the goods or services concerned (e.g., computers or banking services). Because of its lack of intrinsic meaning, from the beginning a fanciful or arbitrary mark attaches exclusively to the owner's goods or services. A descriptive mark, on the other hand, is one such as "DigiBooks" that immediately conveys to the customer exactly what is being offered for sale. Marks that are not merely descriptive but have become indispensable nouns for the goods or services concerned are called "generic" marks. Curiously, most marks that are now generic started out not as descriptive marks but as strong fanciful or arbitrary marks, such as Nylon and Creosote, both of which were once valuable business property. It is to avoid the awful fate of becoming generic that firms spend millions on odd advertising such as "No one makes bandaids—not even Johnson & Johnson." Johnson & Johnson is the maker of Band-Aid® brand bandages, not "bandaids."

As the foregoing discussion suggests, it is (perhaps counterintuitively) the mark that tells you nothing about the product that is strongest, the descriptive mark that is weakest. Indeed, descriptive marks cannot be protected at all, unless and until they acquire what is called "secondary meaning"—that is, a meaning that functions as a brand, separate from its meaning in plain English. An example of this is A-1 Steak Sauce. When the phrase "A-1" was first adopted for that steak sauce, it simply indicated that the manufacturer was touting it as the best steak sauce one could buy. Now, however, decades later, when one hears "A-1" used for steak sauce, one thinks of that odd rectangular bottle and the sauce that comes out of it. Secondary meaning can thus be a powerful and wonderful thing, but it can be acquired only by dint of long use or heavy advertising. Pursuing it is not a recommended strategy for a new business.

This is not always easy advice for publishers, authors, and editors to follow. The founders of journals are peculiarly susceptible to names that are legally worthless. Faced with the need to name a new journal, most will opt for "Journal of the Society for the Preservation of Antipodian Mammals" when "*Aardvark*" would be a much stronger trademark. The scientific urge to convey information conflicts with the legal imperative to withhold it.

In between arbitrary marks and descriptive marks are marks that are "suggestive"—that is, marks that act upon the customer's imagination to convey the general idea of what is being sold, but without actually giving the game away. (Classic examples are Tide for detergent, or Ultra Brite for toothpaste.) A mark such as EtherBooks for an electronic publisher might fall in this category.

An electronic publisher seeking to launch a new business, or a new imprint, must bear these considerations in mind in the task of brand selection. A brand that is strong from the start has a value that will pay off in marketing, in licensing, and (if the fates will have it so) in the eventual sale of the business.

1. Book titles

Titles of individual books are brands too, of course. They are not routinely viewed in this light, because one cliché of trademark law has been that the titles of individual books (as distinct from the titles of repetitive publications such as journals) are not trademarks. As a result, book titles are seldom chosen with the sort of branding considerations that inform other sorts of marketing. And yet there are many titles that have evolved into powerful brands. Lord of the Rings and Winnie-the-Pooh are among the strongest trademarks in our culture. In the opinion of this writer there is scant intellectual basis for discriminating against book titles in trademark law. But the cliché still guides behavior at the Patent and Trademark Office and elsewhere, and must be taken into account. In short, publishers should be alert to the trademark possibilities inherent in their titles, but should not expect easy protection for anything but the most famous titles.

2. Business names and URLs do not guarantee trademarks

Publishers—and especially electronic publishers—need to bear in mind that obtaining ownership of a URL is not the same thing as obtaining ownership of a trademark, and both are different from obtaining the rights to use a corporate name—although the words used in all three may be the same. To illustrate this, take the hypothetical case of a start-up e-publisher that wants to do business as EtherBooks. While this concept is still a gleam in their eye, the entrepreneurs involved go to any one of the Internet domain name registries and reserve the names etherbooks.com, etherbooks.biz, etc. As plans mature, they ask their business attorney to incorporate them. She duly goes to the corporation division of their home state and, finding that EtherBooks, Inc. is available, incorporates the company under that name. Angels are found, money raised, and etherbooks.com launches itself with great fanfare. A week later, a letter arrives from one of the eighty-five in-house lawyers of Incredibly Big Money Corporation, saying that EtherBooks infringes IBMC's exclusive rights in its mark Etherbook. That mark was registered over five years ago in the U.S. Patent and Trademark Office and the registration is now incontestable. If what IBMC sells under its Etherbook mark is close enough to what etherbooks.com sells—namely, publications—that the public might be confused, etherbooks.com will have to abandon its new-hatched name and go back to the drawing board for a new one.

In a sense, etherbooks.com was lucky to hear from IBMC as quickly as it did. How much worse would its name-change experience have been had it been in business for a year or two before getting the deadly missive?

3. The issue of public confusion

Public confusion, by the way, does not mean that a buyer would necessarily assume that etherbooks.com's product was produced by IBMC. It is enough that a reasonable buyer might assume some sort of sponsorship or other relationship between the two entities. In other words, IBMC need not sell "books" or "e–books" under its Etherbook mark in order to shut down etherbooks.com. If it sells, for example, software that enables users to self-publish on-line, a reasonable consumer might be misled into imagining an affiliation between the two product lines. If a judge or jury, putting itself in the shoes of that consumer, finds a likelihood of confusion, etherbooks.com loses.

(ii) AVOIDING TRADEMARK CONFLICTS

What can be done to avoid such problems? Neither the act of registering a URL nor the act of incorporating was likely to give fair warning of this trademark problem. Both the Internet registries and the fifty state corporation departments will permit the use of any name that is not identical to those already in use. Trademark law, on the other hand, protects not only the exact mark but a fairly wide perimeter around that mark, precisely because trademark law's purpose is to prevent public confusion. What etherbooks.com's entrepreneurs, or their lawyer, should have done was to conduct a trademark search before adopting and investing in any name.

Indeed, because of the wide protection given a trademark, it is wise to involve a lawyer who specializes in trademarks, and at the earliest possible stage. He or she will be alert to more ambiguous problems that a search may turn up. One not schooled in such matters might miss the problems that lurk in trademarks such as Ether Publishing or even seemingly unrelated marks such as Ethelbooks.com (named for the owner)—but lurk they do.

1. Not all trademark searches are the same

There are various kinds of searches. The level of search required depends on the level of comfort desired.

1. COMMERCIAL SEARCHES

The most thorough search will examine the databases not only of registered trademarks but also of so-called "common law trademarks"—those that are in use but not registered. If you are seeking the highest level of comfort, there are two or three firms that specialize in searches of huge proprietary databases, designed (though not guaranteed) to find any existing uses of a proposed trademark anywhere in the world of commerce. Such searches can be expensive.

2. INTERNET SEARCHES

For the tight budget, there is a do-it-yourself version: using one's favorite Internet search tool. However, do-it-yourself Internet searches are less reliable than searches outsourced to one of the specialized firms. If they turn up conflicting marks, those conflicts are likely to be serious, and force a search for a new name. The converse, though, is not true. A clean Internet search does not mean that you are free to adopt the trademark you want. The algorithms used in Internet searches are different from those that have been tailor-made for trademark searches, and are less likely to catch conflicts at the perimeter of the law's protection.

3. SEARCHING OFFICIAL REGISTRIES

A narrower form of search will examine only the various official trademark registries—those of the U.S. Patent and Trademark Office and the registries of the fifty states. Such a search is best done using one of the on-line services available for this task—again, because the search algorithms of trademark registries may not spot conflicts that a court might consider important. With this caveat, a registry search in combination with an Internet search provides a fair level of comfort, but less than that of a professional search. (It should be added that where a graphic image mark—a "logo" in common parlance—is concerned, only the commercial search firms can conduct a useful search.)

Had someone performed or commissioned any of the searches described above for our etherbooks.com entrepreneurs, they would have turned up IBMC's mark Etherbook, and the entrepreneurs would have gone searching for a less perilous name.

4. INTERNATIONAL SEARCHES

These commercial searches can be limited to the United States or can be international in scope. Should one search beyond the United States? International searches are substantially more expensive, and in many cases unnecessary. If, say, an English company had registered the trademark Etherbooks in the United Kingdom, that registration would not prevent our entrepreneurs from using the same name in the United States. The English company could, however, prevent expansion outside the United States. As to whether they could prevent the U.S. etherbooks.com from filling orders received from English customers, the answer may depend on the nature of the solicitation and of the fulfillment. Therefore, if a firm has realistic international ambitions, and has the wherewithal to conduct an international search, it should do so. In most cases, though, a U.S. search will give a sufficient level of comfort to a U.S.-based publisher.

(iii) ESTABLISHING THE MARK

Let us now assume that the search for etherbooks.com has come up clean. What step should our entrepreneurs take next?

1. Use, "intent to use," and registration

It used to be that one could acquire trademark rights only by actual use of the mark to be protected. In a sense that is still true, but it is now possible to stake a claim to a mark in advance of use, in a sense to reserve it while one puts together the business that will make use of it. This is the role of so-called ***Intent to use*** trademark registration applications. Anyone lucky enough to have created a good trademark that has not already been adopted, and who anticipates any appreciable lag time between its invention and its actual use in commerce, should apply to register it in the U.S. Patent and Trademark Office on an intent-to-use basis. While no actual registration may issue until the mark has been used, the intent-to-use procedure can reserve the name for several years while the business comes into being. The fees involved in such an application are only modestly higher than for applications based on actual use.

If one does not register a trademark on an intent-to-use basis, one should strongly consider registering it once it has actually gone into use in interstate commerce. While registration does not exactly *create* any legal rights to the mark—those rights accrue only from actual use—it can leverage those rights. Trademark rights based purely on use and not on registration are valid only in the area where actually used, and within a reasonable "zone of expansion" beyond that area. By contrast, a federal registration (i.e., one from the U.S. Patent and Trademark Office) is automatically valid nationwide—subject to any pre-existing uses, which are "grandfathered" but limited to the market where they existed. Thus, once one has got a registration, one can expand across the country at whatever pace suits one's business, without fear that someone else will use the mark first in a territory that one has not yet entered. Having a trademark registered can also give the owner certain procedural advantages should it become necessary to sue an infringer.

2. How to register a trademark

Trademark registration is a relatively simple and inexpensive process. The filing fee is $325 per mark, for each class of goods concerned. (The U.S. Patent and Trademark Office pigeonholes the infinite variety of human commerce into "classes" of goods and services. Class 16 is for printed publications, Class 9 for electronic publications.) It is advisable to engage the help of an attorney experienced in registration. Although this will somewhat increase the expense of the process, it will save a good deal of floundering around, because the rules of trademark registration practice can be quite arcane. A trademark registration needs to be confirmed in the sixth year and renewed every ten years, but may be renewed indefinitely in ten-year increments.

1. PROTECTING BOOK TITLES ON THE WEB

To return briefly to the question of trademarks in book titles: while a trademark may be difficult to establish, it is not at all difficult to establish exclusive URL rights in a book title. A publisher launching an e-book called "The CyberGuide to Fly Fishing" might have a hard time persuading the Patent and Trademark Office that that name is a trademark. But it is the work of minutes to seize "CyberGuidetoFlyFishing.com" and any number of variants (CyberFishing.com, etc.), and thus establish, at least on the Internet, a penumbra of protection around one's title.

3. Trademark notice

Once one has obtained federal registration of a trademark from the U.S. Patent and Trademark Office, one should give notice of that to the public by using the ® symbol. Overuse of the symbol can be annoying to customers, but at the very least it should be used next to the mark—usually to the bottom right or top right of the mark—on all packaging, on the boot-up screen, the first time the mark is used in any promotional piece, and elsewhere where it will catch the customer's eye. DO NOT use the ® symbol except for federally registered marks. For marks that have not been federally registered, the symbol to use is ™ (or ℠, which means "service mark," for services as opposed to products). These symbols have no legal significance but at least warn others that someone has laid claim to the mark.

1. USING AND ACKNOWLEDGING OTHERS' TRADEMARKS

What about using others' trademarks in one's own products or promotional literature? This is acceptable where the use is for informational purposes. For example, it is acceptable to say "Compatible with [software trademark]" or "50% more data entries than [database trademark]" because one is merely conveying information that is of value to the consumer. It is also acceptable to use another party's trademarks in the context of criticism or analysis; the situation is analogous to fair use in the copyright arena. In any case, be sure to use the word mark rather than the logo. For example, it is fine to say that one's product is compatible with Windows 2000, but not to include the famous flying window logo in that statement.

People who use others' trademarks in this manner often include a statement in their publications such as "Windows 2000 is a trademark of Microsoft Corporation." This is a good practice. It is certainly an advisable protection where the fairness of one's use is otherwise open to argument.

4. Use of trademarks in metadata

In the e-publishing context, the fair use debate extends below the surface of information to the use of others' trademarks in metadata or in HTML metatags. Metatags are hidden code; their legitimate function is a sort of indexing function; they are what Internet search engines rely on as an indication of the content of Web material. Misused, they can direct traffic to a Web site that is in competition with the trademark owner's Web site. In one case, a former Playboy "Woman of the Year" was recently permitted to designate herself as such on her Web site, and to use the terms "Playboy" and "Playmate" as metatags, because those uses were factually descriptive or "nominative" uses of those trademarks [*Playboy Enterprises v. Welles,* 279 F.3d 796 (9th cir. 2002)]. In another case, a dissatisfied customer of a company was permitted to use the name of the company as a metatag in the Web sites he had established as vehicles for disparaging the company [*Bihari v. Gross,* 119 F. Supp. 2d 309 (S.D.N.Y. 2000)]. On the other hand, it is equally clear that use of another's trademark as a metatag is trademark infringement if not justified by some supervening policy such as fair use [*Brookfield Communications, Inc. v. West Coast Entertainment Corp.,* 174 F.3d 1036 (9th Cir. 1999)]. Even the former playmate who was entitled to use "Playmate" to describe herself, and as a metatag, was not allowed to use "PMOY" as the "wallpaper" of her Web site. See the chapter on markup for more detail on **HTML metatags** [3.2.1.1] and the chapter on organizing, editing, and linking for details on **metadata** [4.4].

13.3 OTHER LAWS

Publishers are subject to certain other laws, and legal doctrines, that limit what they can publish. Some of these laws give governments the power to punish or even prevent certain publication, others give private individuals the right to sue for damages.

(i) LIBEL

Libel is the publication of false statements of purported fact, that are likely to expose a person to scorn or ridicule in the general community in which he or she lives or works, or any relevant special community such as his or her circle of professional colleagues. Statements of opinion, however scurrilous, cannot be libelous. Neither can true statements, however damaging.

Due in large part to our constitutional guarantee of free speech, U.S. law raises higher barriers to libel actions than any other legal system. This is especially true where matters of public interest are concerned. Where the person claiming to have been libeled is a private citizen, the standard for liability on the defendant's part is one of negligence. (In other words, if a publisher was negligent in ascertaining the truth of something it has published, it will be liable for damages, but not if it had reasonable grounds for believing what it published was correct.) However, where the claimant is a public figure—such as a politician, celebrity, or public official—the plaintiff must show that the author's disregard for the truth was malicious or willful. Furthermore, there is a class of plaintiffs called "limited purpose public figures" who must meet that same high standard of proof even though they are in general unknown to society. For example, a scientist who publishes a paper claiming to have achieved superconductivity at room temperature may in general be an obscure researcher, but he has thrust himself into the public arena for purposes of that one endeavor. Within that narrow scope he is a public figure, and allegations that his research is fraudulent would be subject to the higher standard of malice.

1. Avoiding libel

Publishers should bear in mind that their own ignorance is not a defense. A publisher is entitled to rely on an author whom it knows to be generally thorough and trustworthy, but not on an author whom it knows to be given to invention, exaggeration, or spite. In dealing with the latter type, the publisher may well have a duty to seek confirmation of the truth of the statement to be published. Publishers of newspapers and magazines, which carry the greatest exposure to liability, routinely check facts rather than rely on even their most trusted reporters.

It is thus important for the publisher to be alert to possible libel claims, to seek legal advice when concerned, and to obtain from the author a warranty that the work is not libelous and an agreement to indemnify the publisher if this should prove incorrect. Such a warranty is best secured up front, by the contract between publisher and author, rather than after the fact when the alleged libel has already been published.

1. LINKING

Is there liability for linking to some other Web site that contains defamatory material? (Or for that matter, material that infringes copyright?) Certainly, if a publisher knows or has good reason to suspect that material on another Web site is unlawful in any way, the publisher should not link to that site. Without that degree of knowledge or suspicion, a publisher is free to link to the site. A publisher providing a link has no obligation to verify the linked information independently, and cannot be liable if the content of that other site turns out to be libelous or defamatory.

Liability under copyright law for linking to infringing material may vary—it is too soon to tell—with the nature of the link. If publisher A sets up the link so that no one can tell that publisher B is the source of the framed content, A may well be held liable for direct infringement itself. If, however, the source of the material is clear, then A would not be liable for infringing content unless it knew or had reason to know that the material was unlawful.

(ii) RIGHTS OF PRIVACY AND PUBLICITY

Privacy is an issue of growing importance in the digital age. In a few areas—financial services, medical services, and on-line dealings with minors—laws exist to protect the privacy of citizens. In publishing, however, citizens can rely only on judicial precedents. These precedents are far from uniform, but they tend to side with publishers where there is any plausible argument that the information revealed is "newsworthy." Provided the information disclosed is not of "legitimate concern" to the public, an individual may sue the publisher if the information concerns his or her private life, if disclosure of it would be highly offensive to any reasonable person, and if the disclosure has caused injury such as mental distress.

Courts have not, alas, spoken often or with one voice on the key issue of what standard of care a publisher should be held to when such disclosure has occurred. Some courts say that negligent disclosure is enough to create legal liability; others say that the disclosure must have been intentional. However, the precedents are clear that once the information has been published, anyone other than the original publisher has no liability for further dissemination.

1. Publicity

The right of publicity, on the other hand, while it has its roots in the right of privacy, has become a primarily economic right. It prevents the unauthorized use of someone's name, likeness, voice, or other indicia of personality, for any commercial purpose. It is a creature of state law, and it is far from uniform nationwide, particularly on issues such as whether the right to control exploitation of someone's identity survives that person's death. The right of publicity does not prevent the legitimate publication of items in which someone's identity happens to appear. It does prevent any attempt to use that identity as a trademark or a come-on, or otherwise trade upon the goodwill of that identity. In between these two obvious extremes there is a sometimes uneasy boundary.

2. Foreign laws

Libel laws are universal, although what constitutes libel, and what kinds of statements are immune from prosecution, vary widely from place to place. Thus, a statement that may be protected by the First Amendment in the United States would be actionable *per se* in many other countries. Every country will give protection to its own citizens, within its own borders, against whatever libelous speech it has the power to regulate. Thus, if an American company publishes statements on the Internet about an English citizen, and if under the principles of English law those statements are libelous, the publisher may well be subject to suit in England even though American law might consider the statements privileged, or even nondefamatory. The publisher must in such instances consider whether it has assets in England that it thus is placing at risk, and proceed accordingly.

Obscenity laws are likewise similar in basic approach. But like libel laws they differ substantially from one country to another in the kinds of material they prohibit and the actions that may be taken against the publisher.

1. MORAL RIGHTS

One legal doctrine common to nearly all industrialized countries except the United States is that of so-called ***moral rights***: chiefly the right to have one's authorship acknowledged (and to avoid having authorship of other people's works attributed to oneself), and the right to prevent "distortion or mutilation" of one's work. These two rights are the "right of attribution" (formerly the "right of paternity") and the "right of integrity." U.S. law recognizes these rights, but only as regards an artist's unique or limited-edition artwork, and not even then in many cases. Some state laws are a bit broader in scope but almost toothless in practical effect.

In addition to its quite narrow moral rights laws, the U.S. protects the right of attribution more expansively through federal and state laws that prevent false designation of the origin of goods. Of these, the Lanham Act, which was originally the federal trademark statute but was expanded to include false advertising [15 U.S.C. §1125 et seq.], is a particularly powerful tool due to its nationwide reach. The Lanham Act has been used to prohibit, for example, the false or misleading attribution to an author of the writings of another author. Note that there is considerable overlap on this issue between more traditional laws such as the Lanham Act and the DMCA's prohibition against the knowing use of false "copyright management information." Indeed, because the copyright management information provisions of the DMCA are not limited to digital works but include old-media works as well, those provisions come very close to a broad federal right of attribution.

No U.S. law, however, protects any right of integrity in the arena of publishing. An American publisher is free—if it has proper copyright permission—to publish a substantially altered book, photograph, or other work, so long as it does not misrepresent the origin of the altered version. In this the United States is at odds with many of its closest allies. France and Italy are particularly notable for their expansive definitions of moral rights.

Need a U.S. publisher care about the risk of a right-of-integrity suit in foreign countries? For example, could an author who believes his work has been butchered by his editor bring suit in France to prevent its distribution there?

The answer is, probably not, at least if the author is a U.S. citizen. France would almost certainly not intervene to give an author the protection of its laws when the law of his own domicile does not grant similar protection. If, however, the author were a French citizen, one cannot be certain. When contracting with a non-U.S. author or illustrator, or when obtaining rights to use artworks of foreign nationals, a publisher should be careful to ensure that the law governing the contract is U.S. law, and that the author or artist waives any moral rights that he or she might have. It can then argue, with good chance of success, that a foreign court will find the author is prevented by contract from taking legal action that might otherwise be available.

2. OTHER FOREIGN LAWS

Others laws governing content are particular to certain countries. Certain European countries, for example, have laws against hate speech, and many Muslim countries have laws prohibiting defamation of the Prophet Mohammed. European countries have adopted laws protecting uncopyrightable databases against large-scale extraction and duplication of data.

3. AVOIDING PROBLEMS WITH FOREIGN LAWS

Print publishers can limit their exposure to such foreign laws by refusing to sell to buyers in countries whose laws would be unfriendly. Salman Rushdie's publisher cannot prevent English tourists from carrying copies of *The Satanic Verses* with them when they visit Saudi Arabia. But it can decline to sell copies to any Saudi retailer foolhardy enough to order them.

Electronic publishers do not have this defense mechanism available to them. By definition what they publish is available everywhere, except in those countries like China that manage (at least in part, and for the time being) to control their citizens' access to the Internet.

In practical terms, an Internet publisher has little to fear from foreign countries whose laws differ from U.S. law, so long as it has no physical presence and no assets located in those countries. However, the trend in publishing toward international conglomerates may limit this comfort to smaller U.S. domestic companies.

4. THE YAHOO CASE

What happens when an Internet publisher does become subject to foreign courts was illustrated by the unhappy case of Yahoo. On its auction site, Yahoo's customers in the United States offered certain Nazi memorabilia for sale. In France, it is illegal to offer to sell Nazi memorabilia. Because Yahoo had offices and assets in France, French citizens were able to sue Yahoo seeking to prevent the offering or sale of such things to French Yahoo users [*French Union of Jewish Students v. Yahoo! Inc.,* No. RG 00105308 (County Court of Paris, Nov. 20, 2000)]. In vain did Yahoo argue that such conduct was legal in its home country and the country where the goods were offered, and that Yahoo could not control access to its portal by national origin. (On the latter point, Yahoo conceded that it could perhaps foreclose 60% of its French customers from access to the offending sales.) Before the case could be finally adjudicated, Yahoo threw in the towel and announced it would no longer permit the sale of Nazi memorabilia on its site.

The lesson of this is that foreign governments do not necessarily subscribe to the vision that the Internet is a world without boundaries subject only to its own laws. As a result, every Internet publisher with offices or assets outside the United States should be careful to consult local counsel as to what rules may apply to its content.

13.4 LAWSUITS: IS THERE NATIONWIDE JURISDICTION?

Exposure to legal action outside the United States is not a concern for every electronic publisher. Exposure to legal action within the United States is, however. Internet publishers should assume a fair likelihood of being subject to legal action—for copyright infringement, trademark infringement, or libel—in any state where a plaintiff lives.

The only way to avoid such liability is to limit one's promotion and distribution to what is called a "passive" Web site: a site that does not solicit transactions but merely is up and available for anyone who wants to view and/or purchase what is on the site. For a publisher, though, a passive Web site is not a very useful marketing tool. If instead a publisher sends out promotional e-mails on a nationwide listserv basis, the publisher is probably exposing itself to suit in all the jurisdictions where that e-mail is received. Conceivably, if the number of recipients in that jurisdiction is extremely small relative to the total, and if few or no orders actually come in from that jurisdiction, the publisher can argue that it did not have the "minimum contacts" with the state necessary to subject it to jurisdiction. These are not easy fights to win, however. In the area of copyright, particularly, there is a tendency to uphold jurisdiction where only a single copy or a few copies are actually delivered into the forum state.

In the area of libel, the courts look not only to where sales are made, but also, or instead, to where the injury is done. For example, a court in the District of Columbia recently found it had jurisdiction over a libel claim where the harm occurred principally in that jurisdiction (because the plaintiff was a high-level bureaucrat there). It helped that in that case the plaintiff knew (or by rights should have known) that the impact on interstate commerce would be worst in D.C. [*Blumenthal v. Drudge*, 952 F. Supp. 44 (D.D.C. 1998)].

13.5 CONTRACTING WITH CUSTOMERS

(i) LICENSING THE INDIVIDUAL READER

Electronic publishers are in a unique position vis-a-vis their customers. Print publishers sell copies that require nothing to unlock them but literacy. Unless they sell by direct mail, book publishers have no idea who their customers are. The contract by which a reader acquires a book is simple and unwritten: the reader pays money and walks out of the store with a book.

Even in direct mail situations, and in periodical publishing, no publisher has ever sought a contract from its customers that dictates what they can and cannot do with the printed pages delivered to them. One may safely suppose that no print publisher wishes to be the first to try.

Electronic publishing, in this regard, takes after its forebears in the software industry more than its publishing ancestors. Its customers are inured to the idea that they must click "Agree" on a license in order to have access to published content. Most of them never read the licenses they agree to, but that does not make those licenses illegal. In fact they probably are legal, and enforceable, although there is no small turmoil from state to state as to when, and how. In any event, no one has yet come up with a practical alternative to such "click-through" licenses in the mass market digital environment. The publisher therefore should attempt by contract to stipulate what uses the "licensee" purchaser may make of its product. The customer who wants access to the work has no choice but to agree to those terms, for if he does not he will be denied access. The power this gives publishers has been augmented by the DMCA's prohibition of circumvention technologies, discussed above.

What, then, should such a license or contract provide? There is no one-size-fits-all answer. Points to consider include the following.

1. Keeping copies

Should the user be permitted to store a copy on his or her computer? In most cases this seems reasonable and fair. Indeed, this right could and probably should extend to any computer that belongs to the user.

2. Printing by the user

Should the user be permitted to print the work for his or her own use? This, too, seems reasonable and fair.

3. Using extracts

Should the user be permitted to incorporate extracts from the work in new digital works that the user creates? (Of course, the information contained in the work is free for use; the issue here is whether the user should be able to extract and reuse copyrightable expression.) On this topic, the publisher has in essence four options. One option is to forbid any such reuse, not perhaps in so many words but by a blanket prohibition such as, "All uses not expressly permitted in this license are prohibited." Another is to say nothing that bears on the issue (e.g., by casting the license in terms of express *permissions* and leaving *prohibitions* unspoken). This, in effect, subjects the license to the doctrine of fair use, which will be discussed below. The third option is to say explicitly that any reuse of the content that is within the scope of fair use is acceptable. The fourth, and least practical, is to give explicit quantitative guidelines.

The first option—blanket prohibition—raises interesting legal and philosophical issues, because it allows no room for fair use. Can a contract that denies the reader the benefits of fair use be enforced, especially where it is a "shrink-wrap" or "click-on" license that cannot be negotiated? One's visceral instinct (if one is a consumer) is to say no. However, fair use has never been explicitly cast as a *right* like the right of free speech. Technically, it is classified as a *defense* to a claim of infringement. And even if it were to be regarded as a right, as some judges and scholars have suggested, nothing says that the right of free speech cannot be contracted away. After all, people enter into binding nondisclosure or confidentiality agreements every day. Yet one wonders if a court would uphold a publisher's suit against a customer who, in violation of a shrink-wrap license, reproduced portions of a book in a book review. Of course, no publisher would be so foolish as to bring such an action—and this reality suggests that publishers would do better to earn the goodwill of their customers (those few who bother to read their licenses) by expressly acknowledging fair use in every user contract.

4. Sharing or reselling

To return to the list of contract provisions: Should the user be permitted to share the electronic copy with others? To sell it second-hand?

These questions are more contentious, and perplexing, than might first be imagined.

First there is the legal argument. It is basic doctrine that once a publisher has sold a copy of a book or any other work, it cannot control the further distribution of that copy. The copyright owner controls only the "first sale" of any given copy.

But what if that copy has not been "sold"? A "license" is not a sale, and the shrink-wrap or click-through license may even expressly forbid redistribution of the copy. So the question is whether a court will honor the publisher's demands or the unspoken expectations of the customer. On this point it is too early to generalize with confidence.

Leaving the law aside, what makes sense? The argument in favor of permitting the buyer to share or resell is that this replicates, in the digital environment, what people have done with books and the printed matter since time immemorial. Furthermore, to lend or sell an electronic book does not multiply the number of copies, provided that the person who lends or sells also removes the work from his or her own computer. If a publisher decides to permit lending and sale, it should be sure to stipulate such removal as a quid pro quo. Or at the very least, to stipulate that no one other than the original purchaser can print or store a copy longer than it takes to read it. Furthermore, loans should be permitted if at all only to the user's family and acquaintances, and only if the lender receives no payment.

The argument against permitting lending and sale in such circumstances is purely economic. In the short term at least, a publisher may decide that it will sell more copies of a work if every reader must have his or her own copy. Against this might be set the ill will generated by such attempts to stem the tide of human commerce.

But is it even practical, one may ask, to enforce such a regime? Until the DMCA came into effect, one would have said no. No publisher would sue a customer for lending an e-book. But while the DMCA makes it unlawful to disable copy-protection code embedded in digital works, it also makes it unlawful to create or distribute the disabling technologies. So publishers do not need to sue customers to prevent lending and sale. They need only devise software that locks each copy to a particular computer—as Microsoft has done with Windows XP—and then sue any digital Robin Hood who dares to distribute keys to the lock. Thus, each publisher must decide for itself whether to take the smooth path or the stony—and must decide for itself which is which. (These issues and mechanisms are discussed in more depth in the chapter on **digital rights management** [15].)

(ii) LICENSING THE USER ORGANIZATION

It has become common for publishers of electronic journals and databases, and, to a lesser degree, the publishers of electronic reference works and treatises, to license works to universities, libraries, and other institutions by "site license." The site license replaces multiple subscriptions with a simple contract covering all users at the institution.

Typically, a site license makes the licensed works accessible to any authorized user. The institution is responsible for ensuring that only persons affiliated with it—for example, faculty, research staff, and students—have access passwords.

1. Interlibrary loans

In site licenses, as in individual licenses, the publisher must determine what uses to permit. Since all persons affiliated with the institutions are authorized users, "lending" within the institution is harmless or irrelevant. Whether to prohibit lending outside the institution presents a trickier question. The Copyright Act specifically permits certain copying for purposes of ***interlibrary loans*** (***ILL***s) [17 U.S.C. §108]. However, the statute applies only to copies actually owned by the library that is filing the ILL request. Since a site licensee does not "own" the copies made available to it, unless the publisher otherwise decides, it is not inherently free to fill ILL requests. Furthermore, since a site licensee does not lose access to an electronic work by sending a copy to a sister institution, the concept of a "loan" is somewhat misleading—unless perhaps the "lending" library disables its own copy of the work while the loan is outstanding (not a likely occurrence).

2. Reserve copies

In a similar vein is the issue of so-called "e-reserve" copies. The publisher may therefore decide whether or not to permit the institution's libraries to treat the licensed works like other works in their collections. Whatever the decision, the license should explicitly address this issue. In the absence of contractual permission, does a library have the right under fair use to put a digital work on "reserve"? The answer might be yes if there were some way to assure that the students using the work did not download copies onto their own computers and if only one student could view the work at one time. Otherwise, the answer is almost surely no.

3. Other uses

As for downloading and printing within the institution, site licenses typically permit it. There is no practical way to police it, in any case.

13.6 CONCLUSION

The purpose of this chapter has been to give an overview of the legal landscape in which electronic publishers operate. It is a landscape in which volcanic and tectonic forces still visibly operate, and some of what has been said here may well capture only a moment in time. Nevertheless, there are constants: the desire of content owners to exploit the potential of digital dissemination; the desire of users to do the same; and the desire of courts to mediate between these two by adapting, as best they can, the principles of intellectual property that they have inherited from an earlier and, at least in theory, a simpler time.

14 International Issues

ROBERT E. BAENSCH
Director, Center for Publishing,
New York University

This chapter highlights the twelve key elements that are most important for international communications, online publishing, and e-commerce on the Internet. The size of organization or location of country is irrelevant, because the World Wide Web is a stateless network and framework that goes beyond the physical location of electronic resources and information by connecting millions of computers into a seamless global network. Statistics on Internet users worldwide, with a focus on Europe, Asia, and South America, establish a meaningful framework for what it really means to publish globally. A review of the international publishing activities of professional, legal, scientific, technical, and medical journal publishers offers realistic working examples for publishers who are considering the development of their international on-line business. A concise analysis of geographic, cultural, language, economic, technological, and legal factors provides perspective on the global environment for digital publishing.

14.1 OVERVIEW

Technology is having a significant impact on the publishing industry, but in different ways in different segments of the industry and different parts of the world. Despite the tremendous technological developments, the ever-increasing numbers of PCs around the world, and the dramatic increase in Internet usage, the reality is that a global marketplace is still in the first phase of development. The commercial Web did not exist before 1993, and until 1995 business Web servers numbered only in the hundreds. Only in the past few years has there been a major expansion, and the development of software for browsing the Web that features search functions, faster downloading of text and graphics, integration with Internet e-mail, and discussion groups. The important point is that both large and small publishers have started to develop their on-line businesses; they have established Web sites and are in the process of expanding on-line information services. The benefits of making the major transition from print to electronic publishing are the following:

1. Increased productivity at lower costs
2. Rapid and easier author, editor, translator interaction
3. Speedier publication with immediate global accessibility
4. New ways to add value in combination, composition, presentation, and access to a much wider range of global readers
5. More efficient delivery for librarians and individuals with new services to users
6. Easier accessibility, better searching, deeper archive resources, more applications to information research goals
7. Immediate national, regional, and global delivery and access for searches — anytime and anyplace

The special added value is the ability to search not only the present or current publication but to search the full publication's archival database as well as to use such systems as publishers' CrossRef or librarians' SFX to be able to access related databases for relevant and related information. These are features that are especially important to research institutions and libraries in developing countries where archival collections of printed journals or reference books are very limited or not available. It is the low income levels, limited telephone access, government regulations, and foreign languages that have held back an even more rapid acceptance and use of the Internet throughout the world.

14.2 INTERNET USERS WORLDWIDE

Publishers of traditional printed books, journals, and magazines established a fairly accurate sense of how many copies of their publications can be sold in which parts of the world. They have tracked the royalty income from translation rights to gain an understanding of the market size for a book or magazine published in the language of a market for that market. Few know the number of Internet users and the profile of those users in international regions or countries. The rapid growth rates and changes that continue to take place in different regions and specific countries make that market knowledge even more difficult to obtain. Therefore, it is important to review the number of Internet users on a macro scale and then focus on some specific countries — with the understanding that most of the following numbers are based on 2001 statistics and will change in subsequent years.

The comparative estimates for Internet users worldwide for the 2000 to 2003 time frame, in millions, are shown in Table 1.

Another view of the global market is provided by Simba Information in its forecast of on-line and Internet subscriber growth for the five-years from 2002

TABLE 1. ESTIMATES OF INTERNET USERS WORLDWIDE (MILLIONS)

Source of Estimate	2000	2001	2002	2003
eMarketer	352.2	445.9	529.9	622.9
Computer Industry Almanac (CIA)	413.6	538.5	673.0	825.4
Gartner Dataquest	330.4	403.9	480.3	549.4
Morgan Stanley Dean Witter		400.0	449.0	536.0

Source: © 2001 eMarketer, Inc. www.eMarketer.com

through 2006 (Table 2). The table details the rapid annual growth, region-by-region.

A third perspective is to review the number of Uniform Resource Locators (URLs) that uniquely identify each page of information on the World Wide Web. The URLs serve as Web addresses on an international scale and provide an indicator of the Internet activities for different countries around the world. Network Wizards (http://www.nw.com/) reports the following data as of January 2001 for the number of URLs in the top twenty countries worldwide.

- Japan (.jp): 2,636,541
- United Kingdom (.uk): 1,901,812
- United States (.us): 1,875,663
- Germany (.de): 1,702,486
- Canada (.ca): 1,669,664
- Australia (.au): 1,090,468
- Netherlands (.nl): 820,944
- France (.fr): 779,879
- Italy (.it): 658,307
- Finland (.fi): 631,248
- Taiwan (.tw): 597,036
- Sweden (.se): 594,627
- Brazil (.br): 446,444
- Spain (.es): 415,641
- Mexico (.mx): 404,889
- Norway (.no): 401,889
- Denmark (.dk): 336,928
- Belgium (.be): 320,840
- Switzerland (.ch): 306,073

TABLE 2. FORECAST OF ON-LINE/INTERNET SUBSCRIBER GROWTH BY REGION

Region	2002	2003	2004	2005	2006
Asia-Pacific Rim	19,400,000	42,275,000	65,240,000	82,810,000	96,890,000
Annual Growth		*117.9%*	*54.3%*	*26.9%*	*17.0%*
Europe	30,700,000	39,971,400	48,645,193	56,623,004	64,153,863
Annual Growth		*30.2%*	*21.7%*	*16.4%*	*13.3%*
Latin America	2,626,206	4,294,892	5,995,463	7,692,179	9,169,077
Annual Growth		*63.5%*	*39.6%*	*28.3%*	*19.2%*
Total Core Markets	**52,736,206**	**86,541,292**	**119,880,656**	**147,125,183**	**170,212,940**
Annual Growth		*64.1%*	*38.5%*	*22.7%*	*15.7%*
Noncore Markets	**40,709,926**	**71,941,760**	**103,236,084**	**133,921,118**	**160,839,230**
Annual Growth		*76.7%*	*43.5%*	*29.7%*	*20.1%*
Total Annual Growth	**93,446,132**	**158,483,052**	**223,116,740**	**281,046,301**	**331,052,170**
		74.9%	*40.8%*	*26.0%*	*17.8%*

Source: Simba Information, Inc., International Online Markets 2000

The above statistics include the core countries of China, India, Japan, Hong Kong, Singapore, Australia, Taiwan, U.K., Germany, France, Brazil, Chile, and Mexico. The data does not include North America. The total includes business and consumer dial-up on-line/Internet subscribers for markets where reliable data was available.

TABLE 3. INTERNET USERS, EUROPE (MILLIONS)

Source	2000	2001	2002	2003
eMarketer	108.2	144.4	175.7	196.2
eTForecasts	113.7	146.0	181.2	219.8
Gartner Dataquest	100.2	127.0	149.8	166.8
Morgan Stanley Dean Witter	87.0	121.0	158.0	199.0

Source: © 2001 eMarketer, Inc. www.eMarketer.com

- Korea (.kr): 283,459
- Subtotal for 20 countries: 17,874,822
- Worldwide total: 72,398,092

According to the Internet Software Consortium (http://www.isc.org/) worldwide Internet hosts have increased in number from 56,218,000 in July 1999 to 93,047,785 in July 2000, 125,888,197 in July 2001, and 162,128,493 in July 2002.

(i) EUROPE

It is necessary to move from the global perspective and review the number of Internet users on a region-by-region basis to gain a better understanding of the above noted growth phenomenon. In ranking by number of Internet users, Europe is in first place followed by North America, Asia, and then South America. The economic hesitation of 2002, which Germany as the leading country in the European Union did not want to recognize as a recession, has also had its negative effect on the growth of Internet users in Europe. The compound annual growth rate is projected to be 22 percent between 2001 and 2004 for Internet users in Europe. The number of Internet users in Europe, represented by the core twelve countries for the time frame of 2000 to 2003, is shown in Table 3.

(ii) ASIA

Important factors in Asia are the contrasts between developed and developing countries, due to geography or economics, in relation to the installed telephone line infrastructure. The Asia-Pacific region suffered an extended four-year economic recession from which only a selected number of countries recovered by early 1999. Since mid-1999, the four sectors of government, business, home, and education have all experienced growth in PC sales and Internet subscribers. The deregulation of the telephone and telecommunications industry in the region has also improved the prospects for growth. Table 4 provides information about the number of telephone lines in relation to the number of home PCs and home Internet subscribers in Asia. It shows the status of the installed base in this region as well as the potential for growth.

Asia experienced a rapid development of many small Internet service providers (***ISP***s), which was followed by a period of consolidation because the market could not support so many start-up companies. Asia Online, AT&T WorldNet, China.com, and Pacific Internet are the largest survivors, with several regional companies offering free access to compete. The next phase of growth will depend on further improvements to the region's economies, as well as government investments in telephone and information technology. The single largest driving force in the region will be China, which is expected to have an installed home computer base of 36 million by 2003. In Shanghai, 32 percent of the household PC users access the Internet daily and another 52 percent access the Internet regularly but not daily, according to EuroRSCG Worldwide.

The number of active Internet users in the Asia-Pacific region for the time frame 2000 to 2004 is projected to be 123,300,000 in 2000, 145,900,000 in 2001, 168,000,000 in 2002, 205,000,000 in 2003, and 232,100,000 in 2004, according to eMarketer (www.eMarketer.com).

China—in number of PCs and as a language—will generate the most dramatic growth in the next two to three years simply because of the vast size of its total population and economic growth. China and India represent more than two-thirds of Asia's total population.

(iii) SOUTH AMERICA

South America is a special challenge in view of its two languages and the fact that the Spanish language sites throughout the region are growing more rapidly in number than the Portuguese language sites based in Brazil. The telephone line connections in most of the countries do not provide adequate infrastructure or are too expensive to support a more rapid growth of the installed base of PCs and Internet use. The number of Internet users in South America identified by major country for 2001 to 2004 is shown in Table 5.

Table 5 represents the more conservative estimates of eMarketer; more optimistic numbers are provided by the Computer Industry Almanac, which projects 43.2 million Internet users for South America by 2003. The World Bank is the most conservative, with its estimate of 20.8 Internet users in 2003.

TABLE 4. TELEPHONE LINES, HOME PCS, AND INTERNET SUBSCRIBERS, ASIA, 1999

Country	Population (millions)	Telephone Lines	Home PCs	Internet Subscribers
Australia	19.1	9,600,000	3,200,000	1,500,000
China	1,249.6	123,000,000	12,000,000	7,000,000
Hong Kong	6.9	3,800,000	2,000,000	1,000,000
India	997.5	199,000,000	3,200,000	400,000
Japan	126.5	58,000,000	22,680,000	7,000,000
Philippines	76.8	3,000,000	825,000	240,000
Singapore	3.2	1,820,000	1,200,000	500,000
Taiwan	21.9	14,000,000	4,800,000	2,000,000
Thailand	61.7	9,150,000	1,500,000	500,000
Other		30,000,000	15,000,000	10,000,000
Total		**451,370,000**	**66,405,000**	**30,140,000**

Source: International Online Markets 2000, Simba Information Inc. www.simbanet.com

TABLE 5. INTERNET USERS, SOUTH AMERICA (MILLIONS)

Country	2001	2002	2003	2004
Argentina	1.5	2.0	2.5	3.0
Mexico	2.3	3.2	4.6	6.4
Rest of Region (Spanish Language)	5.5	8.0	11.4	15.0
Total Spanish Language	9.3	13.2	18.5	24.4
Brazil (Portuguese Language)	6.1	8.8	12.5	16.4
Total South America	15.4	22.1	31.0	40.8

Source: © 2001 eMarketer, Inc. www.eMarketer.com

The challenge in Mexico is for Telefonos de Mexico (Telemex) to upgrade the telephone line infrastructure and to add access lines. The second phase is for Telemex to provide the appropriate level of services as the leading ISP. From 1997 to 1999, Telemex relied on U.S.-based ISP Prodigy to maintain their market share. The five major Mexican ISPs during 1999 were the following, as reported by Simba Information based on *Mexicano en Telecommunicaciones* documentation:

1. Telefonos de Mexico, 400,000 subscribers (www.telmex.com.mx)
2. Infosel (Terra Networks), 68,000 subscribers (www.infosel.com.mx)
3. PSINet, 24,000 subscribers (www.psi.com.mx)
4. Acnet, 20,000 subscribers (www.acnet.com.mx)
5. Groupo Empresarial, 1,600 subscribers (www.gemtel.com.mx)

14.3 THE STM INDUSTRY LEADERS

The pioneering efforts of scholarly scientific, technical, and medical (STM) publishers like Academic Press, the ADONIS project, Elsevier Science, LexisNexis, and Springer-Verlag laid the foundation for international publishing on-line. Other publishers and new start-up ventures have joined Westlaw and John Wiley & Sons in building on that foundation to create today's attractive international on-line environment. The Internet offers an unprecedented advantage to smaller companies, substituting for the investment in offices, staff, printed inventory, and global shipments previously required to begin competing in the international business arena. The Internet can be used to develop more effective relationships with present customers, to test new distant international markets, and to communicate (i.e., to be interactive with or to be responsive to new customers) with comparatively low investments and operating costs. In a fundamental sense, all business has become international because of the Internet.

Traditionally it has been and continues to be today the professional, STM, and legal publishers that focus on special market segments and niches around the world. Therefore these types of publishers have been the most successful publishing internationally on-line. Their books, journals, publications, and information services are highly focused for specific niches. An added advantage is that their publications are published in the English language, which is the main language for on-line publishing. It has been difficult and expensive to reach global niche markets with print publications. The Internet, however, is ideally suited to reach niche markets anywhere in the world.

Elsevier Science is a good example: the company's Internet presence has grown from its initial TULIP research and development project, which started in 1978, to the following in 2002:

- Nine million scientists and researchers access the information from around the world
- 1,200 on-line journals
- 1.2 million on-line articles
- 30.0 million article summaries
- 50.0 million indexed Web pages
- Twelve subject-specific databases
- Eight participating publishers and databases (e.g., EconLit, a database of over 440,000 records covering all fields of economics from 1969 to the present)

Elsevier Science is just one of the six major international professional publishers delivering information on a subscription and pay-for-view basis. Professional societies, such as the American Chemical Society, the American Medical Association, the Institute of Electrical and Electronics Engineers (IEEE), and the American Institute of Physics, have created electronic versions of their journals. It is now widely accepted that scholarly journals have to be available in electronic formats to be viable global research and reference tools. An added value is that these organizations are following the models of commercial publishers by converting back issues to database archives for searching and retrieval. This capability is especially valuable for libraries in developing countries, which did not have the financial resources to build and maintain archival collections.

It is best to focus on professional (and specifically STM) publishers and their market segments to understand how these publishers have been able to use their global reach to:

- Increase sales, increase circulation for journals, increase connectivity to sites, and generate revenues, not just "hits"
- Reduce the costs of selling publications or print information services by delivering digital content
- Improve communications with present and new customers to increase sales and reduce costs of doing business on a worldwide basis

14.4 ESTABLISHING THE WEB SITE

The first step toward publishing internationally on-line is establishing an Internet connection or establishing a World Wide Web site. But this needs to be done with a carefully thought out plan—and strategies that include more than just a new way to promote and advertise present print publications. Setting up an identity—a home page and information source on the Web—has become relatively easy. The challenge is how to develop a successful and profitable set of strategies and actions for global marketing and related revenues. The Internet and the World Wide Web are available to every company. What determines competitive advantages are the strategic applications of these capabilities to selected areas of a specific business development plan.

The Internet can be used to achieve all three goals by focusing not only on the Web site but also by really considering the Internet in general for the following:

1. Information distribution. Use the Internet as a global marketing communications tool (advertising, promotion, catalog, publicity, news/ information).
2. Supply chain. Build an interactive channel for direct communications and data exchange with customers, suppliers, and distributors who are based not in one country or the "home" market but around the world.
3. E-commerce. Create new sales and distribution channels, link to a regional distribution channel, or do business with international suppliers, also addressing customer support in different time zones and in different languages.
4. Market research. Carry out very targeted market research by utilizing the interactivity of the Internet, and focus on international market segments by region, country, and then niches therein.

An important point to make—especially in relation to all professional, business-to-business, and STM publishers—is that the ultimate business value of a Web site is not determined by the size of its design budget or even by the number of visits or hits it attracts. It is so important to develop a specific or unique Web application in the context of an overall Internet business strategy. Let us briefly explore each of the six factors.

(i) INFORMATION DISTRIBUTION

Planning for and then implementing a World Wide Web site should include the following:

A careful *internal* assessment of your communication/information sources, publications schedules, promotion, and publicity development—not only for the present core or majority of national customers but with a new global strategy for growth.

A careful *external* assessment to analyze the Internet connectivity, competitors' role on the Web, and what information will make the strongest impact in which parts of the world—especially those parts that are not as sophisticated as the current national or home market customers.

Publishers need to establish an analysis of both the internal and external factors for an integrated and value-added approach to the Web. It is important not to carry out simply a direct conversion of one or two of current print promotions or print publications. There is not one standard or model set of Internet strategies, because each publisher must develop its own unique approach to the digital global marketplace.

Print publishers still think of content development for marketing, promotion, and sales in relation to seasonal or monthly time cycles. It is so important to recruit members of the internal team or external editorial content colleagues to keep the Web server content up-to-date, fresh with news and relevant information. It is not just a matter of preparing the annual catalog/price list or the two seasonal catalogs. The Web site is a news site; it requires continued updates and revisions as well as additions as frequently as possible.

(ii) AN INTERACTIVE COMMUNICATIONS CHANNEL

Connectivity with over 130 countries means that the contents of a Web server will be accessible to millions of network users, and e-mail messages will reach anywhere in the world immediately without added costs. Two-way or multichannel communications is a key Internet feature. Many tools have been developed to facilitate interaction with not millions of network users but that small targeted market segment or niche therein that is the publisher's targeted customer anywhere in the world.

The successful Web sites today have all used the Web's interactive features and customization options to target their very particular customers and respond to their users' suggestions. It has been and continues to be the effective use of a dialogue or *interactivity* on the Internet that best leads to success as an on-line publisher. It is also a challenge to keep content up-to-date on an information rich server with an international audience in mind. Web pages get created to respond to project, program, or publication deadlines and when the deadline passes or the staff person changes, then this content becomes archival history. Some publishers have appointed a person specifically for the international section. The person is responsible for monitoring the content for their subject area, region, country, and language in relation to creating updates and adding new information suitable for the total international arena or for their specific region. They also channel the feedback from the unique or different parts of the world to the appropriate departments of the organization.

(iii) NEW SALES AND DISTRIBUTION CHANNELS

New strategies with related new skills will make effective use of cross-linking of sites and coordinated information management with local, regional, or country sites. Linkage to a publisher's subsidiaries, partners, joint ventures, or key accounts is a form of customization. Information can be maintained centrally on a network server and still be displayed, accessed, and disseminated on an individual or regional basis. Server access can be set to display different levels and kinds of information to different categories and national location of users (i.e., customers).

The Internet's global reach and multinational structure can be used to focus on geographic market segments and open local Web sites directly or in cooperation with a publisher's subsidiary, partner, agent, or distributor.

Once an inquiry or order has been confirmed, it should be possible for the Web site to:

- determine the location of the customer, operating systems, and navigation paths used
- compare that location with the authorized distributors or subscription agencies
- send orders electronically to the closest or most appropriate distributor or agency
- print the order automatically at that location

It is important to use the Web not only as an outward bound communications link with customers but also to interface fully with order processing applications.

(iv) E-COMMERCE

Web-site strategies should include support for on-line ordering, purchase orders, multicurrency payment capabilities, subscription renewals, publication dates, and inventory information. Standards are developing for financial transactions, and for many it is no longer a problem as people all over the world use credit cards. The e-commerce leader in the book publishing industry is Amazon.com, which generates more than 38 percent of its sales outside the U.S. and Canada.

Operating procedures and capabilities need to be set up to link on-line activities with internal/back office order processing for maximum results at minimum cost. Customer interaction, including all functions, is a real opportunity for developing new business. It is a matter of integrating present business practices and taking advantage of the interactive networked opportunities available on the Internet from different time zones, in numerous languages, and with various levels of purchasing power. The other key technical issues include an ability to ship products or publications quickly, safely, and at reasonable cost to international customers and then provide the customer support to those worldwide markets. Currency exchange is a topic that will become an immediate part of billing and collecting for orders generated. Banks and credit card companies will offer different currency exchange rates and service fees, which may vary widely depending on the country and currency. Credit cards are issued in different countries and thus will force adherence to local exchange regulations, with related problems for the U.S. based publisher. The assumption cannot be made that every customer has a credit card from a U.S.-based bank working in U.S. currency.

(v) MARKET RESEARCH

The first step in determining the potential of a region or country is to evaluate the developmental stage and extent of a country's connectivity to the Internet. The second step is to identify the number, type, and content of Web servers in a country. The number of commercial Web servers offering information services and e-commerce products to local or regional customers in specific languages reveals the foundation of a digital marketplace. The third important research step is to identify and analyze selected commercial and educational Web servers' information content that is locally created and to assess the timeliness of such posted information. The Internet and the World Wide Web are growing so quickly that target market countries as well as emerging market profiles are changing dramatically over six or twelve months. Therefore, it is necessary to continue market research including the use of the "interactivity" factor with customers that is so unique for Internet direct customer relationships. During the past few years a number of new and much more sophisticated tracking and reporting systems have been established for Web sites in order to measure not only the number of hits and the number of searches but where in the world the new and growing market potential is. Please note the following key information elements that are gathered and documented daily and accumulated monthly for review, analysis, and proactive action for market development. An effective reporting and management information system should include the following:

1. An overview of general Web server statistics
2. Entry and exit pages, navigation paths
3. Search engines and keywords used, time spent
4. Most requested pages—in descending number of hits
5. Top directories, information, or publications accessed—number of hits and number of user sessions
6. Most active "organization" or "publication"—number of hits, percentage of total user sessions
7. Most active countries visiting the Web—user sessions summarized by country and region
8. Summary of activity by day, hour, month, year-to-date, compared to last year

There are many ways to look at the global market, regions, and selected countries using the power of the Internet. It is easy to think global, but essential to think "local" in developing international marketing, information services, and e-commerce strategies. A publisher needs to assess the level of commercial and educational Internet development on a country-by-country basis to be able to target regions, countries, and finally selected types of customers.

14.5 UNDERSTANDING THE GLOBAL ENVIRONMENT

Technology can provide a presence in any part of the world; however, as publishers of information, in contrast to those selling manufactured products, it is especially important to recognize five key factors in pursuing international business. First and foremost are the cultural and social factors: sufficient research needs to be done to recognize the language, education, religion, reference groups, and work and leisure elements within the social fabric of a country. Relevant data for a country's profile include the installed base of television sets, the number of telephone lines per 100 inhabitants, cellular phone subscribers per 100 inhabitants, and the number of Internet-connected host computers. What is the level of education and the percentage of the population that has attended what levels of the schools and universities? How many publishers, booksellers, and libraries are there in the country? The second factor is the political system within a host country, the government's role in reference to information services, national telecommunications, and changes in the political climate. The third factor is the national economy—GNP, currency revaluation and strength, exchange rates over a 24-month period, and inflation rates—to evaluate the economic strengths and weaknesses on a macro scale. It makes sense to research the Economist Intelligence Unit's Web site (http://www.eiu.com/), which provides business intelligence on 195 countries. A publisher who is planning to take business worldwide on the Internet must determine the average annual income of several different positions relevant to the target customer , and the cost of a telephone call or Internet access in the target 25 or 50 countries. The fourth factor includes all legal aspects of doing business in a country. What are the regulations for copyright protection, international legal agreements, and cooperative or joint venture agreements?

The international publishing and information business is a cross *cultural* business. The seller is expected to adapt to the buyer; therefore, the exclusive use of English on a Web site needs serious consideration (see the **review of languages** [14.7] presented later in this chapter). The visitor is expected to observe the local customs and culture even if the "visit" or delivery is via the Internet. Integrating the different international markets and segments thereof into a marketing strategy requires an understanding of informal versus formal cultures including a rigid time versus fluid time approach to relationships. There are also great differences in "deal" focused versus "relationship" focused cultures. These are a few of the major elements that need to be taken into consideration when one moves direct marketing and direct customer services from the comparatively homogenous American market to the complex global market.

14.6 GEOGRAPHIC AND COUNTRY PRIORITIES

Publishing has been a low-growth business in the United States and Europe, two mature markets. It is in this environment of low growth that technology enables publishers to develop new forms of on-line distribution and reach out for global markets. The U.S. accounts for more than half of the total world use of the Internet. Companies in the U.S. pay less for their connections and have significantly more ISP choices than business customers in any other part of the world. The growth has been dramatic over the past five years and continues at amazing rates after the pause in 2000 and 2001. But more and more nations have an emerging installed base of PCs, with cutting edge network connectivity, and a growing volume of network traffic. They are striving to reach the state of development Europe and the U.S. have achieved. Outside the U. S. over the past five years, connectivity has grown from a few hundred Internet-connected networks to over 20,000 in 2002.

Some publishers have recognized the need for regional or country identities through their subsidiaries, and yet maintain an overall strategy and implementation for their Web sites. But it is possible to build a local identity by establishing local Web servers in such countries as Canada, Britain, or Germany.

The first step in assessing the developmental state of a particular country is to measure its connectivity to the Internet. The National Science Foundation in May 1995 counted the total number of global Internet connected networks and found 50,766 of them, of which 56 percent were within the U.S. and the balance of 44 percent or 22,296 distributed in all other countries. The total number of Internet host computers in July 1995 was 6,642,000 worldwide.

The second step in assessing the Internet development of a particular country is to assess its number of Web sites, that is, commercial Web servers offering products or services. There is usually a transition from an initial pioneer phase of primarily academic and government Web servers to an increasing number of commercial sites. This is a critical indicator for any country as a potential market because there must be enough computer literate and connected buyers and sellers to participate in the new global electronic or digital marketplaces. According to the latest statistics available from eMarketer, there were 476 million Internet users in 2001. Projections are for 793 million Internet users by 2003, worldwide.

The third step is an evaluation of commercial Internet development and use. This indicates how a country is using the capabilities of the Web and thus how well the Web can serve that country as a communications, information, and marketing resource. It is necessary to ask if Web-based communications will reach mainly government, universities, other businesses, or individuals in the selected countries.

The Internet commercial development analysis must be applied to any target country, from the most economically developed to the least connected. Because the Internet and the World Wide Web are growing so rapidly, and changing so dramatically, it is important to review target countries. One cannot approach the Internet as one global information distribution system without targeting regions and countries with specific marketing strategies.

14.7 ENGLISH AND OTHER LANGUAGES

How many of the hundreds of millions of new users expected on the Internet during the next few years, especially in developing countries, will be able to read marketing messages in English? It is not an appropriate assumption that English is the second language in most parts of the world just because textbook publishers refer to ESL as English as a Second Language. In the past five years there has been a growing development of EFL texts and training programs for English as a Foreign Language as the third or fourth if not fifth language learned. Even today people in some countries call it the "English Wide Web." ATM bank machines use bilingual text and give customers choices. Publishers need to consider if there is a need or opportunity to provide language choices for the instructions and for initial text delivered on the Internet. STM and professional publications are in English for sophisticated target customers within their respective market niches. However, it may really help to start with a home page in multiple languages. It is important to note that according to eMarketer studies, confirmed by more recent Global Reach data (www.Glreach.com/globstats), the major languages on the Internet are as given in Table 6.

The real challenge for global information providers and Web-site developers will be creating local language interfaces, as the data show the rapid migration from the English language. Some publishers and services have developed interfaces or opening screens in local languages. It is a matter of establishing local language "front doors" to facilitate entry into a Web site. The actual translation of full content is difficult and expensive. Kinokuniya, the major bookseller and journal distributor in Japan, recognized the requirements of local language interfaces for navigation, access, and ordering when it developed its bilingual on-line bookselling and database information services in English and Japanese. In India the "official" language is Hindi and English is the "associate official" language. However, the rapidly developing software and information technology industry in Mumbai (formerly Bombay) faces sixteen official languages as well as a broad range of other languages on the Internet within that huge country. The introduction and rapid acceptance of standard HTML has certainly helped to support the use of different languages. Also, Microsoft Internet Explorer and Netscape Navigator are now available in over eighteen languages. Microsoft has realized that it is necessary to adapt their software products and Internet services to local languages in order to be accepted by and thus penetrate international markets.

(i) FOREIGN LANGUAGE USE IN EUROPE

In contrast to the U.S., the European community has had a long tradition of learning at least two or three foreign languages in school (see Table 7). The Netherlands, which depends on export business, has the highest rate of teaching and using several foreign languages above and beyond the immediate member countries of the European Union.

TABLE 6. MAJOR LANGUAGES ON THE INTERNET

Language	Year 2002	Year 2003	2003 Rank
English	45.0%	29.0%	1
Japanese	9.8%	7.3%	4
Chinese	8.4%	20.2%	2
German	6.2%	5.8%	5
Korean	4.7%	4.4%	6
Spanish	4.5%	7.6%	3
Italian	3.6%	2.9%	9
French	3.4%	3.8%	8
Portuguese	2.5%	4.0%	7
Russian	1.9%	1.8%	10
Arabic	0.9%	0.8%	11
Other	5.8%	10.8%	

Sources: Global Reach Data, March 2001, June 2001, Inc. www.Glreach.com/globstats; International Online Markets 2000, Simba Information Inc. www.simbanet.com; World Lingo, Inc. April 2001. http://www.worldlingo.com/

(ii) OTHER BARRIERS TO GLOBAL USE

Another aspect of international content is that American publishers' Web pages are often not adapted to global markets. They focus on 1–800 phone numbers, and their ordering forms or forms to request more information require only the name of a state followed by the zip code. It is important to request and provide space for a country with postal zone numbers to appear before the city or between the city and country. On-line forms need to allow for the alphanumeric postal codes used in Canada, Britain, and many other countries. Also, it is essential in the digital world to ask for an e-mail address.

TABLE 7. PERCENT OF POPULATION FAMILIAR WITH THREE CORE LANGUAGES

Country	English	French	German
Belgium (French)	58%	1%	6%
Denmark	92%	8%	58%
France	84%	100%	27%
Germany	93%	23%	100%
Ireland	100%	69%	24%
Italy	61%	33%	3%
Netherlands	96%	65%	53%
Portugal	55%	25%	0.04%
Spain	92%	8%	0.03%
United Kingdom	100%	59%	20%

Source: Eurostat. http://europa.eu.int/comm/eurostat/; Simba Information Inc. www.simbanet.com

14.8 NEW ECONOMICS OF INFORMATION SERVICES

Most professional publishers have a multitier subscription pricing plan based on the number of users for individuals, small group users, large subscribers, academic customers, corporate customers, developed as opposed to developing countries, and complimentary no-fee users. The other very important aspect of these developments is that academic, institutional, government, and industry libraries have all accepted and are subscribing to this tremendous change from print to on-line information services. Pricing according to value has resulted in different prices for different information collections used by different sized institutions in different parts of the world. The subscription prices of electronic information have and will continue to be increasingly settled by negotiations to sign agreements based on the number and type of database users.

The Internet tax moratorium, enacted in the U.S. in 1998, has been extended to November 1, 2003. A publisher needs to be aware of a wide range of taxes in different countries when exploring the economics of doing business in other parts of the world. For example, on May 7, 2002, the European Union approved a plan to begin requiring payment of the European Value Added Tax (VAT) by American companies selling products over the Internet to European customers. It is recommended that publishers carry out research as to the tax regulations and currency revaluation rates in the five, ten, or twenty countries that will represent 80 percent of new international business development.

(i) CONSOLIDATION OF PUBLISHERS AND THEIR CUSTOMERS

The consolidation of publishers as well as that of subscription agencies or aggregators, and of libraries (as consortia), will help make realistic the achievement of equitable results for both the provider and user of digital information. Scholarly and professional publishers continue to consolidate via strategic alliances or the merger and acquisition process. Elsevier Science now is the largest STM publisher, with its acquisition of Academic Press and Harcourt including Saunders and Mosby. This consolidation in the publishing industry across national lines is being challenged by the increase in consolidated subscription agencies and library consortia on a statewide, national, and international scale. In Europe we have experienced the joining of Swets & Zeitlinger (of the Netherlands) and Blackwell Subscription Services (of the United Kingdom) as Swets Blackwell B.V., which thus became the largest journal print subscription and on-line service agency in Europe and a strong service organization in other parts of the world. Meanwhile, costs remain high, as both publishers and libraries have to handle print and digital media at the same time. It is especially the libraries and academic institutions in developing or less-developed countries that encounter the extra mailing postage, distribution, fulfillment and customer service costs for print copies. They do not have the added value of search engines accessing total databases, links to other related publications, and similar on-line services.

14.9 WORLDWIDE ON-LINE ADVERTISING

On-line advertising is an interesting and complex business in the U.S. and even more challenging internationally. Optimistic projections made in the late 1990s are no longer valid, but actual advertising spending through the year 2000 serves as a good base for review of this source of revenue. Web-based advertising did grow dramatically outside of the U.S. and Canada, from $57.0 million in 1997 to $227.2 million in 1998, and then took a huge leap to reach $737.0 million in 1999 and $1,651 million in 2000. But these advertising revenues need to be evaluated in the context of U.S. and Canadian revenues; numbers shown in Table 8 are based on eMarketer data.

TABLE 8. ON-LINE ADVERTISING SPENDING (MILLIONS OF $U.S.)

Year	U.S. and Canada	Other	Total	Percent of U.S. and Canada
1997	$650.0	$57.0	$707.0	92%
1998	$1,667.0	$227.0	$1,894.0	88%
1999	$3,600.0	$737.0	$4,337.0	83%
2000	$6,100.0	$1,651.0	$7,751.0	79%

Source: The eAdvertising Report, eMarketer Inc., June 2000. www.emarketer.com

TABLE 9. WORLDWIDE ADVERTISING REVENUES BY REGION (MILLIONS OF $U.S.)

Region	1999	Percent of Total	2002	Percent of Total
United States	$3,600.0	83%	$13,500.0	71%
Europe	$395.0	9%	$2,871.0	15%
Asia/Pacific	$230.0	5%	$1,692.0	9%
Canada	$43.0	1%	$304.0	2%
Other	$69.0	2%	$627.0	3%
Total	**$4,337.0**	**100%**	**$18,995.0**	**100%**

Source: The eAdvertising Report, eMarketer Inc., June 2000. wwwemarketer.com

Insufficient data is available and too many changes have taken place to project revenue growth for the next three-years. However, it is interesting to review worldwide advertising revenues by region for 1999 and 2002, again as reported by eMarketer, as shown in Table 9.

Europe will remain the leader in total volume and growth generated by e-commerce and on-line spending. Germany leads in Europe with $259.0 million or 28 percent of Web-based advertising spending and is followed by the United Kingdom with $234.0 million representing 25 percent in 2000. Scandinavia is in third place with $223.0 million and thus represents 24 percent of Europe's Web-based ad spending.

For the year 2000, Forrester Research reports that Japan generated $234.0 million in ad spending, China had $16.0 million, and South Korea trailed with only $13.0 million total ad spending.

In South America, Forrester Research reported that in 2000, Web advertising spending in Brazil generated $69.0 million and in Mexico generated $28.0 million. Again, the economic turmoil in Argentina and Brazil combined with the lack of a strong telecommunications infrastructure to depress or restrict on-line advertising spending.

14.10 MARKETING ON THE INTERNET

Before reaching out to on-line services and potential new customers around the globe with marketing messages, publishers should first determine what target markets they are trying to reach and according to which level of priorities. For example, six different and rapidly growing markets with developing connectivity are Brazil, China, Japan, Poland, South Africa, and South Korea. We focus on these six different countries as case studies.

(i) BRAZIL

Population: 174,222,000.
Telephones: 17.6 million main lines in use and an estimated 5.6 million mobile cellular phones in 2002.
ISPs: 58.
Internet users: 11.9 million in July 2001 as reported by eMarketer's *eGlobal.*

The total number of on-line or Internet subscribers, including both home and business customers, grew from 1,748,633 million in 1999 to a new total of 3,759,000 in 2001 according to Simba Information, Inc.

The major players for Internet access services in Brazil are America Online Latin America, Terra Networks, Universo Online, Zaz, PSINet, and Star Media.

(ii) CHINA

Population: 1,244,500,000.
Telephones: 135.2 million main lines and 68 million mobile cellular telephones in 2002.
ISPs: Four in 2001.

Internet users or subscribers: Seven million, and an estimated 12 million home PCs installed in 1999, a number that is projected to grow to 36 million by 2003 according to Simba Information, Inc.

The Ministry of Information Industry (MII) basically has total control and administrative responsibility for the Internet within China. China Telecom has initiated, implemented, and supported the initial Internet access services including Capital Online and NetChina InfoTech.

(iii) JAPAN

Population: 126.5 million.

Telephones: 64 million.

Internet connected networks: 1,847 (United States: 28,470).

Internet connected host computers: 160,000 (United States: 4.2 million).

Internet users: 45.7 million in July 2001, according to eMarketer.

The dominant on-line service is Japan NiftyServe with 1.5 million subscribers.

One of the largest Internet access providers in Japan is IIJ or Internet Initiative Japan (http://www.iij.ad.jp/www/walking-e.html).

The Nippon Tel & Tel site has a searchable directory of several thousand Japanese Web sites, similar to Yahoo (http://www.ntt.jp./).

In second place is Asahi Broadcasting and Publishing Corporation, which provides its newspaper and reference sources on its site (http://www.ashahi.co.jp./).

The speed of Internet access in Asia is still a problem. The infrastructure is not yet in place. Content moving from one Asian country to another is sometimes routed through the U.S..

The average price for 20 hours of Internet access in Japan is $59.12.

(iv) POLAND

Population: 38,780,000.

Internet users: 3.8 million (estimated) for 2001 as reported by eMarketer. The International Telecommunications Union (ITU) also reported 3.8 million, far lower than PriceWaterhouseCoopers' report of 7.6 million users.

Internet hosts: 371,043 in January 2001.

The number of telephone subscribers per 100 inhabitants in Poland is only 55.5. The region's median is 127.5: Denmark has 146.0, Germany 131.8, and Greece 128.1, according to ITU's March 2002 report.

The Telekomunikacja Polska S.A. (TPSA), the Science and Academic Computer Network (NASK), and the Global Systems Group (GTS) are the prime Internet providers in Poland.

The average price for 20 hours of Internet access in Poland is $57.53.

(v) SOUTH AFRICA

Population: 42,150,000.
ISPs: 1,94 million.
Total telephones: 5,075,000 and over 2 million mobile cellular phones.

South Africa is the most networked and most advanced country in Africa.

Internet hosts: 41,329 computers were connected to the Internet in 1995; by 2001 783,000 households had at least one PC connected.
Internet users: 1,755,000 in July 2001, according to eMarketer.
Radios: 13.75 million, 14 AM and 347 FM radio broadcast stations.
Televisions: 5.4 million.

South Africa has been selected as a feature country here because so little information is available on any of the other countries in Africa.

(vi) SOUTH KOREA

Population: 46,850,000.

There are 46.4 telephone lines per 100 people, in comparison to Japan's 55.8 and Taiwan's 54.5 lines per 100 people.

South Korea is the second most networked and advanced country in Asia.

Internet hosts: Seven million computers were connected to the Internet in 1999. The number of Internet users in July 2001 was 26.6 million, ranking in third place after the U.S. and Japan, according to eMarketer.

The average price for 20 hours of Internet access in South Korea is $37.04.

14.11 INTERNATIONAL INFORMATION SOURCES

An overview has been provided of the operational and marketing issues critical to success on the Internet internationally (beyond just establishing a Web site). Now it is important to focus on setting priorities when going global, because the power of the Internet can be overwhelming.

Selected Web sites provide excellent information on the international marketplace so that you can look before you leap (or research before you connect). The Web sites have been selected within three major categories:

1. Financial and economic information for international markets
2. Regional or country information
3. International business and trade sources

URLs for the following Web sites are provided so that readers can pursue their own research.

(i) FINANCIAL AND ECONOMIC INFORMATION FOR INTERNATIONAL MARKETS

Institute of Management and Administration Information for Professionals. (http://starbase.ingress.com/ioma/) Provides overall business information with special data on international market opportunities, international business reports, etc.

International Affairs Resources. (http://www.pitt.edu/˜ian/ianres.html) Categorizes information by area, country, source, and topic.

National Trade Data Bank. (http://www.stat-usa.gov/BEN/services/ntdb-home.html) Has the U.S. government's comprehensive world trade data bank. It is "the" source to use as part of any international marketing research and planning process.

The World Bank. (http://www.worldbank.org/) Provides economic and regional sector reports, which are listed alphabetically by country and include detailed abstracts of country reports.

(ii) REGIONAL OR COUNTRY INFORMATION

Asia Trade. (http://www.asiatrade.com/index.html) Provides information on industry groups, companies, financial trends, trade exhibits, and other resources for Hong Kong, Indonesia, Malaysia, Singapore, Thailand, and Taiwan.

The Embassy Page. (http://www.embpage.org) Provides links to Web sites of embassies and consulates throughout the world.

I*M Europe. (http://www.echo.lu/) The European Commission has gathered information about the EEC market in general and electronic information market specifically. The Web site includes information from the databases of the European Commission Host Organization (ECHO).

Web Digest for Marketers—European Edition. (http://www.spc.nl/WDFM/index.html) The Web Digest for Marketers is a free marketing newsletter distributed around the world. The interest in Europe has been so strong that a European edition has been created.

UT-LANIC (University of Texas, Latin American Network Information Center). (http://lanic.utexas.edu/la/region.html) The Institute of Latin American Studies at the University of Texas in Austin maintains a complete and updated collection of information on academic databases in Latin America as well as information on the economic and commercial developments in all Latin American countries.

(iii) INTERNATIONAL BUSINESS RESOURCES

Michigan State University (http://ciber.bus.msu.edu/busres.htm). A comprehensive business information database including links to international business and country-specific guides maintained by Michigan State University.

14.12 INTERNET PUBLISHING LAW

(i) COPYRIGHT

Federal law in the U.S. protects ***copyright***; copyright laws in other countries vary from those in the U.S.. The Internet presents challenges for copyright law because of its digital and global nature. (See the chapter The Legal Framework for more detail on **copyright** [13.1].)

The digital elements cause problems in the U.S. as well as other countries because most intellectual property laws make assumptions about "writing" and "signatures." Copyright law in the U.S. protects a wide variety of works that can be delivered via the multimedia channels of the Internet, including but not limited to: text, databases, digital images, photographs, films, plays, musical recordings, computer software, compilations of public domain works, and collections of information including catalogs. The digital delivery and retrieval of information at any time and any place around the world makes the act of copying very easy and out of control. In the U.S., the copyright law protects "original works of authorship fixed in any tangible medium of expression," while this principle is more difficult to put into practice in other countries of the world.

Another problem of the Internet for authors, agents, and publishers is the global distribution of information that is in conflict with territory limitations of agreements and most laws. Many trade publishers have limited the purchase or sale of rights to publish and distribute a work to within the U.S. and Canada or North America, in contrast to British Traditional Territories, Commonwealth, or Middle East and African territories. However, if such a work is distributed in digital form via the Internet, such territory restrictions would be unenforceable. The professional, scientific, technical, and medical publishers have pioneered and established a subscription model that includes an agreement between the publisher and the subscriber for copyright protection on a worldwide basis.

The U.S. government established a standing committee in February 1993 to examine the world of "The Information Superhighway." This committee was named the Information Infrastructure Task Force (IITF). From this committee several subcommittees were formed, including the Intellectual Property Working Group, which issued a final report, "Intellectual Property and the National Information Infrastructure," on September 5, 1995. The recommended changes in law address distribution rights, prohibition of devices or methods used to protect copyrighted materials, library exemptions, and copyright management information systems. The report and recommendations should really be considered as the first step, but not a comprehensive solution for the problems and development of laws in the U.S. and global arena. The ***Digital Millennium Copyright Act*** of 1998 outlaws conduct and devices that try to evade technological controls designed to protect copyrighted works. On May 3, 2002, the Electronic Frontier Foundation published a report on the "unintended consequences" of the Digital Millennium Copyright Act (DMCA) over a two-year timeframe. This is another example of the law being developed, applied to digital publishing, and critiqued within the most sophisticated country. It can only serve as a model for other countries to follow.

Much needs to be done to develop laws that address the new technologies of gathering, storing, and delivering information on the Internet. The technology of distributing and making copies has changed, but unfortunately the laws have not. A good review of the current state of copyright protection, licensing, and enforcement of laws to restrict piracy, especially in developing countries, can be found in a report written by Carlo Scollo Lavizzari, legal counsel, for the 5th International Publishers Association Copyright Conference (Accra, Ghana, February 20–22, 2002). The International Publishers Association has 78 member organizations from 65 countries and is based in Geneva, Switzerland (www.ipa-uie.org). The WIPO Copyright Treaty (WCT) became effective on March 6, 2002; however, a truly global framework for copyright protection on the Internet is still in development.

(ii) TRADEMARK

Publishers use logos or imprints to identify the company or organization or service marks to identify information services. A mark can consist of an image, design, word or words, a color, or any combination of these elements. In developing an international role for a publisher, it is important to protect the ***trademark*** or service mark if only for brand extension and to reflect a guarantee of the quality of the publications and/or services. It is important to recognize that a registered domain name is not automatically entitled to trademark protection in the U.S. or any other part of the world. A domain name is protected as a trademark only if the domain name is also used to brand the Web site located at that address. A good example is Amazon.com and its registered offices in the U.S., United Kingdom, Germany, and the Netherlands.

We recommend that, for specific issues or questions, a publisher contact its attorney and related legal counsel, who specialize in media- and computer-related law. See the chapter on **copyright** [13.1] and **trademark** [13.2] issues for a more detailed discussion of trademark as it applies to the U.S.

14.13 CONCLUSION

Distribution of information on a pay-per-use or subscription basis as well as marketing and selling on the Internet has just begun. Companies have launched hundreds or thousands of Web sites on the Internet. Meanwhile, there have been and continue to be dramatic changes. Every year, computing power has doubled and technology prices have fallen, which means that there are opportunities for both the large and small publisher to reach suddenly accessible global markets.

Education will change, marketing will change, on-line shopping will change, money and banking will change, and computers will continue to change. The development of access to the Internet and on-line publishing is also rapidly changing in many countries in *all* parts of the world. Therefore, it is important to focus resources and efforts on very carefully targeted countries, market segments, and computer literate niches therein.

BIBLIOGRAPHY

Afuah, Allan, and Christopher L. Tucci. *Internet Business Models and Strategies*. New York: Irwin/McGraw-Hill, 2002.

"Applied Global Marketing." GLOBMKT. LISTSERV@ukcc.uky.edu

Association of Research Libraries. "Statistics and Measurement Program." 2002. http://www.arl.org/stats/index.html

Cronin, Mary J. *Global Advantage on the Internet: From Corporate Connectivity to International Competitiveness*. New York: Van Nostrand Reinhold, 1997.

Doz, Yves, José Santos, and Pter Williamson. *From Global to Metanational: How Companies Win in the Knowledge Economy*. Boston: Harvard Business School Press, 2002.

Economist, The. *The Economist Guide to Economic Indicators*. London: The Economist, 2001.

eMarketer. *Demographics & Usage, January 2002*. New York: eMarketer, Inc, 2002.

———. *eGlobal: Demographics and Usage, January 2002*. New York: eMarketer, Inc, 2002.

———. *Europe Online: Access, Demograhpics and Usage, May 2002*. New York: e-Marketer, Inc, 2002.

Ginsparg, Paul. "Winners and Losers in the Global Research Village." February 21, 1996. http://arxiv.org/blurb/pg96unesco.html

Grossnickle, Joshua, and Oliver Raskin. *The Handbook of Online Marketing Research: Knowing Your Customer Using the Net*. New York: McGraw-Hill, 2002.

Grycz, Czeslaw Jan, ed. *Professional and Scholarly Publishing in the Digital Age*. New York: Association of American Publishers (AAP), 1997.

Hagel, John, and Arthur G. Armstrong. *Net Gain: Expanding Markets Through Virtual Communities*. Boston: Harvard Business School Press, 1997.

Hart, Jon. *Web Publishing Law*. Washington, D.C.: Dow, Lohnes & Albertson, PLLC, 2002. www.dowlohnes.com

Judson, Bruce. *Net Marketing: Your Guide to Success and Profit on the Net*. New York: Wolff New Media, 1996.

Kahin, Brian, and Hal R. Varian. *Internet Publishing and Beyond*. Cambridge: MIT Press, 2000.

Komenar, Margo. *Electronic Marketing: A Comprehensive Reference to Electronic Marketing Techniques to Help You Reach a Broader Market*. New York: John Wiley & Sons, 1997.

Lavizzari, Carlo Scollo. "Encouraging Creativity through Copyright Protection, The 5th International Publishers Association Copyright Conference." Publishing Research Quarterly 18, no.2 (summer 2002): 41–49.

Liautaud, Bernard, and Mark Hammond. *e-Business Intelligence: Turning Information into Knowledge and Profit*. New York: McGraw-Hill, 2000.

Odlyzko, Andrew. "Competition and Cooperation: Libraries and Publishers in the Transition to Electronic Scholarly Journals." Journal of Electronic Publishing 4, no. 4 (June 1999). http://www.press.umich.edu/jep/04-04/odlyzko0404.html

Opnix. "Internet Traffic Report." 2002. http://www.internettrafficreport.com/main.htm

Rosenblatt, William, William Trippe, and Stephen Mooney. *Digital Rights Management: Business and Technology*. New York: M & T Books, 2002.

Simba Information. *International Online Markets 2000: Strategic Outlook and Forecast.*. Stamford, Ct.: Simba Information, Inc, 2000.

———. *Online Services: Trends and Forecasts—1999 Edition*. Wilton, Ct.: Simba Information, Inc, 1999.

Sterne, James. *World Wide Web Marketing: Integrating the World Wide Web into Your Marketing Strategy*. New York: John Wiley & Sons, 1995.

Tweney, Dylan. "The Defogger: Think Globally, Act Locally." Business 2.0 (November 2001). http://www.business2.com/articles/mag/0,1640,17423,FF.html

15 Digital Rights Management

PAUL HILTS
Former Technology Editor, Publisher's Weekly

Based on a presentation by Bill Rosenblatt, author of *Digital Rights Management: Business and Technology.*

One of the promises of the digital revolution in publishing is that it has the potential to give owners of content—authors, publishers, aggregators—new, robust tools for more intelligent, efficient, and effective management of their content. Nowhere have the benefits of new technology been more eagerly awaited than in the area of rights management. However, content owners have been groping not only for the right technology but for the right applications of competing technologies—as well as dealing with changing business models, customer resistance, legal challenges, and implementation questions. This chapter explores the fundamentals of Digital Rights Management and the different DRM technologies available in order to help publishers and their partners implement the right technology in the right manner.

15.1 OVERVIEW: WHAT IS DRM?

The term "digital rights management" (***DRM***) could be defined as simply as using digital technology to exploit and manage the rights inherent in a work. The reality of the term, though, encompasses not just technology, but a new approach to the whole notion of what we traditionally think of as rights, including issues of copyright, security, sales and distribution, and the impact of these new ideas and technologies on both publishers and their customers.

The concept of digital rights management is central to electronic publishing for commerce. Without a way to protect both the rights of the author by keeping the text safe from piracy and unauthorized modification, and those of the publisher by ensuring the ability to collect revenue from readers, no one would publish on the Internet or in e-books. Back in the days when "publishing" meant going to print only, managing the various rights attached to a book or article was fairly straightforward: someone interested in using the material would license the rights from the holder of those rights—the author, the author's agent, or the publisher. Piracy was a problem, but relatively easy to spot, and the law provided straightforward means to deal with it. However, with the advent of digital publishing processes that often supplemented or even eliminated the print-only products in favor of electronic files, and that made it easy to create perfect copies of those files, new avenues of exploiting content and the rights inherent in the content emerged, along with new concerns about the security of the content and the rights.

This chapter will take a look at three broad areas of DRM:

- controlling access to content, including payment channels, authentication of users and uses of content, and security of content;
- imitating or approximating physical distribution models using largely electronic media;
- inventing new distribution models, including pay-per-view and e-books.

These represent some of the fundamental issues of DRM. The sections of this chapter will deal with these interrelated issues by taking a look at different parts of DRM systems. We'll delve into:

- the background of rights management
- new business models using DRM
- the technology and standards in current or proposed use
- legal issues and some high-profile court cases
- various vendors of DRM systems
- the current state of the market for DRM
- issues relating to actually implementing DRM

(i) CONTROLLING ACCESS TO CONTENT

The principal vehicle for controlling an intellectual property and determining who has the right to print, copy, sell, or otherwise benefit from the use of that content is copyright, a topic that is covered in detail in the chapter **The Legal Framework** [13.1]. The traditional model for dealing with the rights defined by copyright was for the copyright owner to sell or license those rights to a publisher or publishers, usually for an unspecified period of time that amounted to "while it is profitable to print and distribute it," which might be a year or might be several decades. Book authors would typically sell the rights for world or regional publication to a publisher, who might then license subsidiary rights to others, such as first or second serial (magazine or newspaper) rights, paperback publication, foreign-language rights, or audio rights. When the cost of fulfilling orders became greater than the income from those orders, the publisher would cease reprinting the work and declare it "out of print" at which time that publisher's license would end, and the rights would revert to the author or original copyright holder.

The picture today is more complicated, largely due to the new uses to which content can be put and new sales channels made available by digital technology. When publishing was entirely print-based, the vast majority of book sales were whole-book units, with each sale permanent; the same was largely true of a journal or an encyclopedia, and of magazines and newspapers to a great extent as well. Now, a publisher can offer content to other publishers, libraries, aggregators, or consumers in varied ways, with varying licenses: whole text, selected chapters or articles or pages, for varied lengths of time or numbers of viewings, or even published as a database and allowing users to recombine the data. Tracking those uses and securing the content from unauthorized use involves more than just signing a contract and handing over an electronic file. The publisher uses DRM to identify the users of its intellectual property, to take payment from them, to define the ways in which the content may be used and to monitor the use to make sure it is within bounds, and finally to prevent illegal copying and redistribution of the work.

1. Taking payment

Depending on the type of content, there have been a few standard ways to collect money from a sale of that content: book publishers would sell to either a distributor or a bookstore and collect payment, minus unsold returned copies; journal and periodical publishers normally received payment through subscriptions. In sub-rights, the publisher would license the content and collect payment from the licensee. Those avenues for collecting payment still exist and likely will persist, but electronic distribution allows for significant new channels for sales and a variety of ways of collecting revenue. These are discussed in greater detail in **DRM-enabled business models** [15.2.2] below, but briefly they are:

- *Paid downloads:* usually consumer payments by credit card or other on-line payment schemes that allow a person to download the content to his or her own computer or computerlike device (PDAs or e-book readers).
- *Pay-per-view:* payment is made for a single-session use of the content.
- *Subscription:* payment is collected for use or viewing of the content for a specified period of time and is renewable.
- *Usage metering:* payment is made only for the time the content is used or for the amount of content used.
- *Peer-to-peer/Superdistribution:* buyers of content are allowed to "share" the content with others, with payment (if required) being collected at the portal where the sharing occurs. This has not been a particularly successful method of actually collecting money for content; it has been confined so far mostly to audio music.
- *Rights licensing:* in the electronic environment, on-line clearing of permissions, licensing of excerpts, sales of reprints, or licensing of

trademarked content can be done with fewer human interactions and payment can be collected electronically.

2. Identifying and authenticating users

A major part of effective DRM is the ability to know who your users or customers are and to allow them access to the content consistent with the level they pay for—and to do all this as transparently as possible. Systems for identifying and authenticating users vary depending on the type of content, the media of distribution, and the level of access. Identities—including user names, passwords, e-mail addresses, or other personal information—are typically confirmed by information provided by the users or a third party and stored electronically. Digital certificates are one way of using information supplied by third-parties for identifying users. On the horizon, information inherent in and unique to an individual will come into play, such as biometric data (e.g., fingerprints, retina scan, facial features-recognition software). Publishers are only beginning to tackle the privacy and security implications of collecting such information.

Once a user is *identified,* he or she needs to be *authenticated* as being allowed to use the content. Currently most authentication schemes involve either licensing the content to a specific, registered user who must be authenticated at each access irrespective of the hardware platform being used; licensing the content to a specific piece of hardware, regardless of who uses it; or a combination of the two. See **identities and authentication** [15.3.2.1] below for more detail.

3. Specifying valid uses

The ability to distribute content through multiple channels while ensuring that users can only use the content in a way consistent with the access they paid for is a vital part of robust DRM. It is helpful to think of the license to the content as being separate from the content itself. A user is paying not for "the content" but for the *license* or the *right of access* to the content (or part of the content) in a specific way, through a specific medium, for a specific time, and each of those factors may be different for different users. One user might buy multiple sets of rights for a single content item, while another user might license a single set of rights for multiple content items, while a third might license a one-time right to view a content item for a fixed period of time. The content doesn't change, but each situation involves a sale of a different set of rights.

Planners of DRM strategies need to consider what rights might be sold and how valid uses will be determined. Advanced planning in this area will have implications for the architecture of the DRM system affecting both software and hardware. See the section **below** [15.3.1] for more detail.

4. Measuring use

One of the hardest things for publishers to do in electronic publishing is to establish the value of a property that is to be sold and used in parts instead of in whole traditional units like a copy of a book or an issue of a journal or magazine. Publishers have long had the problem of trying to decide what the potential market for a forthcoming work will be, so they can set the first print run: with no hard data from readers, the forecast was little more than guesswork. Even when publishing on CD-ROMs, there was no feedback from customers. But with the advent of the Internet, publishers for the first time can get a very good idea of who's reading what, and can test-market various versions and business plans to see what works best. In publishing electronically, measuring use has been easiest when the content is held at the publishing house in a server, and numbers of times it is accessed or the amount of time allotted is physically counted. Database publishing presents far more complex problems for the rights holder. See **measuring use for market intelligence** [15.3.2.2] for further details.

5. Deterring piracy

Perhaps one of the greatest challenges of DRM is protecting content from unauthorized use and piracy. The electronic medium offers wonderful opportunities for more thorough use of content, but the very aspects of the medium that make it attractive to publishers (nearly instantaneous distribution, easy and near-perfect replication, ability to re-purpose content to new and varied uses, the ability to identify and locate content electronically) also make it ripe for misuse and exploitation. The two technologies that are in current use to deter such misuse or piracy are ***encryption*** and ***watermarking***, both of which have advantages and disadvantages; the are discussed in more detail in the section on **encryption and DRM** [15.3.2.3] below. Finally, new legal tools, such as the Digital Millennium Copyright Act (DMCA), offer legal protection and are discussed below in the section on **legal developments** [15.5] and in the chapter **The Legal Framework** [13.1].

(ii) APPROXIMATING PHYSICAL DISTRIBUTION MODELS

While publishing in the electronic medium has opened up new avenues of publication and distribution, many of those new distribution models are still in their infancy. These new models generate a lot of buzz, but most publishers today are still doing what they know best—perfecting the use of traditional physical distribution models and resolving the attendant rights issues.

1. Disabling infinite perfect copies

Ease of copying a content item is at the core of the computer revolution and the rise of the Internet and World Wide Web. The ability to create any number of identical copies of a content item is a useful tool, but it is also a major stumbling block to realizing the full potential of the medium, because it inhibits publishers from making their content available electronically. Publishers need a robust system of digital rights management that will secure their content such that it cannot easily be copied. Encryption and watermarking (discussed in the section on **encryption and DRM** [15.3.2.3] below) are two technologies that are being used; . these technologies can work either in an on-line environment or in a fixed-media environment (such as ***CD***s or ***DVD***). Further protection schemes are being built into the reading devices, PC hardware and disks, primarily to prevent cracking the protection codes on movies on DVD and audio CDs.

2. Lending, read-only, etc.

The analogy between print and electronic publishing (and the business plans of the publishers) began to break down over lending of copies and pass-along readership. In the early days of ***CD-ROM*** publishing, it became clear that for the majority of trade publishers, CD-ROMs had the worst of both worlds. The disks had to be physically distributed like printed books, so there was little or no saving in distribution; when they included lots of audio, video, and graphical content, they were expensive to produce. Unlike books, which were often acquired and printed for less than $20,000, CD-ROM sub-rights licensing and production often topped ten or even twenty times that amount. This virtually guaranteed that CD-ROM production would be limited to such big-ticket items as dictionaries and encyclopedias. What would happen when the natural market for these CDs (libraries and researchers) began to turn to the Internet for their access?

In the physical world, the equation was simple: one copy equals one use at a time. If you lend that copy to a friend, or a patron of the library, the only way to give another person access at the same time is to buy another copy. But limitless numbers of users can get access to an electronic publication simultaneously via a network. So the site-license was born, charging librarians more than the single-copy price, but less than the full price for every potential reader.

In the late 1990s, when novels and other non-illustrated works became distributable to e-book devices via the Internet, the question arose again: What is the correct price and business model for a work that can be "lent" to millions of readers simultaneously for free? Should libraries store novels on their own servers for download to patrons' e-book devices, and if so, should the book cost more than the print version or the retail single-copy price?

DRM can lock up the text so that it is "read-only," and can't be copied or redistributed, but this has produced a tremendous backlash from librarians who feel this is in conflict with their mission. In 2000, the president of the Association of American Publishers called libraries the enemy of publishers, because they give away free use of texts, thus cutting down on single-copy sales. Clearly, this is an emotionally charged issue that has yet to be resolved.

(iii) INVENTING NEW DISTRIBUTION MODELS

Of course, the real promise of digital rights management is not just to replicate older models of distribution, but to utilize the digital medium to expand the uses of content and fully exploit the rights inherent in it. Some new models are beginning to emerge, and others will follow. Some will fail while others will become the new standards. Here are some of the more promising ideas:

1. Dynamic pricing

Instead of charging one price, as is typically done for a printed version of content, digital distribution offers the opportunity to charge a variety of prices based on a variety of factors, such as how much of the content is used, how long the content is used, whether the content can be copied or printed, etc. Each of these factors represents a different right or set of rights in the content; keeping track of what is sold to whom for what use and for how long is one of the core aspects of DRM.

The first uses of dynamic pricing have been subtly working their way into the market. British publishers have for some time been selling what amounted to unedited galleys of novels, very inexpensively bound, but available long before the actual production run hits the stores—essentially, the customer is paying a premium for first access. Similarly, recognizing the short life span of computer books, McGraw-Hill and other computer publishers have offered "BetaBooks," to which the reader buys a "subscription." The BetaBook costs about half what the finely edited version will cost later, and by registering with the publisher, the user guarantees he will receive updates to the text as the software or the manual itself is modified. Finally, movies on DVD offer a good example of developing dynamic prices: video tapes are generally much less expensive than DVDs, but the "special edition" DVD offers hours of extra footage and ancillary materials.

It is easy to foresee how true dynamic pricing could evolve for publishers, with DRM programs tracking multiple licenses to a single user through credit-card records. The reader could build her own "product" and price structure, taking, for instance, one price for the mass-market paperback alone, and adding (for an additional price) the license to download the e-book to a reading device such as a ***PDA***, and further to download or print out selected chapters of the book, or get marketing "teasers," sections of the book to pass along to friends.

2. Demographics-per-view

An advantage that scholarly, technical, and medical (STM) publishers have over their commercial trade cousins is that they know precisely who their readers are and what kinds of things they want to read. Heart surgeons rarely need information on foot disease, but they need all the latest information on circulation problems. That's what scholarly journals and university presses do—produce highly specialized information for well-defined markets. The products are expensive compared to trade books because their markets are small, but worth the price to their readers because the information is so important to them.

Since a major stumbling block to publishers in determining the proper print run of a book is guessing the real market for an unknown author, a logical extension of the variable license model is to trade value for value—offer lower prices for more demographic information about the reader. The book has value for the reader; the readers' buying and reading habits should definitely have value for the publisher. In order to collect the kind of information that would improve his list, the publisher could offer a small discount off the retail price for the reader's name, address, and phone number or e-mail address; a larger amount off for that information plus the titles of ten books bought recently, and an even larger discount for those plus a questionnaire concerning the book just bought, including likes, dislikes, and suggestions for improvement.

3. Post-PC devices (e-books)

A common belief in the publishing industry is that people are reluctant to pay for content that must be read on a desktop computer screen, and for book-length works this has been largely true in the past. But publishers of journals, market research, and other high-value content have found that people are more than willing to receive, pay for, and read article-length pieces on a computer. As the chapter on **e-books** [11] discusses, there is actually more distribution of books electronically than most people realize, and this is a trend that will only increase as technology evolves. The challenge for all these publishers is how to deliver, secure, manage, and get paid for content distributed to other, non-desktop computers, such as PDAs, e-book readers, or other computer-like devices, such as MP3 players. The convenience of wireless access to the Internet through these devices is certain to build consumer demand in what is currently an infant distribution channel.

4. Business-to-business (syndication)

Selling single books to consumers was a (relatively) easy business—one copy equals one unit of revenue. With electronic books (such as computer manuals) and especially with articles, a new form of business has emerged:

syndication, or business-to-business selling for re-publication. Syndication in newspapers means selling an article or column or photograph to a whole list of publications, bringing the author a much larger audience for less effort than trying to sell to the syndicate members separately, or trying to rewrite the piece for each audience. Syndication in books means selling to an aggregator who will offer collections of works (often on related topics), usually at some reduction in price. Syndication depends on seeing additional value in the relationship of one piece to another. The value of the whole is more than the sum of the parts.

The Internet has also brought about a new type of business model based on the idea of syndication. Syndication on the Internet often means publishing content to "subscribers" who are also publishers and who use the content in their own on-line products and services. The canonical example of on-line syndication is a travel book publisher that syndicates reviews of hotels, restaurants, and tourist attractions to travel websites. In these cases, on-line syndication serves as a convenient way of automating contractually-based derivative-work or secondary publishing arrangements.

15.2 RIGHTS-BASED BUSINESS MODELS

The point of DRM is to enable publishers to take advantage of digital processes to make money in their business. In this section we examine the business models that have driven the means of content distribution in the traditional, pre-DRM world and new models that have been or could be developed using digital processes.

The early DRM systems that concentrated so heavily on copy protection did a disservice to publishers. By putting so much emphasis on the need to prevent piracy, they drowned out the discussions about what business models might make money in a digital world. As a result, people got good copy protection but lost their shirts, and declared loudly and repeatedly in the *Wall Street Journal* and the *New York Times* that there was no money to be made in electronic publishing.

The essence of publishing is to find a market and serve it well. The kinds of products, the means of delivery, and everything else follow from finding customers and discovering what they will pay to have their needs served.

(i) PRE-DIGITAL RIGHTS MANAGEMENT

Given all the talk in recent years about copy protection, a Martian just arriving on Earth could be forgiven for thinking that rights management was invented by computer geeks in the mid-1990s. Actually there have been rights-supporting processes available to protect authors and publishers (such as copyright statutes) since the Enlightenment. These rights management systems from the pre-digital era should not be ignored, because they can teach us a lot about what people thought constituted a business, what made money and what rights were recognized as worth defending.

Rights come about in essentially three ways. There are *legal* rights, those defined by law, such as copyright; *contractural* rights, those you acquire by contract, such as when buying or selling something; and *implicit* rights, those defined by or inherent in the medium the work is distributed in. The first two kinds of rights haven't changed much over the centuries, partly because our notions of what a law can or can't do, and what makes a fair sale, also haven't changed much. The recent changes brought about by digital technologies have added to the rights inherent in traditional media, but they are on the verge of affecting those media to a much greater extent in the near future.

1. Rights management in physical media

The kinds of rights inherent in a print book are so obvious that they are often overlooked in the ways they affect the publishing business: a well-designed, well-printed and bound book is easy to read; a book is easy to carry, to lend or give away. It is hard to change anything in the text, whether a single typographical error or a whole chapter. These facts affect rights management in significant ways that publishers count on to protect their rights and their authors' rights. The large format of a newspaper makes it easy to carry (when folded), but very difficult to copy or reprint. A movie in a theater is easy to see one time; it is difficult to stop and replay particular scenes.

1. PHYSICAL COPIES OF BOOKS ARE IMPERFECT AND EXPENSIVE

Both the convenience and the cost of even rudimentary printing and binding are in most cases superior to illegal copies of books. It is easy to photocopy a single page of a book. It is time-consuming and expensive to photocopy every page of that book. Given the "click charge" on most photocopiers (a fee assessed for each copy made on that machine), someone is paying for the copy, even if the copyright-infringer is not. And even if the person doing the copying plans very well, produces two-sided copies, the paper alone is likely to cost more than a paperback copy of the book, and the copy is still unbound, with the loose sheets likely to get lost or damaged or out of sequence. For all the above reasons, publishers had not been very concerned about ways to prevent photocopying of whole books, until the advent of "infringement technologies" described below. The physical properties of the medium themselves have acted as a deterrent to rights infringement.

2. LIMITING "INFRINGEMENT TECHNOLOGY"

That said, there are new technologies that will help overcome the limitations of copying physical media. Rights management in books got its first big challenge when digital copiers became available with optical character recognition (***OCR***). By allowing copyright infringers to produce both page images and editable files, these copiers make large-scale lawbreaking much simpler. In the mid-1990s, the Association of American Publishers vigorously pursued manufacturers of copiers, which they suspected of developing technologies for copying and OCR scanning entire books without manual intervention. Two new laws are aimed specifically at halting the spread of "infringement technologies" as applied specifically to digital content: The ***Digital Millennium Copyright Act*** (passed in 1998) and the proposed Consumer Broadband and Digital Television Promotion Act (see **legal developments** [15.5] below, and the chapter **The Legal Framework** [13.1.8.1] for more details) are laws intended to address specifically the hardware and software that allow copyright protection cracking.

Another interesting approach to curbing infringement technology is through technology itself. Xerox, in its Palo Alto Research Center (PARC), is experimenting with "smart paper," ordinary-looking paper that carries in it special code that spells out who has the right to copy it. When this smart paper is put on a photocopier, the code will interact with the copier and either stop the copying process or disfigure the copies. As futuristic as this sounds, PARC scientists indicate it may be practical within five years, and commercially available in seven to ten years.

2. Contractual rights

In the pre-digital world, the means of production and distribution were so expensive that content creators rarely did these things for themselves. Instead they would sell their creations to publishers. This agreement would be spelled out in a contract that could include almost anything, from trading a single-format publication right for one-time payment to selling "all rights," with complex reimbursement schemes. In these agreements the contract itself is the "rights management system," with the language crafted by both parties to look after their interests in the intellectual properties.

There are two principal kinds of contracts that were (and are) common under pre-digital conditions. The first kind is between the original creator of the work, who just wants compensation for his efforts, and the first publisher of the piece. The second kind of contract is between the publisher who has bought certain rights and other publishers who can extend the market with different products, such as a trade paperback edition, or a mass-market paperback, or with foreign language publication, either in one specific language or a group of translations.

These secondary contracts are not to be ignored, because the downstream rights can produce many times more revenue than the first publication. In movies, for instance, the U.S. distribution rights are nice, but foreign distribution and videotape rights are where big-budget blockbusters really pay out.

3. Compensation models

As radio, television and, later, photocopying technologies spread, it quickly became apparent to publishers that defending the copyrights and producing fair compensation to content creators presented a problem. There were so many users of copyrighted materials that the cost of negotiating terms, monitoring the uses, and collecting the fees would easily surpass the actual royalties collected. The answer lay in creating clearinghouse organizations where creators and publishers could deposit their works, and users could go to buy licenses to use the materials (texts or music).

The first of these organizations was the American Society of Composers, Authors and Publishers (ASCAP), founded in 1914, followed in 1940 by Broadcast Music International (BMI), to handle music licenses. In 1978, Congress mandated the creation of the Copyright Clearing Center (CCC) to handle similar issues for photocopying copyrighted works.

These organizations came up with different but in effect similar models for compensating their creative members or clients. ASCAP charges fees for any business that uses its music. Because it is based on business, ASCAP bases its fees on the revenue of the business that wants the license. For instance, radio stations that broadcast music frequently are charged on a blanket license, amounting to a little over one percent of annual gross revenues; for talk-radio stations that only use incidental music, ASCAP suggests a per-program license that is .24 percent of gross revenues.

BMI came up with a statistical model based on hours of music played. BMI monitors a scientifically chosen representative cross section of radio and television stations each quarter. The stations being monitored supply BMI with complete information as to all music performed during a certain time period. These lists, known in the industry as logs, are put through an elaborate computer system that multiplies each performance listed by a factor which reflects the ratio of the number of stations logged to the number licensed. BMI monitors approximately 6,000,000 hours of television and 500,000 hours of commercial radio programming annually.

The Copyright Clearance Center also chose a statistical model. CCC determined the prices to charge and the royalties to be paid for each photocopy based on surveys of actual users and the cost of making copies in their particular industry, originally including the number of employees in research and development, but now based on number of employees that are exempt versus the number nonexempt.

4. Government intervention: compulsory licensing

One license-granting arrangement from the pre-DRM days, used in situations where the costs are high relative to the fees likely to be collected, and where the greater good of society is established, is compulsory licensing. Under this arrangement, rightsholders must grant permission to any prospective user who pays an established royalty rate. The Copyright Act mandates four compulsory licensing arrangements—cable TV, phonograph records, broadcasting, and satellite dishes.

With cable or satellite TV delivery, for example, people in remote areas benefit from having the largest number of channels and the widest variety of programming possible. Compulsory licensing prevents these people from being neglected or overcharged just because the cost of providing content to them would not be as profitable as providing content to people in more densely populated areas. The government has declared that rightsholders must deal with system operators at a fee established by the industry but overseen by the government.

While some people have suggested that specific applications of DRM, such as the licensing of music tracks to Web sites not owned by recording companies, be added to the list of compulsory licenses under the Copyright Act, such a move is, at the least, controversial. Proponents say that the rightsholder gets compensated, the user gets his license, and the compulsory nature of the agreement diminishes the likelihood of litigation over the terms. Opponents point out that the fees would be not negotiable in the ordinary sense, but set by a party not involved otherwise in the transaction (which is antithetical to U.S. business practices); that a clear societal greater good is not established with respect to DRM; and finally that the changing nature of digitally based businesses and the related importance of DRM, coupled with the slow reactions of the government bureaucracy, would virtually guarantee that the whole system would be out of sync rapidly and perhaps permanently.

The jury is still out on compulsory licensing for DRM.

5. Unmanaged rights: copyright law

Some rights are not managed at all, but are nonetheless allowed under copyright law to help balance the benefits that accrue to the content creator against "the general benefit derived by the public from . . . the progress of science and the useful arts" (U.S. Constitution, Article I, Section 8). Chief among these unmanaged rights are those bundled under the doctrine of fair use. In some special circumstances, including but not limited to educational use, news reportage, critical commentary, and parody, users may quote from a copyrighted work without paying any license fees or even consulting the rights owner.

It is this last bit that causes trouble for DRM. Fair use is a defense to a charge of copyright infringement rather than a list of "uses that are fair." In other words, it is all about interpretations of the use after the fact; DRM is all about setting rules in advance, allowing automatic enforcement. Many software packages have an End User License Agreement (***EULA***) that prohibits any kind of copying whatsoever. If the user agrees to the terms of the EULA, she is signing a contract that gives away rights that she would have under fair use; if she declines to accept all the terms of the EULA she can't open the software. This is the case due to the well-established legal principle that contract terms trump copyright terms.

Fans of ***Linux*** and other open-source software point to this as one of the program's chief benefits—that it is open, that the software "belongs" to the public that uses it, and the users all have the right to copy, transmit, and modify the code, and all will benefit from the sharing of that code, not just one rights owner. The difference between a license agreement, which is a legally enforceable contract that may contain provisions the user finds onerous but that are required to open the software, and an outright purchase, in which the user can use, sell, give away, or destroy the work because she *owns* it, may well be a deciding factor in whether DRM helps or hurts publishing in the long run. (See the chapter The Legal Framework for detailed discussion of **copyright** [13.1] and **fair use** [13.1.7].)

(ii) DRM-ENABLED BUSINESS MODELS

Up until now we have been discussing those business models and rights management schemes that haven't changed much over the years. Digital technologies have made a difference, though, with the rights inherent in the technologies supporting or challenging new kinds of business models. There are a number of business models currently in use:

- Paid downloads
- Subscriptions
- Pay per view/listen
- Usage metering
- Peer-to-peer/superdistribution
- Rights licensing

1. Paid downloads

One of the oldest DRM-enabled business models is the paid download. Users go to a Web site, browse and select some content, pay for it, usually with a credit card, and finally they get to download the piece. So far, its a direct analog to traditional commerce in physical media. Now comes the DRM part.

The protection from illegal copying is typically encryption, which requires the user to install a client application that can decrypt the work. Sometimes this application can play the decrypted content itself; sometimes it must pass the content to another application for display.

The disadvantages to paid downloads include the complexity of the purchase process, where the user has to own a credit card, the seller has to verify that the card is valid and the purchaser has the right to use it, and the typically awkward DRM technology of applications passing the content back and forth and encrypting and decrypting it.

Examples of products that use one-time paid downloads include e-books; market research studies, such as those from the Gartner Group G2 Computer Intelligence or the Aberdeen Group; and music trials, including Liquid Audio, N2K Encoded Music, and Vivendi Universal's paid MP3s. On-demand delivery of movies from companies like MovieLink, a joint venture of several major film studios, is now a reality.

2. Subscriptions

If one believed all the static in some newspapers about the inability of publishers to make a profit from the Internet, it would be easy to miss one of the most obvious business models in the world—subscriptions. Like paid downloads, this is an old model that abounds with analogs in the non-digital world: neither magazines and newspapers nor cable TV could last long without the money-up-front support from subscriptions, and journals typically totally depend on them.

For a set fee, collected annually or monthly, subscribers to digital content get access to special Web sites or subscriber-only areas of bigger sites; to on-line versions of such print periodicals as the *Harvard Business Review,* and the *Wall Street Journal;* or to music download services such as Pressplay, MusicNet, or FullAudio. Most journals are making the transition from print to electronic; increasing numbers are available only electronically. The same is true of many reference works.

One new idea in on-line subscriptions in the book world comes from computer publishers O'Reilly & Associates and Pearson. In order to combat the short useful life of computer manuals and build up customer loyalty, both Pearson and O'Reilly individually came up with the idea of a subscription to a library of books, then pooled their resources to create a service called Safari. For ten dollars a month users get electronic access to any five books from O'Reilly's or Pearson's lists. Titles are updated automatically, so the user is guaranteed the latest information, and whenever the user is done with a particular title, he can swap it out for a new book.

Subscriptions are the only choice for publishers with either low-value content (such as most newspapers and consumer magazines) or databases and repositories, where the cost of individual transactions would drain the publisher's resources.

3. Pay-per-view/listen

The oldest business model of them all, pay-per-view can be traced supporting live entertainment back to ancient Greece. For more than a century, player pianos and then jukeboxes have had low-cost pay-per-listen music. For the past thirty years cable TV has been charging individually for sporting events like championship boxing matches, big-name live music concerts, and now is delivering first- or second-run movies.

The current state of the art of pay-per-view on computers is languishing because the technology hasn't kept up. The lack of high-speed broadband delivery combined with the equipment problem means that pay-per-view on-line TV is still a ways away. Much closer to reality is the MusicNet/Pressplay/MP3-powered on-line jukebox, followed by MovieLink movies. Providing digital content of text-based media like books, magazines, journals, and reference works is of course straightforward technically; there, the development of business models and effective DRM and payment technology (to lower the cost of transactions and keep the content secure) are the obstacles to pay-per-view.

4. Usage metering

Another business model adapted from the analog world but updated for digital businesses is usage metering. Utility companies have been metering usage of electricity, gas, and water for decades.

Halfway between pay-per-use and subscription services, usage metering is relatively rare on the Internet, but it has worked well for one class of digital businesses: database research services which provide thousands of bits of information that are used only sporadically by any one user. In this category fall the legacy databases Dialog and Lexis-Nexis, and the American Chemical Society's Chemical Abstracts Service Sci Finder.

Because DRM technology can control the flow of information very well and report back to a publisher's server exactly what was used when and by whom, it works well in usage metering applications. The feedback it provides is valuable too: knowing what is of interest to its customers helps a publisher both make available more useful content and set better prices for that content. A word of warning, though—the very usefulness of the demographics and use patterns of customers is bound to raise concerns over privacy and the potential misuse of their information. Tread lightly—or better yet, be willing to trade value for value, and give them the choice of how deeply they will let you into their lives, and what it is worth to them. (See **measuring use for market intelligence** [15.3.2.2] below for more details.)

5. Peer-to-peer/superdistribution

Superdistribution, for all its high-tech sound, merely refers to the repeated passing along of content from one user to another, usually without bothering about licenses or rights agreements. The basic idea of this business model is striking in that it doesn't seem like a business model at all, until you see the effects. Each person in the chain relies on "word of mouth" endorsement of the content from a person they trust. Because of the rapid spread of this kind of information, it is called "viral marketing," and it was used quite successfully in spring 2000 by Seth Godin in his trendy "bestseller" giveaway title, *Unleashing the Ideavirus.* Godin started an e-mail campaign encouraging readers of the book to e-mail copies to all their friends—for free!—and not to bother with telling Godin about the transactions. Soon people wanted something more substantial, and Godin eventually sold more than 30,000 hardcover copies, all pre-ordered by e-mail (no waste), at thirty dollars each.

Godin was sort of done in by his own plan, though. A helpful Frenchman translated the text and began foreign distribution. Unfortunately, Godin had just sold the French-language rights to a publishing house, and it took a while to fix that mess.

Peer-to-peer, which takes its name from the network architecture in which all stations are equals, as opposed to the ***client-server*** relationship in other networks, also depends on multiple pass-along distribution. The difference between superdistribution and peer-to-peer is primarily that the superdistribution process begins with a publisher, while pure peer-to-peer only involves individuals. Used invidiously, peer-to-peer becomes the most anti-business model imaginable. Napster, Aimster, Gnutella, Morpheus, and Kazaa all use variants on the idea of pass-along to make music recordings available on-line for free; FreeNet goes one step further, eliminating the main list-keeping server that tells who ordered what or sent out which files. When the authorities come looking for the original copyright infringer, all they find is thousands of computers linked to the Internet, each claiming that the files came in unbidden, and went out the same way. FreeNet founder Ian Clarke was quoted in the *New York Times* as believing that in the future, people will regard the whole idea of "intellectual property" the way we regard the Salem Witch Trials.

However, when DRM technology evolves to the point where it makes it easy and commonplace for this sort of superdistribution to happen while still compensating the rightsholder—for example, permitting one person to pass a copy to another, but for that copy to be unreadable, or readable for only a short time or incompletely, without payment (a technology that exists today, by the way)—publishers may find this to be one of the most attractive and lucrative ways to distribute and sell their content.

6. Rights licensing

The single most important thing to know about business models is that a lot of success will rely not on selling content, but on selling rights and setting up infrastructure. In books, for instance, as we mentioned earlier, the original publisher may sell tens of thousands of hardcover copies of a text, but the mass-market sales are more likely to be measured in hundreds of thousands, and the seller of that license collects the profit without the risks associated with doing the publishing. Similarly, off-line sales of the film rights, first serial rights, foreign language and geographical distribution rights, facilitated by attending trade shows and rights fairs such as the Frankfurt and London Book Fairs, can produce many times the original revenues from the first edition.

Along with selling the licenses, setting up internal rights and permissions departments to track which licenses have been sold and which remain unexploited can make the publisher vastly more efficient and profitable. DRM is the mechanism for all these sales and and property tracking systems.

In movies, the U.S. distribution might or might not be profitable, but selling the license for foreign distribution almost always is. If the movie is popular at home, selling the associated licenses—the soundtrack, the T-shirt, the themepark, the action figures—produces lots of revenue.

On-line, the book world is just beginning to move into real rights and licensing trading. RightsCenter, for example, is a B-to-B exchange where authors, agents, and publishers all come to do business. Because the business is done on-line, manuscripts can be sent around the world in seconds instead of days, and agents report on-line eBay-style auctions getting bids from as many as thirty countries within five days, a real breakthrough. Serving periodicals, the Copyright Clearance Center RightsLink includes a DRM solution for online viewing, and iCopyright has both an instant copyright clearing service and a new newsclipping service on-line.

15.3 DRM TECHNOLOGY

If copyright is the soul of DRM, then technology is its heart. The first two sections of this chapter described the business and rights models that DRM was invented to support and defend. In this section we will discuss the component parts, the building blocks of the systems that enforce those models. Those building blocks are assembled according to a guiding set of principles, an architecture that will enable the system to do its job well.

Many publishers have been put off by the instability of DRM vendors, and therefore question the viability of the idea of DRM itself. Don't be misled. The individual vendors of DRM products will start up and wither or be consolidated with the passage of time, their products may change, but like the idea of business models and of rights themselves, the guiding principles of how to manage and protect those rights should not change regardless of shifts in the market.

(i) REFERENCE ARCHITECTURE

Good architecture is more than making pretty buildings, it must combine elegant design with a solid underlying structure. The same is true of DRM systems—they are complex in concept, because they handle materials and functions that can reside in a number of places: some must be with the publisher, safe behind the firewall; some must be within the user's system, to allow the best rendering and user-chosen functions; some can be in either of these places or in a third-party server. The systems to handle all the operations necessary can be elegant or awkward, but the best systems all refer back to a basic architecture or set of principles.

Those principles dictate that there are three components to a good DRM system: a *content repository,* with its attendant functions; a *licensing server,* handling rights and identities; and the *client,* where the DRM controller and rendering applications reside.

1. The content server

The name "content server" seems as if it ought to refer to a physical thing, the computer that handles the published materials. In this case, though, the server denotes a system that encompasses both physical places and functions. Since publishers live by selling and protecting content, most publishers will want to keep their content in a repository that is tucked away behind a firewall to keep out intruders. The content server will also have a means of storing information about the products, or their metadata, and the DRM functionality, or packager.

The format used for content storage isn't important, as long as the content can be put into the correct format for DRM handling, delivery, and rendering when necessary. When publishers were primarily concerned with print, PDF seemed a good choice for storage, because it preserved what they valued as one of their functions, the page design. But PDF was difficult to render into XML, for adding digital functionality to the content, while rendering PDF from XML was easy.

Current practice among the most digitally advanced publishers, therefore, is to create and store the content in a content management system (CMS) as XML files that contain both the original content and its metadata. The CMS then can send the file to any of the many destinations publishers now serve, including Web sites for consumer use; B-to-B systems for syndication; the publisher's internal marketing, back office, and support systems; or composing to PDF for sending to print.

1. PRODUCT INFORMATION: METADATA

The content server's product information database is of critical importance to the publisher for two reasons: it is what enables prospective customers to find out what products are available, the way publishers' printed catalogs used to do; and it enables the publisher's sales, marketing, promotion, editorial, production, and rights and permissions departments to coordinate their efforts using information they know is accurate and up-to-date.

There are many kinds of metadata. Some are only important to the publisher's internal systems, such as scheduling information the production department uses. Such things as the title, author, format, and trim size are important to customers as well as the publisher. And some, such as what licenses are available, are only important to other businesses. The server needs to protect sensitive information, so it has to keep straight who is authorized to see what.

Two types of metadata that are important to the DRM system are discovery metadata, to help users find the content within the system, and unique identification numbers, like a license plate on a car.

2. DRM PACKAGER

The DRM packager is the part of the system that prepares the content for distribution. A standard package contains the content, its associated product metadata, and a description of the rights the publisher is giving to the purchaser, all wrapped in a software "envelope."

Sometimes, as might be the case with e-books, the actual digits of the content are included in the package, to be transferred to the user's hard drive or device. With some content, such as streaming media, the content must reside on the publisher's server, so the package only holds the discovery and identification metadata as a link to the place in the publisher's repository where the actual content is being held.

2. The license server

Early DRM systems bundled the actual rights licenses (not just their description) directly in the content package for delivery to the customer. Although this was easy to do, with newer display technologies and more complex rights situations this arrangement became unworkable.

As noted above, for instance, streaming media remain on the publisher's server, but the customer still needs the access rights information. And sometimes publishers want to specify multiple sets of rights, such as for several types of user, for a single content item; or they want to specify a single set of rights to many content items, as with a subscription to a library. All this suggested to technology vendors that they would do better to separate the license from the content and handle each in its own server.

In the license server, a license generator combines the rights specifications and a set of encryption keys produced by the DRM server, with metadata that identifies the content to which the rights apply and the user or device that wants to exercise those rights. The resulting license (sometimes called a permit or ticket) is then sent to the user.

3. The client

The third major component of the DRM architecture is the client, the user's side of the system, which includes the DRM controller, the user's identification mechanism, and the rendering application.

The DRM controller is the brain of the DRM system; it is responsible for several major functions, including receiving the user's request to exercise rights on the content; sending the user's identification to the license server and obtaining a license in return; taking the encryption keys from the license, decrypting the content, and sending it to the rendering application.

There are two principal kinds of rendering applications found in DRM systems these days: standalone applications with DRM built in, and plug-ins to generic rendering applications.

Standalone applications combine content viewing with DRM functionality. This is an older technology, from a time when there was much more proprietary hardware and software around. Because they are purpose built, these applications offer the tightest security, and can restrict the user to only a very few authorized functions. The disadvantages to these standalones include their large size (InterTrust's InterRightsPoint was several megabytes), the need for special distribution and installation, and usability problems including incompatibility with some media formats. The most successful standalone these days is Microsoft's Reader for the PC and the PocketPC handheld, displaying most of the characteristics listed above. An excellent rendering application for e-books, Reader doesn't allow printing of its files; it still has to loaded specially onto even brand new PCs; and it isn't available for the Macintosh. Other older examples of the DRM part of the standalone are InterTrust's DigiBox and the IBM Cryptolope.

The more common kind of rendering application these days is the generic viewing application, such as Adobe Acrobat Reader, with DRM plug-ins to rein in such features Copy, Print, and Save As. The principal advantages are the fact that many more consumers already own the underlying application and the small size of the plug-in (compared to a whole application). The main disadvantage is that the application plus plug-in combination is not as secure as a standalone. Other examples of content viewing with plug-in DRM architecture are the Netscape Web browser and Microsoft Internet Explorer.

The future of client architectures, it seems, will be a family of DRM-enabled rendering applications. These cross-format, cross-device applications are specially designed to work with new cross-device DRM controllers through trusted interfaces. Current examples include the RioPort, for portable music devices, IBM's EMMS (Electronic Media Management System), and coming soon to a device near you, Microsoft's cross-device Black Box DRM controller, working with DRM that is embedded in the OS, part of their future strategy (code-named Mercury).

(ii) DRM FUNCTIONS: IDENTIFICATION, ENCRYPTION

Two of the most important functions performed in the DRM system are easy enough to understand, but difficult to carry out correctly: identification and encryption. Without these two, no transaction is secure, no content adequately protected, no user safe from theft of identity.

1. Identities

The first issue in identification is to determine what the system is trying to identify: a particular person or a particular device. This is an issue because it involves the difference between colloquial use and the legal technicalities of a license, and it shows how digital processes have blurred what used to be clear boundaries between distinct entities.

When a person buys a PC, installs it in a home office, and is the only person who normally has access to that machine, it is natural for that person to think of the PC as being the same as their person: my PC, my laptop, my PDA, my cell phone, my Rio MP3 player. All are extensions of me, tools I use for business—I don't think of them as distinct entities because of the way I use them. I take files from one, put them through a translator that I installed long ago, and read them on another without thinking about it, at least until they fail to transfer or the license to do so is denied.

Because the file formats for those devices are different, it is equally natural for a rights holder to expect that the costs associated with putting their content into a new format, like resetting the type in going from a hardcover book to the mass-market paperback, would be paid by the users of the new format. And it is equally natural to expect, then, that they could claim that the new format both deserves and requires a new license in order to recoup those costs. This is currently the case with e-books and digitally recorded music, but will become much more important in the near future as digital TVs become prevalent. Content holders are sure to see an opportunity to make more revenue from selling all those old movies in digital formats, where consumers are going to want merely to get a translator/recorder and do it themselves. However, balancing those "natural" expectations of rights holders are legal precedents (such as Sony v. Universal in 1984) that establish a consumer's right to "space-shift" content for personal use by converting it to another format for which the consumer has the playback device—such as recording one's own music LPs onto cassette or, more ominously for rights holders, making easy, no-cost copies of audio CDs in MP3 format.

The opposite case, where one device has many users, such as an office computer used for sharing database files and Web access, is equally important. While most rights holders are willing enough to allow site licenses for multiple users (for a higher price), they don't want those users taking their content away from the approved site for use elsewhere.

So being able to identify clearly both the user and the device is critical to making sure that the license that is granted is the one that was sought, and that the actual use is the one for which license was granted.

1. USER AUTHENTICATION

The first task is to identify one person, enabling licenses for one user with an unlimited number of devices. A customer's personal identification can come from any of several means: from information that they volunteer, such as their name, e-mail address, street address, user ID, password, or an account number, such as a credit card number, driver's license, or Social Security Number; from information that is physically part of them (called biometrics), such as a retina scan, a palm print, facial-features recognition, or soon, a DNA printout; or from information supplied by a credential, such as a digital certificate from a trusted third party.

The reliability of any of these means depends both on their relative accessibility to outsiders and their permanence. A name and e-mail address are the least secure, of course. Credit card numbers and Social Security numbers are supposed to be keep secret, but their increasing use for identification has made them prime targets for identity thieves. Passwords would be as secret as Social Security Numbers, but people are careless about their use, storage, and deducibility.

Biometrics are particularly reliable, being inseparable from a person's body, but the devices used to extract them (such as retina scanners) are currently beyond the means of most people. The increasing miniaturization and reliability of digital video promises to help this in the near future.

The third type of personal identification, digital certificates, comes from certificate authorities (CAs) that go to some lengths to verify that the person requesting the certificate is who they say they are before issuing a certificate. A standard technology for carrying a digital certificate is the ***Secure Socket Layer*** (SSL) protocol. The CA will verify the applicant's identity through such trackable numbers as a Federal business tax ID, then encrypt and store the digital certificate in a secure repository, where it is retrievable by DRM systems. RSA Security and Verisign are examples of commercial CAs.

2. DEVICE AUTHENTICATION

Identifying a single device, enabling licenses for one device with an unlimited number of users, is in some ways easier and in some ways harder than establishing user IDs.

Because hard-disk drive manufacturers (and some CPU makers) have been putting unique numbers into their hardware for a very long time, one of the easiest things to do to verify the identity of a machine is to read these numbers.

There are, however, still stumbling blocks on this path. When Intel came late into the game with this idea, it was touted as a way for the government to track improper Internet use by terrorists and child molesters—and the rampant Big-Brotherism raised a storm of protest from privacy advocates.

Just to show that you can't please everybody, and to illustrate what might have happened if Intel's PR department had been a little cleverer about e-commerce, in summer 2001, the opposite condition caused a brouhaha. Microsoft was trying to get people to buy and sell e-books, rather than give them away. But it turned out that there was no way to track usage on a PocketPC (PPC)—there was supposed to be an identifier in the CPU, but in the rush to market a year before, it hadn't happened. So, no device tracking, no highest-level DRM. Publishers could choose to assign lower-level DRM to the files, or give their Microsoft Reader e-books away as special promotions, but publishers didn't want to expose their properties to theft, so they continued to assign the highest level DRM—thus preventing the texts from running on PPCs, enabling only desktop and laptop use. If you had bought a library of e-books intending to run them on your PPC, you could be disappointed.

It turned out, in the end, that the problem could be fixed with a software patch in the next release of the Microsoft Reader software and the more-expensive levels of PPC hardware, both of which came out within a couple of months, but the early PPC adopters were just out of luck.

An alternative to the hardware identifier was the IP address. In the early days of the Internet, all IP addresses were supposed to be permanently assigned to a particular device, and unique around the world. Since then, the huge adoption of the Web and the rapid updates to device hardware has led to network management technologies that either assign IP addresses dynamically, so they change from time to time, or that keep the address unique only within a local sub-network. One way around this might be to add a fifth group of digits to the IP address's current four, like an area code, but we all thought that ten digits was plenty for a phone system once, too.

In recent years, some DRM-implementing companies (including Microsoft and Liquid Audio) have tried combining elements of hardware and user identification to allow licenses for one user with *n* number of devices, where *n* is a fixed, assigned number. Microsoft's plan creates a "persona" for the user, and allows that persona to transfer an e-book to any of three devices. The number three was arrived at by negotiation with publishers, who originally wanted only one device. Microsoft, knowing the reality of the market, with frequent hardware updates, and looking forward to a totally wired population, wanted the number to be four or five. Three devices was seen as a reasonable compromise, not too limiting in the present, and negotiable upward as use data demanded.

2. Measuring use for market intelligence

In order to profit from the ability to sell variable licenses, the publisher must be able to measure and control the use of the content. In publishing a book electronically, measuring use has been easiest when the content is held at the publishing house in a server, and numbers of times accessed or time allotted is explicitly counted. Database publishing presents far more complex problems for the rights holder.

An early attempt at measuring usage on the Web was tracking "cookies," files that combined elements of the user's ID information with data on Web pages visited, products bought, and so on, that were deposited on the user's machine every time they came to a Web site. Cookies have two principal drawbacks, though. First, because they track identity from the user's machine, anyone who can get access to the machine can impersonate that user and skew the data. Second, because they are automatically placed on the user's system unless the user hits a "disable cookies" button on the Web browser, they engender resistance by the user as intrusive, an invasion of privacy. The normal response of many consumers is to disable cookies all the time. If the user's personal and marketing information is of value to the publisher, it oughtn't to be taken involuntarily, but that doesn't mean they won't share it.

A better answer might be to follow the example of STM publishers, and reward customers for voluntarily providing very precise and extensive personal information. While many of the objections to electronic publishing on the Web center on the ballyhooed Internet users' notion that "information wants to be free," in reality the vast majority of people recognize that things of value are rarely free, and they are willing to trade value for value.

Offering many kinds of discounts in exchange for deeper and deeper user information can foster a sense of cooperation and loyalty in the customer. By rewarding this cooperation, publishers can get customers to tell them what is good and bad in the products currently offered, what products are not currently available that they would pay to get, and what products have little value for them. Is a text missing information, or does it contain information that could be better developed? Should the work be longer? Is there too much information, or is it badly edited or organized? Could there be a series of products developed along the same lines as the current product?

The creative use of DRM and variable licensing to invent many levels of users, therefore, can make the content holder more aware of the true value in different bits of their content, leading to more targeted products, more rational pricing, and in the end, a more profitable business. Using DRM as CRM, or customer relationship management, can make the content holder a better publisher.

3. Encryption and DRM

While not all DRM involves ***encryption***, clearly one of the chief concerns of every content rights holder is protecting that content, both from piracy and from tampering. And the chief means of copy protection currently is encryption.

In general, much of the talk in the publishing world about encryption is like a pile of burning leaves, generating more heat than light, and obscuring many of the important issues with smoky debate on emotional topics like privacy or who has the right to know what, and what that knowledge should cost. What a publisher wants from encryption is to keep its content away from the world until the terms of its license are met, to maintain the integrity of the content after the transaction, and to protect the privacy of the transaction partners. To do these things, what the publisher needs to know is, how good is the encryption? The answer, as in many things in the real world, is good enough—and not good enough.

1. HOW GOOD IS ENCRYPTION? YOU DO THE MATH

Encryption is a great deal like a lock on the front door of your house: it is a deterrent good enough to keep out the neighborhood kids, random passing vandals, and other people with little real interest in getting in—but not good enough to keep out professional burglars who've cased the joint and really want your $20,000 stereo system. You can deter a break-in, but you can't totally prevent it.

Much has been made of the relative strength of various encryption algorithms, the procedures used to scramble the text being encrypted. Because we are talking about digital computers, encryption algorithms these days are usually complex mathematical processes.

The two main factors in figuring the strength of an encryption system are

1. How long would it take a hacker to break the code using brute force, that is, trying all the possible combinations until they hit the correct one; and
2. How susceptible the code is to analyzing what the most likely combinations are, so the hacker can try those first.

The key to an algorithm is the number that it is based on; guess the number and you break the code. The length of the key (the number of digits in it) is important because it determines complexity. A password that is composed of five characters, all numbers from 0 through 4, has 5 x 5 x 5 x 5 x 5 or 3,125 possible combinations, beginning with 00000, and ending with 44444. It might take you and me a long time to dial those on a combination lock, but it wouldn't take long for a computer to run through them in a code.

If the password allows up to ten characters, including upper- and lowercase letters and numbers, there are 839,299,365,868,340,224 possible combinations to run through. It has been calculated that even if a computer could run a million attempts each second, it would take more than 13,000 years to run through them all.

Don't be too concerned with the length of the key, though. Remember that these are all averages. A skilled hacker, who knows how to apply various sophisticated mathematical techniques that could greatly reduce the number of possible keys, might get the key on the very first try, or the tenth, or the millionth. Know this: there is no such thing as an unbreakable code that is practical to use. It also probably doesn't matter. In the end, it's usually easier to figure out what the password owner is likely to use to make it easier to remember. Despite warnings, too many people use discoverable bases as their passwords: their wedding anniversary or the name of their favorite ballplayer. Remember the movie *War Games?* The scientist's password was the name of his dead son.

2. NOT GOOD ENOUGH

For a DRM encryption key it's usually easier to find someone who will give it to you if you pay them enough than it is to try to break the code. Which raises the real issue: today's highly complex encryption algorithms are hardly ever the problem in themselves. If a thing has enough value, people will spend what is necessary to get it. Also, popularity (and unreasonable or arrogant claims) attract attention. Very few people want to break the encryption on a single copy of *Great Expectations.* If you can claim that you broke into the new Harry Potter book and distributed a million copies, that notoriety might be worth a lot. Particularly if someone claimed beforehand that the encryption was unbreakable.

A lot of bad press regarding copy protection and the enforcement of the Digital Millennium Copyright Act was generated over a very few cases of high-visibility hacking. CSS (Content Scrambling System) is a weak encryption system for DVD copy protection. The hacker magazine *2600* published code for DeCSS, a system for cracking CSS that the authors claim was only created because the DVD players at the time would work with Windows and Macintosh systems, but not Linux. CSS was implemented despite its weakness because the makers of DVD players refused to pay for the technology necessary to implement stronger encryption.

The more the MPAA (Motion Picture Association of America) decried the obvious illegality of this copyright circumvention technology, trying to get Web sites shut that promoted DeCSS, the more the hackers created new sites to promote it. As of the end of 2002, the case is still moving through appeals courts, the hackers are still having a great time, but as far as we know, there are no computers being sold with commercial copies of DeCSS preloaded, and there has been little if any economic effect on the DVD market.

In summer 2001, a Russian named Dmitry Sklyarov was arrested as he left a hacker convention in Las Vegas. The charge—the first criminal charge filed under the provisions of DMCA—was selling a program that made it easy to break Adobe Acrobat eBook Reader protection. After months of accusations in the press and demonstrations in the streets, Sklyarov was released, not least because the actual selling of the program was done not by Sklyarov, but by his employer, ElcomSoft, a computer security firm in Moscow.

While ElcomSoft still faces large fines if the prosecution is successful (This could be the main DMCA test case before the U.S. Supreme Court), there are loads of questions involved, including two kickers: ElcomSoft was selling the program over the Internet from Moscow, where the software was legal—how do you charge foreign citizens for doing in their own country what is legal there? And second, is there any ordinary citizen anywhere (who is not part of this case) who has used Sklyarov's program to crack an Adobe e-book?

One could be forgiven for thinking that both these cases were more about publicity than the law.

3. GOOD ENOUGH

Even if you believe that both the above cases were about encryption and circumvention, the encryption in use today is good enough mainly because encryption that is hacked once is not necessarily disabled everywhere. There is no known large-scale breaking of e-book or DVD copy protection; the creators of this software don't even seem to be selling very much of it. The numbers just aren't big enough to upset a market as large as DVD movies. Furthermore, the latest encryption research focuses not on the pure strength of the algorithm but on how gracefully it fails. That is, the latest schemes include the ability to minimize the damage once someone hacks the algorithm—for example, by making it easy to update the encryption scheme in the field.

If a content owner avoids the sort of highly publicized, proprietary encryption systems that are likely to draw attention, they will likely get along fine.

And in a part of the business that is less star-struck, there are encryption-related solutions that are working well, too. In addition to being the most important deterrent against copy protection, encryption is well-established as a means of guaranteeing that content has not been changed. One way of verifying the integrity of a file is not to copy-protect the whole file, but only to add to the file a certain number of digits that represent a digest of the text. The digest, or "hash value," acts as a check-sum: only those who know the digest's key can alter the text undetected. There are many types of content whose integrity is worth guaranteeing, such as financial records and scientific research results.

4. Watermarking vs. encryption

An alternative to encrypting content is marking it in a way that lets interested parties tell who it belongs to. This permanent identification of a piece is called ***watermarking***, after the subtle marks makers of fine papers use to identify their products. Digital watermarking, using an unobtrusive portion of a picture or sound file to hide identifying code, won't prevent illegal copying, but if the original owner's identity is detectable, it will certainly put a damper on it. In more general terms, digital watermarking refers to the ability to embed any data (not just ownership information) into content.

Watermarking has some distinct advantages over encryption in DRM. First, encryption requires a special application to render the content usable; watermarking doesn't. Second, because the marking is embedded right into the file, the metadata it contains is bound (mostly) permanently to the file—it is possible to alter the watermarking, but very difficult to do so. With ***encryption***, once the code is broken, it has no effect on the file.

5. Watermarking plus encryption

Combining the strengths of the two technologies is very effective for DRM. The simplest way is to encrypt the watermark but not the whole file. This doesn't disrupt the file, but makes the metadata tamperproof.

The second way to use the technologies to reinforce one another is to encrypt the file and to watermark the whole package. This is the strongest possible protection currently available. It protects the content, and at the same time binds the metadata to it permanently. While there is no perfect encryption, and therefore no perfect copy protection, the combination of physical, technological protection (encryption), and permanent metadata embedding (watermarking) is likely to be the best DRM-based protection for some time to come.

15.4 DRM STANDARDS

Because publishing content electronically is still relatively new, there are some conditions that will greatly affect the future course of the industry. One of the most important is the standardization of the basic technologies. That is, are most of the tools based on open standards that anyone can use and get access to, right down to basic codes, controlled by a public authoring process? Or are those tools entirely the property of a single vendor, who can ignore their faults and change the specs at will?

Open standards are important for an infant industry, because if the members of the industry have to spend their already-limited capital on technology dead ends instead of improving their products, their corporations will be at risk much sooner than necessary. Standardized technology lets the players search for a competitive edge in the right place: better products.

(i) XRML: THE EXTENSIBLE RIGHTS MARKUP LANGUAGE

The eXtensible rights Markup Language (***XrML***) was invented at Xerox PARC in the mid-90s as an extension of Dr. Mark Stefik's work on trusted systems. Among other things, Stefik figured that if rights agreements were to be automated so that computer systems could perform the functions in a rights license, there had to be a formal, standardized language to specify the conditions in the license. Stefik called his language the Digital Property Rights Language, or DPRL.

Xerox patented DPRL, and later spun off a company called ContentGuard, Inc. to commercialize DPRL. Xerox is the principal shareholder in ContentGuard, but significantly, Microsoft has a large minority stake as well. One of the first things ContentGuard did was to take an updated version of DPRL based on XML syntax, rename it XrML, eXtensible rights Markup Language, to reflect its XML heritage, and began to give away free licenses to use the language.

XrML is a very rich, very complex language for describing rights models: it describes not just types of users, and several security levels, but (in the current version, which is Version 2.0) as many as twenty-four different types of rights. This completeness, along with its XML base, bode well for the future of XrML.

In fact, the entire picture of the XrML's future holds some interesting possibilities. It has been finding acceptance among very important standards groups. As of April 2002, XrML has been "contributed to"—and control of its future development ceded to—the Organization for the Advancement of Structured Information Standards (***OASIS***). Born as the original markup language trade association, SGMLOpen, OASIS is a not-for-profit, global consortium that drives the development, convergence and adoption of XML-related e-business standards.

What is not stated in the press releases on this move is that ContentGuard holds patents on the technology on which DPRL/XrML is based: specifically ContentGuard claims patent coverage on *any* rights language. In other words,

ContentGuard could sue other vendors if they try to write a rights language of their own. This is where Microsoft comes in.

As of the summer of 2002, while more than twenty companies, including Adobe and Hewlett-Packard, had expressed support for XrML, Microsoft was the only vendor actually implementing XrML in a commercial setting. And Microsoft has an interesting position re: formerly open standards. A couple of years ago, Microsoft applied for and got a patent on Cascading Style Sheets, a useful technology for adding design to XML documents. And Microsoft has deep pockets. Not to say they *would* sue anybody over a supposedly open standard.

You can find out more details about XrML at www.xrml.org and oasis-open.org.

(ii) DOI: THE DIGITAL OBJECT IDENTIFIER

Copyright management on the Internet has always been a vexing problem for rights holders, trying to find both some permanent means of identification, and some way to track down illegal uses of one's content. The Association of American Publishers set out in 1994 to do something about this problem, and in 1997 announced the Digital Object Identifier (***DOI***), in order to create an e-commerce market for intellectual property on-line and to protect copyright in that market.

The DOI is a persistent, dynamic, customizable, link between customer and content owner, based on an international standard that combines both a unique identifier and an underlying routing system that is an existing part of Internet infrastructure. The DOI is a metascheme capable of incorporating both other ID numbering systems (such as ISBN or ISSN) and any or all metadata standards, thus enabling interoperability across all other numbering and/or metadata schemas. Further, because a DOI encompasses all the existing identification standards, it will allow publishers to update their e-commerce and back office systems without recourse to large, expensive asset management systems.

Like an ISBN, a DOI is made up of groupings of digits, in this case a prefix and a suffix, separated by a slash mark. The prefix is made up of two groups of numbers. The first one names the DOI directory in which to find this particular DOI; although there is only one directory at present, there is room to expand the system. The second group in the prefix is the content owner's identifier, a number issued by the DOI system. Significantly, this portion of the DOI for a given registered digital object stays the same, even if the rights to the object this DOI refers to are sold. Once issued, the DOI is considered a "dumb number"; that way the DOI is guaranteed to remain the same for the life of the object. So although the publisher prefix might have reflected the owner of the rights when the object was originally registered and the DOI was assigned to that object, from that point forward the way to determine the current owner of the rights to the object is not via the publisher prefix but via the DOI system itself. That, in fact, is precisely what it's for.

Unlike an ISBN, the suffix, which is made up by the publisher, can have any number of characters at all, and can include letters as well as numbers. In fact, many publishers have already begun modifying their identification numbers by adding the DOI prefix to their existing ISBNs and ISSNs. The infinitely expandable suffix means a DOI can identify objects of any granularity at all, from a single photo or sentence of type, up to a series of works, and the objects can be of any type, including video, audio, software, or even services. It is not just for electronic publications; by assigning a DOI to a print book, for example, a publisher can make it possible for any on-line mention of that book—in promotional material, in a review, in a reference in another work, in an e-mail from somebody recommending the book to friends, anywhere the DOI appears—to direct potential customers to a host of possible ways to buy that book.

Currently, as a practical matter publishers are assigning DOIs around the level of either a whole book, or else a single book chapter or journal article. There is some debate about whether a DOI should be assigned to a "work" in general (allowing the DOI system to present many possible editions of that work to potential customers who click on the DOI) or to have a DOI for each edition (one for hardcover, one for paperback, one for each kind of e-book, and so forth). The answer is: either or both, whatever works best. There is nothing in the DOI system that requires one or the other of these approaches; and additional DOIs can be registered at any time.

Publishers must register with the International DOI Foundation, or ***IDF*** (http://www.doi.org), to obtain a prefix as their corporate identifier. Then for each DOI it wants to obtain, the publisher submits—generally to a DOI registration agency, such as Content Directions, Inc. (CDI; http://www.contentdirections.com)—an identifying suffix and URL for the object, along with appropriate metadata to help users identify the registered digital object, to be included in a giant look-up table called the DOI directory.

The DOI directory is part of the answer to the problem of "HTTP 404 (File Not Found)" errors. Normally, when a URL goes out of date because the company goes out of business or sells its product lines to other producers, customers reach a 404 dead end. In the DOI system, the URL that the user sees contacts the DOI directory. The DOI system then directs the user to wherever the publisher has specified—often the publisher's own Web site, but including any other appropriate options as well, like distributors or retailers. By having the directory as an intermediate step, the publisher can change the destinations pointed to whenever they want to, while the DOI number remains unchanged.

The current version of the DOI supported by the global DOI Directory and all DOI registration agencies is MultiLinks, the ability to link via a single click from one DOI to any number of different services at the same time. So, for example, when a reader of a review or an e-mail clicks on the DOI, he or she can be presented with an array of options, ranging from "publisher's catalog" to "sample chapter" to "reviews" to "other books by this author" or "other books on this subject" to "buy this book," and the latter can then be subdivided into "Publisher," "Amazon.com," and whatever other sources the publisher chooses.

DOI MultiLinks "travel" wherever the DOI goes, not just on the publisher's own Web site, but anywhere—on authors' Web sites, on publishing partners' Web sites, in bibliographies, e-learning content, in Yahoo or Google or other search engines. DOIs can be embedded directly into a PDF file or an e-book, and they can still reach out over the Web and link the customer back to anything the owner might want to offer. This can include not just books, but additional products, new services, or the ability to e-mail the DOI to others in a viral marketing mode, so that their friends will also be brought to the publisher's services. CDI has more information in a white paper available at http://dx.doi.org/10.1220/whitepaper5.

By far the biggest user of DOIs so far is CrossRef, the cooperative cross-linking service established as a collaborative effort of scientific journal publishers. It enables readers of journal articles to click on the references at the ends of the articles—those with DOIs, that is—and be linked to the publisher of the cited article. Begun in June 2000, CrossRef had registered five million articles (and thus five million DOIs) in its first two years, and continues to add them at a pace of over half a million a year. It has recently expanded its scope to link to books, proceedings, and other works as well. CrossRef has proven that DOI is by no means an experimental technology; it is now a fundamental part of the digital environment. CrossRef is discussed in the chapters **Markup** [3.3.6.3.3] and **Organizing, Editing, and Linking Content** [4.5.5.1].

(iii) ICE: INFORMATION AND CONTENT EXCHANGE

While we have been concentrating on Business-to-Consumer models, B-to-B (business-to-business) will be at least as important for many content holders in a wired world. The Information and Content Exchange (***ICE***) standard is aimed directly at them. ICE is an XML-based protocol for content syndication invented in 1999 by a consortium called IDEAlliance, formerly known as the Graphic Communications Association (GCA), expanding on efforts begun by alliance member Vignette, developers of the StoryServer Web publishing system.

Recognizing that an open standard would face a better reception than another proprietary system, Vignette opened up development of the standard to their customers, one of which was Rupert Murdoch's News Corp. Murdoch's involvement is significant especially because it insured the attention in ICE to newspaper and magazine business models and concerns. Syndication is an excellent way to extend the reach of a publication's content, and to test selectively which pieces have the most demand.

ICE works for both push sales (sent out by the publisher) and pull sales (requested by the recipient) between syndication groups and their customer/subscribers, and puts all subscribers into one of two categories. *Weak* subscribers only receive what they ask for, whether collectively, as in the columns of Drew Pearson, or individually, as in single news items; *Full* subscribers keep the pipeline open twenty-four hours a day, receiving feeds of everything the syndicator chooses to send, whether content or promotional items.

Using ICE, syndicators can put up catalogs that list the content that they want to offer for subscription, with specifications covering updates; they can accept queries from prospective subscribers and negotiate the rights, delivery methods, and prices with them; they can publish, or push content out, on predetermined schedules; and they can do a kind of direct-mail marketing on the Web, sending subscribers unsolicited messages with new offerings and other business communication notes.

For their part, subscribers can look through the syndicators' catalog offerings, select and ask for (pull) the content they want to subscribe to, negotiate the terms of the subscription, and receive content from the syndicator's site.

Another interesting detail about ICE: the communication between syndicator and subscriber includes a description of the rights, but not the license itself. Because it is a B-to-B protocol, it also doesn't have a copy protection scheme attached; it is assumed that business partners will pay for what they buy, and not distribute illegal copies of it. ICE does, however, work with DRM solutions that do those things.

ICE is functioning commercially today in a number of products, all of which are one variety or another of syndication server. Add-ons to current Web-publishing systems or applications servers include Vignette Syndication Server, designed to work with Vignette's content management platform; Interwoven's OpenSyndicate, designed to work with their TeamSite CMS; and HP Bluestone Total e-Syndication, a Java-based application component. ICE support is also built into Context Media's Interchange Suite content integration platform, Stellent's Connection Server, and Quark's avenue.quark (now a feature of Xpress 5 and later).

There is a wealth of detail on the current development of the ICE specification at IDEAlliance's Web site, http://www.icestandard.org.

(iv) OTHER DRM STANDARDS

There are some other open standards and standards organizations that will affect the future growth of DRM for electronic publishing, but on the whole, their influence at this point looks likely to be smaller that those we've discussed this far.

1. ODRL: Open Digital Rights Language

The Open Digital Rights Language (***ODRL***) is an XML-compliant language similar in some respects to XrML. In fact, some people refer to ODRL's rights metadata model as a kind of "XrML Lite."

Though the ODRL language has concepts similar to XrML, ODRL renames them. ODRL's permissions of Usage, Reuse, and Transfer function equivalently to the more common Render, or output format, Derivative work, and Transport or sell, give and loan, which Mark Stefik of Xerox PARC enumerated in his original mid-1990s research. Likewise, ODRL Constraints correspond to Extents (that is, length of time, or number of times accessed) and Requirements is similar to Consideration, what the owner receives in return, such as payment.

The naming differences are significant, considering that ODRL is claimed not to have been influenced by the early form of XrML, DPRL. Perhaps the difference springs from the language's inventor, Dr. Renato Iannella, an Australian consultant working with IPR Systems in Sydney.

In any event, while ODRL has been called "influential" by the Open eBook Forum and Accenture (nee Andersen Consulting), AAP's partner in the e-Book initiative, and a subset of it has been adopted by the Open Mobile Alliance, a standards group for the wireless industry, at this writing there are no known implementations outside the Pacific Rim. The specification is available at http://ww.odrl.net/0.9/ODRL-09.pdf.

2. PRISM: Publishing Requirements for Industry Standard Metadata

The magazine industry is developing its own open standard, called Publishing Requirements for Industry Standard Metadata (***PRISM***) under the auspices of IDEAlliance, the same organization that oversees ICE.

Using the Dublin Core bibliographic metadata set (see the chapters **Markup** [3.3.6.3.1] and **Organizing, Editing, and Linking Content** [4.4.2.3.1] for more information on Dublin Core), PRISM contains a set of text descriptions of the rights available on a given content package. These rights metadata fields, designed to be read by humans rather than by machines, make PRISM a sort of complementary strategy to XrML and similar languages. XrML was invented to make rights transactions machine-readable and thus take humans out of the process where possible. The text rights fields may also contribute to some people's perceptions of PRISM as incomplete or lightweight. Nonetheless, PRISM is generating interest in the periodical world. The standard is young, having debuted in April 2001. More information is available at http://www.prismstandard.org.

3. <indecs>2RDD

At the other end of the scale is ***<indecs>2RDD*** (which stands for the Interoperability of Data in e-Commerce Systems, Rights Data Dictionary), a massively ambitious attempt to build a comprehensive rights metadata description dictionary for B-to-B transactions.

Based on the groundwork of Godfrey Ruse of MUZE Corp., Brian Green of EDItEUR, and others in the U.K., <indecs>2RDD is attempting to define all possible instances of rights metadata language for commercial use, such as contracts, permissions, and licensing, across every medium. The metadata dictionary will then present the complete standardized set of terms in a fashion that will be applicable to other structured approaches, such as those of the Society of Motion Picture and Television Engineers (SMPTE) and create interoperability among them.

Current partners in <indecs>2RRD development include Accenture, ContentGuard, Dentsu (the Japanese advertising giant), EDItEUR, Enpia Systems, the International DOI Foundation, MPAA (the motion picture Academy), and RIAA, the recording industry association, with its international partner, the International Federation of Phonographic Industries (IFPI).

Unquestionably noble in intent, <indecs>2RDD seems doomed by the gargantuan size of the task it has assumed. The huge range of varieties of metadata in any one medium make the term itself hard to define; and finding interoperability among media has long seemed like herding cats. If they can pull it off, more power to them.

4. W3C

A final word about standards bodies and electronic publishing: The World Wide Web Consortium (W3C) is the original governing body for the graphical form of the Internet. As such, it has had a lot of influence on the shape of our conception of what electronic publishing ought to be. But the W3C is in a strange place itself.

One of the reasons there was so much support for the formation of the World Wide Web was that the old ARPANET foundation of the Internet, as administered by the National Science Foundation, was vehemently, radically anti-commercial. Students were getting in trouble in the early '90s for advertising term-paper typing services on the Net.

If Academe was above making a buck, so be it: let there be a second Internet, this one not just allowing commerce, but promoting and promoted by commercial interests. And in case you are still leery of those money-grubbers, we'll give them a ghetto domain, the .com, so no one will be caught there unawares. The Web is far larger and more influential than anyone envisioned even 10 years ago.

No group could have done more to foster the growth of Internet publishing by demanding open, enabling standards than the W3C. But they have done almost nothing. in the direction of promoting DRM standards, apart from a workshop that the organization held in January 2001. It's as if, within the W3C, there is still a feeling, almost a scent on the air, that DRM helps create a wall between knowledge and those who seek it, and therefore DRM might be . . . bad.

Standards are necessary. They will come. If W3C won't back them, that only opens the door for individual vendors to promote their own interests. So far, platform wars have cost us 10 years of potential e-reading. Let's hope that both the standards bodies and the commercial interests can get moving in the right direction now.

15.5 LEGAL DEVELOPMENTS: IMPORTANT LEGISLATION

The chapter **The Legal Framework** [13] discusses at length the law and legal issues for electronic publishers. Mostly, the issues pertaining to Copyright remain unchanged from print days. The troubles only arise when we try to update or interpret ideas developed under a print regime for technologies that move faster and have wider reach than print and other physical products. In this section, we will briefly mention some of the laws, cases, and issues of special interest to or with implications for DRM.

(i) MILESTONES

In print-dominated times, publishers always knew that somewhere over the ocean, beyond the reach of their own government's protection, people were illegally reproducing their works. In the early 1800s, both Charles Dickens and James Fenimore Cooper crossed the Atlantic on tours designed to persuade overseas publishers not to infringe their copyrights.

Since the development of the World Wide Web, publishers' worst fears became realized. Technology outstripped their ability to track and enforce their copyrights because infringers could violate the law and distribute illegal copies around the world in seconds rather than months. In the latter half of the '90s publishers received help from governments to try to have international laws get back on par with worldwide infringers. The following are some of the milestones marking that effort.

1. 1996: WIPO copyright treaties

The Diplomatic Conference held under the auspices of the World Intellectual Property Organization (***WIPO***) in December 1996 led to the adoption of two new Treaties, the "WIPO Copyright Treaty" and the "WIPO Performances and Phonograms Treaty," dealing respectively with the protection of authors and the protection of performers and sound recording producers. Those treaties significantly update the international protection for copyright and related rights begun in the Berne Convention, particularly with regard to digital technologies, and improve the means to fight piracy around the world. The primary intent of the WIPO Copyright Treaty is to bring some degree of uniformity to the many different sets of national copyright laws around the world. Signatory nations had until December 2002 to implement the treaty's provisions.

2. 1998: Digital Millennium Copyright Act (DMCA)

A long document mostly involved with bringing the U.S. into line with the WIPO treaties, ***DMCA*** also included two sections specifically concerning technologies for copyright protection. Section 1201, which includes a section known as the anti-circumvention provision (see the chapter **The Legal Framework** [13.1.8.1] for details), in effect outlaws manufacture or traffic in any technology used to break copyright protection. This provision, which is known as "DMCA 1201 for short, requires the use of, and forbids removal or changing of, what it calls Copyright Management Information, essentially the work's identification or other rights metadata, such as watermarks.

So far there have been three civil suits under DMCA 1201, two concerning attempts to break the encryption on DVDs, and one involving Professor Edward Felten of Princeton, whose research revealed a way of breaking the secure watermarking scheme in the Secure Digital Music Initiative, and decided to publish the results. The RIAA attempted to muzzle the publication by threatening Felten with action under DMCA 1201.

The first criminal case involves a Russian company, ElcomSoft, which in the summer of 2001 was selling a program called the Advanced eBook Processor (AEBPR) over the Internet from Moscow through some U.S.-based Web sites. AEBPR enabled owners of Adobe eBooks to strip off the copy protection and turn the e-book into and ordinary PDF, allowing copying, printing, and other rights not granted by the publisher.

The FBI arrested an ElcomSoft employee, Dmitry Sklyarov, who was in the US to speak at DefCon 9, a hacker convention, under the mistaken impression that Sklyarov owned the program that his research had helped to produce; ElcomSoft actually owned the program. The legal issues got worse from there, and in the process, the case, which went to trial at the end of October 2002, began to look like the first Supreme Court test of DMCA 1201.

The issues are many and varied. The Electronic Frontier Foundation (EFF) is leading the way in a constitutional challenge that claims DMCA 1201 is too vague and broadly written, but the DRM related issues seem to boil down to essentially two. Each of the DMCA 1201 opponents in the cases cited claims the Act restricts Fair Use (and therefore incidentally violates the First Amendment). The second issue hasn't come up yet in public documents, but remains to be examined: the First Sale doctrine, which holds that the content-owner's right to restrict distribution ends with the first sale of the copy under rules approved by the content holder. Specifically, before Adobe Systems bought the company called Glassbook, the Glassbook server had provisions for the user to lend or give away an e-Book; the Adobe e-Books that were the target of ElcomSoft seem not to have allowed that use. It is a good bet that these issues will not be settled in any lower court, and therefore will end up in the Supreme Court.

3. 2000: Electronic Signatures Act

The Electronic Signatures Act, signed into law by President Clinton in June 2000, was a big step forward for e-commerce in general, including DRM. By declaring that contracts in electronic form are as valid and legally binding as those written on paper, the act instantly made electronic rights transactions more acceptable. Wider acceptance of the binding nature of the transactions is sure to encourage more automation of the whole process of rights management and development of better DRM technologies.

4. 2001: European Copyright Directive (ECD)

A near-perfect expression of the philosophical process of dialectic, moving from thesis to antithesis to synthesis, the ECD updates the European Software Directive of 1991 to address issues arising from DMCA 1201.

Most of the act is very enlightened. It explicitly recognizes that private copying is going to increase, and calls for better provision for remuneration to the rights holder, including both new business models and better processes and technologies for their implementation. In addition, it explicitly states that the EC expects there to be more disagreement over copyright issues, and suggests that all parties are likely to be better served by mediation than legal actions. ECD, unlike DMCA, also explicitly reaffirms the First Sale doctrine, and discusses at length the new and different status of redistribution rights in content that is part of a database or third-party redistribution agreement. It also includes definitions of fair use that are more proscriptive—and therefore programmable into systems—than the broad and sometimes ambigous guidelines in fair use doctrine in the U.S.

The main disagreement many people have (Sun Microsystems, for instance, has written a strong position paper on the subject) is with Article 6, which takes DMCA 1201 almost word-for-word, but without some of the exceptions in 1201. In particular, Sun has objected to the lack of an exception to allow circumvention to facilitate reverse engineering, in order to promote interoperability. This is a serious issue because the act also calls for measures to promote interoperability. On the whole, though, ECD is taken to be an improvement over all preceding legislation.

5. 2002 (proposed): Consumer Broadband and Digital Television Promotion Act (CBDTPA)

Originally known as the Security Systems Standards and Certification Act, the Consumer Broadband and Digital Television Protection Act (***CBDTPA***) became an official bill in the U.S. Senate in March 2002, sponsored by Senator Ernest Hollings (D-SC), and was quickly joined by a House bill sponsored by Adam Schiff (D), the representative from Burbank, California.

CBDPTA claims that digital television is lagging development because of rampant illegal copying of copyrighted materials, and proposes to address the problem through technological means. The bill would require copy protection devices (either hardware or software) in all media-playing devices—including PCs, set-top boxes, and handheld devices.

The industry would have one year to set its own standards through a collaboration of media, technology, and consumer groups, with admonitions to employ open source software where possible, and preserve fair use. If the industry could not find its own standard, the Commerce Department, Copyright Office, and FCC would step in with their own mandates.

The CBDTPA has generated a firestorm of controversy, primarily because it was the direct result of lobbying by Disney, News Corp., and other media giants. Technology vendors, led by Intel, have vigorously opposed it, and indeed the CBDTPA is a much-toned-down version of the original SSSCA. Given that Sen. Hollings is retiring from the Senate, and that Congress has more urgent matters with which to occupy itself in the 2003 legislative session, passage of the CBDTPA seems unlikely.

(ii) LEGISLATING DRM?

Attempting to deal with DRM issues through legislation is at best akin to a high-wire act; at worst it resembles a 3-D chess game using hand grenades as pieces. Laws must balance the protection of content owners' rights with the interests of the public. This balance is inherent in the history of copyright law: those rights not reserved for the copyright owner go to the public. But it's difficult to maintain the balance with technology alone.

Fair use, as currently defined in U.S. law, cannot be built into automated systems. The fairness of the use is evaluated on a case-by-case basis after the fact. Because all possible uses and circumstances are not describable beforehand, Fair Use is not conducive to programming.

At the same time it is dealing with rights issues, the law must maintain a balance between current and emerging technologies. It can't be too broad or it hobbles the technology industry unfairly by engendering an uncertain or even hostile environment for development. But a law also can't be too specific, or it will engender easy work-arounds and will soon become irrelevant.

The current US legislation is an inadequate patchwork that tends to favor large media companies at the expense of technology vendors and consumers. The European Copyright Directive is a move in the right direction, especially with its suggestions for mediation and discussion to replace litigation.

(iii) CURRENT CASES

The chapter **The Legal Framework** [13.1.6.1] discusses the following two cases in some depth. In this section, we will merely add some comments on the findings and the issues they raise for DRM.

1. New York Times v. Tasini

In the *Tasini* decision, the Supreme Court found that inclusion of collective works such as newspapers in a database that allowed extraction of single articles destroyed the integrity of the collective work, essentially "de-collecting" them. Anyone who has read an entire issue of the *New York Times* on-line and compared that to reading the physical newspaper knows the truth of that statement: page layout and placement inside the sections are editorial statements, as well as conveniences. This analysis is backed up by the Court's finding no distinction between databases covering only one periodical and those collecting several periodicals: typeface and editorial tone notwithstanding, something essential is still missing. Articles appearing in on-line databases are not "reprints" of the original work, and authors must be compensated separately for the new use.

By not addressing whether the publishers had acquired the display rights in the articles concerned, the Court left unanswered the question of whether that right ought to be included in new contracts with authors, but it's a safe bet that it should. More interestingly, by combining the finding in the *Greenberg* case regarding the addition of retrieval software with *Tasini,* the implication is that the Render right needs to be part of the contract with the author.

1. EFFECTS

The effects of the decision are fairly predictable. It's good for authors, because they not only must be better compensated for their works, but they have new rights they didn't know they had before. The burden on authors, though, is that they will have to become more aware of new technologies and more adept at negotiations—will every reporter now need an agent?

The decision is bad for publishers in several ways. First they must track the use of each part of their collective works much more closely, and better compensate the authors for those uses. Second, they must spend considerable sums to update both their contracts and their tracking abilities and internal systems. The combination of the loss of even the tiny amounts of compensation authors will get from the inclusion in databases (almost all publishers considered this "found money," as did book publishers with sub-rights before they became a standard part of the business model), plus the added expense of legal and systems updates, represent a fair hit to publishers' bottom lines. Unless they can automate the entire publishing and DRM process—which would be good for DRM vendors.

Similarly, the decision will be bad for on-line services—they must now set up complex frameworks for deals with each publisher. In the long run, this will be bad for the public—prices of the databases will go up; usage will decrease to some extent. Some of the services will not be able to manage the changes, and databases will be taken off line. A mixed bag at best, but at least the system will be fairer in the long run.

2. Random House v. RosettaBooks

RosettaBooks published e-book versions of about one hundred old Random House titles, which included still-popular titles from authors like Kurt Vonnegut. Mostly, the court decisions thus far don't change much in the DRM world. But they raise two interesting questions.

First, even after Random House wins (if they ultimately do) and all contracts include e-book rights, how long does a publisher have before deciding that the market is right for publishing the e-book alongside the hardcover? In 1994, book publishers were caught in a similar dispute over publishing in CD-ROM format. Looking at the CD-ROM market, and what the licensing fees would be on video, sound, and graphics to accompany their texts, the publishers waited for the CD publishing market to go quietly away. That is, they did until the movie studios got involved.

The studios were not concerned about music and video costs. They already had agreements with those people, they said, and with their sophisticated production facilities they could work up CD-ROM versions of the book/movie combinations in a trice. They wanted to redefine the electronic book publishing rights as a subset of movie rights.

Nothing doing, cried the publishers. All book rights is all book rights, and we've got 'em.

Then use them, the studios replied, still eager to take advantage of cross-marketing opportunities as they had with Star Wars electronic games.

We will, when the market is right, said the publishers.

In a more timely manner, said the studios, and were preparing to work with authors in the courts to define "timely" when the bottom fell out of the CD-ROM market.

Current practice in the book business is to sell the hardcover for a year or two, then let another publisher bring out a paperback edition, whether trade paper or mass-market. If , two years after first publication, there is no e-book, should the author go back and demand his rights? Is five years timely enough?

The second question involves what happens when RosettaBooks wins (if they ultimately do). What becomes of all books not yet in public domain to which book publishers have the same "all book rights" that Random House had? Does every author need to renegotiate her contract on a twenty year old book? We hope that the chaos that would result from a Rosetta victory would be short lived, but both the above questions need resolution, and seem to present opportunities for DRM developers to work out automated solutions.

15.6 VENDORS: DRM SOLUTIONS FOR PUBLISHERS

Now that we've discussed some of the issues involved, an understanding of the future of DRM probably requires a look at some of the major players in the history of the technology, how they saw their mission in the past and what they look forward to.

(i) ADOBE

Adobe Systems was one of the earliest entries in the market for graphics in electronic publishing. In a way, Adobe could be said to have invented the popular idea of electronic publishing with its PostScript page description language and, later, , Acrobat and PDF, the Portable Document Format.

That doesn't mean that Adobe has had an easy time of things. Some of their internal policy decisions led to a long slow process in maintaining their early leadership. Because Adobe wanted to sell the product they worked so hard to invent, both consumers and Web browser developers were loath to incorporate Acrobat and PDF into their plans. The wariness was natural enough: print suppliers has originally run to PostScript, only to find that, being a proprietary format, it was subject to unannounced revisions. Soon the question was not "Is this document in PostScript?" but *which* version of PostScript—v1, 2.0, 2.1, or some privately modified version that might not run on any other outside systems?

Slowly, PDF gained acceptance as a format for viewing text and graphics, based mainly on its reputation as a reliable read-only format. That read-only quality made it a natural for DRM development; not only that, its plug-in architecture enabled DRM developers to build small applications and add them on, rather than build huge, integrated systems and try to persuade users to opt in. By 1998 there were several third-party solutions all vying to become the main supplier to Adobe.

Late in 1999, Adobe announced plans to release its own DRM system, PDF Merchant, an encryption-based system that tied into a user-side application called Web Buy, which would connect consumers to e-commerce systems to pay for encryption keys to read the document ordered.

But late 1999–early 2000 was an interesting time for e-publishing. Lots of people were developing e-book systems, and Adobe decided that it might be easier in the long run to work with somebody else's accepted system than try to force acceptance of Web Buy. Thus, in 2000, Adobe developed a partnership with (that grew into an outright purchase of) a company called Glassbook that used PDF as a foundation for a nifty e-book reader and had a pretty robust Content Server to boot. Adobe spent 2001 trying to explain that the Glassbook (Adobe) e-book reader was not the same software as their own Adobe Acrobat Reader, and why they needed *two* e-publishing formats in a market that hadn't demonstrated a very strong need for *one*. In the meantime, they also began to use the InterTrust DocBox DRM content packager as a plug-in to Acrobat Reader (DocBox now ships with every copy of Acrobat Reader 5).

The answer to the former question, by the way, points to the future plans for Adobe. The company sees (at least) very two different markets being served. Shorter documents, such as research reports, legal documents, and corporate brochures are well served by the plain old PDF format, with functions such as Print, Copy, and Edit available. The finally-developing e-book market needs to accommodate longer files, but may or may not need Print, and often distinctly avoids Copy. The plans for the coming year are to slowly merge the PDF and e-book formats and consolidate the DRM systems; the company still has to make clear how it will integrate these technologies into a plan to deal with media convergence and their other digital publishing applications. Plans are for Acrobat 6 to include what is now sold separately as the Adobe Acrobat eBook Reader.

(ii) MICROSOFT

Whereas Adobe was shaped in its view of DRM for e-publishing by its history with print reproduction, Microsoft has tried to embrace electronic media first, even naming their first real try at audio and video delivery the Windows Media Player. Alas, the affection was unrequited. Microsoft suffered the fate of many biggest-in-its-industry organizations: it was sniped at from both ends at once. The display end of the Windows Media Player was derided as not being as good as first the Macintosh and the later RealNetworks, while simultaneously the DRM end was made the target of repeated hack attacks through 2000 and 2001.

The second generation of media technologies has fared better. The display technology of Microsoft Reader .lit format with ClearType has been appreciated by almost all who've used it. On the server side, the Digital Asset Server (DAS) is made up of two parts: DAS Server, with the content repository and DRM packaging, and DAS e-commerce functions for tying into the e-book retailer, which can also be run by a third-party ASP (Application Service Provider).

The Reader's DRM system, which is based on a subset of XrML, is tied together and controlled using Microsoft's Passport user identification scheme. Passport creates a unique user ID with password protection, then links the Passport ID to a particular machine to create a "persona," a combination of one person and a small group of machines (two or three) that constitute a "trusted system."

Each time the user buys a new Reader format e-book, he must "activate" the e-book with the Reader display software, which ties the device and the e-book and the user together in the DRM system.

The DRM can provide one of three levels of security (assigned by the publisher) to a Microsoft Reader e-book. Level one, the basic protection, is called Sealed: any Microsoft Reader software can view the text, on any machine, but the contents are "sealed in," that is, certified to be unaltered and unalterable. Level two, called Inscribed, is also sealed, but this time the first page of the e-book has the user's name right on it. You could pass along a pirated copy, but it would be clear who paid for the original, and will presumably be held responsible for the copy. Level three, called Owner-specific, is sealed, inscribed, and encrypted. The key for decrypting the book is the user's persona, so the Reader software must be activated with the user's persona to read the e-book.

1. Third generation: "Unified DRM"

The next generation of Microsoft's DRM was referred to internally for a long time as "Unified DRM," with the code name Mercury. Under unified DRM, there would be a single DRM system that would work across all devices, platforms, and media types, including PCs, video players, music players, and handhelds.

The system would be based on a full implementation of XrML, and would depend on hardware that has a permanent, unique tracking number or digital signature; it would store the user's personal data in an encrypted folder, and include an information sharing agent called "my man."

Reportedly, this system will be included in Microsoft's trusted computing architecture of the future, code-named Palladium, which will monitor all software on the system and check to make sure that any new software is authorized before it can be used. Delivery is supposedly scheduled some time around the end of 2003 or early 2004.

(iii) NOTES ON OTHER SYSTEMS AND VENDORS

1. InterTrust

As this book went to press, InterTrust, one of the oldest companies in DRM—and according to their patent-infringement suit against Microsoft, inventor of many of the industry's basic technologies—was bought by a joint venture of Philips and Sony, called Fidelio Corp., that was created for the purpose. Speculation was rampant concerning the reason for the purchase—whether it was to enhance the company's position in its patent infringement suit against Microsoft, or whether it was a response to feature-film copy protection supplier Macrovision's purchase of Midbar, a music copy protection firm, was hard to say.

What is clear is that InterTrust's chances of staying the course against Microsoft have improved, now that their pockets are a lot deeper.

2. IBM: EMMS

Years ago, IBM developed one of the first security wrappers, the Cryptolope. But the world wasn't as networked, computers were slower, with smaller memories, and a four- to five-megabyte wrapper was too much, and the Cryptolope died.

Though it was originally designed with music delivery and protection in mind, IBM's second entry in the DRM market, the Electronic Media Management System, is testing the e-book market through a partnership with format developer ION Systems. EMMS is the result of several years of research that IBM did under the name Madison Project. The system comprises five modular components that can be sold in a single package or individually, including Content Mastering, covering file conversion and content packaging; Web Commerce Enabler, to sustain e-commerce; Clearinghouse, to clear rights and make reports; Content Hosting, to oversee distribution of content; and Player SDK, to allow publishers to develop their own applications.

3. SealedMedia

UK-based SealedMedia, which has been around since 1996, looks prepared to stay a while longer. While much of the industry withered on the vine in 2001, SealedMedia actually received $16 million in new funding in the fall that year. The DRM is well-established and versatile, able to protect content in PDF, HTML, MP3, JPEG, and QuickTime formats.

4. OverDrive Systems

Another of the long-timers, OverDrive has been in electronic publishing for more than fifteen years. One of the original development partners with Microsoft in creating the Microsoft Reader system, OverDrive has since branched out as a service provider, and supports the Adobe and Palm e-books in addition to Microsoft's. Also, here's a service provider that really provides a useful service: building on the idea of the Digital Asset Server, OverDrive's MiDAS system, resident at OverDrive but run remotely from the e-retailer, gives e-book retailers on a tight budget complete access to server technologies without any heavy investment.

5. Savantech

Though one of the newer companies around, for experience in the right part of the industry it's hard to top Savantech: CEO Prasad Ram was general manager of the Xerox Rights Management Group, developers of products and services based on DPRL. Senior vice president of business development Carol Risher was for many years the AAP's vice president of Copyright and Technology; Risher was the chief shepherdess for such digital foundations for books as the DOI and the ONIX system. Now they are working together in service provider Savantech's enterprise content management, packaging and distribution system product, Photon Commerce. Photon Commerce is not a DRM system per se, but rather a framework that can interoperate with virtually any DRM technology.

15.7 THE STATE OF THE MARKET

"One wild roller-coaster ride" hardly begins to describe the changing state of the DRM market from 2000 to the present. A quick comparison of numbers from surveys just a few months apart in 2001 tells much of the tale.

In June of 2001, IDC surveyed the industry, asking where people thought that DRM revenue would be in 2005, and each year in between. Reports had indicated that for 2000, the actual revenues totaled $96 million. Subjects foresaw that number doubling or more virtually every year, to $218 million in 2001; to $543 million in 2002, $1.18 billion in 2003; $2.13 billion in 2004; and finally $5.36 billion in 2005. People were nothing if not optimistic.

By September of 2001, at the Seybold Seminars and Expo in San Francisco, things had changed, and more than a little. A survey conducted by Advantage Business Research for Seybold queried 1,332 attendees at the show, publishing professionals all, and found a colder, more realistic view of things. On the state of the industry, nine percent reported that they thought DRM was important at that time; only twenty-two percent felt DRM would be important within twelve months. On the implementation timeframe, seven percent reported using DRM at the time; eighteen percent intended to implement DRM within twelve months; twenty-eight percent intended to implement DRM sometime in the future, but didn't know when. Taken together, this means that more than two-thirds of the Seybold attendees, precisely the early-adopting professionals who are the target market for DRM systems, and primary users of the systems then available, thought DRM was still a ways down the road, and nearly forty percent thought they might never implement DRM at all.

Among those respondents who were publishers of paid digital content, only eighteen percent were using DRM at the time, while two-thirds intended to do so in the future. Only twenty percent thought DRM was important at the time, and thirty-nine percent responded that DRM would be important in a year's time. If you're keeping score, that's forty percent of publishers of paid digital content who thought that DRM would still not be important to their business more than a year later.

What was bothering these professionals about the DRM market? Queried about obstacles to adoption, seventy-three percent believed that the standards were not mature or broadly adopted; forty-five percent reported that the revenues involved did not justify the investment in DRM; half said that vendors weren't doing a good job of explaining the value of DRM; seventy-two percent said choosing the right DRM solution is too difficult (at least it sounds as if they were looking at products!); and fifty percent claimed that DRM was irrelevant, that content could not be protected effectively.

Among those who did want to adopt DRM at some point in the future, forty-nine percent wanted to buy the technology tools involved and build their own system in-house; twenty-two percent wanted to adopt an end-to-end solution; and seventeen percent wanted to outsource the whole thing to an ASP.

The number of DRM vendors exhibiting on the show floor went on a rollercoaster, as well: in Spring 1999, there were two DRM exhibitors in the show; in Fall 1999, five; Spring 2000, eight; in Fall 2000, thirteen; in the Spring 2001 Seybold in Boston, DRM exhibitors hit their high of sixteen; by Fall 2001, that number was cut in half, to seven; and fell again in Spring 2002 to five.

For more information, refer to the summary of the survey, available at www.seyboldreports,com/Specials/DRMsurvey/summary.html.

What happened between the IDC and Seybold surveys was a giant technology investment crash, with resulting consolidation of the market. The numbers are pretty devastating, when you keep in mind that report on vendors on the show floor. Five DRM-service providers ceased operation in 2001 or early 2002: Reciprocal, Digital Goods, PublishOne, DigiHub, and Massive Media. Three more vendors—ContentGuard, SealedMedia, and InterTrust—were restructured, with heavy layoffs. Those companies that survived still were acquisition targets: five were acquired, including MediaDNA, by Macrovision; Preview Systems by Aladdin; Vyou by the Copyright Clearance Center; Aegisoft, by RealNetworks; and PassEdge, by InterTrust.

(i) LIKELY MARKET DEVELOPMENT SCENARIO

Looking with a gimlet eye at the current state of the DRM market to find a path ahead, some things start to become apparent. First, format owners have an obvious advantage: Microsoft, Adobe and RealNetworks are far ahead by virtue of the fact that they are collecting revenue from licensing, not losing revenue to it. Pure-play DRM vendors are still at the greatest risk to fail, or to be acquired. SealedMedia, RightsMarket, Aries Systems, and FileOpen are in this category.

Wildcards, with truly unpredictable futures include America Online and such security vendors as VeriSign and RSA. Legal constraints on technology and unauthorized copying are not only not impossible, they loom on the near horizon if the market doesn't begin to police itself somewhat.

The good news is, consolidation precedes growth. In 1915 there were more than 300 auto makers in the US; today there are three. But would anybody want to go back to the pre-World War I market size?

15.8 DRM IMPLEMENTATION ISSUES

If you, like some of the Seybold attendees above, are on the brink of DRM adoption, here are some issues to contemplate, with a suggestion or two for how to proceed.

(i) IS ENCRYPTION NECESSARY?

Because of the resistance of the audience and the cost of implementation, it becomes a very real question for publishers whether encryption is really worthwhile. Different markets will produce different answers, of course. The readers of O'Reilly & Associates manuals on Programming Perl are far more technically adept than the run of Simon & Schuster fiction readers.

Beyond your customers' skills, consider their loyalty: what are the positive and negative aspects of pass-along readership (or bleed, if you prefer)? Seth Godin's *Unleashing the Ideavirus* is only one of many viral marketing campaigns that pointed in the same direction. Rather than think of every copy as a lost sale, consider this: What would you have spent to advertise that title?

This whole question is a great deal like Theory X business management principles versus Theory Y. Can you "go with the flow," let the trust that consumers have in their friends rub off a little on you? And maybe even do a little (careful, subtle) event management to prime the pump, pique consumers' interest in your products? Now compare that approach to marketing to the costs in hardware, media, software and people to try to police your readership, to make certain your dike has no leaks.

(ii) CONSIDER WATERMARKING

Perhaps, rather than bigger locks on your content, all your readers need is a gentle reminder. Watermarking gives you a semi-permanent audit trail. And if your content is valuable enough, you aren't going to stop the determined professional thief anyway. Perhaps, as with Microsoft Reader's "Inscribed" titles, just the notion that you *could* find out where the leak came from would be enough to deter the casual infringer.

(iii) SEEKING A VENDOR: VALIDATION CRITERIA

When it comes time really to implement a DRM solution, to pay your money and take your choice, there are some tried-and-true steps to take. First, make sure everyone in your organization agrees, at least on the business model you want, and the objectives you seek. Next, define a pilot project, a good test of what you seek. Put your expectations down in writing: create a set of vendor requirements, and put them in an official vendor requirements document. The last thing you want to hear afterward is "I never knew you wanted that. Why didn't you tell me?"

This document should list your desired business models; your expected user profile, including client technology; a description of the production and technology environment—what systems will you be using?; and an estimate of the volume of traffic to expect. (For Stephen King's *Riding the Bullet,* people expected a total volume of less than 20,000; when they got 400,000 download requests in the first 24 hours, the ISP couldn't handle the traffic, and broke down.)

Bring vendors into your offices to enable them to evaluate your project and your facilities. Then issue a Request for Proposals, and be prepared to know what you want when the vendors come around.

First, what is the vendor's reputation? How stable or well-funded are they? This is a volatile market. Does the vendor support the business model you want—subscription, piecemeal download, or what ever? How about scalability—can the vendor work with the numbers you expect? Can they adjust if the numbers are significantly different? How do they charge for their services—Flat software license fee? Per transaction royalty? Get the vendor to agree on an acceptable level of customer service.

When you are satisfied that you have the best overall package in one of the vendors, then sign them up.

Glossary

accessibility. In general usage, whether a file or resource on a computer or network is available for access for users; in digital publishing, whether content is available for access, is in a format that can be used with assistive software by people with disabilities, and contains sufficient additional support material to make it comprehensible for them (e.g., alternative text for images that the blind cannot see). *See sections 7.1, 11.2(ii).10.*

Acrobat. A software program created by Adobe Systems for creating, editing, manipulating and annotating PDF files. It has three components: Acrobat Distiller, for creating PDF files from PostScript; Acrobat, for editing and annotating PDF files; and Acrobat Reader, a free utility for viewing and printing PDF files. *See section 6.6.*

Acrobat Distiller. A component program of the Adobe Acrobat software; used for creating PDF files from PostScript files. *See section 6.12.*

Acrobat Reader. A software program created by Adobe Systems for viewing PDF files; typically available free on the Web (www.adobe.com) and used also as a plug-in by most Web browsers. *See sections 7.2(i).4, 6.6, 6.12.*

Active Server Pages (ASP). A programming mechanism for creating and serving dynamic Web pages; generally more efficient and easier to create than CGI, allowing developers to freely mix HTML, scripts, and other programs that could perform discrete, specialized functions, such as querying a database and displaying the results; abbreviated and most commonly used as ASP. *See section 10.1(ii).3.1.*

active-matrix. A type of LCD screen where three transistors are located at each pixel position on the display surface; coupled with backlighting, color filters and a polarizing layer, this allows for bright, color displays. *See section 2.4(ii).2.*

ADA. Americans with Disabilities Act of 1990. U.S. law passed by Congress in 1990 that took effect in 1992, making it illegal for private employers, government, and unions, among other entities, to discriminate on the basis of handicap or disability. *See sections 7.1(ii).2, 9.7(iii).2.*

additive color. Theory and process by which three primary colors—red, green, and blue—are added together in various amounts or degrees to form the colors of the visible spectrum. See also RGB. *See section 6.9(i).1.*

Adobe eBook Reader. Software produced by Adobe Systems for reading electronic books. *See section 7.2(i).4.*

Adobe Type Manager (ATM). A program to manage font handling; images fonts directly from their Type 1 font files to screen bitmaps, allowing for scaling fonts on screen as well as printing PostScript fonts on a non-PostScript printer. *See section 6.7(ii).3.*

ADSL. Asymmetric DSL. A mode of operation of a digital subscriber line in which transmission to a computer is at a higher speed than transmission from that computer. *See section 2.6(iii).2.2.*

AFM. Adobe Font Metrics. An ASCII-based file format used for storing font metric data, used with Adobe Type 1 fonts. *See section 6.7(iv).1.2.*

AFP. Advanced Function Presentation. A page description language used by many IBM printing systems. *See section 6.5(i).*

algorithms. A procedure for solving a mathematical problem, frequently by repetition of an operation, chiefly used in computing to regularize a repetitive task to accomplish an end. *See section 5.5(vi).1.*

Americans with Disabilities Act. See ADA.

Amplitude Modulation (AM) screening. Conventional halftone screening where an image is broken up into halftone dots of differing size. *See section 6.8(vi).5.*

analog. Systems in which change occurs continuously and smoothly through an infinite number of states; see also digital. *See section 2.2(ii).3.*

ANSI. American National Standards Institute. A non-profit organization that administers and coordinates the U.S. voluntary standardization and conformity assessment system. *See sections 2.6(i).2.5, 3.1(ii).2.*

antialiasing. A software technique applied to lines or paths that are not parallel to one of the edges of the display, so as to smooth the jagged edges of such diagonal lines and curves on a bitmapped screen. *See section 2.4(i).4.*

API. Application programming interface. A component to a software system, such as a content management system (CMS), that programmers can use to connect the system with other systems in an organization or otherwise; also the functions programs can use to perform a variety of tasks. *See section 10.2(i).3.*

AppleTalk. A family of network protocols that can run on Ethernet and Token Ring networks as well as Apple's own LocalTalk access protocol. *See section 2.6(iv).1.*

application. A software program that performs tasks at a higher level than the operating system to produce results that are significant to the computer user. *See section 2.3(ii).*

application programming interface. See API.

application servers. The intelligent engines behind a Web site that manage the performance and interplay of diverse applications running in one environment; can be used to integrate portal software, content management software, and other key applications. *See section 10.1(ii).3.3.*

application service provider (ASP). A vendor that serves applications to remote users via the Internet or Web, allowing a customer to use the software or application by subscription rather than purchasing a personal copy. *See section 10.5(ii).1.*

arc. In XLink, meaning information about a traversal (using a link) such as the direction of the link, how it behaves, and what activates it. *See section 3.3(v).1.*

archival DTD. A Document Type Definition for archiving purposes. See also Document Type Definition. *See section 3.3(ii).1.1.*

ARPAnet. Advanced Research Projects Agency Network. Developed by an agency of the U.S. Department of Defense, ARPAnet was the precursor to the Internet, connecting government laboratories and research universities. *See section 2.6(iv).1.*

article-based publishing. Process in which journal publishers electronically publish individual articles in advance of the print issue. *See section 4.3(i).2.*

ASCII. American Standard Code for Information Interchange. A 7-bit character set, which allows for 128 different character encodings. See also Extended ASCII. *See sections 3.3(iii).4, 4.5(iii).4, 5.3(iii).2, 6.8(iii).1.*

ASP. See Active Server Pages or application service provider.

ATM. Asynchronous transfer mode. A highly scalable packet-switching protocol, used to route packets on a WAN; ATM serves the same function in these wide-area circuits as Ethernet does on a local area network. *See section 2.6(iii).2.2.*

ATM. See Adobe Type Manager (ATM).

attribute. In SGML, HTML, and XML, a part of an element that carries metadata about that element and its contents; takes the form of a label and data pertaining to that label; an element can contain more than one attribute. For example, an attribute for a "chapter number" element might be the number itself and would take the form: <CN number="2">. The label is "number" and the value is "2." *See sections 3.2(i).1, 3.3(ii).2.3.*

ATU. ADSL transceiver unit. A device (DSL router) used at the customer or client end of a DSL circuit. *See section 2.6(iii).2.2.*

back-conversion. Process where content is converted to XML or another structure system after traditional production and/or typesetting. *See section 4.2(i).1.*

base DTD. A DTD that defines a restricted set of elements, usually simplified in vocabulary or structure to expedite processing in non-XML systems; best used in conjunction with a reference DTD or archival DTD that provides a more robust model. *See sections 3.3(ii).1.1, 4.2(ii).1.*

Basic Document Vocabulary. In the Open eBook Publication Structure (OEBPS), a set (tagset) of elements and attributes that all OEB Reading Systems must recognize; largely conforms to XHTML 1.0. Also known as Basic OEB. See also Extended OEB. *See section 11.2(ii).1.*

Basic Multilingual Plane (BMP). In the Unicode character encoding system, the first of 32,768 planes that each accommodates 65,536 basic characters; contains virtually all of the encodings thus far defined in Unicode. *See section 3.3(iii).4.1.*

Basic OEB. See Basic Document Vocabulary. *See sections 3.1(iii).3, 3.3(ii).1.3.*

batch processing. A method of processing or executing a task on a computer where the parameters and constraints of the task are specified when the process is started and the operation can proceed without further user intervention; typically used to complete large-scale repetitive tasks or large computational problems; in publishing, frequently used for such tasks as pagination or hyphenation/justification during typesetting. *See section 2.3(i).4.1.*

Berne Convention. International multilateral copyright treaty administered by the World Intellectual Property Organization (WIPO) in Berne, Switzerland; has harmonized copyright law among most countries, and signatories are required to grant each others' citizens the same copyright protection as their own citizens; after relying on other treaty relationships for decades, the United States joined the Berne Convention in 1989. *See sections 13.1(i).3, 13.1(ii).9.1.*

bespoke DTD. A custom-written DTD, as opposed to a standard DTD. *See section 4.2(ii).1.*

BiDi. A protocol for parallel communication between a computer and a printer that is bi-directional, also known as IEEE standard 1284. *See section 2.6(i).2.4.*

binary. Something that is expressed as or contained in a binary system. See also Binary EPS and binary notation. *See section 3.3(vi).2.*

Binary EPS. An image description format that contains a bitmapped preview image and the actual graphic in Encapsulated PostScript; the printable graphic is stored as a stream of numbers representing pixel attributes; suited for outputting images for four-color separation. *See section 6.8(v).1.5.*

binary notation. Expressing a datum, an ASCII character for example, as a series of ones and zeros. *See section 3.3(iii).4.*

binary system. A system that consists of only two states, numerically expressed as a one or a zero, each digit representing a bit.

bit. A contraction of binary digit, representing one of two states in a computer system, usually expressed as a one or a zero. *See section 2.2(ii).1.*

bitmap. A two-dimensional binary array of an object where the object (a line, letter, or graphic) is mapped and described in bits, typically used in computer displays where each pixel is individually addressed with a binary value. See bitmap. *See sections 2.4(i).1, 6.8(ii), 6.8(ii).1.*

bitmapped. A method of display where each pixel on a computer screen is individually addressed. See also bitmap.

Bluetooth. A short-range wireless communications technology; while not specifically a wireless networking technology, it is designed for the transmission of audio and data between wireless and desktop devices. *See section 9.6(iii).2.*

BMP. See bitmap and Basic Multilingual Plane.

Bobby. A software application that examines Web pages and identifies anything on a page that does not conform to the Web Content Accessibility Guidelines; sites that pass the examination and conform to the guidelines are authorized to display the bobby symbol that indicates that the site is accessible to people with visual disabilities. *See section 7.2(i).5.4.*

BRI. Basic Rate Interface. One of the two fundamental speeds at which an ISDN communications line operates; typically used by residential or small business customers who do not require the larger bandwidth of the faster and more expensive Primary Rate Interface (PRI). *See section 2.6(iii).2.2.*

BSD. One of the two main variations of the Unix operating system developed at the University of California at Berkeley. *See section 2.3(i).1.*

byte. A group or sequence of bits (ones or zeros) that represent information; most modern computers group bits 8 at a time, resulting in a 8-bit byte. *See section 2.2(ii).1.*

cable modem. A device used to connect a computer to a wide area network (WAN) utilizing digital (coaxial) cable; the use of "modem" is a misnomer because the signal is already digital, not analog, so no modulation or demodulation are needed. *See section 2.6(iii).2.2.*

CAD. Computer Aided Design. A program or system that combines drawing programs with database and spreadsheet capabilities, typically used by draftsmen and engineers. *See section 2.3(ii).5.2.*

Cascading Style Sheets (CSS). A stylesheet language specifically designed for the Web and HTML. *See sections 5.3(iii).3, 11.2(ii).2, 11.6(v).3.*

CAST. The Center for Applied Special Technology. A non-profit organization that works to increase educational opportunities for people with disabilities through the development and uses of technology. *See section 7.1(iv).*

CBDTPA. Consumer Broadband and Digital Television Protection Act. Proposed legislation, introduced in Congress in 2002 by Sen. Ernest Hollings and Rep. Adam Shiff that would require copy protection technology in all media-playing devices (e.g., computers, television sets, CD and DVD players) to prevent illegal copying of copyrighted content. *See section 15.5(i).5.*

CCD. Charged-coupled device. In digital cameras and scanners, a sensor consisting of three bars with color filters that receives light, samples the color information of the image, and records it digitally. See trilinear arrays.

CD. See compact disc.

CD-R. A type of compact disc (a recordable CD) that can be written one time by consumer drives but read many times thereafter. *See section 2.5(ii).3.2.*

CD-ROM. A type of CD for read-only memory, meaning the disk can be written to only once, usually by the content producer, but read many times thereafter; a medium used for distribution of software and large data sets. *See sections 15.1(ii).2, 2.5(ii).3.1.*

CD-RW. A type of CD for rewritable use, meaning they can be written to and read by consumer disk drives; most such disks can be written to multiple times, but those that can be written once and read many times are called CD-R or CD-ROM.

central processing unit. In a computer, a chip or integrated circuit that is generally the most complex and handles core functions of the machine. *See section 2.2(i).1.*

CEPS. Color Electronic Prepress Systems. Proprietary color production and page composition systems; generally such systems have been replaced by desktop prepress systems, though some are still in use. *See section 6.8.*

CGA. Computer Graphics Adapter. Both a signaling protocol and a type of graphics adapter, which sends signals that address each pixel in a computer display independently. *See section 2.4(ii).5.*

CGI. Common Gateway Interface. A programming mechanism used to generate dynamic Web pages; one of the first such mechanisms used to generate content and run programs through Web pages. *See section 10.1(ii).3.1.*

Chafee amendment. A 1996 amendment to the Copyright Act that provides an exemption from copyright to allow an authorized entity to produce specialized formats of non-dramatic literary works for the blind or other persons with disabilities. *See section 7.2(i).1.1.*

chip. Term for a set of transistors contained in a silicon substrate. *See section 2.2(i).1.*

CIM. See Computer Integrated Manufacturing.

client/server. A network model for accessing remote resources where a client program, typically on a computer or workstation, requests information from a centralized computer called a server, which supplies the data. *See sections 15.2(ii).5, 2.6(ii), 2.6(ii).1, 2.6(iv).2.*

CMM. Color matching method or color management module. Software that transforms or converts color-imaging data from one device to another and is at the heart of a successful color management system. *See section 6.9(v).1.3.*

CMOS. Complementary metal-oxide semiconductors. A type of scanner sensor used in digital cameras and flatbed scanners. *See section 6.11(iii).*

CMS. See color management system.

CMS. Content management system. Any system for electronically managing (creating, editing, managing, and storing) content either on a single computer, a LAN, or on the Web. Most such systems provide for multiple uses of content and some sort of tagging or coding system and combine text processing and database capabilities. *See sections 3.3(ii).1.1, 10.1(i), 10.2, 10.2(ii), 10.5, 10.5(iv).*

CMYK. In printing, the subtractive color process whereby four separate transparent inks—cyan, magenta, yellow, and black—are used to produce all other colors; each color ink is printed using a separate plate; also called process color. *See section 6.9(ii).2.*

CODEC. A compression/decompression (co/dec) algorithm used by multimedia authoring or player software; a wide variety of CODECs for audio and video are in use, each one with specific features and usages such as streaming video, video conferencing, or 3-D animation. *See section 9.6(vi).1.*

color correction. Loosely used for any change in a color in a digital image; more specifically, the process of correcting hue error in ink during the color separation process. *See section 6.9(iii).4.*

color depth. In general, the number of colors that can be represented on a computer screen, expressed both as bits and number of colors; 8-bit color depth provides 256 colors, while 24-bit color depth provides over 16 million colors (more than the human eye can actually distinguish). Color depth is also a specification for digital cameras that specifies the number of bits used to describe each pixel in an image, usually expressed as 24, 36, or 42; also referred to as pixel depth. *See sections 9.3(i).2, 6.11(ii).2.*

color gamut. A specific range of colors out of all possible colors, or the colors that can be described by a color reproduction system out of the millions of colors perceived by the human eye. *See section 8.2(iii).4.*

color management system. CMS. Any system for electronically managing digital color reproduction such that it is predictable and repeatable; most such systems address the standard characteristics and performance of color-imaging hardware and software, the calibration of monitors and scanners for consistent color rendering, and the converting of color data from one device to another; first conceived in the late 1980s, CMS systems are beginning to be used by more designers and publishers. *See section 6.9(v).*

Color-Atlas. A seven-color process designed to use red, green, and blue along with cyan, magenta, yellow, and black to expand the color gamut; used in traditional halftone screening. *See section 6.9(ii).3.*

ColorSync. Color management system for Apple computers, supports ICC profile standard. *See section 6.9(v).3.*

communications buses. A connection, usually by wire, between processors or parts of a computer that transmits information in bits. *See section 2.2(ii).1.*

compact disc (CD). A type of optical storage disk, first introduced by the Sony Corporation for audio recordings; for data storage, CDs were originally used for software distribution and storage of large data sets and could only be read by a computer, not written to, and so they were referred to as CD-ROM, for read-only memory. *See sections 15.1(ii).1, 2.5(ii).3.1.*

compression. The process of minimizing or eliminating redundancy in a digital file to reduce its size for more efficient storage or transmission; most compression technology also allows compression of several discrete files into a single file. *See section 6.8(iv).*

Computer Aided Design. See CAD.

Computer Integrated Manufacturing (CIM). Type of printing or manufacturing where all parts of the manufacturing process or the entire manufacturing plant is completely automated and under computer control, with digital information tying the various manufacturing processes together. *See section 6.12.1.*

computer-to-plate (CTP). Printing process where image content is recorded directly from a computer to the printing plate, rather than first to film. *See section 6.9(iv).*

content management system. See CMS.

continuous tone. Tonal gradation between colors in an image, such as photograph, that is generally gradual and continuous, rather than sharply distinct; also called contone. *See section 6.8(vi).1.*

continuous-inkjet. A type of inkjet printing technology where all nozzles in a print-head emit a constant stream of ink droplets, most of which are electrostatically deflected and recirculated; only those droplets that are not deflected are deposited on paper; this technology allows for faster printing than drop-on-demand inkjet printing. *See section 8.2(ii).2.*

contone. See continuous tone.

contract proofs. Printing proofs used to review and judge critical color, check registration, and determine precise image sizing; such proofs generally require high-quality print reproduction. *See section 6.9(iv).1.*

copyright. Any one or more of a bundle of rights that gives the owner control over the reproduction, distribution, performance, and display of a work of authorship, and over the creation of derivative works of that work; also used to mean the legal system that protects those rights; a statutory system, both domestically and internationally. See also Berne Convention, permission, and fair use. *See sections 13.1(i), 14.12(i).*

Core Media Type. In the Open eBook Publication Structure (OEBPS), a MIME media type that all OEB Reading Devices must support; the OEBPS specifies six such media types. *See section 11.6(iii).6.*

coursepacks. A type of custom publishing or printing (usally using digital printers) where a teacher or professor will select content from different publications or publication types (e. g., journals, books) and have them printed and bound for use by students. *See section 1.2(iii).2.*

CP/M. An operating system for 8-bit computers used on some of the original personal computers; was used by Microsoft as the basis of the DOS operating system; stands for "control program for microprocessors." *See section 2.3(i).3.*

CRC. Camera-ready copy. Content that is prepared for moving directly to printing plates; generally used to refer to physical pages and artwork that are photographed or scanned. *See section 4.2(i).1.*

creator codes. In the Macintosh operating system (before OS X), a four-character text string embedded within a file that identifies the application that created the file and used by the operating system to determine what applications can open it; used along with file type codes. *See section 6.8(v).*

CRM. See customer relationship management.

CrossRef. A cooperative reference linking service, used mostly by STM journal publishers; the first major use of DOI was in CrossRef; robust metadata is central. *See sections 1.2(i).6.1, 3.3(i).3.*

crosswalks. The mapping between two different metadata vocabularies, such as between Dublin Core and MARC. *See section 4.4(iii).2.*

CRT. Cathode Ray Tube. A type of display screen, such as computer monitor or television that consists of a cathode (a negatively charged electrode) that emits a stream of electrons (called a cathode ray) that strikes a fluorescent-coating on the inside of a glass screen to produce photons that make up the visible display; CRTs tend to be large and heavy and are typically found in televisions and desktop computer monitors. *See sections 1.3(iii).4, 2.4(ii), 2.4(ii).1.*

CSS. See Cascading Style Sheets (CSS) *See sections 3.2(iv).1, 3.3(iii).2, 10.1(ii).1.1.*

CTP. See computer-to-plate.

custom color. See spot color.

customer relationship management (CRM). The managing and maintaining of the experience and relationship of users of a Web site, through personalization, usage data capture, and marketing, etc.; often abbreviated as CRM. *See section 10.1(ii).3.4.*

DAISY. Digital Accessible Information SYstem. A series of standards developed by the DAISY Consortium for a digital talking book; the latest standard was approved and published March 2002 as ANSI/NISO Z39.86 - 2002. *See sections 7.2(i).3.1, 11.2(ii).10.*

DAM. Digital asset management. A term that covers a variety of different approaches to using digital methods and processes to store, track, and retrieve content, whether text, images, or multimedia files, usually after publication; sometimes called digital archiving. *See sections 1.2(vii).2, 10.2, 6.12.1.*

database. A computer application optimized for the storage and retrieval of information; includes functions for adding, editing, retrieving, and manipulating that information. See also relational database. *See section 2.3(ii).2.*

database management systems. DBMS or DMS. Programs that are used to interact with and manipulate information in a database. *See section 2.3(ii).2.*

datatyping. In XML, the specification that an element must contain not just data or content, but a specific kind of data or content, as declared in the XML schema; also commonly used in database schemas. *See sections 3.3(ii).2.7, 3.3(ii).4.2.*

DBMS. See database management systems.

DCF. Document Composition Facility. The first commercial implementation of GML in the early 1970s by IBM; a system for formatting generically tagged documents; IBM published the first formal document type defiintion in their *DCF GML User's Guide* in 1978. *See section 3.1(ii).1.*

DCMES. See Dublin Core Metadata Element Set. *See sections 3.3(vi).3.1, 4.4(iii).1.*

DCMI. See the Dublin Core Metadata Initiative. *See sections 3.3(vi).3.1, 4.4(ii).1.*

DCS. Desktop Color Separation. A graphic file format that creates four-color separations by saving images as a set of four Encapsulated PostScript files (for each of the process colors), and a fifth low-resolution preview file. It is used to exchange color information between image editing and page layout programs; developed by Quark; also called five-file EPS or EPS5. *See section 6.12(vii).3.*

decimal notation. The expression or encoding of a datum, such as a character, as a whole number with a predetermined value. *See section 3.3(iii).4.*

default value. As a general term, refers to an understood value where no other value is specified. In SGML, attributes can have default values expressed in a DTD; in XML documents defined by schemas, both elements and attributes can have default values.

derivative work. Content based on or derived from a pre-existing work, in which the original or some part of the original has been recast, transformed, or adapted, including new editions, abridgements, and translations; if made with the permission of the copyright owner of the original, such a work has a separate copyright, which covers only the changes and additions created by the derivative work's author. *See section 13.1(v).2.*

deskewed. The process of aligning or straightening scanned images of printed pages; such pages are usually not precisely straight due to slight variations in the mechanical process of scanning. *See section 8.2(i).1.*

desktop publishing. The process where content is designed and typeset, including adding illustrations and graphics, using a desktop computer operating standard shrink-wrapped software; traditionally these tasks were specialized trades performed by a composition or prepress company. *See section 6.3.*

despeckling. The process of removing flaws in a scanned image of a printed page that are the result of dust or other tiny defects either present in the original documents or introduced during scanning. *See section 8.2(i).1.*

dial-up. A type of connection between a computer and network using a modem for communication over normal telephone lines; so called because the communications software dials a telephone number to establish a network connection. *See section 2.6(iii).2.1.*

DIC Color System Guide. System for matching process color (CMYK) to spot color; primarily used in Japan. *See section 6.9(ii).2.3.*

digital. Usually refers to binary systems where change is expressed as one of two states, commonly ones and zeros; most modern computing technology is digital or binary. See also analog. *See section 2.2(ii).3.*

digital asset management. See DAM.

Digital Millennium Copyright Act (DCMA). Enacted by the U.S. Congress in 1998, the act specifically addresses copyright concerns in the creation and distribution of digital content (text, graphics, audio, and video/film), including prohibiting technology designed to defeat copyright protection schemes (e.g., encryption) and prohibiting the removal of copyright-related information from any work; also grants exemption from infringement liability to Internet Service Providers (ISPs) who are not actively involved in the selection of Web content and who fit certain other criteria. *See sections 13.1(viii).1, 14.12(i), 15.2(i).1.2.*

digital object identifier. See DOI.

digital rights management. See DRM.

digital talking book. A collection of files that conform to the DAISY standard and that thereby allow their content to be accessible to the blind or visually disabled persons; may consist of XML text, text and audio files, or primarily audio files. *See section 7.2(i).3.1.*

digital video disc. See DVD.

Director. Or Macromedia Director Shockwave Studio, currently in version 8.5. A software package for developing multimedia content using Macromedia's Shockwave. *See section 9.6(vi).1.*

disaggregation. The process of using content for other purposes, separate from the work in which it is originally published, such as using chapters from a book in a separate electronic format. *See section 4.3(i).2.*

disk. See compact disc, DVD, fixed disk, floppy disk, laser disk, optical disk, removable disk.

distributed computation. See grid computing.

dithering. The process of mixing pixels of nearby colors or shades of gray to present the optical illusion of colors or grayscale that are not present. *See section 6.8(ii).1.*

DMCA. See Digital Millennium Copyright Act.

DocBook. A widely used standard DTD, originally developed for technical and software documentation. *See section 3.3(ii).3.*

DOCTYPE declaration. In SGML or XML, a notation at the top of a document instance that declares the primary element of the document and the name and location of the DTD that defines the document; must be present for a document to be valid SGML or valid XML. *See section 3.3(ii).5.*

document analysis. An initial process in SGML or XML implementation of selecting the kinds of content to be described, delineating content elements, naming content elements, clarifying how elements relate, recognizing and codifying variants of elements, and determining what non-textual information (metadata) about the content elements might be useful. *See section 3.3(ii).1.*

document instance. A piece of content tagged in SGML or XML that conforms to a DTD or schema specified in a DOCTYPE declaration at the top of the document instance. *See section 3.3(ii).5.*

document management system. A system that manages files that are self-contained documents, especially on a Web site, as opposed to a content management system (CMS) that manages files that are pieces of documents or pieces of Web pages. *See section 10.2.*

document scanner. A specialized type of scanner designed for high-speed image capture of large quantities of paper documents. *See section 6.11(i).*

Document Type Definition (DTD). In SGML and XML, a declaration or formal statement of the rules that define the structure of a particular class of SGML or XML document, including the names of permitted elements, their order, and their frequency of appearance; the permitted contents of each element; the attributes, if any, of each element; and entities that may be used. See also XML schema. *See sections 3.1(ii).2, 3.3(ii).1, 3.3(ii).2, 4.2(ii), 10.4(vi).4.*

DocuTech. A monchrome sheetfed digital printing machnine, produced by Xerox since the early 1990s; current models print at speeds of 180 ppm. *See section 8.4(i).1.3.*

DOI. Digital Object Identifier. An international standard for uniquely and permanently identifying and registering any kind of content—digital or print—the DOI system provides a discovery mechanism for linking to the owner of the rights to the content, even if the ownership has changed over time, and enables that rights owner to control the target or targets of that link and any subsequent transactions; used extensively in the CrossRef linking scheme and elsewhere. *See sections 15.4(ii), 1.2(i).6.1, 1.3(i).5, 3.3(ii).2.3, 4.3(i).2, 4.5(ii).*

domain name. The top-level name of a Web resource, commonly thought of as a site, often starting with a www prefix. Major domains are .com, .org, .net, .gov, etc. *See section 4.5(iii).1.*

dot. A matrix formed of spots; the basic unit of a halftone and often used to express the refinement of resolution of a printing device or sometimes a computer screen. *See section 6.8(vi).2.*

dot gain. In printing, the phenomenon where the tone value of a halftone dot prints at a greater value, making the dot larger than intended; also called tone value increase. *See section 6.8(vi).4.*

double keying. The process of separately keying or typing content, usually from a print-only version to an electronic format, and comparing the two versions to find and correct errors. *See section 5.3(i).1.2.*

DRM. Digital Rights Management. The process of managing access to electronic content and protecting the rights of electronic content in an environment where it is easily copied. See also DOI. *See sections 7.1(v).3, 9.7(iii), 15.1, 1.2(v).2.4, 1.3(ii).3.*

drop-on-demand. A type of inkjet printing technology where droplets of ink are forced out of each nozzle on a printhead as they are needed and deposited on paper; droplets are forced out by heat (thermal drop-on-demand) or pressure (piezoelectric drop-on-demand). See also continuous-inkjet. *See section 8.2(ii).2.*

drum scanner. A scanner in which an original image is held on a cylindrical drum that is rotated in front of a stationary light source and scanning heads. Nearly all drum scanners use photo multiplier tubes (PMTs) for their optics. *See section 6.11(i).*

DS0. A designation of digital data transmission rate or circuit, DS stands for digital service and the zero indicates that it is the basic service, or 64kbps (kilobits per second). *See section 2.6(iii).2.3.*

DSL. Digital Subscriber Line. A digital WAN technology or communications circuit that operates in either a symmetric (same communication speed to and from a computer) or asymmetric mode (higher speed transmitting from a computer than to a computer). *See section 2.6(iii).2.2.*

DSSSL. The Document Style Semantics and Specification Language. A complex ISO standard for transforming and formatting SGML documents. *See section 3.3(iii).3.*

DTD. See Document Type Definition, archival DTD, reference DTD, base DTD.

DTV. Digital Television. Television that uses digital, as opposed to analog, signals; comprises a range of standards, including HDTV. *See sections 2.4(ii).5, 2.6(iii).2.2.*

Dual function scanners. Scanners that can handle both reflective (photographic prints, artwork) and transmissive (transparencies) originals. *See section 6.11(i).*

Dublin Core. See Dublin Core Metadata Initiative or Dublin Core Metadata Element Set.

Dublin Core Metadata Element Set. DCMES. A defined vocabulary of fifteen elements that describe the core metadata that can be assigned to electronic (and physical) resources, established by the Dublin Core Metadata Initiative. *See section 4.4(ii).3.1.*

Dublin Core Metadata Initiative. DCMI. A set of metadata elements that provide a semantic vocabulary for describing core information properties. *See sections 4.4(ii).1, 11.6(v).7, 12.4(v).1.3.*

DVD. Digital video disc. An optical storage medium with higher capacity than conventional CDs, originally pioneered by the entertainment industry for the distribution of motion pictures; when used for data storage or software distribution, sometimes referred to as a digital versatile disc. *See sections 15.1(ii).1, 2.5(ii).3.3.*

dynamic Web pages. A Web page where the elements of the page are stored in systems such as relational databases, and the software collects, organizes, and publishes the pages on the fly; also called dynamically served Web pages. *See section 10.1(ii).3.*

e-book. Short for electronic book. Thought of by most people as an electronic version of a printed book that is downloaded to a reading device, e-books are any type of book that can be read in electronic format, frequently with a variety of interactive digital features (searching, bookmarking, note-taking) and multimedia enhancements. E-books (the electronic content) should not be confused with e-book reading systems or devices. *See sections 1.2(iv).2, 1.3(ii).2, 11.1, 11.3(i), 11.3(ii).*

e-mail. The exchange of computer-stored messages by telecommunications, most often via the Internet. Messages are usually encoded as ASCII text, but HTML encoded messages are becoming more common. Audio, graphic, or other files can also be sent as encoded attachments. *See section 2.6(iv).2.2.*

EGA. Enhanced Graphics Adapter. Both a signaling protocol and a type of graphics adapter, which send signals that address each pixel in a computer display independently. *See section 2.4(ii).5.*

element. In SGML, HTML, and XML, a named portion of content, delimited by a specific pair of start and end tags, typically as defined in a Document Type Definition (DTD) or schema. See also attribute, empty element. *See sections 3.3(ii).2.1, 3.3(ii).2.2, 3.3(ii).2.4.*

embedded system. A computer or computing system that is built into another device, such as a GPS navigation system in a car or a environmental control system inside a refrigerator. *See section 2.3(i).4.2.*

empty element. In SGML, HTML, and XML, an element that does not itself contain content but is used as a vehicle to carry metadata in the form of attributes or to identify something outside the tagged content (such as an image). *See section 3.3(ii).2.4.*

Encapsulated PostScript (EPS). Part of Adobe's Document Structuring Convention that records data about an image, such as size and location within a page, for image files; typically optimized for vector graphics, although an EPS file can contain a bitmapped graphic such as a TIFF as well. *See section 5.5(vi).2.*

encryption. The process or practice of encoding data or content so that it can be read or used only by someone who has the correct algorithmic key. *See sections 15.1(i).5, 15.3(ii).3, 15.3(ii).4.*

entity. In SGML, HTML, and XML, a piece of digital content—text, code, image data—that is given a name and can then be referred to by that name as an alias for that content in the document instance or DTD itself. *See sections 3.3(ii).2.5, 3.3(iii).4.1.*

EPS. See Encapsulated PostScript. *See section 6.8(v).1.5.*

EPS5. See DCS. *See section 6.8(v).2.2.*

EPSI. A format for viewing a preview (a representation of what a graphic looks like) of an Encapsulated PostScript file; the format is platform independent. *See section 6.8(v).1.5.*

Ethernet. A widely used family of LAN protocols for cabled networks that allow communication between computers, developed by Xerox PARC in the 1970s. *See section 2.6(iii).1.*

EULA. End User License Agreement. A legal contract part of most software that delineates the terms under which the software producer will license the product for use by a consumer; typically, a user must agree to abide by the document during the installation process, or by opening the packaging for the software. *See sections 9.3, 9.7(iii).1, 15.2(i).5.*

extended ASCII. An 8-bit character set commonly used in computing today, which accommodates 256 possible encodings. *See section 3.3(iii).4.*

Extended OEB. In the Open eBook Publication Structure (OEBPS), a form of OEB publication that includes tags beyond those defined in the Basic Document Vocabulary, or Basic OEB; style specifications must be provided for each such tag. *See section 3.1(iii).3.*

external link. A hyperlink whose destination is outside of the document or file in which is appears, usually to a separate Web site or resource. *See sections 3.3(v), 4.5(iii).*

extradocument link. See external link.

fair use. A doctrine in copyright law that allows for the reproduction of small portions of content for various, usually culturally beneficial, purposes (e.g., criticism, news reporting, scholarly commentary, parody); quantitative rules of what is and is not fair use are scarce and none of them has the force of law; fair use depends on a variety of factors, including (but not limited to) the ratio of the use to the work as a whole, the nature of the use, and the impact of the use on the market for the original. *See section 13.1(vii).*

fallbacks. In the Open eBook Publication Structure, alternatives that must be provided for features or functions that are beyond the basic requirements of any OEB-compliant system; for example, if a video were part of an e-book, an image file in a format able to be handled by any OEB-compliant system would need to be provided as a fallback for any reading systems unable to handle the video. *See section 11.2(ii).6.*

FAPE. Free and appropriate public education. One requirement of the Individuals with Disabilities Education Act (IDEA) for local school districts in their treatment of disabled students. *See section 7.1(i).3.*

FDDI. Fiber distributed data interface. A LAN protocol developed in the 1990s to provide fast communication between computers. *See section 2.6(iii).1.*

fields. In a database table, a column that contains a specific type of data; a collection of fields comprise a record in that database. *See section 2.3(ii).2.*

file format. A unique method of organizing data for use and storage by software applications; on Windows and Unix systems, the file format is indicated by a dot and a suffix or extension, such as .doc or .jpg that normally consists of three letters, but that can be two or four letters. *See section 6.8(iii).*

file type. In the Macintosh operating system (before OS X), a four-character text string embedded within a file that identifies the type of file to the operating system, so that system knows which applications can open it; used along with creator codes. *See section 6.8(v).*

FireWire. A serial channel communications standard developed by Apple Computer; formalized by the IEEE as standard IEEE 1394. *See sections 9.6(ii), 2.6(i).2.2.*

FIRST. Flexography Image Reproduction Specifications and Tolerances. A specification designed to increase quality control across the flexography printing industry. *See section 6.13(iii).*

five-file EPS. See DCS. *See section 6.8(v).2.2.*

fixed disk. A storage device that is usually intended to be installed as a permanent part of a computer; also called a hard disk; they are normally hermetically sealed in an airtight container. *See section 2.5(ii).1.*

Flash. A software package produced by Macromedia for producing multimedia animations, primarily for the Web; also the animations produced by the software; the Flash player is freely downloadable as a plug-in for Web browsers. *See sections 9.4, 9.6(vi).1.*

flatbed scanners. Scanners that hold an original image on a glass plate parallel to the desk or table that supports the scanner and in which the light source and scanning heads move over the stationary object being scanned. *See section 6.11(i).*

floppy disk. A type of removable storage medium consisting of a semi-rigid, flexible disk housed in a cardboard or plastic sleeve. *See section 2.5(ii).2.*

Focoltone. System for specifying custom colors where the color is defined by process color ink combinations, as opposed to a specific ink formulation. *See section 6.9(ii).2.3.*

formatting objects. In XSL-FO, part of the Extensible Stylesheet Language (XSL), specific elements defined in the vocabulary of XSL-FO that are used to specify the format of a document; an XSLT stylesheet is usually used to transform a document from its original vocabulary or tagset to XSL-FO formatting objects and specific formatting instructions are associated with each resulting formatting object to specify to a rendering engine how to format the document. *See section 3.3(iii).3.1.*

FPO. For Position Only. Used to describe low-resolution graphic images used a placeholders during design or composition; FPO images are replaced with high-resolution graphics prior to printing. *See sections 6.8(v).2.1, 6.12(vii).2.*

frame relay. A type of dedicated data circuit for WAN communication that provides moderate to high-speed service over standard copper telephone cables. *See section 2.6(iii).2.2.*

Frequency Modulated (FM) screening. A halftone screening process where the spots that make up an image are kept at a constant size, but the frequency of those spots and their location is varied to prevent moiré; eliminates the need for screen angles; also called stochastic screening. *See section 6.8(vi).5.*

FTP. File Transfer Protocol. A standard Internet protocol commonly used to transfer files from a server to a client over the Internet or World Wide Web. *See sections 1.3(i).1, 2.6(iv).2.1, 4.5(iii), 4.5(iii).2.*

galleys. The first-run printout of the type set for a book or article, usually on oversize sheets, used for checking and proofing the composition of the content, but not the page makeup. Page proofs show the type in position within the final page design. *See section 6.3.*

gamut. See color gamut. *See section 6.9(ii).*

generated text. Text that is created outside of a source document and that is added to a source document depending on specific circumstances; for example, the numbers in a numbered list, might not be part of the tagged text, but added by a processing system. *See section 3.3(iii).3.1.*

GIF. Graphic Interchange Format. A relatively simple bitmap file format for graphics, popularized by CompuServe Information Service (CIS) in the 1980s; restricted to 8-bit color palettes (256 colors or less); widely used on the World Wide Web for web page graphics. *See sections 5.1(i).4.3, 5.5(vi).1, 6.8(iii).1, 12.4(iii).1.4.*

glyph. A unique character shape or a graphic representation of a character. *See sections 3.3(ii).2.5, 6.7(i).4.*

GML. The Generic Markup Language. A forerunner of SGML, HTML, and XML, among other markup languages, it established the fundamental principles of markup languages; first developed in 1969. *See section 3.1(ii).1.*

GPIB. General Purpose Interface Bus. A communications channel used for connecting a computer to more complex instruments (e.g., motors, medical equipment, data collection instruments); standardized as IEEE 488. *See section 2.6(i).2.6.*

granularity. Term used to denote the level or density at which markup or tagging is applied to content; low granularity implies tagging of major elements only, high granularity implies tagging of many discrete elements and components of elements that constitute the content, often hierarchically nested. *See sections 3.3(ii).1.2, 4.2(ii).3.*

graphics. An element or aspect of a page of content; a representation of an illustration or photograph contained in one of several graphic file formats. See also TIFF, GIF, JPEG, EPS. *See section 6.2.*

gray balance. A criteria for good color reproduction, the ability to reproduce the neutral gray of an original image as a perfect neutral gray by balancing the proportions of cyan, magenta, and yellow in a color separation. *See section 6.9(iii).1.*

grayscale. A bitmap image or display where cells or pixels contain a range of values (i.e., several bits of data for each pixel), resulting in a brightness scale or shades of gray. *See sections 8.2(i).1, 8.4(ii).1.7, 2.4(i).3, 6.8(vi).2.*

grid computing. An approach to computing in which different computers are connected via a network and set to work on the same task or parts of an overall task, also called distributed computation. *See section 2.3(i).4.1.*

GUI. Graphical User Interface. An interface with a computer that allows interaction with a computer in a visual, graphic environment. *See sections 9.3(iv), 2.3(i).2.*

Guide. In the Open eBook Publication Structure (OEBPS), an optional list of files that contain fundamental structural components of the publication, such as table of contents, bibliography, and indexes. *See section 11.6(vi).1.6.*

halftone. An image that has been processed to mimic the continuous tone of an illustration in print by converting it to a matrix of variably sized or shaded dots, or dots with various degrees of color. *See section 8.2(iii).4.*

halftone images. Illustrations or photographs processed with special cameras or scanners to produce an image consisting of a matrix of variably light sized and shaded dots for use in composition copy. *See section 6.3.*

halftoning. A process to allow printing devices to mimic the continuous tone appearance of drawings, paintings, and photographs by representing the images as a range of dots with grayscale or color variations that can be printed or displayed on a screen. *See section 6.8(vi).*

hard disk. See fixed disk. *See section 2.5(ii).1.*

HDTV. High Definition (digital) Television. A digital television standard that uses digital, as opposed to analog, signals to transmit video images to a television. *See section 2.4(ii).5.*

Hexachrome. A Pantone high-fidelity color scheme that uses a six-color process in color reproduction that can achieve a larger color gamut than conventional four-color separations. *See section 6.9(ii).3.*

hexadecimal notation. The expression of a numeric value using base 16, a numbering system of sixteen digits, 0 through 9 and A through F (compared to decimal notation's ten digits, 0 through 9). *See section 3.3(iii).4.*

HiFi Color Project. Established in 1992 to advance the use of high-fidelity color processes for critical and accurate color reproduction. *See section 6.9(ii).3.*

high-fidelity color. Various processes of reproduction of images using more than four colors to achieve a better result than the four-color process. *See section 6.9(ii).3.*

hints. In PostScript using Type 1 fonts, hints maintain the look of type when printing below 600 dpi and in type below 14 point, including making sure all the letters line up, creating visually accurate curves and strokes, and adjusting overall quality. *See section 6.7(i).1.*

host. A computer linked to a network; sometimes called a network node. *See section 2.6(ii).2.*

HTML. The HyperText Markup Language. A fixed set of tags designed to mark up content such that a Web browser can format and display it and execute links. See also XHTML. *See sections 1.2(i), 3.1(i), 3.1(ii).3, 3.3(i), 3.3(i).5, 3.3(ii).1.3, 4.5(iii).1, 5.3(iii).3.*

HTML proofing. A process where content/text is converted to HTML and made available on-line for author proofing, usually between copyediting and typesetting. *See section 4.2(i).3.*

HTTP. HyperText Transfer Protocol. A standard Internet protocol for the transfer of displayable Web pages and related files. *See sections 1.2(i), 3.2, 4.5(iii).1.*

hub. A central point or device on a LAN, linked by cable to other computers or nodes. *See section 2.6(iii).1.*

hue error. Anomalies in the pigments of printing inks due to color contamination by other colors used in the color reproduction process. *See section 6.9(iii).4.*

HyperCard. A comprehensive package of tools hyperlinking text and multimedia content. The last version was 2.4.1 and has not been updated for years; does not run under Windows or Mac OS X. An up-to-date alternative is Revolution, which supports XML, Unicode, and multimedia features. *See section 9.3(iii).1.*

hypertext. A system of interconnecting, or linking, text, devised in the 1960s; the retrieval of documents over the World Wide Web is achieved by using the hypertext transfer protocol (HTTP). *See sections 2.6(iv).2.2, 11.3(iii).7.*

HyTime. An early SGML/HTML standard developed for multimedia and hypermedia use. *See section 3.3(v).1.*

I/O device. Input/Output device. Any device attached to a computer for inputting (e.g., keyboard, mouse) or outputting (e.g., printer, audio speakers) data or information. *See section 2.2(ii).2.*

ICC profile. A standard description of the characteristics and performance of color-imaging hardware and software for input and output devices, developed by the International Color Consortium. *See section 6.9(v).1.1.*

ICE. See Information and Content Exchange. *See sections 15.4(iii), 1.2(vii).1, 6.12.5.*

ICM. Integrated Color Management. Color management system for Microsoft operating systems; supports ICC profile standard. *See section 6.9(v).3.*

IDEA. Individuals with Disabilities Education Act. Federal law that mandates all local school districts must provide disabled students with a free and appropriate public education (FAPE) in the least restrictive environment (LRE). *See sections 7.1, 7.1(i).3.*

identifiers. In text, structural identifiers include explicit identifiers such as headings and subheadings as well as specific call-outs for tables, illustrations, or graphics; implicit identifiers include call-outs or citations to other parts of the text without specifically pointing to them by name or number (e.g., "see table above"); in bibliographic citations in text, a number that links the citation to the reference in the bibliography or to an external reference source. *See sections 5.2(ii), 5.5(viii).*

IDF. International DOI Foundation. Group established in 1998 by the intellectual property community to develop and promote the Digital Object Identifier (DOI) as a content management and rights management infrastructure. *See section 15.4(ii).*

ILL. See interlibrary loan.

IMAA. See Instructional Materials Accessibility Act.

IMAP. Internet Messaging Protocol. A standard protocol for retrieving e-mail from a remote computer. *See section 2.6(iv).2.2.*

imposition. The arrangement of the pages on a large press sheet so that when that sheet is folded into a signature, the pages read consecutively and are right-side-up. *See section 6.3.*

<indecs>2RDD. Interoperability of Data in e-Commerce Systems, Rights Data Dictionary. A DRM standard under development by a consortium founded by the International DOI Foundation (IDF) and EDItEUR that is intended to be a comprehensive rights metadata description dictionary encompassing all possible instances of rights metadata language for commercial use. *See section 15.4(iv).3.*

Information and Content Exchange (ICE). An XML standard largely used in syndication, promoted by IDEAlliance. *See sections 3.3(i).3, 10.4(viii).*

information architecture. Term encompassing the intellectual and creative disciplines behind making on-line material more useful and readable; including many Web-specific issues such as linking, navigation, and personalization, along with more traditional disciplines such as graphic design, indexing, and editing. *See section 10.1(ii).1.6.*

inheritance mechanisms. In XML, elements whose definitions depend on the status or values or definitions of other elements. *See section 3.3(ii).4.1.*

Instructional Materials Accessibility Act (IMAA). Proposed Federal legislation intended to improve access to printed instructional materials used by elementary and secondary school students who are blind, as well as other students who have print disabilities. *See section 7.2(i).1.2.*

integrated circuit. An aggregation of transistors, usually mounted on a chip; a computer chip. *See section 2.2(i).1.*

intent to use. In trademark law, a type of registration with the U.S. Patent and Trademark Office that reserves a trademark before that trademark is actually put into public use. *See section 13.2(iii).1.*

interactive multimedia. Term used interchangeably with multimedia; describes text-based publications that are enhanced with audio and video. *See section 9.2(i).*

interfaces. Connection points between layers of an operating system, or between computing and/or telecommunications devices. *See section 2.3(i).*

interlibrary loan. A system of circulation between libraries in which content (whether physical, such as books, or digital) is shared among them, allowing a client of one library to borrow material owned by another library. *See section 13.5(ii).1.*

internal link. A hyperlink whose destination is within the same document or file; also called intradocument link. *See sections 3.3(v), 4.5(i).*

Internet. A network of computer networks, evolved from the ARPAnet; a variety of different data-transfer protocols support various uses (e-mail, FTP, etc.); the HTTP protocol provides for transmission of the data that makes up the World Wide Web. *See sections 1.3(i).1, 2.6(iv).1.*

Intradocument links. See internal link.

ISDN. Integrated Services Digital Network. A digital WAN technology for connecting computers; operates at two speeds: the Basic Rate Interface (BRI) and the higher-speed Primary Rate Interface (PRI). *See section 2.6(iii).2.2.*

ISO. Short form of the name of the International Organization for Standardization, an international federation of the national standards bodies from 140 countries; ISO is not an acronym, but from the Greek word *isos* meaning equal, and thus is the same in all languages. *See sections 9.6(iii).3, 3.1(ii).2.*

ISO 12083. An international standard set of general reference DTDs for articles, books, serials, and math used for electronic markup, primarily in SGML. *See section 3.1(ii).2.*

ISO 8859. An international standard that expresses a common extended ASCII (8-bit) character set for differing platforms. *See section 3.3(iii).4.*

ISO value. The sensitivity of a digital camera to various light conditions; analogous to photographic film sensitivity or speed, expressed as an ISO value—typically 100 to 800—for non-commercial cameras; in general, the greater the film speed or ISO value, the less ambient light needed to register a reasonable image. *See section 6.11(ii).3.*

ISP. Internet Service Provider. A company that sells connectivity services to business or consumer markets and provides individuals access, via dial-up or a dedicated connection (cable modem, DSL, etc.) to the Internet and Web, usually also providing services such as e-mail. *See section 14.2(ii).*

Java Server Pages. A programming mechanism for creating and serving dynamic Web pages; generally more efficient and easier to create than CGI, allowing developers to freely mix HTML, scripts, and other programs that could perform discrete, specialized functions, such as querying a database and displaying the results; abbreviated and most commonly used as JSP. *See section 10.1(ii).3.1.*

JDF. Job Definition Format. An open, extensible, XML-based print workflow specification that carries a print job from creation to completion. *See sections 1.3(ii).6, 6.12.2.*

JMF. Job Messaging Format. A subset of the Job Description Format (JDF) that handles communications among print MIS systems, computerized workflow control systems, and prepress, press, and post-press equipment. *See section 6.12.2.*

JPEG. Joint Photographic Experts Group. A graphic file format with a compression scheme to minimize the size of graphics files using full-color images (24-bit color) of near-photographic quality; commonly used on the World Wide Web. *See sections 5.1(i).4.3, 5.5(vi).1, 5.5(vi).1, 6.8(iii).1, 6.8(v).1.3, 12.4(iii).1.4.*

JSP. See Java Server Pages.

kernel. The central core piece of an operating system in a computer, containing the most fundamental operating elements. *See section 2.3(i).*

kerning. The selective addition or subtraction of space between individual pairs of letters and between words to make type look better visually. *See section 6.7(v).3.3.*

LAN. Local Area Network. A network of computers where the computers are physically located close to one another. *See section 2.6(ii).2.*

laser disk. Alternate term for an optical disk, so named because lasers are used to read and write information to the disk. *See section 2.5(ii).3.*

LCD. Liquid Crystal Display. A type of display screen, such as a computer monitor or television; semiconductor devices that consist of liquid crystals that either pass or block light through polarization. *See sections 1.3(iii).4, 2.4(ii), 2.4(ii).2.*

LDAP. Lightweight directory access protocol. A protocol for locating and retrieving entries in a phone directory. *See section 2.6(iv).2.2.*

LED. Light-emitting diode. The diode consists of a "bulb" and two wires; the bulb (clear, and often colored) contains a semi-conductor chip with each half holding a positive or negative charge; when energy is applied in the form of electricity, the chip will glow. Most LEDs operate with very low voltage and current. *See section 8.2(ii).1.*

letterspacing. The addition or subtraction of space between letters (usually uniformly to a whole line of type, as opposed to kerning, which applied to individual pairs of letters) to adjust the look; usually used in display type, but some page layout programs add letterspacing to text when a line is justified. *See section 6.7(v).3.2.*

license. In copyright, the transfer of any exclusive right protected by copyright, or the granting of a non-exclusive right by the copyright holder to one or multiple persons. *See section 13.1(vi).*

Lingo. A multimedia programming language of the Macromedia Director authoring software. *See section 9.6(vi).1.*

linkbases. Collections of links (generally using XLink and XPointer), and information about those links, that are maintained outside the documents being linked. *See section 3.3(v).1.*

Linux. A version of the Unix operating system developed by Linus Torvalds in the early 1990s. *See sections 15.2(i).5, 2.3(i).1.*

Lisa. The name of the first Apple workstation and considered the first commercially successful computer to employ a graphical user interface (GUI). *See section 2.3(i).2.*

LocalTalk. A network data access protocol for Apple computers. *See section 2.6(iv).1.*

lossless. A file compression technique where no data is lost or removed during compression. *See section 6.8(iv).*

lossy. A file compression technique where data is lost or removed during compression; the more highly compressed such a file is, the more data is lost. *See sections 9.6(iii).3, 9.6(ix), 6.8(iv).*

lpi. lines per inch. A measure of the size of a halftone screen or its resolution; the higher the lpi, the more refined the resulting halftone. *See section 6.8(vi).1.*

LRE. Least restrictive environment. One requirement of the Individuals with Disabilities Education Act (IDEA) for local school districts in their treatment of disabled students; defined in the Act as: To the maximum extent appropriate, children with disabilities, including children in public or private institutions or other care facilities, are [1] educated with children who are not disabled, and [2] special classes, separate schooling, or other removal of children with disabilities from the regular educational environment occurs only when the nature or severity of the disability of a child is such that education in regular classes with the use of supplementary aids and services cannot be achieved satisfactorily. *See section 7.1(i).3.*

Mac OS. The name of the operating system for the Apple Macintosh computers. *See section 2.3(i).2.*

Machine-Readable Cataloging (MARC). A metadata vocabulary and data format for encoding bibliographic data for search and retrieval over the Internet; developed by the U.S. Library of Congress. *See section 4.4(ii).2.*

Macintosh. One of the first affordable commercial computers designed for desktop use and employing a graphical user interface; developed by Apple and introduced in 1984. *See sections 9.6(i), 2.3(i).2.*

macro. A small file that lists and executes step-by-step instructions that make it possible to automate what an operator might do manually; normally associated with specific software. *See section 3.3(iv).2.*

MARC. See Machine-Readable Cataloging.

markup language. A syntax, or a syntax and a vocabulary (a tagset designed to be used with that syntax), that enables the various parts and features of a given set of content, and the relationships between them, to be distinguished and named, providing a way to label, describe, and delimit these in a publication so that processing systems can tell them apart and know how they relate to each other. Markup languages are used to define specific markup schemes or tagsets. *See sections 7.1(iv), 7.1(v), 3.1, 3.2, 3.3, 4.2, 5.1, 11.6, 12.4(iii).1.2.*

MathML. The Mathematical Markup Language. An XML-based scheme for marking up mathematics, accommodating both presentational and syntactical features; an official W3C Recommendation. *See sections 3.3(i).3, 5.1(i).4.3, 5.5(x).*

MEP. Model Editions Partnership. Developed by a consortium of twelve editorial projects and demonstrating a use of TEI for a specific purpose, the markup of historical documents, it consists of three specific, stable DTDs that are TEI compliant *See section 3.3(ii).3.3.*

metadata. Commonly defined as data about data or information about data. In markup languages and other processing environments, metadata is information that is carried along with or linked to content or data that describes or defines something about that content and allows for more robust use and processing; typically used to define such elements as keywords, authors, identifiers, creation or modification dates; useful in organizing, managing, and searching content. *See sections 3.2(i).1, 3.3(ii).2.3, 3.3(vi), 4.4(i), 11.6(vi).1.2.*

metadata vocabulary. A defined set of metadata elements which are significant to a community of metadata users; examples are the Dublin Core Metadata Initiative, Congress's Machine-Readable Cataloging (MARC), and On-line Information Exchange (ONIX). *See section 4.4(ii).*

metalanguage. In markup, a syntactical system for the creation of markup languages, tagsets, or schemes for specific purposes or specific types of content. *See section 3.3(i).1.*

Microsoft Media Technology. Or Windows Media; a set of digital media components or software packages for creating and playing multimedia in the Windows OS. *See section 9.6(iii).1.*

MIDI. Musical Instrument Digital Interface. A protocol designed for recording and playing back music on digital musical instruments and many PC sound cards; a MIDI file only represents information about the sounds and is far more concise than the sound data itself. Its advantage is very small file size; its disadvantage is a lack of specific sound control. *See sections 9.3(i).2, 9.6(vi).*

modem. A device that converts either digital signals from a computer into analog waveforms for transmission over telephone lines or analog wave forms from a telephone line into digital signals for transmission to a computer; stands for modulation/demodulation. *See section 2.6(iii).2.1.*

moiré. An irregular wavy pattern that can appear in a halftone image. *See section 6.8(vi).3.2.*

monochrome. A pure bitmap where cells contain either a one or zero (i.e., where pixels are either all black or all white) without any shading or intermediate brightness. *See section 2.4(i).3.*

moral rights. A legal doctrine common to Berne Convention countries that includes the right of attribution (the right to have one's authorship of content acknowledged and correctly attributed) and the right of integrity (the right not to have one's work or content distorted or mutilated); U.S. law on this subject is partly in the Copyright Act and partly in other statutes, and satisfies the bare minimum standard required of Berne countries. *See section 13.3(ii).2.1.*

Mosaic. A GUI-based program developed in 1993 for navigating and viewing text and graphics over the Internet; the first Web browser. *See section 2.6(iv).2.2.*

mouse. An input device for a computer that allows users to point at visual objects on a computer screen and thereby activate or manipulate the activity of the computer; a pointing device. *See section 2.3(i).2.*

MP3. MPEG-1 Audio Layer 3. A technology that produces near CD quality music in a compressed file (ratios of 10:1 to 12:1) that can be tranferred over networks quickly and played on any PC with the MP3 software or on a dedicated MP3 player. MP3 is a lossy compression. *See section 9.6(iii).3.*

MPEG. Moving Pictures Experts Group. Named after a working group of the ISO/IEC that is in charge of the development of standards for coded representation of digital audio and video; note that the "M" stands for "moving" not "motion" and refers to all sorts of moving images, not to the motion picture industry. *See section 9.6(ix).*

MTBF. Mean time between failures. A measure of the reliability of digital storage media, such as disk drives. *See section 2.5(ii).*

Multimedia. Term that describes text-based content that is enhanced with audio or video; also interactive multimedia. *See section 11.2(ii).6.*

Multiple Master. A type of font technology introduced by Adobe Systems in 1991 that allows users to create additional fonts from two or more master designs within a single typeface family by varying things like x-height, width, and stroke thickness; Adobe stopped making new Multiple Master fonts in 1999. *See section 6.7(i).3.*

multiprocessor. A computer where individual processors (chips) are linked to work together, to increase computing speed and power, using a technique called parallel processing. *See section 2.3(i).4.1.*

namespace. In XML, a specification that allows a given XML document to use tags that have been created for other unrelated documents and defined in other DTDs or schemas; Namespaces in XML is an official W3C Recommendation. *See sections 3.3(ii).6, 4.5(iv), 11.2(ii).8, 11.6(v).4.*

NCAC. National Center on Accessing the General Curriculum. *See section 7.2(iii).1.*

NewsML. An XML-based scheme used by newspaper publishers. *See sections 1.2(vii).1, 3.3(i).3.*

NISO. National Information Standards Organization. A non-profit, ANSI-accredited organization that develops and publishes technical standards for information technology and management. *See section 7.2(i).3.*

NISO Z39.86. The NISO standard for the DAISY consortium's Talking Book. *See section 11.2(ii).10.*

node. In networking, a computer on a network connected to a central computer or hub; in XML, a point in an XML tree structure where one element branches off from another. *See sections 2.6(iii).1, 3.3(iv).4.*

NT. Short for Windows NT; an operating system; see Windows. *See section 2.3(i).3.*

NTSC. U.S. standard for television signals, named for the National Television Standards Committee; the corresponding European standard is PAL. *See section 2.4(ii).5.*

OAI-PMH. The Open Archives Initiative Protocol for Metadata Harvesting. A standard based on the Dublin Core metadata set for interoperability in the distribution of XML-based metadata. *See section 12.4(v).1.4.*

OAIS. The Open Archival Information System. A reference model and ISO standard that provides a structure for access to and preservation of archived content. *See section 12.4(v).1.2.*

OASIS. Organization for the Advancement of Structured Information Standards. A consortium, founded in 1993 as SGMLOpen, a trade association, that supports the development and adoption of worldwide standards for a wide range of electronic publishing and e-business activities, including XML and related technologies. *See section 15.4(i).*

object-oriented graphics. See vector graphics. *See section 6.8(ii).2.*

OC. A designation of transmission speeds by an optical carrier on a fiber optic cable; the basic OC circuit handles a transmission speed of 51.84Mbps (mega bits per second) *See section 2.6(iii).2.3.*

OCR. Optical character recognition. A process, and a type of software, in which a bitmap image of a printed document (usually captured by a scanner) is converted to text; the individual characters of text are recognized by their graphic shape and stored in a text file; a method of digitizing printed text. *See sections 8.2(i).1, 15.2(i).1.2, 5.3(i).1.3.*

ODRL. The Open Digital Rights Language. An XML-compliant markup language for managing digital rights, similar to XrML. *See section 15.4(iv).1.*

OEBPS. Open eBook Publication Structure. An XML-based specification for the content, structure, and presentation of electronic books; consists of specifications for e-book content as OEBPS Publications and OEBPS Documents and e-book processors as OEBPS Reading Systems *See sections 1.2(iv).2, 3.1(iii).3, 3.3(i).3, 11.1, 11.2(i).1, 11.2(i).6.*

OEBPS Document. An XML document that conforms to the standard of the OEB Publication Structure (OEBPS); can be either Basic (a document that conforms to the Basic Document Vocabulary) or Extended OEB (a document that includes tags beyond the basic set, yet still conforms to the specification). *See sections 11.6(iii).1, 11.6(iii).3.*

OEBPS Package. An XML file that describes an OEBPS Publication; it identifies all the other files that make up a publication and provides information about them. *See sections 11.6(iii).1, 11.6(iii).2.*

OEBPS Publication. A collection of OEBPS Documents, OEBPS Package files, and other files that together constitute a complete publication. *See section 11.2(ii).7.*

ONIX. See Online Information Exchange.

Online Information Exchange (ONIX). A metadata vocabulary and standard used to encode supply-chain metadata when this is being transmitted between publishers, wholesalers, and retailers; developed by EDItEUR, a European group, and maintained and administered in association with the U.S. Book Industry Study Group (BISG) and the British BIC (Book Industry Communication). *See sections 3.3(i).3, 4.4(ii).2, 12.4(v).1.1.*

Open eBook Forum. OeBF. An international trade and standards organization; members consist of companies and people from all areas of the publishing industry; the OeBF is responsible for developing the Open eBook Publication Standard (OEBPS); successor to the Open eBook Initiative. *See sections 11.2(i).3, 11.6(i).2.*

Open eBook Initiative. Forerunner of the Open eBook Forum (OeBF); organization that developed the OEBPS. *See section 11.6(i).2.*

Open Prepress Interface (OPI). A server and prepress production tool that permits use of low-resolution copies of high-resolution images to facilitate workflow, by speeding the transmission of images over a network; high-resolution images are stored on a server while the low-resolution copies are used for FPO purposes in page layout and design programs. *See section 6.12(vii).2.*

open source. Software code that is distributed freely, and that can often be downloaded from the Internet and used or modified without any cost or license. *See sections 3.3(iv).2, 3.3(vi).2.*

OpenType. A new standard for digital type fonts, developed jointly by Adobe and Microsoft, unifying the competing formats of TrueType and Type 1 fonts (including Multiple Masters); uses the Unicode standard for character encoding. *See sections 6.7(i), 6.7(i).4.*

OpenURL. A tagging standard for including metadata in URLs in order to make links. *See section 4.5(ii).1.*

operating system. A program, or group of programs, that form the basic instructions that allow a computer to function. *See sections 2.3, 2.3(i), 2.3(i).2, 2.3(i).3.*

OPI. See Open Prepress Interface (OPI). *See section 6.8(v).2.1.*

optical disk. A storage medium on which data is encoded by modulating an optical property, typically the reflectivity of light from a low-power infrared laser. See also Compact Disc, DVD, and laser disk. *See sections 2.5(i).2, 2.5(ii).3.*

OS. See operating system.

OS X. Fully, Mac OS X; an operating system for Apple Macintosh released in 1999 and based on Unix. *See section 2.3(i).2.*

OSI. Open Systems Interconnection. A standard model for a protocol stack, or layers of protocols for network communication; the OSI model has seven layers. *See section 2.6(iv).*

packet. A segment of information or data transmitted over the network as a collection of bytes that has an enclosing structure containing control data and the information being transmitted. *See section 2.6(ii).1.*

page description language (PDL). A programming language to describe the size, colors, layout, positioning, relationships, and other aspects of the elements of a page—text, graphics, and page geometry; the underlying concept of PostScript. *See section 6.5.*

page layout geometry. An aspect of a page of content that describes the relationship between textual and graphical elements. *See section 6.2.*

PAL. European standard for television signals; stands for phase alternating lines; corresponding U.S. standard is NTSC. *See section 2.4(ii).5.*

Pantone color. See spot color.

Pantone Matching System (PMS). System invented by Lawrence Herbert that identifies each of thousands of spot colors with a specific Pantone color name and/or number and provides the exact ink formula to achieve consistency of color regardless of the printer. *See section 6.9(ii).2.3.*

Pantone Process Guide. System for naming and formulating spot color where color is defined by process color ink combinations, as opposed to specific ink formulas. *See section 6.9(ii).2.3.*

Pantone Solid to Process Guide. System for matching process colors to closest standard Pantone Matching System colors *See section 6.9(ii).2.3.*

parallel. A communications channel in which more than one bit may be transmitted at a time; parallel channels typically move data at a faster rate than serial channels, but also require more wires, connectors, and use more power. *See section 2.6(i).1.2.*

parallel processing. A technique to distribute computing tasks among individual processors (chips) in a multiprocessor computer. *See section 2.3(i).4.1.*

parser. A software program that reads a tagged (generally SGML, HTML, or XML) document, analyzes it against the specified DTD or schema, and flags or reports any aspects of the document that violate the given document definition and rules. *See sections 3.3(ii).2.6, 4.2(ii), 10.4(vi).4.*

PBX. Private Branch Exchange. A digital telephone system typically used by corporations and other businesses, as opposed to traditional analog telephone service. *See section 2.6(iii).2.1.*

PCL. Printer Control Language. A page description language used by many Hewlett-Packard printers. *See sections 8.2(i).2, 6.5(i).*

PCX. A bitmapped graphic file format developed by Zsoft for their PC Paintbrush program in the early 1980s. *See sections 5.5(vi).1, 5.5(vi).1.*

PDA. Personal Digital Assistant. A type of small (usually hand-held) portable computer, used for simple tasks such as making notes, or as an organizer or scheduler, usually with limited multimedia capabilities. There are two primary competing systems: Windows Pocket PC and Palm OS. As they are integrated with global positioning systems (GPS) and wireless telephones, new types of uses are starting to emerge, including enhanced multimedia, Web use, and location-based services. *See sections 1.1(i), 2.3(i).4.2, 5.3(iii).1, 9.6(i), 15.1(iii).1.*

PDF. Portable Document Format. A file format for representing the visual aspects of pages, and vor certain other information about hose pages, independently of the software, hardware, and operating system used to create them and also independently of the output device on which they're to be displayed or printed. Created and maintained by Adobe Systems. *See sections 1.1(i), 1.3(i).4, 3.1(iii), 5.3(iii).1, 6.6, 6.8(v).1.7, 7.2(i).4, 8.2(i), 8.2(i).2, 8.4(ii), 11.5(iii).2.2, 12.4(iii).1.1.*

PDF/X. A file format specification based closely on PDF and designed specifically for file exchange in the graphic arts. *See sections 1.2(vii).1, 6.12.5.*

peer-to-peer. A type of network service that is an evolved version of the client/server model where both client components and server components are built into a single piece of software; examples of peer-to-peer services are Napster, Gnutella, etc. *See section 2.6(ii).1.*

Perl. An open source scripting language for processing and manipulating text and text-oriented tagging. See also Python. *See section 3.3(iv).2.*

permission. A type of non-exclusive license, typically involving the right to reproduce a portion of a work or piece of content in another publication, a fairly routine part of licensing. *See section 13.1(vi).5.*

pica. Originally a type size roughly equal to a 12-point setting; today it is the basic measurement of type, with 6 picas to an inch. *See section 6.7.*

PICT. A metafile graphic file format based on the QuickDraw graphics language for Apple computers; the oldest generic file format for Macintosh; PICT2 is a more robust version that comes in a 24-bit (16.7 million color) version and a more common 8-bit (256 color) version. *See section 6.8(v).1.4.*

pixel. Short form meaning "picture element," a single point in a matrix that makes up a computer display or image file. *See sections 2.4(i).2, 6.8(vi).2.*

pixel depth. See color depth.

pixels per inch (ppi). An expression of digital continuous tone image resolution, whether grayscale or RGB. *See section 6.8(vi).2.*

PMTs. Photomultiplier tube. A type of scanner sensor; used exclusively in drum scanners. *See section 6.11(iii).*

POD. Print on demand or printing on demand. Type of printing where a copy (page, article, or book) is produced for a specific user, such as a book for a customer in a bookstore or a maintenance manual for an airliner when it's delivered. *See sections 1.2(iv).1, 8.3(ii), 8.3(ii).1.*

point size. A fixed number denoting the size in which the characters are rendered (from the top of the highest elements to the bottom of the lowest) in a given setting of a given typeface; an absolute, rather than a relative, measurement based on twelve points per pica. *See section 6.7(v).2.*

point-to-point. A network topology most often used on wide area networks (WANs) to connect two hosts. *See section 2.6(ii).2.*

POP. Post Office Protocol. A standard Internet protocol for retrieving e-mail from a host computer. *See section 2.6(iv).2.2.*

portal software. The software that controls the presentation and delivery of Web site content and applications to the end user. See also application servers. *See section 10.1(ii).3.3.*

POSIX. A variation of the Unix operating system issued as a NIST/IEEE standard in the late 1980s to reconcile differences between System V and BSD. *See section 2.3(i).1.*

PostScript. A programming language (specifically, a page description language) designed for the rendering of graphics, text, and pages; developed in the early and mid-1980s by Adobe Systems, Inc.; now widely used; see also Encapsulated PostScript. *See sections 1.2(ii).1, 3.1(iii), 6.4, 8.2(i), 8.2(i).2, 8.4(i).1.3, 8.4(ii), 11.5(iii).2.2.*

POTS. Plain Old Telephone Service. Analog telephone service, used with a modem for connecting computers over a WAN. *See section 2.6(iii).2.1.*

PPML. Personalized Print Markup Language. Developed by the Print on Demand Initiative, it is an XML-based print language designed to make it faster to print documents that have reusable content, specifically for digital printing. *See section 6.12.4.*

preflight. A structured series of tests a page layout file and its associated files must pass before entering image workflow; used to identify problems, aid solutions, and improve scheduling of the prepress and printing process. *See section 6.12(x).*

preproofs. Printing proofs used during the design and prepress production process to provide feedback on the progress of the job, such as type, page layout, and placement of graphics; such proofs do not usually need high-quality color or graphic reproduction; also called galleys or page proofs and typically printed on laser or desktop printers or viewed on computer monitors. *See section 6.9(iv).1.*

PRI. Primary Rate Interface. One of the two speeds at which an ISDN communications line operates; faster than the less costly Basic Rate Interface (BRI). *See section 2.6(iii).2.2.*

print-on-demand. See POD. *See section 12.1(i).2.1.*

printer font. A type of font designed to be contained in a computer file, either in computer memory or directly in printer memory, for printing, as opposed to screen fonts used for screen display; mostly found in Type 1 fonts, later font schemes simplified font handling by eliminating the dual-font approach. *See section 6.7(ii).*

PrintTalk. An XML standard that provides a single format for printers to collaboratively communicate business transactions and print specifications with their buyers and among themselves; also the name of the organization that developed the standard. *See section 6.12.3.*

PRISM. Publishing Requirements for Industry Standards Metadata. An XML metadata specification and metadata vocabulary for the exchange and preservation of digital content; primarily oriented to periodicals. *See sections 15.4(iv).2, 6.12.5.*

process color. See CMYK.

processing environment. An array of programs collaborating to make a computer function. *See section 2.2(i).1.*

production server. A Web server that contains the final "published" pages of a Web site and that is actively served to the public. See also staging server. *See section 10.3(iii).*

program. A set of instructions for a computer that are executed in groups, enabling productive functionality. Most programs include a user interface, usually a GUI, for ease of use. *See section 2.2(i).1.*

protocol. A rule or standard for communication on a circuit. *See sections 2.2(i).4, 2.6(iv).*

public domain. The body of material, some of it formerly protected by copyright (or patent, etc.), that is free for anyone to use. *See section 13.1(ii).9.2.*

Publication Structure Working Group (PSWG). A working group of the Open eBook Forum, formed in May 2000, and charged with "maintaining and advancing" the Open eBook Publication Structure (OEBPS). *See section 11.6(i).3.*

Python. An open source scripting language for processing and manipulating text and text-oriented tagging. See also Perl. *See section 3.3(iv).2.*

QTVR. QuickTime VR (virtual reality). An imaging technology used to show panorama shots of locations or video or rotating objects; based on Apple's QuickTime technology. *See sections 9.3(i).1, 9.6(ii).*

query. The process of retrieving information from a database through a database management system; a query specifies the source of the data, the type of data, and any constraints; also the expression used in such identification and retrieval. *See section 2.3(ii).2.*

query language. A standard method of creating and refining a query through which data is retrieved from a database. *See section 2.3(ii).2.*

QuickTime. A popular multimedia technology, developed by Apple and available for both Macintosh and Windows platforms; it supports most of the currently used CODECs for audio and video. *See section 9.6(iii).1.*

RAID. Redundant array of independent disks. A disk storage system that utilizes extra disk drives on a stand-by basis to eliminate data loss due to a failure of any single disk. *See section 2.5(ii).*

RAM. See random access memory.

random access memory. Also RAM. A type of computer memory where each of its storage locations can be accessed (addressed) directly rather than in a specific sequence, providing for more efficient and faster retrieval of stored data. *See section 2.2(i).1.*

raster. In general use, a type of graphic or image file that consists of a matrix of pixels (also called a bitmap), as opposed to a vector file, which stores images as mathematical equations; technically, a horizontal line of such image data to be rendered or as rendered on a monitor (computer or television). *See sections 2.4(i).1, 5.5(vi), 6.8(ii).*

Reading Device. In the Open eBook Publication Structure, the physical platform (the hardware and software) on which an electronic publication is rendered. See also Reading System. *See sections 11.2(ii).4, 11.6(iii).8.*

Reading System. In the Open eBook Publication Structure (OEBPS), a combination of hardware and/or software that accepts OEBPS Publications and makes them available to readers; may be a single device or may be split among several computers. See also Reading Device. *See sections 11.2(ii).4, 11.6(iii).7.*

Real Media. A market-leading technology to deliver multimedia content over the Internet and Web; compatible with QuickTime and Microsoft Media Technology, it focuses exclusively on on-line delivery and also offers content as subscription services. *See section 9.6(iii).1.*

Recommendations. A designation of the World Wide Web Consortium (W3C) for a technology standard that has achieved, after a series of publication, comment, and revision rounds, consensus among the group's more-than 500 member organizations; the designation is a sign that the technology is considered stable and reliable. *See section 3.1(iii).2.*

record. In a database table, a row of information that contains different fields pertaining to an item. *See section 2.3(ii).2.*

Red Sage. Fully, the Red Sage Electronic Journal Project. A pioneering effort to implement electronic journal publishing; a collaboration between the University of California, San Francisco; AT&T Bell Laboratories; and Springer-Verlag. *See section 1.2(i).3.*

reference DTD. A Document Type Definition that encompasses a broad range of possible document instances; often characterized by rich structure and generic tag names to accommodate a variety of documents and users; usually publicly available and designed to facilitate interchange between unrelated parties. *See sections 3.3(ii).3, 4.2(ii).2.*

reference linking. The process of linking citations in electronic content to the cited items, usually a direct link to the content of the item or its publisher. *See section 4.5(v).1.*

reference resolver. An application that resolves an incoming query to its proper target reference and returns an identifier from a database to the user. *See section 4.5(v).1.2.*

reflective scanner. A scanner that handles photographic prints and original artwork. *See section 6.11(i).*

relational database. A type of database in which data stored in different tables are related to data in other tables based on a unique field or key. *See section 2.3(ii).2.*

RELAX NG. Regular Language description for XML—Next Generation. Pronounced "relaxing," an XML schema language that unifies the schema languages RELAX (a Japanese national standard), and James Clark's TREX, with the major goal that it be easy to learn and easy to use; it is now a draft international standard (ISO/IEC DIS 19757-2). *See sections 3.3(ii).2, 3.3(ii).4, 3.3(ii).4.4.*

removable disk. A storage device where the storage medium (the disk) can be removed from the drive, such as a floppy disk or an optical disk. *See section 2.5(ii).2.*

resolution. In display technology, a measure of the size of each pixel. *See section 2.4(i).2.*

resolution-independent. A graphic, such as a vector graphic, that allows a printer to produce the image at the highest possible resolution, instead of restricting the printer to a specific arrangement of pixels in a precise matrix. *See section 6.8(ii).2.*

resource description. Alternate term for metadata; data that describes what a given piece of content is. *See section 4.4(i).*

Resource Description Framework (RDF). A standard by which to define metadata to describe resources available on the Web by their properties and values; consisting of a syntax (which is an official W3C Recommendation) and a schema (which is still a working draft as of this writing). *See section 4.4(iii).*

resource discovery. Search process that typically uses metadata to locate and retrieve content. *See section 4.4(i).*

RGB. A color system based on the principles of additive color where many colors can be reproduced by combining various amounts of red, green, and blue light; generally used for digital imaging, scanning, processing, and displaying color information, including on computer monitors and television screens. *See sections 6.8(vi).2, 6.9(i).1, 6.9(ii).1.*

Rich Text Format (RTF). A type of word processing document that is portable between different software yet that retains applied structure and formatting. *See section 4.2(i).1.*

rip. The process or act of converting audio data from a CD to an MP3 file on a computer; technically a format conversion, it has many copyright implications. See also MP3. *See section 9.6(iii).3.*

RIP. Raster Image Processor. A graphics processor that interprets page description files, such as PostScript, and converts them into device-specific instructions for display or output. *See sections 6.5(ii), 6.9(iv).4.*

RS-232. An early, widely adopted serial communications standard; released by the Electronics Industry Association (EIA) in 1969. *See section 2.6(i).2.1.*

RTF. See Rich Text Format (RTF).

sample. A measure of the sensitivity of a scanning device. *See section 6.8(vi).2.*

Scalable Vector Graphics (SVG). An XML-based language for describing graphics, using vectors so that, unlike bitmap formats, the resulting graphics can be imaged at any size and still conform to the available resolution of the rendering device; an official W3C Recommendation. *See section 3.3(i).3.*

scanner. A digital device that takes a physical image—photo, slide, print, transparency, drawing, line art, etc.—and using a light source converts the image to binary data that can be used to manipulate and store that image on a computer. *See sections 5.3(i).1.3, 6.11(i).*

schema. See XML schema. *See section 3.3(ii).1.*

screen angle. The angle at which a halftone screen is turned to minimize the appearance of halftone pattern or moiré; where multiple colors are used, each color in a halftone image is set at a different screen angle. *See sections 6.5(ii), 6.8(vi).3.2.*

screen font. A type of font designed to be displayed on a computer screen, as opposed to printer fonts used for printing; mostly found in Type 1 fonts; later font schemes simplified font handling by eliminating the dual-font approach. *See section 6.7(ii).*

screen ruling. The frequency of a row of dots in a halftone image, usually expressed as lines per inch (lpi); the higher the screen ruling value, the smoother the image, depending on the print medium used. *See section 6.8(vi).3.1.*

screening algorithm. A mathematical formula for arranging halftone dots into halftone screens for optimal reproduction. *See section 6.5(ii).*

script. A file that lists and executes step-by-step instructions that make it possible to automate what an operator might do manually. *See section 3.3(iv).2.*

SCSI. Small Computer Systems Interface. A parallel communications channel that allows communication to a variety of external devices, such as storage devices, printers, scanners, and other peripherals. *See section 2.6(i).2.5.*

SDSL. Symmetric DSL. A mode of operation of a digital subscriber line in which transmission both to and from a computer are the same speed. *See section 2.6(iii).2.2.*

Section 508. A section of the Rehabilitation Act (amended 1998) that requires Federal agencies' electronic and information technology be accessible to people with disabilities. *See sections 7.1(i).1.3, 9.7(iii).2.*

Secure Socket Layer. A standard security protocol for safeguarding information transmission across the Web using a variety of technologies and methods of personal identification, including encryption and digital certificates. *See section 15.3(ii).1.1.*

separations. The process of separating constituent colors in a graphic (RGB or CMYK) for printing, or the resulting representation of the graphic in only one constituent color; also referred to as color separations or sometimes film separations. *See section 6.5(ii).*

serial. A communications channel in which one bit at a time is transmitted; serial channels typically require fewer wires and can be made to operate over greater distances than parallel channels using the same amount of power. *See section 2.6(i).1.1.*

SGML. Standard Generalized Markup Language. A metalanguage that enables the creation of unique and rigorous markup schemes by which to tag particular kinds of content, and that emphasizes the separation of structure and presentation; established as an ISO standard (ISO 8879) in 1986; the parent language of HTML and XML. *See sections 1.2(i).4, 3.1(i).4, 3.3(i), 4.2(ii), 11.5(iii).1.2.*

sharpening. The effect and process of making the transition between tones of an image more distinct. *See section 6.9(iii).6.*

signature. A printed section of a book or magazine that consists of a large sheet of paper that is folded, collected together in proper order with other signatures, bound together, and trimmed to make up the entire publication. *See section 6.12(ix).*

Simple Object Access Protocol (SOAP). An XML protocol that enables programs to request services or functions over the Web. *See sections 2.6(iv).2.3, 3.3(i).3.*

.sit. A file extension for the StuffIt compression software; it is a lossless compression technology; see also .zip. *See section 6.8(iv).1.*

SMIL. Synchronized Multimedia Integration Language. A markup language for use with multimedia that has two design goals: first to define an XML-based language that allows authors to write interactive multimedia presentations (using SMIL 2.0, an author can describe the temporal behavior of a multimedia presentation, associate hyperlinks with media objects, and describe the layout of the presentation on a screen) and second to allow the reuse of SMIL syntax and semantics in other XML-based languages, particularly those that need to represent timing and synchronization. *See section 9.6(ix).*

SMTP. Simple Mail Transfer Protocol. A standard Internet protocol for the transfer of e-mail. *See sections 2.6(iv).2.2, 4.5(iii).2.*

SOAP. See Simple Object Access Protocol.

solid color. See spot color.

SONET. Synchronous optical networking. A type of dedicated data circuit for WAN communications that is used for very high speed digital transmission over optical fiber cables. *See section 2.6(iii).2.2.*

SPC. Statistical process control. The collection and analysis of data to study process capability and performance in the production workflow to make it deliver greater value or efficiency. *See section 6.12.6.*

Specifications for Web Offset Printing (SWOP). A print industry standard specification that defines acceptable levels of dot gain on specific print stocks on Web presses. *See section 6.8(vi).4.1.*

spi. See spots per inch (spi).

Spine. In the Open eBook Publication Structure (OEBPS), a component of the OEBPS Package file; a default, linear reading order for the Publication. *See section 11.6(vi).1.4.*

spot. The smallest addressable image unit on an output imaging device for graphics; a number of spots typically make up a dot that forms a halftone pattern. *See section 6.8(vi).2.*

spot color. In printing, the process of using one specific ink for each color in a design, often referred to as custom color, solid color, or Pantone color. See also Pantone Matching System.

spots per inch (spi). A measure of resolution of a graphic image, sometimes referred to as dots per inch (dpi). *See section 6.8(vi).2.*

spreadsheet. A computer application for bookkeeping or accounting, though frequently used for other purposes, where computational functionality is paramount. *See section 2.3(ii).1.*

ssh. Shorthand for "secure shell"; a terminal emulation program for remotely logging on to other computers. *See section 2.6(iv).2.1.*

staging server. A Web server that contains a pre-publication version of content for a Web site, where it can be added to or edited prior to being published "live" on the production server. *See section 10.3(iii).*

static Web pages. Pages on a Web site that are stored and served whole and complete, with each reader, in effect, viewing the same copy of the same material. *See section 10.1(ii).3.*

STIX. Scientific and Technical Information Exchange. A comprehensive character set for mathematics that is being incorporated into Unicode, with a corresponding font that enables most math characters that currently have to be displayed as graphics on the Web to use a true scalable font. *See section 3.3(iii).4.1.*

STM. Scientific, technical, and medical. An acronym applied to these types of scholarly publishing. *See section 4.2(i).3.*

stochastic screening. See Frequency Modulated (FM) screening.

stylesheet. Primarily in HTML and XML, a separate file that contains presentation specifications for a document or a group of documents. *See section 5.1(i).6.*

subtractive color. Theory and process by which three primary colorants—cyan, magenta, and yellow—absorb or subtract some of the visible spectrum allowing others to pass through to create color on a white surface. See also CMYK. *See section 6.9(i).1.*

superconductor. A material that at very low temperatures allows electric current to flow with virtually no impedance (resistance); superconductors allow for very fast computer processing speeds. *See section 2.3(i).4.1.*

supplementary content. Term usually applied to ancillary content that typically can only be published electronically, such as audio, raw data sets, or moving images. *See section 4.3(i).1.*

SVG. See Scalable Vector Graphics. *See section 1.3(iii).6.*

SVGA. Super Video Graphics Adapter. Both a signaling protocol and a type of graphics adapter, which send signals that address each pixel in a computer display independently; SVGA is the most common and advanced graphics adapter, permitting a large number of pixels to be addressed with a high degree of color definition. *See section 2.4(ii).5.*

System V. One of the two main variations of the Unix operating system developed at AT&T Bell Labs. *See section 2.3(i).1.*

T1. A designation of the equipment used on a DS1 circuit, the DS and T are used interchangeably. T1 circuits operate at a transmission rate of 1.544Mbps (megabits per second). *See section 2.6(iii).2.3.*

T3. A designation of the equipment used on a DS3 circuit, the DS and T are used interchangeably. T3 circuits operate at a transmission rate of 44.74Mbps (megabits per second). *See section 2.6(iii).2.3.*

TabletPC. A slate-form PC, usable in landscape and portrait mode, based on the Windows XP operating system, that can be used with a stylus for writing or drawing as well as being attached to a keyboard or another computer. *See section 9.6(i).*

Tagged PDF. A feature of Adobe Acrobat beginning with version 5.0 that allows tags to be embedded within a PDF document to retain structural infomation such as XML or style names. *See section 12.4(iii).1.1.*

Talking Book. An initiative of the DAISY consortium (NISO standard Z39.86) to provide the blind or visually impaired people access to books. *See section 11.2(ii).10.*

TCP/IP. Transmission Control Protocol/Internet Protocol. A protocol family for networking computers; the TCP layer handles the transport of packets on a local network while the IP layer supports information exchange between networks. *See sections 2.6(iv).1, 4.5(iii).2.*

TEI. Text Encoding Initiative. An international standard scheme, including SGML and XML DTDs and modular DTD fragments with associated guidelines, for the markup of all kinds of textual material, used primarily for scholarly work; commonly used as the basis for custom DTDs. *See sections 3.1(ii).2, 3.3(v).1, 4.4(ii).2.*

TEI Lite. A subset DTD for TEI that offers a simplified version of TEI, with approximately 150 of the 500-some elements of the full TEI. *See section 3.3(ii).3.2.*

telnet. A terminal emulation program for remotely logging on to other computers. *See section 2.6(iv).2.1.*

terabyte. A trillion bytes, or 1,000,000,000,000 bytes. *See section 1.3(iii).1.*

term of copyright. The length of time that a copyright remains enforceable under the domestic law of each particular country; terms are not uniform internationally. *See section 13.1(i).2.*

TeX. A public domain typesetting system especially known for its ability to handle complex mathematical formulas. *See sections 5.1(i).4.3, 5.5(x), 11.5(iii).1.2.*

text. The written portion of an item of content composed of words intended to be read by the ultimate user or consumer, as opposed to the markup, metadata, graphics, or other components associated with them. *See sections 11.5(ii).2.2, 6.2.*

text editor. An application for manipulating words on a computer, typically for creating and editing text documents without formatting capabilities. *See section 2.3(ii).3.*

Text Encoding Initiative. See TEI.

text-to-speech (TTS). A type of software or the process that allows a computer to read text aloud to users; such software can often read text in a manner configured by the user who varies such things as speed, pitch, and type of voice selected (e.g., male, female, young, old). *See section 7.1(iii).*

TFT. Thin-film Transistor. The transistor layer (a thin film of silicon) that is used in active-matrix LCD display screens. *See section 2.4(ii).2.*

TIFF. Tag (or Tagged) Image File Format. A bitmapped graphic file format, originally developed by Aldus Developers Association, and now maintained by Adobe Systems. *See sections 5.1(i).4.3, 5.5(vi).1, 5.5(vi).1, 6.8(iii).1, 6.8(v).1.1, 8.2(i).1, 12.4(iii).1.4.*

TIFF/IT. Tag (or Tagged) File Format for Image Technology. An ANSI IT8.8 bitmap graphic standard that provides an independent transport mechanism for raster images and integrates both high-end and desktop publishing formats, to make data exchange between those two types of systems more efficient and easier. *See sections 1.2(vii).1, 6.8(v).1.2.*

Token Ring. A LAN protocol for cabled networks that allows communication between computers, developed by IBM; see also Ethernet. *See section 2.6(iii).1.*

topology. A designation of the orientation to each other of the various computers on a network. *See section 2.6(ii).2.*

Tours. In the Open eBook Publication Structure (OEBPS), an optional part of the OEBPS Package file that provides alternate reading sequences through a Publication. *See section 11.6(vi).1.5.*

Toyo Color Finder. System for matching process color (CMYK) to spot color; primarily used in Japan. *See section 6.9(ii).2.3.*

tracking. In typesetting, the subtraction of space between the letters in a given group; it is applied to all the letters using the same value; usually used in text rather than display type. *See section 6.7(v).3.4.*

trademark. A brand, in effect: a name, logo, word, or phrase that is closely associated with a company or its product(s) and is protected by law from certain unauthorized uses, especially when applied to competing companies or products; trademarks may be—but are not required to be to gain legal protection—registered with the U.S. Patent and Trademark Office. *See section 14.12(ii).*

transistor. A tiny semiconductor switch used to control the flow of electrons. *See section 2.2(i).1.*

transparency scanner. A scanner that handles transparencies: film negatives and positives (such as slides). *See section 6.11(i).*

trapping. The process of compensating for the mechanical errors that result in misregistration of images on a printing press, done as part of the prepress composition process. *See sections 6.3, 6.5(ii).*

traversal. In XSL, the action of using or following a link. See also arc. *See section 3.3(v).1.*

trilinear arrays. In a scanner or digital camera, part of a CCD that is capable of digitally recording and storing data from the red, green, and blue channels. *See section 6.11(iii).*

TrueType. A scalable font for use in PostScript and for use with both PostScript and non-PostScript printers; developed by Apple and Microsoft—Apple released TrueType in March 1991 while Microsoft introduced TrueType into Windows 3.1 in early 1992. *See sections 6.7(i), 6.7(i).2.*

Trumatch. System for naming and formulating spot color where color is defined by process color ink combinations, as opposed to specific ink formulas. *See section 6.9(ii).2.3.*

TTS. See text-to-speech.

TULIP. An early experiment in electronic journal publishing led by Elsevier in collaboration with several major universities. *See section 1.2(i).3.*

Type 1 fonts. A worldwide standard for digital type fonts (International Organization for Standardization outline font standard, ISO 9541); developed by Adobe Systems for and defined within the PostScript program, this standard is the original file format used for type output on PostScript printers; more than 30,000 fonts in the Type 1 format have been designed by companies around the world. *See section 6.7(i).*

type families. Refers to all the stylistic variations found in a single typeface, usually referenced by one common name; typically includes plain or roman, bold, italic, and bold italic, though a family can contain extensive variations. *See section 6.7(v).1.*

UCS-2. Unicode Character Set 2. In Unicode, a 16-bit encoding form using two 8-bit bytes and accommodating 65,536 possible characters. *See section 3.3(iii).4.1.*

UCS-4. Unicode Character Set 4. In Unicode, a 32-bit encoding form accommodating over 2 billion characters. *See section 3.3(iii).4.1.*

UDL. See Universal Design for Learning.

Unicode. An international standard for encoding the characters used by most of the world's written languages; the fundamental character encoding on which XML is based. *See sections 1.3(i).6, 3.3(iii).4.1, 5.5(i).1, 11.6(v).6.*

Universal Design for Learning (UDL). The application of the concept of universal design—design of buildings and other structures that have built in accommodations for people with special needs, the disabled, and the non-disabled—to learning activities; especially the design of school curricula materials that meet the needs of a wide variety of students including those with disabilities. *See section 7.1(iv).*

Universal Serial Bus (USB). A serial communications channel with an electrical signaling rate that permits a high data transfer rate. *See section 2.6(i).2.3.*

Unix. An operating system made popular in the 1980s for scientific and engineering systems and that is still popular for more complex operating environments; the basis of Linux, Solaris, Mac OS X, and other operating systems. *See section 2.3(i).1.*

URL. Uniform Resource Locator. The address of a file or resource on the World Wide Web; URLs can use different internet protocols, such as HTTP or FTP, and most often contain a domain name and location of the file on the target server. *See section 4.5(iii).1.*

USB. See Universal Serial Bus.

UTF. UCS Transformational Format. In Unicode, a standard that enables the use of Unicode's UCS-2 encoding form while extending its range to include non-BMP characters; essentially the same as UCS-2E. *See section 3.3(iii).4.1.*

valid XML. XML tagging (or the document that is tagged in XML) that conforms to a specific DTD or XML schema. See also well-formed XML. *See section 3.3(ii).5.*

vector. A graphic format that utilizes vectors, where images, fonts, and other graphic elements are mathematically described (as opposed to raster graphics where the image consists of a matrix of pixels), and can thus conform to the resolution of the rendering mechanism; also called object-oriented graphics. *See sections 5.5(vi), 6.8(ii).*

vector graphics. A graphic format that utilizes vectors, where image lines are mathematically described, as opposed to raster graphics where the image consists of a matrix of pixels; also called object-oriented graphics. *See section 6.8(ii).2.*

VGA. Video Graphics Adapter. Both a signaling protocol and a type of graphics adapter that sends signals that address each pixel in a computer display independently. *See section 2.4(ii).5.*

video RAM. (VRAM). Fast memory on the video card of the PC or main memory of the PC, designed for storing the image to be displayed on a computer's monitor; size and speed of the VRAM are critical for video display and games animation; currently 8 MB is minimum and 64 MB to 128 MB is preferred for games. *See section 9.3(i).2.*

virtual journal. An online publication, typically drawing articles and other content from a variety of digital sources and combining them into new thematic publications. *See section 4.3(i).2.1.*

VRAM. See video RAM.

W3C. See World Wide Web Consortium. *See sections 9.6(ix), 3.1(ii).4.*

WAI. See Web Accessibility Initiative. *See sections 7.1(v).3, 7.2(i).5.3.*

WAN. Wide Area Network. A network of computers remote from one another that communicate over commercial telephone and cable systems. *See sections 2.6(ii).2, 2.6(iii).2.*

WAP. Wireless Application Protocol. A specification released in 1997 that forms a networking architecture for cell phones and other wireless, mobile devices. *See section 2.6(iv).1.*

watermarking. The process or practice of permanently marking a piece of content with a code identifying the owner of the rights to that content. *See sections 15.1(i).5, 15.3(ii).4.*

Web Accessibility Initiative. Initiative of the World Wide Web Consortium (W3C) to increase accessibility of the Web for people with disabilities. *See sections 7.1(v).3, 7.2(i).5.3.*

Web Content Accessibility Guidelines. Recommendations published by W3C/WAI that explain how to make Web content accessible to people with disabilities. *See section 7.2(i).5.4.*

well formed. See well-formed XML.

well-formed XML. XML markup (or the document that is marked up in XML) that conforms to the syntax and structure specified by the W3C Recommendation; a well-formed XML document does not have to be valid (i.e., conforming to a specific DTD or schema). A document is not considered XML unless it is well formed. See also valid XML. *See sections 3.3(i).1, 3.3(ii).1, 3.3(ii).5.1.*

WG8. The ISO working group that responsible for the SGML standard. *See section 3.1(ii).2.*

WiFi. Wireless Fidelity. A family of wireless Ethernet standards also known as IEEE 802.11b. *See section 2.6(iii).1.1.*

Windows. The Microsoft operating system employed in so-called PC computers that uses a graphical user interface (GUI); the first version was released in 1985 and was based on the DOS operating system; the Windows operating system has gone through many versions, including Windows NT and Windows XP. *See sections 2.3(i).3, 9.6(i).*

WIPO. The World Intellectual Property Organization. A part of the United Nations system of organizations for promoting and protecting intellectual property; administers twenty-three international treaties related to the protection of intellectual property, including the Berne Convention, WIPO Copyright Treaty, and the WIPO Performances and Phonograms Treaty. *See section 15.5(i).1.*

wireless. Data communication or a network that links computing devices without a physical connection such as a cable; typically using radio as a medium of connection. *See section 2.6(iii).1.1.*

word processor. An application that combines a text editor with composition or page layout functions to allow creating and editing of text as well as formatting capabilities. *See section 2.3(ii).3.*

work for hire. Type of copyright in which the rights to content are owned by the corporation or other entity for which the content was created; typically applied to content created by employees in the course of their work for an employer, persons hired to create such content under close supervision, and certain kinds of commissioned content. *See section 13.1(iii).*

World Wide Web. A system of linked hypertext documents based on the hypertext transfer protocol (HTTP), developed in 1989 by Tim Berner-Lee and others at CERN, a Swiss particle physics laboratory, and made popular by the introduction in the early 1990s of HTML, the HyperText Markup Language, and a GUI-based program called Mosaic, the first Web browser, in 1993. *See sections 1.3(i).2, 2.6(iv).2.2.*

World Wide Web Consortium (W3C). A group comprising over 500 Web-related member organizations that provides governance for the technical evolution of the Web, evaluating and developing new technologies for the Web. W3C does not set standards, but approves recommended technologies by consensus of members. *See sections 3.1(iii).2, 3.3(i).2.*

WORM. Another name for CD-R disks meaning "write once, read many." *See section 2.5(ii).3.2.*

WSDL. Web Services Description Language. A mechanism for discovering services that are available from remote computers on the Internet. *See section 2.6(iv).2.3.*

WYSIWYG. Acronym for "what you see is what you get," meaning the format and look of a document on a computer display will print exactly as it appears, as opposed to, for example, printing with markup tags shown that are invisible on the screen. *See sections 3.2(i).4, 5.3(i).2.2, 6.4.*

XHTML. An implementation of HTML 4 as an XML application, basically using the same element set and designed to be used in the same way as HTML, but expressed in the syntax of XML. *See sections 3.2(iv).2, 11.2(ii).2, 11.6(v).2.*

XLink. The XML Linking language. An XML syntax for describing not only one-directional links but also multidirectional and multiheaded links, for associating metadata with links, for specifying how links are actuated and how they behave, and for enabling links and the information about them to be maintained separately from the documents or resources they connect; issued as a Recommendation by the W3C in July 2001. See also XPointer, XSLT, and XPath. *See sections 1.2(vi).3, 3.3(i).2, 3.3(v).1.*

XML. The Extensible Markup Language. A metalanguage that enables the creation of unique markup schemes (called XML applications, tagsets, or vocabularies) by which to tag particular kinds of content. An official Recommendation of the W3C. The term XML is also often used generically to refer to a family of related technologies. *See sections 1.1(i), 1.2(iii).2, 1.2(vi).3, 3.1(i).2, 3.1(i).4, 3.3(i), 3.3(i).5, 11.5(iii).1.2, 11.6(v).1, 12.2(i), 12.4(iii).1.2.*

XML Schema. The XML schema language officially endorsed as a Recommendation by the W3C.

XML schema. A definition, using any of several XML schema languages, or a particular class of documents or other content; an alternative to DTDs (Document Type Definitions) offering functionality not available in DTDs; unlike a DTD, an XML schema is expressed in XML and is therefore itself an XML document. See also XML Schema and RELAX NG. *See sections 3.3(ii).4, 6.10(ii).2.*

XML-in. A production route where content is structured in XML either before entering the production process or at the beginning of the production process. *See section 4.2(i).2.*

XML-out. A production route where XML is the result of a traditional production process or where XML is created by a process of back conversion on typesetting files. *See section 4.2(i).1.*

XMP. The Extensible Metadata Platform. Created by Adobe but available as an open source, nonproprietary standard, it provides a way to embed XML metadata into binary files such as Adobe Illustrator and Photoshop images. *See sections 1.3(iii).5, 3.3(vi).2.*

XP. Short for Windows XP; an operating system. See also Windows.

XPath. The XML Path Language. The language that provides the syntax and semantics that XSLT, XLink, and XPointer need to be able to address particular parts of actual XML documents based on their structure; published as a Recommendation by the W3C in 1999. *See sections 1.2(vi).3, 3.3(i).2, 3.3(iii).3.1, 3.3(iv).4, 3.3(v).2.*

XPointer. The XML Pointing Language. Based on XPath, it is designed primarily to provide the ability to address almost any point or range in an XML document (or in its external parsed entities), whether or not that point or range is an element or a node on the document tree. Issued as a W3C Candidate Recommendation on September 11, 2001. *See sections 1.2(vi).3, 3.3(i).2, 3.3(v).3.*

XrML. The eXtensible rights Markup Language. A markup language conforming to the XML syntax, developed by Xerox PARC in the mid-1990s, for describing rights models, including types of rights, types of users, and differing security levels. *See section 15.4(i).*

XSL. The Extensible Stylesheet Language. A more powerful and versatile stylesheet language than CCS but easier to use than DSSSL, it is designed to specify the presentation of XML documents, enable them to be transformed, while accommodating both print-based and Web-based presentations; first published as a Recommendation by the W3C in October, 2001. See also XSL-FO, XSLT, and XPath, all of which can considered part of XSL. *See sections 3.3(i).2, 3.3(iii).3.*

XSL-FO. XSL Formatting Objects. Part of the XSL standard, and used in conjunction with XPath and XSLT, XSL-FO is a language (and a vocabulary) for the specification of formatting of XML documents. XSL-FO is not software; it must be interpreted by a rendering engine to create the specified presentation. *See sections 1.3(i).4, 1.3(iii).3, 3.3(i).2, 3.3(iii).3.1.*

XSLT. XSL Transformations. Part of the XSL standard and using XPath, XSLT is a langugae for transforming XML documents into other XML documents or into non-XML documents (such as HTML documents or Quark-XPress-tagged documents); issued by the W3C as a Recommendation in November, 1999. *See sections 3.3(i).2, 3.3(iii).3.1, 3.3(iv).4, 7.2(v).3.*

Z39.50. An ANSI standard protocol for retrieving structured catalog data from remote databases. *See section 2.6(iv).2.2.*

Z39.86. A NISO standard based on DAISY for providing the blind or visually impaired access to books. See also Talking Book.

.zip. A file extension for compression software, such as WinZip or PKZIP, used primarily on Windows PCs; it is a lossless compression technology; see also .sit. *See section 6.8(iv).1.*

Bibliography

"Accessible Textbooks Clearinghouse." Texas School for the Blind and Visually Impaired. 2002. http://www.tsbvi.edu/textbooks/

Addey, Dave, James Ellis, Phil Suh, and David Thiemecke. *Content Management Systems (Tools of the Trade)*. Birmingham, U.K.: Glasshaus, 2002.

Adobe Systems Incorporated. "Color and Color Management." 2000. http://www.adobe.com/support/techguides/color/main.html

———. "eXtensible Metadata Platform (XMP)." 2002. http://www.adobe.com:80/products/xmp/main.html

———. "Introduction to Halftones and Scanning." 2000. http://www.adobe.com/support/techguides/printpublishing/scanning/psscanning.html

Afuah, Allan, and Christopher L. Tucci. *Internet Business Models and Strategies*. New York: Irwin/McGraw-Hill, 2002.

American Foundation for the Blind. "Instructional Materials Accessibility Act Section-by-Section Analysis." American Foundation for the Blind. 2001. http://www.afb.org/info_document_view.asp?documentid = 1704

"Applied Global Marketing." GLOBMKT. LISTSERV@ukcc.uky.edu

Arms, William, Y. "Preservation of Scientific Serials: Three current examples." Journal of Electronic Publishing 5 no. 2 (December 1999). http://www.press.umich.edu/jep/05-02/arms.html

Association of Research Libraries. "Statistics and Measurement Program." 2002. http://www.arl.org/stats/index.html

Baca, Murtha, ed. *Introduction to Metadata, Version 2.0*. Getty Research Institute, 1998. http://www.getty.edu/research/institute/standards/intrometadata/

Bailey, Martin. *PDF/X Frequently Asked Questions*. Global Graphics, 2002. http://www.planetpdf.com/mainpage.asp?webpageid = 1220

Baker, Nicholson. *Double Fold: Libraries and the Assault on Paper*. New York: Vintage Books, 2002.

Beebe, Linda, and Barbara Meyers. "The Unsettled State of Archiving." Journal of Electronic Publishing 4, no. 4 (June 1999). http://www.press.umich.edu/jep/04-04/beebe.html

Boiko, Bob. *Content Management Bible*. Hoboken: John Wiley & Sons, 2001.

Bormans, Jan, and Keith Hill, eds. "MPEG-21 Overview v.4." International Standards Organisation. 2002. http://mpeg/telecomitalialab.com/standards/mpeg-21/mpeg-21.htm

Bradley, Neil. *The XML Comanion,* 3[d] ed. Harlow, England: Addison-Wesley, 2001. http://www.bradley.co.uk

Bringhurst, Robert. *Elements of Typographical Style*. Vancouver: Hartley & Marks, 1992.

Brody, Florian. "Interaction Design: State of the Art and Future Developments." In *Multimedia Graphics: The Best of Global Hyperdesign,* edited by Willem Velthoven and Jorinde Seijdel. Chronicle Books, 1996.

———. "The Medium is the Memory." In *Digital Dialectics: New Essays on New Media,* edited by Peter Lunenfeld. MIT Press, 1999.

Bunting, Fred. *The ColorShop Color Primer: An Introduction to the History of Color, Color Theory, and Color Management*. Light Source Computer Images, Inc., 1998. http://www.xrite.com/documents/mktg/ColorPrimer.pdf

Burk, Alan, James Kerr, and Andy Pope. "Archiving and Text Fluidity / Version Control—The Credibility of Electronic Publishing." The Humanities and Social Sciences Federation of Canada. 2001. http://web.mala.bc.ca/hssfc/Final/Archiving.htm

California Education Code Section 673029. High Tech Center Training Unit of the California Community Colleges, http://www.htctu.fhda.edu/AB422.html

Connolly, Dan. "The XML Revolution." Nature. October 1, 1998. http://www.nature.com/nature/webmatters/xml/xml.html

Coombs, James S., Allen H. Renear, and Steven J. DeRose. "Markup Systems and the Future of Scholarly Text Porcessing." Communications of the Association for Computing Machinery 30, no. 11 (1987): 933–947. http://doi.acm.org/10.1145/32206.32209

Cooper, Alan. *The Inmates are Running the Asylum: Why High Tech Products Drive Us Crazy and How to Restore the Sanity*. Indianapolis: Sams Publishing, 1999.

Corbató, F.J., and V. A. Vyssotsky. "Introduction and Overview of the Multics System." 1965. http://www.multicans.org/fjcc1.html

Cover, Robin. "The Cover Pages: Online Resource for Markup Technologies." Oasis. 2002. http://www.oasis-open.org/cover/sgml-xml.html.

Cronin, Mary J. *Global Advantage on the Internet: From Corporate Connectivity to International Competitiveness*. New York: Van Nostrand Reinhold, 1997.

Day, Michael. "Metadata: Mapping between Metadata Formats." U.K. Office for Library and Information Networking (UKOLN). 1996; updated May 2002. http://www.ukoln.ac.uk/metadata/interoperability/

DCMI. "Dublin Core Metadata Initiative (DCMI)." 2002. http://www.dublincore.org/

DeRose, Steven J., David Durand, Elli Mylonas, and Allan H. Renear. "What is Text, Really?" Reprinted with commentary in ACM Journal of Computer Documentation 21, no. 3 (August 1997). http://doi.acm.org/10.1145/264842.264843

Digital Library Federation. "Andrew W. Mellon Foundation's e-Journal Archiving Program." Council on Library and Information Resources. 2002. http://www.diglib.org/preserve/ejp.htm

Dodds, Leigh. "Eclectic: The XML-DEV weblog." http://weblogs.userland.com/eclectic/

Doz, Yves, José Santos, and Peter Williamson. *From Global to Metanational: How Companies Win in the Knowledge Economy*. Boston: Harvard Business School Press, 2002.

Economist, The. *The Economist Guide to Economic Indicators*. London: The Economist, 2001.

Editeur. "ONIX Product Information Standards." 2002. http://www.editeur.org/

eMarketer. *Demographics & Usage, January 2002*. New York: eMarketer, Inc, 2002.

———. *eGlobal: Demographics and Usage, January 2002*. New York: eMarketer, Inc, 2002.

———. *Europe Online: Access, Demograhpics and Usage, May 2002*. New York: eMarketer, Inc., 2002.

Flynn, Peter, ed. "The XML FAQ." http://www.ucc.ie/xml/faq.xml

Foster, I. "The Grid: A New Infrastructure for 21st Century Science." Physics Today 55, no. 2: 42. http://www.physicstoday.org/pt/vol-55/iss-2/p42.html

Frostig Center, The. *Assistive Technology for Children with Learning Difficulties*. Pasadena: Schwab Foundation for Learning, 2002. http://www.frostig.org/pdf/ATguide.pdf

Garshol, Lars Marius. *Definitive XML Application Development*. Upper Saddle River, N.J.: Prentice Hall PTR, 2000. http://www.phptr.com

Gilbane Report, The. "Content Management, XML, and e-Business News and Analysis." Bluebill Advisors. 2002. http://www.gilbane.com/

Gillam, Richard. *Unicode Demystified: A Practical Programmer's Guide to the Encoding Standard*. Harlow, England: Addison-Wesley, 2002.

Ginsparg, Paul. "Creating a global knowledge network." Paper presented at the Second Joint ICSU Press—UNESCO Expert Conference on Electronic Publishing in Science, UNESCO HQ, Paris. February 20, 2001. http://arXiv.org/blurb/pg01unesco.html

———. "Winners and Losers in the Global Research Village." February 21, 1996. http://arxiv.org/blurb/pg96unesco.html

Goldfarb, Charles F. "XML Times." 2002. http://www.xmltimes.com

Graham, Ian S., and Liam Quin. *XML Specification Guide*. New York: John Wiley & Sons, 1999. http://www.wiley.com/compbooks/graham-quin

Graham, Tony. *Unicode: A Primer*. Foster City, Calif.: M & T Books, 2000. http://www.mulberrytech.com/unicode/primer/

Gross, Phil, and Michael Gross. *Macromedia Director 8.5 Shockwave Studio for 3D: Training from the Source*. Berkeley: Macromedia Press, 2001.

Grossnickle, Joshua, and Oliver Raskin. *The Handbook of Online Marketing Research: Knowing Your Customer Using the Net*. New York: McGraw-Hill, 2002.

Grycz, Czeslaw Jan, ed. *Professional and Scholarly Publishing in the Digital Age*. New York: Association of American Publishers (AAP), 1997.

Guthrie, Kevin M. "Archiving in the Digital Age: There's a Will, but Is There a Way?" Educause Review 36, no. 6 (2001): 56–65. http://www.educause.edu/ir/library/pdf/erm0164.pdf

Hagel, John, and Arthur G. Armstrong. *Net Gain: Expanding Markets Through Virtual Communities*. Boston: Harvard Business School Press, 1997.

Harold, Elliotte Rusty, and W. Scott Means. *XML in a Nutshell*, 2[d] ed. O'Reilly, 2002.

Harold, Elliotte Rusty. "Cafe con Leche XML News and Resource." 2002. http://www.ibiblio.org/xml/

Hart, Jon. *Web Publishing Law*. Washington, D.C.: Dow, Lohnes & Albertson, PLLC, 2002. http://www.dowlohnes.com

Hicks, Tony. "Should We Be Using ISO 12083?" Journal of Electronic Publishing 3, no. 4 (June 1998). http://www.press.umich.edu/jep/03-04/hicks.html

History of the American Printing House for the Blind, The: A Chronology. American Printing House for the Blind, 2001. http://www.aph.org/about/highlite.htm

Hodge, Gail. "Digital Archiving in theNew Millennium: Developing an Infrastructure." Sheridan Press. 2001. http://www.sheridanpress.com/PDF_docs/DigiArchiving.PDF

International Color Consortium. "Information on Profiles." Color.org. 2002. http://www.color.org/info_profiles2.html

InterPlaNet Project. "Interplanetary Internet Special Interst Group." http://www.ipnsig.org/home.htm

Jaeggi, Stephan, and Bern Zipper. *Basics: An Introduction to PDF Technology*. Kiel: Heidelberger Druckmaschinen AG, 1999. http://www.prepress.ch/visionwork/english.html

———. *Creation: The Creation of PDF Documents*. Kiel: Heidelberger Druckmaschinen AG, 1999. http://www.prepress.ch/visionwork/english.html

———. *Management: Economic and Organizational Aspects of PDF*. Kiel: Heidelberger Druckmaschinen AG, 1999. http://www.prepress.ch/visionwork/english.html

———. *Production: Processing*. Kiel: Heidelberger Druckmaschinen AG, 1999. http://www.prepress.ch/visionwork/english.html

Judson, Bruce. *Net Marketing: Your Guide to Success and Profit on the Net*. New York: Wolff New Media, 1996.

Kahin, Brian, and Hal R. Varian. *Internet Publishing and Beyond*. Cambridge: MIT Press, 2000.

Kasdorf, Bill. "XML and PDF—Why We Need Both." Impressions Book and Journal Services. 2000. http://www.impressions.com/resources_pgs/SGML_pgs/XML_PDF.pdf

Kay, Michael. *XSLT Programmer's Reference, 2d ed.* Birmingham, U.K.: Wrox Press, 2001. http://www.wrox.com

Kennedy, Dianne. "ISO 12083 Information." XMLXperts. http://www.xmlxperts.com/12083.htm

Kodak Polychrome Graphics. "The Learning Center." 2002. http://www.kpgraphics.com/gen/prod_support/learning_ctr/index.html

Komenar, Margo. *Electronic Marketing: A Comprehensive Reference to Electronic Marketing Techniques to Help You Reach a Broader Market*. New York: John Wiley & Sons, 1997.

Lassila, Ora, and Ralph R. Swick. "Resource Description Framework (RDF) Model and Syntax Specification." World Wide Web Consortium (W3C). 1999. http://www.w3.org/TR/1999/REC-rdf-syntax-19990222/

Laurel, Brenda, ed. *The Art of Human-Computer Interface Design*. Reading, Mass.: Addiosn-Wesley Longman, 1990.

Lavizzari, Carlo Scollo. "Encouraging Creativity through Copyright Protection, The 5th International Publishers Association Copyright Conference." Publishing Research Quarterly 18, no.2 (summer 2002): 41–49.

Lavoie, Brian. "Meeting the Challenges of Digital Preservation: The OAIS Reference Model." OCLC Newsletter 243 (January/February 2000).

Lawler, Brian. "Index to the Brian Lawler Essays." Brian Lawler. 2002. http://www.thelawlers.com/essays.htm

Levy, David M. *Scrolling Forward: Making Sense of Documents in the Digital Age*. New York: Arcade, 1990.

Liautaud, Bernard, and Mark Hammond. *e-Business Intelligence: Turning Information into Knowledge and Profit*. New York: McGraw-Hill, 2000.

Library of Congress. "MARC Standards." Network Development and MARC Standards Office. 2002. http://www.loc.gov/marc/

Luna, Ben. "Demystifying Graphics File Formats." PC Update 18, no. 4 (May 2001). http://groups.melbpc.org.au/digimage/startingout2.htm

Mariano, Gwendolyn. "Tech giants push MPEG-4 standard." CNET News.com. October 4, 2001. http://news.com.com/2100-1023-273966.htm

Martin, Julia, and David Coleman. "Change the Metaphor: The Archive as an Ecosystem." Journal of Electronic Publishing 7, no. 3 (April 2002). http://www.press.umich.edu/jep/07-03/martin.html

Martínez, José M., ed. "MPEG-7 Overview (version 8)." International Organisation for Standardisation. 2002. http://mpeg.telecomitalialab.com/standards/mpeg-7/mpeg-7.htm

Microsoft Corporation. "Color Management and Windows: An Introduction." December 2001. http://www.microsoft.com/hwdev/tech/color/icmwp.asp

Mulberry Technologies. "XSL-List—Open Forum on XSL." http://www.mulberrytech.com/xsl/xsl-list/

Myers, Barbara, and Linda Beebe. *Archiving from a Publisher's Point of View*. Sheridan Press, 1999. http://www.sheridanpress.com/PDF_docs/archiving.pdf

National Information Standards Organization. *Specifications for the Digital Talking Book (ANSI/NISO Z39.86–2002)*. Bethesda: National Information Standards Organization, 2002. http://www.niso.org/standards/resources/Z39-86-2002.html

National Library of Australia. "Preserving Access to Digital Information (PADI): Emulation." http://www.nla.gov.au/padi/topics/19.html

National Library Service. *NLS Factsheets: Copyright Law Amendment, 1996 PL 104-197*. U.S. Library of Congress, 2001. http://www.loc.gov/nls/reference/factsheets/copyright.html

———. *NLS: That All May Read. Laws and Regulations*. U.S. Library of Congress, 2001. http://www.loc.gov/nls/laws.html

Neilsen, Jakob. *Designing Web Usability: The Practice of Simplicity*. Indianapolis: New Riders Publishing, 1999.

Oasis Technical Committee. "RELAX NG." 2002. http://www.oasis-open.org/committees/relax-ng/

Ockerbloom, John Mark. "Archiving and Preserving PDF Files." RLG DigiNews 5, no. 1 (February 2001). http://www.rlg.org/preserv/diginews/diginews5-1.html#feature2

Odlyzko, Andrew. "Competition and Cooperation: Libraries and Publishers in the Transition to Electronic Scholarly Journals." Journal of Electronic Publishing 4, no. 4 (June 1999). http://www.press.umich.edu/jep/04-04/odlyzko0404.html

Open eBook Forum. "Open eBook Publication Structure Specification." 2002. http://www.openebook.org/oebps/index.htm

Opnix. "Internet Traffic Report." 2002. http://www.internettrafficreport.com/main.htm

Packer, Randall, and Ken Jordan. *Multimedia: From Wagner to Virtual Reality*. New York: W.W. Norton, 2001. http://www.artmuseum.net/w2vr/

Patrick, Michael J. "Demystifying Digital Archiving: Demystifying File Formats." Foreword Magazine (September 2000). http://www.forewordmagazine.com/eword/September/0600demystify.asp

Pine, B. Joseph II, and James H. Gillmore. *The Experience Economy: Work is Theatre and Every Business a Stage*. Boston: Harvard Business School Press, 1999.

Powell, Thomas A. *Web Design: The Complete Reference*. Berkeley: McGraw-Hill Osborne, 2000.

Public Law 101-336. Americans with Disabilities Act of 1990. http://www.usdoj.gov/crt/ada/pubs/ada.txt

Ray, Erik T. *Learning XML*. Sebastopol, Calif.: O'Reilly Associates, Inc., 2001. http://oreilly.com/

Rehabilitation Act Amendments, Section 508 of the Rehabilitation Act of 1973, as Amended (29 USC 794(d)). The Access Board. http://www.access-board.gov/about/Rehab%20Act%20Amend-508.htm

Rehabilitation Act of 1973 (29 USC 701 et seq.). http://www.dot.gov/ost/docr/regulations/library/REHABACT.HTM

Reid, Calvin. "A Little DAB Will Do at Simon & Schuster." Publisher's Weekly (August 5, 2002).

Reinhardt, Robert, and Snow Dowd. *Flash MX Bible*. Indianapolis: John Wiley & Sons, 2002.

Research Library Group. *RLG and OCLC. Trusted Digital Repositories: Attributes and Responsibilities*. Mountain View: RLG, Inc., 2002. http://www.rlg.org/longterm/repositories.pdf

Richie, Dennis M. "The Evolution of the Unix Time-Sharing System." Lucent Technologies. 1996. http://cm.bell-labs.com/cm/cs/who/dmr/hist.html

Roberts, Mary Lou. *Internet Marketing: Integrating Online and Offline Strategies*. New York: Irwin/Mcgraw-Hill, 2002.

Rose, David H., and Anne Meyer. *Teaching Every Student in the Digital Age: Universal Design for Learning*. Alexandria, Va: Association for Supervision and Curriculum Development, 2002. http://www.cast.org/teachingeverystudent/ideas/tes/chapter3.cfm

Rosenblatt, William, William Trippe, and Stephen Mooney. *Digital Rights Management: Business and Technology*. New York: John Wiley & Sons, 2001.

Rosenzweig, Gary. *Special Edition Using Macromedia Director 8.5*. Indianapolis: Que, 2001.

Scott, Ridley. *1984*. Apple Macintosh advertisement. 1984. http://www.apple-history.com/1984.html

Section 504 of the Rehabilitation Act of 1973, as Amended through 1998. The ERIC Clearinghouse on Disabilities and Gifted Education, 1998. http://ericec.org/sect504.html

Seybold Report, The. "Analyzing Publishing Technologies." Seybold Publications. 2002. http://seyboldreports.com

Sidman, David, and Tom Davidson. "A Practical Guide to Automating the Digital Supply Chain with the Digital Object Indentifier (DOI)." Publishing Research Quarterly 17, no. 2 (Summer 2001): 22–23. http://www.contentdirections.com/materials/PRQ-CDIPracticalGuide.htm

Simba Information. *International Online Markets 2000: Strategic Outlook and Forecast*. Stamford, Ct.: Simba Information, Inc., 2000.

———. *Online Services: Trends and Forecasts—1999 Edition*. Wilton, Ct.: Simba Information, Inc., 1999.

Spicklemire, Steve, Kevin Friedly, Jerry Spicklemire, and Kim Brand, eds. *Zope: Web Application Development and Content Management*. Indianapolis: New Riders Publishing, 2001.

St. Pierre, Margaret, and William P. LaPlant, Jr. "Issues in Crosswalking Content Metadata Standards." National Information Standards Organization. 1998. http://www.niso.org/press/whitepapers/crsswalk.html

Stanford University. "Graphic File Formats at a Glance." Academic Computing Publications. 1998. http://acomp.stanford.edu/acpubs/Docs/graphic_file_formats/

Sterne, James. *World Wide Web Marketing: Integrating the World Wide Web into Your Marketing Strategy*. New York: John Wiley & Sons, 1995.

Sutton, Jennifer. *A Guide to Making Documents Accessible to People Who Are Blind or Viusally Impaired*. Washington, D.C.: American Council of the Blind, 2002. http://www.acb.org/accessible-formats.html

Tennison, Jeni. *XSLT and XPath on the Edge*. New York: Hungry Minds/M & T Books, 2001. http://www.jenitennison.com

Text Encoding Initiative. *Web site*. TEI Consortium. 2002. http://www.tei-c.org/

Tweney, Dylan. "The Defogger: Think Globally, Act Locally." Business 2.0 (November 2001). http://www.business2.com/articles/mag/0,1640,17423,FF.html

U.S. Department of Education. "IDEA '97: The Individuals with Disabilities Education Act Amendments of 1997." Office of Special Education and Rehabilitative Services. 2002. http://www.ed.gov/offices/OSERS/Policy/IDEA/

U.S. Department of Justice. "ADA Home Page—Information and Technical Assistance on The Americans with Disabilities Act." U.S. Department of Justice. 2002. http://www.usdoj.gov/crt/ada/adahom1.htm

———. "Americans with Disabilities Act (ADA)." U.S. Department of Justice, Civil Rights Division, Disability Rights Section. 2001. http://www.usdoj.gov/crt/ada/cguide.htm#anchor62335

UKOLN. "Metadata." U.K. Office for Library and Information Networking. Maint Michael Day and Andy Powell. September 2002. http://www.ukoln.ac.uk/metadata/

Unicode Consortium, The. *The Unicode Standard, Version 3.0*. Reading, Mass.: Addison-Wesley, 2000. http://www.unicode.org

Van Herwijnen, Eric. *Practical SGML*, 2d ed. Boston: Kluwer Academic Publishers, 1994. http://www.wkap.nl/prod/b/0-7923-9434-8

Vaughan, Tay. *Multimedia: Making It Work, 5th Edition*. McGraw-Hill Osborne Media, 2001.

Walsh, Norman. "What Is XML?" O'Reilly XML.com. October 1998. http://www.xml.com/pub/a/98/10/guide1.html#AEN58

Watrall, Ethan, and Norbert Herber. *Flash MX Savvy*. Alemeda: Sybex, 2002.

Webopedia. "Network Topologies." Internet.com. 2002. http://www.webopedia.com/quick_ref/topologies.html

World Wide Web Consortium (W3C). "Metadata and Resource Description." 2001. http://www.w3.org/Metadata/

———. "Resource Description Framework." 2002. http://www.w3.org/RDF

———. "Synchronized Multimedia Integration Language (SMIL 2.0)." August 2001. http://www.w3.org/TR/smil20/

———. "W3C Technical Reports and Publications." 2002. http://www.w3.org/TR/

———. "World Wide Web Consortium Issues SMIL 2.0 as a W3C Recommendation." August 2001. http://www.w3.org/2001/08/smil2-pressrelease

———. "XML Schema." Maint. C. M. Sperberg-McQueen and Henry Thompson. 2002. http://www.w3.org/XML/Schema

World Wide Web Consortium. "HyperText Markup Language (HTML) Home Page." http://www.w3.org/MarkUp/

X-Rite, Incorporated. "The Color Guide and Glossary." 2002. http://www.xrite.com/documents/mktg/L11-029.pdf

XML.com. "XML from the Inside Out." O'Reilly. 2002. http://www.xml.com

XMLHack.com. "Developer news from the XML community." 2002. http://www.xmlhack.com

Index